BURT FRANKLIN: BIBLIOGRAPHY AND REFERENCE SERIES #211

American Classics in History & Social Science #41

THE

ISSUES OF THE PRESS

IN

PENNSYLVANIA

1685—1784

VOL. I
1685—1763

A CENTURY OF PRINTING

THE

ISSUES OF THE PRESS

IN

PENNSYLVANIA

1685—1784

BY

CHARLES R. HILDEBURN

VOL. I
1685—1763

BURT FRANKLIN: BIBLIOGRAPHY AND REFERENCE SERIES #211

American Classics in History & Social Science #41

BURT FRANKLIN
NEW YORK

Published By
BURT FRANKLIN
235 East 44th St.
New York, N.Y. 10017

ORIGINALLY PUBLISHED
PHILADELPHIA: 1835
Reprinted 1968

Printed in U.S.A.

TO
MY FRIEND
ISAAC HARVEY, JR.,
I DEDICATE
THESE
VOLUMES.

PREFACE.

THE design of this work is to present, as far as possible, full and strictly accurate descriptions of the titles, with collations, of every book, pamphlet and broadside printed in the Province and State of Pennsylvania, during the first hundred years of the operations of the press within their limits. Nearly six years have been devoted to the work, and within that period every bibliography, library and sale catalogue coming under the compiler's notice from which any information seemed likely to be obtained, has been carefully examined. Every newspaper published in Pennsylvania prior to 1785, as far as access could be had, has been searched. This involved a perusal of each advertisement in from fifty to one hundred and fifty-six newspapers, contained in nearly two hundred and fifty yearly volumes. The principal libraries of America and England have also been visited. The titles which have thus been brought together amount to upwards of forty-five hundred, and probably represent nearly all the issues of the press, with the exception of broadsides, of which a much larger number must have been printed than are now known to exist.

The chronological arrangement of the titles shows

the growth of our literature and development of literary taste. Religion and politics, which engrossed the attention of our local writers during the first forty years, predominate to the end, but the leaven of fancy introduced in 1731, by George Webb and the unknown author of the "Lady Errant Enchanted" worked spasmodically until 1760, when some poem or play came forth at least annually from a native pen. Medicine, in the tracts of Cadwalader, Thomson, Kearsley, Hamilton, Macleane, and others; higher mathematics, in the essays of Grew, Gordon, Abel, and Rittenhouse; philosophy, natural and experimental, in the works of Johnson and Kinnersley, appear with increasing frequency from 1740, and history, in the work of Morgan Edwards, from 1770. Numerous treatises on military affairs were called forth by the Revolution, one of which, "Steuben's Manual," maintained its position as a text-book till well into the present century. Such reprints of English or American publications, as were issued during the first eighty years, were almost all of the same character as those of our local writers. The exceptions being such practical or instructive treatises, as "Every Man his own Doctor," "The Secretary's Guide," and "Fisher's American Instructor."

The elder Bradford's press was most prolific in the productions of one side of a petty schism, known as the Keithian controversy, while the publications of his successor, Jansen, were mainly devoted to the utterances of the opposite side, in a sequel to the earlier quarrel. Beyond establishing a newspaper the issues of Andrew

Bradford's press show no enterprise on his part as a publisher. He was printer to the Province, and with his father joint printer to the Province of New Jersey. The emoluments derived from these positions, with the profits of his newspaper, afforded him a comfortable income, and he printed only such works as local authors brought or the Quaker meeting required, leaving the reading public of his day to depend upon his importations for their acquaintance with contemporaneous literature.

Keimer, remembered mainly through Franklin's sneers, in reprinting " Gordon's Independent Whig " and " Steele's Crisis," was the first proprietor of a press to rise above the mere printer. His press, for its short existence, was very fruitful, and produced, in Sewel's "History of the Quakers," the largest volume printed here prior to 1748, and in " Epictetus his Morals" the first translation of a classic writer issued in America. Franklin's sole deviation from the line adopted by Bradford was the reproduction of Richardson's " Pamela," his other publications not of a strictly practical kind, being the works of local writers or reprints of English tracts on questions of the day. William Bradford, the grandson of the first printer, followed in the same path, and neither Chattin or Dunlap ventured far enough away from it to be worthy of mention. Robert Bell, with, perhaps, the exception of Andrew Steuart—who reprinted a number of popular English works—was the first to present, in home-made garb, a judicious selection from every class of literature current in England. Beginning with "Johnson's Rasselas" in 1768, he published " Lady Montague's Letters and Poems," " Blackstone's Commentaries " in four quarto volumes, " Sterne's Sentimental Journey," " Robertson's History of Scotland " in three volumes, " Leland's History of Ireland " in four volumes, " Robinson Crusoe," " Paradise Lost," travels, plays, poems, and novels innumerable. His success in offering cheap editions soon compelled his fellow printers to enter the same field. James Humphreys, the publisher of " Sterne's Works," in five volumes, and " Chesterfield's Letters," in four, and Robert Aitken, who printed the first American editions of the New Testament and Bible in English, were his most active rivals.

The German presses produced little else than Bibles and Catechisms, Hymn-books and Prayer-books, " Martyr Books " and ghost stories. These volumes are remarkable for their bulkiness, but with the exception of the publications of the Ephrata Community are almost all reprints of European works. The " Zionitischer Weyrauchs-Huegel " printed by Sower, in 1739, was the first book printed in America from German type, and the Bible, issued in 1743 from the same press, was the first printed in a European language in America. The " Martyr Book," printed at Ephrata, in 1748, was the largest work which appeared in America prior to the Revolution.

The first newspaper published in the middle colonies was the " American Weekly Mercury," begun in 1719 by Andrew Bradford. As Franklin says, it "was a paltry thing, wretchedly managed, and no ways entertaining." Keimer's " Universal Instructor," begun in 1728 was not

much better. To Franklin, in the "Pennsylvania Gazette," we owe our first creditable newspaper, and the
publication of the first German newspaper in America,
the "Philadelphische Zeitung," begun in 1732, is also
due to his enterprise. The "Pennsylvania Journal,"
founded in 1742, by William Bradford the 3d, from the
first, more independent in tone than the "Gazette," was
much the best paper published at the time of the Revolution. The "Pennsylvania Chronicle," published from
1767 to 1773, was, however, in every respect, the best
paper ever issued in the Province. Its editor, William
Goddard, a man of some talent and great aggressiveness,
was for a time in the receipt of aid from Joseph Galloway,
Franklin and a number of writers of ability, in both
America and England. The "Pennsylvania Packet,"
begun in 1771, became in 1785 the first daily paper
printed in the United States. Sower's newspaper, begun
in 1739, is said to have reached, about 1760, a circulation
of eight thousand, and Henry Miller is believed to have
been even more successful.

The first magazine which appeared in America—"The
American Monthly Magazine"—came from the press of
Andrew Bradford in February, 1741, but its appearance
was due to John Webbe, its editor, rather than to its
printer. "Ein Geistliches Magazien," begun by Sower in
1764, is believed to have been the first religious periodical published in America.

Among the educational publications may be mentioned
the works of Bell and de Prefontaine on French, and the

German grammars printed by Armbruester in 1748, and Sower in 1751, and Christopher Dock's "Schul Ordnung." There are also several reprints of Latin, Greek, German and French Grammars, etc.

The Almanacs form a class of literature in themselves. Beginning with the very first issue of the press they continued to appear in ever increasing numbers until long after the end of the first century. A marked feature of these publications was the freedom of language, amounting, in many cases, to the broadest indecency, in which the prefaces, tales and verses were written.

The compiler is indebted to Messrs. Samuel W. Pennypacker, Horatio Gates Jones, Frederick D. Stone, Lloyd P. Smith, Henry Phillips, Jr., Charles G. Sower and Oswald Seidensticker, of Philadelphla; A. R. Spofford, of Washington; J. M. W. Lee, of Baltimore; Charles J. Little, of Harrisburg; William S. Stryker, of Trenton; Wilberforce Eames, William Kelby, Samuel S. Purple and Charles H. Kalbfleisch, of New York City; Lindsay Swift, of Boston, and Joseph Smith, of London, for valuable information and assistance promptly and courteously rendered.

CHAS. R. HILDEBURN.

Philadelphia, Oct. 16, 1885.

CHRONOLOGICAL LIST OF PRINTERS IN PENNSYLVANIA BEFORE 1785.

Publishers, whose names appear in the imprints of works described in the following pages, but who were never proprietors of a press, are included in this list and marked with an asterisk (*).

William Bradford, at or near Philadelphia,		1685-1693
Reynier Jansen,	"	1699-1705
Tiberius Johnson,	"	1704-1705
Joseph Reyners,	"	1706
Jacob Taylor,	"	1709-1712
Andrew Bradford,	"	1712-1714
William and Andrew Bradford,	"	1713-1733
Andrew and William Bradford,	"	1739-1740
Samuel Keimer,	"	1723-1729
Benjamin Franklin,	"	1729-1765
B. Franklin and H. Meredith,	"	1729-1732
B. Franklin and D. Hall,	"	1748-1765
B. Franklin and G. Armbruester,	"	1747-1750
B. Franklin and J. Boehm,	"	1749-1751
B. Franklin and A. Armbruester,	"	1754-1758
Hugh Meredith, B. Franklin and	"	1729-1732
David Harry,	"	1729-1730
Christopher Sower, 1st,	Germantown,	1738-1758
William Bradford, 3d,	Philadelphia,	1739-1777
Andrew and William Bradford,	"	1739-1740
William and Thomas Bradford,	"	1766-1777
Cornelia Bradford,	"	1742-1752
Isaiah Warner,	"	1742-1744
I. Warner and C. Bradford,	"	1743-1744
Ephrata Community,	Ephrata,	1745-1792
Joseph Crell,	Philadelphia,	1743-1745
Godhard Armbruester,	"	1747-1750
B. Franklin and G. Armbruester, Philadelphia,		1747-1750
James Coulter,	Lancaster,	1747
David Hall,	Philadelphia,	1748-1772
Franklin and Hall,	"	1748-1765
Hall and Sellers,	"	1766-1772

John Boehm,	Philadelphia,	1748-1751
B. Franklin and J. Boehm,	"	1749-1751
James Chattin,	{ Lancaster, { Philadelphia,	1751 1752-1759
Samuel Holland	Lancaster,	1751
and Henry Miller,	{ Lancaster, { Philadelphia,	1752 1760-1781
Anthony Armbruester,	Philadelphia,	1753-1768
B. Franklin and A. Armbruester,	"	1754-1758
Christopher Sower, 2d,	Germantown,	1754-1778
William Dunlap,	{ Lancaster, { Philadelphia,	1754-1757 1758-1766
Andrew Steuart,	Philadelphia,	1760-1769
Peter Miller and Comp.	"	1760-1762
James Adams,	{ Philadelphia, { Wilmington,	1761 1762-1792
*James Rivington,	Philadelphia,	1761
Nicholas Hasselbach,	{ Chestnut Hill, { Philadelphia,	1761 1762
John Morris,	"	1763-1764
J. Brandmiller,	Bethlehem,	1763-1767
William Sellers,	Philadelphia,	1766-1804
D. Hall and W. Sellers,	"	1766-1772
Hall and Sellers,	{ Philadelphia, { York,	1772-1804 1777-1778
William Goddard,	Philadelphia,	1766-1773
John Dunlap,	"	1767-1795
Robert Bell,	"	1768-1784
Benjamin Mecom,	"	1768-1769
William Evitt,	"	1769-1772
Thomas Bradford,	"	1766-1814
William and Thomas Bradford,	"	1766-1777
Bradford and Hall,	"	1781-1782
Isaac Collins,	"	1769-1770
Joseph Crukshank,	"	1769-1824
Crukshank and Collins,	"	1769-1770
Robert Aitken,	"	1770-1802
Francis Bailey,	{ Lancaster, { Philadelphia,	1771-1778 1778-1800
*John Sparhawk,	"	1771-1775
Hibbert Stewart,	Lancaster,	1771-1774
*John McGibbons,	Philadelphia,	1771
William Mentz,	"	1772-1780
William Laplain,	"	1772-1774
*Samuel Dellap,	"	1772-1776
William Macgill,	"	1772
James Humphreys, Jr.,	"	1772-1778
John Douglas McDougal,	"	1774-1776

Fleury Mesplet,	Philadelphia,	1774-1776
Benjamin Towne,	"	1774-1784
Enoch Story,	"	1775
Story and Humphreys,	"	1775
Daniel Humphreys,	"	1775
Oswald and Humphreys,	"	1783
Charles Cist,	"	1776-1799
Melchoir Steiner,	"	1776-1797
Steiner and Cist,	"	1776-1781
Christopher and Peter Sower,	"	1777-1778
McDonald and Cameron,	"	1778
James Robertson,	"	1778
David C. Claypoole,	"	1779-1800
Jacob Bailey,	Lancaster,	1780-1785
William Hall, ⎫ David Hall, ⎬	Philadelphia,	1772-1821
Hall and Sellers,	⎰ Philadelphia, ⎱ York,	1772-1804 1777-1778
*W. Harris,	Philadelphia,	1780
Peleg Hall,	"	1781-1782
Bradford and Hall,	"	1781-1782
George Kleine, ⎫ Kleine and Reynolds, ⎬	"	1781-1785 1784-1785
Theophilus Coffart,	"	1782-1786
Enoch Story, Jr.,	"	1782-1794
*William Prichard,	"	1782-1784
Eleazer Oswald,	"	1783-1795
Oswald and Daniel Humphreys,	"	1783
*Robert Smith, Jr.,	"	1783
Andrew Brown,	"	1784-1802
Peter Leibert,	Germantown,	1784-1801
Leibert and Billmeyer,	"	1784-1787
Michael Billmeyer,	"	1784-1797

EXPLANATORY.

The initials which precede the numbers of the titles refer to the several public libraries in which the works described can be found.

A. A. S. signifies American Antiquarian Society, Worcester, Mass.
A. P. S.   "   American Philosophical Society, Philadelphia.
B.   "   Bodleian Library, Oxford, England.
B. M.   "   British Museum, London, England.
B. P. L.   "   Boston Public Library, Boston, Mass.
C.   "   Library of Congress, Washington, D. C.
D.   "   Library at Devonshire Meeting House, London.
F.   "   Friends' Library, Philadelphia.
H.   "   Pennsylvania State Library, Harrisburg, Pa.
H. S. P.   "   Historical Society of Pennsylvania.
L.   "   Law Library, Philadelphia.
L. C. P.   "   Library Company of Philadelphia.
M.   "   Massachusetts Historical Society, Boston.
M. S.   "   Library of the Meeting for Sufferings, Philadelphia.
N. J.   "   New Jersey Historical Society, Newark, N. J.
Y. C.   "   Yale College Library, New Haven, Conn.

The works so frequently cited in these pages as "Haven's List," "Seidensticker's Bibliography," and "Weller's Falschen Druckorte" are:

Catalogue of Publications in what is now the United States prior to the Revolution of 1775-6 [By S. F. Haven, Jr.]. Appended to the second edition of *Thomas' History of Printing,* published by the American Antiquarian Society in 1874.

Deutsch-americanische Bibliographie bis zum Schlusse des letzten Jahrhunderts. Von Dr. Oswald Seidensticker. Published in *Der Deutsche Pionier* Volumes VIII to XII.

Die Falschen und fingerten Druckorte. Von Emil Weller. Leipzig, 1864.

| indicates the end of each line on a title page.
. . . . indicate that a line has been omitted.
. . . | . . . . | indicate that one or more lines have been omitted. These omissions are either quotations or lines worded and spaced precisely as in some title previously printed.
[ ] include words or dates which are not on the title page. When brackets [ ] occur in a title they are represented thus ( ).
[n. p. n. d.] means no place, no date.

(xiv)

The size of every work described is given in accordance with the number of pages to the signature.

pp. means pages.

1 leaf means that only one side is printed upon and that the other page is blank.

( ) are used to indicate pages not numbered by the printer. Thus: Half-title, 1 leaf; Title, 1 leaf; Dedication, pp. (2); Preface, pp. i–ix; text, pp. 1–506; Appendix, pp. (15); Index, pp. 1–26; Errata, 1 leaf," means that a short title occupies the first page and that the next page is blank, that this is followed by the full title which occupies a page and that the next is blank. The dedication which follows the full title occupies one leaf both sides of which are printed upon but are not numbered. The preface which follows the dedication fills nine pages, the first of which may or may not be numbered i, but the second and subsequent pages of which are numbered ii to ix. Then follows the work called for by the title page, the pages of which are numbered 1 to 506. To this is added an appendix of eight unnumbered leaves of which the first seven are printed on both sides and the eighth on one side only. The index consists of thirteen leaves printed on both sides and paged 1 to 26, and an unpaged leaf of errata printed on one side only is added.

+. following the number of pages indicate that the only copy met with is imperfect.

.+ following the number of pages indicate that the title omitted is precisely similar to that just given, any variation being given immediately after the .+

? following the place of publication implies a doubt as to whether the work mentioned was printed in that place; following the name of the printer, as to its having come from his press; and following the date, as to the year given being correct.

The use of "*sic*" has been in most cases avoided, and such typographical errors as appear in the titles it is hoped will be generally found to have been reproduced from the originals.

THE ISSUES OF THE PRESS

IN PENNSYLVANIA.

1685.

ATKINS. (S.) Kalendarium Pennsilvaniense, | or, | America's Messinger. | Being an | Almanack | For the Year of Grace, 1686. | Wherein is contained both the English & Forreign | Account, the Motions of the Planets through the Signs, with | the Luminaries, Conjunctions, Aspects, Eclipses; the rising, | southing and setting of the Moon, with the time when she | passeth by, or is with the most eminent fixed Stars: Sun rising | and setting, and the time of High-Water at the City of Phi- | ladelphia, &c. | With Chronologies, and many other Notes, Rules, | and Tables, very fitting for every man to know & have; all | which is accomodated to the Longitude of the Province of | Pennsilvania, and Latitude of 40 Degr. north, with a Table | of Houses for the same, which may indifferently serve New- | England, New York, East & West Jersey, Maryland, and most | parts of Virginia. | By Samuel Atkins. | Student in the Mathamaticks and Astrology. | And the Stars in their Courses fought against Sesera, Judg. 5. 29. | *Printed and Sold by William Bradford, sold also by* | *the Author and H. Murrey in Philadelphia, and* | *Philip Richards in New York;* 1685. | 12mo. pp. (40).   H. S. P.   **1**

It consists of twenty unpaged leaves. The reverse of the title which, in the copy at the Historical Society of Pennsylvania, measures 6 by 3 7-8 inches, the type occupying 5 7-16 by 2 7-8 inches, and half of the succeeding page is filled by Atkins' address "To the Reader," which is followed by Bradford's: "To the Readers" which is given below. The fourth page contains "The Explanation of this ensuing Ephemeris." The fifth, "Chronology" and a list of "Some experienced Medicines, sold by William Bradford at Philadelphia." The sixth, "Common Notes for this Year 1686," the Fairs at Philadelphia, &c. The seventh "A Table of the

Kings of England,'' &c. The eighth, ''A Table of the Moons coming to the South, the first six months of this Year.'' The ninth, the same for ''The last six months of this Year.'' The tenth and eleventh, ''The Eleventh Month (January) hath 31 days.'' The other months, or Moneths as it is most frequently spelt, fill two pages each and end on the thirty-second and third with ''The Tenth Moneth (December) hath 31 days.'' ''A Table of Houses for the Latitude of 40 Degrees North'' fills from the thirty-fourth to the thirty-ninth, and the last page contains ''The Names and Characters of the 12 Signs, 7 Planets, 5 Aspects,'' &c., and a paragraph of errata. The calendar is devoid of the usual ''sayings,'' guesses at the weather, and Saints' days and Holidays, not even the 5th of November being distinguished. The astronomical signs and tidal calculations are ''displayed'' so as to fill the two pages alotted to each month. It was well printed, and the mixture of ''Roman'' and ''Italic'' was no doubt due to the cause assigned by Bradford in excuse for the ''Irregularities.''

The author seems to have been wandering through the Middle colonies, and although his promise of another almanac for the ensuing year indicates an intention to remain in Philadelphia, he probably left the neighborhood soon after the appearance of his ''first Fruits.'' No trace of him appears in the wills, administrations or deeds on record here. In fact, beyond the Kalendarium and the record of his appearing in answer to a summons from the Provincial Council for being so forgetful of the ''plain'' language of the people around him as to speak of ''Lord Penn,'' nothing is known of him. Atkins gives an account of the motives which led to, and his manner of compiling the work in his address.

''TO THE READER.

''I thought good to insirt this short Epistle, that you might understand the cause why I thus ventured to publish this Ephemeris or Almanac, which was truly thus ; I having journied in and through several places, not only in this Province, but likewise in Maryland, and else where, and the People generally complaining, that they scarcely knew how the Time passed, nor that they hardly knew the day of Rest, or Lords Day, when it was, for want of a Diary, or Day Book, which we call an Almanack. And on the other side having in my Travels met with Ingenious Persons, that have been Lovers of the Mathematical Arts, some of which have wanted an Ephemeris to make some Practice thereon : I say, hearing this general complaint from such abundance of Inhabitants, which are here. I was really troubled and did design, according to that small knowledge that I had, to pleasure these my Country men with that which they wanted, although it be not compleated in that Method, which I did intend it should be. Nevertheless I have reduced the Sun and Moons places, according to their mean Motions, to this Meridian, which is five hours West from the City of London : For the other Planets, I have taken them by whole Degrees, from the Ephemerides of that Ingenious and Sollid Artist, Mr. John Gadbury, from whence the Fundamental is derived : The Lunar Aspects I have reduced to the hour that they happen here, as before. As to the Moon's rising and setting, I have used the Method of Mr. Vincent Wing, formerly in his Almanack, that is, the Moons rising from Full to New, and her setting from New to Full, according to her true place in the Ecliptick : for what signifies it to shew you the time of her rising and setting in the day time when you cannot see it. In her Southing, I have something respected her Latitude, and accordingly I have framed a Tide-Table to that Experience that I have made of it here. As to the Moons passing by the fixed Stars, &c. I have generally shewn it at that time when they may be best discerned. Besides the Table of Houses, Table of Kings, &c. I had thoughts to have incerted a figure of the Moons Eclips, a small Draught of the form of this City, and a Table to find the hour of the day by the Shadow of a Staff; but we having not Tools to carve them in that form that I would have them, nor time to calculate the other, I pass it for this year, and not only promise it in the next, but likewise several other more particular Notes and Observations, which shall not only be useful to this Province, but likewise to the neighbouring Provinces on both sides. In the meantime, except this my Mite, being my first Fruits, and you will encourage me, according to my Ability, to serve you in what I may, or can, whilst I am

Philadelphia, the 3d of the ⎫
10th Moneth (December) ⎬   SAMUEL ATKINS."
Anno 1685. ⎭

Bradford's inaugural of "the great Art and Mystery of Printing into this part of America," has been once, but by no means exactly, reprinted. It is here given in *facsimile.*

The Printer to the Readers.

HEreby understand that after great Charge and Trouble, I have brought that great Art and Mystery of Printing into this part of America, believing it may be of great service to you in several respects, hoping to find Encouragement, not only in this Almanack, but what else I shall enter upon for the use and service of the Inhabitants of these Parts. Some Irregularities, there be in this Diary, which I desire you to pass by this year; for being lately come hither, my Matereals were Misplaced, and out of order, whereupon I was forced to use Figures & Letters of various sizes, but understanding the want of something of this nature, and being importuned thereto, I ventured to make publick this, desiring you to accept thereof, and by the next, (as I find encouragement) shall endeavour to have things compleat. And for the ease of Clarks, Scriviners, &c. I propose to print blank Bills, Bonds, Letters of Attourney, Indentures, Warrants, &c. and what else presents it self, wherein I shall be ready to serve you; and remain your Friend,

Philadelphia, the 28th
10th Month, 168⅚.   W. Bradford.

The first issue of the press was not destined to go forth unchallenged. One of the Almanacs fell into the hands of William Markham, the Secretary of the Provincial Council, and at their next meeting he reported, "to Council, that in the Chronologie of the Almanack sett forth by Samll Atkins of Philadelphia and by William Bradford of the same Place, there was these words ' the beginning of Government by ye Lord Penn !' The Council sent for Samll Atkins, and ordered him to blott out ye words Lord Penn ; & likewise for Will Bradford, ye Printer, and gave Charge not to print anything but what shall have lycence from ye Council." (Colonial Records I. 165.) Markham must have obtained an "advance copy," as in those now known the offensive words are not only blotted out by stamping over them a "well-inked three-*em quad*," but the errata on the last page unlike the usual manner of noting an error does not repeat the words to be corrected and only says, among other things, "In the Chronology read the beginning of the Government here by William Penn, Proprietor and Governor 6 years."

But two copies are known to exist. One of these formerly belonged to Mr. Brinley, of Hartford, Conn., at whose sale it realized the sum of $555.00. The other was sold at the dispersion of Dr. King's (of Newport, R. I.) Library for $520.00, and is now in the collection of the Historical Society of Pennsylvania. Fragments of two copies are also known, one of which belongs to the Society just mentioned and the other to Mr. S. Gratz.

BUDD. (T.) Good Order Established | in | Pennsilvania & New-Jersey | in | America, | Being a true Account of the Country; | With its Produce and Commodities there made. | And the great Improvements that may be made by | means of Publick Store-houses for Hemp, Flax, and | Linnen-Cloth; also, the Advantages of a Publick- | School, the Profits of a Publick-Bank, and the Proba- | bility of its arising, if those directions here laid down are | followed. With the advantages of publick Granaries. | Likewise, several other things needful to be understood by | those that are or do intend to be concerned in planting in | the said Countries. | All which is laid down very plain, in this small Treatise; | it being easie to be understood by any ordinary Capacity. To | which the Reader is referred for his further satisfaction. | By Thomas Budd. | [*Philadelphia:*] *Printed* [*by* W. Bradford] *in the Year* 1685. | Sq. 8vo. pp. 40. H. S. P. 2

Mr. F. D. Stone, Librarian of the Historical Society of Pennsylvania, was the first to call in question the heretofore accepted statement, that this work was printed in London. I give his reasons in his own words : "In addition to the similarity there is between the type of Good Order and that of publications which are known to be from Bradford's Press, sheets of the former, used as waste, are in a copy of Keith's Pretended Antidote Proved Poysen, printed by Bradford in

1690, which is preserved in its original binding in the Historical Society of Pennsylvania. Other sheets similarly used were found by a gentleman living in Albany, in the original binding of a Bradford edition of the Presbyterian and Independent Visible Churches. If the late Edward Armstrong's statement in his introduction to Gowan's Reprint of the work is correct, that it was 'given to the printer on the 25th of October, 1685,' all possible doubt about the matter is settled, as Budd is known to have been in Philadelphia so soon afterwards (November 17th, 1685) as to preclude the idea that in the mean while he had crossed the Atlantic." After a careful comparison of its typography with other issues of Bradford's Press, the late John Wm. Wallace, Esq., and the author both concurred in Mr. Stone's opinion. A copy of "Good Order" with all the other available early specimens of Bradford's printing, was then submitted to Mr. Thomas Mackellar, the eminent Type-founder, whose long practical experience with every variety of "letter," makes his opinion conclusive. Mr. Mackellar, after a prolonged and careful examination declared himself convinced, that "Good Order" came from the same "office" as several of the books bearing Bradford's imprint, and enforced his opinion by pointing out peculiarly broken, defective and irregularly formed type in Budd's tract, which re-appeared in one or more of the publications of our first printer.

"Good Order" was going through the press when the publication of the Almanac called forth the order "not to print anything but what shall have lycence from ye Council," and as Budd had recently published in London some strictures on Edward Byllinge, which also reflected on Penn and other Quakers, an application for a license in this case would have met with delay, if not a refusal. These considerations no doubt induced Bradford to omit his name from the imprint.

It was reprinted in New York, 1865, with an Introduction by the late Edward G. Armstrong, in which will be found a very full account of the author and his work. Mr. Rice's copy sold for $155, and was re-sold for $150 at the Menzies Sale. Mr. Brinley's uncut copy sold for $160.

1686.

BURNYEAT. (J.) An Epistle from John Burnyeat to | Friends in Pennsilvania ; | To be disperced by them to the neighbouring Provinces, | which for convenience and dispatch was thought good | to be printed, and so ordered by the Quarterly Meeting | of Philadelphia, the 7th of the 4th Month, 1686. | [Colophon.] *Printed and Sold by William Bradford near Philadelphia*, 1686. | 4to. pp. 4.   H. S. P.   3

The author of this Epistle was a well known Friend. It is dated at " Dublin in Ireland, the 12th of the 8th moneth, 1685," and contains nothing more than the religious platitudes usually found in such publications. One hundred copies were printed by order of the Philadelphia Monthly Meeting, for which Bradford received fifteen shillings. Only three are now known to be extant. These are in the Historical Society of Pennsylvania, the Friends' Library, Philadelphia, and Devonshire Meeting-house, London.

A | GENERAL EPISTLE | Given forth by the People of the Lord, called, | Quakers, That all may know, we own none to be | of our Fellowship, or to be reckoned or | numbered with us, but such as fear the Lord | and keep faithfully to his heavenly Power, | that with a holy Conversation they may | adorn that Truth they profess, otherwise, | what experience soever they have had of the | Truth, and are fallen from it, we account | them as so many Judases or Demasses, and | own such no more than the primitive Chri- | stians owned them; but we testify against | them, and say; such go into perdition | through Transgression, and fall under Dark- | ness into a state of Damnation, twice dead, | pluckt up by the Roots, reserv'd in ever- | lasting Chains, until the Judgement of the | great Day, except it be possible they yet | can find a place of Repentance through | God's great un- limited Mercy.   Read the | general Epistle of Jude. | *Printed and Sold by William Bradford at Phila-* | *delphia in Pennsilvania*, 1686. | Sm. 8vo. pp. 23, (1).   D.   4

  This is the first printed utterance of the Philadelphia Yearly Meeting.   The tract also contains an Epistle from William Penn, and " An Epistle to Friends to be read in their Monthly Meeting, from Frances Taylor."   The last page contains a list of books to be sold by Bradford.   An account of Mrs. Taylor and her husband, who were the parents of Jacob Taylor the printer and Almanac-maker, will be found in the Friend, Vol. XXVII, page 128 *et seq.* The title is now for the first time printed in full.   It occurs three times in Joseph Smith's Catalogue of Friends' Books, but even where most fully given, not more than half of it appears.   I have met with only one copy.

LEEDS. (D.) An Almanack | For the Year of Christian Account 1687. | Particularly respecting the Meridian and Latitude of Burlington, but may indifferently serve all places adjacent. | By Daniel Leeds, Student in Agriculture. | *Printed and Sold by William Bradford, near Philadelphia in Pennsylvania, pro Anno* 1687. | Folio, 1 leaf.   H. S. P.   5

  This almanac is printed on a broadside sheet of paper, divided into twelve parts, for the several months.   At the bottom of the sheet is a short explanation of the Almanac, an account of the eclipses, in which he says, the first "may be seen by us, if the clouds hide not.   I judge it will be a great eclipse, especially to some people."   After this is given the time of holding courts and fairs at Burlington and Philadelphia, and short rules in husbandry, and the whole concludes with these lines :

> " Mind modest reader what thou findest amiss,—
> But let the author know what fault it is :—
> All men have erred since Adam first transgressed :—
> If I commit no fault, I'm one of the best.
> But here my comfort is, though I offend,
> I to my faults can quickly put an end."

Daniel Leeds was married at Burlington Meeting 2d mo. 21st, 1681, and on that occasion is described as late of Shrewsbury in East Jersey, and as being a "Cooper" by trade. He was in New Jersey in 1676, and a resident of Burlington in 1680. In 1682 he was Surveyor General and a member of the Assembly of West Jersey. Two years later he is mentioned as contributing £4 towards a Meeting house in Burlington. His first quarrel with his co-religionists, was about his almanac for 1688 (*infra* No. 7), but he did not withdraw from the Society of Friends until the Keithian schism. He does not seem to have taken a very active part in this quarrel, but having joined the Church of England about the same time as Keith, he became the latter's principal coadjutor in the polemical war, which raged from 1696 to 1706. On the side of the Quakers were Caleb Pusey, Samuel Jenings and Thomas Chalkley. The Episcopalians were Keith, Rev. Evan Evans, Rev. John Talbot and Leeds, of whom Leeds was much the most prolific. He wrote News of a Trumpet, 1697; The Hue and Cry against Error, 1698; A Trumpet Sounded, 1699; The Rebuker Rebuked, 1703; The Great Mystery of Fox-Craft Discovered, 1704; The Second Part of The Great Mystery of Fox-Craft, 1706; as well as a work printed in New York, about 1702, the title of which is unknown. Besides these works, which were always bitter, and frequently contained the most scurrilous charges against prominent Quakers, he filled his almanacs with the controversy, and as he had for a time the field to himself, this was particularly offensive to his opponents. Leeds consequently came in for a large share of the abusive personalities, so freely scattered in this controversy, which was carried on with as little dignity by one side as the other.

Leeds was appointed a member of the New Jersey Provincial Council, November 16th, 1702, but after some years' service, during which several petitions for his removal were presented, was deprived of his seat. He took an active part in organizing St. Anne's, now St. Mary's Church, in Burlington, and was a Vestry man in 1709, which is the last mention of him I have found. His first wife died in 1682, and their only child soon after. By his second wife, he had a large family. Two of his sons, Titan and Felix, were almanac makers.

1687.

LEEDS. (D.) An Almanac for 1688. By Daniel Leeds. *Philadelphia: William Bradford.* 1687.   6

The Minutes of the Philadelphia Quarterly Meeting contain the following :
"5th, of 10th mo., 1687. Ordered by this Meeting, that William Bradford, do bring

in all the Almanacks that he hath printed in Daniel Leeds' name, to the house of Thomas Budd, the which almanack being condemned by the Judgment of Friends of this Meeting, and that there be care taken for ye payment of William Bradford towards his loss therein and that he may use his endeavour to call in those that are already abroad." Mr. Kite gives the following explanation of the cause of this action : "In imitation of the Almanacs published in England, Daniel had added some light, foolish and unsavoury paragraphs, which gave great uneasiness and offence to Friends."

Other entries show that Bradford was ordered "to show what may concern Friends or Truth before printing it to the Quarterly Meeting," and that he subsequently received £4 in payment for the copies destroyed.

The Burlington Meeting also condemned the Almanac, and ordered Leeds not to send anything to be printed, without first obtaining their approval. He acknowledged his error in his own meeting and sent the following apology to that of Philadelphia :

"Friends at Philadelphia Meeting. Concerning my Almanack lately published, and by you disapproved, I say this, that although what is therein be not unsuitable for an Almanack, barely considered ; yet I doe believe there are some particulars in it that are too light and airy for one that is a Christian indeed. And I hope for time to come to write more seriously: and also I intend publiqly to signify as much in the next Almanack I doe wright. This much from me, who am your friend, whilst I am my own,

DANIEL LEEDS"

"Burlington 8th of 12th mo. 1687 "

[PENN. (WM.)] The Excellent Priviledge of | Liberty & Property | Being the | Birth-Right | Of the Free-born Subjects of England. | Containing | I. Magna Charta, with a learned Comment upon | it. | II. The Confirmation of the Charters of the Li- | berties of England and of the Forrest, made in | the 35th, year of Edward the First. | III. A Statute made the 34 Edw. I. commonly called De Tallageo non Concedendo; wherein all | Fundamental Laws, Liberties and Customs are | confirmed. With a Comment upon it. | IV. An Abstract of the Pattent granted by the | King to William Penn and his Heirs and As- | signs for the Province of Pennsilvania. | V. And Lastly, The Charter of Liberties granted | by the said William Penn to the Free-men and | Inhabitants of the Province of Pennsilvania and | Territories thereunto annexed, in America. | Major Hereditas venit unicunq; nostrum a | Jure & Legibus, quam a Parentibus. | [*Philadelphia: William Bradford.* 1687.] 16mo. pp. (8), 63. M. S. 7

Collation : Title, 1 leaf; To the Reader, pp. (2) ; Introduction, pp. (4) ; Magna Charta, pp. 18 ; Comment on Magna Charta, 19–34 ; Confirmation of the Charters, 34–37 ; Sentence of the Clergy against breakers of these Articles, 37–38 ; Curse given by the Bishops against breakers of the Great Charter, 38–40 ; Statute, 34 Edward I, 40–41 ; Comment on the last, 42–43 ; Abstract of the Patent [Penn's], 44–48 ; The Frame of Government, 49–63.

At the foot of the Almanac for 1687, is the following : "There is now in the Press The Excellent Privilege of Liberty and Property, to which is added, A Guide for the Grand and Pettit Jury." The title page looks as if Bradford had set up some sort of an imprint, and had hastily withdrawn it just before printing it. It is the worst specimen of Bradford's work I have seen. In "A Defense of the Legislative Constitution of the Province of Pennsylvania," printed by Andrew Bradford in 1728, it is quoted as the work of William Penn. The defense was no doubt written by David Lloyd, and no objection is raised in any of the several replies which it called forth, to the assertion that Penn was the author of "Liberty and Property." As Lloyd was Attorney General of the Province, and on friendly terms with Penn in 1687, his unchallenged statement is conclusive on such a point.

1688.

ADVERTISEMENT against holding the Annual Fair at the Centre Square. *Philadelphia: William Bradford.* 1688.   8

No copy is known to be extant. The Provincial Council in response to a "Petition of the Inhabitants at the Center of Philadelphia," on April 2, 1688, ordered the next Fair to be held "at the Center," now the site of the New Public Buildings. The location was thought by many people to be too far out of town. A number of persons having signed and circulated some printed strictures on the action of the Council, were summoned to appear before that body, and on doing so, were reproved and graciously pardoned. The Council two days later, to show, no doubt, their appreciation of the "Contemptuous Printing paper," ordered an "Additional Fayr to be kept at Philadelphia, at ye Center." Colonial Records, Vol. I, 218, 224, 226.

BRADFORD. (W.) Proposals for the Printing of a large Bible, | by William Bradford. | [*Philadelphia: William Bradford.* 1688.] Folio, 1 leaf.   H. S. P.   9

The only known copy of this sheet has a curious history. It has been used, by some early binder, Bradford himself perhaps, as the inner lining of the cover of a quarto volume. Here about 1843, it was discovered by Mr. Nathan Kite, who succeeded in removing it almost uninjured. While he lived, Mr. Kite treasured this relic of Bradford's enterprising spirit, above all his other bibliographical possessions. After his death, his widow gave it to a person whom she had employed in moving some of her furniture, in payment, I presume, for his services.

Its new owner left it on exhibition in the Museum, at Independence Hall, for nine years, but finally, in 1883, sold it to the Historical Society of Pennsylvania. It has been reproduced in *facsimile*, and reprinted in Wallace's Commemoration Address.

EATON. (E.) An Almanac for 1688. By Edward Eaton. *Philadelphia: William Bradford.* 1688. 10

Printed by order of the Quarterly Meeting, to take the place of the one by Leeds. No copy is known to be extant. Of the author, it is only known that he was a Friend, and died in Philadelphia, in 1709.

LEEDS. (D.) An Almanac for 1689. By Daniel Leeds. *Philadelphia: William Bradford.* 1688. 11

No copy is known to be extant. Jacob Taylor, in his Almanac for 1706, says: "that unparalleled Plagiary and unreasonable Transcriber, D. Leeds, who hath now for 19 years, with a very large stock of Impudence, filched matter out of other men's works, to furnish his spurious Almanacks." This, and the existence of an Almanac, for the year 1693, is the only evidence I can find of there being an unbroken series of Leeds' Almanacs.

L[EEDS.] (D[ANIEL]) The | Temple of Wisdom | For the Little World, | In Two Parts. | The First Philosophically Divine, treating of | The Being of all Beeings, | And whence everything hath its original, as | Heaven, Hell, Angels, Men and Devils, Earth, | Stars and Elements. | And particularly of all Mysteries concerning the Soul; and | of Adam before and after the Fall. | Also, a Treatise of the four Complexions, with | the Causes of spiritual Sadness, &c. | To which is added, A Postcript to all Students in | Arts and Sciences. | The Second Part, Morally divine, contains | First, Abuses stript and whipt, by Geo. Wither, with his | discription of Fair Virtue. | Secondly. A Collection of divine Poems from Fr. Quarles. | Lastly. Essayes and Religious Meditations of Sir Francis | Bacon Knight. | Collected, Published and intended for a general Good, | By D. L. | *Printed and Sold by William Bradford in Philadelphia,* | *Anno.* 1688. | 12mo. 12

Collation : Title, 1 leaf; Preface, pp. (3); To the Doctors, pp. (3); text, pp. 1-125, (1); Second title, and To the Reader, pp. (2); text, pp. 3-48 ; Third title, 1 leaf; pp. 50-86 ; Errata, 1 leaf.

The postscript to the first part, which occupies the last three pages, is signed "Daniel Leeds."

The second Title reads : Abuses Stript and Whipt, by George Withers. | Treating in a Saterical vein of Man, | with his Passions, namely, | Of Man, 1 | Of Fond Love, 2 | Of Lust, 3 | Of Hate, 4 | Of Envy, 5 | Of Revenge, 6 | Of Chollor, 7 | Of Jealousie, 8 | Of Covetonsness, 9 | Of Ambition, 10 | Of Fear, 11 | Of Despair, 12 | Of Hope, 13 | Of Compassion, 14 | Of Cruelty, 15 | Of Joy, 16 | Of Sorrow, 17 | Conclusion, 18 | As Also | Of Vanity, 2, | Of Inconstancy, 3. Of Weakness, | 4. Of Presumption, &c. | To which is added, | Fair Virtue | The Shepherd's Mistress. | With other Pathetick Poems composed | by G. W. in his Youthful days. | Also, Divine Poems selected from the Works | of Francis Quarle. | The whole concluded with some excellent Essayes, | and Religious Meditations of Sir Francis | Bacon, Knight. | *Philadelphia, Printed and Sold by William Bradford,* | Anno 1688.

The third title reads : Essaies | and | Religious Meditations | Of | Sir Francis Bacon, Knight, | Attorney General to King James | the first. | . . . | . . . | . . . | . . . | . . . | . . . | . . . . | *Printed in the year* 1688. |

Whenever this book has been described, stress is laid upon its containing Bacon's Essays, and the fact that the first part is entirely made up of extracts from the religious vagaries of Jacob Böhm, and more than half of the second part with the forgotten wit (which sent its author to jail) of the youthful days of a round-head thief, is entirely overlooked. That Wither's satires should be selected as a part of the volume is more remarkable than the choice of the common sense of Lord Verulam or the wild speculations of Böhm. The wisdom of the volume is known and recognized to-day ; its folly is perhaps not yet entirely forgotten, but its wit has so passed out of mind that its author was recently mentioned "as perhaps one of the best of the old English poets exhumed by modern literary antiquaries." It has been asserted that the "Temple of Wisdom" was the first *book* printed by Bradford. This honor is now due, if not to Budd's "Good Order," to Penn's "Excellent Privilege of Liberty and Property." There are at least three copies extant, but none of them are in any public institution. Mr. Menzie's copy sold for $190.00, and is now a part of the almost unrivaled collection of early Americana of Mr. Charles H. Kalbfleisch, of New York City.

LETTER from Father La Chaise, Confessor to the French King, to Father Peters, Confessor to the King of England; in which is contained the Project and Design of that Faction to introduce the Prince of Wales. Also a Letter from William Penn to Father LaChaise. *Printed in the City of Philadelphia, in the Land of Promise, by order of Father Penn.* 1688. 4to. 13

The title of this work, which was really printed in England, is from Sabin's Dictionary. I saw a copy for a moment at the Lennox Library, and from its typography was convinced that it never came from Bradford's press. It was probably fabricated by some of Penn's enemies in support of the charge that he was a Roman Catholic.

1689.

BULKELEY. (G.) The People's | Right to Election | Or Alteration of Government in Connecticott, | Argued | In a Letter; | By Gershom Bulkeley Esq; one of their Majesties Justices of the peace | In the County of Hartford. | Together with a Letter to the said Bulkeley, | from a Friend of his in the Bay. | To which is added, The Writing delivered to James Russell of Charlestown | Esq; warning him and others concerned, not to meet to Hold a Court | at Cambridge, within the county of Middlesex. | By Thomas Greaves Esq; Judge of their Majesties Inferior Court of Pleas | and one of their Majesties Justices of the peace within the said County | And also his Answer to Mr. Broadstreete and the Gentlemen mett at the | Town-house in Boston concerning the same. | Published for the Information & Satisfaction of their Majesties loyall | (but abused) Subjects in New England. | *Philadelphia, Printed by Assignes of William Bradford, Anno* 1689. | Sm. 4to. pp. 18.   B. M.   14

Reprinted in the Connecticut Historical Society's Collections, and in the Andros Tracts. For a notice of the author see the latter, and also Colonial Records of Connecticut, Vol. 3, pp. 388–389. An explanation of the imprint will be found in the note to the Frame of Government, *infra* No. 16. Brinley's copy sold for $235.

FOX. (G.)   Religious Papers by George Fox.   *Philadelphia: William Bradford.*   1689.   15

In 1688, Bradford informed the Quarterly Meeting of his having obtained from England, several "Religious Papers, by George Fox," and asked the approval and assistance of the Meeting before printing them. The matter is several times mentioned, for the last time as follows :

"3d of 4th mo. 1689. William Bradford being ordered by the last Monthly Meeting to print George Fox's papers, which is accordingly done, and as many of them remain unsold at amount of seven shillings & 3 d. which the Meeting orders Antho : Morris to pay out of ⸢the Meeting stock. I have been unable to find any trace of this work.

THE FRAME of the Government | of the Province of Pennsil | vania and Territories there- | unto annexed, in America. | [*Philadelphia: William Bradford.* 1689.] Sm. 8vo. pp. 16. F.   16

A careful comparison of this edition with the Charter as printed in the first volume of Colonial Records, shows twenty-nine variations. Twenty-six of these appear to be merely typographical errors. The other three are the omission of the word "Jurisdictions," which appears in the 18th line of page 42, Colonial Records, Vol. 1 ; the omission of the words "officers chosen " in the 39th line of the same page, and the omission of the words " of the Provincial Council," in the 39th line of page 44. The second of these omissions is probably the fundamentally false point to which Blackwell refers. It was printed April 8th, 1689, at the instance of Joseph Growden, and other opponents of the then Governor, John Blackwell, who, supported by a majority of the Provincial Council, was pursuing a line of conduct, which gave rise to the charges, officially denied by the declaration issued 23d of 3d mo. 1689. "That the Governor and some members of the Council had a design or intent to subvert and overturn the frame of Government, and to make voyd the Charter." The Governor on seeing a copy declared "It was high presumption in any man, to promote the publishing of any paper of such concerne without direction, especially for that it was false in as fundamental a point as that was," and, having summoned Bradford to appear before the Council, bound him under £500 penalty not to print anything without a licence. Bradford's account of his examination, in which he boldly asserted the liberty of the press, yet warily avoided committing himself, appears in full in Wallace's Commemorative Address. It was not the first time he had printed the Charter. For, besides the claim he makes of having printed it by Penn's order in England, (presumably the London edition of 1682, which is without a printer's name), he had published it in "Liberty and Property," without exciting any comment. Blackwell no doubt acted under the idea that the Charter had been wilfully distorted in the interest of his opponents.

In addition to the small encouragement in the way of work, Bradford had received since he set up his press, he had now been three times—twice by the Governor and once by the Meeting—taken to task and forbidden to freely follow his trade. His position was more vexatious than it would have been in England, for he found here not only that license he must have, but instead of his "Imprimatur" issuing from Stationers' Hall, the power to grant it was claimed by both the Civil and Religious authorities, the leaders of which were widely at variance. He determined to return to England, applied to the Meeting for a "certificate of removal," and transferred the press to his "assignes," as appears in the imprint of No. 14. He was, however, induced to remain, by the offer of a salary and promise of employment from the Yearly Meeting. The sum offered was £40 per annum. This apparently small stipend becomes a very liberal allowance when compared with the salaries of the Provincial officers. The Chief Justice of the Supreme Court received but £100, the Associate Justice £50, and the Attorney General £60. George Keith's salary as Head Master of the Friends' School was only £50. Just how much business the Meeting was able to "throw in his way," it is impossible to form any definite idea. The four small tracts (Nos. 15, 22, 25 and 30), which are supposed to have been printed by order of the Meeting in 1690 and 1691, would not have afforded him much encouragement. It is most probable that Bradford produced a number of works which have now entirely disappeared.

KEITH. (G.) The | Presbyterian and Independent | Visible Churches | in | New-England | And else-where, | Brought to the Test, and examined accor- | ding to the Doctrine of the holy Scriptures, | in their Doctrine, Ministry, Worship, Consti- | tution, Government, Sacraments and Sabbath | Day, and found to be No True Church of | Christ. | More particularly directed to these in New-Eng- | land, and more generally to those in Old- | England,, Scotland, Ireland, &c. | With | A Call and Warning from the Lord to the People | of Boston and New-England, to Repent, &c. And two | Letters to the Preachers in Boston; and an Answer to the | gross Abuses, Lyes and Slanders of Increase Mather and | Samuel Norton, &c. | By George Keith. | *Philadelphia, Printed and Sold by Will. Bradford*, | *Anno* 1689. | Sm. 8vo.   H. S. P.   17

Collation : Preliminary leaf, *recto* blank, *verso* 5 verses from Revelations ; Title, 1 leaf; A Friendly Epistle, pp. (7); Errata, 1 page ; text, pp. 1-215 ; Post-script ; pp. 215-232.

This work, although written while the author was a member of the Society of Friends, was expressed in such a tone as to cause the Rev. Thomas Barton, an Episcopal Missionary in Central Pennsylvania, to write to the Society for the Propagation of the Gospel, in 1766, that he "often wished that Keith's Presby-terian and Independent Churches brought to the test, could be sent over to every mission." It was answered by Cotton Mather, James Allen, Joshua Moodey and Samuel Willard in "The Principles of the Protestant Religion Main-tained." It was reprinted in London in 1691. Menzies' copy sold for $25 ; Brinley's for $41.

LEEDS. (D.) An Almanac for 1690. By Daniel Leeds. *Phila-delphia: William Bradford.* 1689.   18

No copy is known to be extant.

[PALMER. (JOHN)] .The | Present State of | New-England | Impartially Considered, | In a Letter to the Clergy. | [n. p. n. d.] 4to. pp. 44.   c.   19

The Brinley Catalogue suggests that this tract was printed by Bradford. The copy there described sold for $52.50, and is now in the Library of Congress, where I made a careful examination, and after comparing it with other specimens of Bradford's press, I arrived at the conclusion that it was not printed by Brad-ford. Most of the "letter" is not unlike some of Bradford's, but there is at least one line of type which I never met in any other specimen of his press. Sabin (Dictionary, No. 46,722) erroneously ascribes the authorship to Increase Mather, and gives London as the place of publication. It was an answer to Increase Math-er's "Present State of New English Affairs," and the London edition, printed in 1690 and reprinted in the Andros Tracts, says on the title page, "By John Palmer."

1690.

THE CHRISTIANITY of the Quakers Asserted. *Printed by William Bradford at Philadelphia*, 1690.   20

This title is given as it appears in the Sale Catalogue of Samuel Hazard's library, Lot No. 857. It is no doubt the following tract, described by Joseph Smith, II. p. 454:

"The Christianity of the People commonly called Quakers, asserted by them, against the Unjust charge of their being no Christians, upon several Questions relating to those matters, wherein their Christian belief is questioned. [n. p. 1689?] Folio, pp. (2)."

K[EITH.] (G[EORGE]) A Plain Short | Catechism | for | Children & Youth, | That may be Serviceable to such Others | who need to be instructed in the First Prin- | ciples and Grounds of the | Christian Religion. | To which is added, | A short Paraphrase or Opening, by way | of Meditation on that Prayer which our | Lord Jesus Christ taught his Disciples, com- | monly call'd, The Lord's Prayer. | By G. K. | . . . | . . . | . . . | . . . | . . . | . . . | . . . | . . . . | *Printed and sold by William Bradford at Phila-* | *delphia in Pennsilvania*, 1690. | Sm. 8vo. Title, 1 leaf; Friendly Epistle to the Reader, pp. (4); Catechism, pp. 1-48.   D.   21

KEITH. The Pretended | Antidote | Proved | Poyson: | Or, The true Principles of the Christian | & Protestant Religion Defended, | And the Four Counterfit Defenders | thereof Detected and Discovered; the | names of which are James Allen, Joshua | Moodey, Samuell Willard and Cotton Mather, | who call themselves Ministers of the Gospel | in Boston, in their pretended Answer to my | Book, called, The Presbyterian & Independent | Visible Churches in New-England, and else- | where, brought to the Test, &c. And G. K. | cleared not to be guilty of any Calumnies | against these called Teachers of New-Eng- | land, &c. | By George Keith. | With an Appendix by John Delavall, by way of Animadversion on some Passages in a | Discourse of Cotton Mathers before the ge- | neral Court of Massachusets, the 28th of the | Third Moneth, 1690. | *Philadelphia, Printed by Will. Bradford*, 1690. | Sm. 8vo. pp. (2), 224.   H. S. P.   22

In answer to "The Principles of the Protestant Religion maintained," (see *supra* No. 17, note). It is a plain, forcible, but not intemperate piece of argument. The style is generally clear, and the quotations show an intimate acquaintance with ancient and modern theological and metaphysical writers. Delaval's Appendix is in answer to Cotton Mather's "The Serviceable Man," (see Sabin's Dictionary, No. 46,504). On page 129 occur two words in Greek type—the first I have found in any of Bradford's works. Some of Keith's expressions and illustrations are very quaint. The reasons put forth by the Boston clergymen for refusing a "public dispute" with him, are called "Fig-leaf Reasons." In the Introduction Keith says, "How many Presbyterians have highly commended the Women for throwing their stools at the Bishop reading Common Prayer, in Edinburgh, in Scotland, above fifty years ago, and judged it a noble and heroical act, and some have imputed it to a divine motion." Further on he says (p. 67), "No Rhymes were sung, that I can understand, by the French Protestants in french, till Beza composed them, and translated the Psalms into french metre, and so they were sung at Geneva, hence they were called Geneva Jigs." Menzies' copy sold for $24.

KEITH. A | Refutation | of | Three Opposers of Truth, | By plain Evidence of the holy Scriptures, | viz. | I. Of Pardon Tillinghast, who pleadeth for Water-Baptism, | its being a Gospel-Precept, and opposeth Christ within, as a false | Christ. To which is added, something concerning the Supper, &c. | II. Of B. Keach, in his Book called, A Tutor for Children, | where he disputeth against the Sufficiency of the Light within, in | order to Salvation, and called Christ in the heart, A false Christ | in the secret Chamber. | III. Of Cotton Mather, who in his Appendix to his Book, | called, Memorable Providences, relating to Witchcrafts, &c. doth so | weakly defend his Father Increase Mather from being justly charge- | able with abusing the honest People called Quakers, that he doth | the more lay open his Fathers Nakedness; and besides the Abuses | and Injuries that his Father had cast upon that People, C. Mather, | the Son, addeth New Abuses of his own. | And a few Words of a Letter to John Cotton, called a Minister, | at Plymouth in New England. | By George Keith. | . . . | . . . . | *Philadelphia, Printed and Sold by William Bradford,* | *Anno* 1690. | Sq. 8vo. Title, 1 leaf; pp. 1-73.　　A. A. S.　23

LEEDS. (D.) An Almanac for 1691. By Daniel Leeds. *Philadelphia: William Bradford.* 1690.　　　　　　　　24

No copy is known to be extant.

WILSFORD. (JOHN) An Epistle for General Service. *Philadelphia: William Bradford.* 1690. 25

For a notice of the author, see "The Friend," Vol. 28, pp. 405 *et seq.* This Epistle was printed by order of the Philadelphia Meeting, but I have not been able to find a copy.

1691.

LEEDS. (D.) An Almanac for 1692. By Daniel Leeds. *Philadelphia: William Bradford.* 1691. 26

A | MEMORIAL | between | Jest and Earnest, | From Ignoramus the First, Relating to the | Past and Present State of the Nation. | Presented to all the Honest Ignoramusses of the Lords and Commons of | England. | . . . | . . . . | *At Philadelphia, Printed by Philaletes for the Author.* 1691. | 4to. pp. 7. H. S. P. 27

A Whig tract, relating solely to English politics. It was printed in London.

A MODEST and Impartial | Narrative | Of several Grievances and | Great Oppressions | That the Peaceable and most Considerable Inhabitants | of | Their Majesties Province | of | New-York | in | America | Lie Under, | By the Extravagant and Arbitrary Pro- | ceedings of Jacob Leysler and his | Accomplices. | [*Philadelphia: William Bradford.* 1691.] 4to. pp. 42. N. J. 28

"Dated in New York this 21st. of January, Annoq. Domini 1690," that is 1690–1. Mr. Sabin says it was published at "New York, 1690." It is hardly necessary to remark that the press was not in operation there till 1693. I follow the opinion of John Wm. Wallace, Esq., who had examined the only known copy, in ascribing it to Bradford's press.

WHITEHEAD. (G.) A | Christian Epistle | to | Friends | In General | Of weighty Concern, for their present | and future Peace and Safety from the Soul's | Adversary's subtil Devices and Snares of | Death. | To be carefully Communicated to the Children | of Light, & Professors thereof every where. | Being faithfully given forth, and Recommended from the | Spirit of Christ; By his Servant, | George Whitehead. | . . . | . . . | . . . . | *Printed and Sold by William Bradford at Philadelphia,* 1691. | Sq. 8vo. pp. 15. (1). H. S. P. 29

First printed in London, 1689. The last page contains a list of "Books sold by W. Bradford in Philadelphia." Mr. Brinley's copy sold for $24.

WILSFORD. (J.) A Brief | Exhortation | To all who profess the Truth, | To come clear out of Babylon, and not to joyn with any hurtful | or unseemly Practice, nor make Marriages with Unbelievers, | but be a separate People from every Unclean thing, that | God may receive you. | [_Philadelphia: William Bradford._ 1691.] Sm. 4to. pp. 11.   F. 30

Besides inveighing against Friends marrying out of Meeting, Wilsford was troubled about the "Custom of making great Feasts at Weddings;" "using those immodest Actions of taking the Bride's Garters and Shoestrings," "and shewing of folly in getting them to Bed." He was also troubled about the observance of Christmas and Saint Days. The exhortation, which is dated the "25th of the 1st Moneth, 1691," is followed on page 7 by "A short Testimony for the good Order of Truth, as it is esta- | blished and practiced amongst the People, called Quakers, | shewing how by degrees the Lord in his love led us into it : | Written partly for the opening the Understanding of the weak | and honest hearted, and for convincing of Opposers and | Gainsayers." | It is re-printed in "The Friend," Vol. 28.

1692.

ANTI-CHRIST and Sadducee.   _Philadelphia: W. Bradford._ 1692.   31

Title from Westcott's History of Philadelphia, Chapter LII. This cannot be other than "The Anti-Christs and Sadducees detected among a sort of Quakers ; or Caleb Pusie of Pennsylvania, and John Pennington ; with his Brethren . . . . proved Anti-Christs and Sadducees out of a Printed book lately published by them, falsely called, A modest Account of the principal Differences in point of Doctrine, betwixt George Keith, and those of the People called Quakers in Pensilvania, &c. By George Keith." London. [n. d.] Pusey's book was first printed in London, 1696 ; consequently Keith's reply could not have been printed in Philadelphia.

BLOOD WILL OUT, or an Example of Justice in the Tryal, Condemnation, Confession and Execution of Thomas Southerland, who barbarously Murthered John Clark, of Philadelphia Trader; and was executed at Salem in West-Jersey the 23 February 169$\frac{1}{2}$. _Philadelphia: Printed and Sold by William Bradford._ 1692. 4to. pp. 20.   32

This title is from Watson's MSS. Annals in the Library of the Historical Society of Pennsylvania. It was "the first case of this nature happening in this part of the country." Southerland's confused and contradictory testimony before the Coroner led to his commitment. He was tried before two Justices of the Peace and a jury of 52 persons. There were no witnesses *against* him, nor does he appear to have had the services of counsel for his defense. He confessed having robbed Clark, but said he was with his wife on the night of the murder. She being examined apart testified that he did not come home till early on the following morning. He then declared he had been out in a canoe and landed at a certain time and place where many of the jury had been at the hour named by him without of course seeing him. John F. Watson had met with a copy, and J. R. Smith, of London, in his catalogue No. 52, offers a copy for 7 s. 6 d.

[BUDD. (THOMAS)] A brief Answer to two Papers procured | from Friends in Maryland, the one con- | cerning Thomas Budds favoring John | Lynam, &c. the other concerning his | owning George Keith's Principles and | Doctrine. | [Colophon.] *Printed [by William Bradford] in the Year* 1692. | Sm. 4to. pp. 4.   D.   33

[BUDD.] A | Just Rebuke | to several | Calumnies, Lyes & Slanders | Reported against Thomas Budd. | [*Philadelphia: William Bradford.* 1692.] Sq. 8vo. pp. 6.   H. S. P.   34

In this tract Budd gives a statement of the Keithian doctrines, and recites various stories circulated concerning himself. Two of these, with extracts from his answers are as follows: It was reported "That I did weep so much at a meeting as to wet Two Handkerchiefs of three Quarters of a yard each, and all in deceit. To which I say, this is a great Lye." "It was reported by Arthur Cook that I struck him on the face in the public Meeting in Philadelphia. This is to signifie to all who are desirous to know the truth of the matter . . . that while G. K. was declaring I stept between G. K. and him to keep him off from staring him in the face, but Arthur pressing to get close to G. K. I stood in his way, and Arthur said *Wilt thou* push me? *No* said I, *but I think to stand in the way, and not let thee come close to him,* and withal in a familiar way, I did gently stroke his face, as a nurse would do a sucking child . . . intending no hurt."

CRISP. (S.) A Faithful | Warning & Exhortation | to | Friends | To Beware of | Seducing Spirits, | And to keep on the Armour of Light, in | Sincerity and Simplicity, as their best Armour | in all | Tryals | Written by a Lover of Sincerity, and Traveller for Sion's Re- | demption, and for the Removing of all Oppressions from off the | Souls of them who have believed, | Stephen Crisp. | *Reprinted and Sold by William Bradford at Philadelphia in* | *Pennsilvania, in the Year* 1692. | Sq. 8vo. pp. 20.   35

First printed in London, 1684.

CRISP. An | Epistle | of | Tender Love | and | Brotherly Advice | To All the | Churches of Christ | Throughout the World. | Who are gathered into the one living Faith | and walk in the Light, and therein have their | Fellowship one with another. | From a Friend and Brother in the same Fellowship, who hath | long Travailed, and still Travails for Zions Prosperity, | and for the gathering of Zions Children out of Ægypt and | Darkness, that they may walk and dwell in the Light of Zions | Saviour, which is Christ, the Lord, Whose Outward | Name is, | Stephen Crisp, | *Re-Printed and Sold by William Bradford at Philadelphia in* | *Pennsilvania, in the Year* 1692. | Sq. 8vo. pp. 15.   H. S. P.   36

First printed in London in 1690, and reprinted there as lately as 1848.

AN | EXPOSTULATION | with | Thomas Lloyd, Samuell Jenings, | And the rest of the | Twenty eight Unjust Judges and Signers | of the Paper of Condemnation against | George Keith | And the rest of his Friends. And | Complaint | for a | Public Hearing | and | Tryal | Before all Impartial People. | [*Philadelphia: William Bradford.* 1692.] Sq. 8vo. pp. 7, (1).   H.   37

Reprinted in "The Judgment given forth by Twenty-eight Quakers." London : 1694, and as the second of the "two Answers," in "A true Copy ;" &c., *infra* No. 51. Morgan Edwards in a list of tracts on the Keithian controversy, mentions a "Second Expostulation," referring, no doubt, not to a separate tract, but to this, as found in the last mentioned reprint, calling it "second" to distinguish it from the first of the "two Answers." It contains a curious collection of eight epithets applied by Keith to his opponents, and of twenty-five applied by them to him. Among the former are such terms as Fools, Rotten Ranters, &c., and among the latter, Teller of an Old St. Andrew's Story, Pope, Father Confessor, Lyer, Devil, Wolf, Tyger, Foaming out his own shame, &c. The contents of the last page is the same as in "A true Copy," &c. Murphy's copy sold for $83.

FRAME. (R.) A Short | Description | of | Pennsilvania, | Or, A Relation What things are known, | enjoyed, and like to be discovered in | in [*sic*] the said Province. | Presented (?) as a Token of Good Will to, the | [People?] of England. | By Richard Frame. | *Printed and Sold by William Bradford in* | *Philadelphia,* 1692. | Sq. 8vo. pp. 8.   L. C. P.   38

Mr. S. J. Hamilton reprinted 118 copies, nearly in *facsimile*, with an introduction by Horatio Gates Jones. The reprint, which is now rare, has the following title :

A Short | Description of Pennsilvania. | By Richard Frame. | Re-printed from the supposed unique copy | in the | Philadelphia Library. | [Colophon] | Oakwood Press. | MDCCCLXVII. | 4to. pp. (2), viii, 8.

[KEITH. (George)] An Appeal from the twenty-eight Judges to the Spirit of Truth and true Judg- | ment in all faithful Friends called Quakers that meet at this Yearly Meeting at Burlington, 7 mo. 1692. | *Philadelphia: William Bradford.* 1692. | Folio, 1 leaf.   F. 39

The first edition was a broadside printed in two columns. Keith having been condemned by a meeting of "Public Friends" or ministers and forbidden to preach in meeting, was told by Thomas Lloyd, "if thou thinkest thyself aggrieved by that judgment, thou may appeal to the Yearly Meeting, which is now approaching." Keith accordingly drew up an appeal, in which he "proposed twelve particular heads to be considered," by the Meeting. This having been printed and two copies having' been disposed of by John McComb, a tavern keeper ; he and Bradford were arrested and indicted for publishing and uttering a "Malicious and Seditious Paper." Part of Bradford's types and stock of paper and books were seized, McComb's tavern license was revoked and both men were committed to jail for trial. The trial was postponed first until the October session, and then to the December sitting of the Court. Meantime the prisoners remained in jail, the jailor, however, was so kind as to let McComb "go home an hour or two sometimes in an evening after it was dark." In December Bradford was tried, the jury, however, disagreed and he was remanded until the next session, but in the interval the government changed and the prosecution dropped. McComb, as far as is known, was never brought to trial. In the course of Bradford's trial the Prosecution put the *form* as proof before the jury. "Unable, however, to read the matter from the types, without looking at them closely, the foreman began to pass the *chase* along the panel. Of a sudden the *quoins* got loose and the mass of type fell through a pile of indecipherable *pi*."

[KEITH.] An Appeal from the Twenty eight | Judges, to the Spirit of Truth and true | Judgment in all faithful Friends, called | Quakers, that meet at this Yearly Meeting | at Burlington, the 7 Month, 1692. | [*Philadelphia: William Bradford.* 1692.] Sq. 8vo. pp. 8.   H. S. P. 40

This was the second edition. Besides the display of the title, it differs from the third edition only in the first line of the Postscript. In this it reads "By a Warrant signed by Anthony Morris & Rob. Ewer Justices, the Constable ;" and in the other it is "By a warrant signed by Sam. Richardson & Rob. Ewer, Justices, the Sheriff." In a note to "A true copy of three judgments," Bradford says, of the Appeal, "there happen'd an Error in the Postscript, which pray amend, viz. line 1, for Anthony Morris read Sam. Richardson." It was reprinted in "The Judgment given forth by Twenty-eight Quakers, London : 1694."

[KEITH.]   An Appeal from the Twenty Eight | Judges | to the | Spirit of Truth & true Judgment | In all Faithful Friends, called Quakers, that meet at this Yearly | Meeting at Burlington, the 7 Month, 1692. | [*Philadelphia: William Bradford.* 1692.] Sq. 8vo. pp. 8.   H. S. P.   41

The third edition, in which the error in the first line of the Postscript noted at the end of " A True Copy of Three Judgments " is corrected by the substitution of the name of Samuel Richardson for Anthony Morris, as one of the Justices who issued the warrant against Bradford.

[KEITH.] The | Christian Faith | Of the People of God, called in Scorn, | Quakers | In Rhode-Island (who are in Unity with all faithfull Brethren | of the same Profession in all parts of the World) | Vindicated | From the Calumnies of Christian Lodowick, that formerly | was of that Profession, but is lately, fallen therefrom. | As also from the base Forgeries, and wicked Slanders of | Cotton Mather, called a Minister, at Boston, who hath greatly | commended the said Christian Lodowick, and approved his false | Charges against us, and hath added thereunto many gross, | impudent and vile Calumnies against us and our Brethren, in his | late Address, so called, to some in New-England, the which in | due time may receive a more full answer, to discover his Igno- | rance, Prejudice and Perversion against our Friends in gene- | ral, and G.[eorge] K.[eith] in particular, whom he hath most unworthily | abused. | To which is added, some Testimonies of our Antient | Friends to the true Christ of God; Collected out of their print- | ed Books, for the further Convincing of our Opposers, that it | is (and hath been) our constant and firm Belief to expect Salva- | tion by the Man Christ Jesus that was outwardly crucified without | the Gates of Jerusalem. | *Printed and Sold by William Bradford at Philadelphia in Pennsyl-* | *vania, in the Year* 1692. | Sq. 8vo. pp. 16.   H. S. P.   42

This is a continuation of the controversy with the New England Divines, but it was also the beginning of the Keithian controversy in print.   One of the points at variance between Keith and other Quakers of the Philadelphia Yearly Meeting, was the adoption of a Confession of Faith.   Keith was impressed with the necessity of so doing and had prepared and submitted a form, which was not approved of by the Meeting.   He succeeded, however, in inducing the Rhode

Island Friends to adopt his Confession of Faith, and on his return to Philadelphia, had it printed. Upon its appearance a special sitting of the Monthly Meeting was held at the house of Samuel Carpenter, by which the tract was condemned and Bradford censured for printing it. On this occasion, Keith says in defence of Bradford, that "he was warranted to print by the Monthly Meeting of Rhode Island, which hath as much authority to print without them, as they here have to print without those, unless they here will say, that Philadelphia is the Church of Rome in America, as Samuel Jenings called it the Metropolitan." The reverse of the title contains an abstract of the principles asserted in the six pages immediately following ; and the rest of the tract is taken up with "Testimonies of our Ancient Friends," "Faithfully collected by W. Bradford." Reprinted in More Divisions amongst the Quakers. London. 1693. Menzies' copy sold for $21 ; Brinley's for $30.

KEITH. A Counter Testimonial, Signed by Seventy-eight Persons, disavowing all those concerned in the denial of George Keith. Written by George Keith, A. D. 1692. *Philadelphia: Printed by William Bradford*. 1692. 4to. pp. 4.   43

This title is from Sabin's Dictionary No. 37,188, and is probably inaccurate. It was reprinted in "The Judgment given forth by Twenty Eight Quakers," London : 1694, but with the names of seventy instead of seventy-eight signers.

[KEITH.] A | Discovery | of the | Mystery of Iniquity & Hypocrisie | Acting and Ruling in Hugh Derborough. | [*Philadelphia: William Bradford*. 1692.] Sm. 4to. pp. 12.   B. 44

Reprinted in "More Divisions among the Quakers." London. 1693.

KEITH. The False Judgment of a Yearly Meeting of Quakers in Maryland, condemned by George Keith, Thomas Budd, and other Quakers. To which is added a Discovery of this Mystery of Iniquity. By George Keith. [*Philadelphia: William Bradford*. 1692.] 4to. pp. 24.   45

Sabin No. 37,194 ; probably an inaccurate description of No. 54, *infra*.

[KEITH.] The Fundamental Truths of Christianity | briefly hinted at, by way of Question | and Answer. | [Colophon.] *Printed at London in the Year* 1688. *and Re-printed at Philadelphia* | *by William Bradford, in the Year* 1692. | Sq. 8vo. pp. 8.   F. 46

For the third edition see "Some of the Fundamental Truths," see No. 48, *infra*.

KEITH.   A | Serious Appeal | To all the more Sober, Impar-
tial & Judicious People | in | New-England | To whose hands
this may come, | Whether Cotton Mather in his late Address &c.
hath not | extreamly failed in proving the People call'd Quakers
guilty | of manifold Heresies, Blasphemies, and strong Delusions,
| and whether he hath not much rather proved himself ex-
| treamly Ignorant and greatly possessed with a Spirit of | Per-
version, Error, Prejudice and envious Zeal against them | in
general, and G. K. in particular, in his most uncharit- | able and
rash Judgment against him. | Together with a Vindication of our
Christian Faith | In those Things Sincerely Believed by us es-
pecially respect- | ing the Fundamental Doctrines and Principles of
| Christian Religion. | By George Keith. | *Printed and Sold by*
William Bradford at Philadelphia in Pennsyl- | *vania, in the Year*
1692. | Sm. 4to. pp. (4), 67.   H.   47

In answer to Mathers' "Little Flocks guarded against Grievous Wolves."
Boston : 1691.   Menzies' copy sold for $22 ; Murphy's for $100.

[KEITH.]   Some of the | Fundamental Truths | of | Christi-
anity. | Briefly hinted at, by way of Question and Answer. | With
a Postscript by the Author G. K.   The 3d Edition. | [*Philadelphia:*
William Bradford.   1692.]   Sq. 8vo. pp. 15, (1).   c.   48

At the end is a list of "Books lately Printed and to be Sold by William Bradford in Philadelphia, 1692."

[KEITH.]   Some | Reasons and Causes | of the | Late Separa-
tion | that hath come to pass at Philadelphia be- | twixt us, called
by some the Seperate Meeting, | And Others that meet apart from
us.   More particularly opened to Vindicate and Clear us | and
our Testimony in that respect, viz. That the Sepe- | ration lyeth at
their Door, and They (and not We) are | justly chargeable with it.
| With | An Account of our Sincere Christian | Faith. | . . . |
. . . | . . . | . . . | . . . | . . . | . . . | . . . | . . . | . . . |
. . . . | [*Philadelphia: William Bradford.*   1692.]   Sq. 8vo. pp·
36.   H. S. P.   49

The second tract published on the Keithian Schism.   It begins on the reverse
of the title page with "An Apology for the present Publication of these Things."
This is followed on page 8 by "Some Reasons and Causes of the late Separation

here at Philadelphia." This includes a copy of a condemnation of Thomas Fitzwater and William Stockdale, and an endorsement of "The Christian Faith of the Quakers in Rhode Island," which Keith and his followers had passed at what they called an Adjourned Monthly Meeting, and concludes on page 19 with a list of the signers of these "Judgments ; " in which one of the names has been obliterated by stamping it over with ink from a three-*em* quad. A Postscript beginning on page 20, is followed on page 23 by "Some Testimonies taken out of R. Barclay's Book, called, The Anarchy of the Ranters." This extends to the middle of page 26, the rest of which, and pages 27 and 28, are devoted to account of Keith's efforts towards a reconciliation. The rest of the tract (pp. 29–36) is filled with "An account of the Sincere Christian Faith of some of the faithful people, called in scorn, Quakers, in Pennsilvania, etc." It is temperate in tone and refers to Keith's opponents by the initials of their first names only. Reprinted in "A Farther Account of the Great Divisions among the Quakers in Pensilvania," London. 1693. Brinley's copy sold for $50.

KEITH. A | Testimony | against that | False & Absurd Opinion | Which some Hold, Viz. | That all True Believers and Saints immediately after the Bodily | Death attain to all the Resurrection they expect, and enter | into the fullest Enjoyment of Happiness. | And also | That the Wicked, immediately after Death, are raised up to receive | all the Punishment they are to expect. | Together with a Scriptural Account of the Resur- | rection of the Dead, Day of Judgment, and Christ's last | Coming and Appearance without us. Also, Where, and | What those Heavens are into which the Man Christ is | gone, and entered into. | By George Keith. | [*Philadelphia: William Bradford.* 1692.] Sq. 8vo. pp. 12.   H. S. P.   50

Reprinted as "The Christian Quaker, or George Keith's Eyes opened." London. 1693.

[KEITH.] A true Copy of three Judgments given | forth by a Party of Men, called Quakers | at Philadelphia, against George Keith and | his Friends. With two Answers to the | Said Judgments. | [*Philadelphia: William Bradford.* 1692.] Sq. 8vo. pp. 15, (1).   H. S. P.   51

This tract contains the judgment of the Philadelphia Monthly Meeting in favor of Thomas Fitzwater ; the mild condemnation of William Stockdale by the Meeting of Public Friends, on charges brought against him by Keith ; and the Condemnation and Disownment of Keith by the last named meeting. These, with the title, occupy six pages, four of which are filled by the "Judgment" against Keith. The two replies, the second of which was also printed separately, see No. 37, *supra*, occupy the remainder of the fifteen pages, and the last page contains besides a list of "Books to be Sold by William Bradford in Philadelphia, 1692 ;" the errata noticed under the third edition of "The Appeal from the Twenty eight Judges," and the following : "And whereas it is reported, That the Printer being a favourer of G. K. he will not print for any other, which is the reason that the other Party appear not in Print as well as G. K. These are to signifie, that the Printer hath not yet refused to print any thing for either Party ; and also signifies that he doth not refuse, but is willing and ready to print any thing for the future that G. K's Opposers shall bring to him." Reprinted in "The Judgment given forth by Twenty-eight Quakers." London. 1694. Menzies' copy sold for $19 ; Brinley's for $54.

KEITH. Truth and Innocency | Defended | against | Calumny and Defamation, | In a late Report spread abroad concerning the | Revolution | of | Humane Souls, | With a further Clearing of the Truth, by a | plain Explication of my Sence, &c. | By George Keith. | [*Philadelphia: William Bradford*. 1692. Sq. 8vo. pp. 20.   H. S. P. 52

[KEITH.] A | Vision | Concerning the | Mischievous Seperation | among | Friends | in | Old England. | *Printed and Sold by Will. Bradford at Philadelphia*, 1692. | Sq. 8vo. pp. 7.

H. S. P. 53

"A Vision," &c., signed G. F. occupies two pages, and the rest of the tract is taken up with " A General Epistle against Seperation." " Collected and arranged under this false title," says Joseph Smith, " by George Keith, for an evil purpose, to pass off as George Fox's." Brinley's copy sold for $35.

[KEITH, (GEORGE) AND BUDD. (THOMAS)] False Judgments Reprehended: | And a | Just Reproof to Tho. Everndon, | And his Associates and Fellow-Travellers. | For the False and rash Judgment T. E. gave against G. K. and | his faithful Friends and Brethren, at the publick Meeting | at Philadelphia, the 27. of 10. Mon. 1692. And also for | their bringing with them their Paquet of Letters (Saul-like to Damascus) containing the false judgment of a Faction | of men, calling themselves the Yearly-Meeting at Tredaven | in Maryland the 4 of 8. Mon. 92. And another false Judg- | ment contained in another Letter from William Richardson, | All which will return upon their own heads. | [*Philadelphia: William Bradford*. 1692.] Sq. 8vo. pp. 8.   c. 54

[KEITH, AND BUDD.]   The | Plea of the Innocent | Against The | False Judgment | of the | Guilty | Being a Vindication of George Keith and his | Friends, who are joyned with him in this present | Testimony, from the False Judgment, Calumnies, False | Informations and Defamations of Samuell Jenings, John | Simcock, Thomas Lloyd, and others joyned with them, be- | ing in Number Twenty Eight. | Directed by way of Epistle to faithful Friends of Truth in | Pennsilvania, East and West-Jarsey, and else-where, | as Occasion requireth. | . . . | . . . | . . . | . . . | . . . | . . . | . . . | . . . | . . . . | [*Philadelphia: William Bradford*. 1692.]   Sq. 8vo. pp. 24.   H. S. P.   55

This tract was the joint production of Keith and Budd, and was a more elaborate answer to the Testimony published against Keith by the "Meeting of Public Friends," than the "Appeal from the Twenty-eight Judges." The authors were indicted, tried and fined £5 each for publishing it. (See New England's Spirit of Persecution &c., No. 64, *infra*.) As a part of the controversy it is of the highest importance and it seems to me, supposing the expressions therein assigned to individuals, to be correctly reported that the sentiments expressed by some and at least tacitly approved by a majority of the Quakers of the period, may have justified him in saying, from a Trinitarian point of view, that "More damnable Heresies and Errors were cloaked among the Quakers here than in any Protestant Society in Christendom." It would also seem that the Quaker Meeting of the time countenanced the most puerile questions : For instance, Keith says John Simcock inquired of the Meeting "Did Christ's *bones* rise?" And again, Keith having asserted that "God was present in all His Creatures, even Grass, Herbs, &c." a dispute arose, "Whether God be present in Lice?" Keith says Samuel Jenings called him a "Brat of Babylon." Quere, considering the title (the fourth on page 657, Vol. I. of Smith's Catalogue of Friends' Books) of one of George Fox's books, is this a Quaker rendering of the epithet, which an eminent English writer says is in common use in America, and which he renders for the benefit of ears polite as "the son of a lady dog?" Reprinted in London as "An Account of the Great Divisions amongst the Quakers in Pennsylvania."

NEW HUSBANDRY to New-England, or an Experienced way to raise Quick Hedges and Clover Grass, and the way to make Syder.   *Philadelphia: William Bradford*. 1692.   56

Advertised at the end of "A true Copy of three Judgments."

TO THE | REPRESENTATIVES | of the | Free-Men | Of This Province of | Pennsilvania | And Counties Annexed, | In Assembly Conven'd at Philadelphia the 10th of | the 3d Moneth, 1692. | [*Philadelphia: William Bradford*. 1692.] Folio, pp. 4.   57

A petition against the proposed levy of a tax of 1d. per Pound and 2s. per Head. Signed by about 250 persons.

[WILLARD. (Rev. Samuel)] Some Miscellany | Observations | On our present Debates respecting | Witchcrafts, in a Dialogue | Between S. & B. | By P. E. and J. A. | *Philadelphia, Printed by William Bradford, for Hezekiah Usher,* | 1692. | Sq. 8vo. pp. 16.   M. 58

Reprinted in *facsimile.*

1693.

CLAYPOOLE. (J.) The Spirit of the Hat. By James Claypoole. *Philadelphia: William Bradford.* 1693.   59

Title from Westcott's History of Philadelphia, Chap. LII.

A | CONFESSION of Faith, | In the most Necessary Things of | Christian Doctrine, Faith and | Practice. | According to the Testimony of Holy | Scriptures. | Given forth from the Yearly Meeting at | Burlington the 7th of 7th Moneth, 1692. | by the despised Christian People, called | Quakers. | *Printed and Sold by William Bradford in* | *Philadelphia,* 1693. | Sm. 8vo. Title, 1 leaf; pp. 1–21.   H. S. P. 60

This is the 2nd edition of the Confession of Faith of the Keithian Quakers. A note at the end states that it "hath the Scripture places more truly printed, with the addition of divers others not in the former." Brinley's copy sold for $50.

AN EXHORTATION & Caution | To | Friends | Concerning buying or keeping of Negroes. | [*New York: William Bradford.* 1693.] 4to. pp. 6.   D. 61

"Given forth by our Monthly Meeting in Philadelphia, the 13th day of the 8th Month, 1693, and recommended to all our Friends and Brethren, who are one with us in our Testimony for the Lord Jesus Christ, and all others professing Christianity." In 1688 the settlers of Germantown, to the successive embarrassment of a Monthly, Quarterly and Yearly Meeting, presented a written protest against slavery, which was finally disposed of by the last as "not so proper for this meeting to give a Positive Judgment, It having so general a relation to many other parts, and, therefore, at present they forbore it." It remained for the Philadelphia Meeting of Keithian Quakers, to put forth, in this "Exhortation," the first protest against slavery printed in America. Joseph Smith in his Catalogue of Friends' Books, describes it as having been printed at Philadelphia ; but as Bradford removed to New York about June, 1693, and the "Exhortation" was not "given forth" by the Meeting till October 13th, it must have been printed in New York.

[KEITH. (George)] The | Heresie and Hatred | Which was falsly Charged upon the | Innocent | Justly returned upon the | Guilty. | Giving some brief and impartial Account of the most ma- | terial Passages of a late Dispute in Writing, that hath | passed at Philadelphia betwixt | John Delavall and George Keith, | With some intermixt Remarks and Observations on | the whole. | *Printed and Sold by William Bradford at Philadelphia,* | *Anno Dom.* 1603. | Sq. 8vo. pp. 22, (1).   H. S. P.   62

This is the last of the controversy printed in Philadelphia, and in it Keith says "Notwithstanding the many tedious and vexatious Disputes and Controversies that have been among us of late concerning Doctrines and Principles of Religion, one Party affirming, and the other denying, yet at other times in publick, Thomas Lloyd and Party, have endeavoured to cast a mist before the people to make them believe, that there is no difference in Doctrine betwixt them and George Keith. But on the 11th of the 10th month, 1692 in the Publick Meeting at Philadelphia before several Hundred People, John Delavall silenced that pretence, by accusing me of being guilty of Works of the Flesh, in two particulars, viz. Heresie and Hatred." And he "did further accuse me, That my Heresie and Error was in a Fundamental Doctrine of the Quakers, in saying, The Light within is not sufficient without something else." Keith seems to have made a cautious reply in the meeting and to have endeavored to obtain the charge in writing. Failing in this he at length wrote to Delaval that the logical meaning of the charge brought against him was a denial of the divinity of Christ. To this Delaval replied "that neither he nor his brethren exclude the Man Christ from having a part in our Salvation." Whereupon Keith launches forth into a caustic attack upon the inconsistency of this reply with the charge ; the Unitarian tendency of the charge and Delaval and his doctrines generally. Delaval was a man of wealth and education, a member of the Provincial Council, son-in-law of the Governor, Thomas Lloyd, and a minister of the Society of Friends. The last leaf contains an offer from Bradford to print a reply by Delaval or any one else.

KEITH. The Judgment given by Twenty Eight Quakers against George Keith and his Friends; With Answers to the said Judgment, Declaring those Twenty Eight Quakers to be No Christians: As also an Appeal (for which several were imprisoned, &c.) by the said George Keith, &c. to the Yearly Meeting, Sept. 1692. With a full Account of the said Yearly Meeting. Signed by 70 Quakers [*Philadelphia: William Bradford.*] 1693. 4to. pp. 24.   63

This title is No. 37,200 in Sabin's Dictionary.   It was not printed in Philadelphia but is only an imperfect transcript of the following :

The | Judgment | Given forth by | Twenty Eight Quakers | against | George
Keith, | And his Friends, | With Answers to the said Judgment, declaring those
| Twenty Eight Quakers to be No Christians. | As Also, | An Appeal (for which
several were imprisoned, &c.) by | the said George Keith, &c. to the Yearly
Meeting, Sept. 1692. | With a Full Account of the said Yearly Meeting, | Signed
by Seventy Quakers. | Licensed, | Octob. 28th, | 1693. | Dan. Poplar. | *Printed at
Pensilvania ; and now Re-printed at London, for Richard | Baldwin, near the
Oxford-Arms in Warwick-lane.*   1694. | Sq. 8vo. pp. (2), 22.   It is a reprint of
"A True Copy of Three Judgments," No. 51, *supra ;* "An Appeal from the
Twenty-Eight Judges," Nos. 39–41, *supra ;* and "A Counter Testimonial, signed
by Seventy Persons," No. 43, *supra.*

[KEITH.]   New England's Spirit of Persecution | Transmitted
To | Pennsylvania, | And the Pretended Quaker found Persecuting
the True | Christian-Quaker, | in the | Tryal | of | Peter Boss,
George Keith, Thomas Budd, | and William Bradford, | At the
Sessions held at Philadelphia the Nineth, Tenth and | Twelfth
Days of December, 1692.   Giving an Account | of the most Arbi-
trary Procedure of that Court. | *Printed [by William Bradford] in
the Year* 1693. | Sq. 8vo.   Title, 1 leaf; pp. 1-38.   H. S. P.   64

This is a very far from impartial account of a series of trials, to which, however,
the term persecution is probably not improperly applied.   It begins with a short
narrative of the Keithian controversy, relates the circumstances attending the
arrest and imprisonment of Bradford and McComb (see note to No. 39, *supra*),
and then reports the trial of Peter Boss, upon an indictment for defaming a Magistrate, in a letter containing a variety of charges against Samuel Jenings.   He was
convicted and fined £6.   Boss' charges with half a dozen affidavits in support of
them, and others by Keith and John Philly are printed in full.   Then follow the
proceedings against Keith, upon a similar charge, as one of the authors of the
Plea of the Innocent.   Keith, after much contention with the Court and David
Lloyd who acted as prosecuting attorney, refused to plead in the regular form, and
was recorded *nihil dicit.*   To which he objected as he says "I think I have said
a great deal."   Budd's trial upon the same charge is then briefly reported.   The
jury found "That Thomas Budd was guilty of saying, Samuell Jenings had be-
haved himself too high and imperiously in Worldly Courts."   The court, in spite
of the exception "That it was no verdict, not being found to be a breach of any
Law, fined him £5, and imposed a like penalty on Keith, and refused to allow
an appeal to be taken to the Supreme Court, or to the King and Queen in
Council.   Some comments on the trial and more charges against Jenings are
followed by a report of the proceedings in Bradford's case.   The court was composed of six Quakers ; two were members of the meeting of ministers as well
as signers of the "Judgment" which called forth the cause of the actions,
another was one of the bitterest opponents of Keith and his party, while Jenings

who seems to have acted as president-judge was the subject of the alleged defama-tion, and not only heard the case contrary to ordinary precedure but in direct violation of a resolution of the Assembly. The prosecuting attorney was not the regularly appointed officer, but was specially *engaged* by the court. The juries, it is intimated, were packed with Keith's enemies by the Sheriff, who seems also to have acted as assistant prosecutor.

In the three copies of the tract which I have met with, a sentence on page 7, and two on page 8, have been carefully obliterated with pen and ink. In the London edition these lines are left blank, and a note is added that the same had been done to the copy from which the reprint was made. On page 8 are six or seven words in Hebrew type. Menzies' copy sold for $50 ; Brinley's for $130.

LEEDS. (D.) An | Almanack | and | Ephemerides | For the Year of Christian Account 1693 | Whereunto are Numbered, | From the | Creation of the World, 5660 | Flood of Noah, 3986 | Building of London, 1800 | Building of Rome, 2084 | Death of Alexander the Great, 2016 | Constitution of the Julian Year, 1737 | Death and Passion of Christ, 1660 | Hegyra, or flight of Ma-homet, 1102 | Correction of the Kalender by P. Gregory, 111 | Bessextile, or Leap Year, 1 | Containing matters necessary & useful. | Being fitted to the Meridian of that part of New- | Jersey and Pennsilvania, where the Vertex is distant from | the Equator 4 Degrees; but may, without sensible error | serve all parts adjacent, even from Newfound-Land, to the | Capes of Virginia. | By Daniel Leeds, Philomath. | *Printed and Sold by William Bradford*, 1693. | Sm. 8vo. pp. (51).   65

[PHILLIPS. (John)] A Paraphrastical Exposition on a Letter from a Gentleman in Philadelphia to his friend in Boston, con-cerning a certain Person who compared himself to Mordecai. [*Philadelphia: William Bradford.* 1693.] Sm. 4to. pp. 8.   66

This title is copied from Wharton's Early Poets of Pennsylvania, Memoirs of the Historical Society of Pennsylvania, Vol. II. Part II. p. 58. The name of the author appears in the Minutes of the Philadelphia Monthly Meeting, held 7th Mo. 1693.

A TESTIMONY and Caution to such as do | make a Profes-sion of Truth, who are in | scorn called Quakers, and more especi-ally | such who profess to be Ministers of the | Gospel of Peace, That they should | not be concerned in Worldly Govern- | ment. | [*Philadelphia: William Bradford.* 1693.] Sm. 4to. pp. 12. H. S. P.

"Given forth at the Monthly Meeting of the Christian People called Quakers, at the House of Philip James, the 28th of the 12th Month, 1692-3." With a Postscript signed by Thomas Budd and John Hart.

JENINGS. (Samuel) The State of the Case. Philadelphia.

68

Title from Haven's List. It relates to the Keithian Controversy, and was not printed in Philadelphia, but in London, in 1694.

1699.

DICKINSON. (J.) Gods | Protecting Providence | Man's | Surest Help And Defence | In the times | Of the greatest difficulty and most Imminent danger; | Evidenced in the | Remarkable Deliverance | Of divers Persons, | From the devouring Waves of the Sea, amongst which | they Suffered Shipwrack. | And also | From the more cruelly devouring jawes of the inhumane | Canibals of Florida. | Faithfully related by one of the persons concerned therein, | Jonathan Dickenson. | ... | ... | ... | .... | *Printed in Philadelphia by Reinier Jansen.* 1699. | Sq. 8vo. 69

Collation : Title, 1 leaf; Preface, pp. (10); text, pp. 1-96. This interesting narrative, reprinted in Philadelphia, in 1735, 1751, and 1868; in New York in 1803 ; at Burlington in 1811 ; in London the 2d edition, 1700 ; 3d edition, 1720 ; 4th edition, 1759 ; 5th edition, n. d.; 6th edition, 1787 ; 7th edition, 1790, and more or less abridged, was also frequently printed as a "chap-book." A Dutch translation, with plates and a map, appeared at Leyden about 1700. An edition in German was printed by Sower in 1756, and another appeared in 1774, at "Frankfort und Leipzig." The original manuscript is preserved in the Historical Society of Pennsylvania, which has also nine of the editions above noted. The author was Jonathan Dickinson, not Dickenson, a native of Jamaica, who, with his wife, had joined the Society of Friends a short time before embarking on the voyage, the misfortunes of which are the subject of the book. He was the elder son of the captain of a man-of-war, who, having participated in the capture of Jamaica by the English under Penn and Venables, acquired an estate in that island and settled there. His uncle was Physician to Charles II, his grandfather a clergyman of the established Church, and his great-grandfather chief cook at Eton College. He settled in Philadelphia and became one of the most extensive and successful merchants of the time. He was an alderman, and Mayor of the city; Speaker of the Assembly, Member of the Governor's Council, a Master in Chancery, and a Justice of the Supreme Court. He was buried in the Friends' burying ground June 18, 1722. Fisher's imperfect copy sold for $87.50, and was re-sold at the Brinley sale for the same sum. Mr. Brinley's perfect copy sold for $340.

JENINGS. (S.) Truth Rescued | from | Forgery & Falshood, | being | An Answer to a late Scurrilous piece | Entituled | The Case Put and Decided &c. | Which | Stole into the World without any known Au- | thors name affixed thereto, And renders it the | more like it's Father, Who was a Lyer and | Murtherer from the Beginning. | By | Samuel Jenings. | *Printed at Philadelphia By Reynier Jansen* 1699. | Sq. 8vo. pp. 30, (1).   H. S. P.   70

One hundred copies were reprinted in Philadelphia about 1882. Samuel Jenings appears to have been a man of education and ability, and to have been held in high esteem among his own sect, of which he was a prominent Minister; if a very lauda- tory sketch of him which appeared in "The Friend," Vol. XXVIII., can be trusted. On the other hand if his character be taken from the publications of Keith, he was violent in temper, vindictive in disposition, arrogant in language and demeanor, and unscrupulous in carrying his own cause to a successful issue. This view of Jenings derives support from his conduct in other affairs. He settled in West Jersey in 1680, and soon after received from Edward Byllinge who had purchased the Province and Proprietary rights from the Duke of York, a commision as Gover- nor. This he at first accepted, and acted under till 1683, when he caused himself to be elected Governor by the Assembly, a proceeding which was upon arbitration, adjudged by George Fox, George Whitehead and twelve other prominent Quakers selected to decide the question, to be without a shadow of authority and in direct violation of Byllinge's rights. Jenings refused to acquiesce in this decision and continued the controversy until the government of the Province was surrendered to the Crown. Jenings' pamphlet relates to this affair. He was for some years a member of the Governor's Council and Speaker of the West Jersey Assembly. The Case Put and Decided is said by Joseph Smith and Sabin to have been pub- lished in Philadelphia in 1698 or 1699. If printed in America it most probably came from Bradford's press, but it could certainly not have been issued in Phila- delphia, as Jansen's press belonged to the Quakers and was under the censor- ship of a committee, of which Jenings was a member. Brinley's copy sold for $60.

PROCLAMATION. By the Proprietary of | the Province of Pensilvania, | and Counties annexed | With the Advice of the Council: | A Proclamation | *Philadelphia Printed by Reiner Jansen* 1699. | Folio, 1 leaf.   A. P. S.   71

A proclamation against Pirates, dated the 23d of the Tenth Month, 1699, and signed by William Penn. All persons were to be apprehended who could not "give a Reasonable and Credible Account of their former Abode and Conversa- tion, and about whom is found any such Quantity of East-India, Arabian or other Foreign Goods or Coins, as may render them justly suspected."

1700.

DAVIS. (W.) Jesus | The Crucifyed Man, | the | Eternal Son of God, | or, an | Answer | to | An Anathema or Paper of | Excommunication, of John Wats, en- | tituled, Points of Doctrine preached & | asserted by William Davis. | Wherein the Mystry of Christs Descen- | tion, Incarnation and Crucifixion is | Unfolded. | By William Davis. |

[*Second title.*] Jesus the Crucified Man, | The Eternal Son of God. | Or, | An Answer to an Anathema or Paper of | Excommunication, of John Wats, entituled, | Points of Doctrine preached and asserted by | William Davis. | Wherein the Mystry of Christs Descen- | tion, Incarnation and Crucifixion is Un- | folded. As also, it is made appear by plain | Scripture proof, by Testimonies of the | holy Trinity, Angels and Men (and also of | the very Devils) Acts of Worship done to | him, and Miracles that he wrought; and | Plain Arguments and Reasons drawn from | thence, That the outward and visible | Person or Man Jesus of Nazareth, the Son | of the Virgin Mary, who suffered Death, | and dyed upon the Cross, was (when he did | so dye) and so doth still remain the proper | natural and eternal Son of the living God, | and second Person in the sacred Trinity, & | consequently true God, (tho' not the Fa- | ther) And the Objections answered that | are commonly brought against this Do- | ctrine. In which Answers are explained | divers Scriptures relating to the Person, | Office, Body, Flesh and Blood of Christ. | As also, what is to be understood by that | adorable Expression (Godhead) with several | other useful and pertinent things for such | a Work. | To which is added, A Corollary, shewing | John Wat's Contradictions, Errors and | and Blasphemies. As also, George Keith | Dis-robed. | As also, the Testimonies of the Primitive and | Apostolical Churches, with the Churches | of the succeeding Ages; and also the | Testimonies of the Protestant Churches | since the Reformation, all bearing witness | to this Truth. | By William Davis. | [*Philadelphia:*] *Printed for the Author,* [*by Reynier Jansen*] *in the Year* 1700. | 16mo.

Collation : Preliminary leaf, recto blank, verso, 5 texts from the New Testament ; First title, 1 leaf; Second title, pp. (2) ; The Preface to the Reader, pp. (2) : The Introduction, pp. (32) ; The Contents, pp. (4) ; text pp. 1–34.

"The main doctrine of this book," says the Rev. Morgan Edwards, "is, that the divine nature and the human were so blended in the person of Christ that He was not properly God nor properly man, but a compound of both." For a reply, see No. 94, *infra*, and also note to 78, *infra*. The introduction is of great historical importance, as it contains an account of the Keithian and other religious factions, by one who had been active in several and who at the moment was the leader of a fresh schism.

Davis was a native of Wales. He was sent to Oxford, but left the University on becoming a Quaker. He arrived in Philadelphia in 1684, and was a recognized preacher of the Society, but left it with Keith. In 1697 he joined the Pennepack Baptist Church, from which he was expelled Feb. 17, 1698–9, for heresy. He became a Seventhday Baptist, and acted as minister of a congregation near Frankford until 1711. He then took charge of a Church at Westerly, Rhode Island, where he remained until 1727, when he returned to Pennsylvania. In 1734 he was again in Rhode Island, from whence, ten years later, he led a party of Seventhday Baptists to found a settlement at Squan, New Jersey, of which he became the pastor. He died there in 1745 in his 82d year.

NIESSEN. (G. D.) A Paper by Gertrude Dericks Niessen. *Philadelphia: Reynier Jansen.* 1700. 73

On the 26th of 11th mo. 1699, the following entry was made in the minutes of the Philadelphia Monthly Meeting : "Gertrude Dericks Niessen's Paper, first printed in Dutch and since translated into English, being read in the last Preparatory Meeting and brought hither for the consideration of this Meeting about printing is referred to the next Quarterly Meeting." It was finally approved, and the Meeting paid for printing it. Jos. Smith, in his Catalogue of Friends' Books indicates "An Epistle" printed in English, about 1677, as having been represented by Jansen. But Mrs. Niessen was the author of several tracts which were first printed in Dutch, and it is very doubtful whether Smith is correct.

P[USEY.] (C[ALEB]) | Satan's | Harbinger Encountered, | His False | News of a Trumpet Detected, | His Crooked | Ways in the Wildrnesse | Laid open to the view of the Impartial and Iudicious. | Being | Something by way of Answer to Daniel Leeds | his book, entituled, News of a Trumpet | Sounding in the Wildernesse &c. | Wherein is shewn, | How in several respects he hath grievously wronged and a- | bused divers eminent, worthy and painfull Labourers in the | work of the Gospel, in many places by false Citations out | of their books, and in many other places by perverting their | sayings and expressions; besides his otherwaies basely re- | flecting upon several antient Friends by name. | By C. P. | . . . | . . . | . . . | . . . . | *Printed at Philadelphia By Reynier Jansen* 1700. | Sq. 8vo.   H. S. P.   74

Collation : Title, 1 leaf ; Preface, pp. (2) ; text, pp. 1–114 ; Advertisement, 1 leaf ; Errata, pp. (7). The seven pages of errata, which are printed in double columns, are badly in need of another page or two, to correct the numerous new errors made in the attempt to call attention to the misprints in the text. A notice of the author can be found in "The Friend," Vol. XXIX., page 148 *et seq.* Brinley's copy sold for $170.

A SEASONABLE | Account | Of The | Christian and Dying-Words, | Of Some Young-Men; Fit for the consideration | of all: But Especially of the Youth of this | Generation; viz: | William Fletcher, 17 Years of age, | Tudor Brain, 17 Years of age, | and Richard Manliffe. | With a short Epistle Prefixed. | Published for Instruction and Caution to the Youth | among Friends, called Quakers. | . . . | . . . . | *Printed at Philadelphia by Reynier Jansen.* 1700. | Sq. 8vo. pp. 19.   H. S. P.   75

SOUTHEBY. (WILLIAM) A Testimony against Prophaneness in Philadelphia. *Philadelphia: Reynier Jansen.* 1700.   76

The Philadelphia Monthly Meeting gave their approval of the printing of this tract, 6 mo. 30th, 1700. For a notice of the author see "The Friend," Vol. XXVIII.

UPSHER. (T.) To Friends in Ireland, and elsewhere, a Mournful Word to the Merry-hearted in Zion, with a Word of Comfort to her Bowed-down Mourners. Written in great Exercise of Soul and Spirit in obedience to the Lord. By Thomas Upsher. *Philadelphia: Reynier Jansen.* 1700.   77

First printed in Dublin ? in 1699. Mr. Kite says it was reprinted by Jansen in 1700. An account of the author and a reprint of his "Mournful Word" will be found in "The Friend," Vol. XVII., pp. 29 and 36.

WATTS. (REV. JOHN) A Baptist Catechism. *Philadelphia: Reynier Jansen.* 1700.   78

The Rev. John Watts, says Morgan Edwards (Materials p. 12), composed a catechism or little system of divinity, which was published in 1700.
The Rev. John Watts was born Nov. 3, 1661, at Lydel in the county of Kent, and came to Pennsylvania in 1686. He joined the Baptists, was called to the Ministry in 1688, and had charge of the Pennepack Church from 1690 till his death—Aug. 27, 1702. In addition to the Catechism, he wrote a reply to William Davis' "Jesus the Crucified Man" (No. 72, *supra*). But this was never published.

1701.

AN | ABSTRACT or Abridgment | of the Laws | Made | And Past by William Penn Absolute | Proprietary | And Governour in Chief of the Province of | Pensilvania, | And Territories there unto belonging, with the Advice | and Consent of the Free-Men thereof in General | Assembly mett at | New-Castle | The Fourteenth-day of October and Continued by Ad- | journment till the Twenty-Seventh of November in the | Year 1700. | *Printed at Philadelphia: by Reynier Jansen* 1701. | Sq. 8vo. Title 1 leaf; pp. 42; Table of Contents pp. (2). M. S. 79

The only copy I have met with is imperfect, ending with page 40, but the table contains mention of no page beyond 42. It consists of brief summaries of the 91 laws enacted during the sitting of the Assembly.

AN EPISTLE | To the Quarterly and Monthly-Meeting of Friends in Pensilvania, | and West and East-Jersey: | From our Yearly Meeting in Philadelphia held the 24th. and 25th. | days, of the 7th. Month 1701. | [*Philadelphia: Reynier Jansen.* 1701.] Folio, pp. (2). H. S. P. 80

The Meeting ordered 500 copies to be printed. But one is known to exist.

F[OX.] (G[EORGE]) Gospel | Family-Order, | being a | Short Discourse | concerning the | Ordering of Families, | both of | Whites, Blacks and Indians. | . . . | . . . | . . . | . . . | . . . | . . . | . . . | . . . | . . . | . . . | . . . | . . . . | By G. F. | [*Philadelphia:*] *Reprinted* [*by Reynier Jansen*] *in the Year* 1701. | Sq. 8vo. pp. 23. H. S. P. 81

KEITH. (G.) Mr. George Keith's Account of A National Church, and the Clergy, &c. Humbly presented to the Bishop of London: With some Queries concerning the Sacrament. *Reprinted at Philadelphia by Reynier Jansen,* 1701. 4to. pp. 8. 82

Title from the Brinley Catalogue. It is made up of extracts from Keith's work, written while he was a member of the Society of Friends, and was published in London in 1700, after he had joined the Church of England, by some of his former co-religionists. The Philadelphia Monthly Meeting on 10th mo. 2d, 1700, ordered "four or five hundred of the sheets lately come out of England, called the Defence of the Christianity of the Quakers, by George Keith, printed with as much speed as possible, and brought to the next monthly meeting in order to be dispersed."

M[AULE.] (T[HOMAS]) An Abstract of A | Letter | to | Cotton Mather | Of Boston in | New-England. | By T. M. | [*Philadelphia:*] *Printed by* [*Reynier Jansen*] *in the Year* 1701. | Sm. 4to. pp. 19.

For an account of the author, see the *Maule Genealogy*, Philadelphia, 1868, and *Collections of the Essex Institute*, Vol. III., p. 238.

PASTORIUS. (F. D.) A Primer. By Francis Daniel Pastorius.

The date of publication is uncertain. The minutes of the Philadelphia Monthly Meeting show the purchase of a large number for use in the Friends' schools.

[PENN. (WILLIAM)] The Governour's Speech to the Assembly, at Philadelphia | the 15 September 1701. | *Printed at Philadelphia by Reynier Jansen* 1701. | Folio, pp. (2).   H. S. P.   85

ROGERS. (J.) An Impartial Relation of | An Open and Publick Dispute | Agreed upon | Between Gurdon Saltonstal, Minister of the | Town of New-London, | And | John Rogers of the same place, | With the Circumstances leading thereto, and the Consequences thereof. | As also a Relation of the said Gurdon Saltonstal's recovering a | Judgment of Court, of Six Hundred Pounds, and cost of Court, | against said John Rogers, for saying, the said Saltonstal went to | wave, shun or shift the said Dispute agreed upon. The truth of | which waving, shunning or shifting is here also evidently dem- | onstrated. By John Rogers. | . . . | . . . | . . . | . . . | . . . | . . . | . . . | . . . | . . . | . . . | . . . . | *Printed* [*by Reynier Jansen?*] *for the Author, in the Year* 1701. | Sm. 4to. Title, and To the Reader, pp. (4); A Relation of the Dispute, pp. 15.   86

SHEWEN. (W.) A Brief | Testimony | against | Tale-Bearers, | Whisperers, | and | Back-biters, | Shewing | That where they are given ear unto amongst Friends, | Neighbors, and Relations, or in any Christian So- | ciety, such can never live in Peace, Concord and | Unity. | . . . | . . . | . . . . | By William Shewen. | *Reprinted at Philadelphia* [*by Reynier Jansen*] *in the Year*, 1701. | 8vo. pp. 21.

SHEWEN. Good Advice to Youth. By William Shewen. *Philadelphia: Reynier Jansen.* 1701.   88

This tract is not mentioned by Joseph Smith. The Philadelphia Monthly Meeting, on 28th 12th mo., 1700, ordered 500 copies to be printed at its expense.

1702.

FOX. (G[EORGE]) Instructions | For | Right-Spelling, | and | Plain Directions | For | Reading | and | Writing | True English. | With several delightful | things very Useful and | Necessary, both for | Young and Old, to Read | and Learn. | By G. Fox. | *Reprinted at Philadelphia by | Reynier Jansen* 1702. | 16mo. pp. 104.   89

A | LETTER | from a | Clergy-man in the Country, | to a | Clergy-Man In The City, | Containing | Free Thoughts about the Controversie, | Between | Some Ministers of the Church of England, | and the | Quakers: | With Seasonable Advise to his Brethren, To | Study Peace and Moderation. | *Philadelphia Reprinted by Reynier Jansen* 1702. | Sm. 4to. pp. 12.   H. S. P.   90

PUSEY. (C.) Daniel Leeds, Justly Rebuked for abusing William Penn, and his Folly and Fals-Hoods Contained in his two Printed Challenges to Caleb Pusey, made Manifest; with some remarks also by way of Rebuke on the Author of the Book called News of a Strumpet. *Printed at Philadelphia by Reynier Jansen.* 1702. 4to. pp. 32.?   91

This title is from Joseph Smith's Catalogue of Friends' Books.

TAYLOR. (J.) An Almanac for 1702. By Jacob Taylor. *Philadelphia: Reynier Jansen.* 1702.   92

James Logan writing to Penn, 7th of 3d mo. 1702, says "Jacob Taylor who has wrote a pretty Almanac for this year, one of which comes enclosed," &c. *Penn and Logan Correspondence*, Vol. I., p. 93.

1703.

ADVERTISEMENT calling for the payment of the Proprietary Quit Rents.   93

James Logan writes to William Penn, "24th of 4th Month, 1704. I have endeavoured at a perfect rent-roll for Chester, but not one-half the people have come in ; . . . though by printed bills they had large notice." *Penn and Logan Correspondence*, Vol I., 199.

[KEITH, (George) and EVANS. (Evan)] Some of the many false, scandalous, blasphe- | mous & self-contradictory Assertions of Willam | Davis, faithfully collected out of his Book, printed | Anno 1700, entituled, Jesus the Crucified Man, the | Eternal Son of God, &c. in exact Quotations word | for word, without adding or diminishing. | [*New York: William Bradford.* 1703.] Sm. 4to. pp. 12. H. S. P. 94

Dated, Philadelphia, March 26, 1703, which has misled Joseph Smith and others into stating it was printed here.

M[AULE.] (T[homas]) For the service of Truth, By Phila-lethes or Lover of Truth, T. M. 1703. An Abstract of George Keith's Letter to Thomas Maule, with an Answer by Philalethes there unto. [*Philadelphia:*] *Printed [by Reynier Jansen?] for the Author*, 1703. 4to. pp. 20. 95

[PUSEY. (Caleb)] George Keith | Once More Brought to the Test, | And proved | A | Prevaricator, | Containing something of an Answer to his Book called | The Spirit of Railing Shimei, &c. | And shewing, that George Keith in his attempting, to prove the | Spirit of Railing Shimei &c. to be entred into Caleb Pusey; hath there | by more manifested, that not only the Spirit of Rail-ing, and Envy, | but also of Confusion, about Doctrin's and Prin-ciples of Religion, is | entred in to himself. | . . . | . . . | . . . | . . . . | *Printed at Philadelphia by Reinier Jansen.* [1703] | Sq. 8vo. Title, 1 leaf; Preface, pp. (6); text, pp. 1–32. F. 96

[PUSEY.] Proteus Ecclesiasticus | Or | George Keith | Va-ried in Fundamentalls; | Acknowledged by himself to be such, | and | Prov'd an Apostat, | From his own Definition, Argu-ments, and Reasons. | Contrary to his often repeated false pre-tentions, whereby he | hath Laboured to deceive the People; telling them he is | not varied from any Fundamental Principle, nor any Princi- | ple of the Christian faith, ever since he first came among the | Quakers. | With Remarks on Daniel Leed's abusive Almanack | for the Year 1703. by way of Postscript. | . . . | . . . | . . . . | *Printed at Philadelphia by Reynier Jansen.* [1703.] | Sq. 8vo. H. S. P. 97

Collation : Title, 1 leaf ; The Preface, pp. (5) ; text, pp. 3–60 ; Postscript, pp. 28 ; Additional Postscript, pp. 4 ; Errata, pp. (2).

TAYLOR. (J.) An Almanac for 1703. By Jacob Taylor. *Philadelphia : Reynier Jansen.* 1703.   98

TAYLOR. An Almanac for 1704. By Jacob Taylor. *Phila-delphia : Reynier Jansen.* 1703.   99

1704.

PROCLAMATION. By the Honourable Collonel | John Evans Lieutenant Governour of the Province of | Pensilvania and Counties annexed. | A Proclamation, | Against Immorality and Prophaneness. | *Printed at Philadelphia by Reynier Jansen.* 1704. | Folio, 1 leaf.   H. S. P. 100

[PUSEY. (CALEB)] False News From Gath Rejected. | Containing some Reasons of the People called | Quakers | For their declining to Answer John Talbot's Proposall (at the foot of | F. Bogg's Bomb.) to their last Yearly Meeting at Burlington. | [*Philadelphia : Reynier Jansen.* 1704.] Folio, 1 leaf.   D. 101

Dated "Burlington, 18 7 mo. : 1704," and "Signed in behalf of the People call'd Quakers By us Edward Shippen, George Maris, Anthony Morris, John Redman, Thomas Story, Caleb Pusey, Samuel Jenings, Griffith Owen, Nicholas Waln." See the notice of Pusey in "The Friend," Vol. XXIX.

TAYLOR. (J.) An Almanack for the Year 1705. | An | Ephemeris | of the Motions and Aspects of the | Planets | And the Eclipses of the Luminaries for the Year | of English Account 1705 | Fitted to the Latitude of 40 degrees North, and | the Longitude of 75 degrees west of London ; | serving Pensilvania and the Places adjacent. | By Jacob Taylor. | . . . | . . . | . . . | . . . . | To which is added by C.[aleb] P.[usey] some remarks on D. L[eed]'s abuses | to the Quakers, in his this Years two Almanacks. | *Printed at Philadelphia by Tiberius Johnson.* [1704.] | Sm. 8vo. pp. (32).
                                      A. P. S. 102

A description of this, and other early Almanacs printed in Philadelphia, was read before the American Philosophical Society, by Henry Phillips, Jr., and printed in the Society's Proceedings, Vol. XIX., p. 291.

AN EPISTLE from the Yearly Meeting. *Philadelphia: Reynier Jansen.* 1704.   103

1705.

[PUSEY. (Caleb)] The Bomb Search'd | And found stuff'd
with False Ingredients; being a | Just Confutation of an abusive
Printed Half-Sheet, call'd |·a Bomb, originally published against
the Quakers, | by Francis Bugg. | But | Espoused and Exposed,
and in Print offered to be proved by | John Talbot. | To which is
added, | First: A large Appendix treating of the Real Differences
that | are in divers respects between the Quakers and their Opposers,
| and the Quakers Doctrine, Practice, and Deportment, in those
Points, | Justified from Scripture and the antient Protestants. |
Secondly; divers Testimonies added of those called Fathers of the
| Church, to the Light of Christ, Inspiration; the Spirit's Teach-
ing; | Silent waiting &c. | Thirdly divers of D. L's abuses to the
Quakers; being herein more | fully manifested than hath hitherto
been published. | . . . | . . . | . . . | . . . | . . . . | *Printed at
Philadelphia by Reynier Jansen,* 1705. | Sq. 8vo.   H. S. P.   104

    Collation : Title, 1 leaf ; To the Reader, pp. 3-8 ; The Introduction, etc., pp. 9-32 ;
An Appendix, pp. 33-76. The title next given may have been intended to supply
the "Thirdly" of the title page, and is usually found with it.

[PUSEY.] Some Remarks upon a late Pamphlet signed part
by | John Talbot, and part by Daniel Leeds, called | The Great
Mystery of Fox-Craft. | [*Philadelphia: Reynier Jansen.* 1705.]
4to. pp. 40.   D.   105

TAYLOR. (J.) Ephemeris Sideralis. | A | Mathematical Al-
manack | For the Year of Our Lord | 1706, | Containing the Mo-
tions and Eclipses of the | Luminaries; with the Rising & Setting
of | Sun, the Southing of the Moon, and | the various Motions and
Aspects of the | Moving Stars, | Exactly Calculated according to
the Precepts | of the Ablest Astronomers, and the most | rational
grounds of Art. | For the Vertex of Philadelphia. | By Jacob
Taylor. | *Printed at Philadelphia for the Author.* [1705.] | Sm. 8vo.
pp. (32).   A. P. S.   106

1706.

PUSEY. (Caleb) Some brief Observations | Made on Daniel Leeds his Book, | Entituled | The Second Part of the Mystery of | Fox-Craft. | Published for the clearing the Truth against the false Aspersions | ' Calumnies and Perversions of that often-refuted | Author. | By Caleb Pusey. | With a Postscript by Thos: Chalkly: wherein D. L: is justly rebuked | for falsely citeing him. | . . . | . . . | . . . | . . . | . . . | . . . | . . . . | Printed at Philadelphia by Joseph Reyners. 1706. | Sm. 4to. pp. (4), 28. 4.   M. S. 107

Chalkley's Appendix is entitled : A | Small Broom to sweep away the falshoods which Daniel | Leeds has Thrown into the way of | Thos. Chalkley. | pp. 4.

TAYLOR. (J.) An Almanac for 1707. By Jacob Taylor. *Philadelphia: Tiberius Johnson.* 1706.   108

Mentioned in Haven's List of Ante-Revolutionary Publications under 1707. I have not met with a copy. See No. 102, *supra.*

1707.

TAYLOR. (J.) An Almanac for 1708. By Jacob Taylor. *Philadelphia :* 1707.   109

1708.

TAYLOR. (J.) An | Almanack | For the Year of Christian Account | 1709 | Containing the Motions and Aspects | of the | Planets : | The Eclipses of the Luminaries, | The Rising & Setting of the Sun, the | Lunations, Tydes & Common Notes. | Fitted to the Meridian & Latitude of | The Province of Pensilvania. | By Jacob Taylor. | . . . | . . . | . . . | . . . | . . . | . . . . | [*Philadelphia : Jacob Taylor.* 1708.] Sm. 8vo. pp. (24).   A. P. S. 110

1709.

ANNO Sexto | Annæ Reginæ | An Act for Ascertaining the Rates of Foreign Coins in her Majesties | Plantations in America. | [Colophon.] *London, Printed by Charles Hill &c. and Reprinted at*

Philadelphia. 1709 | [Followed by] Pensilvania ss | Anno Regni Annæ Reginæ Octavo. | An Act for Ascertaining the Rates of Money for Payment of Debts, & Pre- | venting Exactions on Contracts & Bargains made before the First Day of May, | in this present Year One thousand seven hundred & nine. | [Colophon.} *Printed from the Original by J. Taylor.* | Folio, pp. (4).   H. S. P. 111

Each act occupies two pages. The first act was also reprinted by Bradford at New York, 1709. Sabin 53,449.

AN EPISTLE from the Yearly Meeting. *Philadelphia :* 1709.
112

TAYLOR. (J.)   An Almanac for 1710.   By Jacob Taylor. *Philadelphia : Jacob Taylor.* 1709.   113

1710.

[NORRIS. (ISAAC)] Friendly Advice to the Inhabitants of Pennsylvania. *Philadelphia : Jacob Taylor.* 1710.?   114

A prefatory note to the reprint of 1728 says, "The following Paper was wrote, about the Year 1710, by Isaac Norris, Esq ; deceased, by Order, as was said, of the Yearly Meeting, published by the Printer under their Direction, and occasioned by the wild Management of an Assembly led by a Lawyer" [David Lloyd].

TAYLOR. (J.) An | Almanack | For the Year of Christian Account | 1711 | Being the Third after Bissextile or Leap-Year | Fitted to the Meridian & Latitude of | The Province of Pensilvania. | By Jacob Taylor. | . . . | . . . | . . . | . . . | . . . | . . . | . . . | . . . | . . . | . . . | . . . . | *Printed at Philadelphia.* | Sm. 8vo. pp. (24).   A. P. S. 115

1711.

TAYLOR. (J.) An | Almanack | For the Year of Christian Account | 1712. | Being Bissextile or Leap-year | Wherein are Contained | The Motions, and Aspects, of the Planets ; the Lunations | and Eclipses ; the Rising and Setting of the Sun and Moon, | the Time of High-Water, Courts, Fairs and Remarkable | Days. |

Also | Monthly, and Meteorological Observations. | For the Prov-
ince of Pensilvania. | By Jacob Taylor. | . . . | . . . | . . . | . . . |
. . . | . . . | . . . | . . . | . . . | . . . | . . . | . . . | . . . . | *Printed at*
Philadelphia 1711. | Sm. 8vo. pp. (28).   A. P. S.   116

1712.

ACTS of Assembly.   *Philadelphia: Jacob Taylor.*   1712.   117

No copy known to be extant. Mr. Kite says (The Friend, Vol. XVII., p. 44)
"In 1712, he [Jacob Taylor] printed some of the Acts of the Legislature, which
he complains did not sell to afford him any profit."

ADVERTISEMENT. [*Philadelphia: Jacob Taylor.* 1712.]
Folio, 1 leaf.   A. P. S.   118

Dated 15th of 2d Month, 1712. A notice for payment of quit rents.

GOSPEL-TIMES, | Or Oaths Forbidden under the | Gospel. |
Herein being shewn, that the Quaker's Doctrine, Not to | Swear at
all as it is sufficiently Grounded upon the Com- | mands of our Sav-
iour Christ Jesus, & his Apostle | James, so it is Exactly Consistent
with the declared Doctrine | of the Primitive, and many Later
Christians, as appears by | the Writings of divers famous and pious
Men among them, | many of whom were godly Martyrs, and are
to this day by | the Christian world esteem'd and call'd Fathers
in the | Church, and whose Writings & Sayings sufficiently answer
| the most usual Objections brought against us on this Ac- | count,
being briefly abstracted out of larger Instances of | the like kind.
| From a Book call'd a Treatise of Oaths &c. formerly present- |
ed to the King & Parliament & subscribed by our Friends, | William
Penn, Alexander Parker, Stephen Crisp, | George Whitehead,
James Claypool, William Mead, | With some others. | Published
for the Serious Consideration of all, & to clear our Chri- | stian
Doctrine, in this respct, [*sic*] from being esteemed a Novelty of
| Quakerism. | . . . | . . . | . . . | . . . . | *Philadelphia: Printed*
MDCCXII. | Sq. 8vo. Title, 1 leaf; pp. 1–26.   F.   119

[MAULE. (THOMAS)] Tribute | to | Cæsar, | How paid by the
Best Christians, | And to what Purpose. | With | Some Remarks

on the late vigorous Expedition | against Canada. | Of Civil Government, | How Inconsistent it is with the Government of Christ | in his Church, | Compared with the Ancient, Just and Righteous Principles of the Quakers, and their Modern | Practice and Doctrine.   With some Notes upon the Discipline of their Church in | this Province, especially at Philadelphia. | By Philalethes. | [*Philadelphia: about* 1712.]   Sm. 4to. pp. (6), 29.   120

The "Tribute to Cæsar" was the tax for the Canada expedition of 1711.   Title and Author's name from the Brinley Catalogue.

MORGAN. (J.)   Gospel Ordinances.   Sermon at the Ordination of Jonathan Dickinson . . . 29th Sept. 1709.   By Rev. Joseph Morgan, A. M.   *Philadelphia: Printed by William and Andrew Bradford.*   1712.   12mo. pp. 44.   121

Title from Sabin's Dictionary.

TAYLOR. (J.)   An Almanac for 1713.   By Jacob Taylor. *Philadelphia:* 1712.   122

1713.

ACTS and Laws of the Province of Pennsylvania, October 14th, 1712 to March 27, 1713.   *Philadelphia: Andrew Bradford.*   1713. Folio.   123

Probably consisting of about thirty pages, numbered in continuations of the Acts printed by Taylor in 1712.   See collation of "Acts" 1715, No. 131, *infra.* No laws were passed between March 27, 1713, and October, 1714.

TATE, (N.) AND BRADY. (N.)   A New Version | of the | Psalms | of | David, | Fitted to the Tunes | Used in Churches. | By N. Brady, D.D. Chaplain in | Ordinary, & N. Tate, Esq; | Poet-Laureat, to Her Majesty. | *London:* | *Printed in the Year,* 1704. | *Printed, and Sold by William* | *and Andrew Bradford in New-* | *York and Philadelphia,* 1713. | 24 mo. Authorization 1 leaf; Title and Recommendation, pp. (2); pp. 1–212+.   H. S. P.   124

TAYLOR. (J.)   An Almanac for 1714.   By Jacob Taylor. *Philadelphia: Andrew Bradford.*   1713.   125

1714.

CHALKLEY. (T.) Forcing | A Maintenance | Not | Warrantable from the Holy Scripture, | for a Minister of the Gospel. | Being | An Answer to some false and Erroni- | ous pages, writ by Joseph Metcalfe | tending to stir up | Persecution | By Thomas Chalkley. | . . . . | . . . . | . . . . | *Printed at Philadelphia [by Andrew Bradford]* 1714. | 16mo. Title, 1 leaf; Preface, pp. (3); "I Shall now take notice" &c., pp. (2); text, pp. 1–52.   H. S. P.   126

HILL. (H.) A | Legacy for | Children, | Being | Some of the Last Expressions, and | Dying Sayings, | of | Hannah Hill, Junr. | Of the City of Philadelphia, in the Pro- | vince of Pensilvania, in America, Aged. | Eleven Years and near Three Months. | . . . | . . . | . . . | . . . | . . . | . . . | . . . . | *Printed by Andrew Bradford, at the sign of* | *the Bible in Philadelphia.* [1714. ?] | 16mo. pp. 35.   D.   127

THE | LAWS | Of the Province of | Pennsilvania | Collected into | One Volumn, | By Order of the Governour and Assembly of the | said Province. | *Printed & Sold by Andr. Bradford in Philadelphia,* | 1714. | Folio.   H. S. P.   128

Title and "Advertisement to the Reader, pp. (2) ; Contents, pp. (2) ; text, pp. 1–184. Signatures A to Uu, (the latter, pp. 183–184). Pages 14 and 15 are misnumbered 12 and 13. Sheet H, pp. 29 to 32, is followed by I, pp. 34 to 37 ; and I by K, pp. 43, 40, 41 and 42. From L, pp. 43 to 46, the paging is regular up to 55, which is misnumbered 52. Sheet O, pp. 52 (for 55) to 58, is followed by P, pp. 69–72. The paging, except pp. 78 and 79, which are misnumbered 76 and 77, is regular to sheet W, pp. 93 to 96 which is followed by X, pp. 95 * 96 * 93 * 94, * and Y, pp. 99 to 102. The paging is then regular to the end, except page 143, which is misnumbered 132, and 176 misnumbered 172. The "catch-words," run regularly through this erratic pagination.

This is the first printed collection of the Laws of Pennsylvania, and was intended to give in full all the laws then in force, with the titles of such as were obsolete, expired or repealed. Several Acts, and the titles of about a dozen which should have been included, are omitted. The volume is badly printed and full of typographical errors. Mr. Thos. I. Wharton, in Nov. 1827, bought a copy for fifteen cents, which was sold at auction in Nov. 1881, for $200.

TAYLOR. (J.) An Almanac for 1715. By Jacob Taylor. *Philadelphia: Andrew Bradford.* 1714.   129

WATTS. (I.) The Vision of Isaac Watts. *Philadelphia:* 1714. 130

This title is given in Haven's List of Ante-Revolutionary Publications, probably from the Catalogue of the Library Company of Philadelphia. On examination of the volume referred to by the latter, 1714 was found to be a misprint for 1774.

1715.

THE ACTS and Laws | of the | Province | of | Pennsilvania, | Which were Enacted by the General Assembly of | said Province, begun at Philadelphia the 14th October, 1714. | and Continued by Adjournments to the 28th of May, 1715. | being the First Year of the Reign of His present Majesty | King George, Over Great Britain, France and Ireland, | &c. | G. [Royal Arms.] R. | *Printed and Sold by Andrew Bradford at the Sign of the Bible in Philadelphia*, MDCCXV. | Folio. L. C. P. 131

Collation: Title, 1 leaf; Table of Contents, 1 leaf; text, pp. 101–274. Signatures Y to Rr. Signature Ll, pp. 149–152, is followed by Mm. pp. 253–256, and the misnumbering is continued throughout the volume.

CLAESSE. (L.) Morning and Evening Prayer, the Litany, Church Catechism, Family Prayers, &c. Translated into the Mohawk Indian Language. By Lawrence Claesse. *Philadelphia: Printed by Andrew Bradford.* 1715. 8vo. 132

This title is from Haven's list of Ante-Revolutionary Publications. The New York edition printed during the same year is well known to collectors of Americana, and it is not unlikely that this title has been taken from some advertisement by Andrew Bradford offering it for sale.

HILL. (H.) A Legacy for Children. The Second Edition. *Printed by Andrew Bradford, at the Sign of the Bible in Philadelphia.* 1715.? 133

LEEDS. (T.) Leeds, 1716. | The American | Almanack | For the Year of Christian Account 1716. | Unto which is Numbered |
From   { By the Orient & Greek Christians, 7224 |
the   { By the Jews, Hebrews & Rabins, 5476 |
Creation. { By the late Computation of W. W. 5725 |
Being Bessextile or Leap Year. | Wherein is contained | The Lu-

nations, Moons Rising and Setting, the | Eclipses, Judgment of the Weather; Spring | Tydes, the Planets motions & mutual Aspects, | and Symbolical Effects; with the Birthdays of | the Successive Heirs to the Crown of Great | Britain. Time of Sunrise & setting, Day- | Break, Day-light End, Length of the Day, | Time of High-Water, Fairs, Courts, and | Observable Days, &c. | Fitted to a Latitude of 40 Degrees, and | a Meridian of five hours West from London, but | may, without sensible error, serve all the adjacent | places, even from Newfound-land to Carolina. | By Titan Leeds, Philomat. | . . . | . . . | . . . | . . . | . . . | . . . . | *Printed, and Sold by A. Bradford in Philadelphia.* [1715.] | Sm. 8vo. pp. (24). c.   134

SOUTHEBY. (W.) An Anti-Slavery tract. By William Southeby. *Philadelphia: Andrew Bradford.* 1715.   135

Mentioned in "The Friend," Vol. XXVIII., p. 309. In 1717 he published another tract on the same subject.

TAYLOR. (J.) An Almanac for 1716. By Jacob Taylor. *Philadelphia: Andrew Bradford.* 1715.   136

1716.

LEEDS. (T.) Leeds, 1717. | The American | Almanack | For the Year of Christian Account 1717. | Unto which is numbered | . . . | . . . | . . . | Being the first after Leap year. | Wherein is contained | The Lunations, Moons Rising and Setting, the | Eclipses, Judgment of the Weather, Spring | Tydes, the Planets motions & mutual Aspects, | and Symbolical Effects; with the Birth days of | the Successive Heirs to the Crown of Great | Britain. Time of | Sun rise & Setting, Day-Break, Day-light End, Length of the Day, | Time of High-Water, Fairs, Courts, and | Observable Days, &c. | Fitted to the Latitude of 40 Degrees, and | a Meridian of five hours West from London, but | may, without sensible error, serve all the adjacent | places, even from Newfound-Land to Carolina. | By Titan Leeds, Philomat. | . . . | . . . | . . . | . . . | . . . | . . . . | *Printed, and Sold by A. Bradford in Philadelphia.* [1716.] | Sm. 8vo. pp. (24).   H. S. P. 137

P. (G.) Lex Parliamentaria: | or, a | Treatise | of the | Law and Custom | of the | Parliaments | of | England. | By G. P. Esq; | Licensed December 6, 1689. | *London Printed, and Reprinted in New-York* | *and Sold by William and Andrew Bradford* | *in New-York and Philadelphia.* 1716. | 16mo. pp. (6), 184.   H. S. P.   **138**

TAYLOR. (J.) An Almanac for 1717. By Jacob Taylor. *Philadelphia: Andrew Bradford.* 1716.   **139**

1717.

THE CHRISTIANITY of the Quakers asserted. *Philadelphia: Andrew Bradford.* 1717.   **140**

See No. 143, *infra.*

HILL. (H.) A | Legacy for | Children, | Being | Some of the Last Expressions, and | Dying Sayings, | of | Hannah Hill, Junr. | Of the City of Philadelphia, in the Pro- | vince of Pennsylvania, in America, Aged | Eleven Years and near Three Months. | The Third Edition. | . . . | . . . | . . . | . . . | . . . | . . . | . . . . | *Printed by Andrew Bradford, at the Sign of the Bible* | *in the Second Street, in Philadelphia.* 1717. | 16mo. pp. 35.   D.   **141**

LEEDS. (T.) Leeds, 1718. | The American | Almanack | For the Year of Christian Account 1718. | . . . | . . . | . . . | . . . . | Being the Second after Leap Year. | . . . | The Lunations, Moons Rising and Setting, the Eclipses, | Judgment of the Weather, Spring-Tydes, the Planets | motions and mutual Aspects, With the Birth Days of the | Successive Heirs to the Crown of Great Britain. Time | of Sun Rise and Setting, Day-Break, Day-Light End, | Length of the Day, the Seven Stars Southing, Rising | and Setting, Time of High-Water, Fairs, Courts, and | Observable Days. | Fitted to the Latitude of 40 Degrees, and a | Meridian of five hours West from London, but may, | without sensible error, serve all the adjacent places, | even from Newfound-Land to Carolina. | By Titan Leeds, Philomat. | . . . | . . . | . . . | . . . | . . . . | *Printed and Sold by Andrew Bradford, at the Sign of* | *the Bible, in Philadelphia.* [1717.] | Sm. 8vo. pp. (24).   H. S. P.   **142**

[PENN. (WILLIAM)]   A Key opening a way to every common Understanding, How to discern the Difference betwixt the Religion Professed by the People called Quakers, and the Perversions, Misrepresentations and Calumnies of their several Adversaries. *Philadelphia: Andrew Bradford.* 1717.   143

The minutes of the Yearly Meeting begun the 14th. of 7th. mo. 1717, say: "There is printed by Andrew Bradford 1000 small books called The Christianity of the Quakers asserted, and 500 of Penn's Key." See No. 140, *supra.*

SOUTHEBY. (W.)   An Anti-Slavery tract.   By William Southeby.   *Philadelphia: Andrew Bradford.* 1717.   144

TAYLOR. (J.)   An Almanac for 1718.   By Jacob Taylor. *Philadelphia: Andrew Bradford.* 1717.   145

TO | The Honourable | William Keith, Esq; | With the Royal Approbation Lieut. Governour of the Counties | of New-Castle, Kent and | Sussex upon | Delaware, | And the Province of Pennsylvania. | The Humble Address of the Representatives of the said Counties in General As- | sembly met at New-Castle the 13th Day June, Anno; Domini. 1717. | [*Philadelphia: Andrew Bradford.* 1717.]   Folio, pp. 3.   H. S. P.   146

Some copies have three and a half additional lines at the end, beginning "In the present Situation of Affairs, it is Judg'd to be of Service to make the forgoing Address more Publick."

1718.

[KEITH. (WILLIAM)]   A | Letter | to | His Majesty's Justices of the Peace | for the County of | Chester, | With the Governour's | Speech | From the Bench, at a Court of Oyer and Ter- | miner, held at Chester the 15th Day of April, 1718. | Published at the Request of the Represen- | tatives of the Free-men of this Province, in | General Assembly met at | Philadelphia | The 5th Day of May, 1718. | *Philadelphia,* | *Printed, and Sold by Andrew Bradford.* MDCCXVIII. | 4to. pp. 12.   H. S. P.   147

Title in red and black. This is the earliest American example of printing in two colors I have met with.

THE | LAWS | of the | Province | of | Pennsilvania, | Passed by the Governour and General Assemblies of said Pro- | vince, held at Philadelphia in the Years 1715, 1717 and | 1718 being the second and fourth Year of his present Ma- | jesty King George over Great Britain, France and Ireland, &c. | [Royal Arms.] | *Philadel-* *phia.* | *Printed and Sold by Andrew Bradford, at the Sign of the Bible* | *in the Second Street*, MDCCXVIII. | Folio.   L. C. P.   148

Collation : Title and Contents, pp. (2) ; text pp. 275–293, (34), 325–253 [352]. Signatures Ss to Yy, pp. 275–293, p. 282 being repeated ; Aaa to Iii, 17 unpaged leaves, [pp. 34], Kkk to Qqq, pp. 325 to 253, the last being a misprint for 352.

LEEDS. (T.)   Leeds, 1719. | The American | Almanack | For the Year of Christian Account, 1719. | . . . | . . . | . . . | . . . . | Being the Third after Leap Year. | . . . | . . . | . . . | . . . | . . . | . . . | . . . | . . . | . . . | . . . | . . . | . . . . | By Titan Leeds, Philomat. | . . . | . . . | . . . | . . . | . . . . | *Printed and* *Sold by Andrew Bradford, at the Sign of the | Bible, in the second* *Street in Philadelphia.*   [1718.] | Sm. 8vo. pp. (24).   H. S. P.   149

MARYLAND. The | Laws | of the | Province | of | Mary-land, | Collected into one | Volumn, | By Order of the Governour and Assembly of the said | Province, | At a General Assembly begun at St. Mary's the 10th | Day of May, 1692 and continued by several Assemblies | to the Year 1718. | *Philadelphia,* | *Printed by Andrew Bradford, and are to be sold by Evan Jones at* *the* | *City of Annapolis in Maryland*, 1718. | Folio.   Title, 1 leaf ; The Publisher to the Reader, pp. (2) ; Index, pp. (7) ; Laws, pp. 1–220.   L. C. P.   150

PROPOSALS for Traffick and Commerce, | or | Foreign Trade in | New-Jersey, | In Answer to that upbraiding Question, | Why should not We have Trade, as all other | The | Plantations : | Collected | From the Papers of A. and B.   D. U.   A. P.   F. | and G. H. W. and others. | And Humbly Presented to the | General Assembly | By Amicus Patriæ. | . . . . | [*Philadelphia:*] *Printed* [*by Andrew Bradford*] *in the Year* 1718. | 4to. pp. 24.   151

TAYLOR. (J.) An Almanac for 1719.   By Jacob Taylor. *Philadelphia: Andrew Bradford.*   1718.   152

To the Honourable | William Keith, Esq ; Lieut. Governour of the Province of Pennsilvania &c. | The Humble Address | Of the Grand Jury for the City of Philadelphia. | *Philadelphia, Printed and Sold by Andrew Bradford, at the Sign of the Bible, in the second Street,* 1718. | Folio, 1 leaf. H. S. P. 153

1719.

AN ACT | passed in the | General Assembly | Held at | Philadelphia | for the | Province of Pennsilvania | The Twenty Fifth Day of April, in the Fifth Year of His | Majesties Reign Annoq; Domini 1719. | [Royal Arms.] | *Philadelphia* | *Printed and Sold by Andrew Bradford at the Sign of the Bible,* | *in the Second Street.* MDCCXIX. | Folio. L. C. P. 154

Collation : Title, 1 leaf; text, pp. (8). Signatures Rrr to Ttt.

THE AMERICAN | Weekly Mercury, | December 22, 1719. | [Colophon.] *Philadelphia Printed, and Sold by Andrew Bradford, at the Bible in the Second Street* | *and John Copson in Market Street* 1719 | Folio, pp. 2.

No. 2 | The American | Weekly Mercury, | Tuesday December 29, 1719. | *Philadelphia Printed, and Sold by Andrew Bradford, at the Bible* | *in the Second Street and John Copson in the Market Street,* 1719. | pp. [3]–4. L. C. P. 155

The first Newspaper published in the Middle Colonies. For an account of it and its printer, see An Address on Andrew Bradford, by Horatio Gates Jones, 1869, and Thomas' History of Printing, 2d edition.

A BRIEF | APOLOGY | In behalf of the | People | In Derision call'd | Quakers. | Written | For the Information of our | Sober and Well-Inclined Neigh- | bours in and about the Town of | Warminster in the County of Wilts. | By Will. Chandler, Alex. Pyott, | Jo. Hodges. And some others. | . . . | . . . | . . . | . . . . *London Printed, and Re-Printed by* | *Andrew Bradford in Philadelphia.* 1719. | 16mo. pp. 104. H. S. P. 156

LEEDS. (T.)   Leeds, 1720. | The American | Almanack | For the Year of Christian Account, 1720. | . . . | . . . | . . . | . . . . | Being the Bessextile or Leap Year. | Wherein is Contained | The Lunations, Eclipses, Judgment of the Weather, the | Spring-Tydes, the Planets motions and mutual Aspects ; | With the Birth Days of the Successive Heirs to the | Crown of Great Britain. Time of Sun Rise and Set- | ting, Length of the Day, the Seven Stars Southing, | Rising and Setting, Time of High-Water, Fairs, Courts, | and Observable Days. | Fitted to the Latitude of 40 De-grees, and a | Meridian of five hours West from London, but may | without sensible error, serve all the adjacent places | even from Newfound-Land to Carolina. | By Titan Leeds, Philomat. | . . . | . . . | . . . | . . . | . . . . | *Printed and Sold by Andrew Bradford, at the Sign of the | Bible, in the second Street in Philadelphia.* [1719.] | Sm. 8vo. pp. (24).   H. S. P.   157

T[AYLOR]. (J[ACOB])   An | Almanack | For the Year of our Lord 1719. | Or An | Ephemeris | Of the Motions of the Planets, their | Mutual Aspects, and other Phenomena : | the Luna- | tions, Eclipses, the Rising and setting of the Sun (Tydes, | &c.)   Justly calculated for the Meridian and Latitude | of Phil-adelphia ; With other Matters, some Custo- | mary, some Novel, but very Equal in Value, and fit- | ed to the same Elevation of the Pole. | By J. T. | . . . | . . . | . . . | . . . | . . . | . . . | . . . | . . . | . . . | . . . | . . . | . . . . | *Printed and Sold by Andrew Bradford, in the second Street | near the great Meeting-House in Phila-delphia.*   1719. | Sm. 8vo. pp. (30).   A. P. S.   158

1720.

No. 3 | The American | Weekly Mercury, | Tuesday, January 5th, 1719,-20. | [Colophon.]   *Philadelphia Printed, and Sold by Andrew Bradford, at the Bible | in the Second Street and John Cop-son in the Market Street,* 1719.   [1720.] | Folio.   L. C. P.   159

Numbers 3 to 54 (from Tuesday Dec. 20 to Tuesday, Dec. 27, 1720).   Num-bers 13, 20, 21 and 45 consist of four pages, 19, 22, 26, 27, 30–32, 39–41, 44, 46, 48, 49, and 52, of three pages ; and the others of two pages each.   From No. 13, to No. 51, the paper was issued on Thursday, and the others on Tuesday.   In Nos.

14 to 21, "Philadelphia," is prefixed to the date. In No. 4 the year is dropped from the imprint, the second line of which is changed to "Second Street and John Copson in the High Street, and also where Advertisements are taken in." | In No. 9, the words "and also" are omitted. The imprint changes in No. 13 to "Philadelphia Printed, and sold by Andrew Bradford, at the Bible in the Second Street, and | John Copson in the High Street, where Advertisements are taken in." | It changes again in No. 25, to "Philadelphia Printed and Sold by Andrew Bradford at the Bible the [*sic*] second Street, | and may also be had at John Copson in High Street, and William Bradford, | in New York, where Advertisements are taken in." | In No. 50, the spacing of the imprint is slightly changed. Cuts of a mounted Postman on the left and Mercury on the right were added to No. 22, and the spacing of the title was changed to : "The | American | Weekly Mercury." | In No. 33 the position of the cuts was reversed.

JERMAN. (J.) An | Ephemeris | For the Year, 1721 ; | or, an | Almanack. | Containing, | The Motions and Aspects of the Planets ; the | Rising and Setting of the Sun ; the Eclipses | of the Sun and Moon ; Judgment of the | Weather ; Time of High Water at Phila- | delphia ; the Spring Tides ; Remarkable Days : | Time of Courts and Fairs : With other | Useful Observations, | Fitted for the Latitude of 40 Degrees North, and West | from London, the Metropolis of Great Britain, about | 5 Hours ; but may serve, without much Error, from | Boston to the Capes of Virginia. | By John Jerman, A. S. | . . . | . . . | . . . | . . . . | *Philadelphia:* | *Printed by Andrew Bradford in the second Street.* [1720.] | Sm. 8vo. pp. (24). H. S. P. 160

This was the first issue of Jerman's Almanac.

LEEDS. (T.) The American Almanac for 1721. By Titan Leeds. *Philadelphia: Andrew Bradford.* 1720. 161

PENN. (W.) Advice to his Children. By William Penn. *Philadelphia: Reprinted from the 6th London Edition.* 1720. 162

Title from Haven's List. The date is probably an error for 1780, as the 6th London edition did not appear till 1778.

PROCLAMATION. | G. [Royal Arms.] R. | By William Keith, Esq ; | Governour of the Province of Pennsylvania, and Counties of | New-Castle, Kent and Sussex, upon Delaware. | A Proclamation. | *Printed by Andrew Bradford, Printer to the Province of Pennsylvania, &c.* [1720.] | Sm. Folio, 1 leaf. H. S. P. 163

Dated Nov. 5, 1720. Against harboring Robert Moore, who had escaped from Jail in New York, where he was confined under the charge of having killed John Gee in a duel.

T[AYLOR]. (J[ACOB]) An | Almanack | For the Year of our Lord 1720. | Or An | Ephemeris | Of the Motions of the Planets, their | Mutual Aspects, and other Phœnomena, the Lunations, | Eclipses, Rising and setting of the Sun, Time of High- | Water, with Sundry Usual and Useful Observations, | Calculated for the Vertex of Philadelphia. | By J. T. | . . . | . . . | . . . | . . . | . . . | . . . | . . . | . . . . | *Philadelphia Printed and Sold by* | *Andrew Bradford, at the Bible in the Second Street.* | MDCCXX. | Sm. 8vo. pp. (24).   A. P. S.   164

TAYLOR. (J.) An Almanac for 1721. By Jacob Taylor. *Philadelphia: Andrew Bradford.* 1720.   165

1721.

ACTS | of the | Province of Pennsylvania, | pass'd in the | General Assembly | held at | Philadelphia, | The Fourteenth Day of October, and continued by Ad- | journments till the Twenty Fifth Day of February, in | the Seventh Year of His Majesty's Reign, Annoq; | Domini, 1720. | [Royal Arms.] | *Philadelphia:* | *Printed and Sold by Andrew Bradford, Printer to the Province of* | *Pennsylvania, at the Sign of the Bible in the Second Street,* | MDCCXXI. | Folio, pp. 12.   L. C. P.   166

ACTS | of the | Province of Pennsylvania, | pass'd in the | General Assembly | held at | Philadelphia, | The Fourteenth Day of October, and continued by Adjourn- | ments till the Twenty Fifth Day of February, in the Seventh | Year of his Majesty's Reign, 1720. And from thence by | Adjournments to the Twenty Sixth Day of August, 1721, | in the Eighth Year of His Majesty's Reign. | [Royal Arms.] | *Philadelphia:* | *Printed and Sold by An- drew Bradford, Printer to the Province of* | *Pennsylvania, at the Sign of the Bible in the Second Street,* | MDCCXXI. | Folio, Title, 1 leaf; pp. 13-30.   L. C. P.   167

[Two cuts.] No. 55 | THE | AMERICAN | Weekly Mercury, | From Tuesday December 27th, to Tuesday January 3d, 1721. | [Colophon.] *Philadelphia, Printed and Sold by Andrew Bradford at the Bible the Second Street | and also by John Copson in High Street, and William Bradford in New-York, where Adver- | tisements are taken in.* [1722.] Folio, pp. (2). L. C. P. 168

Numbers 55 (from Tuesday, Dec. 27 to Tuesday, Jan. 3, 1721) to 106 (from Tuesday, Dec. 19 to Tuesday, Dec. 26, 1721). The cuts are described under No. 159, *supra*. Numbers 66, 75, 82, 84, 90, 91, 96, 99, 102 and 104 consist of four pages; Numbers 63, 74, 79, 81–83, 85, 95 and 98 consist of three pages, and the others of two pages each. Numbers 63 to 103 were issued on Thursday; the others on Tuesday. In No. 75, the imprint reads: "*Philadelphia, Printed and Sold by Andrew Bradford at the Bible the* [*sic*] *Second Street | and also by William Bradford in New York, where Advertisements are taken in.*" | It also underwent a slight change in No. 78.

LEEDS. (T.) Leeds, 1722. | The American | Almanack | For the Year of Christian Account 1722. | . . . | . . . | . . . | . . . | Being the Second after Leap-Year. | . . . | . . . | . . . | . . . | . . . | . . . | . . . | . . . | . . . | . . . | . . . . | By Titan Leeds, Philomat. | . . . | . . . | . . . | . . . | . . . | . . . . | *Printed and Sold by Andrew Bradford, at the Bible | in the Second Street in, Philadelphia.* [1721.] | Sm. 8vo. pp. (24). L. C. P. 169

A | MEMORIAL, | Humbly shewing the Past and Present State of the Land | lying Waste and Un-inhabited between Nova-Scotia, and | the Province of Main in New-England in America. | [*Philadelphia: Andrew Bradford.* 1721.?] Folio, pp. 2. L. C. P. 170

The Memorial recites : That the said Land was first possessed by the French who were driven from it by the Dutch, and afterwards with New York, it was granted to the Duke of York, who settled 1100 English Families upon it; after the Revolution these settlers were driven out by the French and the land laid waste ; that in 1691 it was granted to the Province of Massachusetts-Bay, and in 1696 given up to the French, from whom it was retaken in 1710 ; that the petitioners had applied in 1716, and in 1718 obtained a recognition of their rights from the Lords of Trade, and had appointed Trustees, who had joined in a petition presented in July, 1718. The petitioners therefore pray that the said Lands and Islands may be erected into a Province by the name of Georgia. Probably printed and circulated with a view to attract settlers.

THE | OFFICE, Duty and Authority | of | Sheriffs, | How and
in what Manner to execute the same, | according to the Common
and Statute Laws | of Great-Britain, which are now in Force | and
Use. | Likewise, | Of Under-Sheriffs and their Deputies ; | and
where the High-Sheriff shall be answerable for | their Defaults,
and where not, &c. | Together with the | Office and Duty of Coro-
ners. | *Philadelphia:* | *Printed and Sold by Andrew Bradford, at the
Bible* | *in the Second Street,* MDCCXXI. | 171

Title from Conductor Generalis, 1722.

THE PARTICULARS of an Indian Treaty at Conestogoe, between His Excellency Sir William Keith, Bart. Governor of Pennsylvania, And the Deputies of the Five Nations. *Philadelphia:
Andrew Bradford.* 1721.   172

Advertised in American Weekly Mercury, July 27, 1721, and reprinted at
Dublin, and London in 1723.

PUGH. (E.)   Annerch | ir | Cymru, | Iw Galw | Oddiwrth y
llawer o bethau at yr un peth angen- | rheidiol er mwyn cadwe-
digaeth eu heneidiau. | Yn Enwedig | At y Tlodion annysgedig,
sef y Crefftwyr, Llafurwyr a Bu- | geiliaid, y rhai o isel radd,
o'm Cyffelyb sy hunan, | Hyn | Er eich Cyfarwyddo i adna-
bod Duw a Christ, (yr hyn yw | bywyd tragwyddol) yr hwn sydd
yn Dduw unig ddoeth. A | Dyseu ganddo ef, fel y deloch yn
ddoethach nach Athrawon. | O Waith Ellis Pugh. | . . . | . . . |
. . . . | *Argraphedig yn Philadelphia, Ymhensilfania, gan Andrew
Bradford,* | MDCCXXI. | 4to.   F. 173

Collation : Title, 1 leaf ; Hanes yr Awdwr, pp. iii-v ; Tystio laeth y Cyforfod
Misol yng-wynedd yn sir Philadelphia Oblegid ein Cyfaill Ellis Pugh, pp. vi-x ;
text, pp. 3–111. The first book printed in Welsh in America. For a translation,
see No. 312, *infra.*

[RAWLE. (FRANCIS)] Some | Remedies | Proposed, | for the
| Restoring the sunk Credit | of the Province of | Pennsylvania ;
| with | Some Remarks on its Trade. | Humbly Offer'd to the
Consideration of the | Worthy Representatives in the General |
Assembly of this Province. | By a Lover of this Country. | . . .
| . . . . | [*Philadelphia:*] *Printed* [*by Andrew Bradford.*] | *in the
Year,* 1721. | 8vo. pp. 20.   L. C. P. 174

Bradford was summoned before the Provincial Council for presuming to publish anything concerning the affairs of the Government without permission, but upon his declaring he knew nothing about the pamphlet, was discharged. For some account of the Author, see *The Penna. Magazine of History and Biography.* Vol. III., p. 118.

TAYLOR. (J.) An Almanac for 1725. By Jacob Taylor. *Philadelphia: Andrew Bradford.* 1721.   175

1722.

ACTS | of the | Province of Pennsylvania, | pass'd in the | General Assembly | held at | Philadelphia, | The Fourteenth Day of October, One Thousand Seven Hun- | dred and Twenty One, and continued by Adjournments | till the Twenty Second Day of May, One Thousand | Seven Hundred and Twenty Two, in the Eighth Year of | His Majesty's Reign. | [*Royal Arms.*] | *Philadelphia:* | *Printed and Sold by Andrew Bradford, Printer to the Province of* | *Pennsylvania, at the Sign of the Bible in the Second Street,* | MDCCXXII. | Folio, Title, 1 leaf; pp. 33-90.   H. S. P.   176

AN ASTRONOMICAL Diary or an Almanac for the year of Christ 1723. *Printed and sold by William and Andrew Bradford in New York and Philadelphia.* Sm. 8vo. pp. (32).   177

THE AMERICAN Weekly Mercury. *Philadelphia: Printed and Sold by Andrew Bradford,* | *at the Bible, in the* | *Second Street; and also by William Bradford in New-York, where Advertisements are taken in.* [1722.] | Folio, pp. (2).   L. C. P.   178

Numbers 107 (from Tuesday, Dec. 26 to Tuesday, Jan. 2, 1721) to 158 (from Tuesday, Dec. 18 to Tuesday, Dec. 26, 1722). The title is spaced as in No. 168, *supra.* Numbers 107-110, 113, 116, 117, 119, 121, 122, 124, 126, 128, 131, 133, 135, 138-140, 142, 146, 147, 149, 150, 153, 155 and 158, consist of two pages ; the others of four pages each, except No. 112, which contains only three. Numbers 116, 118 to 153, and 155 were issued on Thursday, 117 on Saturday, 153 on Friday, and the others on Tuesday.

CONDUCTOR GENERALIS, | Or | The Office, Duty and Authority | of | Justices of the Peace, | High-Sheriffs, Under-Sheriffs, Goalers, Coroners, | Constables, Jury-Men, Over-seers of the Poor, | And Also | The Office of Clerks of Assize | And of the Peace, &c. | Collected out of all the Books hitherto written on those | Subjects, whether of Common or Statute-Law. | To which is Added, | A Collection out of Sir Matthew Hales concerning | The Descent of Lands. | The whole Alphabetically digested under the several Titles, | With a Table directing to the ready finding out the proper | Matter under those Titles. | *Printed and Sold by Andrew Brafdord in Philadelphia*, 1722. | Sq. 8vo. pp. (8.), xii, 299, (1). H. S. P.   179

Page 232 is followed by a separate title page, "The Office, Duty and Authority of Sheriffs," etc., as in 1721.

CRISP. (S.) Two Letters written by Samuel Crisp, about 1702, upon his change from a Chaplain of the Church of England to join with the People called Quakers. *Philadelphia: Andrew Bradford.* 1722. 180

Printed by order of the Yearly Meeting of Friends.

A DISCOURSE upon Heb. 13, ver. 17. By Philobangor. 181

Advertised as "preparing for the Press," in the American Weekly Mercury, Nov. 8, 1722, with a long account of the contents. Probably not printed.

AN EPISTLE of Caution | to | Friends in General | Relating to the | Solemn Affirmation. | From a Meeting held in London the Second of First | Month 1721–22. | [*Philadelphia: Printed by Andrew Bradford.* 1722.] Folio, pp. 3. 182

JERMAN. (J.) An | Almanack | For the Year, 1723, | or, an | Ephemeris, | Containing | The Motions and Aspects of the Planets ; | The Rising and Setting of the Sun ; The Eclipses | of the Sun and Moon ; Judgment of the | Weather ; Time of High-Water at Philadelphia ; | The Spring Tides ; Remarkable Days ; Time of | Courts and Fairs : With some other Observations | necessary to be known. | Fitted for the Latitude of 40 Degrees, and a Meridian | of Five Hours West from London ; but may serve | from Newfoundland to Carolina, without much Error. | By John Jerman. | . . . | . . . | . . . | . . . . | *Philadelphia :* | *Printed and Sold by Andrew Bradford, at the Bible in* | *the Second Street.* [1722.] | Sm. 8vo. pp. (24). L. C. P.   183

"Having accommodated thee with the Planets Places for the Year 1721, I thought to proceed yearly in the said Service, but being absent in Great Britain at the time when the said work should have been composed, I miss'd one year."

A JOURNAL of the Votes and Proceedings of the Honourable House of Representatives of the Province of Pennsylvania. *Philadelphia: Andrew Bradford.* 1722.   184

LEEDS. (T.) The American Almanac for 1723. By Titan Leeds. *Philadelphia: Andrew Bradford.* 1722.   185

THE PARTICULARS of an Indian Treaty at Conestogoe, between His Excellency Sir William Keith, Bart. Governor of Pennsylvania, and the Deputies of the Five Nations, in June, 1722. *Philadelphia: Andrew Bradford.* 1722.   186

THE | SWEDES Petition | to the | House of Representatives | of the | Province of Pennsylvania, | The Governor's Letter thereupon to the | Commissioners of Property, | with | Their Report in Answer to the same. | *Philadelphia:* | *Printed by Andrew Bradford at the Bible in the Second Street,* | MDCCXXII. | Folio, pp. 8.   H. S. P.   187

TAYLOR. (J.) An | Ephemeris, | of the | Planetary Motions | and | Aspects, | For the Year of Our Lord, 1723, | Being the Third after Leap Year. | Containing Also | The Lunations (and Eclipses, tho' there are | none); The Rising and Setting of the Sun and Moon; The Time of High-Water, and other Matters both | Customary and Noval. | Also, | The Rising, Southing and Setting of the most eminent | Fixed Stars. | Calculated for the Vertex of Philadelphia. | By Jacob Taylor. | . . . . | *Philadelphia:* | *Printed and Sold by Andrew Bradford, at the Bible in* | *the Second Street.* [1722.] | Sm. 8vo. pp. (32).   A. P. S.   188

A | TREATY | of | Peace and Friendship | Made and Concluded between His Excellency | Sir William Keith, Bart. | Governor of the Province of Pennsylvania, | For and on Behalf of the said Province, | And the | Chiefs of the Indians of the Five Nations, | At Albany, in the Month of September, 1722. | *Philadelphia:* | *Printed by Andrew Bradford, at the Bible in the Second Street,* | MDCCXXII. | Folio, pp. 8.   B. M.   189

1723.

AN | ACT | pass'd in the | General Assembly | Held at | Phila-
delphia | for the | Province of Pennsylvania. | The Twenty Second
Day of March, in the Ninth Year of | His Majesties Reign
Annoq; Domini 1722 | [*Royal Arms.*] | *Philadelphia:* | *Printed and
sold by Andrew Bradford, Printer to the Province of* | *Pennsylvania,
at the Sign of the Bible in the Second Street,* | MDCCXXIII. |
Folio, pp. 14.   H. S. P. 190

ACTS | passed in the | General Assembly | of the | Province of
Pennsylvania. | Held at | Philadelphia | The Fourteenth Day of
October, One Thousand Seven Hun- | dred and Twenty Two, and
continued by Adjournments | till the Eleventh Day of May, One
Thousand Seven | Hundred and Twenty Three, in the Ninth Year of
His | Majesty's Reign. | [*Royal Arms.*] | *Philadelphia:* | *Printed
and Sold by Andrew Bradford, Printer to the Province of* | *Pennsyl-
vania, at the Sign of the Bible in the Second Street.* | MDCCXXIII.
| Folio, pp. 47.   H. S. P. 191

The last page is printed on the inside of the cover. Two Acts are omitted, both
of which were probably, and one certainly, printed separately. The latter with
the preceding title.

ACTS | passed in the | General Assembly | of the | Province
of Pennsylvania. | Held at | Philadelphia | The Fourteenth Day
of October, One Thousand Seven Hun- | dred and Twenty Three,
and continued by Adjournments | till the Twelfth Day of Decem-
ber next after, in the | Tenth Year of His Majesty's Reign. |
[*Royal Arms.*] | *Philadelphia:* | *Printed and Sold by Andrew Brad-
ford, Printer to the Province of* | *Pennsylvania, at the Sign of the Bible
in the Second Street.* | MDCCXXIII. | Folio, pp. 28.   L. C. P. 192

THE AMERICAN Weekly Mercury.   L. C. P. 193

Numbers 159 (from Tuesday, Dec. 26 to Tuesday, Jan. 1, 1722) to 211 (from
Tuesday Dec. 24 to Tuesday Dec. 31, 1723). Title and imprint as in No. 178, *supra.*
Numbers 159, 161, 165, 167, 171, 174, 176–179, 182, 183, 185, 188, 192, 197, 199,
and 202–404, consist of four pages ; the others of two pages each. From No. 168
to 207, the paper was published on Thursday ; the others on Tuesday. No. 188
is misdated July 24, for 25, and 198 Oct. 4, for 3.

THE | ANTIENT Testimony | of the | People | called | Qua-
kers, | Reviv'd. | By the Order and Approbation of | the Yearly
Meeting held | for the Province of Pennsylvania and | Jerseys.
1722. | *Philadelphia:* | *Printed by Andrew Bradford at the Sign* |
of the Bible in Second-street. 1723. | 16mo. pp. 48.   H. S. P.   194

BURNET. (W.) The | Speech | Of His Excellency | William
Burnet, Esq; | Captain General and Governor in Chief of the
Provinces of New- | Jersey, New-York, and Territories depending
thereon in America, | and Vice-Admiral of the same, To the
Assembly of the Province | of New-Jersey, met at Burlington, the
27th of September, 1723. | [*Philadelphia: Andrew Bradford.* 1723.]
Folio, pp. (2).   L. C. P.   195

The second page contains the Assembly's reply.

THE | CASE | of | Isaac Taylor and Elisha Gatchel, | Two
Officers of Pennsylvania, made Prisoners by the Government | of
Maryland. | [Colophon.] *Printed at Philadelphia,* [*by Andrew Brad-
ford*] *in the Year* 1723. | Folio, pp. 2.   H. S. P.   196

CHALKLEY. (T.) A Letter to a Friend in Ireland, containing
a Relation of some sorrowful Instances of the sad Effects of Intem-
perance as a Warning to Young People. The Third Edition. By
Thomas Chalkley. *Philadelphia: Samuel Keimer.* 1723.   197

Advertised at the end of Eastburn's Doctrine of Absolute Reprobation Refuted.
The first and second editions were printed in London in 1720 and 1722.

EASTBURN. (B.) The | Doctrine | of | Absolute Reprobation,
| According to the Westminster | Confession of Faith, Refuted: |
And the Universality of | the Saving Grace of God asserted. | By
Benjamin Eastburn. | To which is added, | A Postscript by another
Hand, | wherein those several Texts of Scrip- | ture generally per-
verted, to vindicate | the aforesaid Doctrine of Reprobation, | are
set in a true Light. | *Philadelphia:* | *Printed and sold by Samuel
Keimer, in* | *High-street.* 1723. | Sm. 8vo. pp. 66; Advertisement,
1 leaf.   A. A. S.   198

THE HISTORY of the Kingdom of Basaruh; and most sorts of
pleasant Histories, &c. *Philadelphia: Andrew Bradford.* 1723.?

This and several other titles are given as found in a list of "Books Printed and Sold by Andrew Bradford" at the end of Leeds' Almanac for 1724, which is immediately followed by a separate list of "Books to be Sold by Andrew Bradford."

THE HUSBAND-MAN'S Guide, being a Collection of very useful Directions and Receipts for Country People. *Philadelphia: Andrew Bradford.* 1723. ?   200

Advertised in Leeds' Almanac for 1724.

JERMAN. (J.) An Almanac for 1724. By John Jerman. *Philadelphia: Andrew Bradford.* 1723.   201

K[EACH]. (B[enjamin)] War with the Devil, or the Young Man's Conflict with the Powers of Darkness, in a Dialogue. By B. K. *Philadelphia: Andrew Bradford.* 1723. ?   202

These poems seem to have been very popular. Advertised in Leeds' Almanac for 1724. The elder Bradford printed the 12th edition at New York, about 1715, and prefixed a poem of his own.

[KEIMER. (Samuel)] An Elegy On the much Lamented Death of the Ingenious and Well-Beloved Aquila Rose, Clerk to the Honourable Assembly at Philadelphia, who died the 24th of the 4th month, 1723. Aged 28. *Philadelphia: Printed and Sold by Samuel Keimer, in High Street.* 1723. Folio, 1 leaf.   203

Reprinted in Hazard's Register, Nov., 1828, p. 262. Franklin, on his first visit to Keimer, found him employed in setting up these verses. "He could not be said to write them," says Franklin, "for his manner was to compose them in the types directly out of his head." It is the first issue of Keimer's press, and was worked off by Franklin.

LEEDS. (T.) Leeds, 1724. | The American Almanack | For the Year of Christian Account, 1724. | Unto which is Numbered | . . . | . . . | . . . . | Being the Bissextile or Leap Year. | Wherein is Contain'd | The Lunations, Eclipses, Judgment of the | Weather, the Spring-Tides, the Planets Motions, and | mutual Aspects: With the Birth-Days of the | Suc- | cessive Heirs to the Crown of Great Britain. | Time of the Sun's Rising and Setting, Length of the | Day, the Seven Stars Rising, Southing and Setting, | Time of High-Water, Fairs, Courts, and Observable Days. | Fitted to the Latitude of 40 Degrees, and a | Meridian of Five Hours West from London, but may | without sensible Error, serve all the adjacent Places, | even from New-found-land to Carolina. | By Titan Leeds, Philomat. | . . . | . . . | . . . | . . . | . . . | . . . . | *Printed and Sold by Andrew Bradford, at the Sign | of the Bible, in the Second Street, in Philadelphia.* [1723.] | Sm. 8vo. pp. (24). L. C. P. 204

A | LETTER | From one in the Country to his Friend in the City, | On Occasion of the Law of Summons. | [Colophon.] *Philadelphia: Printed and Sold by S. Keimer, in High-street.* [1723.] | Folio, pp. 3. 205

Signed Philadelphos, and dated September 27, 1723.

[LOGAN. (JAMES)] The | Charge | Delivered from the Bench | to the | Grand Jury, | At the Court of Quarter Sessions, | held for the County of Philadelphia, | the second day of September 1723. | Published at the Desire of the said Grand-Jury. | Together with Their Address. | *Philadelphia: | Printed and Sold by Andrew Bradford, at the | Sign of the Bible, in the Second Street,* | MDCCXXIII. | Sq. 8vo. pp. 16. H. S. P. 206

A PARABLE. *Philadelphia: Samuel Keimer.* 1723. 207

The following notice appeared in the American Weekly Mercury, for January 14, 1723–4: "Whereas one Samuel Keimer, who hath lately come into this Province of Pennsylvania, had Printed and Published divers Papers, particularly, one entitled, *A Parable,* &c. in some Parts of which he assumes to use such a Stile and Language, as that perhaps he may be deemed, where he is not known, to be one of the People called Quakers : this may therefore certefie, that the said Samuel Keimer is not one of the said People, nor countenanced by them in the aforesaid Practices. Signed by order of the Monthly Meeting . . . held at Philadelphia, the 29th Day of the Ninth Month, 1733. Samuel Preston, Cl."

SMITH. (J.) The Curiosities of Common Water: Or the Advantages thereof in Preventing and Curing Many Distempers. Written by John Smith, C. M. To which is added some Rules for preserving Health by Diet. *Philadelphia: Samuel Keimer.* 1723

Advertised in the American Weekly Mercury, January 14, 1723–4.

TAYLOR. (J.) An Almanac for 1724. By Jacob Taylor. *Philadelphia: Andrew Bradford.* 1723. 209

THE TESTAMENT of the Twelve Patriarchs, the Sons of
Jacob. *Philadelphia: Andrew Bradford.* 1723.   210

See the History of Basurah, No. 199, *supra.*

THE YOUNG MAN'S Companion, Containing, 1. Directions
for Reading, Writing and Spelling True English. 2. Arithmatick
made Easie and the Rules, thereof explain'd. 3. The method of
Writing Letters upon most Subjects, whether Trade or otherways.
4. Useful Presidents of Bills, Bonds, Letters of Attorney, Wills,
Indentures, Bills of Sale, Deeds of Gift, Assignments, Leases and
Releases, Counter Securities, &c. *Philadelphia: Andrew Bradford.*
1723. ?   211

Advertised in Leeds' Almanac for 1724, and for six or seven years afterwards.

1724.

AN ACCOUNT of the Apprehending, Tryal and Condemnation
of two Grand Criminals, namely, Idleness and Pride. Being a de-
lightful and pleasant, as well as teachable Discourse, designed to
reform those two great Evils of our Day. *Philadelphia: Samuel
Keimer.* 1724.   212

Advertised in No. xi. of the Independent Whig.

THE AMERICAN Weekly Mercury.   L. C. P.   213

Numbers 212 (from Tuesday, Dec. 31 to Tuesday, Jan. 14, 172¾) to 263 (from
Tuesday, Dec. 23 to Tuesday, Dec. 29, 1724). Title and imprint as in No. 178.
Numbers 213, 217, 224, 226, 227, 229, 230, 232, 235, 237, 240, 242, 248 and 256,
consist of four pages, and the others of two pages each. Numbers 221 to 260
were published on Thursday ; the others on Tuesday. No. 242 is misdated Aug.
5, for 6.

[BOCKETT. (ELIAS)] A | Determination | of the | Case | of |
Mr. Thomas Story and Mr. James Hoskins, | Relating to an Affair
of the Pennsylvania | Company, &c. | [*Philadelphia: S. Keimer.*
1724.] Folio, pp. 3.   H. S. P.   214

Smith's Catalogue of Friends' Books describes two editions printed in London.

THE | CASE | Of the People called | Quakers | In the Province of | Pennsylvania, | With respect to the Forms of Declara- | tion of Fidelity to the King, and of Affirmation, | lately granted to their Friends in Great Britain | and Ireland, &c., by Acts of Parliament, briefly | stated and humbly offer'd to the Consideration of | the Governour and Council of the said Province. | [Colophon.] *Phila-delphia: Printed by Andrew | Bradford.* 1724. | Sm. 8vo. pp. 7.

H. S. P.   215

CRISP. (S.) A Short History of a Long Travel, from Baby-lon to Bethel, by that eminent Servant of Christ, Stephen Crisp. *Philadelphia: Samuel Keimer.* 1724.   216

DAVIS. (WILLIAM) A Statement of his quarrel with the con-gregation at Westerly, R. I. *Philadelphia:* 1724.?   217

Partly reprinted, from an imperfect copy, in the Seventhday Baptist Me-morial, Vol. II., p. 107. It is signed William and Elizabeth Davis, and dated Pennsylvania, Nov. 5, 1724.

DELL. (W.) Baptismon Didaches: | Or the | Doctrine | of | Baptisms, | Reduced from its Ancient and Modern | Corruptions; and restored to its Primitive | Soundness and Integtity. [*sic*] | According to | The Word of Truth, | The Substance of Faith, | And | The Nature of Christ's Kingdom. | By William Dell, Min-ister of the Gospel, | and Master of Gonvil and Caius College | in Cambridge. | The Fourth Edition. | . . . | . . . | . . . . | *London, Printed in the Year* 1652, *and re- | printed by S. Keimer in Phila-delphia.* 1724. | Sm. 8vo. pp. v, 54.   F.   218

A DIALOGUE betwixt a Burgomaster of Rotterdam, and Monsieur Jurieu, a French Calvinist Preacher, concerning a Ques-tion of great importance, viz.: Whether the Civil Magistrate ought in Conscience to take Cognizance of Ecclesiastical Disputes, so as to prevent them, or any Ways punish the Authors of them. *Philadelphia: Samuel Keimer.* 1724.   219

A DIALOGUE betwixt a Learned Divine and a Beggar. *Philadelphia: Samuel Keimer.* 1724.   220

DISTINCT Notions of the Plague. *Philadelphia: Samuel Keimer.* 1724.   221

AN | EPISTLE | from our | Yearly Meeting at Burlington, | For the Jerseys and Pennsylvania, &c. Held by Adjournment, | from the Nineteenth to the Twenty third Day of the Seventh | Month 1724. | To the Quarterly and Monthly-Meetings of Friends. | [Colophon.] *Philadelphia, Printed by Andrew Bradford, at the Sign of the Bible in the Second Street,* | MDCCXXIV. | Folio, pp. 4.

THE FARRIER'S Dispensatory. *Philadelphia: Samuel Keimer.* 1724.   223

[GORDON. (THOMAS)] The | Independent | Whig. | [*Philadelphia: S. Keimer.* 1724]. Sm. 4to. pp. (16), 227, (1). H. S. P.   224

Keimer probably began the republication of "The Independent Whig" towards the close of 1723, in weekly numbers of four pages. He published twenty numbers in this form, and then printed off the remainder in book form, using the weekly numbers to make up the complete work. The weekly numbers contain advertisements of works issued by him in 1723, while the last page of the volume offers others which were printed in 1724.

HUGHES. (J.) An Ephemeris for 1725. By John Hughes. *Philadelphia: A. Bradford.* 1724.   225

In the preface to this almanac for 1726 Hughes says "I have adventured this Second time on the Stage to Court Mundane Suffrage."

JERMAN. (J.) An Almanac for 1725. By John Jerman: *Philadelphia.* 1724.   226

KEITH. (W.) New-Castle upon Delaware, May 28. 1724. | This being the Anniversary of His Majesty's Birth-Day, Sir William | Keith, . . . came to the Court-House, . . . | . . . and after having caused the | King's Charter to be publish'd for Erecting the same into a Body Cor- | porate and Politick, with many Valuable Privileges, by the Name of | the City of Newcastle; He made the following Speech to the Cor- | poration. | [Colophon.] *Philadelphia: Printed and Sold by S. Keimer, in High-Street, and W. Read | in the City of Newcastle.* [1724.] | Folio, pp. 3. H. S. P.

Contains also the Address of the Corporation of New Castle in reply to the Governor's Speech.

LEEDS. (T.) [Cut.] | Leeds | 1725. | The American | Alma-nack | For the Year of Christian Account, 1725. | . . . | . . . | . . . | . . . | Being the First after Leap Year | . . . | . . . | . . . | . . . | . . . | . . . | . . . | . . . | . . . | . . . | . . . | By Titan Leeds, Philomat. | *Printed and Sold by Andrew Bradford,* *at the Sign | of the Bible, in the Second Street, in Philadelphia.* [1724.] | Sm. 8vo. pp. (24). N. Y. H. S. 228

The lines omitted are worded and spaced precisely as in the Almanac for 1724, The words "Leeds 1725," are embodied in the fanciful block cut in type metal.

A LETTER from the Presbyterian Ministers of the Association about Boston, to the Baptists at Providence, with the Baptists re-markable Answer. *Philadelphia: S. Keimer.* 1724. 229

Advertised in No. xi. of the Independent Whig.

PROCLAMATION. By | Sir William Keith, Bart. | . . . | . . . . | A | Proclamation. | [*Philadelphia: S. Keimer.* 1724.] Folio, 1 leaf. H. S. P. 230

Dated May 15th, 1724. Announcing the agreement between Lord Baltimore, and Hannah Penn and the Trustees of Pennsylvania, that no person should be molested nor any lands be surveyed or granted by either party within the terri-tory in dispute.

TAYLOR. (J.) An Almanac for 1725. By Jacob Taylor. *Philadelphia: Andrew Bradford.* 1724. 231

WOOLSTON. (T.) A | Free Gift | to the | Clergy : | Or the | Hireling Priests | Of what Denomination soever, | Challeng'd | To a Disputation on this Question, | Whether the Hireling Preachers of this Age, who are all Ministers | of the Letter, be not Worshipers of the Apocalyptical Beast, | and Ministers of Antichrist ? | Very fit to be debated in these latter Times of the Apostacy, in which | - - - Fugere Pudor, Verumque Videsque | In quorum subiere Lo-cum Frandesq ; Doliq; | Infidiæque & Vis, & Amor sceleratus ha-bendi. | By Thomas Woolston, | Sometime Fellow of Sydney-College in Cambridge. | *London : | Printed for the Author, given to* *the Clergy gratis, and | sold by A. Moore near St. Paul's* 1722. (Price One Shilling.) *Reprinted at Philadelphia, and sold by S.* *Keimer.* 1724. | Sm. 4to. pp. 52. 232

1725.

ACTS | passed in the | General Assembly | of the | Province of Pennsylvania. | Held at | Philadelphia | The Fourteenth Day of October, One Thousand Seven Hundred | and Twenty-Four, and Continued by Adjournments till the | Twenty First Day of August next after, being the Twelfth Year | of His Majesty Reign, 1725. | [*Royal Arms.*] | *Philadelphla:* | *Printed and Sold by Andrew Bradford, Printer to the Province of Penn-* | *sylvania, at the Sign of the Bible in the Second-Street.* | MDCCXXV. | Folio, pp. 37.   233

THE AMERICAN Weekly Mercury.   L. C. P.   234

Numbers 264 (from Tuesday, Dec. 22 to Tuesday, Jan. 5, 1724–5) to 314 (from Tuesday, Dec. 21 to Tuesday, Dec. 28, 1725).   Title and imprint as in No. 178. Numbers 265, 274, 286, 290, 292, 297, 301, 305, 308 and 313 consist of four pages, and the others of two pages each.   Numbers 272 to 312 were published on Thursday; the others on Tuesday.   No. 291 is misnumbered 300.   In No. 313 (Dec. 9 to 21), the words "William Bradford in New York," were withdrawn from the imprint.

BURGESS. (D.)   The | Craftsman, | A | Sermon | or | Para-phrase upon several Verses of the 19th Chapter of the | Acts of the Apostles. | Composed by the late Daniel Burgess, and intended to be Preach'd by him | in the High Times, but prevented by the burning of his Meeting-House. | . . . | . . . | . . . | . . . | . . . | . . . . | The Third Edition. | *London:* | *Printed, and re-printed and sold by S. Keimer, in Philadelphia.* | Price Six-pence. [1725.] | 4to. Title, 1 leaf; pp. 1–21.   L. C. P.   235

THE | CHARTER | of | Privileges | Granted by the Honour-able | William Penn, Esq; | to the | Freeholders | And Inhabi-tants of | Pennsylvania. | October 28. 1701. | *Philadelphia:* | *Printed and Sold by Samuel Keimer, in High-Street, near the* | *Market-House.* MDCXXV. [*sic*] | Folio, pp. 8.   L. C. P.   236

A | DIALOGUE | Between Mr. Robert Rich, and Roger Plow-man. | [Colophon.] *Printed by Samuel Keimer, in High-Street. Price Two-Pence.* [1725.] | Folio, pp. 4.   L. C. P.   237

A debate on the Paper Money Question.

AN ENGLISH DICTIONARY, explaining the difficult Terms that are used in Divinity, Husbandry, Physick, Philosophy, Law, Navigation, Mathematicks, and other Arts and Sciences. Containing many Thousands of hard Words, &c. *Philadelphia: Samuel Keimer.* 1725.   238

Advertised by Keimer at the end of "Ways and Means."

THE HISTORY of Diodorus Siculus, containing all that is most memorable, and of the greatest Antiquity in the first Ages of the World, until the War of Troy. *Philadelphia: Samuel Keimer.*

Advertised by Keimer at the end of "Ways and Means."

THE HISTORY of the Wars of his late Majesty Charles XII. King of Sweden, From his first Landing in Denmark, to his return from Turkey to Pomerania. *Philadelphia: Samuel Keimer.*

Advertised by Keimer at the end of "Ways and Means."

HUGHES. (J.) An | Ephemeris | For the Year of Our Lord, 1726. | Or an | Almanack, | Containing | The Motions and Aspects of the Planets, | Eclipses, Lunations, Time of Sun Rising and Set- | ing, Time of High Water, Weather Guesses, and | other observations. Courts, Fairs and other Ob- | servable Days. | Fitted to the Vertex of Philadelphia. | By John Hughes. | . . . | . . . | . . . | . . . | . . . | . . . | . . . | . . . | . . . | . . . | . . . . | *Philadelphia, Printed and Sold by Andrew Bradford, | at the Sign of the Bible in the Second Street.* [1725.] | Sm. 8vo. pp. (32).   H. S. P.   241

The last page contains a list of "Books Printed and Sold by Andrew Bradford, at the Sign of the Bible," and also another of "Books sold at the aforesaid Shop."

JERMAN. (J.) An Almanac for the Year 1726. By John Jerman. *Philadelphia:* 1725.   242

A | JOURNAL | of the | Votes and Proceedings | of the | Representatives of the Province of Pennsylvania. | Anno Domini, 1724. | [Colophon.] *Philadelphia Printed, [by Samuel Keimer] and Sold by Mary Rose in Market-street, below | the Court-House.* [1725.] | Folio, pp. 12.   H. S. P.   243

From Oct. 14, 1724 to Jan. 15, 1724-5, when the House adjourned till Feb. 1st. Bradford printed a continuation to February 6th, with the following heading : A | Journal | of the | Votes and Proceedings | of the | House of Representatives | Of the Province of | Pennsylvania. | February 1, 1724-5 | Folio, pp. 16+. Sheets C and D correspond closely with the same signatures of the volume next described, but on comparing them several differences appear which show this to have been the earlier edition.

A | JOURNAL | of the | Votes and Proceedings | of the | House of Representatives | Of the Province Of Pennsylvania. | [Colophon.] *Philadelphia: | Printed and Sold by Andrew Bradford, at the Sign of the Bible in the | Second-Street. Where any Person may be supplied with whole Setts of | these Proceedings.* MDCCXXV. | Folio, pp. vi, 1–42.   H. S. P.   244

Published in two parts, the first containing the proceedings from Oct. 14, 1724 to March 6, 1725, when the House adjourned to March 15, ends on page 34 with a colophon. The remainder, pp. 35–48, contains the proceedings from March 15th to 20th, when the House adjourned to August 9th.

A | JOURNAL | of the | Votes and Proceedings | Of the Representatives of the Province | of Pennsylvania. | Anno Domini 1725. | [Colophon.] *Printed by Samuel Keimer, who is appointed by Order of a Committee of | the House to print the same.* [1725.] | Folio, pp. (4).   H. S. P.   245

From Oct. 14 to Nov. 2, 1725.

KEITH. (W.) A | Letter | from | Sir William Keith, | Bart. Governour of | Pennsylvania, | To Mr. James Logan, Secretary to | the Proprietorship of the said | Province, | On | Occasion of Mr. Logan's having sent | to Sir William a Copy of his | Printed Paper, called the | Antidote. | *Philadelphia: Printed | and Sold by Andrew Bradford,* 1725. | Sm. 8vo. pp. 16.   H. S. P.   246

KEITH. The | Speech | of | Sir William Keith, Bart. | Governour of the Province of Pennsylvania, and the Counties of | New-Castle, Kent and Sussex upon Delaware, | To the Representatives of the Freemen of the said Province of Pennsylvania, | in General Assembly met, January 5, 1724-5. | [Colophon.] *Philadelphia, | Printed and Sold by Andrew Bradford, at the Sign of the Bible in the | Second-Street,* MDCCXXV. | Folio, pp. (2).   H. S. P.   247

LEEDS. (T.) [Cut.] Leeds | 1726. | The American | Alma-
nack | For the Year of Christian Account 1726. | . . . | . . . |
. . . | . . . . | Being the Second after Leap Year | . . . | . . . |
. . . | . . . | . . . | . . . | . . . | . . . | . . . | . . . | . . . | . . .
| . . . . | By Titan Leeds, Philomat. | *Printed and Sold by Andrew
Bradford, at the Sign | of the Bible in the Second Street, in Philadel-
phia.* [1725.] | Sm. 8vo. pp. (24). N. Y. H. S. 248

A | LETTER | to a | Friend. | [*Philadelphia: Andrew Brad-
ford.* 1725.?] Folio, pp. 4. H. S. P. 249

A criticism on Logan's Memoral, beginning "Dear Roger," and signed "T. T."

[LLOYD. (DAVID)] A Vindication of the Legislative Power, |
Submitted to the Representatives of all the Free-men of the Pro- |
vince of Pennsylvania, now sitting in Assembly. | [*Philadelphia:
Andrew Bradford.* 1725.] Folio, pp. 4. H. S. P. 250

Signed by David Lloyd and dated the 19th of the Month called March, 1724–5.

[LOGAN. (JAMES)] The Antidote. | In some Remarks on a
Paper of David Lloyd's, called | A Vindication of the Legislative
Power. Submitted to | the Representatives of all the Freemen of
Pennsylvania. | [*Philadelphia: Andrew Bradford.* 1725.] Folio,
pp. 8. + [*Ibid.*] Folio, pp. 8. H. S. P. 251

The second edition differs only in having about ten lines added to the closing
paragraph; an "Advertisement" of six and a half lines, and three lines of Errata.

[LOGAN.] A | Dialogue | shewing, | What's therein to be
found. | A Motto being Modish, | For Want of good Latin, are
put | English Quotations. | . . . | . . . | . . . | . . . . | [*Philadel-
phia:*] *Printed [by S. Keimer] in the Year* MDCCXXV. | Sm. 8vo.
pp. 40; Errata, 1 leaf. H. S. P. 252

An Answer to Rawle's "Ways and Means."

LOGAN. A Memorial from James Logan, in behalf of the
Proprietor's Family and of himself, Servant to the said Family.
Philadelphia: 1725. 253

LURTING. (T.) The Fighting Sailor turn'd Peaceable Christian: Manifested in the Convincement and Conversion of Thomas Lurting, with a Short Relation of Many Great Dangers and Wonderful Deliverances he met withal. First written for private satisfaction, and now Published for General Service. *London: Printed, and Re-printed by Samuel Keimer.* 1725. Sm. 8vo. pp. 47.

MARYLAND. The | Charter | of | Maryland, | Together with the | Debates and Proceedings | of | The Upper and Lower Houses of Assembly, | In the Year 1722, 1723 and 1724. Relating to the | Government and Judicature of the Province. | [*Royal Arms.*] | . . . | . . . | . . . | . . . | . . . . | Collected from the Journals, and Published by Order of the Lower-House. | *Philadelphia, Printed and Sold by Andrew Bradford, at the Bible in the | Second-Street.* 1725. | Folio.   A. P. S.   255

 Collation : Title, 1 leaf ; Charter, pp. 1–10 ; Title to Proceedings, 1 leaf ; Preface, pp. iii-iv ; Proceedings, pp. 1–64. The second title is as follows : The | Proceedings | and | Debates | of the | Upper and Lower | Houses of | Assembly | in | Maryland, | In the Years 1722, 1723 and 1724. Relating to the | Government and Judicature of that Province. | . . . | . . . . | Collected from the Journals, and Published by Order of the Lower-House. | *Philadelphia : | Printed and Sold by Andrew Bradford, at the Sign of the Bible in the | Second-Street.* MDCCXXV. |

THE MIRROR of Divine Love unveil'd, in a Poetical Paraphrase of the High and Mysterious Song of Solomon. Whereunto is added a Miscellany of several other Poems, sacred and Moral. *Philadelphia: Samuel Keimer.* 1725.   256

NEW JERSEY. Anno Regni Georgii Regis Magnæ Britanniæ . . . At a Session of the General Assembly of the Colony of New-Jersey, begun . . . and continued by Adjournments to August 23, 1725. *Printed and Sold by William Bradford in New York and by Andrew Bradford in Philadelphia.* 1725. Folio. 257

[RAWLE. (FRANCIS)] Ways and Means | For the Inhabitants of | Delaware | To become Rich: | Wherein | The several Growths and Products of | these Countries are demon- | strated to be a sufficient Fund for a flou- | rishing Trade. | Humbly submitted to the

Legislative Au- | thority of these Colonies. | . . . . | *Printed and Sold by S. Keimer, in Phila- | delphia.* MDCCXXV. | Sm. 8vo. pp. 65, (1), List of Books, pp. (6). H. S. P. 258

This work is believed to have been the first published in the British Colonies of America, upon the general subject of Political Economy. The breadth of view displayed by the Author and the importance of his suggestions called forth the approval of Governor Keith, who, in an Address to the Assembly, said :—"I observe some Ingenious Disinterested Person, bearing an apparent good will to the Prosperity of this Province has lately published some very useful Thoughts relating to the further Improvement of our Product and Commerce : I am of Opinion that such generous Views deserve to be Encouraged, and will become a very proper Subject for the Deliberation of this and future Assemblies, and if by any decent Representation to the Court or Parliament of Great Britain, we can reasonably propose to advance the Trade of this and the Neighboring Provinces, by such means as shall appear to be perfectly consistent with the true Interest of our Mother Country : I shall not only be ready to give all the Assistance that is in my Power, but also to use my best Endeavours to Engage our good Neighbours to concur with us in such Things as evidently tend to our Mutual Advantage, and the Prosperity of the British Trade in General." It is said to have been the first book printed by Franklin (see Mem. Hist. Soc. Pa., Vol. iv., p. 36, and Sparks' Life of Franklin, p. 242). If this is so the type was probably set up during 1724 for Franklin, in his Autobiography written many years afterwards, states that he sailed for London in the Autumn of that year. A small edition of it was privately reprinted in 1878. Brinley's copy sold for $100.

[SCOUGAL. (HENRY)] Vital Christianity: | A Brief | Essay | On the Life of God, | in the | Soul of Man; | Produced and Maintained by a | Christ living in us: | And | The Mystery of a Christ | within, Explained. | With an Exhibition, in which all that | Fear God and give Glory to Him, will be | sanctified. *Printed by Samuel Keimer, for Eleazer Phillips, in Charles-Town in New-England, and Sold at Rice Peter's, in Chestnut-street, Philadelphia.* 1725. | 8vo. pp. (6), 30, (1). B. P. L. 259

SOME Remarkable Proceedings | in | The Assembly of Virginia | Anno 1718. | [*Philadelphia: S. Keimer.* 1725.] Folio, pp. (4).

THE STATE of the Proceedings of the Corporation of the Governors of the Bounty of Queen Anne, for the Augmentation of the Maintenance of the poor Clergy. *Philadelphia: Samuel Keimer.*

STEEL. (R.) The Crisis; Or a Discourse representing from the most authentick Records, the first Causes of the late happy Revolution: And the several Settlements of the Crowns of England and Scotland on her Majesty without Issue, upon the most illustrious Princess Sophia, Electress and Duchess Dowager of Hanover, and the Heirs of her Body being Protestants; by previous Acts of both Parliaments of the late Kingdoms of England and Scotland, and confirmed by the Parliament of Great Britain. With some seasonable Remarks on the Danger of a Popish Successor. By Richard Steel, Esq; *Philadelphia: Samuel Keimer.* 1725.   262

     This and the preceding are advertised at the end of "Ways and Means."

TAYLOR. (J.) An Almanac for 1726. By Jacob Taylor. *Philadelphia: Andrew Bradford.* 1725.   263

TAYLOR. A Compleat Ephemeris For the Year of Christ 1726 . . . . By Jacob Taylor. To Which is added by Another Hand, Calculations . . . on the Eclipse of the Sun, &c. with a brief Introduction towards learning the Hebrew and other Tongues, etc. *Philadelphia: Samuel Keimer.* 1725. Sm. 8vo. pp. (48).   264

     Jacob Taylor disclaimed the authorship in the American Weekly Mercury, January 25, 1725-6; and Aaron Goforth, in same paper, for January 4, threatens the author with a prosecution "as the Law shall direct." The latter says "this man's Religion consisteth only in his Beard and his sham keeping of the Seventh Day Sabbath."

TOMKINS. (J.) A Brief Testimony to the Great Duty of Prayer. By John Tomkins. *London Printed: Re-printed by Samuel Keimer in Philadelphia.* MDCCXXV. Sm. 8vo. pp. 34+.

THE TRIUMVIRATE of Pennsylvania. | In a Letter to a Friend in the Country. | [*Philadelphia: Andrew Bradford.* 1725.?] Folio, pp. 4.   L. C. P.   266

1726.

ACTS | passed in the | General Assembly | of the | Province of Pennsylvania. | Held at | Philadelphia | The Fourteenth Day of October, One Thousand Seven Hundred | and Twenty Five, and continued by Adjournment till the | Twenty-Fifth Day of August next, being the Thirteenth | Year of .His Majesty's Reign, 1726.

| [*Royal Arms.*] | *Philadelphia:* | *Printed and Sold by Andrew Bradford, Printer to the Province of Penn-* | *sylvania, at the Sign of the Bible in the Second-Street.* | MDCCXXVI. | Folio, pp. 28.

THE AMERICAN Weekly Mercury. *Philadelphia: Printed and Sold by Andrew Bradford, at the Bible in the* | *Second Street, where Advertisements are taken in, & all Persons may be supply'd with this Paper.* [1726.] | Folio, pp. (2). L. C. P. 268

Numbers 315 (from Tuesday, Dec. 28th to Tuesday, Jan. 4th, 1725–6) to 365 (from Tuesday, Dec. 20th to Tuesday, Dec. 27th, 1726). Title as in No. 178. Numbers 318, 327, 328, 330, 337, 338, 345, 351, 355, 358 and 361 consist of four pages; the other of two pages each. Numbers 325 to 362 were published on Thursday; the others on Tuesday. In No. 335 the imprint was changed to the form given in No. 297, *infra*. Numbers 349 and 350 are without an imprint. No. 359 was mis numbered 358.

B[ARCLAY]. (R[obert]) A | Catechism | and | Confession of Faith, | Approved of and Agreed unto by the Ge- | neral Assembly of the Patriarchs, Prophets, | and Apostles, Christ himself chief | Speaker In and Among them. | Which containeth a true and faithful Account | of the Principles and Doctrines, which are most surely | believed by the Churches of Christ in Great Britain and | Ireland, who are reproachfully called by the Name of | Quakers; yet are found in the one Faith with the Primi- | tive Church and Saints, as is most clearly demonstrated | by some plain Scripture Testimonies, without Conse- | quences or Commentaries, which are here collected and | inserted by way of Answer to a few weighty, yet easie | and familiar Questions, fitted as well for the wisest and | largest, as for the weakest and lowest Capacities. | To which is added, an Expostulation with, | and Appeal to all other Professors. | By R. B. a Servant of the Church of Christ. | . . . | . . . | . . . . | *London, Printed, and Re-printed and Sold by Samuel* | *Keimer in Second-Street, Philadelphia.* 1726. | Sm. 8vo. Title, 1 leaf; pp. i–vi, 1–99. H. S. P. 269

THE CASE of the Heir at Law and Executrix of the late Proprietor of Pennsylvania. *Philadelphia:* 1726. 270

See No. 279, *infra*.

GORDON. (P.)   The Speech | of the Honourable | Patrick Gordon, Esq; | Lieut. Governour of the Province of | Pennsylvania, | And the Counties of New-Castle, Kent and Sussex, upon | Delaware. | To the Representatives of the Freemen of the said Province of Penn- | sylvania, August 2d. 1726. | [Colophon.] *Philadelphia: Printed and Sold by Andrew Bradford, in Second-Street.* [1726.] | Folio, pp. 4.   H. S. P.   271

GORDON. The Speech | of the Honourable | Patrick Gordon Esq; | Lieutenant Governour of the Province of | Pennsylvania, | And Counties of New-Castle, Kent and Sussex, upon | Delaware. | To the Representatives of the Freemen of the said Province of Penn- | sylvania, November 22d. 1726. | [Colophon.]*Philadelphia: Printed by Andrew Bradford Printer to the Province.* | Folio, pp. 4.

H. (E.)   The Great Love of God manifested in calling men from Death to Life, by the washing of Regeneration.   In a Christian Invitation to all to come to Christ.   By E. H.   *Philadelphia: Printed by Samuel Keimer, in Second Street next door but one to Andrew Bradfords.*   1726.   12mo. pp. 12.?   273

    Title from Smith's Catalogue of Friends' Books.

THE HONEST Man's | Interest | As he claims any Lands in the Counties of | New-Castle, Kent, or Sussex, on Delaware. | [*Philadelphia: Andrew Bradford.* 1726.] Folio, pp. 4.   H. S. P.   274

JERMAN. (J.)   An Almanac for 1727.   By John Jerman. *Philadelphia:* 1726.   275

JOURNAL of the Votes and Proceedings of the House of Representatives of the Province of Pennsylvania.   *Philadelphia: Andrew Bradford.*   1726.   276

A | JOURNAL | of the | Votes and Proceedings | Of the Representatives of the Province | of Pennsylvania. | [*Philadelphia: Printed by S. Keimer.*   1726.] Folio, pp. 50.   277

[KEITH. (W.)]   A Just and Plain | Vindication | of | Sir | William Keith, Bart. | Late Governour of | Pensilvania, | From the Untruths and Aspersions con- | tain'd in a Paper printed at

London, | under the Title of The Case of the | Heir at Law, and Executrix of the late | Proprietor of Pensilvania, &c. | [*Philadelphia:*] *Printed* [*by Samuel Keimer*] *in the Year* 1726. | Sm. 8vo. pp. 31.   L. C. P.   278

[KEITH.]   A Just and Plain | Vindication | of | Sir William Keith, Bart. | Late Governour of Pennsilvania, | From the Untruths and Aspertions contained in | a Paper, Printed at London, and now Reprinting at Phila- | delphia, under the Title of The Case of the Heir at Law and | Executrix of the late Proprietor of Pennsilvania, &c. | [*Philadelphia: Samuel Keimer?* 1726.] Folio, pp. 10.

LEEDS. (F.)   The American Almanac, for 1727.   By Felix Leeds.   *Philadelphia: Andrew Bradford.*   1726.   280

In the Almanac for 1728, F. Leeds says, "The kind acceptance my Almanack met with last Year, has prevail'd with me to pleasure my Friends with another for this Year."

LEEDS. (T.)   Leeds, 1727. | The American | Almanack | For the Year of Christian Account, 1727. | Being the Third after Leap-Year. | . . . | . . . | . . . | . . . | . . . | . . . | . . . | . . . | . . . | . . . | . . . | . . . | . . . | . . . | . . . | . . . | . . . | . . . . | By Titan Leeds, Philomat. | *Printed and Sold by Samuel Keimer, in the* | *Second Street near the Market, in Philadelphia: David Humphreys at Flushing on Long-Island,* | *and Eliezar Phillips at Charles-Town, in New-England.*   [1726.] | Sm. 8vo. pp. (32?).   c.   281

THE LIFE and Character of a Strange He Monster, lately arrived in London from an English Colony in America, and is often to be seen upon the Royal Exchange, Gratis.   *Philadelphia:* 1726. ?   282

A satire upon Andrew Hamilton. See the American Weekly Mercury, No. 344, July 28, 1726, for lines to the most ingenious Pamphleteer author of the he-monster. There is a manuscript copy in the American Philosophical Society.

[LOGAN. (JAMES)]   A more just | Vindication | Of the Honourable | Sir William Keith, Bart. | Against the unparalleled Abuses put upon him, in a Scan- | dalous Libel call'd, A just and plain Vindication of | Sir William Keith, &c. | [*Philadelphia: Andrew Bradford.* 1726.]   Folio, pp. 4.   H. S. P.   283

THE | OBSERVATOR'S | Trip | To America, | in a | Dia-logue | between | The Observator and his Country-man | Roger. | [*Philadelphia:*] *Printed by [Andrew Bradford] in the Year* 1726. | 16mo. pp. 45.   H. S. P.   284

PROCLAMATION.   G. [*Royal Arms.*] R. | By the | Honour-able Patrick Gordon, Esq ; | . . . | . . . | A | Proclamation. | *Philadelphia: Printed by Andrew Bradford, Printer to the Province* 1726. | Folio, 1 leaf.   H. S. P.   285

Dated Oct. 4, 1726.   Against riotous assemblies in Philadelphia.

[PENN. (HANNAH)]   Letter to Sir William Keith.   [*Philadel-phia: Printed by S. Keimer.*   1726.?]   Folio, pp. 4.   H. S. P.   286

Signed Hannah Penn, and dated London 26th of 3d Month, 1724.   Some copies have seven and a quarter lines at the end correcting an omission.

[RAWLE. (FRANCIS)]   A Just Rebuke | to a | Dialogue | be-twixt | Simon and Timothy. | shewing | What's therein to be found. | Namely Levity, Perversion, and De- | traction. All which are detected in | this short Examen. | And that short Treatise, entituled Ways | and Means, &c. rescued from the Dia- | logist's unjust Charge of Inconsistences | and Contradictions. | . . . . | *Philadelphia: Printed by S. Keimer, in Mar-* | *ket-street,* MDCCXXVI. | Sm. 8vo. pp. 31, (1).   H. S. P.   287

In reply to No. 252, *supra.*   Brinley's copy sold for $28.

REMARKS on Sir William Keith's Vindication.   *Philadelphia: Andrew Bradford.*   1726.   Sm. 8vo. pp. 24+.   H. S. P.   288

STIRREDGE. (E.) Strength and Weakness: | Manifest in the | Life, Trials, and | Christian Testimony | of that faithful Servant and Hand- | maid of the Lord | Elizabeth Stirredge, | Who departed this Life at her | House at Hempsted in Hertford-shire, | in the 72d Year of her Age. | Written by her own hand. | Shewing her Pious Care and Council to her Chil- | dren, and according to their Desire made Pub- | lick: Also for the Instruction and Benefit of ma- | ny other Parents and Children concerned. | *Printed at*

London, and Re-printed by Samuel | *Keimer in Philadelphia,*
MDCCXVI. | Sm. 8vo. pp. viii, (10), 150.   A. A. S.   289

TAYLOR. (J.) An Almanac for 1727. By Jacob Taylor.
Philadelphia: 1726.   290

TO | The Honourable | Patrick Gordon, Esq; | Lieut. Gover-
nour of the Province of | Pennsylvania, &c. | The Humble Address
of the Grand-Jury for the City of Philadelphia. | [*Philadelphia:*]
Printed and Sold by Andrew Bradford. [1726.] | Folio, 1 leaf.

TO the Honourable | Patrick Gordon, Esq; | Lieutenant Gov-
ernour of the Province of Pennsylvania, and Counties | of New-
Castle, Kent and Sussex, upon Delaware. | The Address of the
Mayor | And Commonalty of the City of Philadelphia, in Council
the Sixteenth | Day of the Fifth Month (July) Anno. 1726. |
*Philadelphia: Printed and Sold by Andrew Bradford, at the Sign of
the Bible, in the Second Street.* [1726.] | Folio, 1 leaf. H. S. P.   292

WELTON. (R.) The Farewell Sermon of Richard Welton,
D. D. Preached in Christ Church at Philadelphia, Feb. 4th, 1726.

Advertised in the American Weekly Mercury, February 15, 1725–6, as "now
in the Press and will be Published." There is no indication of the Printer.

1727.

ACTS of Assembly.   294

The Assembly which met, Oct. 14, 1726, passed several Laws, which may not
have been printed until published in the collection of Laws, issued in 1728.

ADVICE and Information | To the Freeholders and Freemen
of the Province of | Pensilvania. | And particularly to those of the
County and City of | Philadelphia. | [Colophon.] *Philadelphia,
Printed by Andrew Bradford, September* 1727. | Folio, pp. 4. H. S. P.

AN | ALMANACK | For the Year of Our Lord, 1727. | Being
the Third after Leap-Year. | Or An | Ephemeris | Containing |
The Motions and Aspects of the Planets, | the Eclipses, Lunations,
Rising and Setting | of the Sun, Length of the Days, High- |

Water, and Weather-Guesses, with Courts, | Fairs, and other Remarkable Days. | Fitted to the Vertix of Philadelphia. | . . . | . . . | . . . | . . . | . . . | . . . . | *Printed and Sold by S. Keimer, in Second-Street near* | *the Market, in Philadelphia.* 1727. | Sm. 8vo. pp. (24?). H. S. P. 296

THE AMERICAN Weekly Mercury. *Philadelphia: Printed and Sold by Andrew Bradford, at the Bible in Second Street,* | *where Advertisements are Taken in, and all Persons may be supply'd with this Paper.* [1727.] L. C. P. 297

Numbers 366 (from Tuesday, Dec. 27th to Tuesday, Jan. 3d, 1726–7) to 417 (from Tuesday, Dec. 19th to Tuesday, Dec. 16th, 1727). Title as in No. 178, *supra.* Numbers 380–382, 388, 389, 392, 394, 397, 399, 401, 403, 406–410 and 412 consist of four pages ; the others of two pages each. Numbers 376 to 414 appeared on Thursday ; the others on Tuesday.

THE | CHRISTIAN | Confession | Of the Faith of the harm-less | Christians, in the Ne- | therlands, known by | the name of | Mennonists. | *Amsterdam* | *Printed, and Re-printed and Sold by* | *Andrew Bradford in Philadelphia,* | *in the Year,* 1727. | 16mo. H. S. P. 298

Collation : Title, 1 leaf ; Preface, pp. (2) ; Confession, pp. 5–40 ; Appendix, pp. 44. The appendix has the following title : " An | Appendix | to the | Con-fession of Faith | Of the Christians, called, | Mennonists. | Giving | A short and full Account of them ; because | of the Immagination of the Newness of | our Religion, the Weapon and Revenge- | less Christendom, and its being. | Published | Formerly in the Low-Dutch, and translated | out of the same into High-Dutch, and out | of that into the English Language, 1725. | *Philadelphia : Printed by Andrew Bradford, in the Year,* | 1727. |

A COLLECTION of Elegiac Poems devoted to the Memory of the late virtuous and excellent Matron and worthy elder in the Church of Christ of the Society of Friends, Martha Thomas, late wife of Rees Thomas of Merion of the County of Philadelphia, in the Province of Pennsylvania, and daughter of William Aubrey of Llan Elew in the County of Brecknock in Great Britain, who departed this life on the 7th of 12 mo. 1726–27. *Philadelphia : S. Keimer.* 1727. 299

Reprinted by L. R. Bailey in 1837.

COLLECTION of a Hundred Notable Things. *Philadelphia:*
1727. 4to. pp. 37.   300

Title from Haven's List.

THE | CONSPIRACY | of | Catiline; | Recommended to the
serious Consideration of the Au- | thors of Advice and Information
to the Freeholders and Freemen | of the Province of Pennsylvania:
And Further Information, dated | Octob. 2, 1727. But more especi-
ally to One who stands impeached in | Thirteen Articles, tending to
detain the Rights, infringe on the Pro- | perties, and oppress the
Freemen of this Province. | [*Philadelphia: Andrew Bradford.*
1727.] Folio, pp. (2).   M. S.   301

AN | EPISTLE | from the | Yearly Meeting | Of Friends, held
at | Burlington | The Seventeenth, to the Twenty-First of the
Seventh | Month, 1726. | To the Quarterly and Monthly Meetings
belonging to the same. | [Colophon.] *Philadelphia: Printed by
Andrew Bradford, at the Sign of the Bible in the Second-Street,* |
MDCCXXVII. | Folio, pp. 3.   M. S.   302

GORDON. (P.) The Speech | of the Honourable | Patrick
Gordon Esq; | Lieutenant Governor of the | Counties | of New
Castle, Kent and Sussex | upon Delaware, | and Province of |
Pennsylvania. | To the Representatives of the Freemen of | the
said Counties, October the 21st, 1727. | [*Philadelphia: Andrew
Bradford.* 1727.] Folio, pp. 4.   L. C. P.   303

HORNE. (EDWARD) Philadelphia, 30th 7 br. 1727. | Adver-
tisement. [*Philadelphia: Andrew Bradford.* 1727.] 4to. 1 leaf.

In reply to a charge of defrauding Caleb Cash of a sum of money.

JERMAN. (J.) An Almanac for 1728. By John Jerman.
Philadelphia: 1727.   305

A | JOURNAL | of the | Votes and Proceedings | of the |
House of Representatives | of the | Province of Pennsylvania. |
[*Philadelphia: Andrew Bradford.* 1727.] Folio, pp. 38.   306

Issued at four different times ; the first three parts have the imprint at the end
thus : "Philadelphia : Printed and Sold by Andrew Bradford, Printer to the
Province," which is omitted for want of space in the last.

LEEDS. (F.) [Cut.] Leeds | The American | Almanack | For the Year of Christian Account, 1728. | Unto which is Numbered |

From   { By the Oriental and Greek Christians, 7236. |
the   { By the Jews, Hebrews, and Rabbins, 7488.
Creation { By the late Computation of W. W.   5737. |

Being Leap-Year. | Wherein is Contain'd | The Lunations, Eclipses, Judgment of the | Weather, the Spring-Tides, the Planets Motions, and | mutual Aspects : With the Birth-Days of the Suc- | cessive Heirs to the Crown of Great Britain. | Time of the Moons Rising and Setting, Length of the | Day, the Seven Stars Rising, Southing and Setting. | Time of High-Water, Fairs, Courts, and Observable | Days. | Fitted to the Latitude of 40 Degrees, and | Meridian of five Hours West from London, but may | without sensible Error, serve all the adjacent Places, | even from Newfound-land to Carolina. | By Felix Leeds, Philomat. | *Printed and Sold by Andrew Bradford, at the Sign | of the Bible, in Second Street, Philadelphia.* [1727.] | Sm. 8vo. pp. (28).   H. S. P. 307

The last two pages are partly filled with a list of "Books Printed and Sold by Andrew Bradford, in Philadelphia." Amongst the sayings under November is "In Marriage are two happy things allowed ; a Wife in Wedding Sheets and in a Shroud."

LEEDS. (T.) [Cut.] The Arms of | the Family | of Leeds. | The American Almanack | For the Year of Christian Account, 1728. | . . . | . . . | . . . | . . . | Being the Bissextile, or Leap-Year : | Wherein is contained, | The Lunations, Eclipses, Judgment of the Weather, | the Spring-Tides, Planets Motions and Mutual As- | pects. With the Birth-Days of the Successive | Heirs to the Crown of Great Britain, Time of | Sun and Moon's Rising and Setting, Length | of Days, the Seven Stars Rising, Southing, and | Setting, Time of High-Water, Fairs, Courts, and | Observable Days. | Fitted to the Latitude of 40 Degrees, and a Me- | ridian of Five Hours West from London, but | may without sensible Error, serve all the adjacent | Places, even from New-found-land to Carolina. | By Titan Leeds, Philomat. | *Printed by S. Keimer in Second-street, Philadel- | phia, and sold by W. Heurtin Goldsmith in New- | York, David Humphreys at Flushing on Long- | Island.* (*Beware of the Counterfeit One.*) [1727.] | Sm. 8vo. pp. (32). H. S. P. 308

A MODEST Reply to the Speech of Isaac Norris, Esq ; | delivered from the Bench, in the Court of | Common-Pleas, held for the City and County of | Philadelphia, the 11th Day of September, 1727, | and afterwards Printed. | [*Philadelphia : Andrew Bradford.* 1727.] Folio, pp. 4.   309

[NORRIS. (Isaac)] A Confutation of the Reply to the Speech, &c. | [*Philadelphia : Andrew Bradford.* 1727.] Folio, pp. 4. 310

[NORRIS.] The Speech | Delivered from the Bench in the Court of | Common Pleas held for the City and | County of Philadelphia, the 11 day of | September, 1727. [*Philadelphia : Andrew Bradford.* 1727.] Folio, pp. 3, (1).   311

A Supplement on the fourth page is dated 30th of September, 1727. In some copies the following is substituted : "Some Remarks On a Paper directed to all true Patriots."

PENN. (William)] Fruits of a Father's Love, being the Advice of William Penn, (late Propriétor and Governour of the Province of Pensilvania) to his Children, relating to the Civil and Religious Conduct. Written Occasionally many Years ago, and now made Public for the General Good : By a Lover of his Memory. *Philadelphia : Andrew Bradford.* 1727.   312

Title from Felix Leed's Almanac for 1728.

PUGH. (E.) A | Salutation | to the | Britains, | To Call them | From the Many Things, to the One Thing | needful, for the Saving of their Souls ; | Especially, | To the poor unlearned Tradesmen, Plow- | men and Shepherds, those that are of a low De- | gree like my self, This, in Order to direct you | to know God and Christ, the only wise God, | which is Life eternal, and to learn of him, that | you may become wiser than your Teachers. | By Ellis Pugh. | Translated from the British Language by | Rowland Ellis, Revis'd and Corrected by | David Lloyd. | ... | ... | .... | *Philadelphia : Printed by S. Keimer, for W. Davies,* | *Bookbinder, in Chestnut-Street.* 1727. 16mo. pp. xv, 222.   H. S. P.   313

REMARKS upon the Advice to the Freeholders, | &c.   Paragraph by Paragraph. | [*Philadelphia: S. Keimer.* 1727.]   Folio, pp. 4.   H. S. P.   314

SOME necessary Precautions, worthy to be considered by | all English Subjects, in their Election of Members, | to Represent them in General Assembly ; wherein, | neither Fear, Flattery, nor Gain, ought to byass. | [*Philadelphia: Andrew Brafdord.* 1727.?] Folio, 1 leaf.   315

. . . . Stulta est Clementia, cum tot ubique | Vatibus occurras, perituræ parcere Chartæ. Juv. | [*Philadelphia: S. Keimer.* 1727.]   Folio, pp. 4.   316

A reply to Norris' Speech.

TAYLOR. (J.)   An Almanac for 1728.   By Jacob Taylor. *Philadelphia: Samuel Keimer.*   1727.   317

TO all true Patriots and real Lovers of Liberty | [*Philadelphia: Andrew Bradford.* 1727.]   Folio, pp. 3.   318

A reply to Advice and Information.

TO my respected Friend I. N.   *Philadelphia:* 1727.   319

Signed Jotham, and dated Philadelphia the 16th of the 9th month.   A reply to Norris' Speech, in vindication of Sir Wm. Keith.   Du Simitiere had a copy, but it is not to be found in the Philadelphia Library, which purchased his collection.

TO the | Freeholders & Freemen | A | Further Information. | [*Philadelphia: Andrew Bradford.* 1727.]   Folio, pp. 2.   320

Dated Philadelphia, 2d of October, 1727.

TO the Freeholders, to prevent Mistakes. | A Short Vindication and Explanation of Part | of a late mysterious printed Sheet, called, | Advice and Information to the Freeholders | and Freemen of the Province of Pennsyl- | vania, but particularly to the City of Phi- | ladelphia. | [*Philadelphia: Andrew Bradford.* 1727.] Folio, pp. (2).   321

1728.

THE AMERICAN Weekly Mercury.   L. C. P.   322

Numbers 418 (from Tuesday, Dec. 26 to Tuesday, Jan. 2, 1727–8) to 469 (from Tuesday, Dec. 24 to Tuesday, Dec. 31, 1728). Title and imprint as in No. 297, *supra*. Numbers 422, 431, 433, 435, 437, 439, 441, 444, 445, 447–449, 451, 452, 455, 459, 460, 465 and 468 consist of four pages; the others of two pages each. Numbers 428 to 466 were published on Thursday; the others on Tuesday.

BEISSEL. (C.) Das Büchlein vom Sabbath. Von Conrad Beissel. *Philadelphia:* 1728.   323

See Chronicon Ephratense, p. 35.

BEISSEL. Neun und neunzig Mystische Sprache. Von Conrad Beissel. *Philadelphia:* 1728.   324

See Chronicon Ephratense, p. 35.

BIRKETT. (W.) An | Almanack | For | The Year of Christ, 1729. | And from the Creation | By Holy Scripture, 5678. | Being the First after | Leap-Year. | Wherein is contained | The Lunations, Eclipses, Judgment of the Wea- | ther, Spring-Tides, Planets-Motions and Mutual Aspects, | The Rising, Southing, Setting and Bearing of several Stars, | of the 1st and 2d Magnitude. The Sun Rising and Set- | ting, the Seven Stars Rising, Southing, and Setting, | with the Birth Days of the Successive Heirs to the | Crown of Great-Britain: High-water, Fairs, Courts, and | Observable Days. | Fitted to the Latitude of 40 Degrees, and a Meridian of | Five Hours West from London, but may without | sensible Error, serve all the adjacent Places, even from | Newfoundland to Carolina. | By William Birkett, Philomat. | . . . | . . . | . . . | . . . | . . . | . . . . | *Printed and sold by Andrew Bradford, at the Sign of the* | *Bible, in the Second Street, Philadelphia.* [1728.] | Sm. 8vo. pp. (24).   325

This is the first issue of Birkett's Almanac. "I here present you with an Almanack for the Year 1729. . . . much resembling Mr. Leeds his Almanack, in altho' not altogether dressed in the same Garb; what pleases Madam, disgusts the honest Country Farmer, for whom this is purely intended, and as for the Verses, I made them all *De Novo*, (but that I need not have told you) they being but ordinary and I, no Poet. . . . Next year, if I live, I may, perhaps, pleasure you with Prose, as good as Verse, in my Opinion, ... and with the Unconstant Moon's rising and setting, which is a little troublesome ; but nothing's hard to a willing Mind."

COPIES of some Original Papers, and other Pro- | ceedings, relating to the late Difference in the House of | Representatives of the Province of Pennsylvania, in | General Assembly met the 15th, and continued by | Adjournment to the 20th April, 1728. | [*Philadelphia: Andrew Bradford.* 1728.] Folio, pp. (4).   H. S. P.   326

[BOWNAS. (SAMUEL)] God's Mercy surmounting Man's Cruelty, Exemplified in the Captivity and Redemption of Elizabeth Hanson, Wife of John Hanson, of Knoxmarsh at Keacheachy, in Dover Township, who was taken Captive with her Children and Maid-Servant, by the Indians in New-England, in the Year 1724. In which are inserted, Sundry remarkable Preservations, Deliverances, and Marks of the Care and Kindness of Providence over her and her Children, worthy to be remembered. The Substance of which was taken from her own Mouth, and now published for a general Service. *Philadelphia: Samuel Keimer.* 1728.   327

Advertised in the Pa. Gazette, Dec. 24, 1728.

A DIALOGUE between Freeman and Trusty. *Philadelphia:* 1728.   328

See No. 341, *infra.*

A FEW Words in Favour of Free-Thinking. *Philadelphia: Andrew Bradford.* 1728.   329

Mentioned in an advertisement in the American Weekly Mercury, April 4, 1728.

GORDON. (P.) The Speech | Of the Honourable | Patrick Gordon, Esq ; | Lieut. Governour of the Province of | Pennsylvania, | . . . . | To the Representatives of the Freemen of the said Province | met at Philadelphia, December 17th, 1728. | [Colophon.] *Philadelphia: Printed and Sold by Andrew Bradford, Printer to the Pro-* | *vince.* 1728. | Folio, pp. (4).   H. S. P. 330

Contains also the Assembly's Address to the Governor and his reply.

HALE. (M.) Some necessary and Important Considerations, to be considered of by all sorts of People. Taken out of (that Worthy and Renowned Judge) Sir Matthew Hale's Writings: And therein his own experience of the Inward and Invisible Guidance of the Spirit of God. The Ninth Edition, with Additions. *Philadelphia: S. Keimer.* 1728.   331

JERMAN. (J.) An Almanac for 1729. By John Jerman. *Philadelphia: Andrew Bradford.* 1728.   332

A | JOURNAL | of the | Votes and Proceedings | of the | House of Representatives | of the | Province of Pennsylvania. | [Colophon.] *Philadelphia,* | *Printed and sold by Andrew Bradford, Printer to the Province.* [1728.] | Folio, pp. 22.   333

[KEIMER. (SAMUEL)] Advertisement. [*Philadelphia: Samuel Keimer.* 1728.] Folio, pp. (2).   H. S. P. 334

The Prospectus of the Pa. Gazette. Dated Oct. 1, 1728.

KEIMER. Prospectus of a Lottery. *Philadelphia: S. Keimer.*

"The Board having heard that a Lottery was intended to be erected by Samuel Keimer in this City, during this present ffair, he having sett fforth severall printed papers for that purpose, . . . Ordered that no Lottery be kept during the said ffair." Minutes of Common Council May 16, 1728.

THE | LAWS | of the | Province | of | Pennsylvania: | Now in Force, Collected into One | Volumn. | Publish'd by Order of the General | Assembly of the aforesaid Province. | G. [*Royal Arms.*] R. | *Philadelphia: Printed and Sold by Andrew | Bradford, Printer to the Province,* MDCCXXVIII. | Folio.   H. S. P. 336

Collation : Title, 1 leaf; Table, pp. (4) ; text, pp. 1–352, with a duplicate of pp. 280–281. Edited by Chief Justice David Lloyd.

LEEDS. (F.) The American Almanac for 1729. By Felix Leeds. *Philadelphia: Andrew Bradford.* 1728.   337

LEEDS. (T.) [Cut.] . . . | . . . | . . . . | The American Almanack | For the Year of Christian Account, 1729. | . . . | . . . | . . . | . . . . | Being the first after Bissextile, or Leap-Year. | Wherein is contained, | The Lunations, Eclipses, Judgment of the

Weather, | the Spring-Tides, Planets Motions and Mutual As- | pects, with the Time of the Sun and Moon's | Rising and Setting, Length of Days, the Seven | Stars Rising, Southing, and Setting, Time of | High-Water, Fairs, Courts, and Observable Days. | . . . | . . . | . . . | . . . . | By Titan Leeds, Philomat. | *Printed by S. Keimer in Second-street, Philadel- | phia,* | . . . | . . . | . . . | [1728.] Sm. 8vo. pp. (32).   H. S. P.   338

All the lines omitted are, with the necessary changes in the chronology, and Newfoundland instead of New-found-land, precisely as in the Almanac for 1727.

A LETTER | From a Gentleman in | Philadelphia | To his Friend in | Bucks. | [*Philadelphia: Andrew Bradford.* 1728.] Folio, pp. 4.   L. C. P.   339

A reply to the Representation of the Eight Members.

A LETTER, Occasioned by the Perusal of a Paper | lately published, called, A Dialogue between Free- | man and Trusty. | [*Philadelphia: Andrew Bradford.* 1728.] Folio, pp. (2).   L. C. P.   340

The second page contains an "Advertisement" signed "A. H." and dated Philadelphia, Sept. 30, 1728.

[LLOYD. (DAVID)]   A | Defence | of the | Legislative Constitution | Of the Province of | Pennsylvania. | As it now stands Confirmed and Established, by | Law and Charter. | With some Observations, on the Proceedings published | by Sixteen Members of Assembly, in a Paper, en- | titled, The Votes and Proceedings of the House of Re- | presentatives: Recommended to the Consideration | of all the Free-men of the Province. | [*Philadelphia: Printed by Andrew Bradford.* 1728.]   Folio, pp. 11.   H. S. P.   341

A LOOKING-GLASS, for the Modern Deists or Libertines, called Free-Thinkers.   *Philadelphia: Samuel Keimer.*   1728.   342

Mentioned in an advertisement in the American Weekly Mercury, April 4, 1728.

A | MODEST Apology | for the | Eight Members. | [*Philadelphia: Andrew Bradford.* 1728.]   Folio, pp. (2).   L. C. P.   343

A Satirical apology.

MORRIS Morris's Reasons for his Conduct, in the Present | Assembly, in the Year 1728. | [*Philadelphia: Andrew Bradford.* 1728.] Folio, pp. 2.   L. C. P.   344

Morris, one of the Members for Philadelphia County, had refused to join the other Representatives from the City and County of Philadelphia in withdrawing from the Assembly.

NEW JERSEY. Acts | and | Laws | Of His Majesty's Province of Nova Cæsarea, or | New-Jersey : | As they were Enacted by the Governor, | Council, and General Assembly, at a Ses- | sion held at Perth-Amboy, beginning | the 9th of December, 1727. in the | First Year of the Reign of his Majesty | King George the Second. | [*Royal Arms.*] | *Burlington: Printed and Sold by Samuel Keimer,* | *Printer to the King's Most Excellent Majesty, for* | *the Province of New-Jersey.* MDCCXXVIII. | Folio, Advertisement, 1 leaf, pp. 51 ; Table, 1 leaf.   345

[NORRIS. (Isaac)] Friendly | Advice | To the | Inhabitants of Pensilvania. | [*Philadelphia: Andrew Bradford.*   1726.] | Folio, pp. 3.   H. S. P.   346

First printed about 1710.

THE PROCEEDINGS of some Members of Assembly, at Phi- | ladelphia, April 1728. vindicated from the unfair | Reasoning and unjust Insinuations of a certain Re- | marker. | [*Philadelphia : Printed by S. Keimer.*   1728.] Folio, pp. (4).   H. S. P.   347

See Votes of Assembly, Vol. I., p. 52. Keimer was brought before the Assembly by the Sergeant at Arms in pursuance of an order to that effect. He acknowledged having printed the tract for Edward Horne.

PROCLAMATION.   G. [*Royal Arms.*] R. | By the Honourable | Patrick Gordon, Esq ; | Lieutenant Governor of the Province of Pennsylvania and Counties of | New Castle, Kent and Sussex, upon Delaware. | A | Proclamation. | *Philadelphia : Printed by Andrew Bradford, Printer to this Province,* 2728 [*sic*]. | Folio, 1 leaf.
                                          H. S. P.   348

Some Indians having been murdered, the Governor issued this warning against "abusing" any of the Five Nations.

REMARKS | On the late Proceedings of some Members of Assembly at | Philadelphia: April, 1728. | [*Philadelphia: Andrew Bradford.* 1728.] Folio, pp. (4).   H. S. P.   349

SEWEL. (W.) The | History | of the | Rise, Increase, and Progress, | of the Christian People called | Quakers: | Intermixed with Several | Remarkable Occurrences. | Written Originally in Low-Dutch, and also Tran- | slated into English, | By William Sewel. | The Third Edition, Corrected. | *Philadelphia:* | *Printed and Sold by Samuel Keimer in Second Street.* | MDCCXXVIII. | Folio.   H. S. P.   350

Collation : Title, 1 leaf; Dedication, pp. (2) ; Preface, pp. (8) ; text, pp. 1–694 ; Index, pp. (16). Signatures A to T eight pages, and the others, with b between A and B four pages each. This work, written in Dutch and printed at Amsterdam in 1717, was translated into English by the author and published at London in 1722. A few copies finding their way to America, the Philadelphia Meeting on learning the edition was exhausted, proposed to Andrew Bradford that he should reprint it. Bradford delayed giving a definite answer until after he had arranged with his aunt Tacy Sowle, the English publisher of the work, for 700 copies of the second edition, and then declined. The Quakers then applied to Keimer who readily undertook the work at a much lower price than had been offered Bradford. It proved an unfortunate venture for him as he had not the capital to carry on so large a work, and although he proceeded but slowly with it and received considerable advances of money from the Quakers, as well as subscriptions for 500 copies, he became involved in debt by his purchases of type and paper. The work was begun in 1725, and was not finished till the latter part of 1728, and then only by giving out part of it to Franklin and Meredith. Franklin in his autobiography alludes to his firm's share of the work, thus : "Briental particularly procured for us, from the Quakers, the printing 40 sheets of their history, the rest to be done by Keimer ; and upon this we worked exceeding hard, for the price was low. It was a folio, pro patria size, in pica, with long primer notes. I composed a sheet a day, and Meredith worked it off at press." On this passage Mr. Nathan Kite remarks : "Franklin was at that very time writing against Keimer, and doing everything to injure him in his power ; and with that want of candour, characteristic of a mean mind, does not acknowledge in his memoirs to whom their new office was indebted for its first work. No one would guess from his account that the patronage came from the poor, despised, caricatured Keimer."

The Brinley catalogue claims that the "Title and Dedication, pp. 457 to 674, and the Index (16 pp.) are from Franklin's press." And adds : "These make over *sixty* (instead of forty) sheets of the whole work." In this I cannot agree, as there is no difference in the type, roman or italic, or in the numerals of the pages and marginal dates in the first 532 pages. From page 533 there not only appeared slightly larger and differently shaped numerals in the paging, a new and larger figure in the marginal dates, but the italic letter is not from the same matrices as that used throughout the preceding pages. As to the Title and Dedication, the fact that the first nineteen signatures contain an inset of four pages each was overlooked. The Preface is unquestionably from Keimer's press, and as the Dedication and first two pages of the preface form sheet A 2, the inset of A, which is itself composed of the Title, reverse blank, and the third and fourth pages of the Preface, these two leaves could not have been printed by Franklin and Meredith. In my opinion they printed from page 533 to 694, and the Index (16 pp.), or fourty-four and a half sheets in all. Wight's copy sold for $26; Brinley's for $40.

SHORT-HAND Book. *Philadelphia: S. Keimer.* 1728. 351

Advertised by Keimer in the New Jersey Acts of Assembly for 1728, as just printed and to be given to any one who "shall lay out but Three Shillings in either Bonds, Bills, Indentures, Primmers, or other useful books." He printed a second edition in 1729.

TAYLOR. (J.) An Almanac for 1729. By Jacob Taylor. *Philadelphia:* 1728. 352

TO Morris Morris. | On the Reasons published for his Conduct in Assembly, | in the Year 1728. | [*Philadelphia: Andrew Bradford.* 1728.] Folio, pp. 2. L. C. P. 353

Signed "Timothy Telltruth," and dated Abington the 16th of the 7th Mo. 1728.

TO the | Honourable | Patrick Gordon Esq; | Lieutenant Governour of the Province of | Pennsylvania. | The Representation of the Assembly of the said Province. | [Colophon.] *Philadelphia: Printed and Sold by Andrew Bradford Printer to the Province.* [1728.] | Folio, pp. 10. L. C. P. 354

This Representation in regard to the conduct of the "Eight Members," was drawn up by Andrew Hamilton and Jeremiah Langhorne.

THE TWO following Depositions were laid before the House, | the Ninth Day of August, 1728. | [*Philadelphia: Andrew Bradford.* 1728.] Folio, pp. (2). 355

Depositions of Samson Davis and Thomas Parry concerning Sir William Keith's proposal to appeal to the King for the overthrow of the Proprietary charter in 1726.

TWO | Indian Treaties | the one held at | Conestogoe | In May 1728. | And the other at | Philadelphia | In June following, | between | the Honourable Patrick Gordon Esq; Lieut. | Governour of the Province of Pennsylvania, and | Counties of New-Castle, Kent, and Sussex upon | Delaware, | And | The Chiefs of the Conestogoe, Delaware, Shawanese | and Canawese Indians. | [Colophon.] *Philadelphia:* | *Printed and Sold by Andrew Bradford, Printer to the Province.* [1728.] | Folio, pp. 16, misprint for 17.   L. C. P.   356

Numb. 1. | THE UNIVERSAL Instructor in all Arts and Sciences: | And | Pennsylvania Gazette. | To be continued Weekly. Decemb. 24. 1728. [Colophon.] *Philadelphia: Printed by Samuel Keimer, where Subscriptions are taken | in for this Paper, at Ten Shillings a Year, and Advertisements inserted at Three | Shillings each.* [1728.] | Folio, pp. (4).   H. S. P.   357

Franklin's account of the origin of this paper is that George Webb, a bound servant of his old employer, Keimer, having found means to purchase the remainder of his time from his master, offered his services to Franklin and Meredith. "We could not," says Franklin, "then employ him, but I foolishly let him know as a secret that I soon intended to begin a newspaper, and might have work for him . . . I told him . . . that the then only newspaper . . . was a paltry thing, wretchedly managed, no way entertaining, and yet was profitable. I therefore freely thought a good paper would scarcely fail of good encouragement. . . . Webb . . . told Keimer, who immediately . . . published proposals for one himself. . . . To counteract them . . . I wrote several amusing pieces for Bradford's paper under the title of the Busy Body, which Brientnal continued some months . . . and Keimer's proposals, which we burlesqued and ridiculed, were disregarded. He began his paper, however, and before carrying it on three quarters of a year, with at most only ninety subscribers, he offered it to me for a trifle, and I, having been ready for some time to go on with it, took it in hand directly." In an advertisement in No. 13, Keimer incidentally says: "Two hundred and fifty [copies of the Gazette] are printed every week," and in No. 27, he says: "I had at least at the rate of £120 per Annum, clear of all charges secured to me, by my Newspaper and Leeds' Almanack."

Keimer's paper was better printed than Bradford's Mercury, but in regard to news, it was inferior. Extracts from Chambers' Dictionary, constituting the "Universal Instructor," occupied the first page and a half, and the rest was filled up from the English papers and magazines, with a scanty column of advertisements, and once in a while an original essay or poem. In No. 18, a reprint of De Foe's Religious Courtship was begun. This filled a page or more of each succeeding number, until the paper passed into Franklin's hands, when it was discontinued. Brinley's copy, with numbers 40 to 111 of the Pa. Gazette, sold for $560.

1729.

AN ACT for the better Regulation of Seamen in the Merchants
Service. *Philadelphia: Andrew Bradford.* 1729.   358

Advertised in the Weekly Mercury, Oct. 23, 1729. An Act of Parliament.

ACTS | passed in the | General Assembly | of the | Province of
Pennsylvania. | Held at | Philadelphia, | The Fourteenth Day of
October, One Thousand Seven Hundred | and Twenty Eight, and
Continued by Adjournments till the 11th. | of August, 1729. being
the Third Year of his Majesty's Reign. | [*Royal Arms.*] | *Phila-
delphia:* | *Printed, and Sold by Andrew Bradford, Printer to the
Province.* 1729. | Folio, Title, 1 leaf; pp. 353–387. H. S. P.   359

Intended as a continuation of the Collection of 1728.

ADVERTISEMENT. [*Philadelphia: Andrew Bradford.* 1729.]
4to. 1 leaf.   360

Signed J. Logan, and dated Philadelphia, 22d of the 12th Month (Feb.) 1728–9.
Calling in overdue Quit Rents.

THE AMERICAN Weekly Mercury.   361

Numbers 470 (from Tuesday, Dec. 31 to Tuesday, Jan. 7, 1728–9) to 521 (from
Tuesday, Dec. 23 to Tuesday, Dec. 30, 1729). Title and imprint as in No. 297,
supra. Nos. 473, 490, 518 and 521 consist of two pages ; the others of four pages
each. From No. 486 to 517, the paper was issued on Thursday ; the others on
Tuesday. No. 477 is misnumbered 476, and 513 is misnumbered 512. No. 508
is misdated Sept. 28 to Oct. 5, for Sept. 25 to Oct. 2. This error was detected and
partly corrected before the whole edition was worked off, as I have met with a
copy dated Sept. 28 to Oct. 2.

BIRKETT. (W.) An Almanac for 1730. By William Birkett.
Philadelphia: Andrew Bradford. 1729.   362

DE FOE. (D.) Religious Courtship. By Daniel De Foe. *Philadelphia:* 1729.   363

"As to the Religious Courtship, Part of which has been retal'd [*sic*] to the
Publick in these Papers, the Reader may be inform'd, that the whole Book will
probably in a little Time be printed and bound up by it self." Pa. Gazette,
No. 40.

EPICTETUS | his | Morals. | Done from the original Greek, and the | Words taken from his own Mouth by Arrian. | The Second Edition. | *Philadelphia: Printed by S. Keimer,* | *in Second-street,* MDCCXXIX. | Sm. 8vo. pp. 32.

The first translation of a Greek or Latin classic printed in America.

[FRANKLIN. B.] A Modest | Enquiry | into the | Nature and Necessity | of a | Paper-Currency. | . . . | . . . | . . . . | *Phila-delphia:* | *Printed and Sold at the New Printing-* | *Office, near the Market.* 1729. | Sm. 8vo. pp. 36.   H. S. P.   365

GODFREY. (T.) An Almanac for 1730. By Thomas Godfrey. *Philadelphia: Franklin and Meredith.* 1729. Folio, 1 leaf.   366

[GORDON. (PATRICK)] The Governour's Message to the House of Re- | presentatives, with the Bill, Entituled, An Act for | Emitting Fifty Thousand Pounds in Bills of Cre- | dit, &c. | [*Phil-adelphia: Andrew Bradford.* 1729.] Folio, pp. (2). H. S. P.   367

GORDON. The Speech | of the Honourable | Patrick Gordon, Esq ; | Lieut. Governour of the Province of | Pennsylvania, | . . . . | To the Representatives of the Freemen of the said Province | met at Philadelphia, April the 2d, 1729. | [Colophon.] *Philadel-phia:* | *Printed by Andrew Bradford, Printer to the Province.* 1729. | Folio, pp. (2).   H. S. P.   368

JERMAN. (J.) An Almanac for 1730. By John Jerman. *Philadelphia: David Harry.* 1729.   369

[KEIMER. (SAMUEL)] A Touch of the Times. *Philadelphia: Printed at the New Printing Office.* 1729.   370

The following advertisement appeared in the American Weekly Mercury, for April 24, 1729. "This may inform those that have been induc'd to think other-wise, That the silly Paper, call'd a Touch of the Times, &c. was Wrote, Printed and Published by Mr. Keimer ; and that his putting the Words New Printing Office at the Bottom, and instructing the Hawkers to say it was done there is an Abuse."

LEEDS. (F.) An Almanac for 1730. By Felix Leeds. *Phila-delphia: Andrew Bradford.* 1729.   371

MEREDITH. (J.) A Short | Discourse, | Proving that the | Jewish or Seventh-Day Sabbath | Is Abrogated and Repealed. | By John Meredith. *Philadelphia: Printed at the New Printing-Office in High-Street, near the Market,* 1729. Sm. 4to. pp. 20, (1).   372

MOLLINEUX. (M.) Fruits of Retirement; | or | Miscella-neous Poems, | Moral and Divine. | Being | Some Contemplations, Letters, &c. writ- | ten on Variety of Subjects and Oc- | casions. | By Mary Mollineux, | Late of Leverpool, Deceased. | To which is prefixed, | Some Account of the Author. | . . . | . . . . | *Phila-delphia: | Printed and Sold by Samuel Keimer, in . . . | Second-Street,* 1729. | Sm. 8vo.   373

Numb. XL. | THE | PENNSYLVANIA Gazette. | Containing the freshest Advices Foreign and Domestick. | From Thursday, September 25. to Thursday, October 2. 1729. | *Philadelphia: Printed by B. Franklin and H. Meredith, at the New Printing-Office near the Market, where Advertisements | are taken in, and all Persons may be supplied with this Paper, at Ten Shillings a Year.* | H. S. P.

Numbers xl. to 111 (from Tuesday, Dec. 22 to Tuesday, Dec. 29, 1730), four pages each, except 108–111, two each. Numbers 66, 68, and 70–107 appeared on Thursday ; 69 on Friday ; the others on Tuesday. In Number 89 the imprint assumed the form given in Number 410, *supra.*

PERRY. (E.) A Memorable Account of the Christian Experi-ences and Living Testimonies of that Faithful Servant of Christ, Edward Parry, in his Writings herein collected. *Philadelphia: Samuel Keimer.* 1729. The Second Edition. [*Ibid.*]   375

PROCLAMATION. G. [*Royal Arms.*] R. | By . . . Patrick Gor-don, Esq; | . . . | . . . . | A | Proclamation. | *Philadelphia: Printed by Andrew Bradford, Printer to the Province* 1729. | Folio, 1 leaf.

A | REVISAL | Of the Intreagues of the Triumvirate, with the rest of | the Trustees of the Proprietor of Pennsilvania. | And also, | Of a Warning | To the Inhabitants of the said Province, against the | Guiles of the Devil and Men. | [*Philadelphia: S. Keimer.* 1729.?] Folio, pp. 4.   L. C. P.   377

[SANDIFORD. (Ralph)]   A Brief | Examination | of the | Practice of the Times, | By the Foregoing and the Present | Dispensation: Whereby | is manifested, how the Devil works | in the Mystery, which none can un- | derstand and get the Victory over but | those that are armed with the Light, | that discovers the Temptation and the | Author thereof, and gives Victory o- | ver him and his Instruments, who are | now gone forth, as in the Beginning, | from the true Friends of Jesus, having | the Form of Godliness in Words, but | in Deeds deny the Power thereof; | from such we are commanded to turn | away. | . . . | . . . | . . . | . . . | . . . | . . . | . . . . | [*Philadelphia:*] *Printed for the Author,* [*by Franklin and Meredith,*] *Anno* 1729. | Sm. 8vo.   H. S. P.   378

Collation : Title, 1 leaf; Dedication, signed Ralph Sandiford, and dated Philadelphia, the 1st of the 11th Month, 1728–9, pp. (6) ; Preface, pp. (7) ; text, pp. 1–69 ; To, etc., pp. 71–74 ; Contents, 1 leaf.

Franklin says in a letter dated Nov. 4, 1789, "I printed a book for Ralph Sandiford against keeping negroes in slavery, two editions of which he distributed gratis." *Memoirs of the Historical Society of Pennsylvania,* Vol. I., p. 143, 2d edition.

A SEASONABLE advice to the inhabitants of the Province of Pennsylvania against the guiles of the Devil and Man.   Folio, pp. 3.   379

Mentioned by Du Simetiere in his list of Books, etc., relating to Pennsylvania.

SHORT-HAND Book.   *Philadelphia : S. Keimer.*   1729.   380

In the Pa. Gazette for the 18th of 7th month, 1729, Keimer says he "has reprinted a fresh impression," and offers it gratis as in 1728.

TAYLOR. (J.) An Almanac for 1730. By Jacob Taylor. *Philadelphia: Andrew Bradford.* 1729.   381

[THOMSON. (John)]   An | Overture | Presented to the | Reverend Synod | of | Dissenting Ministers, | Sitting in Philadelphia, in the Month of | September, 1728. | And is now under the Consideration of the | Several Members of the said Synod, in Order | to come to a Determination concerning it at | next Meeting. | Together with a Preface, or an Epistle | containing some further Reasons to strength- | en the Overture, and an Answer to some | Objections against it. | By a Member of the said Synod. | . . . | . . . | . . . | . . . | . . . . | [*Philadelphia:*] *Printed* [*by Franklin and Meredith*] *for the Author.* 1729. | Sm. 8vo. pp. 32.   B. P. L.

TO the Honourable Patrick Gordon, Esq; Governour of the Province | of Pennsilvania, &c. | The humble Address of the Representatives of the Freemen | of the said Province in General-Assembly met. | [*Philadelphia: Andrew Bradford.* 1729.]   Folio, 1 leaf.   383

THE UNIVERSAL Instructor.   H. S. P.   384

Numbers ii (The 2d of the 11th Month, 1728) to xxxix (The 25th of the 7th Month, 1729.) Title and imprint as in Number 357, *supra*, except the change of date to the Quaker style. Number 2 was issued on Jan. 2, 1728-9 ; Number 3 on Saturday, Jan. 7 ; Number 4 on Thursday the 15th ; Number 5 on Tuesday the 21st, and Number 6 on Wednesday, Jan. 29. From Number 7 (Feb. 4) to Number 39, it appeared regularly on Thursdays, except on June 26, no paper being issued between June 19, and July 3, owing to Keimer's having been arrested for debt. In Number 39 he takes leave of his subscribers thus : "It not quadrating with the circumstances of the Printer hereof S. K. to publish this Gazette any longer, . . . he has agreed with B. Franklin and H. Meredith, . . . to continue it to the end of the Year.

A VIEW of the Calumnies lately spread in some scur- | rilous Prints, against the Government of Penn- | sylvania. | [*Philadelphia: Andrew Bradford.* 1729.]   Folio, pp. 4.   385

A VIEW of the Scandals lately spread in some Printed | Libels, against the Government of Pennsyl- | vania. | [*Philadelphia: Andrew Bradford.* 1729. ?]   Folio, pp. 4.   386

A second Edition with slight additions of the preceding.

WATTS. (I.) The Psalms of David, imitated in the Language of the New Testament, and apply'd to the Christian State of Worship. By Isaac Watts, V. D. M. The Seventh Edition. *Philadelphia: Franklin and Meredith.* 1729.   387

WOOLVERTON. (C.) The Spirit's Teaching Man's sure guide : Briefly asserted and recommended to the sober perusal of all Christian believers. By Charles Woolverton, Sen. The Second Edition, corrected and amended by the Author, with large Additions. *Philadelphia: Printed for the Author by Franklin and Meredith.* 1729.   388

1730.

AN | ACT for | Preventing Accidents | that may happen by
Fire. | [*Philadelphia: Franklin and Meredith.* 1730.?] Folio, 1
leaf.   H. S. P.   389

    This Act, passed Aug. 26, 1721, remained in force until the Revolution or later.
The type is Franklin's, but date of publication is uncertain.

THE AMERICAN Weekly Mercury.   390

    Numbers 522 (from Tuesday, Dec. 30 to Tuesday, Jan. 6, 1729) to 574 (from
Tuesday, Dec. 22 to Tuesday, Dec. 29, 1730). Title and imprint as in Number
297, *supra.* Numbers 531, 570 and 572 consist of two pages ; the other of four
pages each. Number 523 was published on Wednesday ; Numbers 528 and 531
to 570 on Thursday ; the others on Tuesday.

    ANNO Regni | Georgii II. | Regis | Magnæ Britanniæ, Franciæ,
& Hiberniæ | Tertio | At a General Assembly of the Pro- | vince
of Pennsylvania, begun and holden at | Philadelphia, the Four-
teenth Day of October, Anno. Dom. | 1729. In the Third Year
of the Reign of our Sovereign | Lord George II. by the Grace of
God, of Great | Britain, France, and Ireland, King, Defender of
the | Faith, &c. | And from thence continued by Adjournments to
the Twelfth of | January, 1729. | [*Penn Arms.*] | *Philadelphia:
Printed and Sold by B. Franklin and H. Meredith, at the | New
Printing-Office near the Market.* | M,DCC,XXX. | Folio, pp. 48.
+ And from thence continued by Adjournment to the Third of |
August, 1730. Being the Third Session of | this Assembly. |
[*Ibid.*] Title, 1 leaf ; pp. 51–57.   391

    For the Acts from Oct. 14, 1730 to Jan. 4, 1730–1, see Number 420, *infra.*

    BALL. (T.) A French School Book. By Thomas Ball. *Phila-
delphia : Franklin and Meredith.* 1730.   392

    Advertised as "now in the Press," in the Pa. Gazette, April 16, 1730.

    BECKETT. (W.) Visitation Sermon ; preached before the
Reverend the Commissary, and the rest of the Clergy of Pennsylvania, in Christ Church. *Philadelphia : Printed by Andrew Bradford.* 1730.   393

This title is from Haven's List, and is probably a misdescription of the followng : The Duty both of Clergy and Laity | to each other. | A | Sermon | Preach'd before the Reverend the | Commissary, | And the rest of the | Clergy | of | Pennsylvania. | In Christ Church, Philadelphia. | On Wednesday, September 24, 1729. | Being the First Visitation held there. | By William Beckett, Missionary at Lewes. | *Annapolis : Printed and Sold by W. Parks.* M, DCC, XXIX. | Sm. 4to. pp. 18. N. Y. H. S.

BEISSEL. C. Ehebüchlein. Von Conrad Beissel. *Philadelphia: B. Franklin.?* 1730. 394

See Chronicon Ephratense, p. 47.

BIRKETT. (W.) An Almanac for 1731. By William Birkett. *Printed and Sold by William Bradford in New York, and Andrew Bradford in Philadelphia.* 1730. 395

COLDEN. (C.) History of the Five Indian Nations. By Cadwallader Colden. *Philadelphia: Printed by Andrew Bradford.* 1730. 396

This title is from Haven's List, and is probably taken from an advertisement by Andrew Bradford of the New York edition of 1727.

CUMMINGS. (A.) Exhortation to the Clergy of Pennsylvania, at Philadelphia, Sept. 24, 1729. *Philadelphia:* 1730. 397

This title is from Haven's List. It is an incorrect description of the following : An | Exhortation | to the | Clergy | of Pennsylvania, | at | Philadelphia. | September 24, 1729. | By the Reverend Archibald Cummings, Commissary, and Rector | of Christ Church, in Philadelphia. | *Annapolis :* | *Printed and Sold by W. Parks.* M.DCC.XXIX. | Sm. 4to. pp. 16 +. N. Y. H. S. Together with Beckett's Visitation Sermon it is advertised as lately published in the Weekly Mercury, Feb. 10, 1729-30. "Both to be sold by Andrew Bradford," who makes no claim to have *printed* them.

AN ELEGY on the Death of that ancient, venerable and useful Matron and Midwife, Mrs. Mary Broadwell, who rested from her Labours, Jan. 2, 1730. Aged A Hundred Years and One Day. *Sold by David Harry, Printer in Philadelphia.* 1730. 398

A second edition was advertised in the Gazette, Jan. 20, 1729-30.

FISHER. (G.) The American Instructor; or Young Man's Best Companion. By George Fisher. To which is added, the

Poor Planter's Physician; with prudent Advice to young Trades-
men. *Philadelphia:* 1730.   399

   Title from Haven's List.   Probably inaccurate.

   GODFREY. (THOMAS) An Almanack for the year 1731.   *Philadelphia: Franklin and Meredith.*   1730.   400

   "Done on a large Sheet of Demi-Paper, after the London Manner."—*Pa. Gazette.*

   GORDON. (P.) The | Speech | of the Honourable | Patrick
Gordon, Esq; | Governor of the Province of Pennsylvania, and
Counties | of New-Castle, Kent and Sussex upon Delaware; To |
the Representatives of the Freemen of the said Pro- | vince, met
at Philadelphia, Jan. 13, 1729–30. | [Colophon.] *Philadelphia:
Printed and Sold by B. Franklin and H. Meredith, at the New |
Printing-Office near the Market.* [1730.] | Folio, pp. (2). H. S. P.   401

   Contains also the Assembly's Address, and the Governor's answer.

   GOETTLICHE | Liebes und Lobes gethöne, | Welche in den
hertzen der Kinder | der Weiszheit zusammen ein | Und von da
wieder ausgeflossen. | Zum Lob Gottes | Und nun von denen schü-
lern der himlischen | weiszheit zur erweckung und auf- | munterung
in ihrem Creutz und | leiden aus hertzlicher lie- | be mitgetheilet. |
Dann | Mit lieb erfü- | ellet sein bringt Gott den besten Preisz |
Und giebt zum singen uns die allerschönste weisz. | *Zu Philadelphia:
Gedruckt bey Benjamin | Francklin in der Marck-strasz.* 1730. |
12mo. pp. 96.   402

   JERMAN. (J.) An Almanac for 1731. By John Jerman.
Philadelphia: Franklin and Meredith.   1730.   403

   LEEDS. (F.) An Almanac for 1731. By Felix Leeds.   *Philadelphia: Andrew Bradford.*   1730.   404

   LEEDS. (T.) [Cut.] The Genuine Leeds Almanack. | For the
Year of Christian Account, 1730 | . . . | . . . | . . . | . . . . |
Being the Second after Bissextile or Leap Year. | . . . | . . . | . . .
| . . . | . . . . | . . . | . . . | . . . | . . . | . . . | . . . | . . . . | By Titan
Leeds, Philomat. | *Printed by D. Harry, in Second-street, Philadel-
| phia,* 1730. | Sm. 8vo. pp. (28).   H. S. P.   405

LEEDS.   Leeds 1731. | The American | Almanack | For the Year of Christian Account 1731. | . . . | . . . | . . . | . . . . | Being the Third after | Bissextile or Leap-Year. | . . . | . . . | . . . | . . . | . . . | . . . | . . . | . . . | . . . | . . . | . . . . | By Titan Leeds, Philomat. | *Printed and Sold by William Bradford in New- | York, and Andrew Bradford in Philadelphia.* [1730.] | Sm. 8vo. pp. (24).   H. S. P.   406

MOLLINEUX. (M.)   Fruits of Retirement; Or, Miscellaneous Poems, Moral and Divine.   Being Some Contemplations, Letters, &c. written on Variety of Subjects and Occasions.   By Mary Mollineux, Late of Liverpool, Deceased.   To which prefixed: Some Account of the Author.   *Philadelphia: Andrew Bradford.*   1730.
       407

Advertised in the Weekly Mercury, June 25, 1730, as lately published, which may refer to the edition printed in the preceding year by Keimer, but it was advertised so steadily for the next six months, I think Bradford probably reprinted it as he did West's Treatise on Mixed Marriages.

MORGAN. (A.) Cyd-Gordiad | Egwyddorawl o'r | Scrythurau: | Neu | Daflen Lythyrennol o'r Prif Eiriau | Yn y Bibl Sanctaidd. | Yn Arwain, dan y Cyfryw eiriau, i fuan | ganfod pob rhyw ddymunol ran o'r | Scrythurau. | A Gyfan-soddwyd Drwy Lafurus Boen | Abel Morgan, | Gwenidog yr Efengyl er lle's y Cymru. | *Argraphwyd yn Philadelphia, gan Samuel Keimer, | a Dafydd Harry.* | MDCCXXX. | Folio,   L. C. P.   408

Collation : Title, 1 leaf; Dedication signed "Enoch Morgan," pp. 2; At y Darl lennydd, signed part by Enoch Morgan and part by John Cadwalader, pp. (4); Cyd-Gordiad, pp. (228).   A Welsh Concordance to the Bible.

NEW JERSEY.   Acts | and | Laws | of His Majesty's Province of Nova Cæsarea, or | New-Jersey: | As they were Enacted by the Governor, | Council, and General Assembly, at a Ses- | sion held at Perth-Amboy, beginning | the 7th of May, 1730, in the Third | Year, and ending July the 8th, in the | Fourth Year of the Reign of his Ma- | jesty King George the Second. | [*Royal Arms.*] | *Philadelphia: | Printed and Sold by Andrew Bradford, in Second-Street,* | MDCCXXX. | Folio, pp. 39; Table, 1 leaf.   409

THE PENNSYLVANIA Gazette. *Philadelphia: Printed by | B. Franklin and H. Meredith, at the New Printing- | Office near the Market, where Advertisements are taken in, and all Persons may be supplied | with this Paper at Ten Shillings a Year. |* H. S. P. 410

Numbers 112 (from Tuesday, Dec. 29 to Tuesday, Jan. 5, 1730-31) to 161 (from Tuesday, Dec. 21 to Tuesday, Dec. 28, 1731). Title as in Number 374, *supra*. Numbers 112-114, 116-120, 155, 158, 160 and 161 consist of two pages ; the others of four pages each. Numbers 120, 156 and 158 were published on Thursday ; the others on Tuesday, except 157, which appeared on Saturday. No paper was issued between the 9th and 23d of September.

[SANDIFORD. (Ralph)] The | Mystery of Iniquity ; | in a brief | Examination | of the | Practice of Times, | By the fore- | going and the present Dis- | pensation : Whereby is manifested | how the Devil works in the Mystery, | which none can understand and get the Victory | over but those that are armed with the Light, | that discovers the Temptation and the Author | thereof, and gives Victory over him and his In- | struments, who are now gone forth, as in the | Beginning, from the true Friends of Jesus, | having the Form of Godliness in Words, but in | Deeds deny the Power thereof; from such we | are commanded to turn away. | Unto which is added in the Postscript, | the Injury this Trading in Slaves doth the | Commonwealth, humbly offer'd to all | of a Publick Spirit. | The Second Edition, with Additions. | . . . | . . . | . . . | . . . | . . . | . . . . | *[Philadelphia :] Printed for the Author, [by Franklin and Meredith,] Anno* 1730. | Sm. 8vo. pp. 111.

[SCOUGAL. (Henry)] Vital Christianity : | A Brief | Essay | On the Life of God, | in the | Soul of Man ; | Produced and Main- | tained by | Christ living in us ; | and | The Mystery of Christ | within, Explained. | With an Exhibition, in which all that | Fear God, and give Glory to Him, will be | satisfied. | . . . | . . . | . . . | . . . . | *Philadelphia: Printed by David Harry.* 1730. | 12mo. pp. (6), 1–26. 412

TAYLOR. (J.) An Almanac for 1731. By Jacob Taylor. *Philadelphia :* 1730. 413

DER TEUTSCHE Pilgrim mitbringende sinen sitten Calender Auf das jahr Nach der gnaden reichen geburt unsers Herrn und

Heylandes Jesu Christi MDCXXXI. (welches ein gemein jahr von 365 tagen ist.) Auf den Pennsylvanischen Meridianum gerichtet jedoch in denen beyliegenden Orten ja von Newfoundland an biss Carolina ohne mercklichen Unterschied gar wohl zu gebrauchen. Zum ersten mahl heraus gegeben. *Zu Philadelphia, Gedruckt bei Andreas Bradford.* [1730.]   414

Title from the Penna. Mag. Hist. and Biog. Vol. vi. p. 370.

VOTES | and | Proceedings | of the | House of Representatives | of the | Province of Pennsylvania, | Met at Philadelphia, on Tuesday the Fourteenth | of October, Anno Dom. 1729, and continued by Adjournments. [to Feb. 13, 1729–30.] | Published by Order of Assembly. | *Philadelphia:* | *Printed and Sold by B. Franklin and H. Meredith, at the New* | *Printing-Office near the Market.* | M,DCC,XXX. | Folio, pp. 38.   H. S. P.   415

WEST. (M.)   A | Treatise | Concerning | Marriage: | wherein | The Unlawfulness of Mixt-Marriages is | laid open from the Scriptures of Truth: | Shewing | That it is contrary to the Will of God, and the | Practice of His People in former Ages, and | therefore of Dangerous Consequence, for Per- | sons of Different Judgments in Matters of Re- | ligious Worship, to be Joyned together in | Marriage. | Written for the Information and Benefit of Christian Pro- | fessors in general and recommended more particularly | to the Youth of either Sex amongst the people called Quakers. | By Moses West. | . . . | . . . | . . . | . . . | . . . | . . . . . . | . . . . | *Philadelphia:* | *Reprinted and Sold by David Harry in Second-Street.* [1730.] | 8vo. pp. 39.   416

1731.

AN ACT for the better Regulation and Government of Seamen in the Merchant Service; and An Act for the more effectual collecting the Duties granted for the Support of the Royal Hospital at Greenwich. *Philadelphia: Andrew Bradford.* 1731.   417

THE AMERICAN Weekly Mercury. *Philadelphia: Printed and Sold by Andrew Bradford, at the Sign of the Bible in Second*

*Street, where | Advertisements are taken in, and all Persons in Town
or Country may be supplyed with this Paper at Ten Shillings | a
Year: Also all sorts of Printing Work done cheap, and Old Books
neatly bound ; likewise Ready Money for Linen Rags. |*   418

Numbers 575 (from Tuesday, Dec. 29, to Tuesday, Jan. 5, 1730) to 626 (from
Tuesday, Dec. 21, to Tuesday, Dec. 28, 1731). Title as in No. 297, *supra*. Numbers 577, 579, 581, 623 and 625 consist of two pages; the others of four pages each.
No. 582 was issued on Wednesday; Numbers 584 to 622 on Thursday; the others
on Tuesday. No. 591 is misnumbered 593, and 600 is misnumbered 500. The
imprint of No. 626 is on the third page, the fourth being filled with a list of books
(in four columns) for sale by Andrew Bradford.

ANNO Regni | Georgii II. | Regis | Magnæ Britanniæ, |
Franciæ, & Hiberniæ | Quarto. | At a General Assembly of the
Pro- | vince of Pennsylvania, begun and holden at | Philadelphia,
the Fourteenth Day of October, Anno Dom. | 1730. In the
Fourth Year of the Reign of our Sovereign | Lord George II. by
the Grace of God, of Great | Britain, France, and Ireland, King,
Defender of the | Faith, &c. | And from thence continued by
Adjournment to the Fourth of | January, 1730. Being the Second
Session of | this Assembly. | [Penn Arms.] | *Philadelphia: |
Printed and Sold by B. Franklin and H. Meredith, at the | New
Printing-Office near the Market.* | M,DCC,XXX. [1731.] | Folio,
Title, 1 leaf; pp. 61-89.   H. S: P.   419

ARSCOT. (A.) Some | Considerations | Relating to the |
Present State | of the | Christian Religion, | Wherein the Nature,
End and Design | of Christianity, as well as the Principal Evi-
dence | of the Truth of it, are explained and recom- | mended out
of the Holy Scriptures, with a ge- | neral Appeal to the Experience
of all Men for | Confirmation thereof. | By Alexander Arscot. |
*Philadelphia: | Printed by B. Franklin, at the New- | Printing-Office
near the Market.* 1731. | Sm. 8vo. pp. 111, (1).   420

Differs from the edition of 1732, only in the imprint, and advertisement on the
last page. In this edition the advertisement, which begins "Books Printed and
Sold at the New Printing-Office near the Market," announces the publication of
"Woolverton's The Spirit's Teaching," and "Meredith on the Sabbath," &c. In
the later edition the advertisement begins "Sold by B. Franklin," &c., and refers
to Barclay's Apology only.

BIRKETT. (W.) An Almanac for 1732. By William Birkett. *Philadelphia: Andrew Bradford.* 1731.   421

GODFREY. (T.) The Pennsylvania Almanack for 1732. By Thomas Godfrey. *Philadelphia: Franklin and Meredith.* 1731.

GODFREY. (T.) A Sheet Almanac for 1732. By Thomas Godfrey. *Philadelphia: Franklin and Meredith.* 1731. Folio, 1 leaf.   423

JERMAN. (J.) The American Almanac for 1732. By John Jerman. *Philadelphia: Franklin and Meredith.* 1731.   424

Advertised with Godfrey's two Almanacs in the Pa. Gazette, Nov. 18, 1731.

THE LADY Errant Inchanted: A Poem. Dedicated to Her Most Serene Highness the Princess Magallia. *Philadelphia: Franklin and Meredith.* 1731.   425

LEEDS. (T.) The American Almanack for 1732. By Titan Leeds. *Printed and Sold by William Bradford in New-York and Andrew Bradford in Philadelphia.* [1731.] Sm. 8vo. pp. (28).
H. S. P.   426

THE PENNSYLVANIA Gazette.   427

Numbers 112 (from Tuesday, Dec. 29, to Tuesday, Jan. 5, 1730–31) to 161 (from Tuesday, Dec. 21, to Tuesday, Dec. 28, 1731.) Title and imprint as in No. 374, *supra.* Numbers 120 to 156 and 158 were issued on Thursday; No. 157 on Saturday; and the rest on Tuesday. Numbers 112–114, 116–120, 155, 158, 160 and 161 consist of two pages: the others of four pages each, except 159, which contains only three pages.

TAYLOR. (J.) An Almanac for 1732. By Jacob Taylor. *Philadelphia:* 1731.   428

DER TEUTSCHE Pilgrim . . . Calender auf das jahr 1732. *Philadelphia: Getruckt bei Andreas Bradford.* 1731.   429

See No. 415, *supra.*

THE VOTES of the House of Representatives. *Philadelphia: Franklin and Meredith.* 1731.   430

Advertised in the Pa. Gazette May 27, and Dec. 14, 1731.

WEBB. (G.) Batchelors-Hall; | A | Poem. | By George Webb. | . . . | . . . | . . . | . . . | . . . | . . . . | *Philadelphia :* | *Printed and Sold [by B. Franklin and H. Meredith] at the New Printing-Office,* | MDCCXXXI. | *Price One Shilling.* | Folio, pp. 12.

A. P. S.   431

1732.

ADVICE and Caution | from | Our Monthly Meeting | At | Philadelphia. | Held the 25th Day of the | Sixth Month, 1732, | Concerning Children and | Servants. | [*Philadelphia : Printed by Andrew Bradford.* 1732.]   Sm. 8vo. pp. 8.   L. C. P.   432

THE AMERICAN Weekly Mercury.   433

Numbers 627 (from Tuesday, Dec. 28, to Tuesday, Jan. 4, 1731–2) to 678 (from Tuesday, Dec. 19, to Tuesday Dec. 26, 1732). Title and imprint as in No. 419, *supra.* Numbers 627, 629, 631, 633, 635, and 675 consist of two pages; the others of four pages each, except 677, in which there are only three. Numbers 637 to 675 were issued on Thursday; the others on Tuesday. No. 653 is misnumbered 652, and 668 is misnumbered 667.

ANNO Regni | Georgii II. | Regis | Magnæ Britanniæ, Franciæ, & Hiberniæ | Quinto. | At a General Assembly of the Pro- | vince of Pennsylvania, begun and holden at | Philadelphia, the Fourteenth Day of October, Anno Dom. | 1731. In the Fifth Year of the Reign of our Sovereign | Lord George II. by the Grace of God, of Great | Britain, France, and Ireland, King, Defender of the | Faith, &c. | And from thence continued by Adjournment to the Tenth of | January, 1731. | [Penn Arms.] | *Philadelphia :* | *Printed and Sold by B. Franklin, at the* | *New Printing-Office near the Market.* | M,DCC,XXXI. [1732.] | Folio, Title, 1 leaf; pp. 93–95. +[*Ibid.*] And from thence continued by Adjournments to the Thirty- | first of July, 1732. | [*Ibid.*] M,DCC,-XXXII. | Title, 1 leaf; pp. 99–102.   H. S. P.   434

ARSCOT. (A.) Some | Considerations | Relating to the | Present State | of the | Christian Religion, | Wherein the Nature, End and Design | of Christianity, as well as the Principal Evidence | of the Truth of it, are explained and recom- | mended out of the

Holy Scriptures ; with a ge- | neral Appeal to the Experience of all Men for | Confirmation thereof. | By Alexander Arscot. | . . . | . . . . | *London Printed: | Reprinted by B. Franklin, at the New- | Printing-Office, in Philadelphia.* 1732. | 16mo. pp. 111. (1).

Some | Considerations | Relating to the | Present State | of the | Christian Religion. | Part II. | Wherein the principal Evidence of | the Christian Religion is explain'd and defended | upon the Principles of Reason, as well as Revela- | tion : With Observations on some Passages in the | Book intituled, Christianity as old as the Creation, | so far as concerns the Doctrine herein advanced. | By Alexander Arscot. | . . . | . . . | . . . . | *London Printed: | Reprinted by B. Franklin, at the New- | Printing-Office, in Philadel- phia.* 1732. | 16mo. pp. 140. (2).   H. S. P.   435

BIRKETT. (W.) An Almanac for 1733.   By William Birkett. *Philadelphia : Andrew Bradford.* 1732.   436

EVANS. (D.)   A Help for Parents and Heads of Families, to instruct those under their Care, in the first Principles of Religion: Being a short plain Catechism, grounded upon God's Word, and agreeable to the Westminster Assembly's excellent Catechisms. By David Evans, a Labourer in the Gospel at Tredyffren in Penn-silvania.   *Philadelphia : B. Franklin.*   1732.   437

Advertised in the Pa. Gazette, No. 174, March 30, 1731-2.

EVANS.   The Minister of Christ and his Flock: As it was delivered in a Sermon at Abington in Pennsylvania, Decem. 30. 1731. at the Ordination of Mr. Richard Treat to the Gospel Ministry there. With an Appendix of the Questions then pub-lickly proposed, and the Charges given.   By David Evans, Minis-ter at Tredyffren.   *Philadelphia : B. Franklin.*   1732.   438

Advertised in the Pa. Gazette, Oct. 5, 1732.

GODFREY. (T[HOMAS]) The Pennsylvania | Almanack | For the Year of Christian Account | 1733. | Fitted to the Latitude of 40 Degrees, | and a Meridian of 5 Hours West from London. | [Penn Arms.] | By T. Godfrey. | *Philadelphia.* | *Printed and Sold by A. Bradford at the Post-Office.* [1732.] | Sm. 8vo. pp. (24).

HOLME. (B.)   A Serious Call in Christian Love to all People, to turn to the Spirit of Christ. . . . By Benjamin Holme. *Philadelphia : Printed by Andrew Bradford.* 1732.   Sm. 8vo. pp. 40.

440

See Magazine of Pennsylvania History,   Vol. iv., p. 442, and J. Smith's Catalogue of Friends' Books.

THE HONOUR of the Gout: Or, a Rational Discourse demonstrating that the Gout is one of the greatest Blessings which can befal Mortal Man; that all Gentlemen who are weary of it are their own Enemies; that those Practitioners who offer at the Cure, are the vainest and most mischievous Cheats in Nature. By way of Letter to an Eminent Citizen. Wrote in the heat of a violent Paroxysm, and now publish'd for the Common Good. By Philander Misiatrus. *London Printed: Reprinted by B. Franklin in Philadelphia,* 1732.   Sm. 8vo.   c.   441

Collation: Title, 1 leaf; The Publisher to the Reader, 1 page; Advertisement, 1 page; text, pp. 5-65 (1 blank); Dedication, pp. (5).

JERMAN. (J.)   An Almanac for 1733.   By John Jerman. *Philadelphia : Andrew Bradford.* 1732.   442

LEEDS. (T.)   The American Almanack for 1733.   By Titan Leeds.   *Printed and Sold by William Bradford in New-York, and Andrew Bradford in Philadelphia.* [1732.]   Sm. 8vo. pp. (28).

NEW JERSEY.   The | Acts | Of the General Assembly | Of the Province of | New-Jersey, | From the Time of the Surrender of the | Government of the said Province, to the | Fourth Year of the Reign of King | George the Second. | Collected and Published by Order of the said | Assembly. | With a Table of the Principal Matters therein contained. | [Royal Arms] | *Philadelphia: Printed and Sold by William and | Andrew Bradford, Printers to the King's Most Excellent | Majesty, for the Province of New-Jersey,* | MDCCXXXII. | Folio, Title, 1 leaf; Table, pp. (12); text, pp. 281.   H. S. P.   444

Edited by John Kinsey, afterwards Chief Justice of Pennsylvania. Brinley's copy sold for $51.

NEW JERSEY.   Anno Regni Georgii II. Sexto.   At a General Assembly of the Province of New Jersey.   *Philadelphia: B. Franklin.*   1732.   Folio.   445

Acts of Assembly passed in 1732.

THE PENNSYLVANIA Gazette.   446

Numbers 162 (from Tuesday, Dec. 28, to Tuesday, Jan. 4, 1731–32) to 213 (Dec. 19 to Dec. 28, 1732). Title and imprint as in No. 374, *supra.* Numbers 162, 175, 177, 196 and 202–213 consist of two pages; the others of four pages each. There are two papers numbered 168, and dated from Feb. 8, to Feb 15th, one of which is the preceding issue (167, Feb. 1, to February 8,) with nothing altered but the name and date. Numbers 162 to 171 were issued on Tuesday; 172 to 185, on Thursday, and 186 to 196, on Monday. The day of the week is omitted after 197, and while the paper appeared once a week, the day of publication was very irregular till the end of the year. Meredith's name is omitted from imprint after No. 179, when it assumed the form given No. 465, *infra.*

PHILADELPHISCHE Zeitung.   *Philadelphia: B. Franklin.* 1732.   447

The Pennsylvania Gazette, of June 15, 1732, announces that on Saturday, June 24, "will be published Philadelphische Zeitung, or Newspaper in High-Dutch, which will continue to be published on Saturdays once a Fortnight. Advertisements are taken by the Printer hereof, or by Mr. Louis Timothee, who translates them."

SAUNDERS. (R.)   Poor Richard, 1733. | An | Almanack | For the Year of Christ | 1733, | Being the First after Leap Year; | And makes since the Creation Years | By the Account of the Eastern Greeks 7241 | By the Latin Church, when ⊙ ent. ♈ 6932 | By the Computation of W. W. 5742 | By the Roman Chronology 5682 | By the Jewish Rabbies 5494 | Wherein is contained | The Lunations, Eclipses, Judgment of | the Weather, Spring Tides, Planets Motions & | mutual Aspects, Sun and Moon's Rising and Set- | ting, Length of Days, Time of High Water, | Fairs, Courts, and observable Days. | Fitted to the Latitude of Forty Degrees, | and a Meridian of Five Hours West from London, | but may without sensible Error, serve all the ad- | jacent Places, even from Newfoundland to South- | Carolina. | By Richard Saunders, Philom. | *Philadelphia:* | *Printed and sold by B. Franklin, at the New* | *Printing-Office near the Market.* [1732.] | Sm. 8vo. + The Second Edition. + The Third Edition. Sm. 8vo. pp. (24).   448

TAYLOR. (J.) An Almanac for 1733. By Jacob Taylor. *Philadelphia: 1732.*   449

DER TEUTSCHE Pilgrim . . . Calender auf das jahr 1733. *Philadelphia: Gedruckt bei Andreas Bradford.* 1732.   450

See No. 415, *supra*.

THE TRADITIONS of the Clergy destructive of Religion; With an Enquiry into the Grounds and Reasons of such Traditions: A Sermon preached at the Visitation held at Wakefield in Yorkshire, June 25, 1731. *London Printed: Reprinted in Philadelphia, by Franklin and Meredith.* 1732.   451

Advertised in the Pennsylvania Gazette, March 30, 1731–2. Dedicated to the Reverend Mr. [Jacob] Henderson [of Maryland], by Athanasius Wildfire, 1731–2.

VORSPIEL | der | Neuen-Welt. | welches sich in der letzten Abendröthe | als ein paradisischer Lichtes-glantz | unter den Kindern Gottes | hervor gethan. | In | Liebes, Lobes, Leidens, Krafft | und Erfahrungs liedern abgebildet, die | gedrückte, gebückte und Creutz- | tragende Kirche auf Erden. | Und wie inzwischen sich | Die obere und Triumphirende Kirche | als eine Paradiesische vorkost her- | vor thut und offenbahret. | Und daneben, als | Ernstliche und zuruffende wächterstimmen | an alle annoch zerstreuete Kinder Gottes, das sie | sich sammlen und bereit machen auf den | baldigen; Ja bald herein brechen- | den Hockzeit-Tag der braut | des Lamms. | *Zu Philadelphia: Gedruckt bey Benjamin | Francklin, in der Marck-strass.* 1732. | Sm. 8vo. pp. 200.   H. S. P. 452

1733.

THE AMERICAN Weekly Mercury. *Philadelphia: Printed and Sold by Andrew Bradford, Post-Master, at the Sign of the Bible | in Second-Street, where Advertisements are taken in, and all Persons in Town or Country | may be supplyed with this Paper. |*   453

Numbers 679 (from Tuesday Dec. 26, to Thursday, Jan. 4, 1732–3) to 730 (from Saturday, Dec. 22, to Saturday, Dec. 29, 1733). Title as in No. 297, *supra*. Numbers 680, 684, 686 and 689 consist of two pages; the others of four pages each, except No. 729, which contains 6 pages. Numbers 679–682, and 692–727 were issued on Thursday; the others on Tuesday, except 728, which appeared on Friday, and 729 and 730, on Saturday. In numbers 680, and 692, the imprint is curtailed for want of space.

ANNO Regni | Georgii II. | Regis | Magnæ Britanniæ, Franciæ, & Hiberniæ | Septimo. | At a General Assembly of the Pro- | vince of Pennsylvania, begun and holden at | Philadelphia, the Four- teenth Day of October, Anno. Dom. | 1733. In the Seventh Year of the Reign of our Sove- | reign Lord George II. by the Grace of God, of | Great Britain, France, and Ireland, King, Defender | of the Faith, &c. | And from thence continued by Adjournments to the Seventeenth | of December, 1733. | [Penn Arms.] | *Philadel- phia:* | *Printed and Sold by B. Franklin, at the* | *New Printing- Office near the Market.* | M,DCC,XXXIII. | Folio, Title, 1 leaf; pp. 105-128. 454

ARTICLES | of | Agreement | made and concluded upon be- tween | The Right Honourable the | Lord Proprietary of Mary- land, | And the Honourable the | Proprietarys of Pensilvania, &c. | touching the | Limits and Boundaries of the Two Provinces. | With | The Commission, | Constituting certain Persons to execute the same. | *Philadelphia:* | *Printed by B. Franklin, at the New Printing-Office* | *near the Market.* M,DCC,XXXIII. | Folio. pp. 19. 1 map. H. S. P. 455

BIRKETT. (W.) An Almanac for 1734. By William Birkett. *Philadelphia: Andrew Bradford.* 1733. 456

BOUCHER. (M.) The American Almanack, for the Year 1734. By Matthew Boucher, Philomath. *Philadelphia: Andrew Brad- ford.* 1733. 457

CATALOGUE of the Library Company of Philadelphia. *Philadelphia: B. Franklin.* 1733. Folio, 1 leaf? 458

In the minutes of the Library Company, occurs the following entry: "May 30, 1733. The Proprietor's Secretary having informed B. Franklin, that if the Directors intended to print their Address, the Proprietor would let them have his Answer in writing." And "desired to see a List of the Library Books, that in his writing for a parcel to present the Company he might not send for what we already have. This lying before me and Mr. Franklin sending a *printed Catalogue,* I added to it the Books given by several hands since the printing of the said Catalogue, and took these Lists to the Proprietor.''

THE SHORTER CATECHISM of the Assembly of Divines, with the Proofs at large. *Philadelphia: B. Franklin.* 1733.   459

Advertised in the Pa. Gazette, March 21, 1733–4.

GODFREY. (T.) The Pennsylvania Almanac for 1734. By Thomas Godfrey. *Philadelphia: Andrew Bradford.* 1733.   460

JERMAN. (J.) An Almanac for 1734. By John Jerman. *Philadelphia: B. Franklin.* 1733.   461

LEEDS. (T.) [Cut.] The Genuine Leeds Almanack. | The American | Almanack | For the Year of Christian Account, 1734. | . . . | . . . | . . . | . . . . | Being the Second after Leap-Year. | Wherein is contain'd, | The Lunations, Eclipses, Judgment of the Weather, the | Spring-Tides, the Planets Motions, and mutual Aspects, | With the Birth-Days of the Successive Heirs to the | Crown of Great Britain: Time of the Suns Rising and | Setting, Length of the Days, Seven Stars Rising, South- | ing and Setting, Time of High-Water, Fairs, Courts, | and Observable Days. | Fitted to the Latitude of 40 Degrees, and | a Meridian of five Hours West from London, but may | without sensible Error, serve all the adjacent Places, | even from New-found-land to Carolina. | By Titan Leeds, Philomat. | *Printed and Sold by Andrew Bradford, Post-Master, at | the Sign of the Bible in Second-Street, Philadelphia.* [1733.] | Sm. 8vo. pp. (24).   H. S. P.   462

[LOGAN. (JAMES)] The Latter Part of | The | Charge | Delivered from the Bench to the | Grand Inquest, | at a Court of Oyer and Terminer and Gaol Delivery, held | for the City and County of Philadelphia, | At Philadelphia the 24th Day of September 1733. | Published at the Request of the said Inquest. | With their Address. | [*Philadelphia: B. Franklin.* 1733.] Folio, pp. 3.   463

NEW JERSEY. Anno Regni | Georgii II. | Regis, | Magnæ Britanniæ, Franciæ, & Hiberniæ | Septimo. | At a General Assem-

bly of the Pro- | vince of New-Jersey, begun and holden at | Bur-
lington, the Twenty-sixth Day of April, Anno Dom. | 1733. In
the Sixth Year of the Reign of our Sovereign | Lord George II.
by the Grace of God, of Great | Britain, France, and Ireland, King,
Defender of the | Faith, &c. | And from thence continued by Ad-
journments to the Sixteenth | of August, 1733. | [Cut.] *Philadel-
phia: Printed and Sold by B. Franklin, at the | New Printing-Office
near the Market.* | M,DCC,XXXIII. | Folio, Title, 1 leaf; pp. 301-
343; Table, 1 leaf.   464

THE PENNSYLVANIA Gazette. *Philadelphia: Printed by
B. Franklin, at the New-Printing- | Office near the Market. Price
10s. a Year. | Where Advertisements are taken in, and Book-Binding
is done reasonably, in the best Manner.* | 465

Numbers 214 (from Dec. 28, to Jan. 4, 1732–3) to 265 (from Dec. 20, to Dec.
31, 1733.) Numbers 214, 234 and 237 consist of two pages; the others of four
pages each. No. 242 is misnumbered 243. Both numbers 243 are dated July 12
to 19, while the correctly numbered issue should be dated July 19 to 26. No.
261 is misdated Nov. 16 to 22, for Nov. 22 to 29. Title as in 374, *supra*.

SAUNDERS. (R.) Poor Richard, 1734. An Almanack . . . .
By Richard Saunders, Philom. *Philadelphia: B. Franklin.* [1733.]
Sm. 8vo. pp. (24).   466

Title, with the necessary changes of dates, etc., as in No. 448, *supra*. A second
edition was published in December, 1733.

TATE, (N.) AND (N.) BRADY. A New Version | of the |
Psalms | of | David, | Fitted to the Tunes Used | in | Churches.
| By | N. Brady, D.D. . . . | and N. Tate, Esq; . . . | . . . . |
*Philadelphia: Printed and Sold by B. Franklin, | at the New Print-
ing-Office, near the | Market. Sold also by A. Bradford, at | the
Bible in Second-Street.* 1733. | 24mo. pp. 286.   H. S. P.   467

TAYLOR. (J.) An Almanac for 1734. By Jacob Taylor.
Philadelphia: 1733.   468

THE TEMPORAL Interest of North America. Shewing the
Causes and Cure of the many Distractions, Wants, Poverty, and
Ill-will to each other, which we are exposed to, in a Country

wherein we might live as happily as any People in the World if it were not our own Fault. Offered to the Consideration of all that love either their Country, their Neighbours, or themselves. Being a continuation of The Nature of Riches. By a Lover of his Country. *Philadelphia: B. Franklin.* 1733.   469

> Advertised in the Pa. Gazette, Aug. 30, 1733.

VOTES of the Assembly. *Philadelphia: B. Franklin.* 1733. Folio.   470

1734.

ADVERTISEMENT. | [*Philadelphia: B. Franklin.* 1734.] Folio, 1 leaf.   H. S. P.   471

> Signed by James Steel, Receiver-General, and dated Philadelphia, the 5th of Sept. 1734. "Whereas in pursuance of divers Warrants issued and granted as well by the late Commissioners of Property, as by the Proprietary Himself, since his Arrival in this Province, sundry Tracts of Land have been surveyed and settled in the several Counties thereof, by Persons who have neglected to account and pay for the same . . . . Therefore Notice is hereby given to all such Persons . . . That in case they do not . . . make payment . . . before the First Day of the Month of March next . . . the several Surveys to them made will be . . . declared void."

ADVERTISEMENT of the Collector of the Excise. *Philadelphia: B. Franklin.* 1734.   472

> By an Act of Assembly passed in 1733, for reviving an Excise on Wine and other Spirits, the Collectors were "required to give public notice by printed Advertisements fixed on convenient public places, of the commencement of this Act, and also the duties hereby imposed, with notice to the Constables of their duty, and full directions how and where entries are to be made."

THE AMERICAN Weekly Mercury.   473

> Numbers 731 (from Saturday, Dec. 29, to Tuesday Jan. 1, 1733-4) to 783 (from Tuesday, Dec. 24, to Tuesday Dec. 31, 1734.) Title and imprint as in No. 433, *supra.* Numbers 731 and 740 consist of two pages; the others of four pages, except 753, 761, 762, 767, 769 and 776, which contain six pages each. No. 747 has a "Postscript" of two pages. Numbers 742 to 780 were published on Thursday; the others on Tuesday.

ANNO Regni | Georgii II. | Regis | Magnæ Britanniæ, | Franciæ & Hiberniæ | Octavo. | At a General Assembly of the Pro- | vince of Pennsylvania, begun and holden at | Philadelphia, the Fourteenth Day of October; Anno Dom. | 1733, in the Seventh Year of the Reign of our Sove- | reign Lord George II. by the Grace of God, of | Great Britain, France, and Ireland, King, Defender | of the Faith, &c. | And from thence continued by Adjournments to the Twelfth | of August, 1734. | [Penn Arms.] | *Philadelphia:* | *Printed and Sold by B. Franklin, at the* | *New Printing Office near the Market.* | M,DCC,XXXIV. | Folio, Title, 1 leaf; pp. 131-133.   474

ANNO Regni | Georgii II. | . . . | . . . | Tertio. | . . . | . . . | . . . | . . . | . . . | . . . | . . . | . . . | . . . | . . . . | [Penn Arms.] | *Philadelphia:* | *Printed and Sold by B. Franklin, at the* | *New Printing-Office near the Market.* | M,DCC,XXXIV. | Folio, pp. 34.   475

A reprint of Acts of Assembly passed from Oct. 14, 1729 to Jan. 12, 1729-30, omitting two Acts, one of which was repealed and the other expired. The title is the same as No. 391, *supra.*

BIRKETT. (W.) An Almanac for 1735. By William Birkett. *Philadelphia: Andrew Bradford.* 1734.   476

BOUCHER. (M.) The American Almanack, for the Year 1735. By Matthew Boucher. *Philadelphia: Andrew Bradford.* 1734.

A SHORT | CONFESSION | of | Faith ; | Being the Substance of all the Funda- | mentals of Our Salvation. | Owned and approved by divers Churches | in London, owning Personal Election and | Final Perseverance. | . . . | . . . | . . . . | *Philadelphia:* | *Printed by Andrew Bradford, for Daniel* | *White,* 1734. | Sm. 8vo. pp. 39.   478

THE | CONSTITUTIONS | of the | Free-Masons. | Containing the | History, Charges, Regulations, &c. | of that most Ancient and and Right | Worshipful Fraternity. | For the Use of the Lodges, *London Printed ; Anno 5723.* | *Re-printed in Philadelphia by special Order, [by B. Franklin,] for the Use* | *of the Brethren in North-America.* | *In the Year of Masonry 5734.* Anno Domini 1734. | Sq. 8vo. pp. 94.   479

DELAWARE.   Anno Regni | Georgii II. | Regis | Magnæ Britanniæ, Franciæ, & Hiberniæ, | Septimo. | At a General Assembly of the Counties | of New-Castle, Kent and Sussex upon Dela- | ware, begun and holden at New-Castle, the Twentieth | Day of October, Anno Dom. 1733.   In the Seventh Year | of the Reign of our Sovereign Lord George II. | by the Grace of God, of Great Britain, France, and Ire- | land King, Defender of the Faith, &c. | And from thence continued by Adjournment to the Seventeenth | Day of March, 1733. | [Arms.] | *Philadelphia:* | *Printed and Sold by B. Franklin, at the | New Printing-Office near the Market.* | M,DCC,XXXIV. | Folio, pp. 24.   H. S. P.   480

AN | EPISTLE | from our | Yearly Meeting held at Burlington, | For New-Jersey and Pennsylvania, &c. from the 14th to | the 18th of the 7th Month, inclusive, 1734. | To the Quarterly and Monthly Meetings of Friends | belonging to the said Yearly Meeting. | [Colophon.]   *Philadelphia: Printed by Andrew Bradford at the Sign of | the Bible in Second-Street.*   MDCCXXXIV. | Folio, pp. 4.   M. S.   481

EVERY Man his own Doctor; or, the Poor Planter's Physician. Prescribing plain and easy Means for Persons to cure themselves of all, or most of the Distempers incident to this Climate, and with very little Charge, the Medicines being chiefly of the Growth and Production of this Country.   The Third Edition.   *Philadelphia: Re-printed and Sold by B. Franklin.*   1734.   8vo. pp. 56.   482

This popular work was probably written by John Tennent, and was first printed at Williamsburg.   It was reprinted by Franklin in 1736, and incorporated in the 9th edition of Fisher's American Instructor, Philadelphia, 1748.

GODFREY. (T.)   The Pennsylvania Almanac for 1735.   By Thomas Godfrey.   *Philadelphia; Andrew Bradford.*   1735.   483

GODFREY.   An Almanac for 1735.   By Thomas Godfrey. *Philadelphia: Andrew Bradford.*   1734.   Folio, 1 leaf.   484

GREW. (T.)   An Almanac for 1735.   By Theophilus Grew. *Philadelphia: B. Franklin.*   1734.   485

Advertised in the Pa. Gazette Jan. 23, 1734–5

THE INDIAN Tale, interpreted and told in English Verse. *Philadelphia: B. Franklin.* 1734.   486

Advertised in the Pa. Gazette, January 16, 1734.

JERMAN. (J.) An Almanac for 1735. By John Jerman. *Philadelphia: B. Franklin.* 1734.   487

LEEDS. (T.) [Cut.] . . . . | The American | Almanack | For . . . 1735. | . . . | . . . | . . . | . . . . | Being the Third after Leap-Year. | . . . | . . . | . . . | . . . | . . . | . . . | . . . | . . . | . . . | . . . | . . . | . . . . | By Titan Leeds, Philomat. | *Printed and Sold by Andrew Bradford, Post-Master, at | the Sign of the Bible in Second-Street, Philadelphia.* [1734.] | Sm. 8vo. pp. (28). 488

THE LIVES and Characters of Sejanus and Protesilaus, Redivivus, with many other noted Politicians. 1. Giving an ample Account of their Political, Metaphysical, Sophystical, and above all their darling Baculine Arguments against that grand Enemy and betrayer of their Craft, Machinations, Intreagues, Avarice, Pride and Ambition, The Press. 2. Shewing how this Potent revealer of Politic Mysteries has rescued the Public from Slavery, and brought these Heroes into the lowest Degree of Contempt. 3. Shewing that the Liberty of the People, and that of the Press are inseparable. *Philadelphia: A. Bradford.* 1734.   489

NEW JERSEY. Anno Regni Georgii II. . . . Septimo. Acts of Assembly. *Philadelphia: B. Franklin.* 1734. Folio, Title, 1 leaf; pp. 347–366.   490

The only copy I have seen lacks the title page.

THE PENNSYLVANIA Gazette.   491

Numbers 266 (from Dec. 31, to Jan. 8, 1733–4) to 316 (from Dec. 19, to Dec. 26, 1734). Title and imprint as in No. 465, *supra*. Numbers 266, 271 and 275 consist of two pages; the others of four pages each, except 299, which contains six pages. No. 305 is misnumbered 304. Issued generally on Thursday, but sometimes on Wednesday.

THE POOR Orphans Legacy: | Being | A Short Collection of | Godly Counsels | and | Exhortations | to a | Young arising

Generation. | Primarily designed by the Author for his | own Children, but published that others may | also reap Benefit by them. | By a Minister of the Gospel. | . . . | . . . | . . . . | *Phila-delphia* : | *Printed by B. Franklin,* 1734. | Sm. 8vo. pp. 38 +.

H. S. P.   492

SAUNDERS. (R.)   Poor Richard, 1735.   An Almanack. . . . By Richard Saunders.   *Philadelphia : B. Franklin.*   [1734.]   Sm. 8vo. pp. (24).

493

TAYLOR. (J.)   An Almanac for 1735.   By Jacob Taylor. *Philadelphia :* 1734.

494

VOTES of the Assembly.   *Philadelphia : B. Franklin.*   1734. Folio.

495

1735.

ADVERTISEMENT.   Philadelphia, January 6.   1734-5. | [*Philadelphia : B. Franklin.*   1735.]   Folio, 1 leaf.   H. S. P.   496

3700 Acres of land in New Jersey, to be sold by John Sikes "in the rights of Joseph Helby."

ADVICE | to the | Free-holders and Electors | of Pennsylvania, &c. | [*Philadelphia : B. Franklin.*   1735.]   Sm. 4to. pp. 7.   497

THE AMERICAN Weekly Mercury.   498

Numbers 784 (from Tuesday, Dec. 31, to Tuesday, Jan. 7, 1734–5) to 835 (from Tuesday, Dec. 23, to Tuesday, Dec. 30, 1735), four pages each.   Title and imprint as in No. 433, *supra.*   Numbers 794 to 833 were issued on Thursday; the others on Tuesday.   In No. 828 the imprint was changed to the form given in No. 530, *infra.*

ANNO Regni | Georgii II. | Regis | Magnæ Britanniæ, Fran-ciæ, & Hiberniæ ; | Octavo. | At a General Assembly of the Pro- | vince of Pennsylvania, begun and holden | at Philadelphia, the Fourteenth Day of October, Anno Dom. | 1734.   In the Eighth Year of the Reign of our Sove- | reign Lord George II. by the Grace of God, of | Great Britain, France, and Ireland, King, De-fender of | the Faith, &c. | And from thence continued by Adjourn-ments to the Seven- | teenth Day of March, 1734.   [1735.] | [Penn

Arms.] | *Philadelphia:* | *Printed, and Sold by B. Franklin at the New* | *Printing-Office, near the Market.* | M,DCC,XXXIV. [1735.] | Folio, Title, 1 leaf; pp. 137–154.   499

ANNO Regni Georgii II. . . . At a General Assembly begun and holden at Philadelphia, the Fourteenth day of October, Anno Dom. 1734. In the Eighth Year of the Reign of our Sovereign Lord George II. . . . And from thence continued to the Seventeenth Day of March, 1734. *Philadelphia: Printed and Sold by B. Franklin . . . .* M,DCC,XXXIV. [1735.] 12mo. pp. 24.   500

A synopsis of the poor laws.—*Sabin.*

BIRKETT. (W.) The American Almanac for 1736. By William Birkett. *Philadelphia: Andrew Bradford.* 1735.   501

BOUCHER. (M.) The American Almanac for 1736. By Matthew Boucher. *Philadelphia: Andrew Bradford.* 1735.   502

BURDON. (W.) The Gentleman's Pocket-Farrier, Shewing how to use your Horse on a Journey, and what Remedies are proper for common misfortunes that may befall him on the Road. By Capt. William Burdon. *London Printed: Re-printed by B. Franklin, Philadelphia,* 1735.   503

CATALOGUE of the Library Company of Philadelphia. *Philadelphia: B. Franklin.* 1735.   504

The minutes of the Directors contain in the early part of 1735, an order for printing a Catalogue, and at the meeting held April 12, 1736, "Benjamin Franklin brought in his account for advertising, receipts and catalogues at several times printed, amounting to £6. 16. 0." In 1741 another catalogue "which shall include *those* formerly printed," was ordered.

CATO'S | Moral | Distichs | Englished in Couplets. | *Philadelphia:* | *Printed and Sold by B. Franklin,* 1735. | 4to. L. C. P.   505

Collation : Title, 1 leaf ; Printer to the Reader, pp. iii-iv; Some Account of the following piece and conjectures concerning its Author, pp. v-vi; Distichs, pp. 7-23; Errata, 1 page. The collection of moral precepts, in Latin Verse, which has come down to us under the name of an unknown "Dionysius Cato," was a standard text book for young scholars in the Middle Ages, and until the last century. If they can be regarded as *classic,* this tract may pass for "the first

translation of a classic which was both made and printed in the British colonies.''
Brinley Catalogue. The Translator was James Logan. Brinley's copy sold
for $125.

DELAWARE. Anno Regni | Georgii II. | Regis | Magnæ
Britanniæ, Franciæ, & Hiberniæ, | Octavo. | At a General Assem-
bly of the Counties | of New-Castle, Kent and Sussex upon Dela-
ware, begun and holden at New-Castle, the Twenty-first | Day of
October, Anno Dom. 1734. In the Eighth Year | of the Reign
of our Sovereign Lord George II. | by the Grace of God, of Great
Britain, France, and Ire- | land King, Defender of the Faith, &c. |
And from thence continued by Adjournment to the * * * of * * * *
[Penn Arms.] | *Philadelphia: | Printed and Sold by B. Franklin, at
the | New Printing-Office near the Market.* MDCCXXXV. | Folio,
pp. 20.   506

DICKINSON. (J.) God's Protecting Providence, Man's surest
Help and Defence in the times of Greatest Difficulty and Danger;
evidenced in the remarkable Deliverance of several Persons, from
the devouring waves of the Sea, amongst which they suffered Ship-
wrack; And also from the more cruelly devouring Jaws of the
inhumane Canibals of Florida. Faithfully related by one of the
Persons concerned therein, Jonathan Dickenson. The Second
Edition. *Philadelphia: B. Franklin.* 1735.   507

Advertised in the Pa. Gazette, April 1, 1736. See No. 69, *supra.*

AN | EXTRACT | of the | Minutes | Of the Commission of
the | Synod, | Relating to the Affair of | The Reverend Mr. Samuel
Hemphil. | Published by Order. | *Philadelphia: | Printed and Sold
by Andrew Bradford, at the Sign | of the Bible in Second-street.*
1735. | 12mo. pp. 13.   B. P. L. 508

A | DEFENCE | Of the Rev. Mr. Hemphill's | Observations: |
Or, An | Answer | to the | Vindication of the Reve- | rend Com-
mission. | . . . | . . . | . . . | . . . | . . . | . . . | . . . | . . . | . . .
. . . | . . . | . . . . | *Philadelphia: | Printed and Sold by B. Frank-
lin at the New Printing- | Office near the Market.* 1735. | Sm. 8vo.
pp. 47, (1).   B. P. L. 509

[FRANKLIN. (Benjamin)] A Letter to a Friend in the Coun-
try, | Containing the Substance of a | Sermon | Preach'd at Phila-
delphia, in the Congregation of | The Rev. Mr. Hemphill, | Con-
cerning the Terms of Christian and | Ministerial Communion. |
. . . | . . . | . . . | . . . | . . . . | *Philadelphia:* | *Printed and Sold
by B. Franklin at the New Printing-* | *Office near the Market.* 1735.
| 8vo. pp. 40.   B. P. L.   510

[FRANKLIN.] Some | Observations | on the | Proceedings |
against | The Rev. Mr. Hemphill; | with a | Vindication of his
Sermons. | *Philadelphia:* | *Printed and Sold by B. Franklin.* 1735.
| Sm. 8vo. pp. 32. + The Second Edition. [*Ibid.*] Sm. 8vo.
pp. 32.   H. S. P.   511

GILLESPIE. (G.) A Treatise | Against the | Deists or Free-
Thinkers, | Proving | The Necessity | of | Revealed Religion. |
By George Gillespie, | Minister of the Gospel at the Head of
| Christiana Creek, in the County of | New-Castle, in America. |
. . . | . . . | . . . | . . . | . . . | . . . | . . . . | *Philadelphia:* |
Printed for the Author by | *A. Bradford, at the* | *Sign of the Bible
in Second Street.* 1735. | 512

GODFREY. (T.) The Pennsylvania Almanac for 1736. By
Thomas Godfrey. *Philadelphia: Andrew Bradford.* 1735.   513

GODFREY. A Sheet Almanac for the Year 1736. By T.
Godfrey. *Philadelphia: Andrew Bradford.* 1735.   514

HIS Majesty's Most Gracious Speech to both, &c: Thursday
Jan. 23, 1734 [1735]. [*Philadelphia: B. Franklin.* 1735.] Folio,
1 leaf.   H. S. P.   515

HUGHES. A Welsh Pamphlet, containing moral reflections
upon Death, Judgment, Heaven and Hell. To which is added,
several very curious pieces of Poetry, esteem'd by the Ingenious,
to be the best extant in that Language. With considerable additions by the Reverend Mr. Hughes. *Philadelphia: Reprinted by
Andrew Bradford.* 1735.   516

Advertised in the Weekly Mercury, Aug. 14, 1735.

JENKINS. (O.) Remarks | upon the | Defence | Of the Reverend | Mr. Hemphill's Observations: | In a Letter | To a Friend. | Wherein the Orthodoxy of his Principles, the | Excellency and Meekness of his Temper, | and the Justice of his Complaints against the | Rev. Commission, are briefly Considered; | and humbly proposed to the Views of his | Admirers. | By Obadiah Jenkins. | . . . | . . . | . . . . | *Philadelphia:* | *Printed and Sold by Andrew Bradford at the* | *Sign of the Bible in Second-street.* | M,DCC,XXXV. | Sm. 8vo. pp. (2), 22.   M. 517

JERMAN. (J.) The American Almanac for 1736. *Philadelphia: B. Franklin.* 1735.   518

LEEDS. (T.) [Leeds Arms.] The Genuine Leeds Almanack | The American | Almanack | For the Year of Christian Account, 1736. | Unto which is Numbered | . . . | . . . | . . . . | Being Bissextile, or Leap-Year. | Wherein is contained | The Lunations, Eclipses, Judgment of the Weather, | Spring Tides, Planets Motions and Mutual Aspects, | Time of Sun and Moons rising and setting, Length | of Days, seven Stars rising, southing and setting, | Time of High-Water, Fairs, Courts and Observ- | able Days. | Fitted to the Latitude of 40 Degrees, and a Meridian | of 5 Hours West from London, but may, without | sensible Error, serve all adjacent Places from New- | foundland to South Carolina. | By Titan Leeds, Philomat. | *Philadelphia: Printed and Sold by Andrew Bradford,* | *at the Sign of the Bible in Second-street.* [1735.] | Sm. 8vo. pp. (28).   H. S. P. 519

A LETTER | From a Countryman to his Friend in the City of | Philadelphia. | [*Philadelphia: B. Franklin.* 1735.] Folio, pp. 2.

On the Governor's acting as Chancellor. By Andrew Hamilton. ?

THE PENNSYLVANIA Gazette.   521

Numbers 317 (from Dec. 26, to Jan. 2, 1734) to 369 (from Dec. 24, to Dec, 30, 1735), four pages each, except numbers 321, 323, 327, 327 for 328, 336 and 337, two pages each. Title and imprint as in No. 465, *supra.* No. 328 is misnumbered 327.

THE REMAINDER of the Observations pro- | mised in the Mercury. [*Philadelphia: Andrew Bradford.* 1735.] Folio, pp. 4.

An answer to a piece against the Governor's acting as Chancellor.

REMARKS | Upon a Pamphlet, Entitled, | A Letter to a Friend in the | Country, containing the Sub- | stance of a Sermon | preached at | Philadelphia, | in the Congregation of the | Rev. Mr. Hemphill. | . . . | . . . | . . . | . . . | . . . | . . . | . . . | . . . | . . . | . . . | . . . | . . . | . . . | . . . . | *Philadelphia : Printed & Sold by Andrew | Bradford at the Bible in Second Street.* | 1735. Sm. 8vo. pp. 32.   M.   523

SAUNDERS. (R.)   Poor Richard, 1736. | An Almanck | For the Year of Christ | 1736, | Being the First after Leap Year. | . . . | . . . | . . . | . . . | . . . | . . . | . . . | . . . | . . . | . . . | . . . | . . . | . . . | . . . | . . . | . . . | . . . | . . . . | By Richard Saunders, Philom. | *Philadelphia:* | *Printed and Sold by B. Franklin, at the New | Printing-Office near the Market.* [1735.] | Sm. 8vo. pp. (24).   H. S. P.   524

TAYLOR. (J.)   Pennsylvania 1736.   An Almanac for 1736. By Jacob Taylor.   *Philadelphia : B. Franklin.*   1735.   525

Advertised in the Pa. Gazette, Nov. 6, 1735.

TENNENT. (G.)   The Necessity of Religious Violence in order to obtain Durable Happiness.   A Sermon preached at Perth-Amboy, June 29, 1735.   By Gilbert Tennent.   *Philadelphia:* 1735.   pp. 45.   526

Title from Haven's List.   There was an edition printed in 1735, by William Bradford in New York, which is not noticed by Haven, and it is not unlikely he has erred in saying it was printed in Philadelphia.

A | VINDICATION | of the | Reverend Commission | of the | Synod : | In Answer to | Some Observations | On their Proceedings against the Reverend | Mr. Hemphill. | . . . | . . . | . . . | . . . | . . . | . . . | . . . | . . . | . . . | . . . | . . . | . . . | . . . . | *Philadelphia :* | *Printed and Sold by Andrew Bradford at the | Bible, in Second-Street.*   MDCCXXXV. | Sm. 8vo. pp. (2), 63.   Y. C.   527

THE VOTES and Proceedings of the House of Representatives of the Province of Pennsylvania.   *Philadelphia: Printed and Sold by B. Franklin, at the New Printing-Office, near the Market.* 1735.   528

1736.

ALMANAC. A large Sheet Almanac for 1737. *Philadelphia:
Andrew Bradford.* 1736.   529

Haven's List, under 1737 and 1738, mentions the "Quaker's Almanac" as
having been printed in Philadelphia. I have not ascertained what it is he refers to.

THE AMERICAN Weekly Mercury. *Philadelphia: Printed
and Sold by Andrew Bradford,* | *Post-Master, at the Sign of the
Bible, in Second-street, where Advertisements* | *are taken in, and all
Persons in Town or Country may be supplied with this Paper.* | 530

Numbers 836 (from Tuesday, Dec. 30 to Tuesday, Jan. 6, 1735-6) to 887 (from
Thursday, Dec. 23 to Tuesday, Dec. 28, 1736), four pages each. Numbers 848
to 886 were issued on Thursday ; the others on Tuesday. Title as in No. 297,
supra.

ANNO Regni | Georgii II. | Regis, | Magnæ Britanniæ, Franciæ,
& Hiberniæ, | Nono. | At a General Assembly of the Pro- | vince
of Pennsylvania, begun and holden | at Philadelphia, the Four-
teenth Day of October, Anno Dom. | 1735. In the Ninth Year of
the Reign of our Sove- | reign Lord George II. by the Grace of
God, of | Great Britain, France, and Ireland, King, Defender of |
the Faith, &c. | And from thence continued by Adjournments to
the | Twelfth Day of January, 1735. [-36.] | [*Penn Arms.*] | *Phila-
delphia:* | *Printed and Sold by B. Franklin, at the New-* | *Printing-
Office, near the Market.* | M,DCC,XXXVI. | Folio, Title, 1 leaf;
pp. 157-169.   531

BIRKETT. (W.) An Almanac for 1737. By William Birkett.
Philadelphia: Andrew Bradford. 1736.   532

BOUCHER. (M.) The American Almanac for 1737. By Matthew Boucher. *Philadelphia: Andrew Bradford.* 1736.   533

CUMMINGS. (A.) The Character of a | righteous Ruler. |
A | Sermon | Upon the Death of the Honorable | Patrick Gordon,
Esq ; | Lieutenant-Governor of the Province | of Pennsylvania, &c.
| Preach'd at Christ's Church | in Philadelphia, Aug. 8. 1736. |
By | Archibald Cummings, M. A. | Rector of the said Church,
and | Commissary to the Bishop of | London. | Published at the

request of several Gentlemen | in this City. | *Philadelphia: Printed and Sold by Andrew Bradford.* | M,DCC,XXXVI. | 8vo. pp. (2), 26.

L. C. P.   534

EVERY Man his own Doctor. Or The Poor Planter's Physician. Prescribing, Plain and Easy Means for Persons to cure themselves of all, or most of the Distempers incident to this Climate, and with very little Charge, the Medicines being chiefly of the Growth and Production of this Country. *Philadelphia: B. Franklin.* 1736.

535

> In a list of "Books, &c. Sold by B. Franklin." in the Pennsylvania Gazette, June 25, 1741, appears the following : "Every Man his own Lawyer, Every Man his own Doctor. (Note, in a short time will be published, *Every Man his own Priest.*)"

JACOBS | Kampff-und Ritter-Platz | Allwo | Der nach seinem ursprung sich sehnende | geist der in Sophiam verliebten seele | mit Gott um den neuen namen | gerungen, und den Sieg | davon getragen. | Entworffen | In Unterschidlichen Glaubens- | u. leidensliedern, uerfahrungs vollen aus- | truckungen des gemuths, darinnen sich | dar stellet, so wol auff seiten Gottes | seine unermuedete arbeit zur rei- | nigung solcher seelen, die sich | seiner fuerung anvertraut. | Als Auch | Auff seiten des Menschen der ernst des | geistes im aus halten unter dem process | der läuterung und abschmeltzung | des Menschen der Sünden samt | dem daraus entspringen- | den lobes-gethön. | Zur | gemüthlichen erweckung derer die das heil | Jerusalems lieb haben. | Verleget | Von einem liebhaber der wahrheit die im ver- | borgenen wohnt. | *Zu Philadelphia, gedruckt bey B. F.* 1736. | Sm. 8vo. pp. 52.   H. S. P.   536

JERMAN. (J.) An Almanac for 1737. By John Jerman. *Philadelphia: Andrew Bradford.?* 1736.

537

THE JURISDICTION of the Court of Chancery in Pennsylvania, vindicated and asserted: with some Remarks upon Mr. Freeman's late Performance, in Franklin's Gazette. *Philadelphia:* 1736.?

538

> Advertised, with a long note, in the Weekly Mercury, March 2, 1735-6, as "Speedily to be Published."

LEEDS. (T.) [Leeds Arms.] . . . | The American | Alma-nack | For the Year of Christian Account, 1737. | . . . | . . . | . . . | . . . . | Being the first after Leap-Year. | . . . | . . . | . . . | . . . | . . . | . . . | . . . | . . . | . . . | . . . | . . . | . . . . | By Titan Leeds, Philomat. | *Philadelphia: Printed and Sold by Andrew Bradford,* | *at the Sign of the Bible.* [1736.] | Sm. 8vo. pp. (28).

[LOGAN. J.] The | Charge | Delivered from the Bench to the | Grand Inquest, | At a Court of Oyer and Terminer | and General Gaol-Delivery, | held for the City and County | of Phila-delphia, April 13. 1736. | *Philadelphia:* | *Printed and Sold by B. Franklin.* | M,DCC,XXXVI. | Sm. 4to. pp. 24.   H. S. P. 540

MOORE. (J.) Of | Religious Melancholy. | A | Sermon | Preached before the | Queen | at | White-Hall, | March the VIth. 169½. | By the Right Reverend Father in God, | John, Lord Bishop of Norwich. | Published by her Majesty's Special Com-mand | The Sixth Edition: | With a Preface, by J[ohn] H[olme]. | *London, Printed* 1703. | *Philadelphia: Re-printed by Andrew* | *Bradford for John Holme.* 1736. | Sm. 8vo. Title, 1 leaf; Pre-face, pp. iv; Sermon, pp. 1-54; Texts, pp. 55-6.   L. C. P. 541

THE PENNSYLVANIA Gazette.   542

Numbers 370 (from Dec. 30, to Jan. 5, 1735-6) to 420 (from Dec. 23, to Dec. 30, 1736), four pages each, except No. 419, which is only two.   Title and imprint as in No. 465, *supra.*

PROCLAMATION. [Penn Arms.] | By the Honourable the | President and Council | . . . . | A Proclamation, | *Philadelphia: Printed by B. Franklin, Printer to the Province.* [1736.] | Folio, 1 leaf.   H. S. P. 543

Against "Three Hundred Men in Arms," from Maryland, who had invaded Chester and Lancaster Counties.

SAUNDERS. (R.) Poor Richard, 1737. | An | Almanack | For the Year of Christ | 1737. | Being the First after Leap Year. | . . . | . . . | . . . | . . . | . . . | . . . | . . . | . . . | . . . | . . . | . . . | . . . | . . . | . . . | . . . | . . . . | By Richard Saunders, Philom. | *Philadelphia:* | *Printed and sold by B. Franklin, at the New* | *Printing-Office near the Market.* [1736.] | Sm. 8vo. pp. (24).

TAYLOR. (J.) Pensilvania, 1737. | An | Almanack, | or | Ephemeris, | For the Year of our Lord, 1737. | Being from the . . . | Building of London, 2844 | Building of Rome, 2489 | Beginning of the Julian Year, 1790 | Destruction of Jerusalem, and 1337490 Jews, 1667 | Invention of Printing, 277 | Birth of Copernicus, 264 | Beginning of the Gregorian Year, 165 | Burning of London, 71 | Royal Grant of Pensilvania, 56 | Arrival of the Proprietary Thomas Penn, 5 | By Jacob Taylor. | . . . | . . . | . . . | . . . | . . . | . . . | . . . | . . . | . . . | . . . | . . . | . . . | . . . | . . . | . . . . | *Philadelphia: Printed and Sold by Andrew Bradford, at | the Sign of the Bible ; Sold also by John Taylor at | Concord, & by several Shopkeepers in Town & Country.* [1736.] | Sm. 8vo. pp. (32).

MR. TRUEMAN'S Observation on Mr. Freeman's Performance against the Court of Chancery in Pennsylvania. *Philadelphia: Andrew Bradford.* 1736.?   546

VOTES of the Assembly. *Philadelphia: B. Franklin.* 1736.

1737.

THE AMERICAN Weekly Mercury.   548

Numbers 888 (from Tuesday, Dec. 28 to Thursday, Jan. 6, 1736–7) to 939 (from Thursday Dec. 22 to Thursday Dec. 29, 1737), four pages each. Title and imprint as in No. 530, *supra.* Numbers 888, 889, 892, and 898 to 939 were issued on Thursday ; the others on Tuesday. Number 912 has a "Postscript" of two pages. In Number 926 the imprint was changed to the form given in Number 571, *infra.*

THE ARTICLES of Agreement made and concluded upon May 10, 1732, between the Right Honourable the Lord Proprietary of Maryland, and the Honourable the Proprietaries of Pennsylvania, &c. touching the Limits and Boundaries of the Two Provinces. . . . Also the Report of the Commissioners. . . . *Philadelphia: B. Franklin.* 1737.   549

Advertised in the Pa. Gazette, Feb. 3, 1736–7. A reprint with additions of Number 455, *supra.*

BIRKETT. (W.) An Almanac for 1738. By William Birkett. *Philadelphia: Andrew Bradford.* 1737.   550

[BLENMAN. (JONATHAN)] Remarks | on | Zenger's Tryal, | Taken out of the Barbados Gazette's. | For the Benefit of the Students in | Law, and others in North America. | [*Philadelphia: Andrew Bradford*. 1737.] Sm. 8vo. pp. 71.   H. S. P.   551

"The Remarks on Zenger's Trial had also been collected together in London, as they likewise were about the same Time at Pennsylvania; both taken from the Barbadoes Gazette." *Caribbeana*, London, 1741, p. vii. The London edition says that the Remarks were written by *two* eminent lawyers in the American Colonies, but Ebenezer Hazard's copy, now in the Library of Congress, is marked in contemporaneous hand "By Johathan Blenman, King's Attorney in Barbadoes." Andrew Hamilton replied to these "Remarks" in a series of articles published in the Pa. Gazette from Nov. 10 to Dec. 8, 1737. This pamphlet has been attributed to Franklin's press, but upon a careful examination, the printer's blocks which appear on page 6, cannot be found in any of his publications, while they appear in the Weekly Mercury, Dec. 28, 1736. All the other blocks are either in the Mercury or some of Bradford's other publications.

BOUCHER. (M.)   The American Almanac for 1738.   By Matthew Boucher.   *Philadelphia: Andrew Bradford*.   1737.   552

CUMMING. (A.)   The danger of breaking | Christian Unity. | In | Two Sermons | Preached at | Christ's-Church, | in | Philadelphia, | June 12, 1737. | By Archibald Cummings, M. A. | Rector of the said Church, &c. | Published by reason of the gross Misrepresentations | made of them, in a public extraordinary manner. | *Philadelphia:* | *Printed and Sold by Andrew Bradford.* M,DCC,XXXVII. | Sm. 8vo. pp. viii. 31.   N. Y. H. S.   553

FROM our | Yearly-Meeting, | Held at Philadelphia, for Pennsylvania and New-Jersey, from the 17th, to the | 21st Day of the 7th Month. 1737. | To the Quarterly and Monthly Meetings. | [Colophon.] *Philadelphia: Printed by Andrew Bradford, at the Sign of the Bible.* 1737. | Folio, pp 3.   M. S.   554

JERMAN. (J.)   An Almanac for 1738.   By John Jerman. *Philadelphia: Andrew Bradford*.   1737.   555

LAY. (B.)   All | Slave-Keepers | That keep the Innocent in Bondage, | Apostates | Pretending to lay Claim to the Pure | & Holy Christian Religion; of what Congregation | so ever; but especially in their Ministers, by whose | example the filthy Leprosy and Apostacy is | spread far and near ; it is a notorious Sin, which | many of the true Friends of Christ, and his pure | Truth, called Quakers, has been for many Years, | and still are concern'd to write and bear Testimo- | ny against; as a Practice so gross & hurtful to Re- | ligion, and destructive to Government, beyond | what Words can set forth, or can be declared of | by Men or Angels, and yet lived in by Ministers | and Magistrates in America. | . . . . | Written for a General Service, by | him that truly and sincerely desires the present | and eternal Welfare and Happiness of all Man- | kind, all the World over, of all Colours, and | Nations, as his own Soul; | Benjamin Lay. | *Philadelphia :* | *Printed* [*by B. Franklin*] *for the Author.* 1737. | Sm. 8vo. pp. 271, (6). L. C. P.

Franklin says, in a letter of Nov. 4, 1789, "About 1736 I printed another [anti-slavery] book . . . for Benj. Lay." See No. 378, *supra.*

LEEDS. (T.) The American Almanac for 1738. By Titan Leeds. *Philadelphia : Andrew Bradford.* 1737. 557

THE PENNSYLVANIA Gazette. 558

Numbers 421 (from Dec. 30 to Jan. 6, 1736–7) to 472 (from Dec, 22 to Dec. 29, 1737), four pages each. Title and imprint as in Number 465, *supra,* until the latter was changed in Number 460 to the form given in Number 584, *infra.* There were two editions of Number 425.

PETERS. (R.) The Two Last | Sermons | Preached at | Christ's-Church | in | Philadelphia, | July 3, 1737. | By Richard Peters. | *Philadelphia:* | *Printed and Sold by B. Franklin.* | M,DCC,XXX-VII. | 4to. pp. xxii. 29. L. C. P. 559

PROCLAMATION. By the Honourable James Logan, Esq ; President of the Council of the Province of Pennsylvania. A Proclamation. *Philadelphia: B. Franklin.* 1737. Folio, 1 leaf.

Against trading with the Spanish West Indies.

SAUNDERS. (R.) Poor Richard, 1738. | An | Almanack | For the Year of Christ | 1738, | Being the Second after Leap Year. | . . . | . . . | . . . | . . . | . . . | . . . | . . . | . . . | . . . | . . . | . . . | . . . | . . . | . . . | . . . | . . . | . . . | . . . . | By Richard Saunders, Philom. | *Philadelphia:* | *Printed and Sold by B. Franklin, at the New* | *Printing-Office near the Market.* [1737.] | Sm. 8vo. pp. (24).

THE | SECRETARY'S Guide, | or | Young Man's Companion. | In Four Parts: | Containing, | Part I. Directions for Spelling, Reading and | Writing true English, with the Pronunciation, &c. | Part II. How to write Letters of Compliment, | Friendship, or Business; with proper directions for exter- | nal and internal Superscriptions, and other Things neces- | sary to be understood in that Affair. | Part III. Arithmetick made Easy, and the Rules | thereof explained and made familiar to the Capacities of | those that desire to Learn.   With a short and easy Me- | thod of Shop and Book-Keeping, Merchant's Ac- | compts, &c. And Tables, how to lay out and mea- | sure Land, Guaging Vessels, Measuring Boards, Glass, round | or square Timber, Buying or Selling any thing by the Hun- | dred: Also a Table of Interest at 6 or 8 per Cent. | Part IV. Forms of the most useful Writings, | such as Bills, Bonds, Letters of Attorney, Indentures, Bonds | of Arbitration, Awards, Umpirages, Deeds of Sale, Deeds | of Gift, Assignments, Leases and Releases, Counter Securi- | ties, Declarations of Trust, with many other useful Writings, | Bills of Exchange, &c. With Monthly Observations in | Gardening, Planting, Grafting, and Inoculating Fruit Trees, | and the best time to prune them. | To which is added, | The Family Companion: | Containing Rules and Directions, how to make Cyder, Mead, | Wines of our own Growth, &c.   With a Collection of choice and safe Remedies, very useful in Families. | The Fifth Edition, greatly Enlarged and carefully Corrected. | *Philadelphia: Printed and Sold by Andrew Bradford*, | *at the Sign of the Bible.* MDCCXXXVII. | Sm. 8vo. Title, 1 leaf; Contents, pp. (8); text, pp. 248.   H. S. P.   562

TAYLOR. (J.) Pensilvania, 1738. | An | Almanack, | or | Ephemeris | Of the daily Motions of the | Sun and Moon ; | The time of their Rising and Setting. | Lunations of Eclipses. | With the | Places and Aspects of the Planets, | Exactly Calculated for the Year 1738. | Being from the | Building of London 2845 | Building of Rome 2490 | Beginning of the Julian Year 1791 | Destruction of Jerusalem and 1337490 Jews 1668 | Invention of Printing 278 | Birth of Copernicus 265 | Beginning of the Gregorian Year 166 | Burning of London 72 | Royal Grant of Pensilvania 57 | Arrival of the Proprietary Thomas Penn 6 | By

Jacob Taylor. | . . . | . . . | . . . | . . . | . . . | . . . . | *Philadel-*
phia: Printed and Sold by Andrew Bradford, at | the Sign of the
Bible ; Sold also by John Taylor at | Concord, & by several Shop-
keepers in Town and Country. [1737.] | Sm. 8vo. pp. (32). A. P. S.

A TREATY of Friendship held with the Six Nations, Philadelphia Sept. and Oct. 1736. *Philadelphia: B. Franklin.* 1737.   564

A TRUE State of the Establishment of the Church of England
in this Province, by the Royal Charter granted to the first Proprietor of Pennsylvania; together with an Examination into the
propriety of calling the Minister who officiates in that Church for
the time being Rector; and of the Rights belonging to a Rector
of a Parish. The whole to be done by way of Dedication, with a
Postscript, after the modern manner. By a Laymen; and Member of the Church of England. *Philadelphia:* 1737.   565

    Advertised in the Pa. Gazette, July 21, 1737, as shortly to be published.

VOTES | and | Proceedings | of the | House of Representatives
| of the | Province of Pennsylvania, | Met at Philadelphia, on the
Fourteenth of October, | Anno Dom. 1737, and continued by Ad-
journments. [to Sept. 2, 1738.] | [*Penn Arms.*] *Philadelphia:* |
Printed and Sold by B. Franklin, at the New Printing- | *Office near*
the Market. M,DCC,XXXVII. | Folio, pp. 36.   H. S. P.   566

WATTS. (I.) Divine Songs Attempted in Easy Language for
the Use of Children. By I. Watts, D. D. . . . The Eighth Edition. *London Printed: Philadelphia: Re-printed and Sold by B.*
Franklin in Market-Street. 1737.   567

WELLFARE. (M.) Die Weissheit Gottes schreyende und
ruffende den Sohnen und Toechtern der Menschen zur Busse, seynde
das Wort des Herren, das Michael Wellfare verkundiget hat dem
Volck. *Zu Philadelphia gedruckt und zu verkauffen bey Benjamin*
Franklin und Johannes Wüster in der Marckt-strass. 1737.   568

WELLFARE. The Wisdom of God crying and calling to the
Sons and Daughters of Men for Repentance. Being the Testimony

deliver'd to the People in Philadelphia Market, Sept. 1734, by Michael Wellfare; Together with some Additional Remarks on the Present State of Christianity in Pennsylvania. *Philadelphia: B. Franklin.* 1737.   569

Advertised in the Pa. Gazette, Jan. 13, 1736–7, with the following note : "About the time when the above Testimony was delivered, the following Paragraph was seen in our Newspapers, viz. Yesterday Morning, Michael Wellfare, one of the Christian Philosophers of Conestogoe, appeared in full Market in the Habit of a Pilgrim, his Hat of Linnen, his beard at full length, and a long Staff in his hand. He declared himself sent by Almighty God to denounce Vengeance against the Iniquity and Wickedness of the Inhabitants of this City and Province, without speedy Repentance."

1738.

ЄЗꞘ А. В. Є. unb Buchſtabierbuch, bey allen Religionen ohne billigen Anſtoß zu gebrauchen. *Germantown: Christoph Saur.* 1738.   570

Advertised in Saur's Almanac for 1740.

THE AMERICAN Weekly Mercury. *Philadelphia: Printed and Sold by Andrew Bradford, at | the Sign of the Bible, where Advertisements are taken in, and all Persons | in Town or Country may be supplied with this Paper. |*   571

Numbers 940 (from Thursday, Dec. 29 to Tuesday, Jan. 3, 1737–8) to 991 (from Thursday, Dec. 21 to Thursday, Dec. 28, 1738), four pages each, except Numbers 960, 962, 965, 968 and 971. There are "Postscripts" of two pages each to Numbers 949, 954 and 981. Numbers 951 to 991 were issued on Thursday ; the others on Tuesday. The imprint was changed in No. 958 to the form given in No. 592, *infra.*

ANNO Regni | Georgii II. | Regis | Magnæ Britanniæ, Franciæ, & Hiberniæ, | Duodicimo. | At a General Assembly of the Pro- | vince of Pennsylvania, begun and holden at | Philadelphia, the Fourteenth Day of October ; Anno Dom. | 1737, in the Eleventh Year of the Reign of our Sove- | reign Lord George II. by the Grace of God, of | Great Britain, France, and Ireland, King, Defender | of the Faith, &c. | And from thence continued by Adjournments to the | Seventh of August, 1738. | [*Penn Arms.*] | *Philadelphia:* |

Printed and Sold by B. Franklin, at the | *New Printing-Office, near the Market.* | M,DCC,XXXVIII. | Folio, Title, 1 leaf; pp. 173-189.

ARSCOT. (A.) Some | Considerations | Relating to the | Present State | of the | Christian Religion. | Wherein | The Principal Evidence of the Christian | Religion is farther Explain'd and Defended ; | In Answer to the Objections made | against It in a late Vindication of the | Bishop'of Lichfield and Coventry : | With an Appendix, | Containing Some Remarks on a Passage in the | Second Volume of Bishop Burnet's History | of his Own Times. | Part III. | By Alexander Arscott. | . . . | . . . | . . . | . . . . | *London ; Printed* 1734. | *Philadelphia : Re-printed by Andrew* | *Bradford, at the Sign of the Bible.* 1738. | 16mo. pp. viii, 175.   573

BIRKETT. (W.) An Almanac for 1739. By William Birkett. *Philadelphia : Andrew Bradford.* 1738.   574

[*Penn Arms.*] BY the | Proprietaries | of | Pennsylvania. | [*Philadelphia : B. Franklin.* 1738.] Folio, 1 leaf. H. S. P. 575

Notice about Proprietary Quit-rents signed Richard Peters, and dated Nov. 23, 1738.

[FENELON. (F. DE SALIGNAC DE LA MOTHE)] The | Archbishop of Cambray's | Dissertation | on | Pure Love, | With | An Account of the Life and Writings of the Lady, for | whose sake the Archbishop was banish'd from Court. | And the grievous Persecutions she suffer'd in France | for her Religion. | Also | Two Letters in French and English, written by one | of the Lady's Maids, during her Confinement in the | Castle of Vicennes, where she was a Prisoner Eight | Years : One of the Letters was writ with a Bit of | Stick instead of a Pen, and Soot instead of Ink, to | her Brother ; the Other to a Clergyman. | Together with an | Apologetic Preface | Containing divers Letters of the Archbishop of | Cambray, to the Duke of Burgundy, the present French | King's Father, and other Persons of Distinction : | Also | Divers Letters of the Lady to Persons of Quality, | Relating to her Religious Principles. | . . . | . . . | . . . | . . . | . . . . | *London :*

Printed, and Re-printed by Andrew | Bradford at the Sign of the Bible, in Front Street Phila- | delphia, MDCCXXXVIII. | 8vo. pp. xcvi., 142+.   H. S. P.   576

DER FRUEHLING ist herbey gekomme, . . . [*Germantown: Christopher Sower.* 1738.] 16mo. size, pp. (2).   H. S. P.   577

DER HOCH-DEUTSCH Amerikanische Calender auf das Jahr 1739. *Germantown: Christopher Sower.* 1738.   578

Of the first issue of Sower's Almanac no perfect copy is known to exist.

[JAMES. (PHILIP)] A Dialogue between a Blindman and Death. Translated out of the British Language, and render'd into familiar English Verse. *Philadelphia: Andrew Bradford.* 1738.   579

JERMAN. (J.) An Almanac for 1739. By John Jerman. *Philadelphia: Andrew Bradford.* 1738.   580

LEEDS. (T.) The American Almanac for 1739. By Titan Leeds. *Philadelphia: Andrew Bradford.* 1738.   581

MEIN Heyland der bist mir, ... [*Germantown: Christopher Sower.* 1738.] 16mo. size, pp. (2).   H. S. P.   582

OFFT hast du mir zugeruffen, ... [*Germantown: Christopher Sower.* 1738.] 16mo. size, 1 leaf.   H. S. P.   583

THE PENNSYLVANIA Gazette. *Philadelphia: Printed by B. Franklin, Post Master | at the New Printing-Office near the Market. Price 10s. a Year. | Where Advertisements are taken in, and Book-Binding is done reasonably, in the Best Manner. |*   584

Numbers 473 (from Dec. 29 to Jan. 3, 1737) to 524 (from Dec. 21 to Dec. 28, 1738), four pages each, except Numbers 490 and 499, which contains six pages. There is a "Postcript" to 497 of two pages. Title as in Number 465, *supra.*

SAUNDERS. (R.) Poor Richard, 1739. | An | Almanack | For the Year of Christ | 1739. | Being the Third after Leap-Year. | . . . | . . . | . . . | . . . | . . . | . . . | . . . | . . . | . . . | . . . | . . . | . . . | . . . | . . . | . . . | . . . | . . . . | By Richard Saunders, Philom. | *Philadelphia :* | *Printed and sold by B. Franklin, at the New | Printing-Office near the Market.* [1738.] | Sm. 8vo. pp. (24).   L. C. P.   585

TAYLOR. (J.) An Almanac for 1739. By Jacob Taylor. *Philadelphia: Andrew Bradford.* 1738.   586

THOMAS. (G.) The | Speech | of the Honourable | George Thomas, Esq; | Lieutenant Governor of the Province of Penn- | sylvania, and Counties of New-Castle, Kent | and Sussex on Dela- ware. | To the Representatives of the Freemen of the | said Province, in General Assembly met. | [Colophon.] *Philadelphia: Printed and Sold by B. Franklin, at | the New Printing-Office, near the Market.* M,DCC,XXXVIII. | Folio, pp. (3).   H. S. P.   587

TO my Friends in Pensilvania. | [*Philadelphia: B. Franklin.* 1738.?] Folio, pp. 3.   L. C. P.   588

Signed Paul Veritt, and dated New York, Sept. 12, 1738. An attack upon Andrew Hamilton.

VOTES | and | Proceedings | of the | House of Representatives | of the | Province of Pennsylvania, | Met at Philadelphia, on the Fourteenth of October, | Anno. Dom. 1738, and continued by Ad- journments [to Sept. 11, 1739.] | [*Penn Arms.*] | *Philadelphia:* | *Printed and Sold by B. Franklin, at the New Printing- | Office near the Market.* M,DCC,XXXVIII. | Folio, pp. 60.   H. S. P.   589

WEST. (M.) A | Treatise | Concerning | Marriage: | Wherein | The Unlawfulness of Mixt-Marriages is | laid open from the Scriptures of Truth: | Shewing | That it is contrary to the Will of God, and the | Practice of His People in former Ages, and | there- fore of Dangerous Consequence, for Per- | sons of Different Judg- ments in Matters of Re- | ligious Worship, to be Joyned together in | Marriage. | Written for the Information and Benefit of Chris- tian | Professors in general; and recommended more par- | ticularly to the Youth of either Sex amongst the Peo- | ple called Quakers. | By Moses West. | . . . | . . . | . . . | . . . | . . . | . . . | . . . | . . . . | *Philadelphia: Reprinted, and Sold by Andrew Bradford,* | *at the Bible in Front-Street.* [1738.] | Sm. 8vo. pp. 39.

WOOLVERTON. (C.) Christ's Eternal Word. A Sermon. By Charles Woolverton. *Philadelphia: B. Franklin.* 1738.   591

See Historical Magazine, 1859, p. 158.

1739.

THE AMERICAN Weekly Mercury.   *Philadelphia: Printed and Sold by Andrew Bradford, at | the Sign of the Bible in Front-street, where Advertisements are taken in, and | all Persons in Town or Country may be supplied with this Paper. |*   592

Numbers 992 (from Thursday, Dec. 28 to Thursday, Jan. 4, 1738) to 1043 (from Thursday, Dec. 20 to Thursday, Dec. 27, 1739), four pages each, except 1015, which contains six pages. Title as in Number 530, *supra.* There is a "Post-script" of two pages to Number 1028. The imprint was changed in Number 1041 to the form given in Number 619, *infra.* Numbers 998, 1000 and 1002 were issued on Wednesday ; the others on Thursday.

ANNO Regni | Georgii II. | Regis, | Magnæ Britanniæ, Fran-ciæ, & Hiberniæ, | Duodecimo. | At a General Assembly of the Pro- | vince of Pennsylvania, begun and holden | at Philadelphia, the Fourteenth Day of October, Anno Dom. | 1738.   In the Twelfth Year of the Reign of our Sove- | reign Lord George II. by the Grace of God, of | Great Britain, France, and Ireland, King, Defender of | the Faith, &c. | And from thence continued by Adjournments to the | First Day of May, 1739. | [*Penn Arms.*] | *Philadelphia: | Printed and Sold by B. Franklin, at the New | Printing-Office near the Market.* | M,DCC,XXXIX. | Folio, Title 1 leaf, pp. 193–228 ; Table 1 leaf.   H. S. P.   593

BIRKETT. (W.)   An Almanac for 1740.   By William Birkett. *Philadelphia: Andrew Bradford.   1739.*   594

THE | BILL | For the better raising | of Money on the In- | habitants of Phila- | delphia for Publick | Uses, and for repeal- | ing a former Act | made to like Purpo- | ses ; | Together with the Governor's | Reasons | For not Passing the same. | [*Philadelphia :*] *Printed [by B. Franklin.]*   1739. | Folio, pp. (2), 16.   H. S. P.   595

[*Penn Arms.*]   BY the | Proprietaries | of | Pennsylvania. | [*Philadelphia: B. Franklin.   1739.*]   Folio, 1 leaf.   H. S. P.   596

Notice about Proprietary Quit-rents, signed "Richard Peters, Secr." and dated June 25, 1739.

DJE EHEMALS verdorrete, nun aber wieder grünende und Frucht-tragende Ruthe Arons. *Germantown: Christopher Sower*. 1739. 597

FALCONAR. (M.) A Choice Collection out of the Psalms of David, the Book of Job, Hale's Contemplation, &c. By Magnus Falconar, of Botness, in Scotland, Mariner. *Philadelphia: Andrew Bradford*. 1739. 598

DER | HOCH-DEUTSCH | Americanische | Kalender, | Auf das Jahr | Nach der Gnadenreichen Geburth unsers Herrn und | Heylandes Jesu Christi | 1740: | (Welches ein Schalt-Jahr ist.) In sich haltende: Die Wochen Tage; Den Tag des Monaths; Tage welche bemerckt | werden; Des Monds Auf- und Untergang; Des Monds Zeichen und Grad; Voll- und | neu Licht; erst und letzt Virtel; Aspecten der Planeten samt Witterung; Der 7 Ster- | nen Aufgang, Sud-Platz und Untergang; Der Sonnen Auf- und Untergang; Nebst | einem Bericht, woher viele, im Calender vorkommende Dinge herstammen; Erklärung | der Zeichen, Adlerlaß-Täff-lein, Anzeigung der Finsternüsse, Courten, Fären, &c. | Eingerichtet vor die Sonnen Höhe von | Pennsylvanien: Jedoch an denen angrentzenden Länden ohne merklichen Unter- | schied zu gebrauchen. | Zum andern mahl herausgegeben. | *Germantown: Gedruckt und zu finden bey Christoph Saur; Auch kœnnen die auswærtige Krœmer solche bey Johannes Wister in Philadelphia haben.* [1739.] | Sm. 4to. pp. (24). H. S. P.

DER | HOCH-DEUTSCH | Pennsylvanische Geschicht-Schreiber | Oder | Sammlung | Wichtiger Nachrichten, aus dem Natur- und Kirchen-Reiche. | Erster Stück August 20, 1739. [*Germantown: Christoph Saur*. 1739.] Sm. 4to. pp. (4). 600

Published, so far as I know, except the first number, on the 16th of each month up to Number 92. Number 93 appeared April 1, 1748, and 94 on April 16, and thenceforth the paper was issued on the first and sixteenth of each month, only the latter however being numbered, those issued on the first of the month being apparently counted as part of the preceding number, up to September, 1756. After that date it was issued semi-monthly but at irregular intervals. In Number 43 the title was changed to "Hoch-Deutsche | Pensylvanische Berichte | . . . | . . . | . . . . | " and in Number 71, this was reduced to "Pensylvanische Berichte | . . . | . . . | . . . . | ." It was a small quarto generally of four, but occasionally of six or even eight pages, until some time between November, 1751 and 1753, when it was enlarged to a folio. It was continued semi-monthly, by the son and grandson of its founder until 1777. The Historical Society of Pennsylvania possesses a file of this paper from April 16, 1743 to Nov. 1, 1751, and from Jan. 16, 1754 to Dec. 18, 1761.

JERMAN. (J.) The American | Almanack, | For . . . . | 1740;
| . . . | . . . | . . . | . . . | . . . | . . . | . . . | . . . | . . . | . . . |
. . . . | By John Jerman, Philomat. | . . . | . . . | . . . | . . . |
. . . | . . . . | *Philadelphia, Printed and Sold by Andrew | Bradford,
at the Sign of the Bible, in Front-street.* [1739.] | Sm. 8vo. pp. (24).

LEEDS. (T.) The American Almanac for 1740. By Titan
Leeds. *Philadelphia: Andrew Bradford.* 1739.   602

NEW JERSEY. Anno Regni | Georgii II. | Regis, | Magnæ
Britanniæ, Franciæ, & Hiberniæ | Duodecimo. | At a General As-
sembly of the Pro- | vince of New-Jersey, begun and holden at |
Perth-Amboy, the Twenty-sixth Day of October, Anno Dom. |
1738. In the Twelfth Year of the Reign of our Sovereign | Lord
George II. by the Grace of God, of Great | Britain, France, and
Ireland, King, Defender of the | Faith, &c. | And from thence
continued by Adjournment to the Thirteenth | of November 1738.
| [*Royal Arms.*] | *Philadelphia:* | *Printed and Sold by B. Franklin,
at the | New Printing-Office near the Market.* | M,DCC,XXXIX. |
Folio, Title, 1 leaf; pp. 369–395, Table, 1 leaf.   603

THE PENNSYLVANIA Gazette.   604

Numbers 525 (from Dec. 28 to Jan. 4, 1738, 9) to 576 (Dec. 27, 1739), four
pages each. Title and imprint as in Number 584, *supra.* There is a "Postscript"
of two pages to Number 566. Number 527 is misnumbered 257, and 573 is misnumbered 572. With Number 564 the paper was reduced to a quarto with
the title and imprint as in Number 648, *infra.*

[ROWE. (ELIZA)] The History of Joseph. A Poem. In
Ten Books. By a Female Hand. *Philadelphia: B. Franklin.*
1739.   605

SAUNDERS. (R.) Poor Richard, 1740. | An | Almanack |
For the Year of Christ? | 1740, | Being Leap Year. | . . . | . . . |
. . . | . . . | . . . | . . . | . . . | . . . | . . . | . . . | . . . | . . .
| . . . | . . . | . . . | . . . | . . . . | By Richard Saunders, Philom. |
Philadelphia: | *Printed and Sold by B. Franklin, at the New |
Printing-Office near the Market.* [1739.] | 12mo. pp. (24).

A Third Edition was advertised in the Pa. Gazette, Jan. 10, 1739-40.

[SMALRIDGE. (GEORGE)] The | Art | of | Preaching, | In Imitation of | Horace's | Art of Poetry. | *London, Printed:* | *Philadelphia, Re-printed, and Sold by* | *B. Franklin, in Market Street.* | M,DCC,XXXIX. | Sm. 8vo. pp. 22.   B. P. L.   607

TAYLOR. (J.) Pensilvania, 1740. | An | Almanack, | or | Ephemeris | Of the daily Motions of the | Sun and Moon; | The time of their Rising and Setting. | Lunations and Eclipses. | With the | Places and Aspects of the Planets, | for the Year, 1740. | . . . | . . . | . . . | . . . | . . . | . . . | . . . | . . . | . . . | . . . | . . . . | By Jacob Taylor. | . . . | . . . | . . . | . . . . | *Philadelphia: Printed and Sold by Andrew Bradford, at* | *the Sign of the Bible, in Front-Street.* [1739.] | Sm. 8vo. pp. (32).   A. P. S.   608

THREE | Letters | to the | Reverend Mr. | George Whitefield. | *Philadelphia: Printed and Sold by An-* | *drew Bradford.* [1739.] | Sm. 8vo. Title, 1 leaf; pp. 1–13.   A. P. S.   609

The letters are from the Rev. Benjamin Colman, Rev. Gilbert Tennent, and the Rev. William Tennent.

VOTES | and | Proceedings | of the | House of Representatives | of the | Province of Pennsylvania, | Met at Philadelphia, on the Fifteenth of October, | Anno Dom. 1739, and continued by Adjournments. [to Sept. 3, 1740.] | [*Penn Arms.*] | *Philadelphia:* | *Printed and Sold by B. Franklin, at the New-Printing-* | *Office near the Market.* M,DCC,XXXIX. | Folio, pp. 131. (1). H. S. P.   610

WHITEFIELD. (GEORGE) An Answer to the Bishop of London's last Pastoral Letter. By the Rev. Mr. Whitefield. *Philadelphia: Andrew Bradford.* 1739.   611

WHITEFIELD. A | Journal | of a | Voyage | from | Gibraltar to Georgia. | By | Geo. Whitefield, A.B. | Of Pembroke College, Oxford. | Containing | Many curious Observations, and Edifying | Reflections, on the several Occurrences | that happen'd in the Voyage. | *Philadelphia,* | *Printed and Sold by B. Franklin,* | in *Market-Street,* 1739. | 24mo. pp. 45.
A | Continuation | Of the Reverend | Mr. Whitefield's | Journal | from | His Arrival at Savannah, | to | His Return to London. |

Philadelphia, | *Printed and Sold by B. Franklin,* | *in Market-Street,* 1739. | pp. [47]–102.

A | Continuation | Of the Reverend | Mr. Whitefield's | Journal | from | His Arrival at London, | to | His Departure from thence, on | His Way to Georgia. | *Philadelphia,* | *Printed and Sold by B. Franklin,* | *in Market-Street.* 1739. | pp. [103]–252.   612

WHITEFIELD.   A | Letter | From the Reverend | Mr. Whitefield, | To the Religious Societies lately | formed in England and Wales. | Printed for the Benefit of | the Orphan House in | Georgia. | *Philadelphia: Printed and Sold by Andrew | and William Bradford, at the Sign of the Bible, in Front-Street.* [1739.] | Sm. 8vo. pp. 19.   L. C. P.   613

WHITEFIELD.   A Sermon, entituled, The Marks of the New Birth.   By George Whitefield, A. B. of Pembroke College Oxford. To which are added Two Prayers.   *Philadelphia: Andrew Bradford.* 1739.   614

WHITEFIELD.   A Sermon, entituled, What think ye of Christ? Preached by Rev. Mr. Whitefield, in this City.   *Philadelphia: Andrew Bradford.* 1739.   615

WHITEFIELD.   A Sermon, entituled, The Wise and Foolish Virgins.   Preach'd by the Rev. Mr. Whitefield, in this City. *Philadelphia: Andrew Bradford.* 1739.   616

ZIONITISCHER | Wehrauchs-Hügel | Oder : | Myrrhen Berg, | Worinnen allerley liebliches und wohlriechen= | des nach Apotheker-Kunst zu bereitetes | Rauch-Werck zu finden. | Bestehend | In allerley Liebes- Würckungen der in Gott | geheiligten Seelen, welche sich in vielen und man= cherley | geistlichen und lieblichen Liedern ausgebildet. | Als darinnen | Der letzte Ruff zu dem Abendmahl des gros= | sen Gottes auf unterschied= liche Weise | trefflich aus gedrücket ist; | Zum Dienst | Der in dem Abend= Ländischen Welt=Theil als | bey dem Untergang der Sonnen erweckten Kirche | Gottes, und zu ihrer Ermunterung auf die | Mitternächtige Zukunfft des Bräutigams | ans Licht ˚gegeben. | *Germantown: Gedruckt bey Christoph Saur.* 1739. | 16mo. pp. (12), 792, (14).   H. S. P.   617

The Weyrauchs Hügel was the first book printed in German type in America, and the first *book* from the press of Christopher Saur. In rather a curious way it led to the establishment of the Ephrata press. The 37th verse of the 400th hymn runs as follows :—

> "Sehet, sehet, sehet, an ! Sehet, sehet an den Mann !
> Der von Gott erhoeret ist, Der ist unser Herr und Christ."

which literally translated is—

> "Look, look, look, Look, look upon the man ;
> He is heard by God ; He is our Lord and Christ."

The compositor asked Saur whether he thought that more than one Christ had appeared. Saur inquired of him why he suggested such an idea ; when the man pointed out this verse and said it appeared to him that by it Conrad Beissel, the founder of the Ephrata Cloister, meant himself. Saur wrote this to Beissel, and asked whether it had any foundation ; whereupon Beissel replied to him that he was a fool. This language did not please Saur, who soon after issued a pamphlet censuring Beissel, saying among other things that his name contained the number 666 of the beast of the Apocalypse, and that he had received something from all the planets—"from Mars his strength, from Venus his influence over women, and from Mercury his comedian trick." Beissel became quite angry, and one of the results of the widening breach was a new press at Ephrata. The Weyrauchs Hügel is the largest and most important collection of the hymns of the Ephrata Cloister. Many of them were written there by Beissel, but unfortunately it is not possible, except in a few instances, to determine the authorship of particular hymns. Christina Hoehn, "a pious and God-fearing woman," who died an inmate of the Cloister at an advanced age, wrote those upon pages 465 and 456, beginning "Wenn mir das Creutz will machen Schmertzen," and "Ich dringe ein in Jesu Liebe." A MSS. volume, beautifully written and illuminated, in the collection of the Historical Society of Pennsylvania, contains the music to which these hymns were sung.

As the edition was small and the book was in common use for devotional pur-poses, it has become extremely scarce, nearly all of the few known copies being imperfect. For accounts of it, see the Deutsche Pionier, Vol. VIII., page 47, and Dr. Seidensticker's paper on "Die Deutsch-Amerikanischer Incunabula," in the same volume, page 475.   s. w. p.

1740.

AN ALMANAC for 1741. *Philadelphia: B. Franklin.* 1740. Folio, 1 leaf.   618

THE AMERICAN Weekly Mercury. *Philadelphia: Printed and Sold by Andrew and William | Bradford, at the Sign of the Bible in Front-street, where Advertisements are | taken in, and all Persons in Town or Country may be supplied with this Paper. |* 619

Numbers 1044 (from Thursday, Dec. 27 to Thursday, Jan. 3, 1739) to 1095 (from Thursday, Dec. 18 to Thursday, Dec. 25, 1740) four pages each, except 1079 and 1082 which contains six pages. There are "Postscripts" of two pages each to Numbers 1050 and 1094. Numbers 1044 and 1055 to 1095 were published on Thursday ; the others on Tuesday. In Number 1080 the old cuts were replaced by three new ones which extend across the page. Mercury on the left ; A view of a city with shipping in the foreground (perhaps intended to represent Philadelphia), in the middle, and the Postman on the right. In Number 1087, William Bradford's name is omitted in the imprint.

BIRKETT. (W.) An Almanac for 1741. By William Birkett. *Philadelphia: Andrew Bradford.* 1740.   620

BULL. (W.) A | Letter | from the Honourable William Bull | Esq ; Lieutenant Governor of the | Province of South Carolina, to the | Honourable Thomas Penn, Esq-Pro- | prietary of Pennsylvania. | Charlestown, South-Carolina, Novemb. 29, 1740. | Sir, | On the 18th. Instant, about two a Clock in the Afternoon, | a Fire broke out in Charlestown, which in about four Hours | Time laid in Ashes the most valuable Part of the Build- | ings, &c. &c. &c. [n. p. n. d.] Folio.   621

A | COLLECTION | of | Charters | and other publick Acts | relating to the | Province of Pennsylvania, | Viz. | I. The Royal Charter to William Penn, Esq ; | II. The first Frame of Government, granted in England, in 1682. | III. Laws agreed upon in England. | IV. Certain Conditions or Concessions. | V. The Act of Settlement, made at Chester, 1682. | VI. The second Frame of Government, granted 1683. | VII. The Charter of the City of Philadelphia, | granted October 25. 1701. | VIII. The New Charter of Privileges to | the Province, granted October 28. 1701. | *Philadelphia: | Printed and Sold by B. Franklin, in Market-Street.* | M,DCC,XL. | Folio, Title, 1 leaf; pp. 46.   H. S. P.   622

CUMMINGS. (A.) Faith absolutely necessary, but not sufficient | to Salvation without good Works. | In Two | Sermons, | Preached at Christ-Church in Philadel- | phia, April 20. 1740. | By Archibald Cummings, M.A. | Commissary to the Bishop of London, &c. | Publish'd in their own Vindication, from the false

| and rash Reflections of the famous Mr. White- | field. | . . . |
. . . | . . . | . . . . | *Philadelphia:* | *Printed by Andrew and William
Bradford at the* | *Sign of the Bible in Front-Street.* [1740.] Sm.
8vo. pp. xvi. 38.   H. S. P.   623

[DEFOE. (DANIEL)] The Family Instructor. In Three Parts.
I. Relating to Fathers and Children. II. To Masters and Servants.
III. To Husbands and Wives. *Philadelphia: B. Franklin.* 1740.?

DEWSBURY. (W.) A | Sermon | on the | Important Doc-
trine | of Regeneration. | Preached at Grace Church-Street, the
Sixth of | the Third Month, 1688. | By William Dewsbury. |
Taken from his Mouth in Short-hand. | William Dewsbury was
one of the first Preachers | among those called Quakers; a very
zealous | Teacher and an eminent Instrument to the Conver- | sion
of many. Sewel's History, page 92. | *Philadelphia:* | *Reprinted
and Sold by B. Franklin,* | *in Market-Street.* M,DCC,XL. | Sm.
8vo. pp. 24.   625

ERSKINE. (R.) Gospel Sonnets, | Or, | Spiritual Songs. | In
Six Parts. | I. The Believer's | Espousals. | II. The Believer's
Jointure. | III. The Believer's Riddle. | IV. The Believer's Lodg-
ing. | V. The Believer's Soliloquy. | VI. The Believer's Principles,
| Concerning, | Creation and Redemption. | Law and Gospel, |
Justification and Sanctification, | Faith and Sense, | Heaven and
Earth. | The Fifth Edition, | With large Additions and great Im-
provements. | By Ralph Erskine, M. A. | *London: Printed.* |
Philadelphia: Re-printed and Sold by | *Benj. Franklin, in Market-
street,* 1740. | 16mo. pp. xvi. 270.   B. P. L.   626

EXTRACTS from the Laws of William Penn; translated into
German for the Use of the Germans in Pennsylvania. *Germantown: Printed by Christopher Sower.* 1740.   627

Title from Haven's List. Probably intended for Number 809, *infra.*

F. (H.) Gespraech zwischen einem fluechtigen Vater aus Rom und
einem Clerico, ans Licht gegeben von H. F.   Erster, zweyter und dritter
Theil. *Gedruckt zu Philadelphia,* 1740. 16mo. pp. 192.   628

FALCONAR. (M.) A Vindication of the Rev. Mr. Whitefield's Doctrine, from several famous Authors. By Magnus Falconar. *Philadelphia: Andrew Bradford.?* 1740.   629

Advertised in the Weekly Mercury July 24, 1740, as "to be printed by subscription."

FINLEY. (S.) A Letter to a Friend, concerning Mr. Whitefield, Messrs. Tennents, &c. and their Opposers. By Samuel Finley. *Philadelphia: B. Franklin.* 1740. 12mo. pp. 12.   630

[GIBSON. (EDMUND)] The Bishop of London's last Pastoral Letter, against Lukewarmness and Enthusiasm. *Philadelphia: Andrew & William Bradford.* 1740.   631

GILLESPIE. (G.) A | Letter | to the | Rev. Brethren of the Presbytery of | New York, or of Elizabeth- | Town ; | In which is shewn | The Unjustness of the Synod's Pro- | test, entered last May at Philadelphia, | against some of the Rev. Brethren. As also | Some of the Causes of the great Decay of | Vital Religion, and Practical Holiness in | our Presbyterial Church ; | With Proof of God's remarkable Appearance, for | the Good of Many Souls, in our Land of late. | By George Gillespie, Minister of the Gospel at | the Head of Christiana Creek, . . . in America. | *Philadelphia: Printed by B. Franklin, for the Author,* 1740. | 12mo. pp. 23. 632

GILLESPIE. A | Sermon | against | Divisions | in | Christ's Churches. | By George Gillespie. | Minister of the Gospel, at the Head of Christiana | Creek, in the County of New-Castle in Ame- | rica. | . . . | . . . | . . . | . . . . | *Philadelphia.* | *Printed by A. and W. Bradford* 1740. | Sm. 8vo.   H. S. P. 633

Collation: Title, 1 leaf ; To the Christian Reader, pp. ii ; text, pp. 31 ; Appendix, pp. xii ; Act against such as withdraw themselves from the publick worship, 1 p.

GORDON. (T.) The Independent Whig; or, a Defence of primitive Christianity against the exorbitant claims and Encroachments of fanatical and disaffected Clergymen. By Thomas Gordon. *Philadelphia:* 1740.   634

Title from Haven's List.

HALE. (M.) Sir Matthew Hale's Sum of Religion. To which is added, a Poem on Zeal. The Real Intercourse. A Hymn. A Morning Hymn. An Evening Hymn. A Midnight Hymn. *Philadelphia: B. Franklin.* 1740.   635

HENRY. (M.) A Method for Prayer, with Scriptural Expressions to be used under each Head. By the late Rev. Mr. Matthew Henry, Minister of the Gospel. *Philadelphia: B. Franklin.* 1740.

Advertised at the end of the second volume of Whitefield's Journal.

𝕯𝕰𝕽 | 𝕳𝕺𝕮𝕳=𝕯𝕰𝖀𝕿𝕾𝕮𝕳 | Americanische | Calender, | Auf das Jahr | Nach der Gnaden=reichen Geburth unsers Herrn und | Heylandes Jesu Christi | 1741; | (Welches ein gemein Jahr von 365 Tagen ist.) | . . . | . . . | . . . | . . . | . . . | . . . . | Eingerichtet auf die Sonnen Höhe von 40 Graden, und zwar vor | Pennsylvanien: Jedoch an denen angrentzenden Länden ohne merklichen Unter= | schied zugebrauchen. | Zum dritten mal heraus gegeben. | *Germantown: Gedruckt und zu finden bey Christoph Saur; Auch kœnnen die auswœrtige Krœmer solche bey Johannes Wister in Philadelphia haben.* [1740.] | Sm. 4 to. pp. (24). H. S. P.

JERMAN. (J.) An Almanac for 1741. By John Jerman. *Philadelphia: B. Franklin.* 1740.   638

KINNERSLEY. (E.) A Letter from Ebenezer Kinnersley, to his Friend in the Country. *Philadelphia:* 1740.   639

First published as a "Postscript" to the Pa. Gazette, Number 606, and perhaps not otherwise printed.

KINNERSLEY. A Letter to the Rev. Jenkin Jones from Ebenezer Kinnersley, occasioned by a late Anonymous Paper, published under the fiction of a Letter to him from his Friend in the Country; but is supposed to be writ by some hackney Writer in Philadelphia, at the instance and by the Instruction of Mr. Jones. *Philadelphia: Andrew and William Bradford.?* 1740.   640

KINNERSLEY. A Second Letter from Ebenezer Kinnersley, to his Friend in the Country, shewing, the Partiality and unjust Treatment he has met with from a Certain Committee whose

Names &c. are inserted in the Pennsylvania Gazette No. 609. *Philadelphia: Andrew and William Bradford.* 1740.   641

LEEDS. (T.)   The American Almanac for 1741.   By Titan Leeds.   *Philadelphia: Andrew Bradford.*   1740.   642

A LETTER to Mr. Ebenezer Kinnersley from his Friend in the Country, in Answer to his two Letters lately published.   *Philadelphia: B. Franklin.*   1740.   643

A NEW and Complete Guide to the English Tongue.   Collected from the best Authors.   In two Books.   The First Containing proper Lessons for Beginners, compos'd chiefly of Scripture Phrases.   The Second for those who have made some Proficiency in Reading: Containing proper Observations and Rules for Accenting of Words and Placing of the Emphasis.   Observations on the Sounds of Letters: Rules for the Division of Syllables.   The Use of true Pointing, with Tables of Abbreviations, and Distinctions of Words.   Intermixed with a Variety of Exercises in Prose and Verse, adapted to the Capacities of Children.   For the Use of Schools.   By an Ingenious Hand.   *Philadelphia: Printed and Sold by B. Franklin.*   1740.   644

NEW JERSEY.   Anno Regni | Georgii II. | Regis, | Magnæ Britanniæ, Franciæ, & Hiberniæ | Tredecimo. | At a General Assembly of the Pro- | vince of New-Jersey, begun and holden at | Burlington, the Tenth Day of April Anno Dom. 1740. | In the Thirteenth Year of the Reign of our Sovereign | Lord George II. by the Grace of God, of Great | Britain, France, and Ireland, King, Defender of the | Faith, &c. | And from thence continued by Adjournment to the Thirty-first | of July 1740. | [*Royal Arms.*] | *Philadelphia:* | *Printed and Sold by Andrew Bradford,* | *at the Sign of the Bible in Front-Street* | M,DCC,XL. | Folio, Title 1 leaf; pp. 397–433; Table 1 leaf.   645

NOBLE. (JOB)   An | Alarm | Sounded: | Desiring it may, by the Power of God, | Answer to the Quotation on Joel II. I. | made use of in the Title Page of the | Book, entitled, The Presumer Detected, and | his Doom display'd; set forth by Gilbert | Tennent, of New-Brunswick in New-Jersey. | By Job Noble. | *Phila-delphia :* | *Printed [by B. Franklin] in the Year* 1740. | 16mo. pp. 19.   H. S. P.   646

THE QUERISTS, or, An Extract of sundry Passages taken out of Mr. Whitefield's printed Sermons, Journals, and Letters : To-gether with some Scruples propos'd in proper Queries raised on Each Remark. By some Church-Members of the Presbyterian Persuasion . . . . *Philadelphia : Printed by B. Franklin.* 1740. Sm. 8vo. pp. 32.   647

January 3. 1739, 40 : Numb. 577. | THE PENNSYLVANIA : Gazette. | Containing the freshest Ad- : vices Foreign and Do-mestick. | *Philadelphia : Printed by B. Franklin, Post-Master,* | *at the New Printing-Office near the Market.   Price 10s. a Year.* | *Where Advertisements are taken in, and Book-Binding is done reasonably, in the Best Manner.* [1740.] | 4to. pp. (4).   648

Numbers 577 to 628 (Dec. 25, 1740), four pages each, except Numbers 597 and 609, eight pages, and 608 and 612, six pages. There is a "Postscript" of two pages to Number 603, and one of four pages to Number 606. A cut of the Penn Arms (first introduced in Number 564) divides the title as indicated by the dotted lines.

REMARKS on several Passages of Mr. Whitefield's Sermons, Journals and Letters, which seem unsound and erroneous and very liable to Exceptions; with several Queries by some Friends to the Truth of the Gospel. *Philadelphia : B. Franklin.* 1740.   649

ROSE. (A.) Poems | On several Occasions, | by | Aquila Rose : | To which are prefixed, | Some other Pieces writ to him, | and to his Memory after | his Decease. | Collected and published by his Son Joseph Rose, | of Philadelphia. | *Philadelphia :* | *Printed at the New Printing-Office, near the* | *Market.* 1740. | 8vo. pp. 56.

On page 45 is the following title : A | Poem | to the | Memory | of | Aquila Rose : | Who died at Philadelphia, August the | 22d, 1723.   Ætat. 28. | By Elias Bockett. | *London : Printed.* | *Philadelphia : Re-printed at the New-* | *Printing-Office.*

SAUNDERS. (R.)   A Pocket Almanac for 1741.   By Richard Saunders. *Philadelphia : B. Franklin.* 1740.   651

SAUNDERS. Poor Richard, 1741. | An | Almanack | For the Year of Christ | 1741, | Being the First after Leap Year. | . . . | . . . | . . . | . . . | . . . | . . . | . . . | . . . | . . . | . . . | . . . | . . . | . . . | . . . | . . . | . . . | . . . | . . . . | By Richard Saunders, Philom. | *Philadelphia: | Printed and sold by B. Franklin, at the New | Printing-Office near the Market.* [1740.] | Sm. 8vo. pp. (24).

SEAGRAVE. (R.) Remarks upon the Bishop of London's last Pastoral Letter. In Vindication of Mr. Whitefield and his particular Doctrines. By Robert Seagrave, M. A. *Philadelphia: Andrew Bradford.* 1740.   653

SMITH. (J[osiah]) The | Character, Preaching, &c. | of the Reverend | Mr. Geo. Whitefield, | Impartially represented and supported, | In a Sermon | Preach'd in Charlestown, South-Carolina, | March 26. Anno Domini 1740. | By J. Smith, V. D. M. | . . . | . . . | . . . | . . . | . . . | . . . | . . . | . . . . | *Philadelphia: | Printed and Sold by B. Franklin.* | M,DCC,XL. | 16mo. pp. 24.

SOME Observations on the Rev. Mr. Whitefield and his opposers. *Philadelphia: B. Franklin.* 1740. ?   655

SOME | Queries, | concerning | The Operation | of the | Holy Spirit, | Answered. | Delivered at a Lecture held at the Baptist-Meet- | ing-House in Charles-Town, South-Carolina: And | now published at the earnest Request of Some of the | Hearers. | *Philadelphia: | Printed by B. Franklin.* 1740. ? | 12mo. pp. 16.

SOME Remarks on Mr. Ebenezer Kinnersley's Two Letters to his Friend in the Country; together with a full Vindication of the Rev. Mr. Jones, and the Committee of the Church under his Care, from the Aspersions and unjust Accusations of the said Mr. Kinnersley. *Philadelphia: B. Franklin.* 1740.   657

[SOWER. (CHRISTOPHER)] Bekanntmachung. [*Germantown: Christoph Saur.* 1740.] 4to. pp. (2).   H. S. P. 658

A prospectus and specimen page of the first "Sower Bible." Issued about 1739 or 1740.

THE SPEECH | Of the Speaker of the House of | Commons, upon Presenting the Money | Bills to His Majesty, April 29, |

1740. | Philadelphia. | In Assembly the 9th. of the 6th month 1740. | [Resolution granting £3000. to the King's use, under certain very great restrictions.] [*Philadelphia: Printed by B. Franklin.* 1740.] Folio, pp. (3).   659

The Speech and Resolution are printed in parallel columns, and at the end are the following lines, headed :

THE CONTRAST.

A Lilliputian, and a Brobdingnag :
A First Rate's Main-Sail, and a Rag :
*JOHN LOCK deceas'd, and † JOHN LOCK here alive :
The Ark of *Noah,* and the smallest Hive :
St. *Peter's,* and the Palace of a *Wren* :
A Ship in Flames, and a lighted Pipe ; What then ?
Why then; If you these different Things revolve,
You may compare the *Speech* and the *Resolve.*

* *The famous Mr. Lock.*   † *A mean Porter of this City.*

TAYLOR. (J.) Pensilvania, 1741. | An | Almanack, | or | Ephemeris | Of the daily Motions of the | Sun and Moon ; | The time of their Rising and Setting. | Lunations and Eclipses. | With the | Places and Aspects of the Planets, | for the Year, 1741. | . . . | . . . | . . . | . . . | . . . | . . . | . . . . | By Jacob Taylor. | . . . . | . . . | . . . | . . . | . . . | . . . | . . . | . . . . | *Philadelphia: Printed and Sold by Andrew Bradford,* | *at the Sign of the Bible, in Front-Street.* [1740.] | Sm. 8vo. pp. (32).   L. C. P.   660

TENNENT. (G.) The | Danger | of an | Unconverted Minis-try. | Consider'd in a | Sermon | On Mark vi. 34. | Preached at Nottingham, in | Pennsylvania, March 8. Anno 1739–40. | By Gilbert Tennent, | A. M. And Minister of the Gospel in | New-Brunswick, New-Jersey. | . . . | . . . | . . . | . . . | . . . . | *Phila-delphia: Printed by B. Franklin,* 1740. + Second Edition.   661

TENNENT. Die | Gefahr bey unbekehrten | Predigern, | Vorgestellt in einer | Sermon | Ueber Marcus am VI. v. 34. | Gepredigt zu Notting=ham in Pensylvania, | den 8ten März, 1740. | Durch Gilbert Tennent, | Diener am Evangelio zu Neu=Braunschwick. | Aus dem Englischen ins Deutsche übersetzt. | . . . | . . . | . . . | . . . . | *Germanton:* | *Ge-druckt und zu finden bey Christoph Saur,* 1740. | 16mo. pp. 45.

TENNENT. A solemn Warning to the secure World, from the God of Terrible Majesty, or the Presumptous Sinner Detected, his Pleas considered, and his Doom displayed &c. By Gilbert Tennent. To which is added, The Life of his Brother, the Rev. Mr. John Tennent, with his two Sermons on the Nature of Regeneration opened, and its absolute Necessity in order to Salvation Demonstrated. *Philadelphia:* 1740.?   663

Advertised in the Weekly Mercury, July 31, 1740. Perhaps printed by William Bradford in New York.

[THOMAS. (George)] Oct. 20, 1740. | My Lords, | . . . . [*Philadelphia: B. Franklin:* 1740.] Sm. 4to. pp. 8. H. S. P. 664

A letter from Gov. Thomas to the Lords of Trade.

VINCENT. (T.) Christ's Certain and Sudden Appearance to Judgment. By Thomas Vincent. *Philadelphia: B. Franklin.* 1740.   665

VOTES of the Assembly. *Philadelphia: B. Franklin.* 1740.

WATTS. (Isaac) The Psalms of David. Imitated in the language of the New Testament, and applied to Christian Churches and Worship. . . . *London Printed: Philadelphia: Re-printed and Sold by B. Franklin, at the New Printing-Office, near the Market.* 1740.   667

WESLEY. (J. & C.) Hymns | and | Sacred Poems. | Published by | John Wesley, M.A. | Fellow of Lincoln College, Oxford ; | And | Charles Wesley, M. A. | Student of Christ-Church Oxford. | . . . | . . . | . . . | . . . | . . . . | *Philadelphia:* | *Printed by Andrew and William Bradford,* | *and sold for the Benefit of the Poor in Georgia.* | MDCCXL. | 12mo. pp. vii. (5). 237.   H. S. P. 668

Printed by Subscription for the Benefit of the Poor in Georgia. Some copies on "a superfine paper."

WHITEFIELD. (G.) A | Brief and General | Account | Of the First Part | of the | Life | Of the Reverend | Mr. Geo. Whitefield, | From his Birth, to his Entering | into Holy Orders. | Written by Himself. | *Philadelphia:* | *Printed and Sold by B. Franklin, in* | *Market-Street.* M,DCC,XL. | 24mo. Title, 1 leaf; Preface, pp. i-iii; text, pp. 1–66.   L. C. P.   669

Andrew and William Bradford also published an edition in Nov. 1740.

WHITEFIELD.   A | Continuation | Of the Reverend | Mr. Whitefield's | Journal | During the Time he was detained | in England, by the Embargo. | Vol. II. | *Philadelphia:* | *Printed and Sold by B. Franklin, in* | *Market-street,* 1740. | 24mo. pp. 63.

A | Continuation | Of the Reverend | Mr. Whitefield's | Journal | from | His Embarking after the Embargo. | To | His Arrival at Savannah in Georgia. | *Philadelphia:* | *Printed and Sold by B. Franklin, in* | *Market-street,* 1740. | pp. [65]-205.   Books sold by B. Franklin, pp. (5).   H. S. P.   670

WHITEFIELD.   A | Continuation | Of the Reverend | Mr. Whitefield's | Journal | from | A few Days after his Arrival at | Georgia, | to | His second Return thither from | Pennsylvania. | *Philadelphia:* | *Printed and Sold by B. Franklin, in* | *Market-Street.* 1740. | 24mo. pp. 96.   L. C. P.   671

A continuation of Vol. II.   See Number 670, and for a further continuation, see 1741, Number 737, *infra.*

WHITEFIELD.   Directions how to hear a Sermon.   By George Whitefield.   *Philadelphia: Andrew and William Bradford.*   1740.

WHITEFIELD.   An Extract of Sundry Passages taken out of Mr. Whitefield's Sermon.   *Philadelphia:* 1740.   12mo.   673

Title from the catalogue of the library of H. A. Brady, of New York.

WHITEFIELD.   The Heinous Sin of Drunkenness. A Sermon. By George Whitefield.   *Philadelphia: Andrew and William Bradford.*   1740.   674

WHITEFIELD.   The Indwelling of the Spirit. A Sermon. By George Whitefield.   *Philadelphia: Andrew and William Bradford.*   1740.   675

WHITEFIELD. A | Journal | of a | Voyage | from | London to Gibraltar. | By | Geo. Whitefield, A. M. | Of Pembroke-College, Oxford. | Containing | Many curious Observations, and Edifying | Reflections, on the several Occurrences | that happen'd in the Voyage. | The Sixth Edition. | *Philadelphia :* | *Printed and Sold by B. Franklin,* | *in Market-Street,* 1740. | 24mo. pp. 64.   L. C. P.   676

This is the first part of Whitefield's Journal and precedes the volume printed in 1739.

WHITEFIELD. A Letter from the Reverend Mr. Whitefield, to a Friend in London, showing the Fundamental Error of the Book, Entitled, The Whole Duty of Man. *Philadelphia : B. Franklin.* 1740.   677

WHITEFIELD. A Letter from the Rev. Mr. Whitefield, to some Church-Members of the Presbyterian Persuasion, in answer to certain Scruples lately proposed in proper Queries raised on each Remark. *Philadelphia: B. Franklin.* 1740.   678

WHITEFIELD. Sermons | on | Various Subjects. | In Two Volumes. | Vol. I. | Containing, | . . . | . . . | . . . | . . . | . . . | . . . | . . . | . . . | . . . | . . . | . . . | . . . | . . . | . . . | . . . | . . . . | By George Whitefield, A. B. | Of Pembroke College, Oxford. | *Philadelphia :* | *Printed and Sold by B. Franklin, in* | *Market-street,* 1740. | 24mo. pp. iv. 223. + Vol. II. | Containing, | . . . | . . . | . . . | . . . | . . . | . . . | . . . | . . . | . . . | . . . | . . . | . . . | . . . | . . . . | By George Whitefield, A. B. | . . . . . | [*Ibid.*]   1740. | 24mo. pp. iv. 224.   H. S. P.   679

WHITEFIELD. Three | Letters | From the Reverend | Mr. G. Whitefield : | viz. | Letter I. To a Friend in London, concerning | Archbishop Tillotson. | Letter II. To the same, on the same Subject. | Letter III. To the Inhabitants of Maryland, | Virginia, North and South-Carolina, concerning | their Negroes. | *Philadelphia:* | *Printed and Sold by B. Franklin, at* | *the New Printing-Office near the Market.* | M,DCC,XL. | Sm. 8vo. pp. 16.   H. S. P.   680

WHITEFIELD. Von | Georg Weitfields | Predigten, | Der | Erste Theil, | Nebst einer Einleitung, und Copia eines | Briefs von

Neu=York. | Aus dem Englischen ins Hoch=Deutsche übersetzt. | ... |
.... | *Germanton:* | *Gedruckt und zu finden bey Christoph Saur,*
1740. | Sm. 8vo. pp. 18.   H. S. P.   681

WHITEFIELD. Von | Georg Weitfields | Predigten, | Der |
Zweyte Theil, | Bestehend aus drey Sermonen. | Aus dem Englischen ins
Hoch=Deutsche übersetzt. | Die Erste: | Von dem Nutzen der Gottseligkeit
in der Jugend. | Die Zweyte: | Von einer Gottseligen Haushaltung. |
Die Dritte: | Von einer Gottseligen Gesellschafft, nebst einem | Anhang, von
Gesellschafften. | *Germanton: Gedruckt und zu finden bey Christoph*
Saur, 1740. | 16mo. pp. 76.   H. S. P.   682

WHITEFIELD. Von Georg Weitfields Predigten, Der Dritte
Theil. *Germantown:* | *Christoph Saur,* 1740.   683

     Advertised in Saur's Almanac for 1741.

WHITEFIELD. Voorbidding ein eider Christen's Plicht en
de Wyze and Dwaaze Maagden, vertoont in twee Predicaties. *J.*
P. Zenger in Niew York en B. Franklin in Philadelphia. 1740.

     This title is from Haven's list.

WHITEFIELD. Worldly Business no Plea for the Neglect of
Religion. A Sermon. By George Whitefield. *Philadelphia :*
Andrew and William Bradford. 1740.   685

[WOOLVERTON. (CHARLES)] The | Upright Lives of the
Heathen | Briefly Noted ; | Or Epistles and Discourses betwixt |
Alexander the Conqueror and | Dindimus King of the Brach- |
mans, giving an Account what sort | of People they are, their Di-
vinity, | and Philosophy, with their manner | of Living, &c. | To-
gether also with the Dying-Words of Ocka- | mickon, an Indian
King. Spoken to Jah- | kursoe, his Brothers Son, whom he ap-
point- | ed King after him. | Collected together, and Published for
a general Service. | ... | ... | ... | ... | ... | ... | ... |
... | ... | ... | ... | ... | .... | *Philadelphia: Printed and Sold by*
A. and W. Bradford. [1740.] | Sm. 8vo. pp. 16.   686

1741.

ALLEIN. (J.) An | Alarm | to | Unconverted Sinners; | In a Serious | Treatise: | Shewing, | I. What Conversion is not, and Correcting | some Mistakes about it. | II. What Conversion is, and wherein it con- | sisteth. | III. The Necessity of Conversion. | IV. The Marks of the Unconverted. | V. The Miseries of the Unconverted. | VI. Directions for Conversion. | VII. Motions to Conversion. | Wherein are annexed divers Practical Cases | of Conscience judicially resolved. | By Joseph Allein, late Minister of | the Gospel at Taunton, in Somersetshire. | *Philadelphia:* | *Printed and sold by B. Franklin, at* | *the New Printing-Office, near the Market.* | M,DCC,XLI. | 16mo. pp. xxiv, 167, 77, (1).   687

THE AMERICAN Magazine, | or | a monthly view of | The Political State | of the British Colonies | For February, 1740–1. | (To be Continued Monthly.) | Containing : | . . . . | *Philadelphia: Printed and Sold by Andrew Bradford: Price One Shilling Pennsylvania Currency, or Eight Pence Sterling.* | 8vo. pp. (2), 35–76. + March, pp. 80–118 imperfect. + Jan. [title not seen] pp. viii. 34.

This was the first Magazine published in the American Colonies, and was projected and edited by John Webbe. The prospectus appeared in the Weekly Mercury, Nov. 6, 1740. The first number was to have been issued in March, 1741, but owing to Franklin's announcing the publication of the General Magazine, the January number was issued February 13, 1741, three days earlier than the first number of Franklin's Magazine. Number 2 was published on March 17th. Number 3 is not advertised in the Weekly Mercury, and was probably the last issued.

Num. 1096 | [Three cuts.] | THE AMERICAN | Weekly Mercury. | From Thursday December 25 to Thursday January 1. 1740–1. | *Philadelphia: Printed and Sold by Andrew Bradford,* | *at the Sign of the Bible in Front-street, where Advertisements are taken in, and* | *all Persons in Town or Country may be supplied with this Paper.* | 689

Numbers 1096 to 1148 (from Thursday, Dec. 24, to Thursday, Dec. 31, 1741), four pages each, except Number 1105, which contains six pages. There are "Postscripts" of two pages each to Numbers 1112, 1114, 1115, 1118, 1125, and 1140.

BALL. (W.) The New-Jersey Almanac for the Year 1742. By William Ball, Philomath. *Philadelphia: Printed and Sold by B. Franklin.* 1741. 690

Advertised in the Pa. Gazette, October 22, 1741.

BIRKETT. (W.) An Almanac for 1742. By William Birkett. *Philadelphia: Andrew Bradford.* 1741. 691

BLAIR. (S.) A Particular | Consideration | of | A Piece, Entituled, | The Querists: | wherein sundry Passages extracted from the | Printed Sermons, Letters and Journals of the | Rev. Mr. Whitefield are vindicated from | the false Glosses and erroneous Senses put upon | them in said Querists; Mr. Whitefield's | Soundness in the true Scheme of Christian | Doctrine maintained; and the Author's | disingenuous Dealing with him exposed. | By Samuel Blair. | . . . | . . . . | *Philadelphia:* | *Printed and Sold by B. Franklin,* 1741. | 16mo. pp. 63. B. P. L. 692

A | CATALOGUE | of | Books | belonging to the | Library Company | of | Philadelphia. | . . . . | *Philadelphia: Printed by B. Franklin,* 1741. | Sm. 8vo. pp. 55. (1). L. C. P. 693

THE | CHARTER | of | Privileges, | Granted by | William Penn, Esq; | to the | Inhabitants of Pennsylvania | and Territories. | [*Penn Arms.*] | *Philadelphia:* | *Printed and Sold by B. Franklin.* | MDCCXLI. | Folio, pp. 8. H. S. P. 694

CHEW. (S.) The | Speech | of | Samuel Chew, Esq; | Chief Justice of the Government of New- | Castle, Kent and Sussex upon | Delaware: | Delivered from the Bench to the | Grand-Jury of the County of | New-Castle, Nov. 21. 1741; and now pub- | lished at their Request. | *Philadelphia:* | *Printed and sold by B. Franklin.* | M,DCC,XLI. | Sm. 4to. pp. 16. + The Second Edition. [*Ibid.*] pp. 16. H. S. P. 695

COLDEN. (C.) An Essay on the Illiac Passion. By Cadwallader Colden. *Philadelphia: B. Franklin.* 1741. 696

DAILY Conversation with God, exemplified in the Holy Life of Armelle Nicholas, a poor ignorant Country Maid in France, commonly known by the name of the Good Armelle, deceas'd in Bretaigne in the year 1671. Done out of the French. . . . . *Philadelphia: Printed and sold by B. Franklin.* 1741.   697

DELAWARE. Laws | of the | Government | of New Castle, Kent and Sussex | Upon Delaware. | Published by Order of the Assembly. | [*Royal Arms.*] *Philadelphia:* | *Printed and Sold by B. Franklin, at the New* | *Printing-Office, in Market-Street* | MDCC-XLI. | Folio, pp. 282, 3.   L. C. P.   698

DIALOGUES, | Between a Minister and an honest | Country-Man, concerning | Election and Predestination, | Very suitable to the Present Times. | To which is annexed, | Divine Prescience consistent with | Human Liberty: Or Mr. Wesley's | Opinion of Election and Reprobation, prov'd | to be not so absurd as represented in a late | Letter, under the Title of Free Grace indeed: | But to be Clear of those destructive Con- | sequences that will forever attend the Cal- | vinistical Doctrine of absolute Fatality. | By an Enquirer after Truth | . . . | . . . . | *Philadelphia Printed: Sold by Andrew Brad-* | *ford, Jacob Duche, William Parsons, and Evan* | *Morgan, Cooper. Price four Pence.* 1741. | Sm. 8vo. pp. 40.

DYLANDER. (J.) Free Grace in Truth. The XXIVth Meditation of Dr. John Gerhard: Translated from Latin into English. With Notes for the better understanding the Author's Meaning. By John Dylander, Minister of the Swedish Church, Wecaco, near Philadelphia. *Philadelphia: Printed and Sold by B. Franklin.* 1741.   700

ERSKINE. (R.) A | Letter | from | The Reverend | Mr. Ralph Erskine | To | The Reverend | Mr. Geo. Whitefield. | *Philadelphia:* | *Printed and Sold by B. Franklin,* 1741. | Sm. 8vo. pp. 14.   701

FALCONAR. (M.) Free Grace with a Witness. By Magnus Falconar. *Philadelphia: Andrew Bradford.*? 1741.   702

Advertised in the Weekly Mercury, March 26, 1740-1, as "Now in the Press and . . . to be sold by Scotch James and none else."

FALCONAR. A Supplement to Free Grace with a Witness. By Magnus Falconar. *Philadelphia.*? 1741.   703

Advertised in the Weekly Mercury, July 2, 1741, as "Now ready for the Press, . . . the Author can't any other way bring it to the Press than by Subscription." Three weeks later he announces "If Subscriptions don't come soon in" it "will not be printed in this Part of the Country. Several Subscriptions are come from New York, and among the rest Three Esqrs. . . . so that they are not all of the Mob kind who are in love with this Ministry." Probably never printed.

FINLEY. (S.) Christ Triumphing | and | Satan Raging. | A | Sermon | On Matth. xii. 28. | Wherein is proven, that the Kingdom of God | is come unto us at this Day. | First preached at Nottingham in Pensilvania, | Jan. 20. 1740, 1, | And now published for the common | Benefit. | By Samuel Finley, Preacher of the Gospel. | . . . | . . . | . . . | . . . | . . . | . . . | . . . | . . . . | *Philadelphia:* | *Printed and Sold by B. Franklin,* 1741. | 16mo. pp. 43.   B. P. L.   704

FREE Grace Indeed! A Letter To the Rev. Mr. John Wesley, Relating to his Sermon Against Absolute Election; Published under the Title of Free Grace. *London, Printed. Philadelphia: Reprinted and Sold by B. Franklin.* 1741.   705

Advertised at the end of A Continuation of Whitefield's Journal, and in the Gazette of Jan. 22, 1740–1. To the latter advertisement is added the following: "Note, This Letter is said, entirely to overthrow the horrid misrepresentation of that sacred Truth of God, the Doctrine of Election, and to reconcile those Scriptures which Mr. Wesley advances in Favour of rotten Free-Will."

THE | GENERAL Magazine, | And | Historical Chronicle, | For all the British Plantations in America. | (To be Continued Monthly.) | January, 1741 | [*Prince of Wales Badge.*] Vol. I. | *Philadelphia:* | *Printed and Sold by B. Franklin.* | 12mo. pp. (2)77. + February, 1741. [*Badge.*] Vol. I. Numb. II. [*Ibid.*] pp. (2) [77 *sic*]–146. No. III. pp. (2). [147]–216. No. IV. pp. (2) [217]– 286. No. V. pp. (2) [287]–356. No. VI. pp. (2) 357–426.

The Pa. Gazette, Feb. 12, 1740–1, announces: "On Monday next will be published The General Magazine for January." Number 2 was published March 24; Number 3, April 27; Number 4, May 24; Number 5, June 27; and Number 6 on July 27. The Magazine then ceased to appear.

[GRUBER. (JOHANN ADAM)] Einfältige | Warnungs= und Wächter=Stimme | An die gerufene Seelen dieser Zeit. | Verfaßt im Jahr 1741. Von einem Geringen. Psalm LXXIV. V. 21. [*German-town: Christoph Saur.* 1741.] 4to. 1 leaf. H. S. P. 707

Reprinted in Fresenius' Nachrichten, Vol. III. p. 297.

DER | HOCH=DEUTSCH | Americanische | Calender, | Auf das Jahr | ... | ... | 1742; | ... | In sich haltende: Die Wochen Tage; Den Tag des Monaths; Tage wel= | che bemerkt werden; Des Monds Auf= und Untergang; Des Monds Zeichen und | Grad; Des Monds Virtel; Aspecten der Planeten samt Witterung; Der 7 Ge= | stirns Auf= gang, Sud=Platz und Untergang; Der Sonnen Auf= und Untergang; | Nebst verschiedenen andern Berichten; Erklärung der Zeichen, Aderlaß= Täfflein, Anzeigung der Finsternisse, Courten, Fären, 2c., 2c. | Eingerich= tet auf die Sonnen Höhe von 40 Graden, und zwar vor | Pennsylvanien: Jedoch an denen angrentzenden Länden ohne | merklichen Unterschied zuge= brauchen. | Zum vierten mal herausgegeben. | *Germantown: Gedruckt und zu finden bey Christoph Saur;* | . . . . [1741.] | Sm. 4to. pp. (24). H. S. P. 708

JERMAN. (J.) The American Almanac for the Year 1742. By John Jerman, Philomath. *Philadelphia: Printed and Sold by B. Franklin.* 1741. 709

LAW. (W.) The Grounds and Reasons of Christian Regenera-tion; or, the new Birth, offered to the Consideration of Christians and Deists. By William Law, M. A. *Philadelphia:* 1741. 710

LEEDS. (T.) The American Almanac for 1742. By Titan Leeds. *Philadelphia: Andrew Bradford.* 1741. 711

[LOGAN. (JAMES)] To Robert Jordan, and others the Friends | of the Yearly Meeting for Business, | now conven'd in Philadel-phia. | [*Philadelphia: B. Franklin.* 1741.] Sm. Folio, pp. 4.

Dated at the end "Stenton, Sept, 22, 1741" and signed "J. L." Thirty copies privately printed, only two of which are known to exist. Reprinted in the Pa. Mag. of History and Biography, Vol. VI. Advising Friends against retaining their seats in the Assembly on account of the necessity of providing for the defence of the Province.

MORGAN. (J.) The General Cause of all Hurtful Mistakes. Sermon from Proverbs iii. 5, 6. By Rev. Joseph Morgan, A. M. *Philadelphia: Printed by B. Franklin.* 1741. 16mo. pp. 24.   713

[NEW-YEAR Verses of the Carriers of the American Weekly Mercury. *Philadelphia: Andrew Bradford.* 1741.] Narrow Folio, 1 leaf.   H. S. P.   714

Headed by a cut of Mercury with his left hand resting upon a snake curled into a circle, in which is a quotation from Ansonius. Thirty-eight lines beginning, "In scenes confus'd the weary Year we've past, | And to our merry Christmas come at last :" |

[*Penn Arms.*] NOTICE is hereby given . . . | . . . That . . . | . . . George Thomas, Esq ; | . . . Governor . . . | . . . | . . . is fully Impowered. . . | . . . | to confirm . . . | the Sale . . . | . . . also to sell . . . | any vacant Lands . . . | [*Philadelphia: B. Franklin.* 1741.] Sm. Folio, 1 leaf.   715

Signed "Richard Peters, Secr." and dated "21st Sept. 1741."

THE PENNSYLVANIA Gazette. *Philadelphia: Printed by B. Franklin, Post-Master, at | the New Printing-Office, near the Market. Price 10s. a Year. |* 4to.   716

Numbers 629 (Jan. 1, 1740–41) to 681 (Dec. 29, 1741), four pages each, except 641, 647, 650, 652 and 673, six pages, and 654, eight pages. Numbers 632 and 633 are misnumbered 932 and 933. Title as in Number 648, *supra.* The price is omitted in the imprint after Number 630.

POOR Robin's Almanac for 1742. *Philadelphia: Andrew Bradford.* 1741.   717

PROCLAMATION. [*Royal Arms.*?] By the Honourable George Thomas, Esq ; Lieutenant Governor and Commander in Chief of the Province of Pennsylvania, and Counties of New-Castle, Kent and Sussex on Delaware ; A Proclamation. *Philadelphia: Printed by B. Franklin.* 1741. Folio, 1 leaf.   718

Dated Sept. 28, 1741. In aid of the officer appointed to collect recruits for the expedition against Havanna.

A | PROTESTATION | presented to | The Synod | of | Philadelphia, | June 1. 1741. | *Philadelphia: Printed and sold | by B. Franklin.* 1741. | Sm. 8vo. pp. 16.   H. S. P.   719

Signed by the Rev. Robert Cross, Francis Alison, John Elder, and nine other Presbyterian Ministers, and eight Elders.

THE QUERISTS, Part III. or an Examination of Sundry Passages taken out of Mr. G. Tennent's Sermon preached at Nottingham, of the Danger of an Unconverted Ministry. Together with some Scruples proposed in proper Queries raised on each remark. By the same Hands as the former. *Philadelphia: Printed and Sold by B. Franklin.* 1741. Sm. 8vo. pp. 150.   720

Advertised as "Just published" in the Pa. Gazette, Sept. 24, 1741.

SAUNDERS. R.   A Pocket | Almanack | For the Year 1742. | Fitted to the Use of Penn- | sylvania, and the neigh- | bouring Provinces. | By R. Saunders, Phil. | *Philadelphia: | Printed by B. Franklin.* [1741.] | 32mo. pp. (16).   721

Title in red and black.

SAUNDERS.   Poor Richard, 1742. | An | Almanack | For the Year of Christ | 1742. | [as in 1738.] *Philadelphia: Printed and Sold by B. Franklin, at the New | Printing-Office near the Market.* [1741.] | 12mo. pp. (24).   L. C. P.   722

A SERMON on Luke, viii. 28.   *Philadelphia:* 1741.   723

Title from Haven List.

A SHORT Reply to Mr. Whitefield's Letter, which he wrote in answer to the Querists; wherein the said Querists testify their Satisfaction with some of the Amendments Mr. Whitefield proposes to make of some of the exceptionable Expressions in his Writings. Together with some other Remarks upon what seems exceptionable in the present Letter; which seem to occur to the Querists. . . . . *Philadelphia: Printed for the Querists, and sold by B. Franklin.* 1741.   724

[SMALRIDGE. (GEORGE)] The | Art | of | Preaching, | In Imitation of | Horace's | Art of Poetry. | *London, Printed:* | *Philadelphia: Re-printed and* | *Sold by B. Franklin, in Market-Street.* | M,DCC,XLI. | Sm. 8vo. pp. 22.   N. Y. H. S.   725

SOME Remarks on a Speech said to have been delivered by Samuel Chew. *Philadelphia:* 1741.   726

SOME Remarks upon the Times, wherein is shewn how, contrary to the Doctrine of Holy Writ most Sects are Hewing out Cisterns which will hold no Water: Or a short Remark on a Letter sign'd by a Person in the Jerseys, who endeavours to prove a Man in the Flesh, or in his carnal State, to be the Child of God. *Philadelphia: Printed for the Author, and Sold by B. Franklin.* 1741.

TAYLOR. (J.) Pensilvania, 1742. | An | Almanack, | or | Ephemeris | Of the daily Motions of the | Sun and Moon ; | The time of their Rising and Setting. | Lunations and Eclipses. | With the | Places and Aspects of the Planets, | for the Year, 1742. | . . . | . . . | . . . | . . . . | By Jacob Taylor. | . . . | . . . | . . . | . . . | . . . | . . . | . . . | . . . | . . . | . . . . | *Philadelphia: Printed and Sold by Andrew Bradford,* | *at the Sign of the Bible, in Front-Street.* [1741.] | Sm. 8vo. pp. (32).   L. C. P.   728

TENNENT. (G.) Remarks | upon a | Protestation | presented to | The Synod of | Philadelphia, | June 1, 1741. | By Gilbert Tennent, A. M. and Minister | of the Gospel in New-Brunswick, New-Jersey, | . . . | . . . | . . . . | *Philadelphia:* | *Printed and Sold by Benj. Franklin.* | 1741. | 16mo. pp. 68.   A. A. S.   729

     The Remarks end on page 36, and are followed by another title page : The | Apology | of the | Presbytery of New-Brunswick, | for | Their Dissenting from Two Acts or New | Religious Laws, which were made | at the last Session of our Synod. | Humbly offer'd to the Consideration of the Synod | now conven'd at Philadelphia. | [*Ibid.*] | 1741. | pp. (2) 39–68.

TENNENT. A | Sermon | upon | Justification : | Preached at New-Brunswick, on the Saturday | before the Dispensing of the Holy Sacra- | ment, which was the first Sabbath in August, | Anno 1740. | By Gilbert Tennent, A.M. | And Minister of the Gospel in the Place aforesaid. | . . . | . . . . | *Philadelphia :* | *Printed and Sold by Benjamin Franklin,* | *in Market-Street.* M,DCC,XLI. | 16mo. pp. 29, (3). + The Second Edition.   730

VOTES | and | Proceedings | of the | House of Representatives | of the | Province of Pennsylvania, | Met at Philadelphia, on the Fourteenth of October, | Anno Dom. 1740, and continued by Adjournments. [to Sept. 22, 1741.] | [*Penn Arms.*] | *Philadelphia :* | *Printed and Sold by B. Franklin, at the New-Printing-* | *Office near the Market.* M,DCC,XLI. | Folio, pp. 33. (1).   H. S. P.   731

VOTES | and | Proceedings | of the | House of Representatives | of the | Province of Pennsylvania, | Met at Philadelphia, on the Fourteenth of October, | Anno Dom. 1741, and continued by Adjournments. [to Aug. 28, 1742.] | [*Penn Arms.*] | *Philadelphia :* | *Printed and Sold by B. Franklin, at the New-Printing-* | *Office near the Market.* M,DCC,XLI. | Folio, pp. 92.   II. S. P.   732

Published in parts at different times.

WATTS. (I[SAAC]) The Psalms of David, imitated in the Language of the New Testament, and apply'd to the Christian State and Worship. By I. Watts. The Thirteenth Edition. *Philadelphia : Reprinted and Sold by B. Franklin.* 1741.   733

WESLEY. (J.) Free Grace. | A | Sermon | Preach'd at | Bristol, | By John Wesley, M.A. | Fellow of Lincoln-College, Oxford. | *Bristol, Printed. by S. and F. Farley,* | *And Re-printed at Philadelphia: [by Andrew Bradford,] and Sold* | *by Edward Pleadwell, in Front-street,* 1740–1. | Sm. 8vo. pp. 32.   H. S. P.   734

WESLEY. Free Grace. | A | Sermon | Preached at | Bristol. | By John Wesley, M.A. | Fellow of Lincoln-College, Oxford. | *Bristol, Printed.* | *Philadelphia :* | *Re-printed and Sold by* | *B. Franklin.* 1741. | Sm. 8vo. pp. 32.   735

WHITEFIELD. (G.) An Account of the Money received and disbursed for the Orphan House in Georgia, by the Rev. Mr. George Whitefield. *Philadelphia : B. Franklin.* ? 1741.   736

WHITEFIELD. A | Continuation | Of the Reverend | Mr. Whitefield's | Journal, | from | A few Days after his Arrival at | Savannah, June the Fourth, | to | His leaving Stanford, the last Town in | New-England, October 29. 1740. | *Philadelphia : | Printed and Sold by B. Franklin,* | M,DCC,XLI. | 24mo. pp. 126. L. C. P.

WHITEFIELD. A Continuation of the Reverend Mr. Whitefield's Journal from his leaving Stanford in New England, to his arrival at Falmouth, Eng. March 11, 1741. Containing an Account of the Work of God at New-York, Pennsylvania and South-Carolina. *Philadelphia : B. Franklin.* 1741. 738

WHITEFIELD. A | Letter | from | The Reverend | Mr. George Whitefield, | To | The Reverend | Mr. John Wesley, | In Answer to his | Sermon, | entitled | Free Grace. | . . . | . . . | . . . . | *Philadelphia : | Printed and Sold by B. Franklin,* M,DCC,XLI. | 16mo. pp. 24. 739

WRIGHT. (J.) The Speech of John Wright, Esq ; | One of the Magistrates of Lancaster | Country, to the Court and Grand-Jury, | on his Removal from the Commission of | the Peace at the Quarter-Sessions held | at Lancaster for the said County in | May 1741. | Published by Order of the Grand-Jury. | [*Philadelphia : B. Franklin.* 1741.] Folio, pp. 4. H. S. P. 740

Wright and others had been active in their opposition to some proceedings of the Assembly, and their names were omitted from a new commission then issued.

1742.

ADVERTISEMENT. *Philadelphia : B. Franklin.* 1742. Folio, 1 leaf. 741

Notice, signed James Logan, and dated 12th of the 12th Month (February) 1742, concerning the payment of quit-rents due to Lætitia Aubrey.

ALSO Sang | Ihrem Gotte aufm Throne, | Und | Dem Lamme in dem Throne, | In der Person Jesu Christi, | die | Gemeine | Zu Bethlehem in Nord-America, | Mit der See-Gemeine vollendet, | Als sie sich am 2ten Junii 1742. st. v. | Als an welchem Tage in

Europa gleich vor zwanzig | jahren ihre Wiederkunft zu ihren
siebenherndert- | jährigen Friedens-Hûtten geschahe, | Der Penn-
sylvanischen | Gemeine Gottes im Geist | Auf der Siebenden | Und
| Schluss-Conferenz | Der Religionen, | In Philadelphia | Dar-
stellete ; und Sie um einen Segen bat. | *Philadelphia, Gedruct bey
Benjamin Franklin.* [1742.] | Sm. 4to, pp. 4.   H. S. P.   742

THE AMERICAN Weekly Mercury.   743

Numbers 1149 (Thursday, Dec. 31 to Thursday, Jan. 7, 1741-2) to 1199 (from
Tuesday, Dec. 21 to Tuesday, Dec. 28, 1742), four pages each except Numbers
1157, 1160, 1163, 1169, 1170, 1183 and 1195, which contain six pages. Title and
imprint as in Number 689, *supra.* On the death of Andrew Bradford the paper
was suspended for one issue, none being published between Nov. 18 and Dec. 2.
In Number 1195 the imprint was changed to the form given in Number 800,
infra.

ANTES. (H).   Herrn Pyrläi Ausruf-Zeddel an die Einwohner in
Penſilvanien, daß Diejenige, ſo Herrn Grafen von Zinzendorf noch
einmal wolten predigen hören, ſich melden ſolten. Unter Henrich Antes
Namen geſchrieben und in Penſilvanien gedruckt. 1742.   744

Title from Fresemius' Nachrichten, Vol. III., p. 715.

AT a Council held at Philadelphia, May 17th 1742. | [*Philadel-
phia: Printed by B. Franklin.* 1742.] Folio, pp. 12.   H. S. P.   745

Contains the Report of a Committee of the Council to whom the Report of a
Committee of the Assembly, in Relation to unhealthy vessels, was referred.

AUSBUND, | Das iſt: | Etliche ſchöne | Chriſtliche | Lieder, | Wie
ſie in dem Ge- | fängnüs zu Baſſau in dem | Schloß von den Schweitzer-
Brüdern, | und von anderen rechtgläubi- | gen Chriſten hin und her | ge-
dichtet worden. | Allen und jeden Chriſten | welcher Religion ſie ſeyen,
un- | partheyiſch faſt nützlich. | *Germantown:* | *Gedruckt bey Christoph
Saur,* 1742. | 16mo.   H. S. P.   746

Collation: Title 1 leaf; Vorede, pp. (8); text, pp. 812; Register, pp. (6);
"Confessio, | oder | Bekantnüsz," | von Thomas von Imbroich, pp. 20; "Ein
| Warhafftiger | Bericht, | Von den Brüdern im | Schweitzerland, in dem |
Zürcher Gebiet, | Wegen der Trübsalen welche über sie | ergangen seyn, um des
Evan- | geliums willen; Von dem 1635sten bis in | das 1645ste Jahr. | pp. 46.

AVTHENTISCHE | Relation | Von dem | Anlass, Fortgang und Schlusse | Der am 1sten und 2ten Januarii Anno 174½ | In Germantown gehaltenen | Versammlung. | Einiger Arbeiter | Derer meisten Christlichen Religionen | Und | Vieler vor sich selbst Gott-dienenden Christen-Menschen | in Pennsylvania; | Aufgesetzt | In Germantown am Abend des 2ten obigen Monats. | *Philadelphia:* | *Gedruckt and zu haben bey B. Franklin.* [1742.] | Sq. 8vo. pp. 15 (1).

Avthentische | Nachricht | Von der | Verhandlung und dem Verlass | Der am 14den und 15den Januarii Anno 174½ | Im sogenannten Falckner-Schwamm | An Georg Hûbners Hause gehalten | Zweyten | Versammlung | Sowol | Einiger Teutschen Arbeiter | Der Evangelischen Religionen | Als | Verschiedener einzelen treuen Gezeugen und | Gottsfürchtiger Nachbarn. | Nebst einigen Beylagen. | *Philadelphia,* | *Gedruckt und zu haben bey B. Franklin.* [1742.] | Title, 1 leaf; pp. 19–40.

Zuverlässige | Beschreibung | Der Dritten | Conferenz | Der Evangelischen Religionen | Teutscher Nation | In Pennsylvania, | Welche am 9. 10. und 11ten Februarii 174½ | In Oley an Johann de Türcks Hause | gehalten worden; | Samt | Denen dieses mahl verfassten | Gemein-Schlûssen. | *Philadelphia,* | *Gedruckt und zu haben bey B. Franklin.* [1742.] | Title, 1 leaf; pp. 43–56.

Vierte | General- | Versammlung | der | Kirche Gottes | Aus allen Evangelischen Religionen | In Pennsylvania, | Teutscher Nation; | Gehalten zu Germantown am 10. 11. und 12ten Martii | im jahr 174½. | An Mr. Ashmeads Hause. | *Philadelphia,* | *Gedruckt und zu haben bey B. Franklin.* [1742.] | Title, 1 leaf; pp. 59–76.

[GRUBER. (JOHANN ADAM)] Gründliche | An-und aufforderung | an die | Ehmahlig erweckte hier und dar zerstreuete | Seelen dieses Landes, | In oder ausser Partheyen, | zur | Neuen Umfassung, | Gliedlicher Vereinigung, | und | Gebets-Gemeinschaft; | Dargelegt aus dringendem Herzen eines um Heilung | der Brüche Zions ängstlich bekümmerten Gemüths, | im jahr 1736. | *Phila-delphia,* | *Gedruckt und zu haben bey B. Franklin,* | MDCCXLII. | Title, 1 leaf, pp. 3–14.

The paging is corrected in the errata on the last page. It should be 79–9?, instead of 3–14. Reprinted in Fresenius' Nachrichten, Vol. III., p. 351.

Extract | aus | Unsers Conferenz-Schreibers | Johann Jacob Müllers | Geführten Protocoll | Bey der | Fünften Versammlung | der | Gemeine Gottes im Geist, | Gehalten in Germantown 1742. den 6ten April und folgende Tage: | Nebst einer Vorrede an die ehrwürdige Conferenz aller | Arbeiter bey der Kirche Jesu Christi in Pennsylvania. | *Philadelphia,* | *Gedruckt und zu haben bey B. Franklin.* [1742.] | Title, 1 leaf, pp. 93–102.

Extract | aus des | Conferenz-Schreibers | Johann Jacob Müllers | Registratur | von der | Sechten Versammlung | der | Evanglischen Arbeiter | In Pennsylvania. | Und | Der Gemeine Gottes im Geist | Siebender | General-Synodus. | Zu Philadelphia am 2. und 3 ten Junii 1742. st. v. | *Daselbst gedruckt und zu haben bey B. Franklin.* [1742.] | Title, 1 leaf; pp. 105–120.   H. S. P. 747

BALL. (W.) The New-Jersey Almanack for the Year 1743. By William Ball, Philom. *Philadelphia: B. Franklin.* 1742.

Advertised in the Pa. Gazette November 11, 1742.

BECHTEL. (J.) Abermaliger Vorschlag desselben wegen gedachter Schule. Von Johannes Bechtel. *Philadelphia:?* 1742.   749

Reprinted in Fresenius' Nachrichten, Vol. III., p. 740.

BECHTEL. Kurzer | Catechismus | Vor etliche | Gemeinen Jesu | Aus der | Reformirten Religion | In Pennsylvania, | Die sich zum alten Berner Synodo halten: | Herausgegeben von | Johannes Bechteln, | Diener des Worts Gottes. | *Philadelphia,* | *Gedruckt bey Benjamin Franklin,* 1742. | 12mo. pp. 42. H. S. P. 750

BIRKETT. (W.) An Almanac for 1743. By William Birkett. *Philadelphia: Andrew Bradford.* 1742.   751

BLAIR. (S.) Animadversions | on | The Reasons of | Mr. Alex. Creaghead's | Receding from the | Judicatures | of this | Church, | Together with its | Constitution. | By Samuel Blair. | . . . | . . . . | *Philadelphia: Printed by Willi-* | *am Bradford, at the Sign of the Bible* | *in Second-Street.* [1742.] | Sm. 8vo. pp. 48+.

BLAIR. The | Doctrines | of | Predestination | Truly & Fairly Stated ; | Confirmed from clear Scripture-Evidence, and | Defended against all the material Arguments | and Objections advanced against it. | By Samuel Blair, late Minister of the Gospel at | Shrewsbury in New-Jersey, and now at London-derry | in Pennsylvania. | *Philadelphia:* | *Printed by B. Franklin for the Author.* M.DCC.XLII. | Sm. 8vo. pp. 79, and Advertisement.   753

BOEHM. (J. P.) Getreuer Warnungs | Brief | an die | Hoch-teutsche Evangelisch Reformirten | Gemeinden und alle deren Glieder, in | Pensylvanien, | Zur getreuen Warschauung, vor denen Leuthen, wel- | che unter dem nahmen von | Herrn-huther | bekandt seyn. | Umb sich vor deren Seelverderblichen und Gewissen- | verwüstenden Lehre zu hüthen und wohl vorzu- | sehen, damit sie nicht | Durch den schein ihres euserlichen scheinheiligen We- | sens, und selbst eingebildeten Gerichtigkeit und | Heiligkeit, zu ihrer Seelen ewigen schaden, | mögen verführt werden. | Nach dem Exempel eines Ehrwürdigen | Kirchen-Raths von | Amster-dam | in Holland. | Und um, vor dem Allmachtigen Gott-tragender Pflicht | und Schuldigkeit halben, geschrieben von mir, | Joh : Ph : Böhm, | Hochteutschen Reform : Prediger, der mir anver-trauten Gemein- | den in Pensylvanien. | *Zu Philadelphia : Gedruckt bey A : Bradford.* 1742. | Sm. 8vo. pp. iv, 96.   754

THE | CHARTERS | of the | Province of Pensilvania | and | City of Philadelphia. | [*Penn Arms.*] | *Philadelphia:* | *Printed and Sold by B. Franklin.* | MDCCXLII. | Folio, pp. 30.   H. S. P.   755

Printed to accompany the Collection of Laws published the same year.

CHEW. (S.) The | Speech | of | Samuel Chew, Esq; | Chief Justice of the Government of New- | Castle, Kent and Sussex upon | Delaware : | Delivered from the Bench to the | Grand-Jury of the County of | New-Castle, Aug. 20. 1742; and now pub- | lished at their Request. | *Philadelphia:* | *Printed and Sold by B. Franklin,* | M,DCC,XLII. | 8vo. pp. 16.   H. S. P.   756

A | COLLECTION | of all the | Laws | Of the Province of | Pennsylvania : | Now in Force. | Published by Order of Assembly. | [*Penn Arms.*] | *Philadelphia:* | *Printed and Sold by B. Franklin,* | M,DCC,XLII. | Folio, pp. 562.   H. S. P.   757

Edited by John Kinsey, who added an appendix which has the following title An | Appendix ; | Containing a | Summary | of such | Acts of Assembly | As have been formerly in Force | within this Province, | For Regulating of Descents, | And Transfering the Property of | Lands, &c. | But since expired, altered or repealed. | [*Penn Arms.*] | *Philadelphia:* | *Printed by B. Franklin.* M,DCC,XLII. | Folio, pp. iv. 24; Table, pp. xi.   H. S. P.

A | COMPENDIOUS Extract | Containing | The Chiefest Articles of Doctrine | and most remarkable Transactions | of | Count Lewis of Zinzendorff | And the | Moravians. | Together with the most natural Objec- | tions of some of their Antagonists. | Collected from the German. | Intended for a Summary of that Contro- | versy, which at present is a matter of Universal | Speculation, in this Part of America. | . . . | *Philadelphia: Printed and Sold by A. Bradford. at* | *the Sign of the Bible in Front-street.* | 12mo. pp. (2). 35.   F.   758

DIE | CONFUSION von Tulpehocken. | [*Philadelphia: B. Franklin.* 1742.] Sq. 8vo. pp. 8.   H. S. P.   759

EDWARDS. (J.) The Distinguishing Mark of a Work of the Spirit of God. Applied to that uncommon Operation that has lately appeared on the Minds of many of the People of this Land : With a particular Consideration of the Extraordinary Circumstances with which this Work is attended. A Discourse delivered at New-Haven, September 10th, 1741, being the Day after the Commencement ; and now published at the Earnest Desire of many Ministers and other Gentlemen that heard it ; with great Enlargement. By Jonathan Edwards, A.M. Pastor of the Church of Christ at Northampton. With a Preface by the Rev. Mr. Cooper, of Boston. *Boston: Printed. Philadelphia: Re-printed and sold by Benjamin Franklin, in Market-Street.* 1742. 8vo. pp. xvi. 84.   760

AN EXAMINATION and Refutation of Mr. Gilbert Tennent's Remarks on the Protestation presented to the Synod of Philadelphia, June 1, 1741. And the said Protest set in its True Light, and justified. By some Members of the Synod. *Philadelphia: B. Franklin.* 1742.   761

[GRUBER. (Johannes Adam)] Liebes=Echo Einiger Verſammel=
ten Seelen, die geruffen ſind und die kommen wollen, auf die gehörte
Warnungs= und Wächterſtimme des Geringen. *Philadelphia:*? 1742.

Title from Seidensticker's Bibliography.

[GRUBER.] Ein Zeugniß eines Betrübten, der ſeine Klage aus=
ſchüttet über die unzeitige, eigenmächtige, übereilte Zuſammen=Berufung
und Sammlung verſchiedener Partheyen und erweckten Seelen, ſo unter
dem Namen Immanuels vorgegeben wird. *Germantown: Christoph
Saur,* 1742.   763

Title from Fresenius' Nachrichten, Vol. III., p. 314.

HILDEBRAND. (J.) Zeugniß der Bruderſchaft in Zion. Von
den wichtigſten Punkten des Chriſtenthums und von dem Bekehrungswerk
der Herrnhutiſchen Gemeinde, nebſt einem ſchriftgemäßen Zeugniß von der
himmliſchen und fleiſchlichen Geburt. Durch Johannes Hildebrand.
Germantown: Christoph Saur, 1742.   764

Title from Seidensticker's Bibliography. Probably intended for No. 827, *infra.*

HIRTENLIEDER von Bethlehem, enthaltend eine kleine Sammlung
evangeliſcher Lieder zum Gebrauch vor Alles was arm iſt, was klein und
gering iſt. *Germantown: Christoph Saur.* 1742. 12mo. pp. 95.

DER | HOCH=DEUTSCH | Americaniſche | Calender, | Auf das
Jahr | Nach der Gnadenreichen Geburth unſers | Herrn und Heylandes
Jeſu Chriſti | 1743; | ... | ... | ... | ... | ... | ... | ... | ... |
.... | Zum fünften mal heraus gegeben. | *Germantown: Gedruckt und
zu finden bey Christoph Saur:* | .... | [1742.] | Sm. 4to. pp. (24).

JERMAN. (J.) The American | Almanack | For the Year of
Christian Account | 1743, | Being the Third after Bissextile or
Leap-Year. | ... | ... | ... | ... | ... | ... | ... | ... |
... | .... | By John Jerman, Philomath. | ... | ... | ... | ...
| ... | .... | *Philadelphia:* | *Printed and Sold by W. Bradford,
at the Sign* | *of the Bible in Second-Street.* [1742.] | Sm. 8vo. pp.
(24).   H. S. P.   767

LEEDS. (T.) The American Almanac for 1743. By Titan
Leeds. *Philadelphia: Andrew Bradford.* 1742.   768

A LETTER from a Gentleman in Philadelphia to | his Friend in the Country. | Philadelphia, Sept. 18. 1742. | [*Philadelphia: B. Franklin.* 1742.] Folio, pp. 2.   H. S. P.   769

In regard to the tenure of office of the Trustees of the General Loan-Office.

LETZTE | Privat-Erklârung | fûr | Pennsylvania, | ûber | Jemands Bericht, | Der sich nicht nur | ûber eine unter seinem Namen, ohne sein Wissen und | Willen, und noch dazu unganz gedruckte | Schrift | beschweret; | Sondern auch | ûber die Gemeine des Herrn | das Urtheil spricht. | *Philadelphia,* | *Gedruckt bey Benjamin Franklin,* MDCCXLII. | Sm. 4to. pp. 12. H. S. P. 770

A MESSAGE | To the Governor from the Assembly. | (In answer to the Governor's Message of the 18th Instant) | [*Philadelphia: B. Franklin.* 1742.] Folio, pp. 4.   H. S. P.   771

Dated "27th of the 3d Mo, 1742," and "Signed by Order of the House, John Kinsey, Speaker." Relates to a quarrel between the Governor and Assembly about the power to appoint a "Doctor to visit unhealthy vessels."

A SHORT | NARRATIVE | of the | Extraordinary Work | at | Cambuslang in Scotland, | In a Letter to a Friend. | With Proper | Attestations, | By Ministers and Others. | *Philadelphia: Printed and Sold by Wil-* | *liam Bradford, at the Sign of the* | *Bible in Second-Street.* 1742. | Sm. 8vo. pp. 36; "Books Sold by William Bradford" pp. (3).   H. S. P.   772

NEISSER. (G.) Aufrichtige | Nachricht | ans | Publicum, | ûber eine | Von dem Hollândischen Pfarrer Joh. Phil. Bôhmen | bei Mr. Andr. Bradford edirte | Lâsterschrift | Gegen | Die so genannten Herrnhuter, | Das ist, | Die Evangelischen Brûder aus Bôhmen, Mâhren. u. f. f. | Welche | Jetzo in den Forks von Delaware wohnen. | Herausgegeben von | Georg Neisser, aus Sehlen in Mâhren, | Schulmeister zu Bethlehem. | Cum Approbatione Superiorum. | *Philadelphia,* | *Gedrukkt und zu haben bei B. Franklin.* MDCCXLII. | Sq. 8vo. pp. 18.   H. S. P.   773

Reprinted in Fresenius' Nachrichten, Vol. III., p. 677. It is there said : "Diese Schrift hat der der Herr Graf von Zinzendorf unter Neissers Namen selbst verfasset."

NEW JERSEY. Anno Regni | Georgii II. | Regis | Magnæ Britanniæ, Franciæ, & Hiberniæ, | Decimo Quinto. | At a General Assembly of the Province | of New-Jersey, begun and holden at Perth-Amboy, the Second Day of October, Anno Domini 1741, | in the Fifteenth Year of the Reign of our Sovereign | Lord George II. by the Grace of God, of Great | Britain, France, and Ireland, King, Defender of the | Faith, &c. | [*Royal Arms.*] *Philadelphia:* | *Printed and Sold by B. Franklin, Printer to* | *the King's Most Excellent Majesty for the Province* | *of New-Jersey:* M,DCC,XLII. | Folio, Title, 1 leaf; pp. 1–17.   774

[NEW-YEAR Verses of the Carriers of the American Weekly Mercury. *Philadelphia: Andrew Bradford.* 1742.] Narrow Folio, 1 leaf.   H. S. P.   775

Headed with the cut of Mercury used in the newspaper, and beginning, "How different are the Lives of Men at Home, | And those that over Lands and Oceans Roam?" |

THE PENNSYLVANIA Gazette. *Philadelphia: Printed by B. Franklin, at the New Printing-* | *Office, near the Market,* | 776

Numbers 682 (Jan. 6, 1741, 2) to 733 (Dec. 30, 1742), four pages each, except Numbers 703 and 716 which contain eight pages. Title, and the imprint of the first four numbers, as in Number 648, *supra.* Imprint after Number 685, as above. Number 683 is misnumbered 684. There is a "Postscript" of two pages to Number 730. With Number 686 the sheet was enlarged and a third column added.

POOR Robin's Almanac for 1743. *Philadelphia: William Bradford.* 1742.   777

PROCLAMATION. By the Honourable | George Thomas, Esq ; | . . . | . . . | A Proclamation. | [*Philadelphia: B. Franklin.* 1742.] Folio, 1 leaf.   H. S. P.   778

Dated Oct. 5, 1742. Against the settlers on land in Lancaster County west of the Blue Mountains.

A PROTESTATION of the Members of the Protestant Lutheran and Reformed Religion . . . about the bad Commotion which happened [at Tulpehocken] on Sunday the 18th of July 1742. *Philadelphia: Andrew Bradford.*? 1742.   779

Title from "Die Confusion von Tulpehocken," which was issued in reply to the above.

SAUNDERS. (R.)   A Pocket | Almanack | For the Year 1743. | Fitted to the Use of Penn- | sylvania, and the neigh- | bouring Provinces. | By R. Saunders, Phil. | *Philadelphia:* | *Printed by B. Franklin.*   [1742.] | 32mo. pp. (16).   c.   780

Title in red and black.

SAUNDERS.   Poor Richard, 1743. | An | Almanack | For the Year of Christ | 1743, | Being the Third after Leap Year. | . . . | . . . | . . . | . . . | . . . | . . . | . . . | . . . | . . . | . . . | . . . | . . . | . . . | . . . | . . . | . . . | . . . . | By Richard Saunders, Philom. | *Philadelphia:* | *Printed and sold by B. Franklin, at the New* | *Printing-Office near the Market.* | [1742.] | Sm. 8vo. pp. (24).

A SERMON on the Resurrection of our Lord.   Preached on Easter-Sunday, from John xi. 25.   *Philadelphia: Andrew Bradford.*   1742.   782

SMITH'S | Animadversions | upon, and | Refutations | Of sundry | Gross Errors, Mistakes and Blunders, | Contained in a certain Pamphlet handed about in this | Government, in the form of a | Sermon or Speech. | . . . | . . . | . . . | . . . | . . . | . . . | . . . | . . . | . . . | . . . . | *Philadelphia: Printed [by Andrew Bradford] for, and Sold by the Au-* | *thor, at Duck-Creek.   Sold also at the Bible in Front-* | *street.   And at several other Places.*   1742. | 16mo. pp. 29.   H. S. P.   783

SPIRITUAL Songs: Or Songs of Praise, with Penitential Cries to Almighty God, upon Several Occasions.   Together with the Song of Songs, which is Solomon's: First turn'd, then paraphras'd in English Verse.   With an Addition of a sacred Poem on Dives and Lazarus.   The Fourteenth Edition.   *London Printed.   Philadelphia: Reprinted and Sold by Isaiah Warner.*   1742.   784

TAYLOR. (J.)   Pensilvania, 1743. | An | Almanack, | or | Ephemeris | Of the | Daily Motions of the Sun and Moon, | The Time of their | Rising and Setting, Lunations, and Eclipses; |

With the | Places and Aspects of the Planets, | For the Year |
1743. | Being from the . . . | Creation of the World 5747 | Landing
of Julius Cæsar in England 1797 | Royal Grant of Pensilvania 63 |
By Jacob Taylor. | . . . | . . . | . . . | . . . | . . . | . . . | . . . |
. . . . | *Philadelphia : | Printed and Sold by Isaiah Warner, almost op-
posite | to Charles Brockden's, in Chesnut-Street.* [1742.] | Sm. 8vo.
pp. (32). H. S. P. 785

TENNENT. (J.) Essay on the Pleurisy. By John Tennent.
Philadelphia : B. Franklin. 1742. 786

Advertised in the Pa. Gazette, September 9, 1742.

THOMSON. (J.) The Government of the Church of Christ,
and the Authority of Church Judicatories established on a Scripture Foundation, and the Spirit of rash judging arraigned and
condemned ; or the Matter of Difference between the Synod of
Philadelphia and the Protesting Brethren justly and fairly stated.
Being an Examination of two Papers brought in by two of the
Protesting Brethren, and read publickly in open Synod in May
1740 : And also an apology brought in, subscribed by the Protesting Brethren, and read also in open Synod in May 1739. By John
Thomson, Minister of the Gospel. *Philadelphia : B. Franklin.*
1742. 787

TO | The Free-Holders | Of the Province of Pennsylvania. |
[*Philadelphia: William Bradford.* 1742.] Folio, pp. 4. H. S. P.

An election address in favor of returning Assemblymen who would take measures for the defence of the Province.

WATTS. (I.) Hymns and Spiritual Songs. By Isaac Watts.
Philadelphia : B. Franklin. 1742. 789

No. (1.) | THE | WEEKLY Advertiser, | or | Pennsylvania. |
Thursday December 2. 1742. | *Philadelphia: Printed and Sold
by William Bradford, at the | Sign of the Bible in Second Street,
where all Persons may be supplied | with this Paper, Price 10 s a Year.
And where Advertisements are taken in.* | Sm. Folio, pp. (4). H. S. P.

Numbers 1 to 4 (Tuesday, Dec. 28, 1742). In No. 3 the title was changed to "The Pennsylvania Journal," as in No. 844, *infra*. See Wallace's "Life of Colonel William Bradford."

WHITEFIELD. (G.) The Marriage of Cana. | A | Sermon | preached at | Black-Heath | and | Philadelphia. | By George Whitefield, A. B. | Late of Pembroke College, Oxford. | *Philadelphia: Printed and Sold by W.* | *Bradford, jun. in Second-Street,* 1742. | Sm. 8vo. pp. 40.   H. S. P.   791

THE YEARLY | Verses | Of the Printer's Lad, | who carrieth a- | bout the Pennsyl- | vania Gazette, | to the Customers | thereof. | Jan. 1, 1741. [1741–2.] | [*Philadelphia: B. Franklin.* 1742.] Narrow folio, 1 leaf.   H. S. P.   792

[ZINZENDORFF. (Nikolaus Ludwig von)] Allen teutſchen Eltern . . . welche ihre Kinder . . . beſorgt ſähen . . . . [*Germantown: Christoph Saur.* 1742.] Sm. 4to. 1 leaf.   H. S. P.   793

Reprinted in Fresenius' Nachrichten, Vol. III., p. 740.

[ZINZENDORFF.] B. Ludewigs | Wahrer | Bericht | De dato Germantown den 20sten Febr. 174½. | An seine liebe Teutsche, | Und | Wem es sonst nützlich zu wissen ist, | Wegen Sein und seiner Brüder | Zusammenhanges | Mit Pennsylvania, | Zu Prüfung der Zeit und Umstände ausgefertiget; | Nebst einem P. S. de dato Philadelphia den 5ten Martii; | Und einigen | Unsre Lehre überhaupt und dieses, Schriftgen insonderheit | Erläuternden Beylagen. | *Philadelphia,* | *Gedruckt bey Benjamin Franklin.* [1742.] | Sq. 8vo. pp. 26.   H. S. P.   794

See Büdengische Sammlung, Vol. III., p. 188.

ZINZENDORFF. Diejenigen | Anmerkungen, | Welche | Der Herr Autor des Kurzen Extracts, &c. | Von | Dem Herrn v. Thurnstein, d. z. Pastore der | Evangel. Luth. Gemeine Jesu Christi | Zu Philadelphia. | In der Vorrede seiner Schrift freundlich begehret hat. | . . . | . . . | . . . . | *Philadelphia:* | *Gedrukkt und zu finden bei Isaias Warner.* | MDCCXLII. | Sm. 4to. pp. 24.

See No. 799, *infra*, for a translation.

[ZINZENDORFF.]   Ludovici a Thûrenstein | in antiqvissima fratrum ecclesia | Ad *taxin kai euschemosynen* | diaconi constituti, | et h. t. | ecclesiæ, qvæ Christo Philadelphiæ | inter Lutheranos colligitur, | Pastoris, | Ad Cogitatus Ingenuos | Pium Desiderium, | h. e. | Epistola | ad | Bonos Pensilvaniæ Cives | Christo non Inimicos, | ob | Conversationis difficultatem taliter qvaliter | Latino Idiomate conscripta, | Et dexteritati cordati interpretis, duce providentia | pie concredita. | *Philadelphiæ, Ex Officina Frankliniana.* [1742.] | Sq. 8vo. pp. 8.   H. S. P.   796

[ZINZENDORFF.]   Etliche | Zu dieser Zeit nicht unnûtze | Fragen | ûber Einige | Schrift-Stellen, | Welche. | Von den Liebhabern der lautern Wahrheit | Deutlich erôrtert zu werden gewûnschet hat | Ein | Wahrheit-forschender in America, | im jahr 1742 : | So deutlich und einfâltig erôrtert als es ihm môglich gewesen ist; und | in folgender klaren und bequemen Form herausgegeben | Von einem | Knecht Jesu Christi. | *Philadelphia,* | *Gedruckt und zu haben bey B. Franklin.* [1742.] | Sq. 8vo. pp. 14.   H. S. P.   797

Reprinted in Fresenius' Nachrichten Vol. III., p. 329.

ZINZENDORFF.   A Pamphlet criticising some of his actions.

The Pa. Gazette for Aug. 26, 1742, contains a long advertisement beginning "The Reverend Lewis of Thurnstein, since his Return from his second Journey to the Indians, has seen a pamphlet without a Name, wherein is contained a story stiled *Species facti.*" The charges contained in the pamphlet are taken up and answered in twelve paragraphs. There seems to have been considerable bitterness of feeling between the Presbyterians and Moravians of the time about the use of "the House on Arch-Street."

[ZINZENDORFF.]   The | Remarks, | which | The Author of the | Compendious Extract, &c. | In the Preface to his Book | Has friendly desired of | The Rev. of Thurenstein, | For the Time Pastor of the Lutheran Congregation | of J. C. in Philadelphia. | . . . | . . . | . . . | . . . . | *Philadelphia:* | *Printed and Sold by B. Franklin.* | M,DCC,XLII. | Sm. 8vo. Title, 1 leaf; Preface, pp. 3–4; Remarks, pp. 5–22; Advertisement, pp. 23–4.   H. S. P.   799

1743.

THE AMERICAN Weekly Mercury. *Philadelphia: Printed and Sold by the Widow Bradford, | at the Sign of the Bible in Front-street, where Advertisements are taken in, and | all Persons in Town or Country may be supplied with this Paper. |*   800

Numbers 1200 (from Tuesday, Dec. 28 to Tuesday, Jan. 4, 1742-3) to 1251 (from Dec. 21 to Dec. 29, 1743), four pages each. There is a "Postscript" of two pages to Number 1214. Title as in Number 689, *supra*. The imprint was changed in Number 1208 to the form given in Number 859, *infra*. After Number 1201 the day of the week is omitted.

ANNO Regni Georgii II. Decimo quarto. Acts of Assembly. *Philadelphia: B. Franklin.* 1743.?   801

The Assembly, in February, 1742-3, enacted six Laws, which may not have been printed otherwise than in the "Laws of the Province," published by Franklin, Number 754, *supra*.

BALL. (W.) The New Jersey Almanac for 1744. By William Ball. *Philadelphia: Isaiah Warner and Cornelia Bradford.* 1742.   802

BECHTEL. (JOHANNES) En kort Catechismus för några Jesu Församlingar, utaf den Reformerta Religionen uti Pennsylvanien som hålla sig til det Berniska Synodo. Först utgifvenidet Tyska Spåket af Johanne Bechtel. *Philadelphia, hos B. Franklin, aohr* 1743. 12mo.? pp. 40.   803

See Acrelius' History of New Sweden, Memoirs of the Historical Society of Pennsylvania, Vol. XI., pp. 330-1. The translation was made by Olaf Mylander, who was then employed in Franklin's office. There is said to be a copy in the Royal Library at Stockholm.

BIBLIA, | Das ist: | Die | Heilige Schrift | Altes und Neues | Testaments, | Nach der Deutschen Uebersetzung | D. Martin Luthers, | Mit jedes Capitels kurtzen Summarien, auch | beygefügten vielen und richtigen Parllelen; | Nebst einem Anhang | Des dritten und vierten Buchs Esrä und des | dritten Buchs der Maccabäer. | *Germantown:* | *Gedruckt bey Christoph Saur,* 1743. | 4to.   H. S. P.   804

Collation : Title, 1 leaf ; Vorrede and Verzeichnisz aller Bücher des Alten und Neuen Testaments, pp. (2) ; text, pp, 1–805 ; Apocrypha, pp. 806–949 ; Anhang, 949–995. New Testament Title and Verzeuchnisz der Bücher des Neuen Testaments, pp. (2) ; text, pp. 3–277 ; Register, pp. (3) ; Kurtzer Begriff, pp. (4). The first title is printed in red and black, and the second in black ink, the latter is as follows : Das Neue | Testament | Unsers | Herrn und Heylandes | Jesu Christi, | Verteutscht | Von | Dr. Martin Luther. | Mit | Jedes Capitels kurtzen | Sumarien, | Auch beygefügten vielen richtigen | Parallelen. | *Germantown :* | *Gedruckt und zu finden bey Christoph Saur,* 1743. | The Historical Society of Penna. has a copy in which the misprint in the 10th line is corrected, "Parallelen," and the 11th line is altered to "Nebst dem gewöhnlichen Anhang." The first Bible printed in America in a European language. See O'Callaghan's American Bibles, p. 22.

A | BILL | For the better Regulating the | Nightly Watch | Within the City of Philadelphia, and | for raising Money on the Inhabitants | of the said City, for defraying the | necessary Expences thereof. | *Philadelphia :* | *Printed by B. Franklin,* M,DCC,-XLIII. | Folio, pp. 11.   H. S. P.   805

BIRKETT. (W.) Poor Will's Almanac for 1744. By William Birkett. *Philadelphia : Isaiah Warner and Cornelia Bradford.* 1743.   806

BLAIR. (S.) A Persuasive to Repentance, in a Sermon preached by the Rev. Samuel Blair. *Philadelphia : William Bradford.* 1743.   807

BOUCHER. (M.) Boucher 1744. | The | Pennsylvania | Almanack, | For the Year of Christ, | 1744. | Being Leap Year. | Wherein is exhibited the daily Motions of the Sun, | Moon and other Planets, the daily rising and set- | ing of the Sun and Moon, the Lunations and | Eclipses, with the mutual Aspects and Judgment | of the Weather. Also a Tide Table fitted to the | Latitude of 40 deg. north, and a Meridian of five | Hours west from London. | By Matthew Boucher, Phil. | . . . | . . . | . . . | . . . | . . . | . . . . | [*Philadelphia :*] *Printed and Sold by W. Bradford at the Sign | of the Bible in Second-Street (at the Corner of Black | Horse Alley).* [1743.] | Sm. 8vo. pp. (20).   H. S. P.   808

DER NEUE CHARTER. | Oder | Schrifftliche Versicherung ; | Der | Freyheiten. | Welche William Penn, Esq : | Den Einwohnern von Penſylvannien und deſſen Territorien gegeben. | Aus dem Engliſchen Original überſetzt. | *Germantown Gedruckt bey Christoph Saur.* 1743. | Sm. 4to. pp. 55.   H. S. P.   809

Translated by Sower and given to the subscribers to his paper in parts of eight pages each.   Although begun in 1743, it was not finished till about July, 1744. It contains the Charter granted by Penn in 1701 ; the Royal Grant of the Province to Penn by Charles II ; The Frame of Government, 1682 ; The Laws agreed upon in England ; Conditions and Concessions agreed upon July 11, 1681 ; Act of Settlement, 1682 ; Extracts from the Charter of Philadelphia ; Abstract of the Poor Laws, and extracts from various Laws.   Number 627, *supra*, is probably intended for this pamphlet, and Number 860, *infra*, is only the last eight pages of it.

A CHOICE Collection of Hymns: With several new Translations from the Hymn-Book of the Moravian Brethren.   *Philadelphia: Isaiah Warner and Cornelia Bradford.*   1743.   810

A | CONFESSION | of | Faith, | Put forth by the | Elders and Brethren | Of many | Congregations | of | Christians | (Baptized upon Profession of their Faith) | In London and the Country. | Adopted by the Baptist Association | met at Philadelphia, Sept. 25, 1742 | The Sixth Edition. | To which are added, | Two Articles viz. Of Imposition of Hands, | and Singing of Psalms in Publick Worship. | Also | A Short Treatise of Church Discipline. | . . . | . . . | . . . . | *Philadelphia: Printed by B. Franklin.* | M,DCC,XLIII. | 16mo. pp. 112, (2) 62.   811

The "Treatise on Church Discipline," written by the Rev. Benjamin Griffith, has the following title : A Short | Treatise | of | Church-Discipline. | *Philadelphia:* | *Printed by B. Franklin,* 1743. | In it the paging is begun anew (pp. 1–62) but the signatures are in continuation of the "Confession."

A DECLARATION of the Presbyteries of New Brunswick and New Castle, judicially met together at Philadelphia, May 26th, 1743.   *Philadelphia: William Bradford.*   1743.   812

DICKINSON. (J.)   A Display of God's special Grace. | In | A familiar Dialogue. | Between | A Minister and a Gentleman of his | Congregation, | About | The Work of God ; in the Conviction and Con- | version of Sinners, so remarkably of late begun | and going on in these American Parts. | Wherein | The Objections against some uncommon Appearances | amongst us are distinctly consider'd, Mis- | takes rectify'd, and the Work itself | particularly prov'd to be from the Holy Spi- | rit. | With | An Addition, in a second Conference, rela- | ting to sundry Antinomian Principles, beginning | to obtain in some Places. | By the Rev'd Mr. Jonathan Dickinson, | Minister of the Gospel at Elizabeth Town in New- | Jersey. | *Philadelphia, Printed and Sold by Willi-* | *am Bradford at the Sign of the Bible* | *in Second-Street,* 1743. | Sm. 8vo. (2), x, 74. (1).

DUTTON. (A.)   A | Letter | from | Mrs. Anne Dutton, | to | The Reverend Mr. | Whitefield. | *Philadelphia, Printed and Sold by William* | *Bradford, at the Sign of the Bible in Second-Street.* [1743.] | Sm. 8vo. pp. 11.   L. C. P.   814

EIN EXTRACT von der Registratur, der Suprem Curt, mit dem Nahmen-Register der letzt hin Naturaliserten, und die Eyde mit dem Quacker Attest. *Philadelphia: Joseph Crellius.* 1743.

Advertised in Sower's Newspaper, Aug. 16, 1743.

EXTRACTS | From The | Minutes and Votes | Of the House of Assembly of | the Colony of New-Jersey ; met in | General Assembly at Burlington, on Satur- | day the 16th of October 1742.   Printed by | Benjamin Franklin, by Order of Andrew | Johnston, Esq ; their Speaker. | To which are added | Some Notes and Observations | Upon the said Votes. | Also the | Governor's Speech | To the Assembly on his Dissolving | of them ; and the Letters and Orders | mentioned and referred to in the Governor's | Speech. | [*Philadelphia :*] *Printed* [*by B. Franklin*] *in the Year* M,DCC,XLIII. | 4to. pp. 56.   L. C. P.   816

FALCONAR. (M.)   A Dialogue between Evangelist and Desperantius.   To which is prefix'd, an Hymn agreeable thereto. Also a Sea-Comparison Spiritualiz'd ; and an Hymn to the Author of the Wandering Spirit, upon his Writing a bitter Satyr against the Rev. Mr. Whitefield, added.   Likewise a spiteful Letter from Scotland and its Answer.   Collected and prefac'd, &c. by Magnus Falconar. *Philadelphia: Isaiah Warner.* 1743.   817

Advertised in the Pa. Gazette, Feb. 17, 1742-3.

FINLEY. (S.) Clear Light put out in obscure | Darkness. | Being an | Examination | and | Refutation | of | Mr. Thompson's Sermon, | Entituled, | The Doctrine of Convictions set | in a clear Light. | By Samuel Finley, | Minister of the Gospel. | . . . | . . . | . . . . | *Philadelphia:* | *Printed by B. Franklin.* 1743. | Sm. 8vo. pp. 71.   H. S. P.   818

FINLEY. Satan stripp'd of his Angelic Robe. | Being an Abridgment of | The Substance of | several | Sermons | Preached at | Philadelphia, January 1742-3. | From 2 Thess. ii. 11, 12. | Shewing the Strength, Nature and Symptoms | of Delusion. | With an Application to the | Moravians. | By Samuel Finley, Minister of the Gospel. | . . . | . . . | . . . | . . . . | *Philadelphia:* | *Printed by W. Bradford, at the Sign of the* | *Bible in Second-Street.* [1743.] | Sm. 8vo. pp. 30.   H. S. P.   819

FLAVEL. (J.) The Teachings of God, opened in their Nature and Necessity. By John Flavel, late Minister of Dartmouth, in Devon. *Philadelphia: William Bradford.* 1743.   820

FLEMMING. (R.) The Fullfilling of the Scriptures, Held Forth In a Discovery of the exact Accomplishment of the Word of God in his Works of Providence, Performed and to be Performed. By Robert Flemming. *Philadelphia.?* 1743.   821

Proposals for printing this work by subscription were advertised in the Pa. Journal for nearly three months.

[FRANKLIN. (Benjamin)] Proposal for Promoting Useful Knowledge among the British Plantations. *Philadelphia: B. Franklin.* 1743. Folio, 1 leaf. ?   822

EJNES GERJNGEN Bericht, was sich zwischen ihm und Herrn Ludwig [Graf Zinzendorff] und andern seiner Zugehörigen, in der Herrnhuter Sache in Jahr und Tag begeben, 1743, samt denen nöthigen Belegen. *Philadelphia:* 1743.   823

Title from Fresenius' Nachrichten, Vol. III., p, 262.

GUELDINS. (S.) Samuel Güldins | Gewesenen Predigers in den Drey | Haupt-Kirchen zu Bern in der Schweitz | Sein | Unpartheyisches

Zeugnüß | Ueber | Die | Neue Vereinigung | Aller | Religions-Par=
theyen | In Penn-Sylvanien. | Wie auch | Von andern nöthigen P u n c-
t e n | Wie die Vorrede und Register | ausweisen. | . . . | . . . . | I Theil.
Gedruckt bey Christoph Saur in Germantown. 1743. | 16mo. pp.
127, (1).   824

Professor Seidensticker includes in his bibliography as a separate work a con-
densation of the titles to the last three parts, "Vom Balsam in Gilead," &c. This
work was an attack upon Zinzendorff's efforts to unite all the German sects in
Pennsylvania. It is divided into five parts. "Balsam in Gilead Auf die Wunden
und Schaeden Aller Religions-Secten und Partheyen in Penn-Sylvanien und in
der gantzen Christenheit. 2ter Theil," begins on page 33. "Von den Falschen
Propheten. Der 3te Theil," begins on page 57. "Von den Wahren Lehren.
und Dienern Christi, an seinem Evangelio. . . . . Der 4te Theil," begins on
page 89. The fifth part. "Wohlgemeynte Reflexionen. Ueber das Verhalten des
James Devanports" begins on page 105. The only known copy is in the collection of Samuel W. Pennypacker, Esq.

GUTHREY. (W.) A | Sermon, | preached | at | Finnick, |
In August, 1662, | By | Mr. William Guthrey, | Upon Matth.
xvi. 25. | . . . | . . . | . . . . | *Philadelphia:* | *Re-printed by B.*
Franklin. | M,DCC,XLIII. | Sm. 8vo. pp. 35.   825

[HANCOCK. (REV. JOHN)] The | Examiner, | or | Gilbert
against Tennent. | Containing a Confutation of the Rev. Mr.
Gilbert | Tennent, and his Adherents: Extracted chiefly from his
Own Writings, and formed upon his Own Plan | of comparing the
Moravian Principles, with the | Standard of Orthodoxy, in dis-
tinct Columns. | Together with some Strictures on the Preface to
the | Rev. Mr. Tennent's Five Sermons and Appendix lately |
published, and subscribed by Six Reverend Ministers | of Boston.
| The whole being an Essay towards answering three | important
Queries, viz. | 1. What is Truth in the present Religious Commo-
tions | in this Land? | 2. What is the shortest method of finding
the whole | Truth? | 3. Whether such as are given to Change,
ought not | in Conscience to make their publick Retractions, ac-
cording to St. Austin? | The whole Essay is submitted to the
Judgment of | Common Sense. | By Philalethes. | . . . | . . . |
. . . | . . . . | *Boston, Printed,* 1743. | *Philadelphia: Re-printed and*
sold by B. Franklin. [1743.] | Sm. 8vo. pp. 31.   826

[HILDEBRAND. (JOHANNES)] Mistisches | und | Kirchliches | Zeuchnüß | Der Brüderschaft | In | Zion, | Von den wichtigsten P u n c t e n des | Christenthums | Nebst einem Anhang | Darinnen dieselbe ihr unpartheyisches | Bedenken an Tag gibt von dem Bekehrungs= | Werck der sogenanten Herrenhutischen | Gemeine in Pennsylvanien, und | warum man ihnen keine Kir= | che zustehen könne. | *Germantown, Gedruckt und zu finden bey C. Saur*, 1743. | 16mo. Title, 1 leaf; pp. 44.

Reprinted in Fresenius' Nachrichten, Vol. III., pp. 410–474. It is there divided into three parts. The first, pp. 410–446, with the title as above ; the second, pp. 446–462, is called, ''Unpartheyisches Bedencken über das Bekehrungs-Werck der Herrnhutischen Gemeine in Pennsylvanien ;'' and the third, pp. 462–474, ''Ein kurtzer Bericht von Ursachen, warendie Gemeinschaft in Ephrata sich mit dem Grafen Zinzendorff und Seinen Leuten eingelassen.''

HILDEBRAND. Schrfftimässiges | Zeuchnüß | Von dem | Himmlischen und Jungfräulichen | Gebährungs=Werck, | Wie es an dem ersten Adam ist mit | Fleisch zugeschlossen, aber an dem zweyten | Adam bey seiner Creutzigung durch | einen Speer wiederum ge= | öffnet worden. | Entgegen gesetzt | Dem gantz ungegründeten Vorgeben | der Herrenhutischen Gemeine von ei= | nem heiligen Ehestand, daraus Sie | das Ebenbild Gottes aus= | zugebähren vorgaben. | Ans Licht gegeben durch | Johannes Hildebrand, | Einem Mitglied der Gemeine Jesu Christi | in Ephrata | Hausvätterlicher Seite. | [*Germantown: Christoph Saur.* 1743.] 16mo. pp. 20.　　　　　　　　　　　　　　　　　　828

THE HIGH-DUTCH Pennsylvania Journal. *Philadelphia: Joseph Crellius.* 1743.　　　　　　　　　　　　　　　829

Title from Thomas' History of Printing. In the Pa. Gazette, June 2, 1743, Crellius announces that he has begun to publish a ''Weekly Newspaper in the German Language.'' Sower in his Newspaper, June 16, 1743, makes some remarks on Crellius' advertisement, in which he says Crellius has printed several numbers in English type, and proposes to continue the paper in ''Holländischer Schrifft, bis er eine Hoch-Deutsche Schrifft bekomme.'' How long Crellius' paper was continued has not been ascertained, but in Sower's paper, Sept. 16, 1746, appeared an announcement of his intention of going to Holland.

DER | HOCH=DEUTSCH | Americanische | Calender, | Auf das Jahr | . . . | . . . | 1744; | (Welches ein Schalt=Jahr von 366 Tagen ist.) | . . . | . . . | . . . | . . . | . . . | . . . | . . . | . . . | . . . | . . . | Zum sechsten mal heraus gegeben. | *Germanton :* | *Gedruckt und zu finden bey Christoph Saur ;* | . . . . [1743.] | Sm. 4to. pp. (28). 830

The title is on the third page, the *recto* of the first leaf being occupied with a full page attempt at an allegorical picture cut in type metal.

HOCHMANN. (E. C.) Ernſt Chriſtoph Hochmanns | von Hoch= enau | Glaubens=Be= | kenntniß, | Geſchrieben aus ſeinem Anrede, | auff dem | Hoch=Gräfl. Lippiſch. Schloß | Detmold, | Samt | Einer an die Juden gehaltenen | Rede. | Auf gnädige Verordnung | Seiner Hoch=Gräfl. Excell. | Des Regierenden Herrn | Graffen zu der Lippe.im | Jahr 1702 gedruckt, und 1703 wieder | aufgelegt, und nun mit einer kurtzen | Vorrede begleithheit. | *Germantown | Gedruckt bey Christoph Sauer* 1743. | 24mo. pp. 24.   H. S. P.   831

THE | INTEREST | of | New-Jersey | Considered, | With re- gard to | Trade and Navigation, | By laying of | Duties, &c. | *Philadelphia: Printed and Sold by William Bradford, | at the Sign of the Bible in Second-Street.* [1743.] | Sq. 8vo. pp. 20.   H. S. P.

JERMAN. (J.) An Almanac for 1744. By John Jerman. *Philadelphia: Isaiah Warner and Cornelia Bradford.* 1743. 833

LEEDS. (T.) The American Almanac for 1744. By Titan Leeds. *Philadelphia: Isaiah Warner and Cornelia Bradford.* 1743.   834

LISCHY. (J.) Jacob Liſchys Reformirten Predigers Declaration ſeines Sinns an ſeine Reformirten Religions? Genoſſen in Penſilvanien. *Germantown: Christoph Saur.* ? 1743.   835

Reprinted in Fresenius' Nachrichten, Vol. III., pp. 731–739.

MATHER. (I.) Soul-Saving Gospel Truths. Deliver'd in sev- eral Sermons : Wherein is shew'd, I. The Unreasonableness of those Excuses which Men make for their Delaying to come to the Lord Jesus Christ for Salvation. II. That for Men to Despair of the Forgiveness of their Sins because they have been Great, is a great Evil. III. That every Man in the World is going into Eternity. By Increase Mather, ... *Philadelphia: Printed by B. Franklin.* 1743. 18mo. pp. 167.   836

MORRIS. (L.) The Speech of His Excellency Lewis Morris, Esq; Captain General and Commander in chief of the Province of New-Jersey, &c. to the Assembly of the said Province, on his Dissolving of them, the Twenty-fifth of Nov. 1742. *Philadelphia: B. Franklin.* 1743.   837

Advertised in the Pa. Gazette, March 31, 1743.

NEW JERSEY. Anno Regni | Georgii II | Regis | Magnæ Britanniæ, Franciæ, & Hiberniæ, | Decimo Septimo. | At a General Assembly of the Province of | New-Jersey, begun and holden at Perth- | Amboy, the Tenth Day of October, Anno Domini 1743. | in the Seventeenth Year of the Reign of our Sovereign | Lord George II. by the Grace of God, of Great | Britain, France, and Ireland, King, Defender of the | Faith, &c. | [*Royal Arms.*] | *Philadelphia:* | *Printed and Sold by B. Franklin, Printer to* | *the King's Most Excellent Majesty for the Province* | *of New-Jersey,* M,DCC,XLIII. | Folio, Title 1 leaf; pp. 21–66.   838

NEW-YEAR Verses of the Carriers of the American Weekly Mercury. *Philadelphia: Cornelia Bradford.* 1743.   839

NEW-YEAR Verses of the Carriers of the Pennsylvania Gazette. *Philadelphia: B. Franklin.* 1743.   840

THE NOTE-MAKER noted, and the | Observer observed upon; | Or, | A Full | Answer | To some | Notes and Observations | Upon the Votes of the House | of Assembly of the Colony of | New-Jersey; | Met in General Assembly at Burlington, on | Saturday the 16th of October 1742. | Being | A Vindication of the | present, and some former Governors, | Councils and Assemblies of the said | Colony, against the unreasonable Cavils | of the said Observer or Note-maker. | By a Lover of True English Liberty. | [*Philadelphia:*] *Printed* [*by B. Franklin.*] *in the Year* M,DCC,XLIII. | 4to. pp. 31.   L. C. P.   841

THE PAPIST'S Curses, or a Vindication of the Roman Catholicks, &c. *Philadelphia:?* 1743.   842

Advertised as "Just Published, and to be Sold by Andrew Farrel," in the Pa. Journal, Nov. 3, 1743.

THE PENNSYLVANIA Gazette.   843

Numbers 734 (Jan. 4, 1742–3) to 785 (Dec. 27, 1743), four pages each, except Number 768, which contains six pages. Title and imprint as in Number 716, *supra*, until the latter was changed, in Number 772, to the form given in Number 891, *infra*.

No. 5. | THE | PENNSYLVANIA Journal, | Or | Weekly Advertiser. | Tuesday January 4, 1742–3. | *Philadelphia: Printed and Sold by William Bradford, at the | Sign of the Bible in Second-street, where all Persons may be supplied | with this Paper, Price 10s. a Year. And where Advertisements are taken in.* | 844

Numbers 5 to 57 (Thursday, Dec. 29, 1743), four pages each, with "Post-scripts" of two pages each to Numbers 22, 42 and 43. In No. 42 the imprint was changed to the form given under No. 891, *infra*.

POOR Robin's Almanack, For the Meridian of the Female Sex, and the Year 1744. *Philadelphia: William Bradford.* 1743.

SAUNDERS. (R.) A Pocket | Almanack | For the Year 1744. | Fitted to the Use of Penn- | sylvania, and the neighbour- | ing Provinces. | With several useful Additions. | By R. Saunders, Phil. | *Philadelphia: Printed by B. Franklin.* [1743.] | 32mo. pp. (24).   c.   846

Title in red and black.

SAUNDERS. Poor Richard, 1744. | An | Almanack | For the Year of Christ | 1744. | It being Leap-Year. | . . . | . . . | . . . | . . . | . . . | . . . | . . . | . . . | . . . | . . . | . . . | . . . | . . . | . . . | . . . | . . . | . . . | . . . . | By Richard Saunders, Philom. | *Phila-delphia: | Printed and Sold by B. Franklin, . . .* | *also by Jonas Greene* . . . . [1743.] | Sm. 8vo. pp. (24).   H. S. P.   847

SHEPHERD. (T.) The Sincere Convert discovering the small Number of True Believers, by Thomas Shepherd. *Philadelphia: William Bradford.* 1743.   848

TAYLOR. (J.) Pensilvania, 1744. | An | Almanack, | or | Ephemeris. | Of the | Motions of the Sun and Moon, | The Time of their | Rising and Setting, Lunations, and Eclipses; | With the

| Places and Aspects of the Planets, | For the Year | 1744. | With some Astronomical Dissertations | at this Time thought highly necessary. | By Jacob Taylor. | . . . | . . . | . . . | . . . | . . . | . . . | . . . | . . . | . . . | . . . | . . . | . . . | . . . . | *Philadelphia:* | *Printed and Sold by I. Warner and C. Bradford, at* | *the Sign of the Bible in Front-Street.* [1743.] | Sm. 8vo. pp. (32). A. P. S.

TENNENT. (G.) The | Examiner, Examined, | or | Gilbert Tennent, | Harmonious. | In Answer to a Pamphlet entitled | The Examiner, | or | Gilbert against Tennent | Being a Vindication of the Rev. Gilbert | Tennent and his Associates, together with | six Rev. Ministers of Boston, from the unjust Re- | flections cast upon them by the Author of that Ano- | nymous Pamphlet, to- gether with some Remarks upon | the Querist's, the third Part, and other of their | Performances. | The Whole being an Essay to vindicate the late | Glorious Work of God's Power and Grace | in these Lands, from the unreasonable Cavils and | Exceptions of the said Pamphlet, and others of like | Nature. | The whole Essay is submitted to the Decision of | Truth and Common Sense. | By Gilbert Tennent, A. M. | . . . | . . . | . . . | . . . | . . . | . . . | . . . | . . . | . . . | . . . . | *Philadelphia: Printed and Sold by* *Willi-* | *am Bradford, at the Sign of the Bible* | *in Second-Street.* 1743. | Sm. 8vo. pp. 146; Errata, 1 leaf. H. S. P. 850

TO | The Free-Holders | Of the Province of Pennsylvania. | [*Philadelphia: William Bradford.* 1743. ?] Folio, pp. 4. 851

An election address. "If these unhappy Differences [about a Militia Law] subsist much longer . . . our excellent Constitution will soon be at an End."

THE | TREATY | Held with the | Indians | of the | Six Na- tions, | at | Philadelphia, | In July, 1742. | [*Arms of Penn.*] | *Phil- adelphia:* | *Printed and Sold by B. Franklin, at the New-Printing-* | *Office, near the Market.* M,DCC,XLIII. | Folio, pp. 25. H. S. P. 852

VOTES | and | Proceedings | of the | House of Representatives | of the | Province of Pennsylvania, | Met at Philadelphia, on the Fourteenth of October, | Anno Dom. 1742, and continued by Ad- journments. [to Aug. 13, 1743.] | [*Penn Arms.*] | *Philadelphia:* |

Printed and Sold by B. Franklin, at the New Printing- | *Office, near*
the Market.   M,DCC,XLIII. | Folio, pp. 73.   H. S. P.   853

[WEBBE. (John)]   A | Discourse | concerning | Paper Money,
| in which | Its Principles are laid open ; | And A Method, plain
and easy, for introducing and | continuing a Plenty, without les-
sening the present | value of it, | Is Demonstrated. | Humbly of-
fered to the Consideration of The Honourable Repre- | sentatives of
the Freemen of the Province of | Pensylvania. | Numb. I. | . . . |
. . . | . . . | . . . | . . . | . . . . | *Philadelphia: Printed for the*
Author, by W. Bradford.   [1743.] | Sq. 8vo. pp. 11.   H. S. P.   854

Advertised as ''Just Published'' in the Pa. Journal, Jan 4, 1742–3.   Probably
no more than one number was issued.

WHEREAS great Quantities of English Copper Half-pence,
have been | lately imported into this Province by the Merchants
who have paid them away. . . . at an advanced | Rate, and now
refuse to receive them back again, . . . | [19 lines.] And it is hum-
bly presum'd, that if our Assembly will order the English Cop-
per Half- | pence to be receiv'd in all Payments in the Loan
Office, at the rate of One Penny | each our currency it will effec-
tually remedy the Evil, . . . | . . . | . . . | . . . | . . . | . . . |
. . . . | Signed in Behalf of Thousands | By Dick Farmer. |
[*Philadelphia: William Bradford.*   1743.?]   4to. 1 leaf.   L. C. P.

𝔚𝔒𝔥𝔏𝔅𝔈𝔊ℜ𝔘𝔑𝔇𝔈𝔗𝔈𝔖 Bedenken vom Wege der Heiligung, wie
derselbe nicht allein in der Versöhnung mit Christo, sondern hauptsächlich
in seiner Nachfolge zu suchen.   *Germantown: Christoph Saur.*   1743.

Advertised in Sower's Newspaper, Sept. 16, 1743.

ZINZENDORFF. (N. L. von)   Every Man's Right to Live.
A Sermon on Ezek. xxxiii. 2. Why will ye die?   Preached at
Philadelphia. by the Rev. Lewis of Thurenstein, Deacon *kata*
Taxin kai' Euschemosyen, of the ancient Moravian Church.
Translated from German into English.   *Philadelphia: B. Frank-*
lin.   1743.   857

Advertised in the Pa. Gazette, May 12, 1743.

ZINZENDORFF. A Letter from Lewis Thurnstein, Deacon of the Moravian Church, to People of all Ranks and Persuasions, which are in Pennsylvania; but more especially to those who are not bigotted to any particular opinion. Translated from the Latin by Philip Reading, A.B. of University College, Oxford. To which will be added an Apology for the Translator. *Philadelphia.?* 1743.   858

Advertised in the Pa. Gazette, February 24, 1742–3, but perhaps not printed.

1744.

THE AMERICAN Weekly Mercury. *Philadelphia: Printed and Sold by Isaiah Warner and Cornelia | Bradford, at the Sign of the Bible, in Front-Street ; where Advertisements | are taken in, and all Persons in Town or Country may be supply'd with this Paper.* |

Numbers 1252 (from Dec. 29 to Jan. 4, 1743–4) to 1303 (from Dec. 20 to Dec. 28, 1744), four pages each. Title as in Number 689, *supra.* Number 1268 is misnumbered 1269. The imprint was changed in Number 1293 to the form given in Number 912, *infra.*

ANHANG oder Appendix zu dem Charter von Verordnungen. *Germanton: Christoph Saur.* 1744.   860

Title from Seidensticker's Bibliography. Probably the last eight pages of Number 809, *supra,* and not a separate publication.

ANNO Regni | Georgii II. | Regis | Magnæ Britanniæ, Franciæ, & Hiberniæ | Decimo Septimo. | At a General Assembly of the Province of | Pennsylvania, begun and holden at Philadelphia, | the Fourteenth Day of October, Anno Dom. | 1743, in the Seventeenth Year of the Reign of our So- | vereign Lord George II. by the Grace of God, | of Great-Britain, France, and Ireland, King, | Defender of the Faith, &c. | And from thence continued by Adjournments to | the Seventh of May, 1744. | [*Penn Arms.*] | *Philadelphia: | Printed and Sold by B. Franklin, at | the New-Printing-Office, near the Market.* | M,DCC,XLIV. | Folio, pp. 22. H. S. P.

BALL. (W.) The New Jersey Almanac for 1745. By William Ball. *Philadelphia: William Bradford.* 1744.   862

BIRKETT. (W.) Poor Will's Almanac for 1745. By William Birkett. *Philadelphia: Cornelia Bradford.* 1744.   863

BLAIR. (S.) A Short and Faithful | Narrative | Of the late Remarkable | Revival of Religion | In the Congregation of New-Londonderry, | and other Parts of Pennsylvania. | As the same was sent in a Letter to the | Rev. Mr. Prince of Boston. | By Samuel Blair, Minister of the Gospel at | New-Londonderry, in Pennsylvania. | . . . | . . . | . . . | . . . . | *Philadelphia: Printed and Sold by Willi- | am Bradford at the Sign of the Bible in Second-street.* [1744.] | Sm. 8vo. pp. 46.   H. S. P.   864

Advertised as "Just Published" in the Pa. Journal, Sept. 27, 1744.

BLAIR. A | Vindication | of | The Brethren who were un-justly and | illegally cast out of the Synod of Phila- | delphia, by a number of the Members, | From | maintaining Principles of Anarchy in | the Church, and denying the due scrip- | tural Authority of Church Judicatures: | Against | The Charges of the Rev. Mr. John | Thompson, in his Piece entituled, The | Government of the Church of Christ, &c. | By Samuel Blair, Minister of the Gospel of Christ at New-Londonderry in Pennsylvania. | *Philadelphia: | Printed by B. Franklin, for the Author.* | MDCCXLIV. | Sm. 8vo. pp. 63.   B. P. L.   865

BOUCHER. (M.) An Almanac for 1745. By Matthew Boucher. *Philadelphia: Cornelia Bradford.* 1744.   866

A CATALOGUE of choice and valuable Books, consisting of near 600 Volumes, on Divinity, History, Law, Physick, Mathematicks, &c., to be sold, for ready money only, by Benj. Franklin, . . beginning April 11, 1744. [*Philadelphia: B. Franklin.* 1744.] 16mo. pp. 16.   867

Distributed gratis. Brinley's copy sold for $60.

CICERO. (M[ARCUS] T[ULLIUS]) M. T. Cicero's | Cato Major, | or his | Discourse | of | Old-Age: | With Explanatory Notes. | *Philadelphia: | Printed and Sold by B. Franklin,* | MDCCXLIV. | 8vo. pp. viii. 159.   H. S. P.   868

Reprinted at London (the 2d ed. ?) 1750; Glasgow, (the 3d ed. ?) 1751 ; The Third Edition, Philadelphia, W. Dunlap, 1758 ; The Fourth Edition, Glasgow, R. Urie, 1758 ; London, Fielding and Walker, 1778; and Philadelphia : W. Duane, [1812. ?] The London edition of 1778 says " With explanatory Notes by Benjamin Franklin, LL. D." The last Philadelphia edition goes a step further and says "Translated, with explanatory Notes by Benjamin Franklin, was intended for insertion in Duane's edition of Franklin's works, but attention having been called to the name of the real translator and annotator it was omitted. The first edition is generally conceded to be the 'finest production of Franklin's press, and a really splendid specimen of the art.' The title page is rubricated." The translator and annotator was Chief Justice James Logan. In "The Printer to the Reader," Franklin incorrectly called it, "this first translation of a classic in this Western World." "Sandys' translation of Ovid" although printed in London, was made in Virginia some ninety years earlier, Keimer in 1729, published in Philadelphia, "Epictetus his Morals," and Franklin himself, in 1735, had printed Logan's translation of "Cato's Moral Distiches." It is (but not uncut) more frequently met with than other specimen of Franklin's press, but nevertheless generally commands a high price. Gilbert's (1873) was sold for $42.50 ; Brinley's for $30 ; Hoffman's for $66 ; Wight's for $73 ; Bruce's $90. Uncut copies are rare. Rice's (uncut?) sold for $155 ; Menzies for $168 ; and one of Brinley's for $260, and the other for $110.

COLMAN. (B.)   A Letter from the Reverend Dr. Colman of Boston, to the Reverend Mr. Williams of Lebanon, upon reading the Confession and Retractions of the Reverend Mr. James Davenport.   *Philadelphia: B. Franklin.*   1744.   869

COUNCIL with the Indians at Philadelphia, in August, 1744. *Philadelphia: B. Franklin.*   1744.   Folio, pp. 16.   L. C. P.   870

DAVENPORT. (J.)   A | Letter | From the Rev. Mr. James Davenport, to Mr. | Jonathan Barber Preacher of the Gospel at | Bethesda in Georgia: Published with the | free Consent of Mr. Davenport. | [*Philadelphia: Printed by William Bradford.*   1744.] Sm. 8vo. pp. 32.   L. C. P.   871

The copy in the Philadelphia Library has no title page, and the tract *may* have been published without one. It is advertised in the Pennsylvania Journal, Dec. 13, 1744, as "Just Published and to be sold by the Printer hereof." It contains several letters from Mr. Barber to Mr. Davenport.

A | DIALOGUE | between | Two Countrymen who met at Brunswick : | One an Inhabitant of Long Island, The Other a

Liver at Gloucester. | The Name of the first was Jonathan Plain, and the | other Obadiah Right. | [*Philadelphia : B. Franklin.* 1743.] 4to. pp. 8.   872

A DIALOGUE between two Gentlemen | in New-York (distinguish'd here by the | Names Josiah, and Sr. Simon) relating to | the publick Affairs of New-Jersey. | [*Philadelphia : W. Bradford.* 1744.] 4to. pp. 7.   L. C. P. 873

[DODSLEY. (ROBERT)] The Chronicles of the Kings of England, written in the Manner of the Ancient Jewish Historians. By Nathan Ben Saddi, A Priest of the Jews. *Philadelphia : B. Franklin.* 1744.   874

ENGELBRECHT. (H.) $\mathfrak{Hans}$ $\mathfrak{Engelbrechts}$ $\mathfrak{Göttliche}$ $\mathfrak{Offenbah}$=$\mathfrak{rungen}$ $\mathfrak{sammt}$ $\mathfrak{einer}$ $\mathfrak{Erzählung}$ $\mathfrak{seines}$ $\mathfrak{wunderbahren}$ $\mathfrak{Lebens}$. *Germantown : Christopher Saur.* 1744.   875

Title from Seidensticker's Bibliography.

ESTAUGH. (J.) A | Call | to the | Unfaithful Professors | of | Truth. | Written by | John Estaugh | In his Life-time ; and now Published | for General Service. | To which is added | Divers Epistles | Of the same Author. | *Philadelphia:* | *Printed by B. Franklin.* | M,DCC,XLIV. | 16mo. pp. 119.   H. S. P. 876

FISHER. (S.) Christ's | Light | Springing, | Arising up, | Shining forth, | And | Displaying it self | through the Whole World. | Being a Treatise wrote | By Samuel Fisher. | *London, Printed in the Year 1660.* | *Philadelphia: Reprinted by William* | *Bradford, at the Sign of the Bible in Se-* | *cond Street.* 1744. | Sm. 8vo. pp. 35.   H. S. P. 877

[FRANKLIN. (BENJAMIN)] An | Account | Of the New Invented | Pennsylvanian | Fire-Places : | Wherein | Their Construction and Manner of | Operation is particularly explained ; | Their Advantages above every other | Method of Warming Rooms de- | monstrated ; | And all Objections that have been raised against | the Use of Them, answered and obviated. | With Directions for putting them up, and for Using | them to the best Advantage. With a Copper-Plate, | in which several Parts of the Machine | are exactly laid down, from a Scale of equal Parts. | *Philadelphia:* | *Printed and Sold by B. Franklin.* 1744. | 8vo. pp. (2), 37, (1), 1 folded plate.   H. S. P. 878

[FUNCK. (Heinrich)] Ein | Spiegel | der | Tauffe | mit Geiſt, | mit | Waſſer | und mit | Blut. | Verfaſſet in neun Theil, | Aufs neue augsgeſetzt und ausgezogen aus dem | Heiligen Fundament-Buch, des | Neuen und Alten Teſtaments, der | Cononiſchen Bucher. | ... | ... | ... | [*Germantown :*] *Gedruckt im Jahr* 1744. | 16mo. pp. 94.

GILLESPIE. (G.) Remarks upon Mr. Geo. Whitefield, Proving him a Man under Delusion. By George Gillespy, Minister of the Gospel, in the County of New-Castle, in America. *Philadelphia: Printed [by B. Franklin?] for the Author, and sold by John Stevens, at the Harp & Crown, in Third Street, opposite the Work-House.* 1744.   880

DER | HOCH | DEUTSH | Americkaniſche | Calender, | Auf das Jahr | ... | ... 1745 ; | (Welches ein gemein Jahr von 365 Tagen iſt.) | ... | ... | ... | ... | ... | ... | ... | ... | ... | ... | .... | Zum ſiebenden mal heraus gegeben, | *Germantown : Gedruckt und zu finden bey Christopher Saur ; | Auch kœnnen die auswœrtige Krœmer solche bey David Tœschler, in Philadelphia haben.* [1744] | Sm. 4to pp. (32).

JERMAN. (J.) An Almanac for 1745. By John Jerman. *Philadelphia: Cornelia Bradford.* 1744.   882

JUST arrived from London, | For the Entertainment of the Curious and Others, | ... | ... | The Solar or Camera Obscura Microscope, | Invented by the Ingenious Dr. Liberkhun. [*Philadelphia: B. Franklin.* 1744.] Folio, 1 leaf.   A. P. S. 883

The exhibition also included a Musical Clock.

LEEDS. (T.) The American Almanac for 1745. By Titan Leeds. *Philadelphia: Cornelia Bradford.* 1744.   884

LUTHER. (M.) Der | kleine | Catechismus | D. Martin Luthers. | Mit Erläuterunger | herausgegeben | zum Gebrauch | der Lutheriſchen Gemeinen | in | Pennſylvanien | *Germantown* | *Gedruckt bei Christoph Saur.* | 1744. | 16mo. pp. 83.   H. S. P. 885

MORRIS. (L.) The | Speeches | Of His Excellency | Lewis Morris, Esq; | Governor of New-Jersey, &c. | To the House of Assembly of the said Province, | met in General Assembly at Burlington, on | the 22d of June, 1744. | With | The Assembly's Address and Message | to His Excellency. | To which is added | An Abstract of the Bill, entitled, An Act for | Settling and better Regulation of the Militia of | the Province of New-Jersey, and for making | Provision in Cases of Insurrection, Rebellion or | Invasion; as sent down from the Council to | the House of Assembly, upon the 30th of | June. | And | Some Observations from the | Votes of the Assembly. | *Philadelphia:* | *Printed by B. Franklin,* 1744. | 4to. pp. 36.   L. C. P.   886

THE | NATURE | and | Design | of | Christianity. | Extracted from a late Author. | *Philadelphia :* | *Printed by W. Bradford, in* | *the Year* MDCCXLIV. | 16mo. pp. 34.   H. S. P.   887

A German translation was published by C. Sower. It is advertised in his newspaper, Sept. 16, 1744, and is mentioned by Seidensticker as a "Tractätgen von der Geringshätzung . . . Lebens," etc.

THE | NEW-ENGLAND Psalter; | or, | Psalms of David. | With the | Proverbs of Solomon, | and | Christ's Sermon on the Mount. | Being a proper Introduction for the Train- | ing up Children in the Reading of the Holy | Scriptures. | [*Royal Arms.*] | *Philadelphia:* | *Printed and Sold by B. Franklin.* 1744. | 16mo. pp. (176).   H. S. P.   888

NEW-YEAR Verses of the Carriers of the American Weekly Mercury. *Philadelphia: Isaiah Warner and Cornelia Bradford.* 1744.   889

NEW-YEAR Verses of the Carriers of the Pennsylvania Gazette. *Philadelphia : B. Franklin.* 1744.   890

THE PENNSYLVANIA Gazette. *Philadelphia: Printed by B. Franklin, Post-Master, at the New-* | *Printing-Office, near the Market.* | 4to.   891

Numbers 786 (Jan. 3, 1743) to 837 (Dec. 25, 1744), four pages each, except Numbers 801 and 826, which contain six pages. Title as in Number 648, *supra*. Number 815 is misnumbered 814.

THE PENNSYLVANIA Journal.   *Philadelphia: Printed and Sold by William Bradford at the Sign | of the Bible, the Corner of Black Horse Alley in Second Street, where Persons | may be supply'd with this Paper at 10 s. a Year.   And where Advertisements are | Taken in. |*   H. S. P.   892

Numbers 58 (Tuesday, Jan. 3, 1743-4) to 109 (Dec. 29, 1744), four pages each, with "Postscripts" of two pages each to Numbers 61 and 85, and one of four pages to Number 72 ; and "Supplements" of two pages each to Numbers 93, 98 and 100.   Title as in Number 844, *supra*.

POOR Robin's Almanac for 1745.   *Philadelphia: William Bradford.   1744.*   893

PROCLAMATION. [*Penn Arms.*]   By the Honourable | George Thomas, Esq ; | . . . | . . . | A Proclamation. | [*Philadelphia: B. Franklin.   1744.*]   Folio, 1 leaf.   H. S. P.   894

Dated June 11, 1744.   Announcing the Declaration of War with France, enjoining the inhabitants of Pennsylvania to provide themselves with arms, &c., &c.

PSALTERSPIEL. Das Kleine | Davidische | Psalterspiel | Der | Kinder Zions, | Von | Alten und Neuen auserlesenen | Geistes | Gesängen ; | Allen wahren Heyls=begieri= | gen Säuglingender Weisheit, | Insonderheit aber | Denen Gemeinden des Herrn, zum | Dienst und Gebrauch mit Fleiß zusammen | getragen, | Und in gegenwärtig=beliebiger Form | und Ordnung, | Nebst einem doppelten darzu nützlichen und der | M a t e r i e n halben nöthigen | Register, | aus Licht gegeben. | *Germantown Gedruckt bey Christoph Saur.   1744.* | 24mo.   H. S. P.   895

Collation : Title, 1 leaf ; Vorrede, pp. (4); text, pp. 1-530 ; Register, pp. (15); Errata, 1 page.

[RICHARDSON. (SAMUEL)]   Pamela : or Virtue Rewarded. In a Series of Familiar Letters from a beautiful young Damsel, to her Parents.   *Philadelphia: B. Franklin.   1744.*   896

Advertised in the Pa. Gazette, Oct. 11, 1744.

SAUNDERS. (R.) A Pocket | Almanack | For the Year 1745. | Fitted to the Use of Penn- | sylvania, and the neighbour- | ing Provinces. | With several useful Additions. | By R. Saunders, Phil. | *Philadelphia:* | *Printed by B. Franklin.* [1744.] | 32mo. pp. (24). c. 897

Title in black only.

SAUNDERS. Poor Richard, 1745. An Almanac for 1745. By Richard Saunders. *Philadelphia: B. Franklin.* 1744. 898

SMITH. (J.) Curiosities of Common Water, or the Advantages thereof in preventing and curing many distempers. Gathered from the Writings of several Eminent Physicians, and also from more than Forty Years Experience. By John Smith. To which is added, some Rules for preserving Health by Diet. *Philadelphia: William Bradford.* 1744. 899

Advertised in the Pa. Journal, April 26, 1744, as "to be publish'd by subscription." Benjamin Lay, who was probably the author of the Rules for preserving Health, was the projector of this edition which may not have been printed.

TAYLOR. (J.) Pennsylvania, 1745. | An | Almanack, | and | Ephemeris | of the | Motions of the Sun and Moon, | The true Places, and Aspects of the | Planets. | The Rising and Setting of the Sun. | The Rising, Setting, and Southing of the | Moon. | For the Year | 1745. | With some Dissertations on the Abuses | of Astronomy. | By Jacob Taylor. | . . . | . . . | . . . | . . . | . . . | . . . | . . . | . . . . | *Philadelphia:* | *Printed and Sold by William Bradford at the Sign* | *of the Bible in Second-street.* [1744.] | Sm. 8vo. pp. 32. L. C. P. 900

TENNENT. (G.) Love to Christ a necessary Qualification | in Order to feed his Sheep. | A | Sermon | Preach'd at Neshaminie, December 14. 1743. | Before the Ordination | Of the Reverend | Mr. Charles Beatty. | By Gilbert Tennent, A.M. | Published at the Desire of the People of the | Place aforesaid. | . . . | . . . | . . . . | *Philadelphia: Printed by William Brad-* | *ford, at the Sign of the Bible in Second Street.* | 1744. | 16mo. pp. 37, (1). H. S. P.

TENNENT.   The Necessity of Studying to be Quiet and Doing our own Business. A Sermon preach'd at Philadelphia, September 30th, 1744, on I Thessalonians vi. ii. with some enlargement.   By G. Tennent, A. M., Minister of the Gospel in Philadelphia. *Philadelphia: William Bradford.*   1744.   902

TENNENT.   The Necessity of Thankfulness for Wonders of divine Mercies. | A | Sermon | Preached at Philadelphia April 15th 1744. | On Occasion of the important and glorious Victory | obtain'd by the British Arms in the Mediterranean, | under the Conduct of | Admiral Matthews, | Over the united Fleets of | France and Spain, | And likewise the frustrating a detestable Attempt | to invade | England, | by a | Popish Pretender. | By Gilbert Tennent, A.M. | Published at the Desire of the Hearers. | . . . . | *Philadelphia: Printed by William Bradford, | at the Sign of the Bible in Second-Street.*   1744. | 4to. pp. 16.   H. S. P.   903

TENNENT.   Twenty-Three | Sermons | upon the | Chief End of Man. | The | Divine Authority of the sacred | Scriptures, | The | Being and Attributes of God, | and the | Doctrine of the Trinity. | Preach'd at Philadelphia, Anno Dom. 1743. | By Gilbert Tennent, A. M. | . . . | . . . | . . . | . . . | . . . | . . . | . . . . | *Philadelphia: Printed and Sold by William | Bradford, at the Sign of the Bible in Second Street.* | MDCCXLIV. | Sq. 8vo.   H. S. P.

Collation : Title, 1 leaf; Preface, pp. (4); Contents, pp. (3); Sermons, pp. 3–465.

[TERSTEEGEN. (GERHARD)] Der Frommen Lotterie, oder Geist=liches Schatz=Kästlein.   *Germantown: Christoph Saur.*   1744.

" It consists of 381 tickets, printed on stiff, white paste-board, 2¼ inches in size, and numbered like lottery tickets, each containing a poetic gem composed by the celebrated Gerhard Tersteegen, and a verse or passage from the Scriptures. These tickets were enclosed in neat cases, some made of leather, and others of wood nicely dove-tailed.   The good people in olden time enjoyed themselves, generally on Sunday afternoons, by drawing prizes out of this sacred or spiritual treasury, and often when they felt gloomy or despondent they would resort to it in the hope of drawing some promise or consolation to cheer their drooping spir-its."—*A. H. Cassel in the Official Record of the Montgomery County Centennial Celebration.*

TRACTÄTGEN von der Geringschätzung und Nichtigkeit unseres na-türlichen und zeitlichen Lebens und wie wichtig und nothwendig es ist, das man sich zu der unendlichen Glückseligkeit und ewigem Leben zubereiten lasse in der wahren Wiedergeburt. (Aus dem Englischen übersetzt.) *Germantown : Christoph Saur.* 1744.   906

     Title from Seidensticker's Bibliography. See No. 887, *supra* (Nature & Design).

A | TREATY | Held at the Town of | Lancaster, in Pennsylvania, | By the Honourable the | Lieutenant-Governor of the Province, | And the Honourable the | Commissioners for the Provinces | of | Virginia and Maryland, | with the | Indians | of the | Six Nations, | In June, 1744. | *Philadelphia: | Printed and Sold by B. Franklin, at the New-Printing-Office, | near the Market.* M,DCC,XLIV. | Folio, pp. 39.   907

VERSCHIEDENE alte und neuere Geschichten von Erscheinungen der Geister, und etwas von dem Zustande der Seelen nach dem Tode. Nebst verschiedenen Gesichtern solcher die auch jetzo noch am Leben sind. *Germanton: bey Christoph Saur,* 1744.   12mo.   908

     Title from Seidensticker's Bibliography.

THE VERSES of the Printer's Boy that | carries about the Pennsylvania Jour- | nal, 1743–4. | [*Philadelphia: W. Bradford.* 1744.]   Narrow Folio, 1 leaf.   H. S. P.   909

VOTES | and | Proceedings | of the | House of Representatives | of the | Province of Pennsylvania, | Met at Philadelphia, on the Fourteenth of October, | Anno Dom. 1743, and continued by Adjournments. [to Aug. 11, 1744.] | [*Penn Arms.*] | *Philadelphia: | Printed and Sold by B. Franklin, at the New Printing- | Office near the Market.* M,DCC,XLIV. | Folio, pp. 54.   H. S. P.   910

WATTS. (I[SAAC])   A Preservative from the Sins and Follies of Childhood and Youth, written by way of Question and Answer. To which are added some Religious and Moral Instructions, in Verse. By I. Watts, D. D. The Fourth Edition. *Philadelphia: B. Franklin.* 1744.   911

1745.

THE AMERICAN Weekly Mercury. *Philadelphia: Printed and Sold by Cornelia Bradford, at the | Sign of the Bible, in Front-Street; where Advertisements are taken in, and | all Persons in Town or Country may be supply'd with this Paper. |*   912

Numbers 1304 (from Dec. 28 to Jan. 1, 1744, 5) to 1355 (from Dec. 17 to Dec. 24, 1745), four pages each, except 1317, which contains six pages. Title as in Number 688, *supra.* There is a "Postscript" of two pages to Number 1344.

[ARMSTRONG. (JOHN)] The | Art | of preserving | Health : | A | Poem. | [Cut.] *London, Printed: | Philadelphia, Re-printed, and Sold by | B. Franklin.* M.DCC.XLV. | 4to. pp. 88.   H. S. P.

BALL. (W.) The New Jersey Almanac for 1746. By William Ball. *Philadelphia: William Bradford.* 1745.   914

BEISSEL. (C.) Myſtiche Abhandlung über Die Schöpfung und von des Menſchen Fall Und Wiederbrinung durch des Weibes Saa= men. *Ephrata: Druckt der Bruederschaft im Jahr* 1745. Sm. 4to. pp. 92+.   915

Author and date of publication on the authority of Mr. Abraham H. Cassel.

[BIESSEL.] Urſtändliche und Erfahrungs=volle | Hohe | Zeuguüſſe | Wie man zum | Geiſtlichen Leben | Und deſſen Vollkommenheit, | ge= langen möge. | Welche | Ein Hoch=Erleuchteter und Gott=Ergebener Zeuge Jesu Christi, In | Seinem Geiſtlichen Tage=Werck erlernet; Und die= ſelbe, bey unterſchie= | denen Umſtänden, an Seine Geiſtliche Kinder, und Anverwandte, eröffnet ; | Von Denſelben aber | Um Jhrer Vortrefflich= keit willen, geſammlet, und, zum Unterricht Anderer, | ans Licht gegeben. | *Ephrata, in Pensylvanien, Drucks der Bruederschafft,* 1745. | 4to. pp. (8), 294.   H. S. P. 916

The same work as is next described but with a new title and preface ; and a new second title at p. 59, as follows : Mystiche | Und | Erfahrungs-volle | Episteln, | In sich enthaltend, | Wie man zum | Geistlichen Leben | Und | dessen Vollkommenheit, | gelangen möge. | Page 283 has been reprinted, and the 68th to the 73d Epistle, pp. 284–294, added.

[BEISSEL] Zionitischen Stiffts I. Theil. | Oder eine | Wolrich= ende Narde, | Die nach einer langen Nacht in der herrlichen Mor= gen=Röthe ist auf gegan= | gen auf dem Gefielde Libanons, und hat un= ter den Kindern der | Weißheit einen Balsamischen Geruch von sich gege= ben. | Des von Gott hoch begnadigten und beadelten fürtrefflichen | Theo- logi der Mystichen Gottes=Gelärtheit. | Irenici | Theodicai. | Als welcher durch die Stimme des Bräutigams die Gesandschaft des aller= | reinsten Geistes der Himlischen Sophia empfangen zur Offenbarung | der Paradisischen Jungfrauschaft: und ist gesalbet worden zum | Priester- lichen Amt der Verföhrung in seiner Ihme von | Gott anvertrauten Ge= meine. | Bestehend in einer Sammlung geistlicher Gemüts=Bewegun= | gen und Erfahrungs=voller Theosophischer Sendschreiben, | welche von Demselben | An seine vertraute Freunde und geistliche Kinder sind gestellet, und nun um ihrer Vor= | trefflichkeit willen den Kindern der Weißheit zu einem geistlichen | Unterricht gesammlet, und ans Licht gegeben worden. | *Ephrata in Pensyvanien Drucks und Verlags der Bruederschaft.* 1745. | Sq. 8vo. pp. (16), 283.   **917**

The preceding work as first issued. The general title, preface and second title at p. 59, were suppressed and burned by order of Beissel, on account of their being written by Israel Eckerlin. See note to Number 925, *infra* and also Chron- icon Ephratense, p. 156. The second title begins: Die Wiederdarstellung | Der reinen Paradisischen Menschheit, oder des Jungfräulichen | Ebenbildes Gottes, welches in Adams Schlaf ist verblichen, und | in Christi Leiden und Sterben wieder aufwerckt worden. | vorgestellt | In einer Sammlung geistlicher und | Theosophischer | Episteln. | [18 lines.]

BERJCHTE oder Sammlnng wichtiger Nachrichten aus dem Natur= und Kirchenreich. *Germantown: Christoph Saur.* 1745.   **918**

Title from Seidensticker's Bibliography.

[BERKELEY. (George)]   An abstract from Dr. Berkeley's Treatise on Tar-Water, with some Reflections thereon, adapted to Diseases frequent in America. By a Physician. *Philadelphia:?* 1745.   **919**

Mr. Thompson Westcott, in the Historical Magazine, 1860, p. 75, quotes this title from an advertisement in the Pa. Gazette, March 26, 1744–5, adding "Frank- lin, printer." The advertisement begins "To be sold by B. Franklin," and I think refers to the New York edition.

𝕰𝕴𝕹𝕰 𝕭𝕰𝕾𝕮𝕳𝕽𝕰𝕵𝕭𝖀𝕹𝕲 ber wahren Kirche, was unb wo ſie lag.
Germantown: Christopher Saur.   1745.   920

Title from Seidensticker's Bibliography.

BIRKETT. (W.)   Poor Will's Almanac for 1746.   By William
Birkett.   *Philadelphia: Cornelia Bradford.*   1745.   921

[CADWALADER. (Thomas)]   An | Essay | On the West-
India | Dry-Gripes ; | with the | Method of Preventing and
Curing | that | Cruel Distemper. | To which is added, | An Extra-
ordinary Case in Physick. | *Philadelphia :* | *Printed and sold by B.*
Franklin. | M.DCC.XLV. | 8vo.   H. S. P.   922

Collation : Title, 1 leaf ; Preface, pp. iii.–v. ; text, pp. 1–42.   The copy in the
Library of the College of Physicians has inserted a suppressed "Preface," which
is paged iii.–vi., and begins "It was neither Thirst after Gain, nor the Desire of
Applause, but the Welfare of Mankind alone, which excited me to publish this
Essay."   The published Preface is entirely re-written and in much better taste.
The same Institution possesses the original manuscript.

CATALOGUE of Books to be sold at Auction.   *Philadelphia :*
B. Franklin.?   1745.   923

Advertised in the Pa. Gazette, March 5, 1744–5, "given gratis."   The collection consisted of over 600 volumes.   A supplement was advertised as "just published," in the paper for March 19th.

THE | CONFESSION of Faith, | The Larger and Shorter |
Catechisms, | with the | Scripture Proofs at Large. | Together with
| The Sum of Saving Knowledge (contain'd in | the Holy Scrip-
tures, and held forth in the said Con- | fession and Catechisms) and
Practical Use there- | of; Covenants National and Solemn | League
Acknowledgement of Sins and | Engagement to Duties, Directories,
| Form of Church Government, &c. | Of Publick-Authority in the
| Church of Scotland. | With | Acts of Assembly and Parliament,
rela- | tive to, and approbative of the same. | . . . | . . . | . . . |
. . . | . . . . | *Philadelphia :* | *Printed and Sold by B. Franklin.*
| M.DCC.XLV. | 16mo.   H. S. P.   924

Collation : Title and Contents, pp. (2) ; To the Christian Reader, pp. 3–13 ; An
Ordinance, &c. pp. 14–20 ; Confession of Faith, Title and Contents, pp. (2) ; text,

pp. 23–164 ; Larger Catechism, Title and Act, pp. (2) ; text, pp. 167–366 ; Shorter Catechism, Title and Act, pp. (2) ; text, pp. 369–410 ; The Sum of Saving Knowledge, Title and Contents, pp. (2) ; text, pp. 413–446 ; National Covenant, Title, 1 leaf ; text, pp. 449–462 ; The Solemn League and Covenant, Title, 1 leaf ; text, pp. 465–470 ; Acknowledgment of Sins, Title and Act, pp. (2) ; text, 473–482 ; The Directory for Publick Worship, Title, 1 page ; text, pp. 484–521 ; Form of Church Government, Title, 1 leaf ; text, &c. pp. 525–557 ; Directory for Family Worship, Title, 1 page ; text, &c. pp. 560–567 ; Table, pp. (24). The several title pages, in order noted in the collation, are as follows :

The | Confession of Faith, | Agreed upon by the | Assembly of Divines | at | Westminster, | With the Assistance of | Commissioners | from the | Church of Scotland, | as | A Part of the Covenanted Uniformity in Religion be- | twixt the Churches of Christ in the Kingdoms of | Scotland, England, and Ireland. | Approved by the General Ass embly 16 4 7, and Ratifiedand Established by Act of Parliament 1649, as the | Publick and Avowed Confession of the | Church of Scotland. | With the Scripture-Proofs at large. | *Philadelphia* : | *Printed and Sold by B. Franklin.* | M,DCC,XLV. | —The | Larger Catechism, | Agreed upon by the | Assembly of Divines | at Westminster, | With the Assistance of | Commissioners | from the | Church of Scotland, | as | A Part of the Covenanted Uniform-ity in Religion | betwixt the Churches of Christ in the Kingdoms | of Scotland, England and Ireland. | And | Approved Anno 1648, by the General Assembly | of the Church of Scotland, to be a Direc- | tory for the Catechising such as have made some Pro- | ficiency in the Knowledge of the Grounds of Re- | ligion. | With the Proofs from Scripture. | *Philadelphia* : | *Printed by B. Franklin, in Market-Street,* | M,DCC,XLV. | —The | Shorter Catechism, | . . . | . . . | . . . | . . . | . . . | . . . | . . . | . . . | . . . | . . . | . . . | . . . . | And | Approved Anno 1648, by the General Assem- | bly of the Church of Scotland, to be a Di- | rectory for Catechising such as are of weaker Ca- | pacity. | . . . . | *Philadelphia:* | *Printed by B. Franklin,* M,DCC,XLV. | —The | Sum | of | Saving Knowledge ; | Or, a brief Sum of | Christian Doctrine, | Contained in the | Holy Scriptures, | And holden forth in the foresaid | Confession of Faith and Catechisms : | Together with | The Practical Use thereof. | . . . | . . . | . . . . | *Philadelphia* : | *Printed by B. Franklin,* M,DCC,XLV. | —The | Confession of Faith | of the | Kirk of Scotland ; | Or, the | National Covenant. | With | A Designation of such Acts of Parliament, as | are expedient for Justifying the Union af- | ter-mentioned. | . . . | . . . | . . . | . . . | . . . | . . . | . . . | . . . | . . . | . . . . | *Philadelphia* : | *Printed by B. Franklin,* M,DCC,XLV. | —The | Solemn League | and | Covenant | for | Reformation and Defence of Reli- | gion, the Honour and Happiness of | the King, and the Peace and Safety of | the Three Kingdoms of Scotland, Eng- | land, and Ireland. | Taken and Sub-scribed several Times by King | Charles II. and by all Ranks in the said | Three Kingdoms. | With | An Act of the General Assembly, 1643, and an Act | of Parliament 1644, Ratifying and Approving the | said League and Covenant. | . . . | . . . | . . . | . . . | . . . | . . . | . . . | . . . . | *Philadelphia* : | *Printed by B. Franklin,* M,DCC,XLV. | —A | Solemn Acknowledgment | of | Publick Sins, | and | Breaches of the Covenant ; | and a | SolemnEngagement | To all the | Duties contained therein, | Namely, | Those, which do in a more special Way relate |

unto the Dangers of these Times. | Together with | The Act of the Commission of the General | Assembly 1648, and Act of Parliament in 1649, | for Renewing the League and Covenant. | *Philadelphia :* | *Printed by B. Franklin,* M, DCC, XLV. | —The | Directory | for the | Publick Worship of God, | Agreed upon by the | Assembly of Divines | at | Westminster, | . . . | . . . | . . . | . . . | . . . | . . . | . . . | . . . . | With | An Act of the General Assembly, and Act of Parlia- | ment, both in Anno 1645, Approving and Establish- | ing the said Directory. | . . . | . . . . | *Philadelphia :* | *Printed by B. Franklin,* M, DCCXLV. | —The | Form | Of Presbyterial | Church-Government, | and of | Ordination of Ministers ; | Agreed upon by the | Assembly of Divines | at | Westminster, | . . . | . . . | . . . | . . . | . . . | . . . | . . . . | With | An Act of the General Assembly, Anno 1645, Approv- | ing the same. | . . . | . . . | . . . | . . . | . . . . | *Philadelphia :* | *Printed by B. Franklin,* M, DCC, XLV. | —The | Directory | for | Family-Worship, | Approved by the | General Assembly | of the | Church of Scotland, | for | Piety and Uniformity in Secret and | Private Worship, and mutual Edi- | fication. | With | An Act of the General Assembly, Anno 1647, | for Observing the same. | *Philadelphia :* | *Printed by B. Franklin,* M, DCC, XLV. |

[ECKERLIN. (ISRAEL)]   Part of an Anti-Moravian tract. *Ephrata :* 1745.   925

The Chronicon Ephratense, p. 129, says : "A book against the Moravians, written by one of the Ephrata brethren by order of the 'Vorsteher' Conrad Beissel, with an appendix by the brother Prior (Israel Eckerlin), and an essay by Johannes Hildebrand showing marriage to have been the cause of man's fall, was printed in English as well as in German, by Eckerlin's order, soon after the arrival of the press at Ephrata. When Eckerlin, not long afterwards, withdrew from the 'brotherhood,' both editions of this book, as well as others in which he was concerned, were burned."

ECKERLIN.   Die Regul und Richt-schnur eines Streiters Jesu Christi.   Von Israel Eckerlin.   *Ephrata :*   1745.   926

Burned by order of Beissel, as above.

ECKERLIN.   Der Wandel eines Einsamen.   Von Israel Eckerlin.   *Ephrata :*   1745.   927

Burned by order of Beissel, after Eckerlin's withdrawal from the Ephrata community. See Chronicon Ephratense, p. 156.

DIE | ERNSTHAFFTE | Christen= | Pflicht, | Darinnen | Schöne Geiſtreiche | Gebetter, | Darmit | Sich fromme Chri= | ſten=Hertzen zu allen | Zeiten und in allen | Nöhten tröſten | können. | Nebſt einem Anhang | Einer | Aus dem blutigen Schau= | Spiel überſetzter Geſchich=

| te zweyer=Blut= | zeugen der | Wahrheit, Hans von Ober= | dam u. Valerius des | Schulmeisters. | *Gedruckt in Ephrata* | *im Jahr* 1745. | 24mo. pp. 166.   H. S. P.   928

ERSKINE. (E. AND R.) A Collection of Sermons, preach'd some by the Rev. Ebenezer Erskine, M.A. Minister of the Gospel at Sterling; and others by the Rev. Ralph Erskine, M.A. Minister of the Gospel at Dumferling, and Author of the Gospel-Sonnets: With a Preface by the Rev. Thomas Bradbury. *Philadelphia: B. Franklin.* 1745.   929

FREJMUTHJGE und unpartheyische Gedanken von der Religion, Kirche und Glückseligkeit der Englischen Nation unter der gegenwärtigen Regierung. Zu anderer christl. Völker nützlichem Gebrauch, Warnung und Vorsicht. (Aus dem Englischen übersetzt.) *Germantown bey Christoph Saur.* 1745.   930

THE FRIENDLY Instructor: Or, a Companion for Young Ladies and Young Gentlemen. In which their duty to God, and their Parents, their Carriage to Superiors and Inferiors, and several other very useful and instructive Lessons are recommended, in Plain and Familiar Dialogues. With a Recommendatory Preface, by the Rev. Dr. Doddridge. *London Printed: Philadelphia Re-printed and Sold by B. Franklin, in Market-Street.* 1745.   931

GUELDENE | Aepffel | Jn | Silbern Schalen | Oder: | Schöne und nützliche | Worte und Wahrheiten | Zur Gottseligkeit. | Enthalten | Jn Sieben Haupt=Theilen, | die in diesem Buch zusam̃en gestellet sind; | Mit sonderbarem Fleiß von denen in der vorigen | Edition häufig einge= schlichenen | Druckfehlern gereiniget. | Nebst angehänten Vorreden, | und einem Zweyfachen . . . ster. | *Efrata, Im Jahre des Heils* 1745, *verlegt durch etliche Mitglieder der Mennonisten-Gemeine.* | 16mo. pp. 519, (14).   932

DER | HOCH=DEUTSH | Americanische | Calender, | Auf das Jahr | . . . | . . . | 1746; | . . . | . . . | . . . | . . . | . . . | . . . | . . . | . . . | . . . | . . . . | Zum achten mal heraus gegeben. | *Germantown: Gedruckt und zu finden bey Christoph Saur;* | . . . . | [1745] | Sm. 4to. pp. (22).   H. S. P.   933

JERMAN. (J.) The American | Almanack, | For the Year of Christian Account | 1746 ; | Being the Second after Leap-Year. | Wherein is contained, | The Lunations, Eclipses, Planets-Mo- | tions and Aspects, Judgments of the Weather, | the Time of the Sun's and Moon's Rising and | Setting, Seven Stars Rising, Southing and Setting, | High-Water, Spring-Tides, Fairs, Courts, Meet- | ings, and other observable Days. | Fitted to the Latitude of Forty Degrees | North, and a Meridian of Five Hours West from | London, but may without much Error serve | from New-foundland to South-Carolina. | By John Jerman, Philomath. | . . . | . . . | . . . | . . . . | *Philadelphia:* | *Printed and Sold by Cornelia Bradford, at the* | *Sign of the Bible in Front-street.* [1745.] | Sm. 8vo. pp. 20.   H. S. P.   934

LEEDS. (T.) The American Almanac for 1746. By Titan Leeds. *Philadelphia: Cornelia Bradford.* 1745.   935

A | MODEST Vindication | of the late | New-Jersey Assembly, | In | Answer | To a printed Paper against them, | Call'd A | Representation. | [*Philadelphia:*] *Printed [by W. Bradford] in the Year* MDCCXLV. | 4to. pp. 32.   H. S. P.   936

MORE. (T.) An Almanac for 1746. By Thomas More. *Philadelphia: B. Franklin.* 1745.   937

DAS NEUE | Testament | Unsers | Herrn und Heylandes | Jesu Christi, | Verteutscht | Von | D. Martin Luther. | Mit | Jedes Capitels kurtzen | Sumarien, | Auch beygefügten vielen richtigen | Parallelen. | *Germantown :* | *Gedruckt und zu finden bey Christoph Saur,* 1745. | 16mo. pp. (4), 592, (4).   H. S. P.   938

See O'Callaghan's List of American Bibles.

NEW-YEAR Verses of the Carriers of the American Weekly Mercury. *Philadelphia: Cornelia Bradford.* 1745.   939

NEW-YEAR Verses of the Carriers of the Pennsylvania Ga-zette. *Philadelphia: B. Franklin.* 1745.   940

NEW-YEAR Verses of the Carriers of the Pennsylvania Journal. *Philadelphia: William Bradford.* 1745.   941

A PAPER concerning some Disturbances in Christ Church. *Philadelphia:* 1745.   942

An answer to the above was published in the Weekly Mercury, April 4, 1745.

THE PENNSYLVANIA Gazette.   943

Numbers 838 (Jan. 1, 1745) to 890 (Dec. 31, 1745), four pages each, except Numbers 849, 854, 859, 860, 861, 876, 878 and 882, which contain six pages, and 862, which contains eight pages. There are "Supplements" of two pages each to Numbers 841, 851 and 868, and one of 1 leaf to 867. Title and imprint as in Number 891, *supra.*

THE PENNSYLVANIA Journal.   H. S. P.   944

Numbers 110 (Jan. 1, 1744) to 162 (Dec. 31, 1745) four pages, with "Postscripts" of two pages each to Numbers 113, 126, 132, 134, 143, 150 and 151; "Advertisement," of two pages to Number 144, and "Supplement" of two pages each to Numbers 148 and 154. Title as in Number 844, *supra;* imprint as in Number 892, *supra,* to Number 133, when it was changed to the form given in Number 944, *infra.*

POOR Robin's Almanac for 1746. *Philadelphia: William Bradford.* 1745.   945

ROWE. (E.) Devout Exercises of the Heart in Meditation and Prayer and Praise. By Mrs. Elizabeth Rowe. *Philadelphia: B. Franklin.* 1745.?   946

SAUNDERS. (R.) A Pocket | Almanac | For the Year 1746. | Fitted to the Use of Penn- | sylvania, and the neighbour- | ing Provinces. | With several useful Additions. | By R. Saunders, Phil. | *Philadelphia:* | *Printed by B. Franklin.* [1745.] | 32mo. pp. (24).   c.   947

SAUNDERS. Poor Richard, 1746. | An | Almanack | For the Year of Christ | 1746, | It being the Second after | Leap-Year. | [as in 1738.] *Philadelphia:* | *Printed and Sold by B. Franklin.* [1745.] | 12mo. pp. (24).   L. C. P.   948

TAYLOR. (J.) Pensilvania, 1746. | An | Almanack | or | Ephemeris | Of the | Motions of the Sun and Moon . . . Pla- | ces and Aspects of the Planets, the Rising and | Setting of the Sun: The Rising, Southing and Sett- | ing of the Moon: For the Year | 1746. | . . . | . . . | . . . | . . . | . . . | . . . | . . . | . . . . | With the Origin, Progress and Character of Soothsayers, | Sorcerers, Astrologers, Fortune-tellers, and Wizards.   Col- | lected from the most illustrious Authors of the present | Century, and the last preceeding. | By Jacob Taylor. | . . . | . . . | . . . | . . . | . . . | . . . . | *Philadelphia: Printed and sold by William | Bradford at the* *Sign of the Bible in 2d Street.*   [1745.] | Sm. 8vo. pp. (32).   949

Jacob Taylor was a school teacher in 1701, and Surveyor General of Pennsylvania from Nov. 20, 1706 to Aug. 22, 1733, when he resigned. He died in Chester Co., March 2, 1745-6.

TENNENT. (G.)   All Things come alike to All : | A | Sermon, | On Eccles. ix, 1, 2 and 3 Verses. | Occasioned by a Person's being struck by the | Lightning of Thunder. | Preached at Philadelphia, July the | 28th, 1745. | By Gilbert Tennent, A. M. | Minister of the Gospel in Philadelphia. | . . . | . . . | . . . | . . . | . . . . | *Philadelphia : | Printed by William Bradford at the | Bible* *in Second-Street.*   1745. | Sm. 8vo. pp. 40.   H. S. P.   950

TENNENT.   The Danger of Spiritual Pride represented. | A | Sermon | preach'd at | Philadelphia, | December the 30th, 1744. | On Romans XII. 3. | With some Enlargements. | By Gilbert Tennent, A. M. | Minister of the Gospel at Philadelphia. | . . . | . . . | . . . | . . . . | *Philadelphia: Printed by William | Bradford,* *at the Sign of the Bible in Second-Street.*   [1745.] | Sm. 8vo. pp. 30 ; Corrigenda, 4 lines.   H. S. P.   951

Printed with the "Necessity of keeping the Soul ; " the signatures run A to G through the two.

TENNENT.   Discourses, | on several | Important Subjects. | By Gilbert Tennent, A. M. | Minister of the Gospel in Philadelphia. | *Philadelphia : | Printed by W. Bradford at the | Bible in* *Second-street.*   MDCCXLV. | Sm. 8vo.   952

Collation : Title, 1 leaf; Contents, pp. (2) ; Sermons, pp. 1–358 ; Corrigenda, 1 leaf. Contains six sermons, which have the three following title pages :

THE NATURE of Justification opened : | A | Sermon. | Preach'd at | Phila-delphia, | January the 27th, 1744–5. | On Galations II. 16. | With Enlargements. | By Gilbert Tennent, A. M. | Minister of the Gospel in Philadelphia. | Publish'd at the Desire of the Hearers. | . . . | . . . | . . . | . . . | . . . | . . . | . . . | . . . . . . | . . . | . . . . | *Philadelphia : Printed by W. Bradford, at* | *the Bible in Second Street,* 1745. | pp. 95.

VINDICÆ LEGIS : | or, the | Law established by Faith. | Three | Sermons, | preach'd at | Philadelphia, | February the 24th, and March the 10th, | 1744–5. | On Romans III. 31. | By Gilbert Tennent, A. M. | Minister of the Gospel in Phila-delphia. | . . . | . . . | . . . | . . . | . . . | . . . . | *Philadelphia . Printed by W. Brad-ford, at* | *the Bible in Second Street,* 1745. | Title, 1 leaf , pp. 99–246.

VINDICÆ OPERUM : | or, the | Necessity of Good Works Vindicated. | Two | Sermons, | On Phil. ii. 12, 13. | Preach'd at | Philadelphia, | March 24th, 1744–5. | By Gilbert Tennent, A. M. | Minister of the Gospel in Philadelphia. | . . . | . . . | . . . | . . . | . . . | . . . | . . . | . . . . | *Philadelphia : Printed by W. Bradford, at* | *the Bible in Second Street,* 1745. | Title, 1 leaf; pp. 299–358.

TENNENT. A Funeral | Sermon | Occasion'd by the | Death | Of the Reverend | Mr. John Rowland, | Who departed this Life | April the 12th, 1745. | Preach'd at Charles-Town, in Chester | County, April the 14th, 1745. | By Gilbert Tennent, A. M. U. D. M. | . . . | . . . . | *Philadelphia : | Printed by William Bradford at | the Bible in Second-Street,* M,DCCXLV. | Sm. 8vo. pp. 72. H. S. P.

To this work, with a separate title-page but with a continuous paging, is added "A | Narrative | of the | Revival and Progress | of | Religion | in the | Towns of Hopewell, Amwell and Maiden- | Head, in New-Jersey, and New-Providence | in Pennsylvania. In a Letter to the | Rev. Mr. Prince, Author of the Christian | History. | By the Rev. Mr. John Rowland. | Being the last Work of that faithful Servant | of Jesus Christ, which he compos'd a little | before his Decease, and is now publish'd for the | Benefit and Consolation of God's People. | By Thomas Bourne. | . . . | . . . | . . . | . . . | . . . | . . . . | *Philadelphia : | Printed by William Bradford at the | Bible in Second-Street.* M,DCCXLV. | pp. [49]–72.

TENNENT. The Necessity of praising God for Mercies | receiv'd. | A | Sermon | occasion'd | By the Success of the late Ex-pedition, (un- | der the Direction and Command of Gen. | Pepperel and Com. Warren,) | in reducing the City and Fortresses of | Louis-burgh, on Cape-Breton, | To the Obedience of His Majesty, King | George the Second. | Preach'd at Philadelphia July 7, 1745. |

By Gilbert Tennent, A.M. | Minister of the Gospel in Philadel-phia. | . . . | . . . | . . . . | *Philadelphia: Printed and Sold by Will-iam* | *Bradford at the Bible in Second Street.* [1745.] | Sm. 8vo. pp. (2), 40.   H. S. P.   954

TENNENT.   The Necessity of keeping the Soul. | A | Sermon | preach'd at | Philadelphia, | December the 23d, 1744. | On Deu-teronomy iv. 9. | By Gilbert Tennent, A.M. | Minister of the Gospel at Philadelphia. | . . . | . . . | . . . | . . . . | *Philadelphia: Printed by William* | *Bradford, at the Sign of the Bible in Second-Street.* | [1745.]   Sm. 8vo. pp. 24.   H. S. P.   955

TILLOTSON. (J.)   The Usefulness of Consideration in order to | Repentance. | A | Sermon. | By the Most Reverend | Dr. John Tillotson, | Late Lord Arch-Bishop of Canterbury. | *Philadelphia:* | *Printed by William Bradford at the Bible* | *in Second-Street.* M,DCC,XLV. | 4to. pp. 20.   956

A note written on page 3 of the copy in the Philadelphia Library says, "This sermon was given at the Funeral of Clement Plumsted, Esq." Mr. P. died in May, 1745, and as the Sermon was not advertised for sale it was probably printed for distribution at his funeral.

VOTES | and | Proceedings | of the | House of Representatives | of the | Province of Pennsylvania, | Met at Philadelphia, on the Fourteenth of October, | Anno Dom. 1744, and continued by Ad-journments, [to   .] | [*Penn Arms.*] | *Philadelphia:* | *Printed by B. Franklin, at the New Printing-* | *Office near the Market.*   M,DCC,XLV. | Folio.   957

Probably about sixty pages.   I have met with nothing more than the title page.

WHITEFIELD. (G.)   A | Letter | To the Reverend | Dr. Chauncy, | On Account of some Passages relating | to the | Revd. Mr. Whitefield, | In his Book intitled Seasonable Thoughts on the | State of Religion in New-England. | By George Whitefield, A. B. | Late of Pembroke-College, Oxon. | . . . . | *Philadelphia: Printed and Sold by W.* | *Bradford at the Bible in Second-street,* | MDCC-XLV. | Sm. 8vo. pp. 32.   H. S. P.   958

1746.

AN | ACCOUNT | of the | Treaty | Held at the City of | Albany, in the Province of New-York, | By His Excellency the | Governor of that Province, | And the Honourable the | Commissioners for the Provinces | of | Massachusetts, Connecticut, | and | Pennsylvania, | with the | Indians | of the | Six Nations, | In October, 1745. | *Philadelphia: Printed by B. Franklin, at the New-Printing-Office, | near the Market*, M,DCC,XLVI. | Folio, pp. 20.   L. C. P.   959

AN ACT for the more effectual Suppressing Profane Cursing and Swearing. *Philadelphia: B. Franklin.* 1746. Folio, 1 leaf.   960

By the third section of this Act, which was passed March 7, 1745–6, it was ordered that "a copy of the same, printed on a single Sheet of Paper" be sent to every Constable in the Province "Who shall forthwith . . . affix the same in the most Publick Place in their respective Wards and Districts."

THE AMERICAN Weekly Mercury.   A. A. S.   961

Number 1356 (from Dec. 24 to Jan. 1, 1745, 6) to 1375 (for May 15 to May 22, 1746).

ANNO Regni | Georgii II. | Regis | Magnæ Britanniæ, | Franciæ, & Hiberniæ, | Decimo Octavo. | At a General Assembly of the Province of | Pennsylvania, begun and holden at Phi- | ladelphia, the Fifteenth Day of October, Anno Dom. | 1744, in the Eighteenth Year of the Reign of our So- | vereign Lord George the II. by the Grace of God, | of Great-Britain, France and Ireland, King, De- | fender of the Faith, &c. | And from thence continued by Adjournments. | [*Penn Arms.*] | *Philadelphia:* | *Printed and Sold by B. Franklin, at | the New Printing-Office, near the Market,* | M,DCC,XLVI. | Folio, Title, 1 leaf; pp. xxv.–xxvi. H. S. P.   962

ANNO Regni | Georgii II. | Regis | Magnæ Britanniæ, Franciæ, & Hiberniæ | Decimo Nono. | At a General Assembly of the Province of | Pennsylvania, begun and holden at Phi- | ladelphia, | the Fourteenth Day of October; Anno Dom. | 1745, in the Nineteenth Year of the Reign of our So- | vereign Lord George

II. by the Grace of God, | of Great Britain, France and Ireland, King, | Defender of the Faith, &c. | And from thence continued by Adjournments to the | Seventh Day of March, 1745. | [*Penn Arms.*] | *Philadelphia:* | *Printed and Sold by B. Franklin, at* | *the New-Printing-Office, near the Market.* | M,DCC,XLVI. | Folio, Title, 1 leaf; pp. 25–59. + And from thence continued by Adjournments | to the Ninth Day of June, 1746. | [*Ibid.*] Title, 1 leaf; pp. 61–69.   H. S. P.   963

BALL. (W.) The New-Jersey | Almanack, | For the Year of Christian Account | 1747. | Unto which is Numbered from the Creation, | By the Oriental and Greek Christians, 7255 Years. | By the Jews, Hebrews and Rabies, 7957 | By the Computation of W. W. 5756 | Being the Third after Bissextile or Leap-Year. | Wherein is contained: The Lunations, E- | clipses, Judgment of the Weather, Planets, Motions and | Aspects, time of the Sun and Moon's rising and Seting | the length of the Days, a Table shewing the Moon's age eve- | ry Day in the Year, a Table of the Moon's southing, a Tide | Table shewing the Time of High Water at Philadelphia, Bur- | lington, Bordentown, and Trenton landings, the Time of the | Seven Stars southing, setting and rising, and also the south- | ing of several other Stars, the Part of the Body where the | Sign is every Day for such as observeth the same: Courts, | Fairs, and Quaker General Meetings; with several other | Things. With a Meridian of five Hours W. from London, | and calculated for the Meridian of Trenton, where the Pole | Arctic is elevated above the Horizon 40 Deg. 20 Min. but | may without much Error serve all the adjacent Places from | Newfoundland to South-Carolina. | By William Ball, Philomath. | . . . | . . . | . . . | . . . . | *Philadelphia: Printed and Sold by W. Bradford, at the* | *Sign of the Bible in Second-Street.* [1746.] | Sm. 8vo.   c.   964

𝖉𝖎𝖊 𝖀𝕸𝕲𝕰𝖂𝕰𝕹𝕯𝕰𝕿𝕰 𝕭𝕴𝕭𝕰𝕷.   Ein Traktätlein.   *Germantown: Christoph Sower.*   1746.   965

Advertised in Sower's Almanac for 1747.

BIRKETT. (W.) An Almanac for 1747.   *Philadelphia: Cornelia Bradford.*   1746.   966

BLAKENEY. (WILLIAM) AND HUMPHRY BLAND. The New Manual Exercise. By General Blakeney. To which is added The Evolutions of the Foot. By General Bland. *Philadelphia: B. Franklin.* 1746. 967

BRAINERD. (D.) Mirabilia Dei inter Indicos, | Or the | Rise and Progress | Of a Remarkable | Work of Grace | Amongst a Number of the | Indians | In the Provinces of New-Jersey | and Pennsylvania, | Justly Represented in | A Journal | Kept by Order of the Honourable Society | (in Scotland) for propagating Christian | Knowledge. | With some general Remarks. | By David Brainerd, Minister of the Gospel, | and Missionary from the said Society. | Published by the Rev. & Worthy Correspondents | of the said Society. With a Preface by them. | . . . | . . . | . . . | . . . | . . . | . . . | . . . | . . . | . . . | . . . . | *Philadelphia: Printed and Sold by William | Bradford in Second-Street.* | [n. d.] 8vo. pp. viii. 253.

At page 81 is a separate title page beginning "Divine Grace Display'd . . . Printed by William Bradford."

THE | CHARTER | of the | Library Company | of | Philadelphia. | *Philadelphia: | Printed by B. Franklin,* M,DCC,XLVI. | Sm. 8vo. H. S. P. 969

Collation : Title, 1 page ; Charter, pp. 2–8 ; Laws, Title, 1 leaf ; text, pp. 3–15 ; Books | Added to the | Library | Since the Year 1741. [n. p. n. d.] | pp. 1–28 ; Rules, pp. (3) ; Advertisement, 1 page. The second part has the following title : Laws | of the | Library Company | of | Philadelphia. | Made, in Pursuance of their | Charter, | At a General Meeting, | held in the Library, on the Third Day | of May, 1742. | *Philadelphia : | Printed by B. Franklin,* M,DCC,XLVI. |

CHUBB. (T.) An Examination of Mr. Barclay's Principles, . . . as laid down in his Book, intitled, An Apology for the . . . Quakers. . . . . To which is added, The Glory of Christ. By Thomas Chubb. *London: Printed by J. Darby and T. Browne.* . . . 1746. 8vo. pp. 99. 970

Ascribed to Franklin's press, under the year 1746, in my "List of the Publications issued in Pennsylvania. Philadelphia, 1882," and in the "Bulletin of the Boston Public Library, Vol. V. No. 7. The copy from which I took the title for my "List" is in the Philadelphia Library, and proves to be an imperfect copy of Chubb's two tracts printed at London in 1726.

𝔙𝔬𝔪 ℭ𝔬𝔪𝔢𝔱𝔢𝔫. *Germantown : Christoph Saur.* 1746. 971

Title from Seidensticker's Bibliography.

CRASSHOLD. (K.) The Modern Poemander; Or the wise honest and moral Krishtian Crasshold's Disertation on the Deity, in a Letter to his Friend Joseph Wills. *Philadelphia: Cornelia Bradford.?* 1746.   972

Title mainly from Haven's List. Crasshold was a tailor; he died in 1759, and his tombstone, with a Latin inscription, still stands in the burying grounds of Christ Church, in this city.

DUSS. (J. F.) Die merkwürdige Geschichte der Belehrung von Jacob Friedrich Duß, ein Bäcker in Würtemberg. *Germantown : Christoph Saur.* 1746.   973

Title from Seidensticker's Bibliography. It is advertised in Sower's Paper, May 16, 1746.

AN | EPISTLE | from our | Yearly-Meeting, | Held at Burlington, for New-Jersey and Pennsylvania, | by Adjournment, from the 20th Day of the Seventh | Month, to the 23d Day of the same, inclusive, 1746. | To the several Quarterly and Monthly Meetings of | Friends belonging to our said Yearly-Meeting. | [*Philadelphia: Printed by B. Franklin.* 1746.] Folio, pp. 4. M. S.

FINLEY. (S.) A Charitable Plea for the Speechless ; Or, The Right of Believers-Infants to Baptism vindicated. And the Mode of it by Pouring or Sprinkling Justified. By Samuel Finley, Minister of the Gospel at Nottingham in Pennsylvania. *Philadelphia: William Bradford.* 1746. pp. viii. 115.   975

[FRANKLIN. (Benjamin)] Reflections | on | Courtship and Marriage: | In | Two Letters | to a | Friend. | Wherein a Practicable Plan is laid down for | Obtaining and Securing | Conjugal Felicity. | *Philadelphia:* | *Printed and Sold by B. Franklin,* | M,DCC,XLVI. | Sm. 4to. pp. vii. 68.   H. S. P. 976

Dr. Rush's copy now in the L. C. P. has noted on the title page "By Benjamin Franklin, B. R."

DER | HOCH-DEUTSH | Americauische | Calender, | Auf das Jahr | ... | ... | 1747; | ... | ... | ... | ... | ... | ... | ... | ... | ... | .... | Zum neunten mal heraus gegeben. | *Germantown: Gedruckt und zu finden bey Christoph Saur:* | ....[1746] | Sm. 4to. pp. (32).   977

JERMAN. (J.) An Almanac for 1747. By John Jerman. *Philadelphia: B. Franklin.* 1746.   978

LEICHENPREDIGT eines berühmten Geistlichen in Georgien über Offenbarung VII. 13. *Germantown: Christoph Saur.* 1746. 979

Title from Seidensticker's Bibliography.

LUTHER (M.) Der Psalter des Königs und Propheten Davids verteutscht von D. Martin Luther, mit jedes Capitels Kurtzen Summarien auch beygefügten vielen richtigen Parallelen. *Germantown gedruckt und zu finden bey Christoph Saur.* 1746. 24mo. pp. 252.

This title is from a manuscript copy made by Mr. A. H. Cassell.

MORE. (T.) An Almanac for 1747. By Thomas More. *Philadelphia: B. Franklin.* 1746.   981

NEU-Eingerichteter Americanischer Geschichts-Kalender, auf das Jahr 1747. *Philadelphia: Gedruckt bey B. Francklin.* 1746.   982

NEW JERSEY. Anno Regni | Georgii II. | Regis | Magnæ Britanniæ, Franciæ & Hiberniæ, | Decimo Nono. | At a General Assembly of the Pro- | vince of New-Jersey, holden the | Eight Day of May, Anno Domini 1746, | and in the Nineteenth Year of our Sovereign | Lord George II. by the Grace of God, | of Great Britain, France, and Ireland, | King, Defender of the Faith, &c. | [*Royal Arms.*] | *Philadelphia:* | *Printed and Sold by B. Franklin, Printer to the | King's most Excellent Majesty for the Province of | New-Jersey,* M,DCC,XLVI. | Folio, pp. 14.   983

NEW JERSEY. Anno Regni | Georgii II. | Regis | . . . | Vigesimo. | At a General Assembly of the Pro- | vince of New-Jersey, holden the | Twenty eighth Day of June, Anno Domini 1746, | and in the Twentieth Year of our Sovereign | Lord George

II. . . . | . . . | . . . . | [*Royal Arms.*] | *Philadelphia:* | *Printed and Sold by B. Franklin, Printer to the* | *King's most Excellent Majesty for the Province of* | *New-Jersey,* M,DCC,XLVI. | Folio, pp. 22.   984

NEW-YEAR Verses of the Carriers of American Weekly Mercury. *Philadelphia: Cornelia Bradford.* 1746.   985

NEW-YEAR Verses of the Carriers of the Pennsylvania Gazette. *Philadelphia: B. Franklin.* 1746.   986

THE | NEW-YEAR'S Verses, | Of the Printer's Lad who carries about the | Pennsylvania Journal to the | Customers thereof | January 1, 1746. | [*Philadelphia: W. Bradford.* 1746.] Folio, 1 leaf.   H. S. P.   987

THE PENNSYLVANIA Gazette.   L. C. P.   988

Numbers 801 (Jan. 7, 1745–6) to 942 (Dec. 30, 1746), four pages each, except Numbers 906, 925, 927, 928 and 931, which contain six pages, and Number 905, which contains eight pages. There are "Supplements" of two pages each to Numbers 891, 917 and 922, and one of 1 leaf to Number 916. Title and imprint as in Number 891, *supra.*

THE PENNSYLVANIA Journal. *Philadelphia: Printed and Sold by William Bradford at the Sign of the Bible,* | *the Corner of Black Horse Alley in Second Street, where Persons may be supply'd with* | *this Paper at 10 s. a Year. And where Advertisements are taken in.* | 989

Numbers 163 (Jan. 7, 1745–6) to 215 (Dec. 30, 1746), four pages each, with "Supplements" of two pages each to Numbers 163, 170, 178 and 179. Title as in Number 844, *supra.* Number 209 is misdated Nov. 10 for Nov. 20.

POOR Robin's Almanac for 1747. *Philadelphia: William Bradford.* 1746.   990

PROCLAMATION. G. [*Royal Arms.*] R. | By the Honourable | George Thomas, Esq; | . . . | . . . | . . . | A Proclamation. | *Philadelphia: Printed by B. Franklin, Printer to the Province.* [1746.] Folio, 1 leaf.   991

Dated July 14, 1746. Appointing a day of Thanksgiving for the victory at Collenden.

SAUNDERS. (R.) A Pocket | Almanack | For the Year 1747. | Fitted to the Use of Penn- | sylvania, and the neighbour- | ing Provinces. | With several useful Additions. | By R. Saunders, Phil. | *Philadelphia:* | *Printed by* **B.** *Franklin.* [1746.] | 24mo. pp. (24).   c.   992

SAUNDERS. Poor Richard, 1747. | An | Almanack | For the Year of Christ | 1747, | It being the Third after | Leap-Year. | [as in 1738.] *Philadelphia:* | *Printed and Sold by B. Franklin.* [1746.] | 12mo. pp. (24).   L. C. P.   993

TENNENT. (G.) A | Sermon | preach'd | In Greenwich, September 4. 1746. | At the | Ordination | of | Mr. Andrew Hunter. | By Gilbert Tennent, A.M. | *Philadelphia: Printed by William | Bradford, at the Sign of the Bible | in Second-street.* [1746.] | Sm. 8vo. pp. 42.   H. S. P.   994

UNTERRICHT von der Einsammlung des Willens der Seelen. Ein stilles Herzensgespräch. *Germanton: Christoph Saur.* 1746.   995

Advertised in Sower's Newspaper, April 16, 1746.

VOTES of the Assembly. *Philadelphia: B. Franklin.* 1746.

WHITEFIELD. (G.) Britain's Mercies, | And | Britain's Duty, | Represented in | A | Sermon | Preach'd at the New-Building | in | Philadelphia, | On Sunday August 24, 1746. | Occasion'd by the Suppression of the late | Unnatural Rebellion. | By George Whitefield, A.B. | Late of Pembroke College, Oxon. | *Philadelphia:* | *Printed and Sold by W. Bradford, at | the Bible in Second-street*, MDCCXLVI. | 8vo. pp. 27.   H. S. P.   997

WHITEFIELD. Five Sermons on the following Subjects, viz: I. Christ the Believer's Husband. II. The Gospel Supper. III. Blind Bartimeus. IV. Walking with God. V. The Resurrection of Lazarus. With a Preface of the Rev. Mr. Gilbert Tennent. *Philadelphia: Printed and Sold by B. Franklin,* MDCCXLVI. 8vo. pp. xiv, 169.   998

WHITEFIELD. A Further | Account | Of God's dealings with the Reverend | Mr. George Whitefield, | From the Time of his Ordination to | his embarking for Georgia. | To which is annex'd | A brief Account of the Rise, Pro- | gress, and Present Situation | of the | Orphan-House in Georgia. | In a Letter to a Friend. | By George Whitefield, A.B. | Late of Pembroke College Oxon. | . . . | . . . | . . . . | *Philadelphia:* | *Printed and Sold by W. Bradford,* at | *the Bible in Second-street.* MDCCXLVI. | 16mo., pp. 64, 1 leaf, 2 folded leaves.   H. S. P.   999

At page 49 is a second title, as follows : " A Brief | Account | of the | Rise, Progress, and Present | Situation | of the | Orphan-House, in Georgia. | In a Letter to a Friend. | By George Whitefield, A.B. | Late of Pembroke College, Oxon. | . . . | . . . . | *Printed in the Year,* 1746. | pp. [49]–64.

1747.

AN ACCOUNT of the Apparition of the late Lord Kilmarnock, to the Rev. Mr. Foster.   With what passed between them in this Interview, the next Morning after his Execution.   To which is added, the Second Appearing of the late Lord Kilmarnock, to a Clergyman of the Church of England, in the Evening of the same Day ; The Account of which is given in the Close of a Dialogue between a Clergyman and a Sea-Captain, occasioned by the Rev. Mr. Foster's Account of the late Lord Kilmarnock.   *Philadelphia :* *B. Franklin.*   1747.   1000

AN ACCOUNT of the Births | and Burials in Christ-Church Parish, in | Philadelphia, from December 24, 1746, to | December 24, 1747.   By Caleb Cash, | Clerk, and Charles Hughes, Sexton ; | [n. p. n. d.]   Folio, 1 leaf.   L. C. P.   1001

ANNO Regni | Georgii II. | Regis | Magnæ Britanniæ, | Franciæ & Hiberniæ | Vigesimo. | At a General Assembly of the Province of Penn- | sylvania, begun and holden at Philadelphia, the | Fourteenth Day of October; Anno Domini 1746, in the | Twentieth Year of the Reign of our Sovereign Lord | George II. by the Grace of God, of Great Bri- | tain, France, and Ireland, King, Defender of the | Faith, &c. | And from thence continued by Adjournments to the | Third Day of May, 1747. | [*Penn Arms.*] | *Philadelphia:* | *Printed and Sold by B. Franklin, at the New-* | *Printing-Office, near the Market.* MDCCXLVII. | Folio, Title, 1 leaf; pp. iii-iv.   H. S. P.   1002

BALL. (W.) The New Jersey Almanac for 1748. By William Ball. *Philadelphia: William Bradford.* 1747.   1003

BIRKETT. (W.) An Almanac for 1748. By William Birkett. *Philadelphia: William Bradford.* 1747.   1004

BLAKENEY, ([William]) and Humphry BLAND. The New Manual Exercise. By General Blakeney. To which is added, The Evolutions of the Foot. By General Bland. The Second Edition. *Philadelphia: B. Franklin.* 1747.   1005

Advertised in the Pa. Gazette, Dec. 29, 1747.

[BURGH. (James)] Britain's | Remembrancer. | Being | Some Thoughts on the proper | Improvement of the present | Juncture. | The Character of this Age and | Nation. | A brief View from History, of | the Effects of the Vices which | now prevail in Britain, upon | the greatest Empires and States | of former Times. | Remarkable Deliverances this | Nation has had in the most | imminent Dangers; with | suitable Reflections. | Some Hints, shewing what is | in the Power of the several | Ranks of People, and of every | Individual in Britain, to do to- | ward securing the State from | all its Enemies. | The Fifth Edition. | *London: Printed.* | *Philadelphia: Re-printed, and Sold* | *by B. Franklin, at the New Printing-Office* | *near the Market.* [1747.] | Sm. 8vo. pp. 47.   c.   1006

Advertised in the Pa. Gazette, Oct. 1, 1747.

A COPY of a Letter from Quebeck in Canada, to a | Pr - - e M - - - e in France, dated October 11, 1747. [*Philadelphia: B. Franklin.* 1747.?] Folio, pp. (3).   H. S. P.   1007

Under the disguise of a French scheme to procure an Act of Parliament forbidding the issue of colonial Bills-of-Credit, the advantages, etc., of the paper currency are set forth.

EDWARDS. (J.)   An Humble Attempt to promote an Explicit agreement and visible Union of God's People, in Extraordinary Prayer, &c.   By Jonathan Edwards.   *Philadelphia.?* 1747.   1008

Printed at Boston in 1747, and by Haven said to have been reprinted in Philadelphia. It is advertised in the Pa. Journal, April 14, 1748, together with Edward's Sermon on the Rev. David Brainerd, which was also printed at Boston in 1747, as "Lately Published and to be Sold by the Printer hereof," probably referring in both cases to the Boston editions.

[FRANKLIN. (Benjamin)] Die | Lautere Wahrheit, | Oder | Ernſtliche Betrachtung | des gegenwärtigen Zuſtandes | Der | Stadt Philadelphia, | und der | Provinß Penſylvanien. | Von einem Handwercksmann in Philadelphia. | [*Cut.*] | Aus dem Engliſchen überſeßt durch J. Crell. | *Gedruckt, und zu finden bey Gotthard Armbruester.* [1747.] | 8vo. pp. 20.   H. S. P. 1009

[FRANKLIN.]   Plain Truth: | Or, | Serious Considerations | On the Present State of the | City of Philadelphia, | and | Province of Pennsylvania. | By a Tradesman of Phiadelphia. | . . . | . . . | . . . | : . . | . . . | . . . | . . . | . . . | . . . | . . . | . . . | . . . | . . . | . . . | . . . . | [*Philadelphia:*] *Printed* [*by B. Frankin*] | *in the Year* MDCCXLVII. | 8vo. 22, (2).   H. s. p.   1010

A second edition was advertised in the Pa. Gazette, Dec. 29, 1747.

FREILINGHUYSEN. (T. J.)   Versamelinge | van eenige | Keur-Texten, | Meest by byzondere geleegentheeden gedaan | I. De Eerste Ebenhaezer, dat is Gedenk- | steen der hulpe; uyt, I. Sam. vii. 21. | II. De Pligten van Zions Wagteren, zynde | een bevestigings Predikatie; uyt, Ezech. iii. 17, 18, 19. | III. De Derde bevattende Christi weemoe- | dige klagte, over de ongelovighyd van | Jerusalems Inwoonderen; uyt, Mat. xxiii. | 37. | IV. Een Christens bemoediging, in den | Geestelyken Stryd; uyt, Luc. xxii. 31, 32. | En uytgegeven door | Theod. Jac. Freilinghuysen. | Bedienaer des H. Evangeliums, in de Herformde Neder- | duytsche Gemeyntens, te Rariton, Niew-Bronswick, &c. | in Niew-Jersey, eertyds Niew-Nederland. | *Gedruckt tot, Philadelphia, door W. Bradford.* | [n. d.]   Sm. 8vo. pp. vi, 73.   H. s. p.   1011

The date is that assigned by Col. W. Bradford. The last date I can find is Dec., 1745.

𝕰𝕴𝕹 | 𝕲𝕰𝕽𝕴𝕹𝕲𝕰𝕽 Schein | Des | Verachteten Lichtleins, | Der Warheit die in Christo ist; | Beleuchtet etliche Gründe, welche auf das neue | an das Licht getreten, in einem Tractätlein genant : | Ein ernstlicher Ruf, in Christlicher | Liebe an alles Volck 2c. | Und damit der Leser solches Tractätlein | mit desto grösserem Nutzen lesen möge, wird ihm | auch all= hie in diesem Geringen Schein, ein | Schriftmässiges Zeugnus von drey | Puncten vor Augen geleget. | I. Von der Heiligen Schrift. | II. Von der wahren Bekehrung. | III. Von der Taufe Christi. | Herausgegeben von einem Liebhaber der | Warheit, auf Gutfinden und Kosten der | Brü= derschafft die solches Zeugnus träget. | . . . | . . . . | *Germanton, ge- druckt [bey Christoph Saur] im Jahr* 1747. | 16mo. pp. (4), 28.

𝕯𝕬𝕾 | 𝕲𝕰𝕾𝕬𝕰𝕹𝕲 | Der einsamen und verlassenen | Turtel= | Taube | Nemlich der Christlichen | Kirche. | Oder geistliche u. Erfahrungs=volle Leidens u. Liebes=Gethöne, | Als darinnen beydes die Vorkost der neuen Welt als | auch die darzwischen vorkommende Creutzes=und Leidens= | Wege nach ihrer Würde dargestellt, und in | geistliche Reimen gebracht | Von einem Friedsamen und nach der | stillen Ewigkeit wallenden | Pilger. | Und nun | Zum Gebrauch der Einsamen und Verlassenen zu Zion | ge= sammlet und ans Licht gegeben. | *Ephrata.* | *Drucks der Brueder- schafft im Jahr* 1747. | Sq. 8vo.   **1013**

There are two or more editions. Collation of one edition : Title and An- them, pp. (2); Vorbericht, pp. (5); Eine Sehr deutliche Beschreibung, [oder] Vorrede über die Sing-Arbeit, pp. (14), (1); Der Geistliche Braut-Schmuck, &c., (60 Hymns), pp. 1–44 ; Das Kirren der Turtel-Tauben (62 Hymns), pp. 45–139 ; Die Braut des Lamms, pp. 140–144 ; Nun folget die Abend-ländische Morgen- Röthe (88 Hymns), pp. 144–294 ; Gilfende Hertzens-Bewegungen, &c. (35 Hymns), pp. 295–325 ; 31 additional hymns, pp. 326–356 ; Nachrede des Gesangs der Turtel Taube, pp. 357–359 ; Register, pp. (5); Collation of a later edition : As above to p. 294. Gilfende Hertzens-Bewegungen, &c. Reprinted (7th, 8th and 9th lines differently spaced, and a different "tail-piece"), pp. 295–419 (114 hymns, *i. e.*, 29, of those in the 1st edition, and the 31 additional hymns of the same, with 54 new ones interspersed. The first hymn of the earlier edition is the 6th, and the 31st of the additional hymns of the same, the 114th of the later edition. The 13th, 21st and 27th hymns of the first are omitted in the second edi- tion); Vonder Zerfallenen Hütte Davids (47 Hymns), pp. 420-495, with a slip in- serted between pp. 456 and 457, containing five additional verses to the 26th Hymn; Three additional hymns, pp. (2); Ein Geistliches Denckmal, pp. (2); Nachrede, pp. (4); Rocks Bruder Lied, pp. (4); Register, pp. (7); Ein Geistliches Denckmahl u. Lobspruch, &c., pp. (2).

"This was the first collection of the hymns of the Ephrata cloister issued from their own press, and was printed on paper manufactured by the brethren. Many of the hymns were written by Conrad Beissel, or Vater Friedsam who was the "Vorsteher." It well illustrates their peculiarities in bookmaking. Most of their publications being intended only for their own use they issued them in such shape as best answered their purpose at the time, and variations in the text are numerous. One of the remarkable features of the cloister was the great number of hymn books written and published there. Beissel was an expert musician and composer. Fahnestock says: "In composing sacred music he took his style from the music of nature, and the whole, comprising several large volumes, are founded on the tones of the Æolian Harp. The singing is the Æolian Harp harmonized. It is very peculiar in its style and concords and in its execution. The tones issuing from the choir imitate very soft instrumental music conveying a softness and devotion almost superhuman. In a 'Vorrede über der Sing Arbeit' Beissel, in this volume, gives a full and technical description of his method and views of music."

S. W. P.

DER | HOCH-DEUTSCH | Americanische | Calender, | Auf das Jahr | . . . | . . . | 1748 | (Welches ein schalt Jahr von 366 Tagen ist.) | . . . | . . . | . . . | . . . | . . . | . . . | . . . | . . . | . . . | Zum zehenten mal heraus gegeben. | *Germantown: Gedruckt und zu finden bey Christoph Saur.* | . . . .[1747.] | Sm. 4to. pp. (32). H. S. P. 1014

HOLME. (B.) Ein | Ernstlicher | Ruff | In | Christlicher Liebe | An alles Volck, | Sich zu dem | Geist Christi in ihnen | Zu bekehren, | Auf daß sie zu einem rechten Verstand dessen, das aus | Gott ist, gelangen, und dadurch vermögend gemacht | werden mögen, Ihm auf eine angenehme Weise | zu dienen. | Nebst einigen Anmerckungen | über folgende Puncte: | I. Die Allgemeinheit der Liebe Gottes, daß | er seinen Sohn gesandt hat und in den | Todt gegeben für alle Menschen. | 2. Die heilige Schrifft. | 3. Den Gottes-Dienst. | 4. Die Tauffe. | 5. Das Abendmahl. | 6. Die Christliche Vollkommenheit. | 7. Die Auferstehung von den Todten. | . . . | . . . | . . . . | In Englischer Sprache heraus gegeben | von | Benjamin Holme, | und ins teutsche übersetzt | 1744. | *Und nochmal gedruckt zu Germanton* [*bey Christoph Saur.*] 1747. | 16mo. pp. 77. Auf Kosten der Freunde. H. S. P. 1015

JERMAN. (J.) An Almanac for 1748. By John Jerman. *Philadelphia: B. Franklin.* 1747. 1016

KINNERSLEY. (E.) A | Letter | To the Reverend | The Ministers | of the | Baptist Congregations, in | Pennsylvania, and the New-Jerseys; | Containing Some | Remarks, | On their Answers to certain | Queries, proposed to them, at their | Annual Association Phila- | delphia, September 24. 1746. | By Ebenezer Kinnersley. | ... | .... | *Philadelphia: Printed by W. Bradford,* | *at the Sign of the Bible, in Second-street.* [1747.] | 16mo. pp. 24.

𝔎𝔏𝔄ℜ𝔈 und | 𝔊ewiffe | 𝔚ahrheit, | 𝔓f. 119. v. 160. 𝔗itum 1. 9. | Betreffend den eigendlichen | 𝔷uftand, | fo wohl der 𝔚ahren Friedliebenden Ehriften | und 𝔊ottesfürchtigen, als auch der verfal= | lenen Streit= oder 𝔎riegs=Süchtigen, | 𝔷ufammt ihrer behder Hoffnung | und 𝔄usgang. | Schrifftmäßig dargelegt | von einem 𝔗eutfchen 𝔊eringen Handwercks Mann. | ... | ... | ... | ... | ... | ... | ... | ... | .... | *Gedruckt in Germanton bey Christoph Saur.* 1747. | 8vo. pp. 15.   L. C. P.   1018

LETTERS | between | Theophilus and Eugenio, | on the | Moral Pravity of Man, | and the | Means of His Restoration. | Wrote in the East-Indies, | And now First Published from the Original Manuscript. | *Philadelphia: Printed and Sold by B. Franklin.* | MDCCXLVII. | 4to. pp. iv. 64.   H. S. P.   1019

These letters have been attributed to Franklin, but this cannot be correct as there is a copy printed in 1720, in the Bodleian Library.

LOVIGNY. (J. B.) 𝔍oh, 𝔅erniers 𝔏ovigny, 𝔙erborgenes 𝔏eben mit 𝔈hrifto in 𝔊ott. *Germantown: Gedruckt bey Christoph Saur.* 1747.

Title from Seidensticker's Bibliography. From Sower's paper of June 1 and August 16, 1749, and October 1, 1751, I think Sower did not publish this work, but only solicited orders for "die letzte und verbesserte edition gedruckt 1747," which in the last mentioned paper he says "Kurtzlich ist aus Teutschland ankommen"

MORE. (T.) . . . Almanack, | for | the Year of Christian Account, | 1748. | And | From the Creation, by Scripture, 5757. | Being Bissextile, or Leap-Year. | Wherein is contained. | The Lunations, Eclipses, Judgment of the | Weather, (in this uncertain Climate) Planets places in | the Ecliptick, and Mutual Aspects, Sun and Moon's rising | and setting, Seven Stars rising and setting,

Tide-Table, | Fairs, Courts, and observable Days. | Calculated from Caroline Tables, according | to Art, and fitted for the Province of Pennsylvania, but | may without sensible Error serve all the Provinces | adjacent. | By Thomas More, Philodespot. | . . . | . . . | . . . | . . . . | *Philadelphia :* | *Printed and Sold by B. Franklin, at the New-Printing* | *Office in Market-street.* [1747.] | Sm. 8vo. pp. (24).   H. S. P.   1021

The preface is cynical and coarse enough to have been written by Franklin.

MORGAN. (A.) Anti-Pædo-Rantism ; | or | Mr. Samuel Finley's | Charitable Plea for the Speechless | Examined and Refuted : | The Baptism of Believers | Maintain'd ; | And | The Mode of it, by Immersion, | Vindicated. | By Abel Morgan, at Middletown, | in East-Jersey. | . . . | . . . | . . . | . . . | . . . . | *Philadelphia :* | *Printed by B. Franklin, in Market-Street.* | M,DCC,XLVII. | 16mo.   H. S. P.   1022

Collation : Title, 1 leaf ; Preface, pp. iii-ix ; text, pp. 11–160 ; Appendix, Title, 1 leaf ; text, pp. 163-174 ; Errata, 1 leaf. The Appendix, which was written by the Rev. Benjamin Griffith, has the following title : An | Appendix | To the Foregoing Work ; | being | Remarks | On some Particulars in a late Pamphlet, | Entituled, | Divine Right of Infant-Baptism &c. | Written by another Hand. | *Philadelphia :* | *Printed by B. Franklin,* | M,DCC,XLVII. |

𝕹𝔈𝔘-eingerichteter Americanischer Geschichts-Kalender, auf das Jahr 1748. *Gedruckt bey B. Francklin und J. Boehm.* 1747.   1023

NEW-YEAR Verses of the Carriers of the Pennsylvania Gazette. *Philadelphia : B. Franklin.* 1747.   1024

NEW-YEAR Verses of the Carriers of the Pennsylvania Journal. *Philadelphia : William Bradford.* 1747.   1025

𝕹𝔒𝔠𝕳 mehr Zeugnüsse der Wahrheit, von einem Bauersmann im Busch. *Germantown : Christoph Saur.* 1747.   1026

OBSERVATIONS upon Beauty, Coquetry, Jilting, Jealousy, &c. With some Reflections on a Married State. *Philadelphia : William Bradford.* 1747.   1027

A PAPER containing Exceptions against some things in the present mode of administering & Receiving the Lord's Supper in most of our Presbyterian Societies laid before the Synod of Philadelphia in May 1747. Together with a Preface . . . by the Presbytery of New-Castle. *Lancaster: Printed by James Coulter.* MDCCXLVII. 16mo. pp. 17.   1028

THE PENNSYLVANIA Gazette.   H. S. P.   1029

Numbers 943 (Jan. 6, 1746-7) to 994 (Dec. 29, 1747), four pages each, except Numbers 956, 957, 963, 964, 966, 970, 971, 976, 978, 980, 981, 983 and 984, which contain six pages. There is a "Supplement" of two pages to Number 977. I have not seen Numbers 947-949, 960-962, and 990. Title and imprint as in Number 891, *supra.*

THE PENNSYLVANIA Journal.   H. S. P.   1030

Numbers 216 (Jan. 6, 1746-7) to 267 (Dec. 29, 1747), four pages each, with "Supplements," of two pages each to Numbers 225, 246 and 256. Title and imprint as in Number 989, *supra.*

POOR Robin's Almanac for 1748. *Philadelphia: William Bradford.* 1747.   1031

POPE. (A.) An Essay on Man, in Four Epistles. By Alexander Pope, Esq; enlarged and improved by the Author. *Philadelphia: William Bradford.* 1747.   1032

PROCLAMATION. G. [*Royal Arms.*] R. By the . . . President and Council of the Province of Pennsylvania. A Proclamation for a General Fast. *Philadelphia: Printed by B. Franklin.* MDCCXLVII. Folio, 1 leaf.   1033

"I proposed to them (the Council) the proclaiming a fast, . . . They embraced the motion, but as it was the first fast ever thought of in the province, the Secretary had no precedent from which to draw the proclamation. I drew it . . . it was translated into German and printed in both languages."—*Memoirs of Benjamin Franklin*, Phila., McCarty and Davis, 1840. Vol. I. p. 45.

RAY. (J.) The Acts of the Rebels, written by an Ægyptian: Being an Abstract of the Journal of Mr. James Ray, of Whitehaven, Volunteer under his Royal Highness the Duke of Cumberland. To which is added, The Lamentations of Charles, the Son of James, With the Farewell Speech which he made to the Rebels, held at Lord L——'s the Night after the Battle of Culloden ; and by his Order distributed among the Remains of his shatter'd Army before they dispersed. *Philadelphia: Printed and Sold by B. Franklin.* 1747.   1034

> Advertised in the Pa. Gazette, April 23, 1747. In the same paper for Sept. 10, Franklin announces "The Sixth Edition."

EJNE RUFENDE Wächter Stimme An alle Seelen die nach Gott und seinem Reich Hungerend sind. Oder eine vorstellung, wie der arme mensch dem göttlichen Leben erstorben und im 4 Elementischem Leben auf= gewacht Nebst einer anweisung, wie man noch hier in der zeit demselben Leben loß werden und bey leibes=leben die wahre Rühe erlangen und der Künfftigen ewigen Seeligkeit genitz werden kömme.... *Germantown: Gedruckt und zu finden bey Christoph Saur im Jahr* 1747. 16mo. pp. 159.   H. S. P.   1035

SAUNDERS. (R.)   A Pocket | Almanack | For the Year 1748. | Fitted to the Use of Penn- | sylvania, and the neighbour- | ing Provinces. | With several useful Additions. | By R. Saunders, Phil. | *Philadelphia :* | *Printed by B. Franklin.* [1747.] 24mo. pp. (24).   c.   1036

SAUNDERS. Note, This Almanack us'd to contain but 24 Pages, and | now has 36 ; yet the Price is very little advanc'd. | Poor Richard improved: | Being an | Almanack | and | Ephemeris | of the | Motions of the Sun and Moon ; | the true | Places and Aspects of the Planets ; | the | Rising and Setting of the Sun ; | and the | Rising, Setting and Southing of the Moon, | for the | Bissextile Year, 1748. | Containing also, | The Lunations, Con- junctions, Eclipses, Judg- | ment of the Weather, Rising and Setting of the | Planets, Length of Days and Nights, Fairs, Courts, | Roads, &c. Together with useful Tables, chro- | nological Obser- vations, and entertaining Remarks. | Fitted to the Latitude of Forty, Degrees, and a Meridian of near | five Hours West from London; but may, without sensible Error, | serve all the Northern Colonies. | By Richard Saunders, Philom. | *Philadelphia:* | *Printed and Sold by B. Franklin.* [1747.] | 8vo. pp. (36).   H. S. P.   1037

THE SCOTCH Psalms. *Philadelphia: B. Franklin.* 1747.

[TERSTEEGEN. (GERHARD)] Geiſtliches | Blumen=Gärtlein | Inniger Seelen ; | Oder kurtze | Schluß=Reimen | Betrachtungen und Lieder | Ueber allerhand Warheiten des | Inwendigen Chriſtenthums; | Zur Erweckung, Stärckung, | und Erquickung in dem | Verborgenen Le= ben | mit Chriſto in Gott. | Nebſt der | Frommen Lotteri. | *In Teutsch- land zum 4ten Mahl gedruckt ; | und nun in America das erste Mahl | Gedruckt zu Germanton | bey Christoph Saur,* 1747. | 24mo. pp. 486, (6).   H. S. P. 1039

TERSTEEGEN. Glückliche Genügſamkeit der Stillen im Lande! Brüderlich Lehr=Troſt= und Vermahnugsſchreiben, von Gerhard Ter= ſteegen. *Germanton: Christoph Saur.* 1747.   1040

  Title from Seidensticker's Bibliography.

EINE TEUTSCH und Engliſche Grammatic, beſonders geignet vor Teutſche die Engliſch lernen wollen. *Germantown: Gedruckt bey Chri= stoph Saur.* 1747.   1041

  Title from Seidensticker's Bibliography.

TREAT. (R.) A Sermon Preach'd at the Ordination of Mr. Daniel Lawrence, at the Forks of the Delaware, in Pennsylvania, April 2d Anno Domini 1747. Together with the Charges and Exhortation, both to the Minister and Congregation on said Occa- sion. By Richard Treat, A.M. *Philadelphia: William Bradford.* 1747.   1042

VOTES and Proceedings of the House of Representatives of the Province of Pennsylvania, met at Philadelphia, on the Fourteenth of October, Anno Dom. 1746, and continued by Adjournments. *Philadelphia: Printed and Sold by B. Franklin, at the New Print- ing-Office near the Market.* MDCCXLVII. Folio, pp. 36. (1).

[ZUBLY. (JOHANNES JOACHIM)] Eine Leicht=Predig, welche ein Reformirter Prediger in Savanna in Georgien gehalten über die Worte Apoc. 7, Wer ſind dieſe in Weiſen Kleidern, ꝛc. *Germantown: Chri= stoph Saur.* 1747.   1044

_____ Advertised in Sower's Newspaper, June 16, 1747.

1748.

AN ACCOUNT of the Births | and Burials in Christ-Church Parish, in Philadelphia, from December 24, 1747, to | December 24, 1748. By Caleb Cash, | Clerk, and Charles Hughes, Sexton. | [n. p. n. d.] Folio, 1 leaf. L. C. P. 1045

BALL. (W.) The New Jersey Almanac for 1749. By William Ball. *Philadelphia: William Bradford.* 1748. 1046

DIE BESCHREIBUNG | Des | Evangeliums Nicodemi. | Von dem | Leyden unsers Herren | Jesu Christi, | Wie er von den Juden, als | Ein Uebelthäter Zauberer, etc: vor | Pilato fälschlich verklagt, und un= | schuldig zum Tod verurtheilt worden. | Wie auch | Von seiner Begräb= nuß, | Auferstehung u. Himelfahrt ect: | Welches beschrieben worden in dem | dreyßigsten Jahr des Kay= | serthums Tyberii. | *Ephrata Verlags M: M:* | *im Jahr* 1748. | 16mo. pp. 88. H. S. P. 1047

BIRKETT. (W.) An Almanac for 1749. By William Birkett. *Philadelphia: William Bradford.* 1748. 1048

BOEHM. (J. P.) Der reformirten Kirche in Pennsylvanien Kirchen= ordnung, welche im Jahre 1725 von Johannes Philipp Böhm aufgestellt und von den Gliedern der Gemeinde angenommen ist. *Philadelphia, Ge- druckt bey Gotthard Armbruester in der Archstrasze.* 1748. 1049

BRAGHT. (T[IELEMAN] J[ANS] V[AN]) Der | Blutige Schau= Platz | oder | Märtyrer= | Spiegel der Tauffs Gesinten | oder | Wehr= losen=Christen, | Die um des Zeugnuß Jesu ihres Seligmachers willen | gelitten haben, und seynd getödtet worden, von Christi Zeit an | bis auf das Jahr 1660. | Vormals aus unterschiedlichen glaubwürdigen Chronicken, Nachrichten und Zeugnüssen gesam= | let und in Holländischer Sprach her= aus gegeben | von T. J. V. Braght. | Nun aber sorgfältigst ins Hoch= teutsche übersetzt und zum erstenmal ans Licht gebracht. | [Cut.] | *Ephrata in Pensylvanien,* | *Drucks und Verlags der Bruederschafft. Anno* MDCCXLVIII. | Folio. H. S. P. 1050

Collation : Title and preliminary matter, pp. 56; text, pp. 1–478; Register, pp. (6). 2d volume. Title, 1 leaf; An meine geliebte Freunde, &c., pp. (2); Vorrede, pp. (10); text, pp. 1–949; Errata, 1 page; Register und Anweisung, pp. (8); Nach- rede, pp. (2). 1 plate. The title to the second volume is as follows: Des |

Blutigen Schau–Platzes | oder | Martyrer-Spiegels | der | Tauffs | Gesinnten | oder | Wehrlosen Christen. | Zweyte Theil. | Vormals in Holländischer Sprache heraus gegeben, | und mit vielen glaubwürdigen Urkunden vermehrt, | nun aber aus dem Holländischen in das Hochteutsche getreulich, über- | setzet, und mit einigen neuen Nachrichten vermehret. | *Ephrata in Pensylvanien | Drucks und Verlags der Bruederschafft. Anno* MDCCXLIX. | There are copies with the titles in red and black, but as generally met with they are printed in black only. The edition consisted of 1200 copies, of which a large part were issued without the plate, the design of which was offensive to the Mennonite purchasers. It is the largest, as well as the most frequently to be met with issue of the Ephrata press. For an account of it, see the Pennsylvania Magazine of History and Biography, Vol. V, p. 276.

ℰℐℛ ℭℌℛℐℒℐℒ | besuchet | oft und gerne | Die | Zions=Kinder | nach und ferne, | Und im Geist bey Tag | und Nacht, | Um allgemeines Wohlergehen | Den Bundes=Engel anzuflehen, | Trotz allem Secten= Reid! | bedacht. | Er seufzt bey seinem stillen Wandern, | Er singt und bettelt auch mit andern, | Er schallt auch auf der | Hohen Wacht. | [*Germantown: C. Saur.* 1748.] Sm. 8vo. pp. (8). H. S. P. 1051

THE CONGRESS between the Beasts, under the mediation of the Goat, for negotiating a peace between the Fox, the Ass wearing a Lion's skin, the Horse, the Tigress, and other quadrupeds at war: A farce in two Acts, now in rehearsal at a new grand Theatre in Germany. Written originally in High-Dutch, by the Baron Huffumbourghausen; and translated by J. J. H—— D—— G—— R, Esq; The Second Edition, corrected and amended in the print. *Philadelphia: Godhard Armbruster.* 1748. 1052

[CRISP. (STEPHEN)] Eine | Kurtze | Beschreibung | einer | langen Reise | aus | Babylon | nach | Bethel. | Offenb. 18, 4. | In Englischer Sprache geschrieben, im Noem. 1691. | und aus dem 5ten Druck ins Teutsche übersetzt 1748. | mit Beyfügung einiger Schrifftstellen, zu | mehrerer Erläuterung. | *Germanton gedruckt bey Christoph Saur,* | 1748. | 16mo. pp. 38. 1053

[CURRIE. (W.)] A | Sermon, | Preached in | Radnor Church, | On | Thursday, the 7th of January, 1747. | Being the Day ap- pointed by the | President and Council of the | Province of Penn- sylvania, | To be observed as a | General Fast. | By a Presbyter of the Church of England. | *Philadelphia:* | *Printed and Sold by* | *Benjamin Franklin,* | *and David Hall.* MDCCXLVIII. | 8vo. pp. 23.   H. S. P. 1054

CURRIE. A | Treatise | On the Lawfulness of | Defensive War. | In Two Parts. | By William Currie. | . . . | . . . | . . . | . . | . . . | . . . | . . . | . . . | . . . | . . . | . . . | . . . | . . . | . . . | . . . | *Philadelphia:* | *Printed and Sold by B. Franklin and* | *D. Hall,* | *at the New Printing-Office, in Market-street.* | MDCC-XLVIII. | 8vo. pp. xviii. 102.   H. S. P. 1055

DAVIES. (S.) A | Sermon | On Man's | Primitive State; | And | The First | Covenant. | Delivered before the Reverend Presbytery | of New-Castle, April 13th 1748. | By Samuel Davies, Minister of the Gospel. | . . . | . . . | . . . | . . . | . . . | . . . | . . . | . . . | *Philadelphia:* | *Printed by William Bradford, at the* | *Sign of the Bible, in Second-street.* 1748. | 8vo. pp. 42. L. C. P.

EDWARDS. (J.) A Treatise concerning Religious Affections, &c. By Jonathan Edwards, A.M. *Philadelphia:? William Brad-ford.* 1748.   1057

Printed at Boston in 1746. Proposal for re-printing it by Subscription were advertised by Bradford for nearly five months.

AN EPISTLE from the Yearly Meeting. *Philadelphia: B. Franklin, and D. Hall.* 1748.   1058

ERSCHEINUNGEN der Geister, u. ſ. w. Zweite Auflage. *Ger-mantown: Christoph Saur.* 1748.   1059

Title from Seidensticker's Bibliography. See No. 908, *supra.* It is advertised in Sower's paper, May 16, 1748.

EVANS. (D.) Law and Gospel : | Or, | Man wholly Ruined by the Law, | and | Recovered only by the Gospel. | Being | The Substance of some Sermons preached at | Tredyffryn, in Pennsyl-vania, in the Year | 1734, and again at Piles-Grove, in New- | Jersey, in the Year 1745. | By David Evans, A.M. and Minister of the Gospel, | formerly at Tredyffryn, and now at Piles-Grove. | Published at the Importunity and Charges of a Number | of his

People at the abovesaid Piles-Grove. | . . . | . . . | . . . | . . . |
. . . . | *Philadelphia:* | *Printed by B. Franklin and D. Hall, at the*
| *New Printing-Office, near the Market.* 1748. | Sm. 8vo. pp. 52.

FINL[E]Y. (S.) A | Vindication | of the | Charitable Plea | for
the | Speechless: | In | Answer | to | Mr. Abel Morgan's | Anti-
pædorantism. | Wherein | The Points in Controversy | are more
largely opened, and his Objec- | tions particularly considered and
refuted. | The Whole is freely submitted to the Judg- | ment of
Common Sense. | By Samuel Finly, V. D. M. at Nottingham, | in
Pennsylvania. | . . . | . . . . | *Philadelphia:* | *Printed and Sold by*
William Bradford, at the Sign of | *the Bible in Second-street.* |
MDCCXLVIII. | 8vo. pp. viii, 113.   L. C. P.   1061

FISHER. (G.) The American | Instructor: | Or, | Young
Man's Best Companion. | Containing, | Spelling, Reading, Writ-
ing, and Arithmetick, | in an easier Way than any yet published;
and how to qua- | lify any Person for Business, without the Help
of a Master. | Instructions to write Variety of Hands, with Copies
| both in Prose and Verse. How to write Letters on Bu- | siness
or Friendship. Forms of Indentures, Bonds, Bills | of Sale,
Receipts, Wills, Leases, Releases, &c. | Also Merchants Accompts,
and as short and easy Me- | thod of Shop and Book-keeping;
with a Description of the several | American Colonies. | Together
with the Carpenter's Plain and Exact Rule: Shew- | ing how to
measure Carpenters, Joyners, Sawyers, Bricklayers, Plai- | sterers,
Plumbers, Masons, Glaziers, and Painters Work. How to | un-
dertake each work, and at what Price; the Rates of each Com- |
modity, and the common Wages of Journeymen; with Gunter's
Line; | and Coggeshal's Description of the Sliding-Rule. | Like-
wise the Practical Guager made Easy; the Art | of Dialling, and
how to erect and fix any Dial; with Instructions for | Dying,
Colouring, and making Colours. | To which is added, | The Poor
Planters Physician. | With Instructions for Marking on Linnen;
how to Pickle | and Preserve; to make divers Sorts of Wine; and
many excellent | Plaisters, and Medicines, necessary in all Fami-
lies. | And also | Prudent Advice to young Tradesmen and Dealers.
| The whole better adapted to these American Colonies, than | any

other Book of the like Kind. | By George Fisher, Accomptant. | The Ninth Edition Revised and Corrected. | *Philadelphia: Printed by B. Franklin, and | D. Hall, at the New-Printing-Office, in Market-Street, 1748.* | 12mo. pp. v, 378, 5 plates.   H. S. P.   1062

" MR. FRANKLIN, The absolute and obvious Necessity of Self-Defence, in the present Conjuncture," &c. [*Philadelphia: Franklin and Hall.* 1748.] Folio, pp. 2.   H. S. P.   1063

In support of Tennent's Sermons on Defensive War.

FRELL. (G.) Von dem | wahren, ewigen | Friedsamen Reiche | Christi, | Und aller seiner Glieder, das hie auf Erden, im | Glauben und Liebe mit Leiden und Geduldt, die Welt und | alle ihre Feinde überwindet, und nach dieser Zeit ewig mit | Gott und Christo sieget, und triumphiret über den | Teuffel, Welt, Sünde und Todt. | Allen | Chatholisch-Evange= lisch-Friedfer= | fertigen-Guthertzigen Christen zu weiterer Nachtrachtung | Ermahnung, diesem Friedsamen König Christo | nachzufolgen, und ihm zu dienen, über welche sey | Friede, Trost und ewige Barmhertzigkeit von | Gott, durch Jesum Christum im | Heiligen Geiste. | Aufgesetzt durch Georg Frell, von Chur in Graubünd= | ner Land. | . . . | . . . | . . . . | *Germanton, gedruckt bey Christoph Saur,* 1748. | 8vo. pp. 15.   1064

THE FRENCH Convert :   Being a true Relation of the Happy Conversion of a Noble French Lady, from the Errors and Superstitions of Popery to the Reformed Religion, by means of a Protestant Gardener, her Servant.   Wherein is shewn, her great and unparalleled Sufferings on the Account of her said Conversion ; as also her wonderful deliverance from two Assassins, hired by a Popish Priest to murder her ; and her miraculous Preservation in a Wood for two Years ; and how she was at last providentially found by her Husband, who, together with her Parents, were brought over by her means to the embracing the true Religion, as were divers others also. The Tenth Edition. To which is added, A brief Account of the present severe Persecutions of the French Protestants.   *Philadelphia: B. Franklin, and D. Hall.* 1748. 1065

FREY. (A.) Andreas Freyen | seine | Declaration, | oder: | Er= klärung, | Auf welche Weise, und wie er | unter die sogenante | Herrn=

huter | Gemeine ge= | kommen ; | Und warum er wieder davon abge=
gangen | Nebst der Beweg=Ursache, warum ers publicirt. | *Germanton
gedruckt bey Christoph Saur*, | 1748. | 16mo. pp. 88.   H. S. P.   1066

EIN GEHEIMER Seelenspiegel, worinen sich ein Mensch besehen
kan wieter in der Wiedergeburt kommen sey.   *Germantown : Christoph
Saur*.   1748.   1067

Advertised in Sower's Newspaper, June 16, 1748.

GERMAN Newspaper.   *Philadelphia : Godhard Armbruster.*
1748.   1068

"Godhard Armbruster, German Printer, in Arch-street, Philadelphia, Hereby
gives notice . . . that he publishes a News-paper in that language once a Fortnight." Pa. Gazette, Feb. 2, 1747-8. In May he began to issue his paper weekly.
See Sower's Newspaper, May 16, 1748.

GILBERT. (B.)   Truth Vindicated, | And the | Doctrine of
Darkness | manifested : | Occasioned by the Reading of Gilbert
Tennent's late Composure, | intituled, | Defensive War Defended.
| Dedicated to the Service of the | Christian Reader. | By Benja-
min Gilbert. | . . . | . . . | . . . | . . . | . . . | . . . | . . . | . . . | . . . .
| *Philadelphia :* | *Printed for the Author [by Franklin and Hall] in
the Year* | M,DCC,XLVIII. | 8vo. pp. iv, 48.   M. S.   1069

GRAMMATICA Anglicana | Concentrata, | Oder | Kurtzge=
faßte | Englische Grammatica. | Worinnen | Die zur Erlernung dieser
Sprache | hinlänglich=nöthige | Grund=Sätze | Auf eine sehr deutliche und
leichte Art | abgehandelt sind. | [*Cut.*]   *Philadelphia, gedruckt und zu
finden bey Gotthard Armbruster.*   [1748.] | 8vo. pp. (8), 118.   1070

GRÜNDLICHE Anweisung zu einem Heiligen Leben. | Von einem
Geistlich=gesinneten lang verstorbenen Lehrer.   Uebersetzt 1747. | *Ger-
manton gedruckt bey Christoph Saur*, 1748. | Folio, 1 leaf.   1071

EIN | GRUENDLICHES | Zeugnüß | Gegen das kürtzlich | her=
ausgegebene | Büchlein, | Genannt Pläin Truth. | Oder: | Lautere Wahr=
heit. | Von einem Teutschen Bauers=Mann, | in Pennsylvanien 1748. |
. . . | . . . | . . . | . . . | . . . | . . . | . . . | . . . | . . . | . . . . | *German-
ton, gedruckt bey Christoph Saur*, 1748. | 8vo. pp. 24.   L. C. P.   1072

HOBURG. (C.) Kurtzer | und erbaulicher | Auszug | oder: | Denck= | würdige | Sprüche | Aus | Christian Hoburgs | Postilla Mystica | über die Evangelium. | Mit kurtzen Summarien vor jeden | Text, und einem dienlichen Register | versehen, dem Lehr= und Heyls= | begierigen zu Nutz und | Aufmerckung. | *Germanton gedruckt bey Christoph Saur,* | 1748. | 16mo. pp. 311.   H. S. P.   1073

DER | HOCH=DEUTSCH | Americanische | Calender, | Auf das Jahr | . . . | . . . . | 1749 | (Welches ein gemein Jahr von 365 Tagen ist.) | . . . | . . . | . . . | . . . | . . . | . . . | . . . | . . . | . . . . | Zum eilff= ten mal heraus gegeben. | *Germantown: Gedruckt und zu finden bey Christoph Saur.* | . . . . [1748.] | Sm. 4to. pp. (36). H. S. P.   1074

HOCHREUTNER. (J. J.)   Schwanen Gesang | Oder | Letzte Arbeit, | Des | Weiland Ehrwürdigen und Hochgelehrten | Herrn | Johann Jacob Hochreutner | Bestimmten Prediger | Der | Ehrsamen Reformierten Gemeinde | zu Lancäster, | Welcher | Auf eine ausserordent= liche Weise nach Gottes allweiser | Zulassung durch einen Büchsen= Schuß aus dem Zeitlichen in das ewige Leben | den 14 October 1748. im 27sten Jahr seines Alters hingerücket wurde. | Zum Trost der betrübten Gemeinde in Lancäster zu dem Druck befördert | und mit einer Zuschrifft versehen | Von | Michael Slatter, V. D. M. zu St. Gallen in der Schweitz, | gegenwärtig Reform. Prediger in Philadelphia und Ger- mantown | in Pennsylvanien | *Philadelphia, gedruckt bey Johan Boehm, wohnhafft in der Arch-Strasse,* 1748. | 4to. pp. (4). 15.

H[UME.] (S[OPHIA])   An | Exhortation | to the | Inhabitants | Of the Province of | South-Carolina, | To bring their Deeds to the Light of | Christ, in their own Consciences. | By S. H. | In which is inserted, | Some Account of the Author's Expe- | rience in the Important Business of | Religion. | . . . | . . . | . . . | . . . | . . . | . . . | . . . | . . . . | *Philadelphia:* | *Printed by William Bradford.*   [1748.] | 8vo. pp. 158.   H. S. P.   1076

Dated 30th o' 10th Month [December], 1747, and therefore not printed till 1748, although this edition has been generally catalogued as printed in 1747.

H[UME.]   Exhortation to the inhabitants of the Province of South Carolina.   *Philadelphia: Printed by B. Franklin and D. Hall.*   1748.   B. P. L.   1077

JERMAN. (J.) An Almanac for 1749. By John Jerman. *Philadelphia: B. Franklin, and D. Hall.* 1748.   1078

EJNE | KURTZE | Vermittelungs= | Schrift | In sich haltende, | Eine | Ansprache | An alle Menschen | Doch | Ins | Besondere | An die, die um Gott und Göttlicher | Dinge wegen mit Eiffer angezogen sind | Als mit Kriegs= | Waffen, | für Göttliche Wahrheiten zu streiten. | Aufgesetzt | Von einem Liebhaber der Göttlichen | Warheit. | *Gedruckt zu Germanton bey Christoph Saur.* | Im Jahre da die Gerichte Gottes augen= scheinlich mit | Macht anfangen einzubrechen, zum Nutzen und Ver= | besser= ung des menschlichen Geschlechts. 1748. | 16mo. pp. 35. H. S. P. 1079

KURTZE | Verteidigung | Der | Lautern Wahrheit | gegen die so ge= nannte | Unterschiedliche Christliche | Wahrheiten, | Welche der Buchdrucker C. S. in Ger= | mantown ohnlängst ausgestreuet. | Vorgestellet | in einem | Brief | Von einem 3ten Handwercksmann in Phi= | ladelphia an seinen Freund im Lande geschrieben, | und | Welche beyde Wahrheiten der Author | dieses Briefs denen Verständigen Teutschen | zur Beurtheilung in Druck vorleget; | . . . | . . . | . . . | . . . | . . . . | [*Philadelphia:*] *Gedruckt im Jahr* 1748. | 8vo. pp. 19.   H. S. P. 1080

LEWIS. (J.) The Church Catechism Explained, by Way of Question and Answer; and confirmed by Scripture Proofs; Divided into five Parts, and Twelve Sections. Wherein a brief and plain Account is given of, I. The Christian Covenant. II. The Christian Faith. III. The Christian Obedience. IV. The Christian Prayer. V. The Christian Sacraments. Collected by John Lewis, Minister of Margate, in Kent. The Thirteenth Edition. *Philadelphia: B. Franklin, and D. Hall.* 1748.   1081

LISCHY. (J.) Jacob Lischy's Zweyte Deklaration oder Erklärung seines Sinnes an seine Ruf Religionsgenossen in Pennsylva. und was der Unterschied sei zwischen ihm und den sogenannten Mährischen Brüdern. *Germantown: Christoph Saur.* 1748. 4to. pp. 20.   1082

MORE. (T.) An Almanac for 1749. By Thomas More. *Philadelphia: B. Franklin, and D. Hall.* 1748.   1083

𝔑𝔈𝔘-eingerichteter Americanischer Geschichts-Calender, auf das Jahr 1749. *Philadelphia: Gedruckt bey B. Francklin und J. Boehm.* 1748.   1084

NEW JERSEY. Anno Regni | Georgii II. | Regis | Magnæ Britanniæ, Franciæ, & Hiberniæ, | Vigesimo Primo. | At a General Assembly of the Colony of | New-Jersey, continued by Adjournments to | the 17th Day of November, Anno Dom. | 1747, and then begun and holden at Bur- | lington, being the fifth Sitting of the second | Session of this present Assembly. | [*Royal Arms.*] | *Philadelphia:* | *Printed by B. Franklin, Printer to the King's* | *most excellent Majesty, for the Province of New-Jersey.* | M,DCC,-XLVIII. | Folio, pp. 53, (1).   1085

NEW-YEAR Verses of the Carriers of the Pennsylvania Gazette. *Philadelphia: B. Franklin.* 1748.   1086

NEW-YEAR Verses of the Carriers of the Pennsylvania Journal. *Philadelphia: William Bradford.* 1748.   1087

THE PENNSYLVANIA Gazette. *Philadelphia: Printed by B. Franklin, Post-Master, and D. Hall,* | *at the New-Printing-Office, near the Market.* | 1088

Numbers 995 (Jan. 5, 1747-8) to 1046 (Dec. 27, 1748), four pages, except Numbers 1002, 1008, 1009, 1010, 1011, 1013, 1016, 1017, 1030 and 1031, which contain six pages. The imprint of the first number is as in Number 891, *supra*, and afterwards as above. Title as in Number 648, *supra*.

THE PENNSYLVANIA Journal.   H. S. P.   1089

Numbers 268 (Jan. 5, 1747-8) to 319 (Dec. 27, 1748), four pages each, with "Supplements" of two pages each to Numbers 273, 275 and 279. Number 290 is misnumbered 280. Title and imprint as in Number 989, *supra*.

POOR Robin's Almanac for 1749. *Philadelphia: William Bradford.* 1748.   1090

POPE. (A.) An Essay on Man. In Four Epistles, By Alexander Pope, Esq; Enlarged and Improved by the Author. To which is added the Universal Prayer. *Philadelphia: William Bradford.* 1748.   1091

Advertised in Pa. Journal, Aug. 4, 1748. The second edition printed by Bradford.

SAUNDERS. (R.) A Pocket | Almanack | For the Year 1749. | Fitted to the Use of Penn- | sylvania, and the neighbour- | ing Provinces. | With several useful Additions. | By R. Saunders, Phil. | *Philadelphia:* | *Printed and sold by B. Franklin,* | *and D. Hall.* [1748.] | 24mo. pp. (24).   H. S. P.   1092

SAUNDERS. . . . | . . . . | Poor Richard improved: | Being an | Almanack | . . . | . . . | . . . | . . . | . . . | . . . | . . . | . . . | . . . | For the | Year of our Lord 1749. | . . . | . . . | . . . | . . . | . . . | . . . | . . . | . . . | . . . . | By Richard Saunders, Philom. | *Philadelphia:* | *Printed and Sold by B. Franklin,* *and D. Hall.* [1748.] | Sm. 8vo. pp. (36).   1093

SCHMIEDLEIN. (J.) Kurtze | Beschreibung, | des | Lebens und Todtes | von | Jacob Schmiedlein, | aus | Wollhausen | im Lutzerner Gebiet in der Schweitz, | welcher im Jahr 1747 im Monath May die | Woche vor Pfingsten zu Lutzern | verbrandt worden. | *Germanton gedruckt bey Christoph Saur,* | 1748. | 16mo. pp. 16.   H. S. P.   1094

SEAGRAVE. (R.) The | True Protestant: | A | Dissertation, | Shewing | The Necessity of asserting the Principles | of Liberty in their full Extent. | By Robert Seagrave, A.M. | . . . | . . . | . . . . | *London Printed:* | *Philadelphia Re-printed, and Sold by W. Bradford,* | *at the Sign of the Bible in Second-Street.* | MDCCXLVIII. | Sm. 8vo. pp. (2), 35, (1).   L. C. P.   1095

SERMON to the Indians at the Funeral of the Rev. David Brainerd. *Philadelphia:* 1748.   1096

Title from Haven's List.

DER SÆIGENISCHE Katechismus oder ein Auszug aus dem Heidelberger Catechismus. *Germantown: Christoph Saur,* 1748.   1097

Advertised in Sower's Newspaper, Aug. 1, 1748.

[SMITH. (John)] The | Doctrine of Christianity, | As held by the People called | Quakers, | Vindicated: | In Answer to | Gil-

bert Tennent's Sermon | On | The Lawfulness of War. | . . . | . . .
| . . . | . . . | . . . | . . . | . . . | . . . | . . . | . . . | . . . | . . . .
Philadelphia: | *Printed by Benjamin Franklin,* | *and David Hall.*
MDCCXLVIII. | 8vo. pp. iv. 56.+ The Second Edition. [*Ibid.*]
8vo. pp. iv. 56.　　　　　　　　　　　　　　　H. S. P.　1098

[SMITH. (Samuel)] Necessary | Truth: | Or | Seasonable |
Considerations | for the | Inhabitants of the | City of Philadelphia,
| and | Province of Pennsylvania. | In Relation to the Pamphlet
call'd | Plain Truth: | And Two other Writers in the | News-
Papers. | . . . | . . . | . . . | . . . | . . . | . . . . | *Philadelphia:* |
Printed [*by W. Bradford*] *in the Year* MDCCXLVIII. | 8vo. pp.
16.　　　　　　　　　　　　　　　　　　　　　H. S. P.　1099

The author was Samuel Smith, the historian of New Jersey. The following
extract from the manuscript diary of John Smith, gives the names of both author
and printer: "Nov. 30, 1747. Received from Bro. Samuel, Necessary Truth,
wch he designs as some Remarks on Plain Truth. I carried it to W. Bradford,
and agreed with him to print 500." It was distributed gratis.

[SOWER. (Christopher)] Verſchiedene | Chriſtliche | Wahrheiten,
| Und | Kurtze Betrachtung | Uber das kürtzlich herausgegebene | Büch-
lein, | Genannt: | Lautere Wahrheit. | Aufgeſeßt zur Uberlegung, | Von
einem Handwerksmann in Germanton. | . . . | . . . | . . . | . . . | . . . |
. . . | . . . | . . . | . . . . | *Germanton gedruckt bey Christoph Saur,*
1748. | 8vo. pp. 32.　　　　　　　　　　　　　　H. S. P.　1100

TENNENT. (G.)　Brotherly Love recommended, by the Ar- |
gument of the Love of Christ. | A | Sermon, | Preached at | Phil-
adelphia, | January, 1747–8. | Before the | Sacramental Solemnity.
| With some Enlargement. | By Gilbert Tennent, A.M. | . . . | . . .
| . . . | . . . | . . . . | *Philadelphia:* | *Printed and Sold by Benja-*
min Franklin | *and David Hall.*　MDCCXLVIII. | 8vo. pp. 36.

TENNENT.　The late Association for Defence, encourag'd, |
or | The lawfulness of a Defensive War. | Represented | in a |
Sermon | preach'd | At Philadelphia December 24. 1747. | By
Gilbert Tennent, A.M. | . . . | . . . | . . . | . . . | . . . | . . . | . . .
| . . . | . . . | . . . | . . . | . . . | . . . . | Published at the request
of the Hearers. | *Philadelphia: Printed by William Bradford.*
[1748.] | 8vo. pp. Half-title, 1 leaf; pp. 46; Corrigenda, 1 leaf.

TENNENT. The late Association for Defence, encourag'd, | or | The Lawfulness of a Defensive War. | Represented | in a | Sermon | preach'd | At Philadelphia December 24, 1747. | By Gilbert Tennent, A. M. | . . . | . . . | . . . | . . . | . . . | . . . | . . . | . . . | . . . | . . . | . . . | . . . | . . . . | Published at the request of the Hearers. | The Second Edition. | *Philadelphia:* | *Printed by William Bradford.* [1748.] | 8vo. pp. 45.   H. S. P.

The half title reads : The Reverend | Mr. Tennent's | Sermons | on | defensive War. |

TENNENT. The late Association for Defence, farther | encourag'd, | or | The Consistancy of Defensive War, with True | Christianity. | Represented | in two | Sermons | preach'd | At Philadelphia, January 24. 1747–8. | By Gilbert Tennent, A.M. | . . . | . . . | . . . | . . . | . . . | . . . | . . . | . . . | . . . | . . . . | *Philadelphia:* | *Printed and Sold by William Bradford,* | *at the Sign of the Bible in Second-Street.* [1748.] | 8vo. pp. iv, 56.   L. C. P.   1104

TENNENT. The Late Association for Defence | Farther Encouraged: | Or, | Defensive Warfare Defended; | and | Its Consistancy with True Chri- | stianity Represented. | In a | Reply | To some | Exceptions against War, in a late | Composure, intituled, | The Doctrine of Christianity, as held by the People | called Quakers, vindicated. | By Gilbert Tennent, A.M. | . . . | . . . | . . . | . . . | . . . | . . . | . . . | . . . | . . . | . . . | . . . | . . . . | *Philadelphia:* | *Printed and Sold by B. Franklin and D. Hall.* | MDCCXLVIII.   Price 2s. 6d. | 8vo. pp. iv, 183.   H. S. P.

TENNENT. A | Sermon | Preach'd | At Philadelphia, January 7. 1747–8. | Being the Day appointed by The | Honourable | the | President and Council, | To be observed throughout this Province, | As a Day of | Fasting and Prayer. | With some Enlargement. | By Gilbert Tennent, A.M. | . . . | . . . | . . . | . . . | . . . . | *Philadelphia:* | *Printed by W. Bradford, at the Sign of* | *the Bible in Second-street.* MDCCXLVIII. | 8vo. pp. 34.   L. C. P.

The half title reads : " The Reverend Mr. Tennent's Sermon on Fasting and Prayer."

TERSTEEGEN. (G.) Warnungs=Schreiben | wider die | Leicht=
sinigkeit, | Worin | die nothwendige Verbindung | der | Heiligung | mit
der | Rechtfertigung, | Wie auch | was Evangelisch ist, | kurtzlich ange=
zeiget wird durch | Geret Te Stegen. | Aus dem Holländischen übersetzt.
Germanton gedruckt bey Christoph | Saur, 1748. | 24mo. pp. 48.
                                                                    1107

TO the Inhabitants of the Province of Pennsylvania. | [n. p.
n. d.] Folio, 1 leaf.   1108

In favor of raising troops for the defense of the Province, signed " Ebenezer
Durham."

A | TREATISE | Shewing | The Need we have to rely upon
| God as sole Protector of this Province; | And | The Reason of
Man's degenerating from his | State of Purity, and the Means
whereby he may be re- | established again. | Also, | Some Re-
marks made on those two Passages in Gilbert | Tennent's Sermon,
viz. Swearing, and Sabbath- | Breaking; with a Reply thereunto. |
Together with | Something in Answer to a late Performance, inti-
tuled, Plain Truth; discovering the Falsity therein con- | tained,
with Remarks on the Authors Irreligion. | Containing wholesome
Advice to the Faithful, to hold | on their Way, and shewing the
woful Effects of transpi- | ring with strong Liquor, and the Way
set forth how to | answer the End of our Creation; | With | A
Call to the Inhabitants of this Province to Amendment | of Life.
| By one that wisheth well to all Mankind. | *Philadelphia:* |
Printed by Godhard Armbrister. | *in Arch-Street.* 1748. | Sm. 8vo.
pp. (26).   L. C. P. 1109

A | TREATY | between the | President and Council | of the
| Province of Pennsylvania, | and the | Indians of Ohio, | Held
at Philadelphia, Nov. 13, 1747. | [*Penn Arms.*] | *Philadelphia:* |
*Printed and Sold by B. Franklin, at the New | Printing-Office, near
the Market.* MDCCXLVIII. | Folio, pp. (8).   B. M. 1110

A | TREATY | held by | Commissioners, | Members of the
Council of the | Province of Pennsylvania, | At the Town of
Lancaster, | With some Chiefs of the Six Nations at Ohio, and
| others, for the Admission of the Twightwee Nation into the |

Alliance of his Majesty, &c., in the Month of July, 1748. | [*Penn Arms.*] *Philadelphia:* | *Printed and Sold by B. Franklin, at the New* | *Printing-Office, near the Market.* MDCCXLVIII. | Folio, pp. (10).   B. M.   1111

VOTES | and | Proceedings | of the | House of Representatives | of the | Province of Pennsylvania. | Met at Philadelphia, | on the Fourteenth of October, | Anno Dom. 1747, and continued by Adjournments. [to Sept. 3, 1749.] | [*Penn Arms.*] | *Philadelphia:* | *Printed and Sold by B. Franklin, at the New* | *Printing-Office, near the Market.* MDCCXLVIII. | Folio, pp. 55, (1). B. M.   1112

WATTS. (I.) The Assembly's Catechism, with Notes: Or the Shorter Catechism, composed by the Assembly of Divines at Westminster: With a brief Explication of the more difficult Words and Phrases contained in it, for the Instruction of Youth. By the late I. Watts, D. D. The Fifth Edition. *Philadelphia: B. Franklin, and D. Hall.* 1748.?   1113

WHITEFIELD. (G.) A | Letter | From the Reverend | Mr. Whitefield, | to | A Reverend Divine in Boston; | Giving a Short Account of his late Visit to | Bermuda. | *Philadelphia:* | *Printed by B. Franklin and D. Hall.* | MDCCXLVIII. | Sm. 8vo. pp. 7.

1749.

ACCOUNT of the Births and Burials in Christ Church Parish. *Philadelphia:* 1749.   1115

ANNO Regni | Georgii II. | Regis | Magnæ Britanniæ, Franciæ & Hiberniæ, | Vigesimo Secundo. | At a General Assembly of the Province of | Pennsylvania, begun and holden at Phi- | ladelphia, the Fourteenth Day of October; Anno Dom. | 1748, in the Twenty-second Year of the Reign of our | Sovereign Lord George II. by the Grace of God, | of Great-Britain, France and Ireland, King, Defender | of the Faith, &c. | And from thence continued by Adjournments to the Second | Day of January, 1748, 9. | [*Penn Arms.*] | *Philadelphia:* | *Printed and Sold by B. Franklin, at the New-* | *Printing-Office, near the Market.* M,DCC,XLIX. | Folio,

Title, 1 leaf; pp. 73–88.+ . . . Vigesimo Tertio. | And from
thence continued . . . to the Seventh | Day of August, 1749. |
[*Ibid.*] Title, 1 leaf; pp. 91–105.   H. S. P.   1116

BALL. (W.) The New Jersey Almanac for 1750. By William
Ball. *Philadelphia: William Bradford.* 1749.   1117

THE | BEGGAR, and no Beggar: | Or | Every Man a King if
he Will. | A | Parable. | Containing an Example of a Perfect |
Man in Christ. | To which is added, | The Hidden Manna; being
an En- | couragement to the Spiritual Progress; in a | Letter to
a well-disposed Friend. | Also | A Word of Comfort to the Poor
and Infirm. | *Philadelphia:* | *Re-printed [by Franklin and Hall] in
the Year* MDCCXLIX. | Price Sixpence. | 8vo. pp. 30.   N. Y. H. S.

BIRKETT. (W.) Poor Will's Almanac for 1750. By William
Birkett. *Philadelphia: Cornelia Bradford.* 1749.   1119

THE SHORTER CATECHISM of the Reverend Assembly of
Divines, with the Proofs thereof out of the Scriptures in Words
at Length. Which are either some of the former quoted Places,
or others gathered from their other Writings: All fitted both for
Brevity and Clearness, to this their Form of sound Words. For
the Benefit of Christians in general, and of Youth and Children
in Understanding, in Particular; that they with more ease may
acquaint themselves with the Truth according to the Scriptures,
and with the Scriptures themselves. *Philadelphia: B. Franklin,
and D. Hall.* 1749.   1120

Advertised at the end of Letters on the Spirit of Patriotism.

CHALKLEY. (T.) A | Collection | of the | Works | of |
Thomas Chalkley. | In Two Parts. | . . . | . . . | . . . | . . . . |
Philadelphia: Printed by B. Franklin, and D. Hall, | MDCCXLIX.
| 8vo.   H. S. P.   1121

Collation: Title, 1 leaf; Testimony, pp. v-xiii, Contents, 1 page; 2d title, 1
leaf; Journal, pp. 1–326; 3d title, 1 leaf; Works, pp. cccxxix—590. The second
and third title pages are as follows: A | Journal, | or, | Historical Account, | of
the | Life, Travels, and Christian Experiences, | of that | Antient, Faithful
Servant of Jesus Christ, | Thomas Chalkley; | Who departed this Life in the

Island of | Tortola, the fourth Day of the Ninth | Month, 1741. | . . . | . . . |
. . . | . . . | . . . . | *Philadelphia:* | *Printed by B. Franklin, and D. Hall,* |
MDCCXLIX. |

The | Works | of | Thomas Chalkley. | Part II. | Containing | His Epistles,
and other Writings. | *Philadelphia:* | *Printed by B. Franklin, and D. Hall.* |
MDCCXLIX. |

CONDUCTOR GENERALIS: | Or, the | Office, Duty and Au-
thority | of | Justices of the Peace, | High-Sheriffs, Under-Sheriffs,
Gaolers, Coroners, | Constables, Jury-Men, and Overseers of the
Poor. | As Also | The Office of Clerks of Assize, | And of the
Peace, &c. | Collected out of all the Books hitherto written on
those Subjects, | whether of Common or Statute-Law. | The whole
Alphabetically digested under the several Titles; with a | Table
directing to the ready finding out the proper Matter under | those
Titles. | To which is added, | A Collection out of Sir Matthew
Hales, concerning The Descent of | Lands; with several choice
Maxims in the Law, and the Office of Mayors, &c. | The Second
Edition, with large Additions. | *Philadelphia:* | *Printed and Sold
by B. Franklin, and D. Hall, at the New-* | *Printing-Office, near the
Market,* 1749. | 16mo. Title, 1 leaf; Preface, pp. (2); Table, pp.
12; Introduction, pp. xvi; text, pp. 1–464. H. S. P. 1122

CONSTITUTIONS | of the | Publick Academy, | in the | City
of Philadelphia. | [*Philadelphia: B. Franklin, and D. Hall.*
1749.] Folio, pp. 4. H. S. P. 1123

DAVIS. (J.) Some Queries sent to the Rev. G. Whitefield, by
Jonathan Davis, in the Year 1740, which remain as yet Unan-
swered. *Philadelphia: B. Franklin, and D. Hall.* 1749. 1124

Title from Haven's List.

𝕯𝕬𝕾 𝕰𝕹𝕿𝕯𝕰𝕮𝕶𝕿𝕰 Geheimnüß der Boßheit der Herrenhutischen
Sekte. *Philadelphia. Johann Boehm.* 16mo. pp. (8), 124+. 1125

AN EPISTLE from the Yearly Meeting. *Philadelphia: B.
Franklin, and D. Hall.* 1749. 1126

DER FAMA. *Philadelphia: Johannes Boehm.* 1749. 1127

This was a periodical publication of some kind, not one of which is now known to exist. I am indebted to Professor Seidensticker for a reference to an article in Sower's newspaper for Feb. 16, 1750, in answer to a "Schmähscrifft" which appeared "in Mr. Böhm Fama" of the 10th of February. When this periodical began or ended is not known, but as Böhm died in July, 1751 (See Sower's paper for Aug. 16, 1751), it was probably discontinued before or about that time.

FINLEY. (S.) The approved Minister of God. | A | Sermon | Preach'd at the | Ordination | of the Reverend | Mr. John Rodgers: | at St. Georges, in Pennsylvania, March 16, 1749. | By Samuel Finley, | Minister of the Gospel at Nottingham. | Publish'd at the Request of the Hearers, with | some Enlargements. | . . . | . . . | . . . | . . . . | *Philadelphia:* | *Printed by William Bradford in Second-Street.* | *For Messrs. David Stewart, and Isaac Dushane.* [1749.] | 8vo. pp. 23; Errata, 1 leaf. c. 1128

[FRANKLIN. (BENJAMIN)] Proposals | Relating to the | Education | of | Youth | in | Pennsylvania. | *Philadelphia:* | *Printed* [*by B. Franklin, and D. Hall,*] *in the Year,* M.DCC.XLIX. | 8vo. pp. 32. H. S. P. 1129

𝕯𝕰𝕽 | 𝕳𝕺𝕮𝕳=𝕯𝕰𝖀𝕿𝕾𝕳 | Americanifche | Calender, | Auf bas Jahr | . . . | . . . | 1750. | . . . | . . . | . . . | . . . | . . . | . . . | . . . | . . . | . . . | . . . . | Zum zwölfften mal heraus gegeben. | *Germantown: Gedruckt und zu finden bey Christoph Saur.* | . . . .[1749.] | Sm. 4to. pp. (36). H. S. P. 1130

THE IMPENETRABLE Secret. *Philadelphia: B. Franklin, and D. Hall.* 1749. 1131

Advertised as "Just published," in the Pa. Gazette, May 11, 1749.

JAMES. (T.) A Short | Treatise | on the | Visible Kingdom of Christ, | and | The great Charter Privileges granted | by Him to His Subjects. | Wherein it is proven, That his . . . | is, and was, the same in Substance . . . | the Old and New Testament, and the | Subjects the same, viz. Believers, and their Infant-seed; and that it was under | the same Covenant. viz. The Covenant | of Grace. | And likewise proven, That .Water-baptism | is come in the Room of Circumcision, | and the Lord's Supper in the

Room of | the Passover. | By Thomas James. | *Philadelphia:* *Printed by B. Franklin and D. Hall.* | MDCCXLIX. | Sm. 8vo. pp. 30. c. 1132

JANEWAY. (J.) A | Token | for | Children. | Being | An exact Account of the Conver- | sion, Holy and Exemplary Lives, | and Joyful Deaths of several young | Children. | By James Janeway, Minister of the Gospel. | To which is added, | A Token for the Children | of New-England. | Or, | Some Examples of Children, in whom the | Fear of God was remarkably Budding be- | fore they died, in several Parts of New- | England. | Preserved and published for the Encouragement of Piety | in other Children. | With New Additions. | *Boston, Printed:* | *Philadelphia, Re-printed, and sold by* | *B. Franklin, and D. Hall,* MDCCXLIX. | 12mo. pp. xii, 108. B. P. L. 1133

EIN JEDER | Sein eigener Doctor, | oder | Des armen | Land= Mannes Artzt. | In sich haltend: | Wie sich jedermann durch schlechte, | und leichte Mittel von allen, oder doch von | den meisten Kranckheiten, die in diesem Climate | gemein sind, curiren kan, und das mit we= | nigen Kosten, weil die Mittel mei= | stens in diesem Lande wachsen. | Zu erst in Englischer Sprache geschrie= | ben und zum öfftern gedruckt, nun aber um seiner | Vortrefflichkeit willen ins Teutsche übersetzt, | worden durch P. M. | *Philadelphia: Gedruckt und zu finden bey Benjamin Francklin und* | *Johann Boehm,* 1749. | 16mo. pp. 40. H. S. P. 1134

JERMAN. (J.) An Almanac for 1750. By John Jerman. *Philadelphia: B. Franklin, and D. Hall.* 1749. 1135

KEMPIS. (T. à) The | Christian Pattern, | or the | Imitation | Of | Jesus Christ, | being an | Abridgment | of the | Works | of | Thomas à Kempis. | By a Female Hand. | *London Printed* M.DCC,XLIV. | *Germantown:* | *Re-printed, by* | *Christopher Sowr* 1749. | 8vo. Title, 1 leaf; pp. 1–278. H. S. P. 1136

KEMPIS. Thomas a Kempis Vier Bücher von der Nachfolge Christi. *Germantown: Christoph Sauer.* 1749. 1137

LISCHY. (J.) Eine | Warnende | Wächter= | Stimm | An alle Gott und Jesum liebende Seelen. | Hergenommen | Aus dem überaus

wichtigen Evangelio | Von den Falschen Propheten | Zuerst in einer Pre=
digt am 8 Sontag nach Trinitatis | Der Reformirten Gemeinde an der
kleinen Catores mündlich | Zugeruffen | Und hernach solches mit kurtzen
doch gründlichen | Anmerckungen | von den sogenandten | Mährischen Brü=
dern | oder | Zinzendörffern | Bekräfftiget: | Und auf vielfältiges Begehren,
zu desto allgemeinerer | Warnung und Erbauung | Zum Druck übergeben
durch | Jacob Lischy V. D. M. | Prediger der Reformirten Gemeinden
uber der Susquehanna in Pennsylvanien. | *Germantown gedruckt bey
Christoph Saur* 1749 | Sq. 8vo. pp. 48.   H. S. P.   1138

LUTHER. (M.)   Der kleine Catechismus des seligen D. Martin
Luthers.   *Philadelphia: B. Franklin, und J. Boehm.*   1749.   1139

Prepared for publication by the Rev. Peter Brunnholtz.   See the "Hallische
Nachrichten," p. 384.   Dr. Reynold's in his Introduction to Acrelius "Nachrichten, pp. 384 and 867, as authority for his statement that the Rev. C. M. von
Wrangel, "Published (in Dr. Franklin's printing-office) a translation of Luther's
Shorter Catechism into English."   As von Wrangel did not arrive in this country
till 1759, and the first reference is to a passage in a letter written in 1749 which
contains a distinct statement that Brunnholtz prepared the catechism for the
press, and the second reference is to a catechism printed by Henry Miller in 1761
or 1762, Dr. Reynolds is at least unfortunate in his citations.

MORE. (T.)   An Almanac for 1750.   By Thomas More.   *Philadelphia: B. Franklin, and D. Hall.*   1749.   1140

NEU=eingerichteter | Americanischer | Geschichts= | Calender, | Auf
das Jahr | Nach der Gnadenreichen Geburt unsers | Herrn und Heylandes
Jesu Christi | 1750. | (Welches ein gemeines Jahr von 365 Tagen ist.) |
Darinen | Ordentlich angezeiget werden die Wochen=Tage, der Tag | des
Monats, der Sonntags=Buchstaben, samt denen Evangelien, die Neue
Zeit, | der Monds Viertel, der Planeten Lauff, und muthmaßliche Witter=
ung, der Son= | nen Auf= und Untergang, der Venus (des Morgen= oder
Aben=Sterns) Auf= | und Untergang, des Monds=Zeichen und Grad,
dessen Auf= und Untergang, des | 7 Gestirns Aufgang, Sud=Platz und
Untergang, Erklärung der Zeichen, Auf= | lauffung der Fluth (oder Deit)
Anzeigung der Finsternissen, Aderlaß=Ta= | sel, Courten, Fären, nebst
andern Nachrichten und Begebenheiten. | Eingerichtet von 40 Grad Nord=
Breite, sonderlich vor | Pennsylvanien, doch auch in denen angräntzenden
Landen ohne sonderlichen | Unterschied zu gebrauchen. | Zum drittenmal

anß Licht gegeben. | *Philadelphia, gedruckt und zu finden bey Benjam. Francklin, und Joh. Boehm.* [1749.] | Sm. 4to. pp. (36).
H. S. P. **1141**

NEW JERSEY. Acts | and | Laws | Of His Majesty's Province of Nova-Cæsarea, or | New Jersey : | As they were Enacted by the Gover- | nor, Council, and General Assembly, | in several Sessions. The first of | which was held at Perth-Amboy, | and begun on the Tenth Day of | October, 1743. and continued to | the Tenth Day of December, 1743. | The following Act was passed the | Second Day of December, 1743. | [*Royal Arms.*] | *Philadelphia : Printed and Sold by William | Bradford, Printer to the King's Most Excellent Ma- | jesty, for the Province of New-Jersey,* MDCCXLIX. | Folio, pp. 56; Table, 1 leaf.
1142

Contains various Acts passed between October 10, 1743 and August 10, 1748.

NEW JERSEY. Acts | and | Laws | Of His Majesty's Province of Nova Cæsarea, or | New-Jersey: | At a General Assembly of the | Colony of New-Jersey, begun Feb- | ruary 20th. 1748–9. at Burlington, | and continued to the 28th of | March 1749. being the first set- | ting of this present Assembly : | On which Day the following | Acts were passed. | [*Royal Arms.*] | *Philadelphia : Printed and Sold by William | Bradford, Printer to the King's Most Excellent Ma- | jesty, for the Province of New-Jersey,* MDCCXLIX. | Folio, pp. 11, (1).
1143

NEW-YEAR Verses of the Carriers of the Pennsylvania Gazette. *Philadelphia : B. Franklin, and D. Hall.* 1749.
1144

NEW-YEAR Verses of the Carriers of the Pennsylvania Journal. *Philadelphia : William Bradford.* 1749.
1145

THE PENNSYLVANIA Gazette.
1146

Numbers 1047 (Jan 3, 1748–9) to 1098 (Dec. 26, 1749), four pages each, except Numbers 1071, 1089, 1091, 1092, 1093 and 1094, which contain six pages. There is a "Supplement" of 1 leaf to Number 1059. The size of the page varies frequently throughout the year. Title and imprint as in Number 1088, *supra.*

THE PENNSYLVANIA Journal.
H. S. P. **1147**

Numbers 320 (Jan. 3, 1748-9) to 371 (Dec. 26, 1749), four pages each, with a "Supplement" of two pages to No. 340. Title and imprint as in Number 989, *supra*.

POOR Robin's Almanac for 1750. *Philadelphia: William Bradford.* 1749.   1148

A | PRESENT | for an | Apprentice: | Or, | A Sure Guide | To gain both | Esteem and Estate. | With Rules for his Conduct to his | Master, and in the World. | By a late Lord Mayor of London. | The Fourth Edition. | *Philadelphia: | Printed and sold by B. Franklin, and | D. Hall,* MDCCXLIX. | 24mo. pp. 103, (4).   L. C. P.   1149

PROCLAMATION. G. [*Royal Arms.*] R. | By the Honourable | James Hamilton, Esq; | . . . | . . . | . . . | A Proclamation. | *Philadelphia: Printed by B. Franklin, Printer to the Province.* [1749.] | Folio, 1 leaf.   H. S. P.   1150

Dated Aug. 11, 1749. Against selling liquor to the Indians, who visit Philadelphia to hold Treaties.

PROCLAMATION. G. [*Royal Arms.*] R. | By the Honourable | James Hamilton, Esq; | . . . | . . . | . . . . | A Proclamation. | *Philadelphia: Printed by B. Franklin, Printer to the Province.* | Folio, 1 leaf.   H. S. P.   1151

Dated July 18, 1749. Warning "Squatters" to leave the Indians' lands west of the Blue Hills.

[ST. JOHN. (HENRY, VISCOUNT BOLINGBROKE)] Letters | on the | Spirit of Patriotism: | On the | Idea of a Patriot King: | And | On the State of Parties, | At the Accession of | King George the First. | *London Printed: | Philadelphia Reprinted, and Sold by | B. Franklin and D. Hall, at the Post- | Office, near the Market.* MDCCXLIX. | 8vo. pp. 86; Books lately published, 1 leaf. L. C. P.

SAUNDERS. (R.) A Pocket | Almanack | For the Year 1750. | Fitted to the Use of Penn- | sylvania, and the neighbour- | ing Provinces. | With several useful Additions. | By R. Saunders, Phil. | *Philadelphia: | Printed and sold by B. Franklin. | and D. Hall.* [1749.] | 24mo. pp. (24).   C.   1153

SAUNDERS. Poor Richard improved: | Being an | Alma-nack | . . . | . . . | . . . | . . . | . . . | . . . | . . . | . . . | . . . | . . . . | For the | Year of our Lord 1750. | . . . | . . . | . . . | . . . | . . . | . . . | . . . | . . . | . . . . | By Richard Saunders, Philom. | . . . | . . . . | *Philadelphia:* | *Printed and Sold by B. Franklin,* *and D. Hall.* [1749.] | Sm. 8vo. pp. (36).   **1154**

SOME Remarks on Abel Morgan's Answer to Samuel Finley; and a Note to the People called Quakers. *Philadelphia: B. Franklin, and D. Hall.* 1749.   **1155**

TENNENT. (G.) Irenicum Ecclesiasticum, | or | A Humble Impartial | Essay | upon the | Peace of Jerusalem, | wherein | The Analogy between Jerusalem and the visible Church is in some | Instances briefly hinted. | The Nature, the Order, the Union, of the visible Church, | together with her Terms of Com-munion, are particularly | considered, and their Excellency opened. | Moreover the following important Points are largely explain'd. | 1. What is to be understood by the Peace of Jerusalem. | 2. What by praying for the Peace of Jerusalem. | 3. How, and why we should pray for its Peace and Prosperity. | Under the afore-said General Heads, the following Particulars are | discuss'd, viz. The Nature, Kinds, Hindrances, Means and | Motives of Peace and Union, together with an Answer to | Objections. | Also | A Prefatory Address to the Synods of New-York & Philadelphia. | By Gilbert Tennent, A.M. | . . . | . . . | . . . | . . . | . . . . | *Philadelphia.* | *Printed and Sold by W. Bradford, at the Sign of the* *Bible* | *in Second-Street.* MDCCXLIX. | 8vo. pp. viii, 141, (1).

TENNENT. A | Sermon | Preach'd at Burlington in New-Jersey, November 23. | 1749. Being the Day appointed by his Excellency | the Governor, with the advice of His | Majesty's Council, | for a | Provincial Thanksgiving. | Before the Governor and others, upon Texts | chosen by his Excellency. | With a Prefatory Address to Philip Doddridge, D. D. | By Gilbert Tennent, A. M. | . . . | . . . | . . . | . . . . | *Philadelphia.* | *Printed by W. Bradford at the Sign of the Bible* | *in Second-Street,* MDCCXLIX. | Sq. 8vo. pp. 28.   H. S. P.   **1157**

TENNENT. A | Sermon | Preach'd at Philadelphia, July 20.
1748. | On a | Funeral Occasion, | Wherein the absolute certainty,
and great Moment, of the | Doctrine of the | Resurrection | Are
proved and illustrated; with a Reply to the principal Ob- |
jections against it. | By Gilbert Tennent, A.M. | ... | ... | ...
| ... | ... | .... | *Philadelphia:* | *Printed and Sold by W.
Bradford, in Second* | *Street,* 1749. | 8vo. pp. 16.   c.   1158

TENNENT. The Substance and Scope of both Testaments, |
Or, | The Distinguishing Glory of the Gospel. | A | Sermon | on
| The Displays of Divine Justice, | in | The Propitiatory Sacrifice
of Christ : | Representing the Nature, Necessity, and Sufficiency,
of his | Satisfaction, the Imputation of his Righteousness, in |
consequence of it, together with an Answer to the most impor- |
tant Objections. | Preach'd at Philadelphia, in April 1749. | By
Gilbert Tennent, A.M. | ... | ... | ... | ... | ... | ... | ... |
.... | *Philadelphia:* | *Printed and Sold by William Bradford in* |
Second-Street, 1749. | 8vo. pp. 27.   H. S. P.   1159

TENNENT. The Terrors of the Lord. | A | Sermon | upon
the | General Judgment, | Preach'd at Maidenhead, in New-Jersey,
May the 17th 1749. | Before | The Synod of York. | By Gilbert
Tennent, A.M. | ... | ... | .... | *Philadelphia:* | *Printed and Sold
by William Bradford in Second-Street,* 1749. | 8vo. pp. 10.   c.

TENNENT. Two | Sermons | Preach'd at Burlington, | in New-
Jersey, April 27th, 1749. | The Day appointed by His Excellency
the Governor, | and the Honourable the Council, | for a | Provin-
cial Fast, | Before the Governor and others, upon Texts | Chosen
by His Excellency. | By Gilbert Tennent, A.M. | ... | ... | ... |
... | .... | *Philadelphia:* | *Printed and Sold by W. Bradford, in
Second* | *Street.* [1749.] | 8vo. pp. 40.   c.   1161

𝕿𝕽𝕰𝖀𝕳𝕰𝕽𝕿𝟛𝕵𝕲𝕰 und einfältige Anweifung, wie fich folche gut=
willige Seelen zu verhalten haben, welche theils von den groben Weltgei=
ftern und Lockvögeln zum Mittwachen, theils von den unlautern
Seelenwerbern und Nebenbuhlern unter gutem Schein zu ihrer Nachfolge

gereißet, gelocket, angefochten und überlauffen werden. Von einem durch
Schaden gewißigten Gemüth. *Germantown. Christoph Saur.* 1749.

Title from Seidensticker's Bibliography.

A | TRUE and Particular | Relation | Of the Dreadful | Earth-
quake, | Which happen'd | At Lima, the Capital of Peru, and |
the neighbouring Port of Callao, | On the 28th of October, 1746.
| With an Account likewise of every Thing mate- | rial that
passed there afterwards to the End of | November following. |
Published at Lima by Command of the Viceroy, | And Trans-
lated from the Original Spanish, | By a Gentleman who resided
many Years in those | Countries. | *London Printed :* | *Philadelphia
Reprinted, and Sold by B.* | *Franklin, and D. Hall, at the New-* |
Printing-Office, near the Market. 1749. | 8vo. pp. 52.   H. S. P.

VOTES of the Assembly. *Philadelphia : B. Franklin,* 1749.

WATTS. (I.) Divine Songs, attempted in easy Language, for
the Use of Children. By the late Isaac Watts, D. D. The
Eleventh Edition. *Philadelphia : B. Franklin, and D. Hall.* 1747.

WHITEFIELD. (G.) Some | Remarks | on a | Pamphlet, |
entituled. | The Enthusiasm of Methodists and Papists | compar'd ;
| Wherein several Mistakes in some Parts of | his past Writings
and Conduct are ac- | knowledged, and his present Sentiments |
concerning the Methodists explained. | (In a Letter to the Author.)
By George Whitefield, late of Pemb. | Coll. Oxon. Chaplain to
the Rt. Honourable | the Countess of Huntingdon. | . . . . |
London Printed: | *Philadelphia Re-printed, and Sold, by* | *W. Brad-
ford in Second-Street,* 1749. | Sm. 8vo. pp. 46.   H. S. P. 1166

[ZUBLY. (JOHANNES JOACHIM)] Eine Predigt welche ein Schwei=
ßer, ein Reformirter Prediger in Sud Carolina bey Charleßtaun gehalten,
über die Worte des Propheten Hosea: Sie bekehren sich, aber nicht recht.
Germantown : Christoph Saur. 1749.   1167

Advertised in Sower's Newspaper, Sept. 1, 1749.

1750.

AN ACCOUNT of the Births and Burials in Christ-Church Parish, in Philadelphia, from Dec. 1749 to Dec. 1750. *Philadelphia.* 1750.   1168

ANLEITUNG zur Englischen Sprache für die Teutschen um das Englische zu lernen. *Germantown: Christoph Saur.* 1750.   1169

Title from Seidensticker's Bibliography.

ANNO Regni | Georgii II. | Regis, | Magnæ Britanniæ, Franciæ & Hiberniæ, | Vigesimo Tertio. | At a General Assembly of the Province of Penn- | sylvania, begun and holden at Philadelphia, the | Fourteenth Day of October, Anno Domini 1749, in the | Twenty-third Year of the Reign of onr Sovereign | Lord George II. by the Grace of God, of Great- | Britain, France and Ireland, King, Defender of the | Faith, &c. | And from thence continued by Adjournments to the First | Day of January, 1749. | [*Penn Arms.*] | *Philadelphia:* | *Printed and Sold by B. Franklin, at the New-* | *Printing-Office, near the Market.* MDCCL. | Folio, Title, 1 leaf; pp. 107–119. + And from thence continued by Adjournments to the | Sixth Day of August, 1750. | [*Ibid.*] Title, 1 leaf; pp. 123–125.   H. S. P.   1170

BALL. (W.) The New Jersey Almanac for 1751. By William Ball. *Philadelphia: William Bradford.* 1750.   1171

BIRKETT. (W.) An Almanac for 1751. By William Birkett. *Philadelphia: Cornelia Bradford.* 1750.   1172

CONDUCTOR Generalis. The Second Edition. *Philadelphia: B. Franklin, and D. Hall.* 1750. 8vo. pp. (116), xvi, 464.   H. S. P.

See Number 1122, *supra*, from which this differs only in the date.

[FENELON. (F. SALIGNAE DE LA MOTHE)] The | Archbishop of Cambray's | Dissertation | on | Pure Love, | With | An Account of the Life and Writings of [Madame Guion] the Lady, for | whose sake the Archbishop was banish'd from Court. | And the grievous Persecutions she suffer'd in France | for her Religion, |

Also | Two Letters written by one of the Lady's Maids, | during her Confinement in the Castle of Vicennes, | where she was a Prisoner Eight Years: One of the | Letters was writ with a Bit of Stick instead of a Pen, | and Soot instead of Ink, to her Brother; the Other | to a Clergyman. | Together with an | Apologetic Preface. | Containing divers Letters of the Archbishop of | Cambray, to the Duke of Burgundy, the present French | King's Father, and other Persons of Distinction. | Also | Divers Letters of the Lady to Persons of Quality, | Relating to her Religious Principles. | . . . | . . . | . . . | . . . | . . . . | *London: Printed, and Re-printed by Christophor* | *Sowr at Germantown* 1750. | 8vo. pp. xcvii. 120.   H. S. P.   1174

THE FRIENDLY Instructor; or, A Companion for young Ladies, and young Gentlemen: In which their Duty to God, and their Parents, their Carriage to Superiors and Inferiors, and several other very useful and instructive Lessons are recommended, In plain and familiar Dialogues. With a recommendatory Preface by the late Rev. Dr. Doddridge. The Sixth Edition. *Philadelphia: B. Franklin, and D. Hall.* 1750.   1175

𝕲𝔒𝔈𝖙𝖙𝕷𝕴𝕮𝕳𝔈 | Liebes-Andacht | mit einer | Anweisung | Und | Unterricht: | Wie man die Liebes-Andacht in der | Stille und Ruhe des Gemüths | üben soll vor Gott. | Samt einer Erklärung, worinnen die | Wahre und Falsche Gemüths- | Ruhe bestehe. | Und worin die wahre Gemeinschafft der Heiligen | mit der Christlichen Kirchen bestehe. | Beschrieben von einem Schüler in der Uebung | dieser Gemüths-Ruhe in Gott: | Aus geringer Erfahrung durch | Gottes Gnade. | *Germantown* | *Gedruckt bey Christoph Saur,* 1750. | 16mo. Title, 1 leaf; Vorrede, pp. (9); text, pp. 1–53.   H. S. P.   1176

𝕯𝕬𝕾 𝕲𝖀𝔈𝕷𝕯𝔈𝕽𝔈 𝔄. 𝔅. 𝔈. oder die Schule der Weisheit in Reimen. *Germantown: Gedruckt und zu finden bey Christoph Saur* 1750. 16mo. pp. 144.   H. S. P.   1177

HERVEY. (J.) Meditations | and | Contemplations. | In Two Volumes. | Containing, | Vol. I. | Meditations among | the Tombs. | Reflections on a | Flower Garden; | And, A Descant on | Creation. | Vol. II. | Contemplations | on the Night. | Contemplations

| on the Starry | Heavens; And, | A Winter Piece. | By James Hervey, A.B. | Late of Lincoln-College, Oxford. | The Seventh Edition. | Vol. I. | *London Printed:* | *Philadelphia Re-printed, and Sold by W. Brad-* | *ford, at the Sign of the Bible in Second-street.* | M,DCC,L. | 16mo. pp. xvi. 234.+Vol. II. | [*Ibid.*] pp. xv. 237.

𝕯𝕰𝕽 | 𝕳𝕺𝕮𝕳=𝕯𝕰𝖀𝕿𝕾𝕮𝕳 | Americaniſche Calender, | Auf das Jahr | . . . | . . . | 1751. | . . . | . . . | . . . | . . . | . . . | . . . | . . . | . . . | . . . | . . . | . . . . | Zum dreyzehnten mal heraus gbgeben. | *Germantown: Gedruckt und zu finden bey Christoph Saur.* | . . . . [1750.] | 4to. pp. (36). H. S. P. 1179

Title and Monthly Calendars in red and black.

JAMES. (P.) A Dialogue between a Blind Man and Death. Translated out of the British Language and render'd into familiar English Verse. By Philip James. The Third Edition. *Philadelphia: B. Franklin, and D. Hall.* 1750. 1180

JAMES. (T.) A short Treatise on the Visible Kingdom of Christ, And the great Charter Privileges granted by Him to His Subjects: Wherein it is proven, That his Kingdom is, and was, the same in Substance under the Old and New Testaments, and the Subjects the same, viz. Believers, and their Infant-seed; and that it was under the same Covenant, viz. The Covenant of Grace. And likewise proven, That Water-baptism is come in the Room of Circumcision, and the Lord's Supper in the Room of the Passover. By Thomas James. *Philadelphia: B. Franklin, and D. Hall.* 1750. 1181

JERMAN. (J.) The American | Almanack | For the Year of Christian Account | 1751, | . . . | . . . | . . . | . . . | . . . | . . . | . . . | . . . | . . . | . . . | . . . . | By John Jerman, Philom. | . . . | . . . | . . . | . . . | . . . | . . . | . . . . | *Philadelphia:* | *Printed by B. Franklin and D. Hall.* [1750.] | Sm. 8vo. pp. (24). 1182

"It was for the Year 1721, that I first published Almanacks, and have so continued yearly (excepting some intervals that happened)."—*Preface.*

KEMPIS. (Thomas à) Der Kleine | Kempis, | Oder | Kurtze Sprüche | und | Gebätlein, | Aus denen meiſtens unbekann= | ten Werck=

lein | des | Thomæ à Kempis | zusammen getragen | zur | Erbauung der Kleinen. | Vierte, und vermehrte Edition. | *Germantown* | *Gedruckt bey Christoph Saur*, 1750. | 24mo. pp. 162; 1 plate.   H. S. P.   1183

LETTERS | from the | Dead | to the | Living. | By Philaretes. | *Philadelphia :* | *Printed by B. Franklin, and D. Hall,* | *at the Post-Office, in Market-street.* | MDCCL. | 8vo. pp. 43, (5?). H. S. P.   1184

LIEBREICHER Zuruf der Väter, Freunden u. Göner in Europa, gethan an die, von Ihnen gesandte, Hirten in Pensylvania, an ihrem Lob= und Danck=Fest, wegen derer glücklichen Ankunfft, so jährlich fället auf den 15. Ianuarü. *Ephrata: Typis Sociatatis.* 1750. Sm. 4to. pp. 28.   1185

MORGAN. (A.) Anti-Pædo-Rantism Defended : | A | Reply | to | Mr. Samuel Finley's | Vindication of the Charitable Plea | for the Speechless. | Wherein | His Repeated Objections against the Baptism | of Believers only, and the Mode of it by | Immersion, are again Examined and | Refuted. | By Abel Morgan, | At Middletown, in East-Jersey. | . . . | . . . | . . . | . . . | . . . . | *Philadelphia:* | *Printed by B. Franklin, and D. Hall,* | *in Market-street.* MDCCL. | Large 16mo. pp. 230.   H. S. P.   1186

MOORE. (T.) An Almanac for 1751. By Thomas Moore. *Philadelphia: B. Franklin, and D. Hall.* 1750.   1187

    The name of the compiler of the Almanac for 1748 is printed "More," but in all the subsequent advertisements it is given "Moore."

NEU=eingerichteter Americanische Geschichts Calender, auf das Jahr 1751. *Philadelphia: B. Franklin und G. Armbruster.* 1750.

NEW JERSEY. Anno Regni | Georgii II. | Regis | Magnæ Britanniæ, Franciæ & Hiberniæ. | Vigesimo Primo. | At a General Assembly of the Colony of New-Jersey, | begun and holden at Burlington, November the 17th, 1747. | and continued to February 18, 1747. On which Day | the following Act was passed. | [*Royal Arms.*] | *Philadelphia:* | *Printed by William Bradford, Printer to the King's* | *Most Excellent Majesty, for the Province of New-Jersey.* [1750.] | Folio, pp. 18.   1189

NEW–YEAR Verses of the Carriers of the Pennsylvania Gazette. *Philadelphia: B. Franklin, and D. Hall.* 1750.   1190

NEW–YEAR Verses of the Carriers of the Pennsylvania Journal. *Philadelphia: William Bradford.* 1750.   1191

THE PENNSYLVANIA Gazette.   1192

Numbers 1099 (Jan. 2, 1749–50) to 1150 (Dec. 25, 1750), four pages each, except Numbers 1116, 1117, 1119, 1120, 1123–1126 and 1128, which contain six pages. Title and imprint as in Number 1088, *supra*, until Number 1129, when the paper was enlarged, and the imprint changed to the form given in Number 1233, *infra*.

THE PENNSYLVANIA Journal.   H. S. P.   1193

Numbers 372 (Jan. 2, 1749) to 423 (Dec. 25, 1750), four pages each. Title and imprint as in Number 989, *supra*. There is a "Supplement" of two pages to Number 413.

POOR Robin's Almanac for 1751. *Philadelphia: William Bradford.* 1750.   1194

PROCLAMATION. G. [*Royal Arms.*] R. | By the Honoura- ble | James Hamilton, Esq ; | Lieutenant Governor, and Comman- der in Chief, of the Province of | Pennsylvania, and Counties of Newcastle, Kent and Sussex, on | Delaware. | A Proclamation. | *Philadelphia: Printed by B. Franklin, Printer to the Province.* MDCCL. | Folio, 1 leaf.   H. S. P.   1195

Announcing the passage of an act of Parliament to prevent "the erection of any mill or other engine for slitting or rolling of iron, or any plating Forge to work with a Tilt Hammer, or any Furnace for making Steel, in any of the Colonies."

REASON against Coition. A discourse (as it is said) preached at St. Patrick's Church in Dublin, by the reverend and most cele- brated Dean Swift; calculated for the latitude of Hibernia, but may, without sensible error, serve some other places. *Philadel- phia: Godhard Armbruster.* 1750.   1196

Advertised in the Pa. Gazette, May 10, 1750, as published at the request of Mr. Ebenezer Tomlinson.

SAUNDERS. (R.) A Pocket Almanac for 1751. By Richard Saunders. *Philadelphia: B. Franklin, and D. Hall.* 1750.   1197

SAUNDERS. Poor Richard improved: | Being an | Alma-nack | and | Ephemeris | of the | Motions of the Sun and Moon; | the true | Places and Aspects of the Planets ; | the | Rising and Setting of the Sun ; | and the | Rising, Setting and Southing of the Moon, | For the | Year of our Lord 1751. | Containing also, | The Lunations, Conjunctions, Eclipses, Judg- | ment of the Weather, Rising and Setting of the | Planets, Length of Days and Nights, Fairs, Courts, | Roads, &c. | Together with useful Tables, chro- | nological Observations, and entertaining Remarks. | Fitted to the Latitude of Forty Degrees, and a Meridian of near | five Hours West from London; but may, without sensible Error, | serve all the Northern Colonies. | By Richard Saunders, Philom. | . . . | . . . . | *Philadelphia:* | *Printed and Sold by B. Franklin, and D. Hall.* [1750.] | Sm. 8vo. pp. (36). H. S. P.   1198

THOMPSON. (A.) A | Discourse | on the | Preparation of the Body | for the | Small-Pox: | And | The Manner of receiving the Infection. | As it was deliver'd in the Publick Hall of the Acad-emy, | before the Trustees, and others, on Wednesday, | the 21st of November, 1750. | By Adam Thomson, Physician in Philadel-phia. | . . . | . . . | . . . | . . . . | *Philadelphia :* | *Printed by B. Frank-lin, and D. Hall.* | MDCCL. | 4to. pp. 24.   A. A. S.   1199

Thomson was originally from Edinburg, and came to Philadelphia in Nov. 1748, having practised in Maryland for some years. He died in New York, in 1767 or 1768.

VOTES | and | Proceedings | of the | House of Representatives | of the | Province of Pennsylvania, | Met at Philadelphia, on the Fourteenth of October, | Anno Dom. 1749, and continued by Adjournments. [to June 18th 1750.] | [*Penn Arms.*] | *Philadelphia :* | *Printed and Sold by B. Franklin, at the New | Printing-Office near the Market.* MDCCL. | Folio, pp. 77, (1).   H. S. P.   1200

1751.

AN ACCOUNT of Births | and Burials in Christ-Church Parish, | in Philadelphia, from December 24, 1750, | to December 24, 1751. By Caleb Cash, | Clerk, and Samuel Kirke, Sexton. | [n. p. n. d.] Folio, 1 leaf.   L. C. P.   1201

An | Account | Of the | Robberies | Committed by | John Morrison, | And his Accomplices, in and near Philadelphia, 1750. | Together with | The Manner of their being discover'd, their Behaviour on their | Tryals, in the Prison after Sentence, and at the Place of | Execution. | [*Cut.*] | *Philadelphia, Printed [by Anthony Armbruster] in the Year* 1750–1. | 8vo. pp. 14 +.   H. S. P.

ANNO Regni | Georgii II. | Regis, | Magnæ Britanniæ, Franciæ & Hiberniæ, | Vigesimo Quarto. | At a General Assembly of the Province of Penn- | sylvania, begun and holden at Philadelphia, | the Fourteenth Day of October, Anno Domini, 1750, in | the Twenty-fourth Year of the Reign of our Sovereign | Lord George II. by the Grace of God, of Great- | Britain, France and Ireland, King, Defender of the | Faith, &c. | And from thence continued by Adjournments to the | Seventh Day of January, 1750–1. | [*Penn Arms.*] | *Philadelphia:* | *Printed and Sold by B. Franklin, at the New-* | *Printing-Office, near the Market.* MDCCLI. | Folio, Title, 1 leaf; pp. 129–151. + And from thence continued by Adjournments to the | Sixth Day of May, 1751. | [*Ibid.*] Title, 1 leaf; pp. 155–158.   H. S. P.   1203

ARNDT. (J.) Des Hocherleuchteten Theologi, Herrn Johann Arndts, | Weiland General=Superintendenten | des Fürstenthums Lüne= burg, 2c. | Sämtliche | Sechs geistreiche Bücher | Vom | Wahren | Christenthum, | Das ist: | Von heilsamer Buße, | Hertzlicher Reue und Leid über die | Sünde, wahrem Glauben, auch heiligem | Leben und Wandel der rechten wahren | Christen. | Neue Auflage mit Kupfern, | Samt | Richtigen Anmerckungen, kräfftigen Gebetern | über alle Capitel, | und | Einem sechsfachen Register. | *Philadelphia, gedruckt und verlegt bey Benjamin Franklin* | *und Johann Boehm,* 1751. | 8vo. Title, 1 leaf; Preliminary matter, pp. (32); text, pp. 1–1356 ; 65 plates.
                                                      H. S. P.   1204

AUSBUND, | Das ist: | Etliche schöne | Christliche | Lieder | Wie sie in dem Ge= | fängnüß zu Bassau in dem | Schloß von den Schweitzer= Brüdern | und von anderen rechtglaubigen | Christen hin und her ge= | dichtet worden. | Allen und jeden Christen | welcher Religion sie seyen, un= | partfjevifdj faft nußlidj. | *Germanton : | Gedruckt bey Christoph Sauer*, 1751. | 16mo. pp. (10), 812, (6), 20, 46.   H. S. P.   1205

BALL. (W.) The New-Jersey | Almanack, | For the Year of Christian Account | 1752. | . . . | . . . | . . . | . . . . | Being Bissextile or Leap-Year. | . . . | . . . | . . . | . . . | . . . | . . . | . . . | . . . | . . . | . . . | . . . | . . . | . . . | . . . | . . . | . . . . | By William Ball, Philomath. | *Philadelphia : Printed and sold by W. Bradford at | the sign of the Bible in Second-Street.* [1751] | Sm. 8vo. pp. (32?).   1206

BIRKETT. (W.) An Almanac for 1752. By William Birkett. *Philadelphia : Cornelia Bradford.* 1751.   1207

A CATALOGUE of Books to be sold at Auction, beginning April 20. 1751. *Philadelphia: William Bradford.* 1751.   1208

A CATALOGUE of Books which will begin to be sold by Auction on Nov. 25, at Mr. Vidal's long Room in Second Street. *Philadelphia: William Bradford.* 1751.   1209

[CRISP. (Stephen)] A | Short History | of a | Long Travel, | from | Babylon, | to | Bethel. | Written the 9th Month, 1691. | The Seventh Edition. | *London : Printed and Sold by J. Sowle, | and Re-printed by Cornelia Bradford | in Philadelphia*, 1751. | Sm. 8vo. pp. 23.   H. S. P.   1210

THE DEED of Settlement of the | Society for insuring of Houses, in and | near Philadelphia. | [*Philadelphia : B. Franklin, and D. Hall.* 1751.] 4to. pp. 8.   L. C. P.   1211

DICKINSON. (J.) God's Protecting Providence, | Man's Surest Help and Defence, | in | Times of greatest Difficulty, and most | eminent Danger. | Evidenced, | In the remarkable Deliverance of Robert Barrow, | with divers other Persons, from the devour- | ing Waves of the Sea; among which they suf- | fered | Shipwreck: | And also, | From the cruel, devouring Jaws of the inhuman | Canibals of Florida. | Faithfully related by Jonathan Dickinson, one | of the Persons concerned therein. | The Fourth Edition. | . . . | . . . | . . . | . . . . | *Philadelphia:* | *Printed and Sold by William Bradford, at the Sign of the Bible in Second-Street.* | M,DCC,LI. | 8vo. Title, 1 leaf; Preface, pp. (6); text, pp. 80.

[DODSLEY. (ROBERT)] The Oeconomy of Human Life. Translated from an Indian Manuscript, written by an ancient Brahmin. To which is prefixed, an Account of the Manner in which the said Manuscript was discovered. In a Letter from an English Gentleman, now residing in China, to the East of * * * *. The Sixth Edition. *Philadelphia: B. Franklin, and D. Hall.* 1751.   1213

ELLWOOD. (T.) Davideis: The Life of David, King of Israel: A Sacred Poem, in Five Books. By Thomas Ellwood. The Fourth Edition, Corrected. *Philadelphia: B. Franklin, and D. Hall.* 1751.   1214

AN EPISTLE from the Yearly Meeting. *Philadelphia: B. Franklin, and D. Hall.* 1749.   1215

[FRANKLIN. (BENJAMIN)] Idea of the English School, | Sketch'd out for the Consideration of the Tru- | stees of the Phil- adelphia Academy. | [*Philadelphia: B. Franklin, and D. Hall.* 1751.] 8vo. pp. 8.   H. S. P.   1216

Generally found appended to Peters' Sermon on Education, Number 1234, *infra.*

THE FRENCH Convert: Being a true Relation of the Happy Conversion of a Noble French Lady from the Errors and Super- stitions of Popery to the Reformed Religion, by Means of a Pro- testant Gardener, her Servant. The Eleventh Edition. *Philadel- phia: B. Franklin, and D. Hall.* 1751.   1217

For a fuller title see the 10th edition, Number 1129, *supra.* There was a copy in the Burlington Library, according to the catalogue of 1758, which cannot now be found.

G. . . (G.) An | Almanack, | For the Year of our Lord, | 1752: | Being Bissextile, or Leap-Year: | Wherein is contained, | The Lunations, Eclipses, Judgment of the Weather, | Sun and Moon's rising and setting, fixed Stars rising, | setting and southing, with Fairs, Courts, and obser- | vable Days; interspers'd with several remarkable | Prodigres in Nature. | Calculated to suit the Meridian (as well as the Pockets | of the good People) of Lancaster; but | may, without sensible Error, serve all Pennsylvania, | and the neighbouring Provinces. | By G. G. Astronomical Professor. | . . . | . . . | . . . | . . . . | *Lancaster:* | *Printed and Sold by James Chattin,* | *at the New-Printing-Office, near the Mar-* | *ket,* . . . | . . . | . . . . | Sm. 8vo. pp. (16).   1218

  The Almanac begins immediately after the imprint, about three-fourths of the way down the title page. The author introduces it as his "First Attempts in This Way."

GERMAN and English Gazette.   *Philadelphia: Godhard Armbruster.*   1219

  In the Pa. Gazette, Sept. 26, 1751, it is announced that "At the German Printing-Office, in Arch-street, is now printed every fortnight, a Dutch and English Gazette, containing the freshest Advices . . . . in both Languages." Thomas, in his History of Printing, says the paper was called "Die Zeitung." This may be correct, but the title given by Prof. Seidensticker is certainly wrong, as it is that of a paper which was not begun till about 1755, and was printed entirely in German.

GREW. (T.) The Barbadoes Almanac for 1752. By Theophilus Grew. *Philadelphia: B. Franklin, and D. Hall.* 1751. Folio, 1 leaf.   1220

  Printed in red and black. There was at one time a copy in the Library Company of Philadelphia, but it cannot now be found.

HAMILTON. (A.) A Defence of Doctor Thompson's Discourse on the Preparation of the Body for the Small-pox, etc. Wherein everything that has been yet advanced against it is fairly examined; particularly Dr. Mead's Censure of Dr. Boerhaave's Opinion concerning a specific Antidote, and Mr. Kearsley's Remarks. In a letter to a Physician in Philadelphia. By Alexander Hamilton, Physician at Annapolis, in Maryland. *Philadelphia: William Bradford.* 1751. 1221

DER | HOCH-DEUTSCH | Americanische | Calender, | Auf das Jahr | ... | ... | 1752. (Welches ein schalt Jahr von 366 Tagen ist.) | ... | ... | ... | ... | ... | ... | ... | ... | ... | ... | .... | Zum vierzehenten mal heraus gegeben. | *Germantown: Gedruckt und zu finden bey Christoph Saur.* | .... [1751.] | 4to. pp. (36). H. S. P. 1222

JERMAN. (J.) An Almanac for 1752. By John Jerman. *Philadelphia: B. Franklin, and D. Hall.* 1751. 1223

[KEARSLEY. (John)] A | Letter | to a | Friend: | Containing | Remarks | on a | Discourse | Proposing a Preparation of the Body | for the | Small-Pox: | And | The Manner of receiving the Infection. | With some Practical Hints relating to the Cure of the Dumb | Ague, Long Fever, | the Bilious Fever, and some | other Fevers, incidental to this Province. | ... | .... | *Philadelphia:* | *Printed by B. Franklin, and D. Hall.* MDCCLI. | 4to. pp. 16. H. S. P. 1224

MOORE. (T.) The American Country Almanac, for the Year 1752. By Thomas Moore. *Philadelphia: B. Franklin, and D. Hall.* 1751. 1225

NEU-eingerichteter | Americanischer | Geschichts- | Calender, | Auf das Jahr | ... | .... | (Welches ein Schalt-Jahr von 355 Tagen ist.) | ... | ... | ... | ... | ... | ... | ... | ... | ... | ... | ... | .... | .... | Zum Fünfftenmal ans Licht gegeben. | *Philadelphia, gedruckt und zu finden bey Benj. Franklin. in der Buchdruckerey in der Arch-Strasse.* [1751.] | Sq. 8vo. pp. (40). 1226

NEW JERSEY. Anno Regni | Georgii II. | Regis | Magnæ Britanniæ, Franciæ, & Hiberniæ. | Vigesimo Quarto. | At a General Assembly of the Province of New-Jersey, | summoned to be held at Perth-Amboy on the sixth Day | of April, 1751, and from thence continued by several Pro- | rogations to the Twentieth Day of May, 1751, and then | begun and holden, being the first Session

of the present | Assembly. | The following Acts were passed by
His Excellency | Jonathan Belcher, Esq ; on the 6th of June, 1751.
| [*Royal Arms.*] | *Philadelphia :* | *Printed by W. Bradford, Printer
to the Kings Most Ex-* | *cellent Majesty, for the Province of New-Jersey.*
[1751.] | Folio, pp. 15.   1227

NEW JERSEY. Anno Regni | Georgii II. | Regis | Magnæ
Britanniæ, Franciæ, & Hiberniæ. | Vigesimo Quinto | At a Gen-
eral Assembly of the Province of New-Jersey | summoned to be
held at Burlington, in September and | October 1751, being the
second Session of this present As- | sembly. | The following Acts
were passed by His Excellency | Jonathan Belcher, Esq ; on the
23th of October, 1751. | [*Royal Arms.*] | *Philadelphia :* | *Printed by
W. Bradford, Printer to the King's Most Ex-* | *cellent Majesty, for
the Province of New-Jersey.* [1751.] | Folio, pp. 21.   1228

NEW-YEAR Verses of the Carriers of the Pennsylvania Gazette. *Philadelphia: B. Franklin, and D. Hall.* 1751.   1229

NEW-YEAR Verses of the Carriers of the Pennsylvania Journal. *Philadelphia: William Bradford.* 1751.   1230

EJNE | NUETZLICHE | Oder Beyhülfe | Vor die Teutschen | Um
| Englisch zu lernen: | Wie es vor Neu-Ankommende und andere | im
Land gebohrene Land- und Handwercks-Leute, | welche der Englischen
Sprache erfahrne und geüb- | te Schulmeister und Preceptores ermange-
len, | vor das bequemste erachtet worden ; | mit ihrer gewöhnlichen Arbeit
| und Werckzeug erläutert. | Nebst einer | Grammatic, | Vor diejenigen,
| Welche in andern Sprachen und deren | Fundamenten erfahren sind. |
Germanton, | *Gedruckt und zu finden bey Christoph Saur,* 1751. |
16mo. Title, 1 leaf; Vorrede, pp. (2) ; text, pp. 1–285 ; Register, pp.
(3); A Short | Appendix | of a | German Gramar, | pp. (4).   1231

THE PENNSYLVANIA Gazette. *Philadelphia : Printed by
B. Franklin, Post-Master, and D. Hall, at the New-* | *Printing-Office,
near the Market.* | 1232

Numbers 1151 (Jan. 1, 1750–1) to 1203 (Dec. 31, 1751), four pages each, except
Numbers 1172–1175, and 1185, which contain six pages. Title as in Number 648,
supra.

THE PENNSYLVANIA Journal.   H. S. P.   1233

Numbers 424 (Jan. 1, 1750–1) to 476 (Dec. 31, 1751), four pages each. Title and imprint as in Number 989, *supra*, up to Number 447, when the former was changed to the form given in Number 1273, *infra*. There is a "Supplement" of two pages to Number 439. Number 452 is misnumbered 451.

PETERS. (R.) A | Sermon | on | Education. | Wherein | Some Account is given of the | Academy | Established in the | City of Philadelphia. | Preach'd at the Opening thereof, on the Seventh | Day of January, 1750–1. | By the Reverend Mr. Richard Peters. | *Philadelphia:* | *Printed and Sold by B. Franklin, and D. Hall,* | *at the Post-Office.* MDCCLI. | 8vo. H. S. P.   1234

Title, 1 leaf; Dedication, pp. iii.–vii. (1) ; Sermon, pp. 41 ; Constitutions of the Publick Academy, pp. 42–48 ; Idea of the English School, pp. 8.

POOR Robin's Almanac for 1752. *Philadelphia: William Bradford.* 1751.   1235

PROCLAMATION. By the Honourable James Hamilton, Esquire, Lieutenant Governor . . . . A Proclamation. [n. p. about 1751.] Folio, 1 leaf.   1236

Title from Sabin's Dictionary, Number 59,942.

RULES | for the | St. Andrew's | Society | in | Philadelphia. | *Philadelphia:* | *Printed by B. Franklin, and D. Hall.* | MDCCLI. | 8vo. pp. 16.   L. C. P.   1237

SAUNDERS. (R.) A Pocket | Almanack | For the Year 1752. | . . . | . . . | . . . | . . . . | By R. Saunders, Phil. | *Philadelphia:* | *Printed and sold by B. Franklin,* | *and D. Hall.* [1751.] | 24mo. pp. (24).   H. S. P.   1238

SAUNDERS. Poor Richard improved: | Being an | Almanack | . . . | . . . | . . . | . . . | . . . | . . . | . . . | . . . | . . . | . . . . | For the | Year of our Lord 1752: | Being Bissextile, or Leap-Year. | . . . | . . . | . . . | . . . | . . . | . . . | . . . | . . . | . . . | By Richard Saunders, Philom. | *Philadelphia:* | *Printed and Sold by B. Franklin, and D. Hall.* [1751.] | Sm. 8vo. pp. (36).   H. S. P.

SHORT. (T.) Medicina Britannica: | Or a | Treatise | on such | Physical Plants; | as are | Generally to be found in the Fields or Gardens | in Great-Britain: | Containing | A particular Account of their Nature Vir- | tues, and Uses. | Together with the Observations of the most learned Physicians, | as well ancient as modern, communicated to the late ingeni- | ous Mr. Ray, and the learned Dr. Sim. Pauli. | Adapted more especially to the Occasions of those, whose Condition or Situation | of life deprives them, in a great Measure, of the Helps of the Learned. | By Tho. Short, of Sheffield, M. D. | To which is added, | An Appendix: | Containing | The true Preparation, Preservation, Uses and Doses of most | Forms of Remedies necessary for private Families. | The Third Edition. | With a Preface by Mr. John Bartram, Botanist of | Pennsylvania, and his Notes throughout the Work, shewing the Places | where many of the described Plants are to be found in these Parts of | America, their Differences in Name, Appearance and Virtue, from those | of the same Kind in Europe; and an Appendix, containing a Description | of a Number of Plants peculiar to America, their Uses, Virtues, &c. | *London Printed:* | *Philadelphia Re-printed, and sold by B. Franklin, and* | *D. Hall, at the Post-Office in Market-street.* MDCCLI. | 8vo. pp. xx, 339, 40, 7.   1240

In the Library of Congress, there is a copy of this work with a slightly different title page. The first three words above given are omitted. It begins: A | Treatise | on such | Physical Plants, | &c.

TERSTEEGEN. (G.) Der Frommen Lotterie. Von Gerhard Tersteegen. *Germantown: Christoph Saur.* 1751.   1241

Advertised in Sower's Newspaper, Oct. 1, 1751.

VOTES and Proceedings of the House of Representatives. *Philadelphia: B. Franklin.* 1751. Folio.   1242

ZUBLEY. (J. J.) Evangelisches Zeugnuß. | Vom | Elend und Erlösung | Der Menschen, | in zwey Predigten abgelegt | Und auf hofnung Mehrer Erbauung | dem Druck überlassen | Vom | Johann Joachim Zublin | Prediger bey einer englischen gemeinde ohnweil Carles stade | in Sud Carolina. | *Germanton, gedruckt bey Christoph Saur* 1751. | Sq. 8vo. Title, 1 leaf; pp. 32.   M. S.   1243

1752.

AN ACCOUNT of the Births | and Burials in Christ-Church Parish. | in Philadelphia, from December 24, 1751, | to December 24, 1752. By Caleb Cash, Clerk, and Samuel Kirke, Sexton. | [n. p. n. d.] Folio, 1 leaf.   L. C. P.   1244

ANNO Regni | Georgii II. | Regis, | Magnæ Britanniæ, Franciæ & Hiberniæ, | Vigesimo Quinto. | At a General Assembly of the Province of Penn- | sylvania, begun and holden at Phila-delphia, | the Fourteenth Day of October, Anno Domini 1750, in | the Twenty-Fourth Year of the Reign of our Sovereign | Lord George II. by the Grace of God, of Great- | Britain, France, and Ireland, King, Defender of the | Faith, &c. | And from thence continued by Adjournments to the | Sixth Day of August, 1751. | [*Penn Arms.*] | *Philadelphia :* | *Printed and Sold by B. Franklin, at the New-* | *Printing-Office, near the Market.* MDCCLII. | Folio, Title, 1 leaf; p. clxi.   L. C. P.   1245

ANNO Regni | Georgii II. | Regis, | Magnæ Britanniæ, Franciæ & Hiberniæ, | Vigesimo Quinto. | At a General Assembly of the Province of Penn- | sylvania, begun and holden at Phila-delphia, | the Fourteenth Day of October ; Anno Domini, 1751, in | the Twenty-fifth Year of the Reign of our Sovereign | Lord George II. by the Grace of God, of Great- | Britain, France and Ireland, King, Defender of the | Faith, &c. | And from thence continued by Adjournments to the | Third Day of February, 1752. | [*Penn Arms.*] | *Philadelphia :* | *Printed and Sold by B. Franklin, at the New-* | *Printing-Office, near the Market.* MDCCLII. | Folio, Title, 1 leaf; pp. 161–184. + And from thence continued by Adjournments to the | Tenth Day of August, 1752. | [*Ibid.*] Title, 1 leaf; pp. 187–208.   H. S. P.   1246

BALL. (W.) The New Jersey Almanac for 1753. By Wil-liam Ball. *Philadelphia: William Bradford.* 1752.   1247

BEATTY. (C.) A | Sermon | preached | In | Woodbury, | At the Ordination of the Reverend Mr. | Chesnut there, | By Charles

Beatty, Minister of the | Gospel at Neshaminey. | *Philadelphia :* *Printed and Sold by W.* | *Bradford, in Second Street.* | M.DCC.LII. | Sm. 8vo. pp. 55.   H. 'S. P.   1248

[BEISSEL. (Conrad)] Erſter Theil | Der | Theoſophiſchen | Lectionen, | Betreffende die Schulen des einſamen | Lebens. | *Ephrata* *gedruckt im Jahre* 1752. | Sq. 8vo. pp. (4), 432.   H. S. P.   1249

CIRCULAR SCHREIBEN der Vereinigten Reformirten Prediger in Pennſylvanien an die dieſige ſamtliche Reformirten Gemeinden darin ſie kurtzlich der lagen, wie der groſſe Jehovah die von S. E. Mich. Slatter, V. D. M. an unſere Chriſti Kirchenreiter übernommenen Commiſſion zu ihrer Kultung und Hülfe in Gnaden geſegnet und wie ſolches von ſolchen Gemeinen ſolle gebührend erkant mit denkſagung an genommen werden. In Allgemeinen Nachricht heraus gegeben von J. M. Maiß, J. P. Ley= dick, J. Leppy. *Lancaster: Gedruckt bey H. Miller und S. Holland.* 1752. 4to. pp. 11.   1250

DAVIES. (R.) An | Account | of the | Convincement, Exer- cises, | Services and Travels, | Of that Ancient Servant of the Lord, | Richard Davies: | With | Some Relation of Ancient Friends, | and the Spreading of Truth in | North-Wales, &c. | The Second Edition. | *London: Printed.* | *Philadelphia: Reprinted and* *Sold by* | *James Chattin, next Door to the Pipe,* | *in Church-Alley.* M,DCC,LII. | 24mo. pp. (18), 233, (1).   1251

On the last page Chattin solicits subscriptions for "The Pennsylvania Intelli- gencer," to be issued "whenever a proper Number of Subscribers have entered."

DELAWARE. Laws | of the | Government | of | New-Castle, Kent and Sussex, | Upon Delaware. | Published by Order of the Assembly. | [*Royal Arms.*] | *Philadelphia:* | *Printed and Sold by B.* *Franklin and D. Hall,* | *at the New Printing-Office, in Market-* *Street.* | MDCCLII. | Folio, pp. 363 ; Table, xvii.   H. S. P.   1252

[DODSLEY. (R.)] The | Oeconomy | of | Human Life. | Part the Second. | Translated from an Indian Manu- | script, found soon after that | which contain'd the Original of | the First Part ; and written by | the same Hand. | In | A Second Letter from an | English Gentleman residing at China, | to the Earl of * * * |

The Third Edition. | *London, Printed :* | *Philadelphia, Re-printed,* *and sold by* | *B. Franklin, and D. Hall, at the* | *New-Printing-Office.* MDCCLII. | 16mo. pp. viii, 112.   H. S. P.   1253

"The Seventh Edition" of the first part was published by Franklin and Hall in 1752. I have not met with a copy, nor of the sixth edition, see Number 1214, *supra*.

EVANGELISCHES Zeugnuß | von der | Falschen | Fleisches= | Religion | in allen Secten der Christen= | heit, nach ihrem Ursprung, eigentli= | chem Wesen und dreyfa= | cher Stütze; | In einer Versam= lungs= | Rede am IX. Sonntag | nach Trinitatis öffentlich abgelegt | über den Text: | Actor. XIX, 23–fin. | Biß zu end des Capitels. | *Germanton Gedruckt bey C. Saur.* 1752. | 16mo. pp. 16.   H. S. P.   1254

FINLEY. (S.)   Faithful Ministers the Fathers of the | Church. | A | Sermon | preached | at | Fogs-Mannor. | On Occasion | Of the Death of the Reverend Mr. Samuel | Blair, who departed this Life July 5. | 1752. | By Samuel Finley, A. M. Minister of | the Gospel at Nottingham in Pensylvania. | . . . | . . . . | *Philadelphi ;* [sic] | *Printed and sold by W. Bradford in Second-Street.* | MDCCLII. | 1255

F[RY] (J[OHN])   An Essay on Conduct.   A Poem.   By J. F. The Third Edition.   *Philadelphia: James Chattin.*   1752.   1256

FÜNFF | schöne Geistliche | Lieder | Das erste | Tobias war ein fromer | Mann. | Das andere, | Kürtzlich vor wenig | Tagen | Das dritte | Es ist ein wunder= | schöne Gab. | Das vierte, | Mein fröhlich Hertz | das treibt mich an. | Das fünffte, | Es war ein Gottes= | fürchtiges und christliches Jungfräulein. | [*Germantown:*] *Gedruckt* [*bey Christoph Saur*] *im Jahr* 1752. | 16mo. pp. 40.   H. S. P.   1257

Printed as part of the supplementary matter to the edition of the Ausbund, published in 1751.

GEISTREICHE LIEDER.   Kern | Alter und neuer, in 700. be= stehender, | Geistreicher, | Lieder, | Welche sowohl | Bey dem öffentlichen Gottesdienste | in denen | Reformirten Kirchen | der Hessisch=Hanauisch= Pfälzisch=Pennsylvanischen | und mehrern andern angräntzenden Landen | Als auch zur | Privat=Andacht und Erbauung | nützlich können gebraucht

werden. | Nebſt | Joachimi Neandri | Bundes=Liedern | Mit beygefüg=
ten | Morgen= Abend= und Comunion Gebätern, | wie auch Catechiſmo
und Simbolis. | Nach dem neueſten Geſangbuch, welches gedruckt zu Mar=
burg, | bey Johann Heinrich Stock, nun zum erſten mal gedruckt | zu
Germanton bey Christoph Saur. 1752. | 16mo.   H. S. P.   1258

Collation : Title and text, pp. 562 ; Register, pp. (10) ; Heidebergischer
Catechimus, pp. 1–21 ; Morgen-und-Abend-Gebäter, pp. 21–29 ; Evangelia und
Episteln, pp. 29–113 ; Historie der Zerstörung Jerusalem, pp. 114–120 ; Andäch-
tige Kirchen-Gebäte, pp. 120–123. This is part of the Reformed Hymn Book,
issued in 1753, see Number 1301, *infra.*

HERVEY. (J.)   Remarks on Lord Bolingbroke's Letters. By
James Hervey. *Philadelphia: William Bradford.* 1752.   1259

DER | HOCH=DEUTSCH | Americaniſche | Calender, | Auf das
Jahr | ... | ... | 1753. | (Welches ein gemein Jahr von 365 Tagen
iſt.) | ... | ... | ... | ... | ... | ... | ... | ... | ... | ... |
Zum fünffzehenten mal heraus gegeben. | *Germantown: Gedruckt und zu
finden bey Christoph Saur.* | ....[1752.] | 4to. pp. (40). H. S. P. 1260

JERMAN. (J.)   An Almanac for 1753. By John Jerman.
Philadelphia: B. Franklin, and D. Hall. 1752.   1261

[JOHNSON. (Samuel)] Elementa Philosophica : | Containing
chiefly, | Noetica, | Or Things relating to the | Mind or Under-
standing : | And | Ethica, | Or Things relating to the | Moral
Behaviour. | *Philadelphia:* | *Printed by B. Franklin, and D. Hall,
at the | New-Printing-Office, near the Market.* 1752. | 8vo. H. S. P.

Collation : Title, 1 leaf ; Half-title to Noetica, 1 leaf ; Title to Noetica, 1 leaf ;
Dedication, 1 leaf ; Advertisement, pp. vii.–viii.; Introduction, pp. ix.–xix.;
Contents, pp. xx.–xxiv.; Noetica, pp. 1–103 ; Half-title to Ethica, 1 leaf ; Title
to Ethica, 1 leaf ; Advertisement, pp. v.–vii ; Contents, 1 page ; Ethica, pp.
1–103 ; Errata, 1 leaf. The title to Noetica is as follows : Noetica : | Or the First
Principles of | Human Knowledge. | Being a | Logick, | Including both | Meta-
physics and Dialectic, | Or the Art of Reasoning. | With a brief Pathology, and
an Account of the | gradual Progress of the Human Mind, from | the first Dawn-
ings of Sense to the highest | Perfection, both Intellectual and Moral, of | which
it is capable. | To which is prefixed, | A Short Introduction | To the | Study of
the Sciences. | ... | ... | ... | .... | *Philadelphia :* | *Printed by B. Franklin,
and D. Hall, at the | New-Printing-Office, near the Market.* 1752. | The title to
Ethica is as follows : Ethica : | Or the First Principles of | Moral Philosophy ;

| And especially that Part which is called | Ethics. | In a Chain of necessary Consequences | from certain Facts. | . . . | . . . | . . . | . . . | . . . | . . . | . . . | . . . | . . . | . . . | . . . . | The Second Edition. | *Philadelphia:* | *Printed by B. Franklin, and D. Hall, at the* | *New-Printing-Office, near the Market.* 1752. | In a list of the "Printed Works of William Smith, D.D." (Horace W. Smith's Life, &c. of Rev. William Smith, Vol. II. p. 534), is the following title : "A Compendium of Logic, including Metaphysics, and one of Ethics, by Samuel Johnson, D.D.; with a Philosophical Meditation and Religious Address to the Supreme Being, for the use of young students in Philosophy, by William Smith, A.M. *Published in Phila., in* 1753, *by B. Franklin, and in London,* 1754." No doubt this is intended for the title above given. The Philosophical Meditation, appended to "Noetica," is by Fenelon, as translated by Bishop Berkeley. The "Religious address" seems to be "Mr. Wolleston's Prayer" which is appended to "Ethica." Smith seems to had something to do with the re-publication of the work in London in 1754, but the Philadelphia edition was undertaken by Franklin a year before Smith came to America. See Beardley's Life of Johnson, p. 180.

2tes Stück. | DIE | LANCASTERISCHE | Zeitung: | Oder | Ein Kurzer Begriff | Der | Hauptſächlichſten Aus= | ländiſch= und Einhei= | miſchen Neuigkeiten. | Den 29ſten Jenner, 1752. | [*Hamilton Arms.*] | Numb. 2. | The | Lancaster | Gazette: | or, | A Compendium | of the | Most material Foreign | and Home News. | January 29, 1752. | *Lancaster, Printed by H. Miller and* | *S. Holland, at the* *New-Printing-Office in* | *King's-Street: where all Sorts of Printing* *Busi-* | *ness is done at a reasonable Rate.* [1752.] | Sm. Folio, pp. (4).   H. S. P.   1263

Published fortnightly. The last issue I have met with is Number 31, June 5, 1753, but it was no doubt continued for some time longer. It was printed in German and English in parallel columns. From or before Number 12, the imprint was changed to *Lancaster, Printed by S. Holland, at the Post-Office, in King's Street; where all* | *Sort of Printing Work is done at reasonable* | *Rate.* |

LUTHER. (M.)   Der Kleine | Catechismus | Des ſel. | Dr. Martin Luthers | Nebſt | den gewöhnlichen Morgen= Tiſch= und | Abend= | Ge= beten. | Wobey | Die Ordnung des Heils in | einem Liede, in kurtzen Sätzen in | Frage und Antwort, und in | einer Tabelle; | wie auch | der Inhalt der heiligen Schrift | in Verſen | hinzugefüget | Zum gebrauch der Jugend. | Nebſt einem | Anhang der ſieben Buß=Pſalmen, | einem geiſtli= chen Liede und das Einmal Eins. | *Germantown* | *Gedruckt und zu haben bey* | *Christoph Saur.* | [1752.] | 24mo. pp. iii, 139, (1).   1264

MOONEY. (N.) The Life of Nicholas Mooney: Wherein is contained, His Parentage and Education; an Account of his join- ing the Rebel Army at Carlisle, and the Part he acted therein, 'till the Defeat thereof at Culloden Moor; the Adventures he met with before and after this, 'till he took to the Highway, with a brief Account of his vicious Life 'till he committed the Robbery at Bristol, for which he was executed on Friday, April 24th, 1752. Together with his moral and religious Reflections upon the most remarkable Passages of his whole Life; and an Account of his Conversion the Sunday before his Trial. Taken from his own Mouth, by a friend; and publish'd at his Request. *Philadelphia: William Bradford.* 1752.   1265

MOORE. (T.) An Almanac for 1753. By Thomas Moore. *Philadelphia: B. Franklin, and D. Hall.* 1752.   1266

𝕹𝕰𝖀=eingerichteter Americanifche Gefchichts=Calender, auf das Jahr 1753. *Philadelphia: B. Franklin und G. Armbruster.* 1752. 1267

NEW JERSEY. The | Acts | Of the General Assembly | Of the Province of | New-Jersey, | From the Time of the Surrender of the Government in the Second | Year of the Reign of Queen Anne, to this present Time, be- | ing the Twenty Fifth Year of the Reign of King George the | Second. | Collected and Published by Order of the General Assembly | of the said Province. | With Proper Tables; and an Alphabetical Index containing all the | Principal Matters in the Body of the Book. | By Samuel Nevill Esq; | Second Justice of the Supreme Court of Judicature of the | said Province. | [*Philadelphia:*] | *Printed by William Bradford, Printer to the Kings Most | Excellent Majesty for the Province of New-Jersey,* | MDCCLII. | Folio, Title, 1 leaf; Dedication, 1 leaf; pp. 507.   H. S. P.   1268

NEW JERSEY. Anno Regni | Georgii II. | Regis | Magnæ Britanniæ, Franciæ, & Hiberniæ. | Vigesimo Quinto. | At a Ses- sion of General Assembly of the Province of New-Jersey; begun and held at Perth-Amboy, on the | Twenty Fifth Day of January 1752; and ended on the | Twelfth of February following, being the Second Session | of this present Assembly; on which Day the following | Act was passed. | [*Royal Arms.*] | *Philadelphia:* | *Printed by W. Bradford, Printer to the King's Most Ex-* | *cellent Majesty, for the Province of New-Jersey.* [1752.] | Folio, pp. 27.

NEW-YEAR Verses of the Carriers of Pennsylvania Gazette. *Philadelphia: B. Franklin, and D. Hall.* 1752.   1270

NEW-YEAR Verses of the Carriers of the Pennsylvania Journal. *Philadelphia: William Bradford.* 1752.   1271

THE PENNSYLVANIA Gazette.   1272

Numbers 1204 (Jan. 7, 1752) to 1253 (Dec. 26, 1752), four pages each, except Numbers 1217–1226, 1236–1238, 1241, and 1246–1251, which contain six pages. Number 1218 is misnumbered 1291. Title and imprint as in Number 1232, *supra.*

THE | PENNSYLVANIA Journal | and Weekly Advertiser. |

Numbers 477 (Jan. 7, 1752) to 525 (Dec. 26, 1752), four pages each. Only 49 pages were issued during the year. Imprint as in Number 989, *supra.*

POOR Robin's Almanac for 1753. *Philadelphia: William Bradford.* 1752.   1274

𝕽𝕰𝕱𝕺𝕽𝕸𝕵𝕽𝕿𝕰𝕽 oder Heidelberger Katechismus. *Germantown: Christoph Saur.* 1752.   1275

Title from Seidensticker's Bibliography.

RELIGION | of the | Ancient Brachmans; | manifested, | In Epistles and Discourses | between | Alexander the Great, | and | Dindimus King of the Brachmans. | With a short Account of their Manner of Living: As also, of the | Religion of the Eastern Magi, and some Hints, | of the Belief of the Ancient Chinese, and Phi- | losophers concerning God, and the Fall of Man. | Collected and Published for General Service. | . . . | . . . | . . . | . . . | . . . . | *Philadelphia:* | *Printed and Sold by James Chattin, next Door* | *to the Pipe, on Church-Alley.* 1752. | 8vo. pp. 24.   H. S. P.   1276

ROBERTS. (D.) Some Memoirs of the Life of John Roberts. Written by his Son Daniel Roberts. The Third Edition. *Philadelphia: James Chattin.* 1752.   1277

SAUNDERS. (R.)　A Pocket | Almanack | For the Year 1753. | . . . | . . . | . . . | . . . . | By R. Saunders, Phil. | *Philadelphia:* | *Printed and sold by B. Franklin,* | *and D. Hall.* [1752.] | 24 mo. pp. (24). 　　　　　　　　　　　　　　H. S. P.　1278

SAUNDERS.　Poor Richard improved. | Being an | Almanack | . . . | . . . | . . . | . . . | . . . | . . . | . . . | . . . | . . . | . . . . | For the | Year of our Lord 1753: | Being the First after Leap-Year. | . . . | . . . | . . . | . . . | . . . | . . . | . . . | . . . | . . . . | By Richard Saunders, Philom. | *Philadelphia:* | *Printed and Sold by B.* *Franklin, and D. Hall.* [1752.] | Sm. 8vo. pp. (36). H. S. P.　1279

STEINER. (J. C.)　J. Conrad Steiner Ref. Pred. in Germantown, Wächter-Stimm aus den verwüsteten Reformirten Sion in Pennsylvanien an dessen lehrer und Wächeter ins besonder und des gesamte noch ins gemein. *Germantown: Gedruckt bey Chr. Saur.* 1752. 4to. pp. 16.

TENNENT. (G.)　The Divine Government over all considered, | and | The necessity of Gratitude, for Benefits con- | ferred, (by it,) | Represented, in two | Sermons, | Preach'd June the 7th. 1752. in the Presby- | terian Church lately erected in Arch-Street, | in the City of Philadelphia. | On Occasion | Of the first Celebration of religious Wor- | ship there. | By Gilbert Tennent, A. M. | . . . | . . . | . . . | . . . | . . . | . . . | . . . | . . . | . . . | . . . | . . . . | *Philadelphia:* | *Printed by William Bradford in Second Street.* [1752.] | 8vo. Half title, 1 leaf; Title, 1 leaf; text, pp. 3–79.

UNPARTHEYISCHE | Gedancken | in Reimen | bey Einweyhung einer Evangelischen Kirche | in Germanton, | Mitgetheilt von einem Fremdlinge unter Mesech | Den 1 October 1752. | [*Germantown: Christoph Saur.* 1752. ?] Folio, pp. (4). 　　　　　　H. S. P.　1282

VOTES and Proceedings of the House of Representatives. *Philadelphia: B. Franklin.* 1752. Folio. 　　　　　　　　1283

VOTES | and | Proceedings | of the | House of Representatives | of the | Province of Pennsylvania. | Beginning the Fourth Day of December, 1682. | Volume The First. | In Two Parts. | [*Penn*

Arms.] | *Philadelphia:* | *Printed and Sold by B. Franklin, and D. Hall, at the* | *New-Printing-Office, near the Market.* MDCCLII. | Folio.   H. S. P.   1284

Collation : Title, 1 leaf; Preface, iii–iv; Grants, Charters, &c., pp. v–xxxviii; Votes, pp. 1–164 ; Appendix, pp. i–xxix; Title to Part II., 1 leaf; Charter of 1701, &c., pp. i–viii; Votes, pp. 1-187.

1753.

AN ACCOUNT of the Births | and Burials in Christ-Church Parish, | in Philadelphia, from December 24, 1752, | to December 24, 1753. By Caleb Cash, | Clerk, and Samuel Kirke, Sexton. | [n. p. n. d.] Folio, 1 leaf.   L. C. P.   1285

DIE NEUE ACTE enthaltend, was ein jeder Beamter, als der Feld= messer, Sheriff, Constabel, Coroner und die übrigen zu Lohn haben sollen. *Germantown : Christoph Saur.* 1753.   1286

Title from Seidensticker's Bibliography.

ALLENS. (J.) Useful | Questions, | whereby | A Person may examine himself | every Day. | Composed by the Rev'd. Joseph Allen : | And | Introduced with this General Direction, | viz. | Every Evening before you sleep (unless you find | some other Time of the Day more for your | Advantage in this Work) sequester yourself | from the World, and, having set your Heart | in the Presence of the Lord, charge it | before God to answer the follow- ing Inter- | rogatories. | *Philadelphia:* | *Printed and Sold by William Bradford,* | *at the Sign of the Bible, in Second-Street.* | MDCCLIII. | 8vo. pp. 8.   H. S. P.   1287

BALL. (W.) The New Jersey Almanac for 1754. By William Ball. *Philadelphia: William Bradford.* 1753.   1288

B[ARCLAY.] (R[OBERT]) A | Catechism | and | Confession of Faith | Approved of, and agreed unto, by the | General Assembly of the Patriarchs, Prophets, and | Apostles, Christ himself Chief Speaker in and a- | mong them. | Which containeth a true and faithful Account of | the Principles and Doctrines, which are most | surely believed by the Churches of Christ in | Great-Britain, Ireland, &c. who are reproach- | fully called by the Name of Quakers ; yet are | found in the One Faith with the Primitive | Church and Saints, as is most clearly demon- | strated by some plain Scripture-Testimonies | (without Consequences or Commentaries) which | are here collected and inserted by Way of An- | swer to a few weighty, yet easy and familiar | Questions, fitted as well for the wisest and lar- | gest, as for the meanest and lowest Capacities. | To which is added, An Expostulation with, and | Appeal to, all other Professors. | The Eighth Edition. | By R. B. a Servant of the Church of Christ. | . . . | . . . | . . . | . . . . | *London, Printed. Philadelphia : Reprinted and | Sold by James Chattin, in Church-Alley.* 1753. | Sm. 8vo.   H. S. P.   1289

Collation : Title, 1 leaf ; Preface, 4 leaves ; Catechism, pp. 200 ; Contents, pp. (3) ; List of Books, pp. (2).

BENKENDORFF. (H.) Seliger | Marter=Stand | Der erften Chriften, | Oder von den Zehen | Haupt=Verfolgungen | der erften Chri= ften Neues=Te=ftaments ; | In den erften dreyhundert Jahren, unter | den heidnifchen Keyfern, bis auf den erften Chriftli= | chen Kayfer Conftan= tinum Magnum : | Wie auch | Von den vielfältigen Märterern und ftand= | hafftigen Bekennern Chrifti felbiger Zeit, und | derer fchwerer und graufa= men Marter. | Nach eines jeden gottfeligen Belieben wie ein an= | muth= iges im Chriftenthum zur Ubung der Geduld | wohl dienfames Hand= Büchlein, dergleichen | hiebevor in unferer Mutter=Sprache nicht gar | viel zu finden, nützlich zu gebrauchen. | Aus den älteften Scribenten mit fleiß zufamen ge= | tragen, und dem gemeinen Mann zum Beften in | Deutfcher Sprache befchrieben | Von | Henrico Benkendorff, | von Ultzen. | *Philadelphia, gedruckt und zu finden bey Anton Armbruester wohn- hafft in der Dritten-Strasse, dessglei- | chen bey David Limbeck Buch- binder, Anno* 1753. | 16mo. pp. 326.   H. S. P.   1290

BOLTON. (R.) Twenty | Considerations | against Sin, | by | The eminently pious, greatly learned, and venerable | Divine | Mr. Robert Bolton. | Extracted from that judicious, close, and practical Treatise | of His, entituled, | Instructions for a right | comforting afflicted Consciences. | . . . | . . . | . . : | . . . . | *Phila-*

delphia: | *Printed and Sold by William Bradford,* | *at the Sign of the Bible, in Second-Street,* | MDCCLIII. | 8vo. pp. 27.   H. S. P.   1291

THE CASE of the German Protestant | Churches settled in the Province of Pensyl- | vania, and in North America. | [*Philadelphia: B. Franklin, and D. Hall.* 1753.?] Folio, 1 leaf.   H. S. P.

C[RISP.] (S[TEPHEN]) A short History of a long Travel, from Babylon to Bethel. By S. C. The Ninth Edition. *Philadelphia: James Chattin.* 1753.   1293

DAVIES. (S[AMUEL]) A | Sermon, | Preached before the | Reverend Presbytery | of | New-Castle, | October 11. 1752. | By S. Davies, V. D. M. | In Hanover, Virginia. | Published at the Desire of the Presbytery and | Congregation. | *Philadelphia:* | *Printed by B. Franklin, and D. Hall, at the* | *New Printing-Office, in Market-street.* | M,DCCLIII. | 8vo. pp. v, 38.   c. 1294

[DOVER. (WILLIAM)] Useful | Miscellanies: | Or, | Serious Reflections, | Respecting | Mens Duty to God, and | One towards Another. | With | Advices, Civil and Religious, | Tending | To regulate their Conduct in the various | Occurrences of Human Life. | Published for general Service, | By a Well-Wisher to all Mankind. | . . . | . . . . | *London: Printed.* | *Philadelphia: Reprinted and* | *Sold by James Chattin, in Church-Alley,* | 1753. | 8vo. pp. 96.   L. C. P.   1295

ELLWOOD. (T.) Davideis: The Life of David, King of Israel: A sacred Poem, in Five Books. By Thomas Ellwood. The Fourth Edition. *Philadelphia: James Chattin.* 1753.   1296

THE FATAL | Consequences | of the | Unscriptural Doctrine | of | Predestination | and | Reprobation; | With | A Caution against it. | Written in High-Dutch by M. K. and translated | by Desire. | *Germantown,* | *Printed and Sold by Christopher Sowr,* 1753. | 16mo. pp. 14.   1297

FISHER. (G.) The American | Instructor: | Or, | Young Man's Best Companion. | Containing, | Spelling, Reading, Writing, and Arithmetick, | in an easier Way than any yet published;

and how to qua- | lify any Person for Business, without the Help of a Master. | Instructions to write Variety of Hands, with Copies | both in Prose and Verse. How to write Letters on Bu- | siness or Friendship. Forms of Indentures, Bonds, Bills of | Sale, Receipts, Wills, Leases, Releases, &c. | Also Merchants Accompts, and a short and easy Me- | thod of Shop and Book keeping; with a Description of the | several American Colonies. | Together with Carpenter's Plain and exact Rule: Shew- | ing how to measure Carpenters, Joyners, Sawyers, Bricklayers, Plaisterers, | Plumbers, Masons, Glasiers, and Painters Work. How to undertake each | Work, and at what Price; the Rates of each Commodity, and the com- | mon Wages of Journeymen; with Gunter's Line, and Coggeshal's De- | scription of the Sliding-Rule. | Likewise the Practical Guager made Easy; the Art of | Dialing, and how to erect and fix any Dial; with Instructions for Dying, | Colouring, and making Colours. | To which is added, | The Poor Planter's Physician: | With Instructions for Marking on Linnen; how to Pickle and | Preserve; to make divers Sorts of Wine; and many excellent Plaisters, and | Medicines, necessary in all Families. | And also, | Prudent Advice to young Tradesmen and Dealers. | The whole better adapted to these American Colonies, than any | other Book of the like Kind. | By George Fisher, Accomptant. | The Tenth Edition, Revised and Corrected. | *Philadelphia: Printed by B. Franklin and | D. Hall, at the New-Printing-Office, in Market-Street*, 1753. | 12mo. pp. v. 1–384, (2), 6 plates.　　　H. S. P.

F[RY.] (J[OHN]) An Essay on Conduct and Education; Recommended to the People called Quakers. A Poem. By J. F. . . . . The Fourth Edition, Corrected. To which is added Poems, on several Subjects, by another Hand. *London: Printed. Philadelphia: Reprinted and Sold by James Chattin.* 1753.　　　　　　　　　　　1299

FULLER. (S.) Some Principles and Precepts of the Christian Religion, by way of Question and Answer. Recommended to Parents and Tutors for the Use of Children. By Samuel Fuller. *Philadelphia: James Chattin.* 1753.　　　　　　1300

𝕲𝕰𝕾𝕬𝕹𝕲-𝕭𝖀𝕮𝕳. Neu-vermehrt und vollständiges | Gesang Buch, | Worinnen sowohl die | Pfalmen Davids, | Nach | D. Ambrosii Lob= waffers | Uberfetzung hin und wieder verbeffert, | Als auch | 700 auser= lefener alter und neuer | Geiftreichen Liedern | begriffen find, | Welche anjetzo fämtlich | in denen Reformirten Kirchen | der Heßifch=, Hanau= ifch= Pfältzifchen und vielen | andern angrentzenden Landen zu fingen gebräuchlich, | in nützliche Ordnung eingetheilt, | Auch | Mit dem Heydel= bergifchen Catechifmo und | erbaulichen Gebätern verfehen. | *Germanton,* | *Gedruckt und zu finden bey Christoph Saur*, 1753. | 16mo. pp. (2), 1–214, (2), 1 plate.   H. S. P.   1301

See Number 1258 *supra,* for the larger part of this Hymn book.

GREW. (T.) The | Description | and | Use | of the | Globes, | Celestial and Terrestrial ; | With | Variety of Examples | For the Learner's Exercise : | Intended for the Use of such Persons | as | would attain to the Knowledge of those | Instruments ; | But | Chiefly designed for the Instruction | of the young Gentlemen at the Aca- | demy in Philadelphia. | To which is added | Rules for working all the Cases in Plain and | Spherical Triangles without a Scheme. | By Theophilus Grew, | Mathematical Professor. | *Germantown,* | *Printed by Christopher Sower*, 1753. | 16mo. pp. 60, 1 leaf.   H. S. P.   1302

HABERMANN. (J.) Das grosse Gebet-Buch. Von Johann Habermann. *Philadelphia : Godhard Armbruster.* 1753.   1303

HALL. (D.)   A | Compassionate | Call, | and | Hand reached forth | in | Tender Gospel Love, | To˜ all such Persons, as having once made | Profession of the blessed Truth, | yet by some Mis- conduct or other have | unhappily forfeited their Unity with | the Society of Friends, in what | Capacity, Post or Station soever in the | Church they may have been ; or in | what Circumstance of Life soever they | now stand in their present disunited | Situation. | By David Hall. | *London : Printed.* | *Philadelphia : Reprinted and Sold* | *by James Chattin, in Church-Alley*, 1753. | Sm. 8vo. pp. 20. + The Second Edition. [*Ibid.*] + The Third Edition. [*Ibid.*]

HALL. (D.) A | Compassionate | Call, | And | Hand Reached Forth | in | Tender Gospel Love, | To all such Persons, as having

once made | Profession of the blessed Truth, yet by | some Mis-
conduct or other have unhappily | forfeited their Unity with the
Society of | Friends, in what Capacity, Post or | Station soever in
the Church they may have | been ; or in what Circumstances of
Life soever | they now stand in their present disunited | Situation.
| By David Hall. | The Fourth Edition. | *London : Printed.* |
Philadelphia: Reprinted and Sold | *by James Chattin, in Church-
Alley,* 1753. | Sm. 8vo. pp. 12.   H. S. P.   1305

𝔇𝔧𝔢 𝔎𝔩𝔢𝔧𝔫𝔢 𝔥𝔞𝔯𝔣𝔢. *Germantown.   Christoph Saur.* 1753

Title from Seidensticker's Bibliography.

THE HERMIT. A Poem. [*Philadelphia: James Chattin.*
1753.] Sm. 8vo. pp. 8.   H. S. P.   1307

𝔇𝔢𝔯 𝔥𝔬𝔠𝔥=𝔇𝔢𝔲𝔱𝔰𝔠𝔥 Americanifche Kalender, auf das Jahr
1754. *Germantown: Christoph Saur.* 1753.   1308

JEFFRYS. (J.) A Serious | Address | to the | People | of the
| Church of England, | In some | Observations upon their own |
Catechism. Tenderly recom- | mended to their Consideration. |
By John Jeffrys. | To which are prefix'd, | Some Passages of his
Life, writ- | ten by himself. | *London : Printed.* | *Philadelphia :
Reprinted and Sold* | *by James Chattin, in Church-Alley.* 1753.
| Sm. 8vo. pp. 45, (3).   H. S. P.   1309

JERMAN. (J.) An Almanac for 1754. By John Jerman.
Philadelphia : B. Franklin, and D. Hall. 1753.   1310

JOHNSON. (S.) A Short | Catechism | for | Young Children,
| Proper to be taught them before | they learn the Assembly's
or | after they [have] learned the | Church Catechism. | By S.
Johnson, D.D. | *Philadelphia, Printed by Ant. Armbruster* | *in Arch-
Street.* 1753. | Sm. 8vo. pp. 18.   1311

MOORE. (T.) An Almanac for 1754. By Thomas Moore.
Philadelphia : B. Franklin, and D. Hall. 1753.   1312

MORE. (T.) The | Common-Wealth | Of | Utopia. | Contain-
ing a learned and pleasant Dis- | course of the best State of a

Pub- | lick Weal, as it is found in the new | Island called Utopia. | Written by the Right Honourable Sir Thomas | Moore, Lord Chancellor of England. | *London : Printed.* | *Philadelphia : Reprinted and Sold* | *by James Chattin, in Church-Alley.* 1753. | 8vo. Title, 1 leaf; pp. 1–126. H. S. P. 1313

NEW JERSEY. Anno Regni | Georgii II | Regis | Magnæ Britaniæ, & Hiberniæ, | Vigesimo Sexto | At a Session of General Assembly of the Province of New- | Jersey ; begun and held at Burlington, on the Sixteenth | Day of May 1753 ; and ended on the 8th of June fol- | lowing, on which Day the following Acts were passed. | [*Royal Arms.*] | *Philadelphia :* | *Printed by W. Bradford, Printer to the King's Most* | *Excellent Majesty, for the Province of New-Jersey.* [1753.] | Folio, pp. 59, (1), 2 leaves folded.

NEW-YEAR Verses of the Carriers of the Pennsylvania Gazette. *Philadelphia : B. Franklin, and D. Hall.* 1753. 1315

NEW-YEAR Verses of the Carriers of the Pennsylvania Journal. *Philadelphia : William Bradford.* 1753. 1316

OWEN. (J.) The Youth's Instructor in the English Tongue: Or a Spelling Book, containing more Words, and a greater Variety of very useful Collections than any other Book of this Kind. By John Owen. The 3d Edition. To which is added, a practical English Grammar. By Thomas Dilworth. *Philadelphia : James Chattin.* 1753. 1317

THE PENNSYLVANIA Gazette. 1318

Numbers 1254 (Jan. 2, 1753) to 1305 (Dec. 25, 1753), four pages each, except Numbers 1268, 1269, 1272, 1274, 1275, 1285, 1287 and 1291–1303, which contain six pages. Title and imprint as in No. 1232, *supra.*

THE PENNSYLVANIA Journal. H. S. P. 1319

Numbers 526 (Jan 2, 1753) to 577 (Dec. 20, 1753), four pages each. Title and imprint as in Number 989, *supra,* up to Number 548, when the paper was enlarged and a third column added, and the imprint changed to the form given in Number 1379, *infra.*

POOR Robin's Almanac for 1754. *Philadelphia: William Bradford.* 1753.   1320

RIMIUS. (H.) A Candid | Narrative | of the | Rise and Progress | of the | Herrnhuters, | commonly call'd | Moravians, or Unitas Fratrum; | With a short Account of their Doctrines, | drawn from their own Writings. | To which are added, | Observations on their Politics in general, and | particularly on their Conduct whilst in the | County of Budingen, in the Circle of the | Upper-Rhine, in Germany. | By Henry Rimius, | Aulic Councillor to His late Majesty the King of Prussia, | and Author of the Memoirs of the House of Brunswick. | *London, Printed: | Philadelphia, Re-Printed and Sold by | William Bradford, at the Sign of the | Bible in Second-Street,* MDCCLIII. | 8vo. pp. 112.   H. S. P.

ROBERTS. (D.) Some | Memoirs | Of the Life of | John Roberts. | Written by his Son | Daniel Roberts. | The Fourth Edition. | . . . | . . . | . . . . | *Bristol: Printed | Philadelphia: Reprinted | and Sold by James Chattin, | next Door to the Pipe in Church Alley.* | 1753. | Sm. 8vo. pp. 69. Ad. pp. (2). H. S. P. 1322

THE ROYAL Primer improved: Being an easy and pleasant Guide to the Art of Reading. With 28 Cuts adapted to Children. The Second Edition. *Philadelphia: James Chattin.* 1753.   1323

SAUNDERS. (R.) A Pocket | Almanack | For the Year 1754, | . . . | . . . | . . . | . . . . | By Richard Saunders, Phil. | *Philadelphia: | Printed and sold by B. Franklin, | and D. Hall.* [1753.] 24mo. pp. (24).   H. S. P. 1324

SAUNDERS. Poor Richard improved: | Being an | Almanack | . . . | . . . | . . . | . . . | . . . | . . . | . . . | . . . | . . . | . . . . | For the | Year of our Lord 1754: | Being the Second after Leap-Year. | . . . | . . . | . . . | . . . | . . . | . . . | . . . | . . . | . . . . | By Richard Saunders, Philom. | *Philadelphia: | Printed and Sold by B. Franklin, and D. Hall.* [1753.] | Sm. 8vo. pp. (36).   H. S. P.

SIEGVOLCK. (P.) The | Everlasting | Gospel, | Commanded to be preached by | Jesus Christ, | Judge of the Living and Dead, | Unto | All Creatures, Mark xvi. 15. | Concerning | The Eternal

Redemption | found out by Him, | Whereby Devil, Sin, Hell, and Death, shall at | last be abolished, and the whole Creation | restored to its primitive Purity ; | Being | A Testimony against the present Anti- | christian World. | Written in German by Paul Siegvolck, | and translated into English by John S. | *Germantown*, | *Printed by Christopher Sower*, | MDCCLIII. | 16mo. pp. viii. 152.   H. S. P.   1326

[SMITH. (WILLIAM)]   A | Poem | On visiting the | Academy | of | Philadelphia, June 1753. | . . . | . . . | . . . . | *Philadelphia:* | *Printed [by Franklin and Hall] in the Year* MDCCLIII. | 4to. pp. 16.   1327

A | TREATY | held with the | Ohio Indians, | at | Carlisle, | In October, 1753. | [*Penn Arms.*] | *Philadelphia:* | *Printed and Sold by B. Franklin, and D. Hall, at the | New-Printing-Office, near the Market.* MDCCLIII. | Folio, pp. 12.   L. C. P.   1328

TURFORD. (H.)   The Grounds of a Holy Life ; to which is added, Paul's Speech to the Bishop of Crete, &c.   By Hugh Turford.   *Philadelphia : James Chattin.*   1753.   1329

THE VALUE of a Child ; or, Motives to the Good Education of Children.   In a Letter to a Daughter.   *Philadelphia : B. Franklin, and D. Hall.*   1753.   16mo. pp. 30.   1330

[VENN. (HENRY)]   The Art | of | Contentment, | By the Author | of | the Whole Duty of Man, &c. | . . . | . . . | . . . . | [Cut.] | *Oxford : Printed.* | *Philadelphia : Reprinted and Sold | by James Chattin, in Church-Alley,* 1753. | Sm. 8vo. pp. 133.   H. S. P.

VOTES | and | Proceedings | of the | House of Representatives | of the | Province of Pennsylvania, | Met at Philadelphia, on the Fourteenth of October, Anno | Domini 1752, and continued by Adjournments. | [*Penn Arms.*] | *Philadelphia:* | *Printed and Sold by B. Franklin, at the New-Printing-Office, | near the Market.* MDCCLIII. | Folio, pp. 52.   H. S. P.   1332

VOTES | and | Proceedings | of the | House of Representatives | of the | Province of Pennsylvania | Beginning the Fourteenth

Day of October, 1707. | Volume The Second. | [*Penn Arms.*] | *Philadelphia:* | *Printed and Sold by B. Franklin, and D. Hall, at the* | *New-Printing-Office, near the Market.* MDCCLIII. | Folio, Title, 1 leaf; pp. 1–494.   H. S. P.   1333

WATTS. (I[SAAC]) The | Psalms | of | David, | Imitated in the Language of the | New Testament: | And apply'd to the | Christian State and Worship. | By I. Watts, D.D. | The Sixteenth Edition. | . . . | . . . | . . . | . . . | . . . | . . . | . . . . | *Philadelphia, Sold by J. Chattin, Printer, W.* | *Muir, Book-binder near Market Wharf, W.* | *Schippius, Book-binder in Strawberry Alley ;* | *and by Garret Noel, Bookseller, New-York.* [1753. ?] | 12mo. Title, 1 leaf; pp. 1–320; Index, pp. (18); Table of First Lines, pp. (12).   1334

WHITEFIELD. (G.) An | Expostulatory | Letter | Addressed to | Nicholas Lewis, | Count Zinzendorff, | And | Lord Advocate of the Unitas Fratrum. | By | G. Whitefield, A.B. | Late of Pembroke College Oxford; and Chap- | lain to the Right Hon. the Countess of | Huntingdon. | . . . . | The Third Edition. | *London, Printed:* | *Philadelphia, Re-Printed and Sold by* | *William Bradford, at the Sign of* | *the Bible in Second-Street,* MDCCLIII. | 8vo. pp. 15.   L. C. P.   1335

𝕯𝕰𝕽 𝕷𝕰𝕿𝖅𝕿𝕰 𝖂𝕴𝕷𝕷𝕰 des hochfürstlichen Printzen Diederichs | von Anhalt Dessau, des alten Regierenden Fürsten von Dessau und Preussischen | Genral = Feld = Marschall sein Sohn, geschrieben im Jahr 1753. | [n. d. v. p.] Folio, 1 leaf.   H. S. P.   1336

𝕯𝕰𝕽 𝖂𝖀𝕹𝕯𝕰𝕽𝕭𝕬𝕳𝕽𝕰 bußfertige Seelensorger, wie er zur Erkenntniß seiner Sünden kommen ist, und sie bereut hat. *Germantown: Christopher Sower.* 1753. 16mo. pp. 36.   H. S. P.   1337

1754.

AN ACCOUNT of the Births | and Burials in Christ-Church Parish, | in Philadelphia, from December 24, 1753, | to December 24, 1754. By Caleb Cash, | Clerk, and Samuel Kirke, Sexton. | [n. p. n. d.] Folio, 1 leaf.   L. C. P.   1338

BALL. (W.)   The New-Jersey | Almanack, | According to the New Stile ; | For the Year of Christian Account | 1755. | [24 lines.] | By William Ball, Philomath. | *Philadelphia: Printed and Sold by W. Bradford,* | *at the Corner of Front and Market-Streets.* [1754.] | Sm. 8vo. pp. (32 ?).   L. C. P.   1339

HOLY BIBLE in Verse.   *Philadelphia: James Chattin.*   1754.

Advertised in the Pa. Gazette, Oct. 17, 1754.

BLAIR. (S.)   The Works of the Reverend Samuel Blair, Late Minister of the Gospel at Foggs-Manor, in Chester County, Pennsylvania, ... *Philadelphia: William Bradford.*   1754.   8vo.

Title from Sabin's Dictionary.

BOWNAS. (S.)   God's Mercy surmounting Man's Cruelty, exemplified in the Captivity and Redemption of Elizabeth Hanson, wife of John Hanson, of Knoxmarsh at Kecheachy, in Dover Township, who was taken a captive with her children, and Maid-Servant, by the Indians in New England, in the Year 1724. In which are inserted, Sundry Remarkable Preservations, Deliverances, and Marks of the Care and Kindness of Providence over her and her children, worthy to be remembered. The substance of which was taken from her own Mouth, and is now published for general service, by Samuel Bownas. The Second Edition. *Philadelphia: Printed and sold by James Chattin.* Sm. 8vo. pp. 24.

Title from Sabin's Dictionary, Number 30,264. See Number 327, *supra.*

BUNYAN. (J.)   Eines Christen | Reise | Nach der seeligen | Ewigkeit, | Welche | In'unterschiedlichen artigen | Sinnen-Bildern, | Den gantzen Zustand | Einer bußfertigen und Gott-suchenden | Seele | Vorstellet ; | In Englischer Sprache beschrieben | Durch | Joh: Bunian, | Lehrer in Betford, | Um seiner Fürtrefflichkeit willen in | die Hoch-Teutsche Sprache übersetzt. | *Ephrata in Pennsylvania.* | *Drucks und Verlags der Bruederschafft* | *Anno* 1754. | 16mo. pp. 280.   H. S. P.   1343

BUNYAN.   Eines Christen Reise | Nach der seeligen | Ewigkeit | Anderer Theil, | Worinnen unter artigen | Sinn-Bildern | fortgesetzet wird, | Wie | Des Christen Weib u. Kinder die gefährliche Reise | auch

angetreten, unb bas erwünſchte Land ver= | gnügt erreicht ḥaben. | Vor=
mals burch | Joh: Bunian | Jn Engliſcher Sprache beſchrieben, | Nun
aber inš Hoch=Teutſche überſetzet | Durch | Christ. Mart. Seibeln |
Past. unb Brobſten zu Berlin. | *Ephrata in Pennsylvania* | *Drucks
und Verlags der Bruederschafft* | *Anno* 1754. | 16mo. pp. (8), 264.

(BOURBON. [Armand de] Prince of Conti) Extracts | of |
Several Treatises | Wrote by the | Prince of Conti, | with the |
Sentiments of the Fathers, | And some of the | Decrees of the
Councils, | concerning | Stage Plays; | Recommended to the
Perusal and | serious Consideration of the | Professors of Christian-
ity in the City | of Philadelphia. | *Philadelphia,* | *Printed by
William Bradford, at the Sign of* | *the Bible, in Second-Street,*
MDCCLIV. | 8vo. pp. 47. (1).   h. s. p.   1345

A | CATALOGUE | of Books | belonging to the | Union-
Library-Company | of Philadelphia. | To which is prefixed, |
the Articles of the Company, with the Names of | the present
Members, and Rules observed by the | Clerk in letting out Books,
&c. | *Philadelphia :* | *Printed by James Chattin.* 1754. | Sm. 8vo.
pp. 50.   h. s. p.   1346

THE ASSEMBLY'S CATECHISM With Notes; which
briefly Explain the more difficult Words and Phrases contained
in it, for the Instruction of Youth. By the late Dr. Watts.
Lancaster: W. Dunlap. 1754.   1347

THE LARGER CATECHISM &c. Agreed Anno. 1648. by
the General Assembly of the Church of Scotand, to be a Directory
for Catechising such as have made some proficiency in the Knowledge of the Grounds of Religion. *Lancaster: W. Dunlap.* 1754

THE SHORTER CATECHISM of the Reverend Assembly of
Divines at Westminster; for the Instruction of Youth. *Lancaster: W. Dunlap.* 1754.   1349

THE SHORTER CATECHISM with the Proofs thereof out of
the Scriptures in Words at Length. *Lancaster: W. Dunlap.*

    These four catechisms are advertised at the end of Rowe's Devout Exercises.

CHALKLEY. (T.) A | Collection | of the | Works | of | Thomas Chalkley. | In Two Volumes. | . . . | . . . | . . . | . . . | . . . . | Vol. I. | The Second Edition. | *Philadelphia : | Printed and Sold by James Chattin,* | *in Church-Alley.* 1754. | Sm. 8vo. H. S. P.

Collation. General Title, 1 leaf; Contents, &c., pp. (2) ; Title to Journal, 1 leaf; "Testimony of the Philadelphia Meeting," pp. iii–viii ; pp. 1–325. Vol. II. Title, 1 leaf; Preface, pp. iii–iv ; Epistles, &c. pp. 1–244 ; Index, pp. vii. The title of the second volume is : The | Works | of | Thomas Chalkley. | Vol. II. | Containing | Epistles and other Writings. | *Philadelphia : | Printed and Sold by James Chattin.* | 1754. |

CHRISTIAN | Education | Exemplified under the Character of | Paturnus | Instructing his only Son | [Cut.] | *Germantown : | Printed by Christopher Sower Junior,* 1754. | Sm. 8vo. pp. 8.

C[RISP.] (S[TEPHEN]) A Short History of a Long Travel from Babylon to Bethel. By S. C. The Tenth Edition. *Philadelphia: James Chattin.* 1754. 1353

DAILY Conversation with God, | Exemplify'd in the | Holy Life | of | Armelle Nicolas, | A Poor ignorant Country Maid in France ; | Commonly known by the name of the | Good Armelle, | Deceas'd at Bretaigne in the Year 1671. | Done out of French. . . . | . . . | . . . | . . . | . . . | . . . | . . . | . . . | . . . | . . . | . . . . | *Germantown : | Printed by Christopher Sower Junior.* 1754. | Sm. 8vo. pp. 16. H. S. P. 1354

DAWSON. (W.) The Youth's entertaining Amusement, or a plain Guide to Psalmody ; being a Collection of the most usual and necessary Tunes sung in the English Protestant Congregations in Philadelphia, &c. In two Parts, viz. Treble and Bass ; with all proper and necessary Rules adapted to the meanest Capacities. By W. Dawson, Writing Master and Accomptant, at the Hand and Pen, in Third-street. *Philadelphia : B. Franklin, and D. Hall.* 1754. 1355

Advertised in the Pa. Gazette, Jan. 14, 1755.

DELAP. (S.) Remarks | On Some | Articles | Of the | Seceders New Covenant, | And Their | Act of Presbytery, |

Making it the Term of Ministerial | and Christian Communion. | By Samuel Delap, A.M. | and Dissenting Minister at Letterkenny. | . . . | . . . | . . . | . . . | . . . | . . . | . . . | . . . | . . . | . . . | . . . | . . . . | *Belfast Printed:* | *Lancaster: Re-printed and Sold by W.* | *Dunlap, at the New-Printing-* | *Office in King-Street.* 1754. | Sm. 8vo. pp. 47.   c. 1356

ELLWOOD. (T.) Davideis. The Life of David, King of Israel. A Sacred Poem; in Five Books. By Thomas Ellwood. The Fifth Edition, Corrected. *London Printed: Philadelphia, re-printed by James Chattin.* 1754. Sq. 16mo. pp. viii, 248.   1357

AN EPISTLE from the Yearly Meeting. *Philadelphia: B. Franklin, and D. Hall.* 1754.   1358

AN | EPISTLE | of | Caution and Advice, | concerning the | Buying and Keeping | of | Slaves. | *Philadelphia:* | *Printed and Sold by James Chattin,* | *in Church-Alley.* 1754. | Sm. 8vo. pp. 8.

From the Yearly Meeting of Friends held 9 mo. 1745 at Burlington.

FINLEY. (S.) The Madness of Mankind, | Represented | in a | Sermon | preached | in the | New Presbyterian Church | in Philadelphia, | on the 9th of June, 1754. | By Samuel Finley, A. M. | Minister of the Gospel at Nottingham. | Published at the Desire of many of the | Audience, with a few Enlargements. | *Philadelphia,* | *Printed and Sold by William Bradford,* | *at the Corner-House of Front-and Market-Streets.* [1754.] 8vo. pp. 30.

FOR the Benefit of | Miss Hallam, and her two Brothers, | By a Company of Comedians from | London, | At the New Theatre, in Water-street, | This present Evening (being the Tenth of June, 1754) will | be presented a new Tragedy, called, | The Gamester. | [12 lines.] To which will be added, a Farce called, | Miss in her Teens. | . . . . | [*Philadelphia: Franklin and Hall.* 1754.] Folio, 1 leaf.   H. S. P. 1361

FOTHERGILL. (J.) An | Account | of the | Life and Travels, | in the | Work of the Ministry, | of | John Fothergill. | To which are added, | Divers Epistles to Friends in Great-Britain |

and America, on various Occasions. | *London: Printed.* | *Philadel-phia: Reprinted and Sold* | *by James Chattin, in Church-Alley,* | 1754. | Sm. 8vo. pp. iv, 280.   H. S. P.   1362

[FRANKLIN. (BENJAMIN)] Some | Account | of the | Penn-sylvania Hospital; | From its first Rise, to the Beginning | of the Fifth Month, called May, 1754. | *Philadelphia:* | *Printed by B. Franklin, and D. Hall.* MDCCLIV. | 4to. pp. 40.   H. S. P.   1363

FREAME. (J.) Scripture-Instruction; | Digested into several Sections | By Way of | Question and Answer. | In Order to pro-mote | Piety and Virtue | And discourage Vice and | Immoral-ity. | With a preface relating to | Education | By John Freame. | . . . | . . . | . . . . | *London: Printed* 1713. | *Reprinted at Ephrata in Pennsylvania.* | 1754. Price 1 Shilling. | 16mo. pp. 162. (2).   1364

F[RY.] (J[OHN]) An | Essay | on | Conduct. | Recommended | To the People called Quakers. | A Poem. | By J. F. | . . . | . . . . | The Fourth Edition, Corrected. | To which is added, | Poems, on several Subjects, | by another Hand. | *London: Printed.* | *Philadelphia: Reprinted and Sold* | *by James Chattin, in Church-Alley.* 1754. | Sm. 8vo. pp. ix, [misprint for iv.] 20.   H. S. P.   1365

[HILDEBRAND. (JOHANNES)] Ein Geſpräch zwiſchen einem | Jüngling und einem Alten | von dem Nutzen der Gottſeeligen | Gemein-ſchaften. | [*Germantown. Christoph Saur.* 1754.] 16mo. pp. 24.

DER | HOCH-DEUTSCH | Americaniſche | Calender, | Auf das Jahr | . . . | . . . . | 1755 | . . . | . . . | . . . | . . . | . . . | . . . | . . . | . . . | . . . | . . . . | Zum Siebenzehenten mal heraus gegeben. | *Germantown: Gedruckt und zu finden bey Christoph Saur.* | *Auch koennen die auswaertige Kraemer solche bey David Taeschler in Phila-delphia haben* | *oder in Lancéster ley Henrich Walter.* [1754.] | 4to. pp. (48).   H. S. P.   1367

JERMAN. (J.) The American | Almanack | For the Year of Christian Account | 1755, | Being the Third after Leap-Year. | . . . | . . . | . . . | . . . | . . . | . . . | . . . | . . . | . . . | . . . |

. . . . | By John Jerman, Philom. | . . . | . . . | . . . | . . . | . . .
| . . . . | *Philadelphia:* | *Printed by B. Franklin and D. Hall.*
[1754.] | Sm. 8vo. pp. (24).   1368

[KENNEDY. (ARCHIBALD)] Serious Considerations on the
Present State of the Affairs of the Northern Colonies. *Philadel-*
phia: B. Franklin, and D. Hall. 1754.   1369

Advertised in the Pa. Gazette, May 23, 1754.

A | LETTER | From | Benjamin Jones, | In Alexandria in
Virginia, | To | John Jones, | In Pennsylvania. | Taken from a
late News-Paper. | [*Philadelphia:*] *Re-printed* 1754. | Sm. 8vo.
pp. 7.

MORE. (T.) The American | Country Almanack | for the |
Year of Christian Account | 1755. | [13 lines.] | By Thomas More.
| . . . | . . . | . . . | . . . . | *Philadelphia:* | *Printed and Sold by*
B. Franklin and D. Hall, at | *the New-Printing-Office near the Mar-*
ket. [1754.] | Sm. 8vo. pp. (24).   L. C. P.   1371

NAKSKOW. (P. S.) The Articles of Faith, of The Holy
Evangelical Church, According to the Word of God and the Aus-
burg Confession. Set forth in Forty Sermons. By Magist. Pet-
rus Sachariæ Nakskow, ... Translated from the Original into
English, By Jochum Melchior Mages. *Philadelphia:?* 1754. 1372

Advertised in the Pa. Journal, Sept. 12. 1754, as to be published in monthly
parts, the first of which is "just published, and to be sold by William Bradford."
Probably referring to the edition printed in New York in 1754.

𝔑𝔈𝔘=eingerichteter Americanischer Geschichts=Calender, auf das Jahr
1755. *Philadelphia: Gedruckt bey B. Francklin und A. Armbruster.*
1754.   1373

NEW–JERSEY. Anno Regni | Georgii II. | Regis | Magnæ
Britaniæ, et Hiberniæ, | Vigesimo Septimo. | At a Session of
General Assembly of | the Province of New-Jersey; begun and held
| at Perth-Amboy, on the Seventeenth Day of April, One | Thou-
sand Seven Hundred and Fifty-four, and ended the | Twenty-first
Day of June following; on which Day the | following Acts were

passed. | [*Royal Arms.*] | *Philadelphia : | Printed by W. Bradford, Printer to the King's Most | Excellent Majesty, for the Province of New-Jersey.* [1754.] | Folio, pp. 36.   1374

NEW-YEAR Verses of the Carriers of the Pennsylvania Gazette. *Philadelphia: B. Franklin, and D. Hall.* 1754. 1375

NEW-YEAR Verses of the Carriers of the Pennsylvania Journal. *Philadelphia: William Bradford.* 1754.   1376

PENN. (W.) Some Fruits of Solitude in Reflections and Maxims, Relating to the Conduct of Human Life. *Philadelphia : James Chattin.* 1754.   1377

Advertised as "Penn's Maxims," in the Pa. Gazette, Oct. 17, 1754.

THE PENNSYLVANIA Gazette.   H. S. P. 1378

Numbers 1306 (Jan. 1, 1754) to 1358 (Dec. 31, 1754), six pages each, except Numbers 1306, 1317 and 1319, which contain four pages. The cut of the snake divided in eight pieces with the motto "Join or Die," appeared on May 9. Title and imprint as in Number 1232, *supra.*

THE PENNSYLVANIA Journal. *Philadelphia : Printed and Sold by William Bradford, at the Sign of the Bible, the Corner of | Black Horse Alley, in Second-Street, where Persons may be supplied with this Paper at 10 s. a Year. And | where Advertisements are taken in.* | Folio.   H. S. P. 1379

Numbers 578 (Jan. 3, 1754) to 630 (Dec. 31, 1754), four pages each. Title as in Number 1273, *supra.* The imprint was changed in Number 604 to the form given in Number 1429, *infra.* The paper for April 18th is misdated April 81.

POOR Robin's Almanac for 1755. *Philadelphia: William Bradford.* 1754.   1380

ROWE. ([ELIZABETH]) Devout Exercises of the Heart, in | Meditation and Soliloquy, | Prayer and Praise. | By the late Pious and Ingenious | Mrs. Rowe. | Review'd and Published at her Request, | By I. Watts, D.D. | *Edinburgh Printed: | Lancaster, Re-printed, and Sold by W. | Dunlap at the New-Printing-Office | in King Street,* 1754. | Sm. 8vo. pp. 126 ; Contents, pp. (2) ; Advertisement, 1 leaf ; Books, &c., 1 leaf.   H. S. P. 1381

SAUNDERS. (R.) A Pocket | Almanack | For the Year 1755. | Fitted to the Use of Penn- | sylvania, and the neighbour- | ing Provinces. | With several useful Additions. | By Richard Saunders, Phil. | *Philadelphia: | Printed and sold by B. Franklin,* | *and D. Hall.* [1754.] | 24mo. pp. (24).   c. 1382

SAUNDERS. Poor Richard improved : | Being an | Almanack | . . . | . . . | . . . | . . . | . . . | . . . | . . . | . . . | . . . | . . . | For the | Year of our Lord 1755 : | Being the Third after Leap-Year. | . . . | . . . | . . . | . . . | . . . | . . | . . . | . . . | . . . . | | By Richard Saunders, Philom. | *Philadelphia: | Printed and Sold by B. Franklin, and D. Hall.* [1754.] | Sm. 8vo. pp. (36). H. S. P.

SMITH. (W.) Personal Affliction and frequent Reflection upon human Life, of great Use to lead Man to the Remembrance of God. A Sermon, preached on Sunday Sept. 1, 1754, in Christ-Church, Philadelphia; Occasioned by the Death of a beloved Pupil, who departed this Life August 28, 1754, in the 16th Year of his Age. By W. Smith, M. A. Professor of Philosophy in the Academy of Philadelphia. *Philadelphia: B. Franklin, and D. Hall,* 1754. 8vo. pp. viii, 16, (1).   1384

> Verses by Francis Hopkinson, J. Duché, Paul Jackson, and others, are prefixed. The pupil was William Thomas Martin, son of Josiah Martin, who was afterwards Governor of North Carolina.

TOBLER. (J.) The Pennsylvania Town and Countryman's Almanac for 1755. By John Tobler. *Germantown: Christopher Sower.* 1754.   1385

VOTES | and | Proceedings | of the | House of Representatives | of the | Province of Pennsylvania, | Met at Philadelphia, on the Fifteenth of October, Anno | Domini 1753, and continued by Adjournment. | [*Penn Arms.*] | *Philadelphia: | Printed and Sold by B. Franklin, at the New-Printing-Office,* | *near the Market.* MDCCLIV. | Folio, pp. 78, (1).   H. S. P. 1386

VOTES | and | Proceedings | of the | House of Representatives | of the | Province of Pennsylvania. | Beginning the Fourteenth Day of October. 1726. | Volume The Third | [*Penn Arms.*] |

Philadelphia: | *Printed and Sold by B. Franklin, and D. Hall, at the* | *New-Printing-Office, near the Market.* MDCCLIV. | Folio, pp. 591.   1387

A | WARNING | Of the | Presbytery of New-Castle, | To the People under their Care, | Against | Several Errors and evil Practices | Of | Mr. John Cuthbertson: | With an Appendix relating to the | Seceders. | *Lancaster:* | *Printed and Sold by W. Dunlap, at the* | *New-Printing-Office, in King-Street,* | M,DCC,LIV. | Sm. 8vo. pp. 55.   c. 1388

The appendix begins on page 39, with a separate title page, as follows : An Appendix | To the Foregoing : | Being | Remarks | On the Doctrine and Practice | Of the | Seceders. | *Lancaster: Printed by W. Dunlap.* | M,DCC,LIV. |

WOOLMAN. (J.) Some | Considerations | On the Keeping of | Negroes. | Recommended to the Professors | of Christianity of every | Denomination. | By John Woolman. | *Philadelphia:* | *Printed and Sold by James Chattin,* | *in Church-Alley.* 1754. | Sm. 8vo. Title, 1 leaf; Introduction, pp. (4); text, pp. 1–24. Advertisement, pp. (2).   H. S. P. 1389

1755.

AN ACCOUNT of the Births | and Burials in Christ-Church Parish, | in Philadelphia, from December 24, 1754, | to December 24, 1755. By Caleb Cash | Clerk, and Samuel Kirke, Sexton. | [n. p. n. d.] Folio, 1 leaf.   L. C. P. 1390

AN | ACCOUNT | Of the | Distances | From the City of | Philadelphia, | Of all the Places of Note within the | Improved Part of the Province of | Pennsylvania. . . . | . . . | . . . | . . . | . . . | . . . | . . . . | *Philadelphia:* | *Printed by William Bradford, at the* | *Corner House of Front and Market-Street.* [1755.] 8vo. pp. 15.   L. C. P. 1391

AN ACT for Granting £60,000 to the King's use [passed Nov. 27, 1755]. [*Philadelphia: B. Franklin, and D. Hall.* 1755.] Folio.   1392

Title from Sabin's Dictionary, No. 59,780.

ADDITIONAL | Charter | of the | College, | Academy, | and | Charity School | of | Philadelphia, in Pennsylvania. | [*Penn Arms.*] *Philadelphia:* | *Printed by B. Franklin, and D. Hall.* 1755. | Folio, Half-title, 1 leaf; pp. 13.   H. S. P.   1393

ADVERTISEMENT. | Lancaster, April 26, 1755. | [n. p. n. d.] Folio, 1 leaf.   1394

Signed B. Franklin, calling for 150 four horse wagons for the use of Braddock's Army.

ANNO Regni | Georgii II. | Regis, | Magnæ Britanniæ, Franciæ & Hiberniæ, | Vigesimo Octavo. | At a General Assembly of the Province of Penn- | sylvania, begun and holden at Philadelphia, | the Fourteenth Day of October, Anno Domini, 1754, | in the Twenty-eighth Year of the Reign of our Sove- | reign Lord George II. by the Grace of God, of | Great-Britain, France and Ireland, King, Defender of | the Faith, &c. | And from thence continued by Adjournments to the Seven- | teenth Day of March, 1755. | [*Penn Arms.*] | *Philadelphia:* | *Printed and Sold by B. Franklin, at the New-* | *Printing-Office, near the Market,* MDCCLV. | Folio, Title, 1 leaf; pp. 211–214. + And from thence continued . . . to the Thir- | teenth Day of June, 1755. | [*Ibid.*] Title, 1 leaf; pp. 217–222. + And from thence . . . to the | Twenty-third Day of July, 1755. | [*Ibid.*] Title, 1 leaf; pp. 225–235. + [*Ibid.*] And from thence . . . to the Fif- | teenth Day of September, 1755. | [*Ibid.*] Title, 1 leaf; p. 239.   H. S. P.   1395

ANNO Regni | Georgii II. | Regis, | Magnæ Britanniæ, Franciæ & Hiberniæ, | Vigesimo Nono. | At a General Assembly of the Province of Penn- | sylvania, begun and holden at Philadelphia, | the Fourteenth Day of October, Anno Domini, 1755, | in the Twenty-ninth Year of the Reign of our Sove- | reign Lord George II. by the Grace of God, of | Great-Britain, France and Ireland, King, Defender of | the Faith, &c. | And from thence continued by Adjournments to the Third | Day of November, 1755. | [*Penn Arms.*] | *Philadelphia:* | *Printed and Sold by B. Franklin, at the New-* | *Printing-Office, near the Market.* MDCCLV. | Folio, Title, 1 leaf; pp. 243–260.   H. S. P.   1396

BALL. (W.)   The New Jersey Almanac for 1756.   By William
Ball.   *Philadelphia: William Bradford.*   1755.   1397

BARTON. (T.)   Unanimity and Public Spirit. | A | Sermon,
| Preached at | Carlisle, | And some other Episcopal Churches,
in the | Counties of York and Cumber- | land, soon after General
Brad- | dock's Defeat. | Published by particular Request. | By the
Reverend Mr. Thomas Barton, | Missionary to the said Churches.
| To which is prefixed, | A Letter from the Reverend Mr. Smith,
Provost of the College of Philadelphia, concerning | the Office
and Duties of a Protestant Ministry, espe- | cially in Times of
public Calamity and Danger. | *Philadelphia:* | *Printed and Sold by
B. Franklin, and D. Hall, at | the New-Printing-Office; by W.
Dunlap, in Lan- | caster; and in York County by the Author.*
1755. | 8vo. Title, 1 leaf; Preface, pp. iii–iv; Smith's Letter, pp.
v–xx; Sermon, pp. 1–16.   H. S. P.   1398

EJN BETTLER | und doch kein | Bettler, | Ein jeder ein König |
wann er will. | Ein Gleichnis, in sich haltend ein Exem= | pel eines voll=
kommenen Mannes in Christo; | Wozu noch beygefüget | Das | Verbor=
gene Manna | Als eine Anfrischung zum Geistlichen Fort= | gang: In
einem schreiben an einen | wohlgesinnten Freund; | Wie auch, ein Wort
des Trostes an die Arme | und Unvermögende. | In Englischer sprach
gedruckt zu Philadelphia | 1749. Und zur Erwägung und nutzen der |
Deutschen übersetzt. | *Germanton.* | *Gedruckt und zu finden bey
Christoph Saur 1755.* | 16mo. pp. 45, (1).   H. S. P.   1399

A BILL, entituled, An Act for raising Fifty Thousand | Pounds
for the King's Use, by a Tax of Twelve-pence per | Pound, and
Twenty Shillings per Head, yearly, for two | Years, on all the
Estates Real and Personal, and Taxables, | within this Province.
[*Philadelphia: B. Franklin.* 1755.] Folio, pp. 4.   H. S. P.   1400

BOOKS | Just Imported from London, and to be Sold by |
William Bradford, | At his Shop, adjoining the London Coffee-
House in Market-Street. [*Philadelphia: William Bradford.*
1755.] Folio, 1 leaf.   H. S. P.   1401

BUNYAN. (J.)   Das angenehme Opfer | oder | Die Vortrefflichkeit eines | Zerbrochenen Herzens: | Vorstellende die Kenn-Zeichen, Eigen- | schafften und wahre Würckungen | eines zerschlagenen Geistes, | Verfasset von dem berühmten Prediger und | treuen Diener Jesu Christi. | Johann Bunian. | Als welche seine letzte Schrifft war, und | zu Londen von Johann Gwittim Anno 1702 | außgegeben worden: und nun aus der 4ten Auf- | lage um seiner Wichtigkeit willen, als zu diesen | hart-hertzigen Zeiten nicht unnöthig, ins Deut- | sche übersetzt, von einem Gutmeynen- den. | *Germantown.* | *Gedruckt und zu finden bey Christoph Saur,* 1755. | 16mo. pp. 151, (1).   H. S. P. 1402

Printed with the 3d part of Bunyan's Pilgrim's Progress, with continuous signatures, but separate paging.

BUNYAN.   Johann Bunians | Pilgrims- | oder | Christen | Reise | auß dieser Welt nach der Zukünfftigen | Der dritte Theil. | Dargelegt unter dem Gleichnis eines | Traums: | Zeigende, die mancherley Be- schwernisse | und Gefahren, die Ihm begegnet: Und die | viele Siege, die Er erhalten über Welt, | Fleisch und den Teufel; | Wie auch dessen glückliche Ankunfft in | der Himlischen Stadt, und der Herrlichkeit und | Freude, die er da gefunden zu seinem ewigen | vergnügen. | Uebersetzt aus der 13ten Englischen Auflage. zur Er- | munterung der Liebhaber solcher Reise; von einem | Geringen Mit-pilger. | *Germanton.* | *Gedruckt und zu finden bey Christoph Saur* 1755. | 16mo. pp. 144. H. S. P.

BURR. (A.)   A Fast Sermon at Newark. 1755. By Aaron Burr. *Philadelphia:* 1755.   1404

Title from Haven's List. Sabin gives a New York edition, which is also mentioned by Haven, and is probably the only one printed.

CHAMBERLAIN. ([THOMAS])   England's Timely Remembrancer, or the Minister preaching his own Funeral Sermon, containing many wonderful Things seen in a Vision, by the Rev. Mr. Chamberlain. *Philadelphia: James Chattin.* 1755.   1405

CLARK. (T.)   Remarks | upon the | Manner and Form | of | Swearing | By Touching and Kissing the Gospels: | In a Letter to a Friend. | Being partly Excerpts from an anonymous Book, | entituled The New Mode of Swearing, | Tactis et Deosculatis

Evangeliis, published 33 | Years ago. | By the Rev. Mr. Thomas Clark, | Minister at Ballibay, in the County of Mo- | naghan, Ireland. | . . . | . . . . | *Glasgow Printed :* | *Lancaster Re-printed by W. Dunlap,* | *in Queen-Street, for Mr. Alexander Mure, in* | *Chestnut-Level.* 1755. | Sm. 8vo. pp. 30 ; Advertisement, 1 leaf.

[CLARKE. (W.)] Observations on the late and present Conduct of the French, with regard to their Encroachments upon the British Collonies in North America. Together with Remarks on the Importance of these Colonies to Great Britain. To which is added, wrote by another hand, Observations concerning the Increase of Mankind, &c. *Philadelphia : ?* 1755. 1407

Title from Haven's List. First printed at Boston, and re-printed in London. The existence of a Philadelphia edition is doubtful,

[CRISP. (STEPHEN)] Eine | Kurtze | Beschreibung | einer | Langen Reise | aus | Babylon | nach | Bethel. | Offenb. 18, 4. | In Englischer Sprache geschrieben, im Novem. 1691. | und aus dem 5ten Druck ins Teutsche übersetzt 1748. | mit Beyfügung einiger Schrifftstellen, zu | mehrerer Erläuterung. | *Und nun das Zweyte mal zu* | *Germanton gedruckt bey Christoph Saur,* | 1755. | 16mo. pp. 38, (8). H. S. P. 1408

DAVIES. (S.) Religion | and | Patriotism | the | Constituents | of a good | Soldier. | A Sermon preached to Captain Over- | ton's Independant Company of Volunteers, | raised in Hanover County, Virginia, Au- | gust 17, 1755. | By Samuel Davies, A. M. Minister of the | Gospel there. | *Philadelphia :* | *Printed by James Chattin.* 1755. | Sq. 8vo. pp. 24. H. S. P. 1409

This Sermon is rendered remarkable by the following prophetic note on page 9 :—" As a remarkable Instance of this, I may point out to the Public that heroic Youth, Col. Washington, whom I cannot but hope Providence has hitherto preserved in so signal a Manner, for some important Service to his Country."

EATON. (I.) The Qualifications, Characters and Duties of a good Minister of Jesus Christ, considered. A Sermon preached at the Ordination of Rev. Mr. John Gano, Anno Domini 1754. By Isaac Eaton, Minister of the Baptist Church, in Hopewell, New-Jersey. *Philadelphia : B. Franklin, and D. Hall.* 1755. 8vo.

Ascribed to John Gates in Haven's List, probably following T. Westcott, in the Historical Magazine, for 1860, p. 236. The title above given is from the Pa. Gazette, Sept. 25, 1755, which Westcott quotes as his authority for ascribing it to John Gates.

AN | EPISTLE | from our | General Spring Meeting of Ministers | and Elders for Pennsylvania and New- | Jersey, held at Philadelphia, from the | 29th of the Third Month, to the 1st | of the Fourth Month, inclusive, 1755. | To Friends on the Continent of America. | [*Philadelphia: Printed by James Chattin.*? 1755.] Folio, pp. 4.   M. S.   1411

EVANS. (L.) Geographical, Historical, | Political, Philosophical, and Mechanical | Essays. | The First, Containing | an | Analysis | Of a General Map of the | Middle British Colonies | in | America ; | And of the Country of the Confederate Indians : | A Description of the Face of the Country ; | The Boundaries of the Confederates ; | And the | Maritime and Inland Navigations of the several Rivers | and Lakes contained therein. | By Lewis Evans. | *Philadelphia :* | *Printed by B. Franklin, and D. Hall.* MDCCLV. | 4to. pp. iv. 32. + The Second Edition. [*Ibid.*]   1412

𝕯𝕰𝕽 | 𝕳𝕺𝕮𝕳=𝕯𝕰𝖀𝕿𝕾𝕮𝕳 | Americanifche | Calender, | Auf das Jahr | . . . | . . . | 1756. | (Welches ein Schalt Jahr von 366 Tagen ift.) . . . | . . . | . . . | . . . | . . . | . . . | . . . | . . . | . . . . | Zum Achtzehenten mal heraus gegeben. | *Germantown : Gedruckt und zu finden bey Christoph Saur.* | . . . | . . . . [1755.] | 4to. pp. (48). H. S. P. 1413

JERMAN. (J.) The American | Almanack | For the Year of Christian Account | 1756, | Being Leap-Year | . . . | . . . | . . . | . . . | . . . | . . . | . . . | . . . | . . . | . . . | . . . . | By John Jerman, Philom. | . . . | . . . | . . . | . . . | . . . | . . . | . . . . | *Philadelphia :* | *Printed* [*by Franklin and Hall*] *for the Author.* [1755.] | Sm. 8vo. pp. (24).   1414

[KEMPER. (HENRY)] Treuhertzige | Erinnerung und | Warnung, | beftehend | in vielen Klag=Reden | vom Verfall des Chriften= | thums, | im äufferlichen Gottes=dienft. | Mit famt einer Anweifung von dem wah= | ren bleibenden und ewigen Gottes=Dienft, | ohne welchen niemand feelig ift, auch nicht | ohne folchen feelig werden kan. | Heraus gegeben auß

Liebe zu aller Menschen | Seeligkeit, von einem auf der Wacht | stehenden Ermahner. | *Germanton.* | *Gedruckt bey Christoph Saur* | *im Jahr* 1755. | 16mo. pp. (12), 78.   1415

DAS | KINDER= | BÜCHLEIN | In den | Brüder=Gemeinen. *Gedruckt* | *zu Germanton bey* | *Christoph Saur.* 1755. | Sm. 16mo. pp. (16), 210, (62).   1416

THE LIFE and Confession of John Myrick, who was executed for the Murder of his Wife and Children. *Philadelphia: James Chattin.* 1755. Sm. 4to.   1417

MOORE. (T.) An Almanac for 1756. By Thomas Moore. *Philadelphia: B. Franklin, and D. Hall.* 1755.   1418

NACHKLANG | Zum | Gesang der einsamen | Turtel Taube, | Ent= haltend eine neue Sammlung | Geistlicher Lieder. | *Ephrata Drucks der Bruederschafft* | *Im Jahre* 1755. | Sq. 8vo. pp. 112. H. S. P. 1419

NEU=eingerichteter Americanischer Geschichts Calender, auf das Jahr 1756. *Philadelphia: B. Francklin und A. Armbruester.*   1420

DAS NEUE | Testament. | Unsers | Herrn und Heylandes | Jesu Christi, | Verteutscht | Von | D. Martin Luther. | Mit | Jedes Capitels kurtzen | Sumarien. | Auch beygefügten vielen richtigen | Parallelen. | *Germanton.* | *Gedruckt und zu finden bey Christoph Saur,* 1755. | 16mo. pp. (4), 562, (4).   H. S. P. 1421

   The second edition. Title in red and black.

NEW JERSEY. Anno Regni | Georgii II. | Regis | Magnæ Britaniæ et Hiberniæ, | Vigesimo Octavo. | At a Session of General Assembly of | the Province of New-Jersey; begun and held | at Elizabeth-Town, on the Twentieth Day of February, | One Thousand Seven Hundred and Fifty-five, and ended | the Third Day of March following; on which Day the | following Acts were passed. | [*Royal Arms.*] | *Philadelphia:* | *Printed by W. Bradford, Printer to the King's Most* | *Excellent Majesty, for the Province of New-Jersey.* [1755.] | Folio, pp. 8.   1422

NEW JERSEY. Anno Regni | Georgii II. | Regis | Magnæ Britaniæ, Franciæ and Hiberniæ, | Vigesimo Octavo. | At two Sessions of General Assembly of | the Province of New-Jersey ; held at Eliza- | beth-Town, the one begun the Seventh Day of April | 1755, and ended the Twenty Third Day of the same | Month ; the other begun the Twenty Fourth of April | 1755, and ended on the Twenty Sixth of the same Month, | being the Third and Fourth Sessions of this present | Assembly, during which Time the following | Acts were passed. | [*Royal Arms.*] | *Philadelphia : | Printed by W. Bradford, Printer to the King's Most | Excellent Majesty, for the Province of New-Jersey.* [1755.] | Folio, pp. 24.   1423

NEW JERSEY. Anno Regni | Georgii II. | Regis | Magnæ, Britaniæ, et Hiberniæ, | Vigesimo Nono | At a Session of General Assembly of the Province of | New-Jersey ; begun at Elizabeth-Town, on the First | Day of August 1755 ; and held by Adjournment at | Perth-Amboy, and ended the Twentieth Day of the | same Month, on which Days the following Acts were | passed. | [*Royal Arms.*] | *Philadelphia : | Printed by W. Bradford, Printer to the King's most | Excellent Majesty for the Province of New-Jersey.* [1755.] | Folio, pp. 64.   1424

NEW JERSEY. Anno Regni | Georgii II. | Regis | Magnæ Britaniæ, Franciæ, and Hiberniæ, | Vigesimo Nono. | At a Session of General Assembly of the Province of | New-Jersey ; begun and holden at Elizabeth-Town, | the Sixteenth Day of December 1755, being the sixth | Sessions of this present Assembly ; during which | Time the following Law was pass'd. | [*Royal Arms.*] | *Philadelphia : | Printed by William Bradford, Printer to the | Province of New-Jersey.* [1755.] | Folio, pp. 17.   1425

THE | NEW-YEAR | Verses | Of the Printers Lads, who carry the Penn- | sylvania-Gazette to the Customers. | for 1755. | [*Philadelphia : B. Franklin, and D. Hall.* 1755.] Folio, 1 leaf. L. C. P.

NEW-YEAR Verses of the Carriers of the Pennsylvania Journal. *Philadelphia : William Bradford.* 1755.   1427

THE PENNSYLVANIA Gazette.   H. S. P.   1428

Numbers 1359 (Jan. 7, 1755) to 1409 (Dec. 25, 1755), six pages each, with a "Supplement" of two pages to Number 1384. Title and imprint as in Number 1232, *supra*.

THE PENNSYLVANIA Journal. *Philadelphia: Printed and Sold by William Bradford, at the Sign of the Bible, the Corner- | House of Front and Market-Streets, where Persons may be supplied with this Paper at 10 s. a Year. And | where Advertisements are taken in. |*   H. S. P.   1429

Numbers 631 (Jan. 6, 1755) to 681 (Dec. 25, 1755), four pages each. Title as in Number 1273, *supra*.

THE PENNSYLVANIA Primer, . . . for the Use of Country Schools; . . . . *Lancaster: W. Dunlap.* 1755. 12mo.   1430

𝔓𝔥𝔦𝔩𝔞𝔡𝔢𝔩𝔭𝔥𝔦𝔰𝔠𝔥𝔢 Zeitung von allerhand auswärtigen und einheimischen merkwürdigen Sachen. *Philadelphia: gedruckt und zu haben bey B. Francklin, General Postmeister, und A. Armbruester, in der 4ten Strasse.* 1755. Folio.   1431

Prof. Seidensticker places this title under the year 1751, but judging from the only number I have met with (see Number 1549, *infra*), I think it was not begun until about June, 1755.

POOR Robin's Almanac for 1756. *Philadelphia: William Bradford.* 1755.   1432

READING. ([PHILIP]) The Protestant's Danger, and the Pro- | testant's Duty. | A | Sermon, | On Occasion of the present | Encroachments | Of the | French. | Preached at | Christ-Church, Philadelphia, | On Sunday, June 22, 1755. | By the Reverend Mr. Reading, Mis- | sionary at Apoquiniminck, in New-Castle | County, on Delaware. | Published at the Request of several of the Congre- | gation before whom it was delivered. | *Philadelphia: | Printed by B. Franklin, and D. Hall, | at the New-Printing-Office.* 1755. | 8vo. pp. 28.   H. S. P.   1433

A RELATION of a remarkable Providence, which fell out at the time of the Great Earthquake at Jamaica, very proper to be reflected on at this Time of immenent Danger, and after having lately had a warning from God, by a smaller Shock of the like kind in this Place. A Paper proper to be given away. *Philadelphia: James Chattin.* 1755.   1434

SAUNDERS. (R.) A Pocket | Almanack | For the Year 1756. | Fitted to the Use of Penn- | sylvania, and the neighbour- | ing Provinces. | With several useful Additions. | By R. Saunders, Phil. | *Philadelphia:* | *Printed and sold by B. Franklin,* | *and D. Hall.* [1755.] | 24mo. pp. (24).   c.   1435

SAUNDERS. Poor Richard improved: | Being an | Almanack | . . . | . . . | . . | . . | . . | . . | . . | . . | . . | . . . | For the | Year of our Lord 1756 : | Being Bissextile or Leap-Year. | . . . | . . . | . . | . . | . . | . . | . . | . . | . . . | . . . . | By Richard Saunders, Philom. | *Philadelphia:* | *Printed and Sold by B. Franklin, and D. Hall.* [1755.] | Sm. 8vo. pp. (36).   H. S. P.

SCOUGAL. (H.) Das Leben Gottes in der Seele des Menschen. Von Henry Scougal. Mit 2 Vorreden von Gilbert Burnett und William Wisshart. Erste Americanische Auflage. *Germantown. Gedruckt und zu finden bey Christoph Saur im Jahr 1755.* 16mo. pp. (21), 77.   H. S. P.   1437

     From a manuscript title added to an imperfect copy by Mr. A. H. Cassel.

[SMITH. (WILLIAM)] A Brief | History | Of the Rise and Progress of the | Charitable Scheme, | Carrying on by a | Society of Noblemen and Gentlemen | in | London, | For the Relief and Instruction of poor Ger- | mans, and their Descendents, settled in Penn- | sylvania, and the adjacent British Colonies in | North-America. | Published by Order of the Gentlemen appointed Trustees-General, | for the Management of the said Charitable Scheme. | *Philadelphia:* | *Printed by B. Franklin, and D. Hall.* | MDCCLV. | 4to. pp. 18.   H. S. P.   1438

SMITH. A Letter on the Office and Duties of a Protestant Ministry. By William Smith. *Philadelphia:* 1755. 8vo.   1439

     Title from Haven's List. See Number 1398, *supra.*

SMITH.   A | Sermon, | Preached in | Christ-Church, | Phila-
delphia; | before the | Provincial Grand Master, | and | General
Communication | of | Free and Accepted | Masons. | On Tuesday
the 24th of June, 1755, being the Grand | Anniversary of St. John
the Baptist. | . . . | . . . . | By William Smith, M. A. Provost
of | the College and Academy of Philadelphia. | *Philadelphia:* |
Printed and Sold by B. Franklin, and D. Hall. [1755.] | 8vo. pp.
24.   A. P. S.   1440

TOBLER. (J.)   [Cut.] | The Pennsylvania | Town and Country-
| man's Almanack, | For the Year of our Lord 1756. | Being
Bissextile or Leap-Year. | Containing almost ₂every Thing usual
in Almanacks. | By John Tobler, Esq.; | *Germantown: printed and
sold by C. Sower jun.   And | in Philadelphia to be had of Thomas
Maule in Second-Street, and | several other Shops where they formerly
were sold.* | [1755.]   [Cut.]   16mo. pp. (40).   H. S. P.   1441

A TRUE | State of the Case | Of R[ebecca] R[ichardson] Widow.
[*Philadelphia: Printed by William Bradford.*? 1755.]   16mo. pp.
15.   L. C. P.   1442

𝕭𝕰𝕽𝕾𝕮𝕳𝖅𝕰𝕯𝕰𝕽𝕰 | alter und neuere | Geſchichten | Von Erſchein=
ungen | der | Geiſter, | Und etwas | von dem | Zuſtand der Selen | Nach
dem Tode | Nebſt verſchiedenen | Geſchichtern | ſolcher die auch jeßo noch im
Leben ſind. | Dritte und vermehrte Auflage. | *Germanton gedruckt bey
Christoph Saur* | 1755. | 16mo. pp. 201.   H. S. P.   1443

VOTES | and | Proceedings | of the | House of Representatives
| of the | Province of Pennsylvania, | Met at Philadelphia, on the
Fourteenth of October, Anno | Domini 1754, and continued by
Adjournments. | [*Penn Arms.*] | *Philadelphia:* | *Printed and Sold by
B. Franklin, at the New-Printing-Office,* | *near the Market.* | MDCC-
LV. | Folio, pp. 187, (1); Appendix, pp. 4.   H. S. P.   1444

WHITEFIELD.   (G.)   A brief Account of some Lent and
other extraordinary Processions and Ecclesiastical Entertainments
seen last Year at Lisbon.   By George Whitefield, late of Pembroke College; and Chaplain to the Right Honourable the
Countess of Huntingdon.   *Philadelphia: James Chattin.*   1755.

1756.

AN ACCOUNT of the Births | and Burials in Christ-Church Parish, | in Philadelphia, from December 24, 1755, | to December 24, 1756. By Caleb Cash, | Clerk, and Samuel Kirke, Sexton. | [n. p. n. d.] Folio, 1 leaf.   L. C. P. 1446

ACRELIUS. (I.) A | Sermon, | explaining | The Duties of Christian Subjects | to their Sovereign ; | Preached in | Christiana Church, | In New-Castle County, and Christiana Hun- | dred, upon Delaware, on the Twenty-fourth | Sunday after Trinity, in the Year 1755. | By Israel Acrelius, M.A. | Commissary of the Swedish Congregations upon | Delaware, and Missionary at Christiana. | *Philadelphia: | Printed and Sold by B. Franklin, and | D. Hall, at the New-Printing- | Office, in Market-street.* MDCC-LVI. | 16mo. pp. 23.   H. S. P. 1447

ACRELIUS. Der Tod eine Seligkeit. Rede bey der am 12. Februar 1756 geschehenen Beerdigung Hrn. Matthias Heinzelmanns, von Magister Acrelius. Aus dem Englischen übersetzt von Joh. Fr. Handschuh. *Philadelphia: Francklin und Armbruester.* 1756.   1448

Title from Seidensticker's Bibliography.

AN | ADDRESS | to those | Quakers, | Who perversely refused to pay any Regard to | the late provincial Fast, May 21, 1756. | To which is added, | A celebrated Paper, reprinted from The Mo- | nitor, or British Freeholder, Numb. 28. | on Occasion of the Quakers refusing to keep | the General Fast appointed in England, Feb. | 6. 1756. | . . . | . . . | . . . | . . . | . . . . | *Philadelphia: | Printed and Sold by James Chattin, at the Newest-Printing-Office, | on the South Side of the Jersey Market.* 1756. | (*Price Six-pence.*) | 4to. pp. 16.   1449

This tract gave great offence to the Quakers, and Chattin, two weeks after he first advertised it, gave notice in the Pa. Gazette, that he desired "to be excused by the Publick from selling any more of the late Address to the Quakers." It was then sold by "Black Harry Bookbinder, in Lætitia-Court."

EIN | ANGENEHMER Geruch der | Rosen und Lilien | Die im Thal der Demuth unter | den Dornen hervor gewachsen. | Alles aus der

Schwesterlichen Gesell= | schaft in Saron.   [*Ephrata:*] *Im Jahr des Heils* 1756. | Sq. 8vo. pp. (2), 26, 18.   H. S. P.   1450

ANNO Regni | Georgii II. | Regis, | Magnæ Britanniæ Franciæ & Hiberniæ, | Vigesimo Nono. | At a General Assembly of the Province of Penn- | sylvania, begun and holden at Phila- delphia, | the Fourteenth Day of October, Anno Domini 1755, in | the Twenty-ninth Year of the Reign of our Sovereign | Lord George II. by the Grace of God, of | Great-Britain, France and Ireland, King, Defender of | the Faith, &c. | And from thence continued by Adjournments to the Third | Day of February, 1756. | [*Penn Arms.*] | *Philadelphia:* | *Printed and Sold by B. Franklin, at the New-* | *Printing-Office, near the Market.*   MDCCLVI. | Folio, Title, 1 leaf; pp. 263–266.+And . . . continued . . . to the Fifth | Day of April, 1756. | [*Ibid.*]   Title, 1 leaf; pp. 269– 270.+And . . . continued . . . to the Tenth | Day of May, 1756. | [*Ibid.*]   Title, 1 leaf; pp. 273–274.+And . . . continued . . . to the Six- | teenth Day of August, 1756. | [*Ibid.*]   Title, 1 leaf; pp. 277–316.   H. S. P.   1451

AN ANSWER to Lewis Evans' Letter on the Impropriety of sending Forces to Virginia.   *Philadelphia:* 1756.   1452

AN | APOLOGY | For the People called Quakers, | Contain- ing some Reasons, for their not complying with human Injunc- tions | and Institutions in Matters relative to the Worship of God. | Published by the Meeting for Sufferings of the said People at Philadelphia, in pursuance of | the Directions of their Yearly Meeting, held at Burlington, for Pennsylvania and New- | Jersey, the 24th Day of the Ninth Month, 1756. | [*Philadelphia: James Chattin.*   1757.]   Folio, pp. 3.   L. C. P.   1453

Signed James Pemberton, Clerk, and dated 29th of the 6th Month, 1757. It was republished by order of the Meeting in 1776.

AT the Cockpit, | Before the Lords of Trade and Plantations. | One of the Petitions from the Province of Pennsylvania, signed by a great | number of the chief inhabitants, was read, setting forth the defenceless | State of the Colony; The Cruelties and Ravages daily committed within it, and the further Danger to which it is exposed by the Inactivity of the As- | sembly; and praying his Majesty to take these things into his wise and | princely Consideration, and to afford them such Relief as to his Wisdom | shall seem proper. | [*Philadelphia: B. Franklin, and D. Hall.* 1756.] Folio, pp. 9.   H. S. P.   1454

The speeches of Mr. Yorke (Lord Hardwicke) and Mr. Forester for the petition, and Messrs. Henly and Pratt (Lord Camden) against it.

BALL. (W.) The New Jersey Almanac for 1757. By William Ball. *Philadelphia: William Bradford.* 1756.   1455

𝕯𝕬𝕾 𝕭𝕽𝖀𝕯𝕰𝕽𝕷𝕵𝕰𝕯 oder ein Ausfluß Gottes und seiner Liebe aus der Himmlischen und Paradiesischen Gold-Ader, oder Brunnen des Lebens entsprungen. Aus der Brüderlichen Gesellschaft in Bethania entsprossen und herfürgebracht, betreffend den Inhalt von der unschätzbaren vom Himmel gebrauchten Brüder-Liebe; als welche Jesus auf Erden gelehrt und dargethan, u. s. w. | *Ephrata. Drucks der Bruederschafft im Jahr des Heils* 1756. Sq. 8vo. pp. (2), 30.   1456

BURR. (A.) A Sermon preached before the Synod of New-York, convened at Newark, in New-Jersey, the 30th of September, 1756, on these words (Isai. xxi. 11, 12,) The Burden of Dumah: He calleth to me out of Seir, Watchman, What of the Night? &c. &c. By Aaron Burr, A.M. President of the College of New-Jersey. *Philadelphia: William Bradford.* 1756.   1457

A CATALOGUE of a very curious Collection of Prints consisting of several Hundred Representations of Trees, Shrubs, Plants, Herbs, Fruits, Flowers, &c. To be sold cheap, the lowest Price being mark'd in the Catalogue. *Philadelphia: James Chattin.?* 1756.   1458

CHAMBERLAIN. (T[HOMAS]) Eine Erinnerung | An die Englische Nation | Daß ein Jeder die rechte Zeit | wahrnehmen soll, | Geschehen von | Einem Prediger | Welcher seine eigene Leichen Predigt | gehalten: | Enthält in sich | Eine Warnung | Vom Himmel | an alle boßhaffte Sünder auf Erden, | samt einer besondern Nachricht verschiedener | bewunderungs-würdiger Dinge, welche der | Ehrwürdige Mr. Chamberlain kurtz | vor seinem Abschied auß dieser Welt | in einem Gesicht gefeben, deffen | eigentliche Zeit ihm ebenfalls | gezeiget wurde; | Gedruckt zu London und Philadelphia | Anno 1755. | und auß dem Eng= lifchen ins Teutfche überfetzt. | *Germanton* | *Gedruckt und zu finden bey Christoph Saur* 1756. | 16mo. pp. 14.   H. S. P.   1459

THE | CHRISTIAN'S Duty | To | Render to Cæsar the Things that are Cæsar's, | Considered ; | With Regard to the Payment of the present | Tax of Sixty Thousand Pounds, granted | to the King's Use. | In which all the Arguments for the Non-payment | thereof are examined and refuted. | Addressed to the Scrupulous among the People | called Quakers. | By a Lover of his King and Country. | *Philadelphia :* | *Printed [by Franklin and Hall] in the Year* MDCCLVI. | 8vo. pp. 27.   H. S. P.   1460

DAVENPORT. (J.)   The Faithful Minister Encouraged.   A Sermon at the Opening of the Synod of New York, met at Phila- delphia, Oct. 1, 1755.   By James Davenport.   *Philadelphia :* 1756. 8vo. pp. 35.   1461

Title from Haven's List.

DICKINSON. (J.)   Die | Göttliche Befchützung | Ift der Menfchen gewiffefte Hülffe und | Befchirmung zu allen Zeiten, auch in den | gröffeften Nöthen Gefahren. | Aus Erfahrung gelernet. | Bey einer merckwürdigen Gefchichte da | verfchiedene Perfonen aus der grofen Waf= | fers Gefahr errettet worden, in dem fie nicht | nur Schiffbruch erlitten | fondern auch aus den | noch graufamern Rachen der unmenfchlichen | Canibalen oder Menfchen= | freffern | in Florida find befreyet worden. | Getreulich aufge= zeichnet | Von einem welcher felbft perfohnlich dabey | gewefen, nemlich von | Jonathan Dickinfon. | ... | ... | ... | .... | Die 4te Edition. | Zu Philadelphia gedruckt und nun zum erften mal | in Teutfch heraus gegeben. | *Germanton.* | *Gedruckt und zu haben bey Christoph Saur* 1756. | 16mo. pp. 32 for 98.   H. S. P.   1462

EVANS. (L.)   Geographical, Historical, | Political, Philoso- phical and Mechanical | Essays. | Number II.   Containing, | A | Letter | Representing, | the Impropriety of sending Forces to Virginia : | The Importance of taking Frontenac ; | And that the Preservation of Oswego was owing to General Shirley's | Proceeding thither. | And containing Objections to those Parts of Evans's General Map and | Analysis, which relate to the French Title to Country, on the | North-West Side of the St. Laurence River, between Fort Frontenac | and Montreal. &c. | Published in the New-York Mercury, No. 178, Jan. 5, 1756. | With an | Answer, | To so much thereof as concerns the Public; | And the several Articles set in a just Light. | By Lewis Evans. | *Philadelphia:* | *Printed for the Author; and Sold by him in Arch-Street:* | *And at New-York by G. Noel, Bookseller near Counts's Market.* | MDCC-LVI. | 4to. pp. 42, (1).   H. S. P.   1463

FENELON. The | Uncertainty | of a | Death-Bed | Repentance, | Illustrated under the Character of | Penitens. | [*Germantown: Christopher Sower.* 1756.] 16mo. pp. 16.   H. S. P.   1464

FLEMING. (W. AND E.) A Narrative of the Sufferings and Surprising Deliverance of William and Elizabeth Fleming, Who were taken captive by . . . the Indians, . . . as related by Themselves. *Lancaster: William Dunlap.* 1756.   1465

This edition is mentioned in an advertisement in the Pa. Journal of the edition "Printed for the Benefit of the unhappy sufferers," which is also advertised in the Pa. Gazette as containing additions and amendments, not in the first or second editions before published. It is also advertised in the Pa. Gazette, Jan. 8, 1756.

FLEMING. A Narrative of the Sufferings and Surprising Deliverance of William and Elizabeth Fleming, Who were taken Captives by Captain Jacobs, in a late Excursion by him and the Indians under his Command, on the Inhabitants of the Great-Cove, near Conecochieg, in Pennsylvania, as related by themselves. The Second Edition. *Philadelphia: James Chattin.* 1756.

FLEMING. A Narrative of the Sufferings and Surprising Deliverance of William and Elizabeth Fleming, Who were taken captive by Capt. Jacob, Commander of the Indians, who lately made an Excursion on the Inhabitants of the Great Cove, near Conecochieg, Pennsylvania, as related by themselves. *Philadelphia: Printed for the Benefit of the Unhappy Sufferers.* [1756.] 12mo. pp. 28.   1467

FLEMING (W. and E.) Eine | Erzehlung | von den | Trübsalen | und
der | Wunderbahren Befragung | so geschehen an | William Flemming | und
dessen | Weib Elisabeth | Welche bey dem verwichenen Einfall | der Indi-
aner über die Einwohner im | großen Wald (Grät Grob) bey Can- | nagod-
schick in Pensilvanien sind | gefangen genommen worden. | Nach ihrer
eigenen Aussage. | ... | .... | *Zu Laencester gedruckt von W. Duglas*
| und ins Teutsche uebersetzt und Gedruckt zu | Germantown bey
Christoph Saur 1756. | Auch zu haben bey David Daeschler zu
Philad. | 16mo. pp. 28, (1).   H. S. P.   1468

GALERM. (J. B.)   A Relation of the Misfortunes of the
French | Neutrals, as laid before the Assembly of the Pro- | vince
of Pennsylvania by John Baptiste Galerm, on the | said People.
[*Philadelphia:* 1756.]   Folio, 1 leaf.   H. S. P.   1469

GELLATLY. (A.)   A Detection of Injurious Reasonings and
Unjust Representations.   In Two Parts.   By the Rev. Alexander
Gellatly.   *Lancaster: W. Dunlap.*   1756.   8vo. pp. 240.   1470

   In reply to Delap's Remarks, No. 1744, *supra.*   A portion of the second part
was written by the Rev. Andrew Arnot.   See Sprague's Annals of the American
Pulpit, Vol. IX.

DER | HOCH-DEUTSH | Americanische | Calender, | Auf das
Jahr | ... | ... | 1757. | (Welches ein gemein Jahr von 365 Tagen
ist.) | ... | ... | ... | ... | ... | ... | ... | ... | ... | ... |
Zum Neunzehenten mal heraus gegeben. | *Germantown: Gedruckt und*
zu finden bey Christoph Saur. | .... | .... [1756.] | 4to. pp. (48).
                                                            H. S. P.   1471

[HOLLATZ. (David)]   Die gebahnte Pilgerstraße nach dem Berg
Zion und himmlischen Jerusalem, der Stadt Gottes.   *Philadelphia:*
B. Franklin und A. Armbruester.   1756.   1472

   Title from Seidensticker's Bibliography.

IMRIE.   A Letter from the Reverend Mr. David Imrie,
Minister of the Gospel at St. Mingo, in Annandale, to a Gentleman in the City of Edinburgh.   Predicting the speedy Accomplishment of the great, awful and glorious Events which the

Scriptures say are to be brought to pass in the Latter Times. Published for detecting the spurious Papers that have been imposed on the World in Mr. Imrie's Name. *Edinburgh, printed* 1755: *Boston, re-printed* 1756, *and now re-printed by James Chattin, in Philadelphia.* 1756.   1473

IMRIE. (D.) Des Ehrenwürdigen Lehrers | David Imries | Predigers in St. Mongo in Schottland | Send Schreiben | An seinen Freund in Edenburg | Verkündigend | Die baldige Erfüllung der großen und schröck= | lichen und auch herrlichen Erfolgungen, . . . | von die H. Schrift sagt, daß sie in | Den | Letzten Tagen | geschehen sollen: | Bekant gemacht um die eingeschobene | Schrifften zu entdecken, womit die Welt | intergangen worden unter Mr. | Imries Nation. | . . . . | *Erstlich zu Edinburg gedruckt, hernach in Boston,* | *ferner zu Philadelphia bey J. Chattin.* | *Und nun ausz dem Englischen ins Teutsche uebersetzt,* | *und gedruckt in Germanton bey Chr. Saur.* 1756. | 16mo. pp. 26.
                                                    H. S. P. 1474

JERMAN. (J.) An Almanac for 1757. By John Jerman. *Philadelphia: B. Franklin, and D. Hall.* 1756.   1475

KAWANIO Che Keeteru: | A true | Relation | of a | Bloody Battle Fought | between | George and Lewis, | In the Year | 1755. | [*Philadelphia:*] *Printed* [*by William Bradford*] *in the Year* M,DCC,LVI. | 8vo. pp. 16. + Second Edition. *Philadelphia: James Chattin.* 1756.   H. S.P. 1476

Said to have been written by Nicholas Scull.   A poetical attack on the Quakers for preventing proper measures being taken to defend the Province from the French and Indians.

KURTZER Begriff oder leichtes Mittel zu Gott zu beten oder mit Gott zu reden. *Philadelphia: B. Franklin and A. Armbruester.* 1756.

Title from Seidensticker's Bibliography.

LIDENIUS. (J. A.) The | Lawfulness | of | Defensive War. | A | Sermon | Preached before the Members of the Church, at Chie- | chester, in the County of Chester, and Province of Penn- | sylvania, upon their Association for | Defence, February 14.

1756. | By John Abr. Lidenius, | Itin. Miss. to the Swede Congregations. | . . . . | *Philadelphia:* | *Printed and Sold by James Chattin, at the Newest-Print-* | *ing-Office, on the South Side of the Jersey Market.* | 1756. | 4to. pp. 16.   L. C. P.   1478

THE | LIFE, | Adventures, | and surprizing | Deliverances, | of | Duncan Cameron. | Private Soldier in the Regiment | of Foot, late Sir Peter Halket's. | The Third Edition. | *Philadelphia :* | *Printed and Sold by James Chattin, at the Newest-* | *Printing-Office, on the South Side of the Jersey* | *Market.* 1756. | 8vo. pp. 16.   1479

LIVINGSTON. (W.) A Funeral Eulogium on the Reverend 'Mr. Aaron Burr, Late President of the College of New-Jersey. By William Livingston, ... *Philadelphia: B. Franklin.* 1756.? 4to.   1480

Title from H. A. Brady's Catalogue, lot 2127. As Burr did not die till 1757, the date, as well as other parts of this title, is inaccurate.

MACLEANE. (L.) An Essay | on the Expediency of | Inoculation | and | The Seasons most proper for it. | Humbly inscribed | to | The Inhabitants of Philadelphia, | By Lauchlin Macleane, M.D. | . . . | . . . . | *Philadelphia,* | *Printed by William Bradford, at the Corner-* | *House of Market-and Front-Streets* 1756. | 8vo. pp. 39.   H. S. P.   1481

MOORE. (T.) An Almanac for 1757. By Thomas Moore. *Philadelphia: B. Franklin, and D. Hall.* 1756.   1482

A BRIEF | NARRATIVE | of the | Case and Trial | of | John Peter Zenger, Printer of the | New-York Weekly-Journal. | *New-York Printed :* | *Lancaster Re-printed, and Sold by* *W. Dunlap,* | *at the New-Printing-Office, in Queen-Street,* 1756. | Folio, pp. 39.   H. S. P.   1483

THE | NATURE and Design | of | Christianity. | Extracted from a late Author. | . . . | . . . | . . . | . . . | . . . | . . . | . . . . | *Germantown:* | *Printed by Christopher Sower, junior,* 1756. | 16mo. pp. 16.   H. S. P.   1484

NEU=eingerichteter Americanischer Geschichts Calender, auf das Jahr 1757. *Philadelphia: B. Franklin und A. Armbruster.* 1756.

                                                             1485

NEW JERSEY. Anno Regni | Georgii II. | Regis | Magnæ Britaniæ, Franciæ, & Hiberniæ. | Vegesimo Nono. | At a Session of General Assembly of | the Province of New-Jersey; held at | Elizabeth-Town, in March 1756, on the 16th Day | of which Month the following Act was passed. | [*Royal Arms.*] | *Philadelphia:* | *Printed by W. Bradford, Printer to the King's Most* | *Excellent Majesty for the Province of New-Jersey.* [1756.] | Folio, pp. 12.
     1486

NEW JERSEY. Anno Regni | Georgii II. | Regis | Magnæ Britanniæ, Franciæ, et Hiberniæ, | Vigesimo Nono. | At a Session of General Assembly of the Province | of New-Jersey, held at Elizabeth-Town, by Ad- | journments May 20, 1756, and continued till the | second Day of June following, on which Days the | the following Acts were passed. | [*Royal Arms.*] | *Philadelphia:* | *Printed by W. Bradford, Printer to the King's Most* | *Excellent Majesty, for the Province of New-Jersey.* [1756.] | Folio, pp. 78.
     1487

NEW JERSEY. Anno Regni | Georgii II. | Regis | Magnæ Britanniæ, Franciæ, et Hiberniæ, | Trigesimo | At a Session of General Assembly of the Province | of New-Jersey, held at Elizabeth-Town, December 17, | 1756, and continued till the twenty fourth Day of the | same Month, on which Day the following Act was | passed. | [*Royal Arms.*] | *Philadelphia:* | *Printed by W. Bradford, Printer to the King's Most* | *Excellent Majesty, for the Province of New-Jersey.* [1756.] | Folio, pp. 5.   1488

THE | NEW-YEAR | Verses | Of the Printers Lads, who carry | the Pennsylvania Gazette to | the Customers. | For 1756. | [*Philadelphia: Franklin and Hall.* 1756.] Folio, 1 leaf. L. C. P.

NEW-YEAR Verses of the Carriers of the Pennsylvania Journal. *Philadelphia: William Bradford.* 1756.   1490

A PATERN of Christian | Education | Agreeable to the Precepts and Practice of our | Blessed Lord and Saviour Jesus Christ. | Illustrated under the Characters of | Patterus & Eusebia. | Extracted from a late pious Author. | . . . | . . . | . . . | . . . | . . . | . . . . | *Germantown:* | *Printed by Christopher Sower, Junior,* 1756. | 16mo. pp. 16.   H. S. P. 1491

PENNSYLVANIA : | A | Poem. | By a Student of the College of Philadelphia. | *Philadelphia :* | *Printed by B. Franklin, and D. Hall.* | MDCCLVI. | Folio, pp. 11.   L. C. P. 1492

THE PENNSYLVANIA Gazette.   1493

Numbers 1410 (Jan. 1, 1756) to 1462 (Dec. 30, 1756), six pages each, except Numbers 1428, 1451, 1459 and 1460, which contain four pages. Title and imprint as in No. 1272, *supra.*

THE PENNSYLVANIA Journal.   H. S. P. 1494

Numbers 682 (Jan. 1, 1755) to 734 (Dec. 30, 1756), four pages each, with a two page "Supplement" to No. 694. Title and imprint as in No. 1429, *supra.* No. 688 is misnumbered 679.

POOR Robin's Almanac for 1757.   *Philadelphia: William Bradford.*   1756.   1495

PROPOSALS | For Printing by Subscription, | The Second Edition of "A Voyage to the South | Sea," in the Years 1740–1, in the Wager Man of War . . . | . . . . | [By] . . . John Bulkeley and John Cummins, . . . [*Philadelphia: Printed by James Chattin.* 1756.]   Folio, 1 leaf.   H. S. P. 1496

Dated "Philadelphia, July 5, 1756."

PROCLAMATION. G. [*Royal Arms.*] R. | By the Honourable | Robert Hunter Morris, Esq ; | . . . | . . . | A Proclamation. | *Philadelphia: Printed by B. Franklin, and D. Hall.* MDCCLVI. | Folio, 1 leaf.   H. S. P. 1497

Dated April 14, 1756. Against the Delaware Indians.

SAUNDERS. (R.) A Pocket | Almanack | For the Year 1757. | Fitted to Use of Penn- | sylvania, and the neighbour- |

ing Provinces. | With several useful Additions. | By R. Saunders, Phil. | *Philadelphia:* | *Printed and sold by B. Franklin,* | *and D. Hall.* [1756.] | 32mo. pp. (24).   c. 1498

[(SAUNDERS.)] Poor Richard improved: | Being an | Almanack | . . . | . . . | . . . | . . . | . . . | . . . | . . . | . . . | . . . | . . . . | For the | Year of our Lord 1757: | Being the First after Leap-Year. | . . . | . . . | . . . | . . . | . . . | . . . | . . . | . . . | . . . . | By Richard Saunders, Philom. | *Philadelphia:* | *Printed and Sold by B. Franklin, and D. Hall.* [1756.] | Sm. 8vo. pp. (36).   H. S. P. 1499

[SCOUGAL. (Henry)] Das | Leben Gottes | in | der Seele des Menschen | oder | die Natur und Vortrefflichkeit | der | Christlichen Religion, | den | Zerstreuten Kindern Gottes und verlohrnen Scha- | fen vom Hause Israel in und aufier den mancherley | Partien zum Dienst, | auf | Veranstaltung der von einer löblichen Ge= | sellschaft in London ernanten General | Trustees aus dem englischen ins teutsche | übersetzt; | Nebst | einer in ihren Namen gestellten Vorrede, | worin | so wohl das Vor= haben dieser löblichen Ge= | sellschaft als auch die eigentliche Absicht | dieser gegenwärtigen Uebersetzung vor= | geleget wird. | *Philadelphia: Gedruckt und zu haben bey Benjamin* | *Francklin, Post-Meister und Ant. Armbruester,* 1756. | 8vo. pp. (21), 78, (1).   H. S. P. 1500

SMITH. ([William]) The Reverend Mr. Smith vindicated from the Im- | putation of Perjury, in a Letter to a Friend. | [*Philadelphia: Printed by William Bradford.?* 1756.] Folio, pp. (2).   1501

TENNENT. (G.) The good Mans Character and Reward repre- | sented, and his Loss deplor'd, together with Re- | flections on the Presages of approaching Calamities. | In a | Funeral Discourse, | with some Enlargements | Occasioned by the Death of Captain William | Grant of the City, who departed this Life, | September 30, 1756. | Preached | In Philadelphia | on the following Sabbath. | And now published, at the Desire of the | Hearers. | By | Gilbert Tennent, A. M. | . . . | . . . | . . . | . . . | . . . |

. . . . | *Philadelphia,* | *Printed by William Bradford, at the Cor-* | *ner-House of Front-and Market-Streets.* [1756.] | Sm. 8vo. Half-title, 1 leaf; pp. 39.   H. S. P.   1502

TENNENT. The Happiness of Rewarding the Enemies | of our Religion and Liberty,| Represented | in a | Sermon | Preached in Philadelphia, Feb. 17, 1756. to | Captain Vanderspiegel's Independent | Company of Volunteers, at the Request of | their Officers. | By Gilbert Tennent, A.M. and Minister | of the Gospel of Christ. | . . . | . . . . | Published at the Desire of said Officers and | Company. | *Philadelphia:* | *Printed by James Chattin, at the Newest-* | *Printing-Office, on the South Side of the* | *Jersey Market.* 1756. | 4to. pp. 32. + Second Edition.   L. C. P.   1503

A | TREATY | Between the Government of New-Jersey, | and the | Indians, | Inhabiting the several Parts of said Province, | Held at | Croswick, | In the County of | Burlington | On Thursday and Friday the eighth and ninth Day of January, 1756. | [*Royal Arms.*] | *Philadelphia:* | *Printed by William Bradford, Printer to the Province of* | *New-Jersey.* | [1756.] Folio, pp. 11.

TOBLER. (J.) The Pennsylvania Town and Countryman's Almanac for 1757. By John Tobler. *Germantown: Christopher Sower.* 1756.   1505

TREUHERTZIGE Erinnerung und Warnung. Klagreden vom Verfall des Christenthums. *Philadelphia: B. Franklin und A. Armbruester.* 1756.   1506

Title from Seidensticker's Bibliography.

VOTES | and | Proceedings | of the | House of Representatives | of the | Province of Pennsylvania, | Met at Philadelphia, on the Fourteenth of October, Anno | Domini 1755, and continued by Adjournments. | [*Penn Arms.*] | *Philadelphia:* | *Printed and Sold by B. Franklin, at the New-Printing-Office,* | *near the Market.* MDCCLVI. | Folio, pp. 174.   H. S. P.   1507

WHITEFIELD. (G.) A Short | Address | To | Persons of all Denominations, | occasioned by the | Alarm of an Intended

Invasion. | By George Whitefield, | Chaplain to the Right Honourable the Countess of Huntingdon. | . . . . | The Third Edition. | *London Printed:* | *Philadelphia Re-printed, and Sold by B. Frank-* | *lin, and D. Hall, at the New-Printing-Office,* | *in Market-street.* | MDCCLVI. | 8vo. pp. 16.   1508

ZUBLY. (John Joachim) The | Real Christians | Hope | in | Death ; | or | An Account of the edi- | fying Behaviour of several Persons | of Piety in their last Moments, | With a Preface recommendatory by the | Rev. Mr. Clarke, Rector of St. Philips | Charlestown, | Collected and published | By | J. J. Zubly. | Minister of the Gospel in South Carolina. | *Germantown.* | *Printed by Christopher Sower.* MDCCLVI. | 16mo. Title, 1 leaf; Dedication and Preface, pp. ix; text, pp. 1–187.   1509

1757.

AN ACCOUNT of the Births | and Burials in Christ-Church Parish, | in Philadelphia, from December 24, 1756, | to December 24, 1757. By Caleb Cash, | Clerk, and Samuel Kirke, Sexton. | [n. p. n. d.] Folio, 1 leaf.   L. C. P.   1510

AN ACT for Forming and Regulating the Militia of | the Province of Pennsylvania; which passed the House of | Assembly at their Session in March, 1757; together with | the Amendments proposed by the Governor. | [*Philadelphia: Printed by B. Franklin and D. Hall.* 1757.] Folio, pp. 12.   H. S. P.   1511

ADVERTISEMENT. | [n. p. 1757.] 4to. 1 leaf.   H. S. P.   1512

Signed Richard Hockley and Edmund Physick, and dated January, 24, 1757. Calling for arrears of Proprietary Quit-rents.

THE | AMERICAN Magazine | and | Monthly Chronicle for the British Colonies. | Volume I. | Containing | From October 1757 to October 1758 | inclusive. | By a Society of Gentlemen. | . . . . | *Philadelphia:* | *Printed and Sold by William Bradford, at the Corner House in* | *Front and Market-Streets.* [1757–58.] | 8vo.

Collation, Title and Directions, pp. (2); text, pp. 1–656; Index, pp. (6). Edited by the Rev. William Smith, D.D. The Historical Society of Pennsylvania has a copy on thick paper.

ANNO Regni | Georgii II. | Regis, | Magnæ Britanniæ, Franciæ & Hiberniæ, | Tricesimo. | At a General Assembly of the Province of Penn- | sylvania, begun and holden at Philadelphia, | the Fourteenth Day of October, Anno Domini 1756, in | the Thirtieth Year of the Reign of our Sovereign | Lord George II. by the Grace of God, of | Great-Britain, France and Ireland, King, Defender of | the Faith, &c. | And from thence continued to the Fourth of No- | vember, 1756. | [*Penn Arms.*] | *Philadelphia:* | *Printed and Sold by B. Franklin, at the New-* | *Printing-Office, near the Market.* MDCCLVII. | Folio, Title, 1 leaf; pp. 319–321. +And from thence continued by Adjournments to the Twen- | ty-second Day of November, 1756. | [*Ibid.*] Title, 1 leaf; pp. 325–334. + And . . . continued by Adjournments to the Third | Day of January, 1757. | [*Ibid.*] Title, 1 leaf; pp. 337–344. + And . . . continued . . . to the Third | Day of January, 1757. [April 9. 1757.] | [*Ibid.*] Title, 1 leaf; pp. 347–361. + And . . . continued . . . to the Thir- | tieth Day of May, 1757. | [*Ibid.*] Title, 1 leaf; pp. 365–372.   H. S. P.   1514

BALL. (W.) The New Jersey Almanac for 1758. By William Ball. *Philadelphia: William Bradford.* 1757.   1515

BARCLAY. (R.) The | Anarchy | of the | Ranters, | And other Libertines; | The | Hierarchy | of the | Romanists, | and other | Pretended Churches, equally refused and re- | futed, in a two-fold Apology for the Church | and People of God, called in Derision, Quakers. | Wherein | They are vindicated from those that accuse them of Disorder | and Confusion on the one Hand, and from such as calumniate | them with Tyranny and Imposition on the other; shewing, that | as the true and pure Principles of the Gospel are restored by | their Testimony; so is also the antient Apostolick Order of | the Church of Christ re-established among them, and settled | upon its right Basis and Foundation. | By Robert Barclay. | . . . | . . . | . . . | . . . . | *Philadelphia:* |

Re-printed, and Sold by B. Franklin, and | *D. Hall,* 1757. | Sm. 8vo. Title, 1 leaf; Preface. iii to viii; text, pp. 1–111; Contents, 1 page.   H. S. P.   1516

BEATTY. (C.) Double Honor due to the Laborious Gospel Minister. Represented in a Sermon preached at Fairfield, in New Jersey, the 1st of December, 1756, at the Ordination of the Reverend Mr. William Ramsey. Published at the Desire of the Hearers, By Charles Beatty, Minister of the Gospel at Neshaminey. *Philadelphia: William Bradford, at the Corner House of Front and Market Streets.* [1757.] 8vo. Half Title, 1 leaf; pp. 56.   1517

𝖣𝖨𝖤 𝖡𝖤𝖲𝖢𝖧𝖱𝖤𝖩𝖡𝖴𝖭𝖦 von dem Friedensſchluß zwiſchen unſerm government und dem Jndianerkönig Tiediuskung.   *Germantown: Christoph Saur.* 1757.   1518

Title from Seidensticker's Bibliography.

BULKELEY. (J.) AND J. CUMMINS. A | Voyage | to the | South Seas, | In the Years 1740–1. | Containing, | A faithful Narrative of the Loss of his Majesty's Ship the | the [*sic*] Wager on a desolate Island in the Latitude 47 | South, Longitude 81: 40 West: With the Proceedings and | Conduct of the Officers and Crew, and the Hardships they | endured in the said Island for the Space of five Months, their | bold Attempt for Liberty, in Coasting the Southern Part of | the vast Region of Patagonia; setting out with upwards of | Eighty Souls in their Boats, the Loss of the Cutter, their | Passage through the Streights of Magellan; an Account of | their Manner of living in the Voyage on Seals, Wild Horses, | Dogs, &c. and the incredible Hardships they frequently un- | derwent for Want of Food of all Kinds; a Description of | the several Places where they touch'd in the Streights of | Magellan, with an Account of the Inhabitants, &c. and their | safe Arrival at the Brazil, after sailing one thousand Leagues | in a Long-Boat; their Reception from the Portugese, an | Account of the Disturbances at Rio Grand, their Arrival at | Rio Janeiro, their Passage and Usage on Board a Portugese | Ship to Lisbon, their Return to England, their Confinement | for the Loss of the Ship, and their Releasement; the Arri- | val of the Captain, who had been left behind by his own | Request where the Ship was lost; the Officers second Con- | finement, Trial and Acquittance; the Arrival of three of | the Crew, who had been left with five others on the unin- | habited Part of Pategonia, &c. Interspersed with many enter- | taining and curious Observations, not taken Notice of by Sir | John Narborough, or any other Journalist, with many | Things not published in the First Edition. | By John Bulkeley and John Cummins, | Late Gunner and Carpenter of the Wager. | The Second Edition, with Additions. | . . . | . . . | . . . | . . . . | *London, Printed. Philadelphia: Reprinted by James Chat-* | *tin, for the Author.* 1757. (*Price 10s.*) | 8vo. pp. xxxii, 306. H. S. P. 1519

CATALOGUE of Books to be sold by James Chattin. *Philadelphia: James Chattin.* 1757. 1520

THE | CHARTER, | Laws, | and | Catalogue of Books, | of the | Library Company | of | Philadelphia. | . . . . | *Philadelphia:* | *Printed by B. Franklin, and D. Hall.* | MDCCLVII. | 8vo. pp. 23, 132. H. S. P. 1521

THE CHILD'S New Play-Thing, or best Amusement, intended to make the Learning to Read a Diversion, instead of a Task. *Philadelphia: James Chattin.* 1757. 1522

"Dedicated to the School Masters and Mistresses of Pennsylvania and New Jersey." "More complete than any Book with this title in Europe." Pa. Gazette, Dec. 8, 1757.

DILWORTH. (T.) A New Guide to English Tongue. By Thomas Dilworth. *Philadelphia: James Chattin.* 1757. 1523

ELIXIR Magnum: | The | Philosophers Stone | found out. | Being a certain Method to Extract Sil- | ver and Gold out of the Earth in | great Plenty. | By Way of Address to the Legisla- | tive Powers of all the British Colo- | nies in North America. | *Philadelphia:* | *Printed and Sold by James Chattin, at* | *the Newest-Printing-Office, the South Side* | *of the Jersey Market,* 1757. | 8vo. pp. 29. 1524

EVERARD. (J.) Some | Gospel Treasures, | or the | Holiest of all Unvailing ; | Discovering yet more the | Riches of Grace and Glory | To The | Vesels of Mercy, | Unto whom it is given to know the Mysteries of that | Kingdom, and the Excellency | Of | Spirit | Power | Truth | above | Letter | Forms | Shadows | In several Sermons, preached at Kensington and elsewhere, | By John Everard D. D. | *London printed in the Year* 1653. *And now Reprinted in* | *Germantown by Christopher Sower.* 1757. | Sq. 8vo. pp. xi, 268, 280.   H. S. P.   1525

FINLEY. (S.) The Curse of Meroz ; | Or, | The Danger of Neutrality, in the | Cause of God, and our Country. | A | Sermon, | Preached the 2d of October, 1757. | By Samuel Finley, A. M. Minister of | the Gospel, in Nottingham, Pennsylvania. | Published at the Desire of many. | . . . | . . . | . . . | . . . . | *Philadelphia :* | *Printed and Sold by James Chattin, at the Newest-* | *Printing-Office, on the South Side of the Jersey-* | *Market.* 1757. | 8vo. pp. 32.   H. S. P.   1526

HARRIS. (M.) A | Sermon | Preached in the Church of St. Peters in Lewis, | in Sussex County on Delaware, on July 18, 1757. | Being | The Day appointed by the Honourable Wil- | liam Denny, Esq; to be observed as a | Day of Fasting and Humiliation, to implore | the Blessing of God on his Majesty's Arms, | especially on the Expedition now carrying | on under his Excellency John Earl | of Loudon. | By Matthias Harris, offici- ating Minister | to the several Congregations of the Church | of England, in Sussex County on Delaware. | *Philadelphia :* | *Printed and Sold by James Chattin,* 1757. | 8vo. pp. 54, (1). A. P. S.   1527

DER | HOCH=DEUTSCH | Americanische | Calender, | Auf das Jahr | . . . | . . . | 1758. | . . . | . . . | . . . | . . . | . . . | . . . | . . . | . . . | . . . | . . . | . . . . | Zum Zwanzigsten mal heraus gegeben. | *Ger- mantown : Gedruckt und zu finden bey Christoph Saur.* | . . . | . . . . [1757.] | 4to. pp. (48).   H. S. P.   1528

HONESTY. (O.) A Remonstrance of Obadiah Honesty, in the Case | of the Reverend Mr. Sm[i]th, with some Remarks on his being | called before the House of A[ssembl]y. | [*Philadelphia: William Bradford.* 1757.] Folio, pp. (4).   H. S. P.   1529

HONESTY. The Second Edition, with Additions, of, | A | Remonstrance, | By Obadiah Honesty, | In the Case of the Reverend Mr. Sm-th, with some Remarks on | his being call'd before the House of A[ssembl]y. | [*Philadelphia: Printed by William Bradford.* 1757.] Folio, pp. (4).   H. S. P.   1530

HOPKINS. ([SAMUEL]) An | Abridgment | of | Mr. Hopkins's | Historical Memoirs, | Relating to the | Housatunnuk, or Stockbridge Indians: | Or, | A brief Account of the Methods used, and | Pains taken, for civilizing and propagating the | Gospel among that Heathenish Tribe, | and the Success thereof, under the Ministry of | the late Rev. Mr. John Sergeant. | *Philadelphia:* | *Printed and Sold by B. Franklin, and D. Hall.* | M,DCC,LVII. | 8vo. pp. 40.   H. S. P.   1531

HOPKINS. An | Address | to the | People of New-England. | Representing | The very great Importance of attaching the | Indians to their Interest; not only by | treating them justly and kindly; but by using pro- | per Endeavours to settle Christianity among them. | By Samuel Hopkins, A.M. | Pastor of a Church in Springfield. | . . . | . . . | . . . . | Printed in Boston, 1753. Being a conclusion to the | Historical Memoirs relating to the Housatunnuk In- | dians; with an Account of the Methods used for the | Propagation of the Gospel amongst the said Indians, by | the late reverend Mr. John Sergeant. | Now recommended to the serious Consideration of the Inhabi- | tants of Pennsylvania, and the other Colonies. | *Philadelphia:* | *Printed by B. Franklin, and D. Hall.* 1757. | 8vo. pp. 27.   1532

DER INHALT | Von den verſchiedenen | Conferentzen, | Welche mit den | Indianern | gehalten worden | Zu | Eſton. | In dem Monath July und Auguſt. | *Germanton.* | *Gedruckt und zu finden bey Christoph Saur* 1757. | 4to. pp. 36.   H. S. P.   1533

DER INHALT | Von den verſchiedenen | Conferentzen, | Welche einige Freunde zu Philadelphia mit et= | lichen Indianern gehalten, um eine

Vorbereitung zum | Frieden zu machen; nach dem der Krieg gegen die Indianer schon | würcklich erkläret und publiciert war: | Samt der Bottschafft, welche der Governor auf Genral Jansens | Order an die Indianer an der Susquehanna gesandt durch eben dieselbe | Indianer und was die Bottschaffter daselbst ausgerichtet. | Wie auch | Der Inhalt von den | Conferentzen | Mit den Indianern zu Esten in den Monathen | July und November 1756. | Nebst dem Bericht, welche die Glieder des Haußes, die den | Govenor nach Esten zu den Conferentzen begleitet; dem Hauß | überbracht haben. | *Theils* | *Gedruckt zu Philadelphia bey B. Franck-lin und D. Haal, und aus dem englischen | uebersetzt und gedruckt zu Germanton bey Christoph Saur*, 1757. | 4to. pp. 55.   1534

JERMAN. (J.)   An Almanac for 1758.   By John Jerman. *Philadelphia: B. Franklin, and D. Hall.*?   1757.   1535

A | LETTER | From a Gentleman in Philadelphia, to a Freeholder in the County Northampton. [*sic*] | [*Philadelphia: W. Bradford.*?   1757.]   Folio, pp. 2.   H. S. P.   1536

Concerning W. Plumsted's election to the Assembly from Northampton Co.

A | MEMORIAL, | containing | A summary View of Facts, | with their | Authorities, | In Answer to the Observations sent by | the English Ministry to the Courts of | Europe. | Translated from the French. | *Philadelphia:* | *Printed by James Chattin*, 1757. | 8vo. Half-title, 1 leaf; Title, 1 leaf; Advertisement to the Reader, pp. iii–iv; text, pp. 1–338.   H. S. P.   1537

A translation of the "Mémoire contenant le Précis des Faits," published by the French Government in 1756, several copies of which were found in French vessels captured by American privateers early in 1757. Three or more editions were published in Paris, one in quarto and two duodecimo volumes. Proposals for publishing, by subscription, a translation appeared in the Pa. Gazette, Feb. 17, 1757. In May the subscribers were informed that the volume was ready for delivery. Two editions (of the same translation) were also printed in New York in 1757 under the same title, while another appeared in London as "The Conduct of the late Ministry." Part of it was appended to the edition of Livingston's Review of the Military Operations in North America, printed in Dublin, 1757. A translation appeared in London in 1759 as "The Mystery Reveal'd." It was also reprinted in Craig's "Olden Time," Vol. II. The memorial occupies the first 58 pages, and is based upon the captured papers of Washington and Braddock, which form a large part of the remainder of the volume.

MINUTES | of | Conferences, | held with the | Indians, at Easton, | In the Months of July and November, 1756; | Together with | Two Messages sent by the Government to the | Indians residing on Sasquehannah; and the Report of the Com- | mittee appointed by the Assembly to attend the Governor at | the last of the said Conferences. | [*Penn Arms.*] | *Philadelphia:* | *Printed and Sold by B. Franklin, and D. Hall, at the | New-Printing-Office, near the Market.* MDCCLVII. | Folio, pp. 32.   H. S. P.

MINUTES | of | Conferences, | held with the | Indians, | at | Easton, | In the Months of July, and August, 1757. | [*Penn Arms.*] | *Philadelphia:* | *Printed and Sold by B. Franklin, and D. Hall, at the | New-Printing-Office, near the Market.* MDCCLVII. | Folio, pp. 24.   H. S. P.   1539

MINUTES | of | Conference, | held with the | Indians, | At Harris's Ferry, and at Lancaster, | In March, April, and May, 1757. | [*Penn Arms.*] | *Philadelphia:* | *Printed and Sold by B. Franklin, and D. Hall, at the | New-Printing-Office, near the Market.* MDCCLVII. | Folio, pp. 22.   H. S. P.   1540

MOORE. (W.)   A | Preface | To A | Memorial | Delivered in to the Assembly of the Province of Pennsylvania, September 22, 1757. | By William Moore, Esq; of Chester County. | [followed on p. 2. by] | The Memorial of William Moore. | To the Honourable the Representatives of the Freemen of the Province of Pennsylvania, in As- | sembly met. | [*Philadelphia: James Chattin.* 1757.] Folio, pp. 4.   H. S. P.   1541

𝔑𝔈𝔘=eingerichteter Americanifcher Gefchichts=Calender, auf das Jahr 1758. *Philadelphia: B. Franklin, und A. Armbruester.*   1757.

THE NEW-ENGLAND Primer. *Philadelphia: James Chattin.* 1757.   1543

NEW JERSEY.   Anno Regni | Georgii II. | Regis | Magnæ Britanniæ, Franciæ, et Hiberniæ, | Tricesimo | At a Session of General Assembly of the Province | of New-Jersey, . . . | and continued till the thirty-first Day of March, 1757, the following Acts were passed | [*Royal Arms.*] | *Philadelphia:* | *Printed by*

W. Bradford, Printer to the King's Most | *Excellent Majesty, for the Province of New-Jersey.* [1757.] | Folio, pp. 56.   1544

NEW JERSEY. Anno Regni | Georgii II. | . . . | . . . | Tricesimo. | . . . | . . . | and continued till . . . 1757, the following Acts were passed | [*Royal Arms.*] | *Philadelphia:* | *Printed by W. Bradford, Printer to the King's Most* | *Excellent Majesty, for the Province of New-Jersey.* [1757.] | Folio, pp. 27.

NEW JERSEY. Anno Regni | Georgii II. | . . . | . . . | Tricesimo Primo. | . . . | . . . | and continued till October 22, 1757. | [*Royal Arms.*] | *Philadelphia :* | *Printed by W. Bradford, Printer to the King's Most* | *Excellent Majesty, for the Province of New-Jersey.* [1757.] | Folio, pp. 30.   1546

THE | NEW-YEAR | Verses | Of the Printers Boys, who carry about the | Pennsylvania Gazette to the Customers. | [*Philadelphia : Franklin and Hall.* 1757.] Folio, 1 leaf.   1547

NEW–YEAR Verses of the Carriers of the Pennsylvania Journal. *Philadelphia : William Bradford.* 1757.   1548

THE PENNSYLVANIA Gazette.   H. S. P.   1549

Numbers 1462 (Jan. 6, 1757) to 1514 (Dec. 29, 1757), six pages each, except 1476, and from 1496 to 1514, four pages each. From 1496 to 1514 each number has a half sheet (two pages) of which the first two have the regular imprint. Title and imprint as in No. 1232, *supra*.

THE PENNSYLVANIA Journal.   H. S. P.   1550

Numbers 735 (Jan. 6, 1757) to 786 (Dec. 29, 1757), four pages each, with a two page "Supplement" to No. 769, and one of 1 leaf to No. 782. Title and imprint as in No. 1273, *supra*, up to No. 772, when the paper was slightly enlarged, and the imprint changed to the form given in No. 1601, *infra*.

𝔓𝔥𝔦𝔩𝔞𝔡𝔢𝔩𝔭𝔥𝔦𝔰𝔠𝔥𝔢 Zeitung, | von allerhand | Auswär=tigen und einheimischen merckwürdigen Sachen. | Den 31ſten December, 1757, Num. XLVIII. | *Philadelphia, gedruckt und zu haben bey B. Francklin, General Postmeister und A. Armbruester in der 4ten Strasse, . . .* | . . . . | Folio, pp. (4).   H. S. P.   1551

This is only number of this paper I have met with, and it is particularly interesting as being the one on which the prosecution against the Rev. William Smith, and William Moore, was founded. It is said to have been issued twice a month, and was edited by Dr. Smith. The facts that Franklin's name appears in the imprint, and that Moore's petition was printed in the Gazette and Journal, were entirely ignored in the proceedings of the Assembly.

PIKE. (J.) An | Epistle | to the | National Meeting | of | Friends, | in | Dublin, | concerning good Order and Discipline | in the Church. | Written by Joseph Pike. | *Philadelphia: | Reprinted, and Sold by B. Franklin, and | D. Hall,* 1757. | Sm. 8vo. pp. 23.   H. S. P.   1552

Generally found with Barclay's Anarchy of the Ranters.

PREFONTAINE. (P. P. DE)   A Direct Guide to the French Language.   By Peter Papin de Prefontaine.   *Philadelphia.*? 1757.   1553

Proposals for printing it by subscription appeared in the Pa. Gazette, Oct. 28, 1756, "Subscriptions will be taken in till the first of January next," and "the Book will be published as soon as possible after the Subscription is closed."

𝕯𝕰𝕽 𝕻𝕾𝕬𝕷𝕿𝕰𝕽 Davids. *Philadelphia: B. Francklin und A. Armbruester.*   1554

Title from Seidensticker's Bibliography.

POOR Robin's Almanac for 1758.   *Philadelphia: William Bradford.*   1757.   1555

𝕽𝕰𝕲𝕰𝕷𝕹 und Articuls zu besserer Regierung und Anführung Ihro Majestät Garden zu Pferde und zu Fuße und aller dero anderer Kriegs=völker in Grosbritanien und Irland Herrschaften jenseits des Meeres und in den auswärtigen Ländern. Vom 24. März 1755. Auf Ihro Majestät Befehl öffentlich herausgegeben uud auf Veranstaltung der General Trustees, so zur Aufrichtung englischer Schulen unter den Teutschen in Pennsylvanien verordnet sind, zum Besten der unter Ihrer Majestät regulären und Provincial=Truppen in Nord Amerika stehenden Teutschen aus dem Englischen in's Teutsche übersetzt. *Philadelphia. Gedruckt von B. Francklin und A. Armbruester im Mertz* 1757.   pp. 41.   1556

Title from Seidensticker's Bibliography.

SAUNDERS. (R.) A Pocket | Almanack | For the Year 1758. | Fitted to the Use of Penn- | sylvania, and the neighbour- | ing Provinces. | With several useful Additions. | By R. Saunders, Phil. | *Philadelphia:* | *Printed and sold by B. Franklin,* | *and D. Hall.* [1757.] | 24mo. pp. (24). 1557

SAUNDERS. Poor Richard improved: | Being an | Alma- nack | . . . | . . . | . . . | . . . | . . . | . . . | . . . | . . . | . . . | . . . . | For the | Year of our Lord 1758 : | Being the Second after Leap-Year. | . . . | . . . | . . . | . . . | . . . | . . . | . . . | . . . | . . . . | By Richard Saunders, Philom. | *Philadelphia:* | *Printed and Sold by B. Franklin, and D. Hall.* [1757.] | Sm. 8vo. pp. (36). H. S. P. 1558

The almanac contains the sayings of Poor Richard collected in the form of "Father Abraham's Speech."

SERIOUS Reflections on the Times. A Poem. By a Minister of the Gospel. *Philadelphia: James Chattin.* 1757. 1559

SMITH. (R.) Detection Detected, | or | A Vindication of the | Revd. Mr. Delap, and New-Castle | Presbytery, from the Charges of injurious | Reasonings, and false Representa- | tions, exhibited against them by the Rev. | Messieurs Gellatly and Arnot. | By Robert Smith, Minister of | the Gospel at Pequea. | To which is prefixed a Letter to | the Author on the same Subject, from the Rev. | Samuel Finley, A. M. Minister of the | Gospel at West-Nottingham. | . . . | . . . | . . . | . . . | . . . | . . . . | *Lancaster :* *Printed and Sold by W. Dunlap,* | *at the New-Printing-Office in Queen-Street.* 1757. | 8vo. pp. iv, 138 +. H. S. P. 1560

SMITH. (W.) A | Charge | Delivered May 17, 1757, | at the first | Anniversary Commencement | in the | College and Aca- demy | of | Philadelphia, | To the young Gentlemen who took their | Degrees on that Occasion. | By W. Smith, M. A. Provost of the said | College and Academy. | To which is added, in Latin | A | Salutatory Oration, | Delivered on the same Occasion. | By Paul Jackson, Professor of Languages in | the said College and Academy, on taking his Degree | of Master of Arts. | *Philadel- phia:* | *Printed by B. Franklin, and D. Hall.* 1757. | 8vo. pp. 16.

SMITH. The Christian Soldier's Duty; the | Lawfulness and Dignity of his Office; | and the Importance of the Protestant | Cause in the British Colonies, stated and | explained. | A | Sermon, | Preached April 5, 1757. | In | Christ-Church, Philadelphia, | To the first Battalion of his Majesty's Royal | American Regiment; at the Request | of their Colonel and Officers. | By William Smith, A. M. Provost of the | College and Academy of Philadelphia. | To which is annexed, A Prayer on | the same Occasion. | *Philadelphia:* | *Printed and Sold by James Chattin.* 1757. | 8vo. Title, 1 leaf; Dedication, 1 leaf; pp. 1–38.   A. P. S. 1562

SMITH. Four Discourses, September 1, 1754; June 24, 1755; May 21, 1756; and April 5, 1757. By William Smith, D. D. *Philadelphia:* 1757.   1563

Title from the Catalogue of the Loganian Library, Philadelphia, 1837. On examination this proves to be pages 1–128. (Signatures B to I), of "Discourses on Several Public Occasions During the War in America," &c. "By William Smith, D. D., Provost of the College and Academy of Philadelphia. London, 1759."

DJE TEUTSCHEN Kriegsartifel. *Philadelphia: B. Franklin und A. Armbruester.* 1757.   1564

Title from Seidensticker's Bibliography.

TO | William Denny, Esquire | Lieutenant Governor and Commander in Chief of the | Province of Pennsylvania, &c. | The Address of the Trustees and Treasurer of the Friendly Association for re- | gaining and preserving Peace with the Indians by Pacific Measures. | [*Philadelphia: B. Franklin, and D. Hall.* 1757.] Folio, pp. 4.   H. S. P. 1565

Dated at the end "Philadelphia, the 14th of the Seventh Month, 1757."

TOBLER. (J.) [Cut.] 1758. | The Pennsylvania | Town and Country-Man's | Almanack, | For the Year of our Lord 1758. | Being the second after Leap-Year. | Containing almost every Thing usual in Almanacks. | By John Tobler, Esq: | *Germantown: printed and sold by C. Sower jun. And | to be had in Phila-*

*delphia of Solomon Fussell, at the Sign of the | Hand-Saw over
against the Church in Second-Street, and also, | of Christopher Mar-
shall and Thomas Say.* [1757.] | [Cut.] 16mo. pp. (40). H. S. P.

𝕍𝔼ℝ𝕳𝔸ℕ𝔇𝕷𝕌ℕ𝔊𝔼ℕ 𝔡𝔢𝔰 ℭ𝔬𝔢𝔱𝔲𝔰 𝔳𝔬𝔫 ℙ𝔢𝔫𝔫𝔰𝔶𝔩𝔳𝔞𝔫𝔦𝔢𝔫. *Philadelphia: B. Franklin und A. Armbruester.* 1757.   1567

The Rev. Dr. Jos. Henry Dubbs possesses a letter of the Rev. J. P. Böhm,
which says the writer had been for some time engaged in revising the proofs of
this work.

VOTES and Proceedings of the House of Representatives.
Philadelphia: B. Franklin. 1757. Folio.   1568

WATTS. (I.) Divine Songs, attempted in easy Language, for
the Use of Children. By Isaac Watts, D. D. *Philadelphia:
James Chattin.* 1757.   1569

WATTS. The Psalms of David, imitated in the Language of
the New Testament. By Isaac Watts, D.D. The Seventeenth
Edition. *Philadelphia: James Chattin.* 1757.   1570

WEISER. (C.) Translation | of a | German Letter, | wrote by
| Conrad Weiser, Esq ; | Interpreter, on Indian Affairs, for the |
Province of Pennsylvania. | [*Philadelphia: B. Franklin, and D.
Hall.* 1757.] 8vo. pp. 7.   H. S. P. 1571

Probably printed with Hopkins' Address or the Abridgment of his Historical
Memories. It was written in 1746.

1758.

AN ACCOUNT of the Births | and Burials in Christ-Church
Parish, | in Philadelphia, from December 24, 1757, | to Decem-
ber 24, 1758. By Caleb Cash, | Clerk, and Samuel Kirke, Sexton.
| [n. p. n. d.] Folio, 1 leaf.   L. C. P. 1572

ALISON. (F.) Peace and Union Recommended. A Sermon
preached at Philadelphia, before the Reverend Synod of New
York, May 24th, 1758. By Francis Alison, D. D. *Philadelphia:
Printed by W. Dunlap.* M.DCC.LVIII.   1573

ANNO Regni | Georgii II. | Regis, | Magnæ Britanniæ, Franciæ & Hiberniæ, | Tricèsimo Primo. | At a General Assembly of the Province of Penn- | sylvania, begun and holden at Philadelphia, | the Fourteenth Day of October, Anno Domini 1757, in | the Thirty-first Year of the Reign of our Sovereign | Lord George II. by the Grace of God, of | Great-Britain, France and Ireland, King, Defender of | the Faith, &c. | And from thence continued by Adjournments to the Se- | cond Day of January, 1758. | [*Penn Arms.*] | *Philadelphia:* | *Printed and Sold by B. Franklin, at the New-* | *Printing-Office, near the Market.* MDCC-LVIII. | Folio, Title, 1 leaf; pp. 375–390. + And . . . continued . . . to the | Second Day of January, 1758. [April 22, 1758.] | [*Ibid.*] Title, 1 leaf; pp. 393–407 + [Continued to May 3, 1758 n. p. n. d.] pp. 409–427. + And . . . continued . . . to the | Fourth Day of September 1758. | [*Ibid.*] Title, 1 leaf; pp. 431–436.

H. S. P. 1574

BALL. (W.) The New Jersey Almanac for 1759. By William Ball. *Philadelphia: William Bradford.* 1758. 1575

BOSTWICK. (D.) Self Disclaimed and Christ Exalted; a Sermon preached at Philadelphia, before the Reverend Synod of New York, May 25th, 1758. By David Bostwick, A.M. Published at the Request of the Members of the Synod. . . . *Philadelphia: Printed by W. Dunlap.* M.DCC.LVIII. 12mo. pp. 54.

Title from Sabin's Dictionary.

THE CHARTER | Laws | and | Catalogue of Books of the Library Company | of | Burlington. | *Philadelphia:* | *Printed by William Dunlap, at the* | *newest Printing Office on the* | *South Side of the Jersey-Market.* | 1758. | 8vo. pp. 32, 72. H. S. P. 1577

CICERO. (M[ARCUS] T.) Cato Major; or, a Treatise on Old Age, by M. Tullius Cicero. With Explanatory Notes from the Roman History. *Philadelphia: Printed by William Dunlap.* 1758. 16mo. pp. 168. 1578

See No. 868, *supra.*

[DOVE. (DAVID JAMES)]   The Lottery. | A | Dialogue | Between | Mr. Thomas Trueman and | Mr. Humphrey Dupe. | [*Germantown : Christopher Sower.* 1758.] 16mo. pp. 16.   **1579**

Containing also two poems, viz. "The Academy Garland" and "The Lottery."

DURHAM. (EBENEZER)   To the Inhabitants of the Province of Pennsylvania. | [n. p. 1758.?] Folio, 1 leaf.   L. C. P.   **1580**

An address on the defenceless state of the Province.

EASTBURN. (R.)   A   Faithful | Narrative, | Of | The many Dangers and Sufferings, as well as | wonderful Deliverances of Robert East- | burn, during his late Captivity among the | Indians : Together with some Remarks | upon the Country of Canada, and the | Religion, and Policy of its Inhabitants ; the | whole intermixed with devout Reflections. | By Robert Eastburn. | Published at the earnest Request of many | Friends, for the Benefit of the Author. | With a recommendatory Preface, by the | Rev. Gilbert Tennent. | . . . | . . . | . . . | . . . | . . . | . . . . *Philadelphia : | Printed by William Dunlap.*   1758 | 8vo. pp. 45. (1).   H. S. P.   **1581**

A | FRAGMENT | of the | Chronicles | of | Nathan Ben Saddi ; | A Rabbi of the Jews. | Lately discovered in the Ruins of | Herculaneum : | And Translated from the Original, into the | Italian Language. | By the Command of the King of the Two-Sicilies. | And | Now first publish'd in English. | *Constantinople :* | [*Philadelphia :*] *Printed* [*by James Chattin*] *in the Year of the Vulgar Æra,* 5707. | 8vo. Title, 1 leaf; pp. (12).   L. C. P.   **1582**

Of the characters presented in this piece, which is an allegorical account of the arrest of the Rev. Dr. Smith and Wm. Moore of Moon Hall, I have identified several: Isaac, the Judge, is Isaac Norris, Speaker of the Assembly ; Adonis, the Scribe, is Benjamin Franklin; Daniel, the Etheopean, Daniel Roberdeau ; Gruban, Nathaniel Grubb, of Chester Co.; Sheptol, Thomas Leech, of Philadelphia ; Hughall, John Hughes, of Philadelphia; Masteral Abber, William Masters, of Philadelphia; Asber, George Ashbridge, of Chester Co.; Tochal, John Douglas, of Lancaster Co.; Asa, the Butcher, Joshua Ash, of Chester Co.; Wa-Nereth, the Stupid, Isaac Wayne, of Chester Co.; Peronal, the beastly, Richard Pearne, of Philadelphia; Shimei, Rev. Wm. Smith, D. D.; Morat, William Moore; Kerak, Edward Kelly, Doorkeeper of the Assembly.

[FRANKLIN. (BENJAMIN)] Reflections on Courtship and Marriage; In Two Letters To a Friend. Wherein a Practicable Plan is laid down for Obtaining and Securing Conjugal Felicity. To which is added A Letter from the late Dean Swift, to a very young Lady on her Marriage, containing salutory Advice relating to her conduct thro' Life. The Third Edition. *Philadelphia: Printed and Sold by William Dunlap, at the Newest-Printing-Office, on the South Side of the Jersey Market.* 1758.   1583

FREDERICK II. The Relaxation of War; or the Hero's Philosophy. A Poem, written by the King of Prussia, during his Residence at Breslau. *Philadelphia: W. Dunlap.* 1758. 1584

GELLATLY. (A.) Some | Observations | Upon | A late Piece entitled, The Detection detected or | a Vindication, &c. | Containing a Discovery of the Manner | how the Rev. Mess. S. Finley & R. Smith | the Authors of said Piece, handle the Obliga- | tion of the National and Solemn | League, the Nature of Faith, the | Gospel-Offer and Some Other | Points. | And | Shewing that the Detection is not de- | tected in the Manner they pretend. | By Alexander Gellatly | Minister of the Gospel and Member of the | associate Presbytery in Pennsylvania. | . . . | . . . | . . . | . . . | . . . | . . . | . . . | . . . | . . . | . . . . | *Germantown. | Printed by Christopher Sower.* 1758. | Sm. 8vo. pp. 204.   c. 1585

GORDON. (J.) John Gordon's | Mathematical | Traverse Table, &c., | *Printed in the Year* 1758, *and | Sold by Mr. W. Dunlap, in | Philadelphia, Mr. G. Noel, | in New-York, Mr. B. Mecom, | in Boston, and by the Author.* | Sm. 12mo. pp. (66), 2 plates. A. P. S.

GRANT. (T.) Thomas Grant, Second Lieutenant of the Privateer Ship Britannia, thinking himself highly | Reflected upon, in the last Week's Gazette: Publishes the following Depositions, in Vindication of his strik- | ing the Colours on Board the said Ship. | [*Philadelphia: William Bradford.* 1758.] Folio, pp. 3.

HALL. (D.) A | Mite | into the | Treasury; | or, | Some serious Remarks on that solemn and | indispensible Duty of duly attending Assemblies | for divine Worship, incumbent upon all

Persons | come to the Years of Understanding (especially the | Professors of Truth) whilst favoured with Health, | Strength and Liberty; together with some due | Animadversions upon the Neglect thereof; as | also a Word of Consolation to such sincere hearted ¦ Friends, as are rendered incapable of personally | attending them, by reason of Old Age, some | bodily Disorder, or Confinement, &c. | To which is subjoined, | An Epistle to Friends of | Knaresborough Monthly-Meeting. | By David Hall. | . . . | . . . | . . . | . . . | . . . | . . . | . . . | . . . . | *London Printed:* | *Philadelphia, Re-printed by B. Franklin,* | *and D. Hall.* 1758. | 8vo. pp. x, 53.   H. S. P.   1588

𝕯𝕰𝕽 | 𝕳𝕺𝕮𝕳=𝕯𝕰𝖀𝕿𝕾𝕮𝕳 | Americanische | Calender, | Auf das Jahr | . . . | . . . | 1759. | . . . | . . . | . . . | . . . | . . . | . . . | . . . | . . . | . . . | . . . | . . . . | Zum Ein und Zwantzigsten mal heraus gegeben. | *Germantown: Gedruckt und zu finden bey Christoph Saur.* | *Auch koennen die auswaertige Kroemer solche bey David Taeschler in Philadelphia haben* | *oder in Lancester bey Ludwig Laumann, und in Newyorck bey Michel Hoffmann.* [1758.] | 4to. pp. (48).

JERMAN. (J.) An Almanac for 1759. By John Jerman. *Philadelphia: W. Dunlap.* 1758.   1590

LABOUR in Vain, or an attempt to wash the Black Moore White, humbly inscribed to the author of the chronicle. *Philadelphia:* 1758.   1591

"Ornamented with a caricature print. Written in Verse, and is a Satyr of the person that adhered to Moore and Smith in their disputes with the assembly."
—*Du Simitiere MSS. relating to Pennsylvania,* p. 239.

MESSAGE of Gov. Barnard to the Minisink Indians; and a Conference in consequence thereof, held at Burlington, August, 1758. *Philadelphia: William Bradford.* 1758. Folio, pp. 6.

MINUTES | of | Conferences, | held at | Easton, | In October, 1758, | With the Chief Sachems and Warriors of the Mohawks, | Oneidoes, Onondagoes, Cayugas, Senecas, Tuscaroras, Tuteloes, Skaniada- | radigronos, consisting of the Nanticokes and Conoys, who now make one | Nation; Chugnuts, Delawares, Unamies,

Mahickanders, or Mohickons ; | Minisinks, and Wapingers, or Pumptons. | [*Penn Arms.*] | *Philadelphia:* | *Printed and Sold by B. Franklin, and D. Hall, at the* | *New-Printing-Office, near the Market.* MDCCLVIII. | Folio, pp. 31.   H. S. P. 1593

Neu-eingerichteter Americanifcher Gefchichts-Calender, auf das Jahr 1759. *Philadelphia: B. Franklin und G. Armbruester.* 1758. 1594

NEW JERSEY. Anno Regni | Georgii II. | Regis | Magnæ Britanniæ, Franciæ, et Hiberniæ, | Tricesimo Primo. | At a Session of General Assembly of the Province | of New-Jersey, | held at Burlington, ... and continued to April 4, 1758. | [*Royal Arms.*] | *Philadelphia:* | *Printed by W. Bradford, Printer to the King's Most* | *Excellent Majesty, for the Province of New-Jersey.* [1758.] | Folio, pp. 28. + And continued to April 15th 1758. [*Ibid.*] Folio, pp. 8.   1595

NEW JERSEY. The | Grants, Concessions, | And | Original Constitutions | Of the Province of | New-Jersey | The | Acts | Passed during the Proprietary Governments, and other ma- | terial Transactions before the Surrender thereof to | Queen Anne. | The Instrument of Surrender, and Her formal Acceptance | thereof. | Lord Cornbury's Commision and Instructions conse- | quent thereon. | Collected by some Gentlemen employed by the General Assembly. | And Afterwards | Published by Virtue of an Act of the Legislature of the said | Province. | With proper Tables alphabetically digested, containing the principal Matters in | the Book. | By Aaron Leaming and Jacob Spicer. | *Philadelphia:* | *Printed by W. Bradford, Printer to the King's Most Excellent* | *Majesty for the Province of New-Jersey.* [1758.] | Folio, pp. (4), 763.   H. S. P. 1596

This handsome volume, generally known as *Leaming and Spicer's Laws*, was prepared under the authority of an act of Assembly passed in 1752, and is the largest work issued from the press of Wm. Bradford. Subscribers' names were first solicited in February, 1755, the compilers having spent nearly two years in its preparation. Three years more were consumed in printing, and it was not until May, 1758, that it was ready for delivery. Up to that time 170 copies had been subscribed for, and the editors say in the Pa. Journal May 11, 1758, "a number of copies yet remain not subscribed for " and "any person may be supplied " until " the 17th of July next, after which we will not further extend the sale." It was reprinted about 1880. Kent Gilbert's (1873) copy sold for $34 ; Brinley's, $44, and Murphy's, $30.

THE NEW Rules of His Royal Highness the Duke of Cumberland, to be observed in the Army. *Philadelphia: W. Dunlap.* 1758.   1597

THE | NEW-YEAR | Verses, | Of the Printers Lads, who | carry the Pennsylvania Gazette, | to the Customers. | [*Franklin and Hall.* 1758.]   Folio, 1 leaf.   1598

NEW-YEAR Verses of the Carriers of the Pennsylvania Journal. *Philadelphia: William Bradford.* 1758.   1599

THE PENNSYLVANIA Gazette.   H. S. P.   1600

Numbers 1515 (Jan. 5, 1758) to 1566 (Dec. 28, 1758), four pages each, with an extra half sheet (two pages) to each number. Title and imprint as in No. 1272, *supra.*

THE PENNSYLVANIA Journal. *Philadelphia: Printed and Sold by William Bradford at the Corner-House of | Front and Market-Streets, where Persons may be supplied with this Paper at 10s. a Year. And where Advertise- | ments are taken in. |* H. S. P.   1601

Numbers 787 (Jan. 5, 1758) to 831 (Dec. 28, 1758), four pages each. Title as in No. 1429, *supra.* No. 822 is misnumbered 821.

THE POLITE Philosopher: Or, an Essay on that Art which makes a Man happy in himself, and agreeable to others. *Philadelphia: W. Dunlap.* 1758.   1602

Reprinted by Bradford and Hall in 1781.

SAUNDERS. (R.) A Pocket | Almanack | For the Year 1759. | Fitted to the Use of Penn- | sylvania, and the neighbour- | ing Province. | With several useful Additions. | By R. Saunders, Phil. | *Philadelphia:* | *Printed and sold by B. Franklin,* | *and D. Hall.* [1758.] | 24mo. pp. (24).   c. 1603

SAUNDERS. Poor Richard improved: | Being an | Almanack | . . . | . . . | . . . | . . . | . . . | . . . | . . . | . . . | . . . | . . . . | For the | Year of our Lord 1759: | Being the Third after Leap-Year. | . . . | . . . | . . . | . . . | . . . | . . . | . . . | . . . | . . . | By Richard Saunders, Philom. | *Philadelphia:* | *Printed and Sold by* *B. Franklin, and D. Hall.* [1758.] | Sm. 8vo. pp. (36).   H. S. P.

THE GREAT SCOTS Prophet; or some remarkable Passages of the Life and Death of Mr. Alexander Peden, late Minister of the Gospel at New Glenluce, in Galloway; singular for Piety, Zeal and Faithfulness, but especially who exceeded most to be heard of in our late Ages in that Gift of Foreseeing of Events, and Foretelling what was to befall the Church and Nations of Scotland and Ireland, particular Families and Persons, and of his own Life and Death. *Philadelphia: James Chattin.* 1758. 1605

SCOURGE. (H.) Tit for Tat, | or the | Score wip'd off. | By Humphrey Scourge, Esq; | Number 1. | To be continued Occasionally. | [*Philadelphia: Printed by James Chattin.* 1756.] Folio, pp. 4.   H. S. P. 1606

TENNENT. (G.) Sermons | on | Important Subjects; | adapted | To the perilous State of the | British Nation, lately | preached in Philadelphia. | By Gilbert Tennent, A.M. | Minister of the Gospel. | . . . | . . . | . . . | . . . . | *Philadelphia:* | *Printed* *by James Chattin, at the Newest-* | *Printing-Office, on the South Side* *of the* | *Jersey-Market.* 1758. | Sm. 8vo. pp. xxxvii, 1–425. H. S. P.

TOBLER. (J.) [Cut.] 1759. | The Pennsylvania | Town and Country-Man's | Almanack, | For . . . 1759. | . . . | . . . | By John Tobler Esq: | *Germantown: Printed and Sold by C. Sower* *jun. And* | . . . | . . . | *of Christopher Marshall and Jonathan Zane,* [1758.] [Cut.] 16mo. pp. (40).   H. S. P. 1608

TRYON. (T.) The Way to Health, Long-Life and Happiness. By Thomas Tryon. *Philadelphia:* 1758. 1609

Proposals for printing a limited edition were advertised in the Pa. Gazette in October, 1757, and for the next three months or longer. In the Gazette, Dec. 15, 1757, is a poem " On the Author " &c. to which is added a statement " that the subscription has been opened by a Gentleman of Note in this City, who subscribed £20 : And as divers others . . . have subscribed largely, it is expected the Book will soon be committed to the Press. No more will be printed than what may be subscribed for." Probably not published till 1761; see No. 1775, *infra*.

VOTES | and | Proceedings| of the|House of Representatives | of the | Province of Pennsylvania, | Met at Philadelphia, on the Fourteenth of October, Anno | Domini 1757, And continued by Adjournments|[*Penn Arms.*] | *Philadelphia: Printed and Sold by B. Franklin, at the New-Printing-Office, | near the Market.* MDCCLVIII. | Folio, pp. 94.   H. S. P.   1610

WEATHERWISE. (A.) Father Abraham's | Almanack, | (On an entire New Plan.) | For the Year of our Lord, 1759. | Being the third after Leap-Year. | Containing, | Eclipses, Judgment of the Weather, Festivals, and other | remarkable Days, Length of Days and Nights, Moons | Age, Suns Rising and Setting, High-water at Philadel- | phia, Tables of Interest at six per Ct. Tables of Coins | as they pass Current in this and the neighbouring Govern- | ments. An Account of Fairs, Courts, Roads, and Qua- | kers Yearly Meetings: The whole interspersed with | a variety of entertaining and useful Remarks both in | Prose and Verse. | To which is added, | An exact and nice Representation of his Majesty the King|of Prussia, done on a Folio Copper plate, by an eminent | Hand, with a compendious Account of his Life and | late memorable Actions. | Likewise, | An exact Plan of Louis-bourg, with a succinct Account | of its antient Right, its Product, its excellent Fisheries, | and the Value it is of to the English Nation; with a | Journal of the Siege and Surrender thereof. | Together with | A compendious Account of the Author's Travels over the vast Con- | tinent of America, with his Remarks on the Climate, Customs, | manners, Religion and Product of each Place, particularly of Mexi- | co, Grenada, Florida, Canada, Terra-Firma, Peru, the Land of the | Amazons, Brazil and Chili ; with the Land of the Negroes, of | Barbary and the great Desart of Africa, &c. &c. | By Abraham Weatherwise, Gent. | *Philadelphia : | Printed and Sold by W. Dunlap, | at the Newest-Printing-Office, on the South Side of the Jersey-Mar- | ket, and but three Doors from the Corner of Second-Street.* [1758.] | Sm. 8vo. pp. (40).   H. S. P.

Some copies have the following imprint : *Printed at Philadelphia by W. Dunlap, for G. Noel, | Bookseller, in New York.* |

1759.

AN ACCOUNT of the Births | and Burials in Christ-Church Parish, | in Philadelphia, from December 24, 1758, | to December 24, 1759.   By Caleb Cash, | Clerk, and Samuel Kirke, Sexton. | [n. p. n. d.] Folio, 1 leaf.   1612

AN ACT for granting His Majesty the sum of one hundred thousand pounds, passed at a General Assembly begun . . . October, 1758, and . . . continued . . . to the 5th February, 1759. *Philadelphia: Printed and Sold by B. Franklin*, ... MDCCLIX. Folio, Title, 1 leaf; pp. 45.   1613

AGREEMENT between William Smith and others as William Smith & Co. and certain adventurers and proposed settlers concerning 1,000,000 acres of land in Nova Scotia. [*Philadelphia: about* 1759.]   Folio, pp. 4.   1614

AGUECHEEK. (A.)   The | Universal American Almanack: | Or, Yearly Astronomical Magazine. | Fitted to the Lat: of 40 Degrees and a Meridian of near five Hours West from | London; but may without sensible Error, serve all the Northern Colonies. | For the Year of our Lord, 1760; | And from the Creation, according to Prophane History, 5706 | But by the Eastern and Greek Christian, 7268 | By the Jews, the Hebrews and the Rabbies, 5520 | And by the Account of Holy Scripture, 5769 | Being Bissextile, or Leap-Year. | Containing, (More in Quantity and greater Variety than any | Almanack of the Kind and Price ever published heretofore) | The Motions of the Sun and | Moon; the true Places and | Aspects of the Planets; the | Rising and Setting of the Sun; | the Rising, Setting, and South- | ing of the Moon; the Luna- | tions, Conjunctions, and | Eclipses; Judgment of the | Weather; Rising and Set- | ting of the Planets; Rising, | Setting and Southing of the | Seven Stars; Length of the | Days and Nights; Time of | High-Tide at Philadelphia; | Difference betwixt the Julian | and Gregorian Stile: An | exact List of all the Courts | of Justice in the Provinces | of Pennsylvania, New Jer- | sey, New York, Maryland | and Virginia; Account of | the Roads, from one End of |

the Continent to the other, &c. | Evans's Tables of the Distance | of all the noted Places on the | Continent ; Quaker's yearly | Meetings ; List of the present | Royal Family ; of the Kings | and Queens of England, since | the Conquest ; Time of the | Fairs in this and the neighbour- | ing Provinces ; the exact Dis- | tance of Places from Louis- | bourg round to Mississippi, with | a Description of the River | Ohio ; a Table of the Weight | and Value of Gold and Silver | Coin ; Tables of Interest ; List | of his Majesty's Forces in Ame- | rica ; a brief Table of memo- | rable Things ; a Table of Ex- | pence ; Rates and Hire of the | Stage-Boats and Wagons. | With many entertaining Pieces, | useful Directions, valuable Re- | ceipts, solid Maxims, &c. &c. | To the whole is added, by Way of Appendix, | An authentic History of Quebec, the River St. Lawrence, &c. | By Andrew Aguecheek, Esq ; Philom. | *Philadelphia : Printed by William Bradford, at the* | *London Coffeehouse ; and Andrew Steuart in Lætitia-Court.* [1759.] | Sm. 8vo. pp. (40).   H. S. P.   1615

ANNO Regni | Georgii II. | Regis, | Magnæ Britanniæ, Franciæ & Hiberniæ, | Tricesimo Secundo. | At a General Assembly of the Province of Penn- | sylvania, begun and holden at Philadelphia, | the Fourteenth Day of October, Anno Domini 1758, in | the Thirty-second Year of the Reign of our Sovereign | Lord George II. by the Grace of God, of | Great-Britain, France and Ireland, King, Defender of | the Faith, &c. | And from thence continued by Adjournments to the | Fifth Day of February, 1759. | [*Penn Arms.*] | *Philadelphia :* | *Printed and Sold by B. Franklin, at the New-* | *Printing-Office, near the Market.* MDCCLIX. | Folio, Title, 1 leaf ; pp. 439–483. + And . . . continued . . . to the | Twenty-first Day of May, 1759. | [*Ibid.*] Title, 1 leaf, pp. 487– 513. + And . . . continned . . . to the | Tenth Day of September, 1759. | [*Ibid.*] Title, 1 leaf ; pp. 517–526.   H. S. P.   1616

ANNO Regni | Georgii II. | Regis, | Magnæ Britanniæ, Franciæ & Hiberniæ, | Tricesimo Secundo. | At a General Assembly of the Province of Penn- | sylvania, begun and holden at Philadelphia, | the Fifteenth Day of October, Anno Domini 1759, in | the Thirty-third Year of the Reign of our Sovereign | Lord

George II. by the Grace of God, of | Great-Britain, France and Ireland, King, Defender of | the Faith, &c. | And from thence continued by Adjournments [to Nov. 20, 1759.] | [*Penn Arms.*] | *Philadelphia :* | *Printed and Sold by B. Franklin, at the New-* | *Printing-Office, near the Market.* MDCCLIX. | Folio, Title, 1 leaf; pp. 529–530.   H. S. P.   1617

[BENEZET. (A.)]   Observations | On the Inslaving, importing and purchasing of | Negroes | With some Advice thereon extracted form the | Yearly Meeting Epistle of London for the pre- | sent Year | Also | Some Remarks on the absolute Necessity of | Self-Denial, renouncing the World, and true | Charity for all such as sincerely Desire to be | our blessed Saviour's Disciples. | *Germantown.* | *Printed by Christopher Sower.*   1759. | 16mo. Title, 1 leaf; pp. 2–15.   H. S. P.   1618

BISSET. (J.)   Abridgment and Collection | of the | Acts of Assembly | Of the Province of | Maryland, | At present in Force. | With | A small choice | Collection of Precedents | in | Law and Conveyancing. | Calculated for the Use of the Gentlemen of the Province. | By James Bisset, Attorney at Law. | . . . . | *PPiladelphia:* [*sic*] | *Printed by William Bradford, Printer, in Mar-* | *ket-* | *Street, for the Author,* 1759. | 8vo. Title, 1 leaf; Dedication, 1 leaf; Preface, pp. (4); Charter of Maryland, pp. 10; Abridgment, &c. pp. 11–366.   H. S. P.   1619

BOOKS | Imported in the last Vessel from London, and to be sold by | David Hall, | At the New-Printing-Office, in Market-Street, Philadelphia. | [*Philadelphia : B. Franklin, and D. Hall.* 1759.]   Folio, 1 leaf.   1620

BROMLEY. (T.)   The Way to the | Sabbath of Rest. | Or the | Soul's Progress in the Work | of the | New-Birth. | With | Two Discourses of the Author never before Printed viz. | The Journeys of the Children of Israel, as in their | Names and historical Passages, they comprise the | great and gradual Work of Regeneration: | And | A Treatise of extraordinary divine Dispensations, | under the Jewish and Gospel Administrations. | By Mr. Thomas Bromley. | To which are added | A Discourse on

Mistakes concerning Religion, Enthu- | siasm, Experiences &c. By Thomas Hartley Rector | of Winwick. | *London Printed.* | *Germantown Reprinted and sold by Christopher Sower,* | *Also sold by* *Solomon Fussell and Jonathan Zane in* | *Philadelphia.* 1759. | 8vo. pp. viii, 280.   H. S. P.   1621

The Way to the Sabbath of Rest ends on page 60, and is followed by "The Journeys of the Children of Israel," pp. 61–187, and An Account of an Extraordinary Dispensation, pp. 188–280. See No. 1629, *infra.*

A CATALOGUE of above 2000 Volumes of valuable Books, mostly new. Which will begin to be sold by Auction on the 17th of January, 1759. *Philadelphia: William Bradford.* 1759.

CLARKE. (R.) The Prophetic Numbers of Daniel and John calculated; In order to show the Time when the Day of Judgment for this First Age of the Gospel, is to be expected: And the setting up The Millennial Kingdom of Jehovah and his Christ. By Richard Clarke, Minister of the Gospel of Jesus Christ. The Third Edition. *Philadelphia: William Bradford.* 1759.

Advertised in the Pa. Journal, April 12, 1759. The Fourth Edition was announced May 17.

DAVIES. (S.) The Curse of Cowardice. A Sermon to the Militia of Hanover County, in Virginia, at a General Muster, May 8, 1758. By Samuel Davies. *Philadelphia:* 1758. 8vo.? pp. 36.   1624

Title from Haven's List. Sabin notices editions printed at London, 1758, and Boston and Woodbridge, N. J., 1759.

DELL. (W.) The | Doctrine of | Baptisms, | Reduced from its | Ancient and Modern Corruptions ; | And restored to its | Primitive Soundness | And | Integrity : | According to the Word of Truth; the Sub- | stance of Faith, and the Nature of | Christ's Kingdom. | By William Dell, | Minister of the Gospel, and Master of Gonvil and Caius | College, in Cambridge. | . . . | . . . . | The Fifth Edition. | *London Printed:* | *Philadelphia, Reprinted,* *by B. Frank-* | *lin, and D. Hall.* 1759. | 8vo. pp. 43. H. S. P. 1625

𝖣𝖩𝖤 𝖤𝖱𝖅𝖀𝖤𝖧𝖫𝖀𝖭𝖦𝖤𝖭 von Maria le Roy und Barbara Leininger, welche vierthalb Jahr unter den Indianern gefangen gewesen und am 6ten May in dieser Stadt angekommen. Aus ihrem eigenen Munde niedergeschrieben und zum Druck befördert. *Philadelphia, gedruckt und zu haben in der teutschen Buchdrueckerey, das Stueck vor 6 Pentz.* 1759.

Title from Seidensticker's Bibliography. A translation will be found in the Pa. Archives 2d Series, Vol. VII, p. 401.

FROM our Yearly Meeting at Philadelphia, | for Pennsylvania and New-Jersey, | from the 22d Day of the Ninth Month to the 28th of | the same (inclusive) 1759. | To the Quarterly and Monthly Meetings of Friends belong- | ing to the said Yearly Meeting. | [*Philadelphia: B. Franklin, and D. Hall.* 1759.] Folio, pp. 3.   H. S. P. 1627

HARTLEY. (T.) A | Discourse | on | Mistakes concerning Religion, | Enthusiasm, Experiences, &c. | By Thomas Hartley, A. M. | Rector of Winwick in Northamptonshire. | *London Printed.* | *Germantown reprinted by Christopher* | *Sower.* 1759. | 16mo. pp. 71.   H. S. P. 1628

See Dell's Christ's Spirit, No. 1668, *infra.*

𝖣𝖤𝖱 | 𝖧𝖮𝖢𝖧=𝖣𝖤𝖀𝖳𝖲𝖢𝖧 | Americanische | Calender, | Auf das Jahr | ... | ... | 1760. | (Welches ein schalt Jahr von 366 Tagen ist.) | ... | ... | ... | ... | ... | ... | ... | ... | ... | .... | Zum Zwey und zwanzigsten mal heraus gegeben. | *Germantown: Gedruckt und zu finden bey Christoph Saur.* | ... | ....[1759.] | 4to. pp. (48).

JERMAN. (J.) The American | Almanac. | For the Year of Christian Account, | 1760. | Wherein is contained, | The Rising and Setting of the Sun; the Rising, Setting, | and Southing of the Moon; the Lunations, Conjunctions, | Eclipses, Rising, Setting, and Southing of the Planets; | Length of Days; Judgment of the Weather; Festivals, | and other remarkable Days; High Water at Philadelphia; | Quakers Yearly Meetings, Fairs, Courts, Roads, &c. | To which is added, | The History of Abdallah, Prince of Indostan: A beautiful | Eastern Tale. | Fitted to the Latitude of Forty Degrees North, and a | Meridian of five Hours

West from London, and may without | much Error, serve from Newfoundland to South-Carolina. | By John Jerman, Philomat. | . . . | . . . | . . . | . . . . | *Philadelphia :* | *Printed and Sold by W. Dunlap, at the* | *Newest-Printing-Office, on the South Side of the* | *Jersey-Market.* [1759.] | Sm. 8vo. pp. (28).   H. S. P.   1630

This is probably the last of Jerman's Almanacs. John Jerman was born in Radnor Township, Chester Co., Nov. 12, 1684, and died there July 16, 1769.

THE | JOURNALS | of the | Lives and Travels | of | Samuel Bownas, | and | John Richardson. | *London Printed :* | *Philadelphia, Reprinted, and Sold by William* | *Dunlap, at the Newest Printing-Office, in* | *Market-Street,* 1759. | 8vo. 1 leaf.

Second title. An | Account | of the | Life, Travels, | and | Christian Experiences | in the | Work of the Ministry | of | Samuel Bownas. | *London Printed :* | *Philadelphia, Reprinted, and Sold by William* | *Dunlap, at the Newest Printing-Office, in* | *Market-Street,* 1759. | 8vo. pp. viii, 242.

Third title. An | Account | of the | Life | of that | Ancient Servant of Jesus Christ, | John Richardson, | Giving a Relation of many of his Trials | and Exercises in his Youth, and his Services | in the Work of the Ministry, in England, | Ireland, America, &c. | . . . | . . . | . . . . | *London Printed :* | *Philadelphia, Reprinted, and Sold by William* | *Dunlap, at the Newest Printing-Office, in* | *Market-Street,* 1759. | 8vo. pp. vi, 220.   H. S. P.   1631

LEECHMAN. (W.) The | Wisdom of God | in the | Gospel Revelation. | A | Sermon, | Preached at the opening of the General | Assembly of the Church of Scot- | land, in May 1758. | By Dr. William Leechman, | Professor of Divinity in the University of Glasgow. | *Philadelphia :* | *Printed by William Bradford, at the London Coffee-House in* | *Front and Market-Streets,* MDCC,LIX. | 8vo. Half title, 1 leaf; pp. 42.   H. S. P.   1632

The half title reads : A | Sermon | Preached before His Majesty's | High Commissioner, at the opening | at the General Assembly of the Church | of Scotland 1758. |

𝕍𝕆𝕃𝕃𝕊𝕋𝔄𝔈ℕ𝔇𝕀𝔊𝔈𝔖 | 𝔐𝔄ℝ𝔅𝕌ℝ𝔊𝔈ℝ | Gesang=Buch, | Zur | Uebung der Gottseligkeit, | in 649 Chriſtlichen und Troſtreichen | Pſal= men und Geſängen | Hrn. D. Martin Luthers | und anderer | Gottſeliger

Lehrer, | Ordentlich in XII. Theile verfaffet, | Und mit nöthigen Regis=
tern auch einer Verzeichniß verfehen | unter welche Titul die in Anhang
befindliche Lieder gehörig: | Auch zur Beförderung | des fo Kirchen=als
Privat=Gottesdienftes, | Mit erbaulichen | Morgen=Abend=Buß=Beicht=
und | Communion=Gebätlein vermehret. | *Germanton,* | *Gedruckt und
zu finden bey Christoph Saur* 1759. | 16mo. pp. (12), 527, (16), 14.

MINUTES | of | Conferences | held at | Easton | In October,
1758, | With the Chief Sachems and Warriors of the Mohawks,
| . . . | . . . | . . . | . . . . | [*Penn Arms.*] | *Philadelphia:* | *Printed
and Sold by B. Franklin, and D. Hall, at the* | *New-Printing-Office,
near the Market.* MDCCLIX. | Folio, pp. 31.   1634

See No. 1593, *supra.*

Neu=eingerichteter Americanifcher Calender, auf das Jahr 1760. *Philadelphia: Anton Armbruester.* 1759.   1635

THE | NEW–YEAR | Verses | Of the Printers Lads, who
carry | about the Pennsylvania Gazette to | the Customers. |
[*Philadelphia: B. Franklin, and D. Hall.* 1759.]   Folio, 1 leaf.

NEW-YEAR Verses of the Carriers of the Pennsylvania Journal.
Philadelphia: William Bradford. 1759.   1637

THE PENNSYLVANIA Gazette.   H. S. P.   1638

Numbers 1567 (Jan. 4. 1759) to 1618 (Dec. 27, 1759), four pages each, with
an extra half sheet (two pages) to each. Title and imprint as in No. 1272, *supra.*

THE PENNSYLVANIA Journal.   H. S. P.   1639

Numbers 839 (Jan. 4, 1759) to 890 (Dec. 27, 1759), four pages each, with a
"Supplement" of 1 leaf to No. 851, and one of two pages to No. 872. Title and
imprint as in No. 1601, *supra*, up to No. 871, when the latter was changed to the
form given in No. 1693, *infra.* No. 840 is misnumbered 830.

THE PENNSYLVANIA Pocket Almanac for 1760. *Philadelphia: William Bradford.* 1759.   1640

ROMAINE. (W.) The Knowledge of Salvation precious in
the Hour of Death, prov'd in a Sermon, occasion'd by the Death
of the Rev. Mr. James Hervey. By William Romaine, A. M.
The Seventh Edition. *Philadelphia: W. Dunlap.* 1759.   1641

RUTTY. (J.) The | Liberty | of the | Spirit | and of the | Flesh | distinguished : | In an Address to those Captives in Spirit | among the People called Quakers, who are | commonly called Libertines. | By John Rutty, | An unworthy Member of that Community. | . . . | . . . | . . . | . . . | . . . | . . . | . . . | . . . | . . . | . . . | . . . . | *Dublin, Printed:* | *Philadelphia, Re-printed by B. Franklin,* | *and D. Hall.* 1759. | 8vo. pp. 64.   H. S. P.   1642

SAUNDERS. (R.) A Pocket Almanac for 1760. By R. Saunders. *Philadelphia : B. Franklin, and D. Hall.* 1759.   1643

SAUNDERS.   Poor Richard improved. | Being an | Almanack | . . . | . . . | . . . | . . . | . . . | . . . | . . . | . . . | . . . | . . . . | For the | Year of our Lord 1760: | Being Bissextile or Leap-Year. | . . . | . . . | . . . | . . . | . . . | . . . | . . . | . . . | . . . | . . . . | By Richard Saunders, Philom. | *Philadelphia :* | *Printed and Sold by B. Franklin, and D. Hall.* [1759.] | Sm. 8vo. pp. (36). H. S. P.   1644

SMITH. (R.) A Wheel in the Middle of a Wheel: | Or, | The Harmony and Connexion of | the various Acts of Divine Providence. | A | Sermon | Delivered before the second Rev. Pres- | bytery of New-Castle, and their Correspon- | dents, met at White-Clay-Creek, January 2d, | 1759. | By Robert Smith, | Minister of the Gospel at Pequea. | Published at the Request of the Hearers. | *Philadelphia:* | *Printed by W. Dunlap, at the Newest- Printing-Office,* | MDCCLIX. | 8vo. pp. 57, 1 leaf.   c.   1645

The half title reads : Mr. Smith's Discourse | on Divine Providence. |

EJN | SPJEGEL der Eheleute | Nebst schönen Erinnerungen vor | Ledige Personen, | Welche willens sind, sich in den Stand der Ehe | zu begeben. | Wie auch | Etwas von den Ursachen, warum viele | Menschen aus einer Religion in die andere | übergehen. | Vorgestelt in einem Ge= spräch zwischen einem | Jüngling und Meister. | [*Germantown:*] *Gedruckt under der Presse* [*Christoph Saur.*] 1758. | 16mo. pp. 32.   1646

THOMAS. (T.) The Pennsylvania | Almanac. | Or | Ephemeris, | Of the daily Motions of the Sun and Moon, | For 1760: Being Leap-Year. | Wherein is contained, | The Rising and Setting of the Sun; the Rising, Setting, | and Southing of the Moon;

the Lunations, Conjunctions, | Eclipses, Rising, Setting, and Southing of the Planets; | Length of Days; Judgment of the Weather; Festivals, | and other remarkable Days; High Water at Philadelphia; | Quakers Yearly Meetings, Fairs, Courts, Roads, &c. | Fitted to the Latitude of Forty Degrees North, and a | Meridian of near five Hours West from London, and may | without sensible Error, serve all the Northern Colonies. | By Thomas Thomas, Philomat. | . . . | . . . | . . . | . . . . | *Philadelphia: | Printed by W. Dunlap, for the Author.* [1759.] | Sm. 8vo. pp. (32). 　　　　　　　　　　　　　　　　H. S. P. 1647

TOBLER. (J.) [Cut.] | The Pennsylvania | Town and Country-Man's Almanack, | For the Year of our Lord 1760. | Being the third after Leap-Year. | . . . . | By John Tobler, Esq; | *Germantown: printed and sold by C. Sower jun.* | . . . | . . . | . . . . [1759.] | Sm. 8vo. pp. (40). 　　　　　　　　　　　　H. S. P. 1648

A | TRUE and Impartial State | Of the Province of | Pennsylvania. | Containing, | An exact Account of the Nature of its Government; the Power | of the Proprietaries, and their Governors; as well those | which they derive under the Royal Grant, as those they have | assumed in manifest Violation thereof, their Father's Char- | ter, and the Rights of the People: Also, the Rights and | Privileges of the Assembly, and People, which they claim | under the said Grant, Charter, and Laws of their Country, | confirmed by the Royal Approbation. | With a true Narrative of the Dispute between the Governors | and Assemblies, respecting the Grants of Supplies so often | made by the Latter, and rejected by the Former. In which | is demonstrated, by incontestable Vouchers, that arbitrary | Proprietary Instructions, have been the true and only Cause | of the Refusal of such Supplies, and the late defenceless State | of the Province. | The whole being a full Answer to the Pamphlets intitled A | Brief State, and A Brief View, &c. of the | Conduct of Pennsylvania. | . . . | . . . | . . . | . . . | . . . | . . . | . . . | . . . | . . . | . . . . | *Philadelphia: | Printed by W. Dunlap, at the Newest-Printing- | Office,* M,DCC,LIX. | 8vo. Title, 1 leaf; Dedication, pp. i-v; text, pp. 1–173; Appendix, pp. 1–34; Advertisement, 1 leaf. 　　　　　H. S. P. 1649

This tract was probably inspired, if not wholly written by Franklin. Dr. William Smith is known to have been the author of "A Brief State, and A Brief View, &c. of the Conduct of Pennsylvania." In the list of his published works, appended to his "Life, &c.," by Horace W. Smith, he is said to have been the author of this reply to his two former publications. Dr. Smith's relations with the Assembly just at that time renders any such claim ridiculous. The Assembly would hardly have rewarded him for procuring an order from the "King in Council," annuling some of their resolves with a request to act as their apologist.

VOTES | and | Proceedings | of the | House of Representatives | of the | Province of Pennsylvania, | Met at Philadelphia, on the Fourteenth of October, Anno | Domini 1758, and continued by Adjournments. | [*Penn Arms.*] | *Philadelphia:* | *Printed and Sold by B. Franklin, at the New-Printing-Office,* | *near the Market.* MDCCLIX. | Folio, pp. 111, (1).   H. S. P.   1650

WAGNER. (M. T.) 𝔐. 𝔗𝔬𝔟𝔦𝔞𝔰 𝔚𝔞𝔤𝔫𝔢𝔯'𝔰 𝔄𝔟𝔰𝔠𝔥𝔦𝔢𝔟𝔰=𝔑𝔢𝔟𝔢 𝔞𝔫 𝔰𝔢𝔦𝔫𝔢 𝔏𝔲𝔱𝔥𝔢𝔯𝔦𝔰𝔠𝔥𝔢 𝔊𝔢𝔪𝔢𝔦𝔫𝔟𝔢𝔫 𝔦𝔫 𝔓𝔢𝔫𝔫𝔰𝔶𝔩𝔳𝔞𝔫𝔦𝔢𝔫, 𝔴𝔢𝔩𝔠𝔥𝔢 𝔢𝔯 𝔷𝔲 𝔲𝔫𝔱𝔢𝔯𝔰𝔠𝔥𝔦𝔢𝔟= 𝔩𝔦𝔠𝔥𝔢𝔫 𝔷𝔢𝔦𝔱𝔢𝔫 𝔞𝔩𝔰 𝔓𝔯𝔢𝔟𝔦𝔤𝔢𝔯 𝔞𝔩𝔩𝔢 14 𝔗𝔞𝔤𝔢 𝔬𝔟𝔢𝔯 4 𝔚𝔬𝔠𝔥𝔢𝔫 𝔟𝔢𝔟𝔦𝔢𝔫𝔱. *Ephratæ Typis Societatis.* pp. 9.   1651

WEATHERWISE. (A.) Father Abraham's Almanac, | (On an entire New Plan.) | For the Year of our Lord, 1760. | [33 lines.] | By Abraham Weatherwise, Gent. | *Philadelphia: Printed by W. Dunlap, at the Newest-* | *Printing-Office, on the South Side of the Jersey-Market.* [1759.] | Sm. 8vo. pp. (40).   H. S. P.   1652

WEBB. ([THOMAS]) A | Military Treatise | on the | Appointments of the Army. | Containing | Many useful Hints, not touched | upon before by any Author: | And | Proposing some new Regulations in | the Army, which will be particularly useful in | carrying on the War in North-America. | Together with a | Short Treatise on Military Honors. | By Lieutenant Webb, of His | Majesty's Forty-eighth Regiment, | . . . . | *Philadelphia: Printed by W. Dunlap, at the Newest-Printing-Office,* | MDCCLIX. | Sm. 8vo. pp. xiii, iii, 2 folded plates.   1653

There is a Second title at page 91, as follows: A | Treatise | on | Military Honors. | By Lieutenant Webb. | . . . . | *Philadelphia:* | *Printed by W. Dunlap.* The Author, who lost an eye at the siege of Quebec, is better known as one of the earliest Methodist preachers in America, than as a soldier or writer on Military subjects.

1760.

AN ACCOUNT of the Births and Bu- | rials in Christ-Church Parish, in Philadelphia, | from December 24, 1759, to December 24, 1760. | By Caleb Cash, Clerk, and Samuel Kirke, Sexton | to the Seventh of August last, now William Sheed, | Sexton. | [n. p. n. d.] Folio, 1 leaf.　　　　　　　　　　　　　　 L. C. P. 1654

AGUECHEEK. (A.) The | Universal American, | Almanack, | Or, Yearly | Astronomical, Historical and Geographical | Magazine. | . . . | . . . | . . . . | For the Year of Our Lord 1761 ; | [22 lines.] By Andrew Aguecheek, Philom. | *Philadelphia:* | *Printed by W. Bradford, at the London-Coffee-House,* | *And A. Steuart, at the Bible-in-Heart, the Corner* | *of Black-Horse-Alley, in Second-Street.* [1760.] | Sm. 8vo. pp. (40).　　　　　　　　　　　　　　 H. S. P. 1655

ANNO Regni | Georgii II. | Regis, | Magnæ Britanniæ, Franciæ & Hiberniæ, | Tricesimo Tertio. | At a General Assembly of the Province of Penn- | sylvania, begun and holden at Philadelphia, | the Fifteenth Day of October, Anno Domini 1759, in | the Thirty-third Year of the Reign of our Sovereign | Lord George II. by the Grace of God, of | Great-Britain, France and Ireland, King, Defender of | the Faith, &c. | And from thence continued by Adjournments to the | Eleventh Day of February, 1760. | [*Penn Arms.*] | *Philadelphia:* | *Printed and Sold by B. Franklin, at the New-* | *Printing-Office, near the Market.* MDCCLX. | Folio, pp. 45.　　　　　　　　　　　　　　 H. S. P. 1656

BAPTISM. A tract against Water-Baptism. *Philadelphia:* ? 1760.　　　　　　　　　　　　　　　　　　　　　　　1657

See No. 1725, *infra.*

[BENEZET. (ANTHONY)] Observations | On the Inslaving, importing and purchasing of | Negroes ; | With some Advice thereon, extracted from the | Epistle of the Yearly-Meeting of the People called | Quakers, held at London in the Year 1748. | . . . | . . . | . . . | . . . | . . . | . . . | . . . | . . . . | Second Edition. | *Germantown:* | *Printed by Christopher Sower.* 1760. | 16mo. pp. 16.　　　　　　　　　　　　　　 H. S. P. 1658

Contains also "The Uncertainty of a Death-Bed Repentance."

DJESE NEUE | BUECHER und Waaren | sind bey | Christoph Lochner, | Buchdrucker und Handelsmann, von Basel kommend, | Um einen billigen Preis bey der Quantität oder Einzehn zubekommen, | In seinem Laden, bey Mr. Dietrick, Tobackspinner in der | Zweiten-Strasse, zu Philadelphia. | [n. p. n. d.] Folio, pp. (2).   1659

CATALOGUE | of | Books. | Just Imported from | London, | And to be Sold by | W. Bradford, | At the London-Coffee-House, | Philadelphia. | Wholesale and Retaile. | With good Allowance to those | that take a Quantity. | [*Philadelphia: William Bradford.* 1760.?] 8vo. pp. 16.   H. S. P.   1660

CATALOGUE of Books to be sold at Auction, by William Dunlap. *Philadelphia: William Dunlap.* 1760.   1661

CATALOGUS | Bibliothecæ Loganianæ: | Being | A choice Collection of Books, | as well in the Oriental, Greek and | Latin, as in the English, Italian, | Spanish, French and other Lan- | guages. | Given by the late | James Logan Esq; | Of Philadelphia for the Use of the Publick. | Numbered as they now stand in the | Library ; | Built by him, in Sixth-street, over against the | State-house Square. | *Philadelphia, Printed by Peter Miller & Comp.* | *in the Year* 1760. | 8vo. pp. (2), 116.   H. S. P.   1662

THE | SHORTER CATECHISM. | Presented by the | Assembly of Divines | at Westminster, | to both | Houses of Parliament, | and | by them approved. | Containing | The Principles of the Christian | Religion. | With | Scripture Proofs. | *Philadelphia:* | *Printed by William Bradford, at* | *the Corner of Front and Market-Streets,* 1760. | Sm. 8vo. pp. 48.   H. S. P.   1663

CERTAIN | Agreements | and | Concessions, | Made concluded and agreed on by and between the | Contributors to a Sum of Money for erecting and | establishing a School House and School in Ger- | mantown, this twenty fifth Day of January | in the Year of our Lord one thousand Seven | Hundred and Sixty. [*German-town: Christopher Sower.* 1760.] 4to. pp. 8.   L. C. P.   1664

A | COLLECTION | of the | Laws | of the | Province of Penn-syl- | vania, now in Force. | Vol. II. | *Philadelphia,* | *By P. Miller and Company at the German-Print-* | *ing Officein Race-Street,* MDCC-LX. | 16mo. Title, 1 leaf; Index, pp. xii; text, 464.   1665

A DECLARATION | of what God has done | for our Souls. | By some Baptist People, called Quakers, | in New-London County, in Con- | necticut Colony. | March 25, 1760. | [n. p. n. d.] Sm. 8vo. pp. 4.   L. C. P. 1666

DELL. (W.) Christ's Spirit, | a | Christian's Strength. | Or, | A Plain Discovery of the Mighty and | Invincible Power, that all Believers | receive through the Gift of the | Spirit. | First held forth in Two Sermons, on Acts | I. viii. and after Published for the Instruction | and Use of those that are Spiritual, Anno | MDCXLV. | By William Dell, Minister of the Gospel of Jesus | Christ; at Yelden in the County of Bedford. | . . . | . . . | . . . | . . . | . . . . | *Germantown.* | *Printed by Christopher Sower.* 1760. | H. S. P. 1667

Collation : Title, 1 leaf; Christ's Spirit, pp. 75–121 ; The Stumbling Stone, by W. Dell, pp. 122–168. Printed with Hartley's Discourse on Mistakes concerning Religion, 1759, the paging and signatures being continuous.

DELL. The | Trial | of | Spirits, | Both in | Teachers and Hearers. | Wherein is held forth | The clear Discovery, and certain Down- | fal, of the Carnal and Anti-Christian | Clergy of these Nations. | Testified from the Word of God, to the | University Congregations in Cambridge. | By William Dell, Minister of the | Gospel, and Master of Gonvil and Caius College, in | Cambridge. | *London:* | *First printed in the Year* 1666. | *Philadelphia:* | *Re-printed by* | *B. Franklin, and D. Hall.* MDCCLX. | 8vo. pp. 55.

AN EPISTLE from the Yearly Meeting. *Philadelphia.* 1760.

EVANGELIA | und | Episteln. | Auf alle Sonntage, | wie auch | Auf die hohe Feste, | Andere Feyer= und Apostel Tage | durchs gantze Jahr. | Hiebevor | Aufs neue eingerichtet, und mit Fleiß | corrigiret ; | Nunmehro aber, auf vieler Verlangen, | Mit denen aus den Evangeliis gezogenen Kir= | chen Gebäten. | zur Beförderung des Gottesdienstes, |

Nebſt der Hiſtorie | Von der Zerſtöhrung der Stadt Jeruſalem | vermeh=
ret und verbeſſert. | *Germanton* | *Gedruckt und zu finden bey Christoph*
Saur. 1760. | 16mo. pp. 94. H. S. P. **1670**

FALGATE. (I.) The Dealer's Companion and Trader's Assistant, in a new Order. Containing, I. A New Set of Tables, for shewing the Value of any Number or Quantity of Goods or Wares, at
any Rate under Twenty Shillings per Yard, Stone, Ell, Pound,
Ounce, Gallon, Pint, &c. And of any Weight under half a Tun.
. . . Tables of Interest, . . . at 5 and 6 per Cent. By Israel Falgate. Concluding with a Perpetual Almanack. *Philadelphia :*
Andrew Steuart. 1760. **1671**

FENELON. (F. Salignac de la Mothe) The Uncertainty of
a | Death-Bed | Repentance, | Illustrated under the Character of
Penitens. | [*Germantown :* *Printed by Christopher Saur.* 1760.]
Sm. 8vo. pp. 16. L. C. P. **1672**

HERVEY. (J.) The Ministry of Reconciliation: Representing
the | benign tendency of the Gospel ; and that 'tis | the friendly
Office of Ministers, as the Embassa- | dors (or Agents) of Christ,
to press Men with | all imaginable Tenderness, Humility, and
Ear- | nestness to accept the Treaty of Reconcilia- | tion, as es-
tablished in Him, and urged by Him, | while on Earth. | A |
Sermon, | Preached at the Parish-Church of | All-Saints, in
Northampton. | By James Hervey, A. M. | Late Rector of Wes-
ton-Favell, in Northamptonshire. | . . . | . . . | . . . . | *Phila-*
delphia : | *Printed by W. Dunlap, in Market-Street.* | M,DCC,LX.
| 8vo. pp. 23. L. C. P. **1673**

DER | HOCH=DEUTSCH | Americaniſche | Calender, | Auf das
Jahr | . . . | . . . | 1761. | (Welches ein gemein Jahr von 365 Tagen
iſt) | . . . | . . . | . . . | . . . | . . . | . . . | . . . | . . . | . . . | . . . |
Zum Drey und zwantzigſten mal heraus gegeben. | *Germanton : Gedruckt*
bey Christoph Saur. | . . . | . . . . [1760.] | 4to. pp. (48). **1674**

HOECHSTMERKWUERDIGE | Prophezeyung | von wichtigen |
Kriegs=und Welthändeln: | In welcher vornemlich | von dem glorwürdigen
| Könige von Preuſſen | geweiſſagt wird. | Aus einer uralten Lateiniſchen

Handſchrift, ſo in einem berühm= | ten Europäiſchen Bücherſaale verwahrt wird. | Mit einem | Verſuch einer Erklärung. | *Philadelphia,* | *Gedruckt und zu haben bey Henrich Miller, in Second-striet,* | *im zweyten Hause auf der linken hand von Rees-striet,* | 1760. | Sm. 4to. pp. 8.   1675

AN INDUCEMENT to Right Thinking; Wherein is contained Many Turns, both diverting and instructing: In Prose and Verse. *Philadelphia: William Dunlap.* 1760.   1676

THE INSTRUCTOR: Or, Young Man's best Companion. *Philadelphia: Andrew Steuart.* 1760.   1677

[JACKSON. Richard] The | Interest | of | Great Britain | considered, | With Regard to her | Colonies, | And the Acquisitions of | Canada and Guadaloupe. | To which are added, | Observations concerning the Increase of Mankind, | Peopling of Countries, &c. | *London Printed:* | *Philadelphia Re-printed, and Sold by William* | *Bradford, at the London-Coffee-House.* | MDCC-LX. | 8vo. pp. 47.   H. S. P. 1678

Commonly attributed to Franklin when first published, but now known to have been written at his instance by Richard Jackson, who was assistant Agent of Pennsylvania. Chief Justice Edward Shippen, in a letter dated "Oct. 2, 1760," says, "I have seen B. Franklin's Pamphlet, and think it the best book that has been published in England concerning American Affairs. He appears to have thoroughly understood his subject and has done justice to the cause he espouses. Certainly we should be dupes to give up Canada."

[KEARSLEY. (John)] The Case of Mr. T.[homas] L.[awrence] with regard to the Method pursued | therein by J.[ohn] K.[earsley, Senior Surgeon, with the uncommon Treatment the | Said J. K. hath met with, in his Proceedure therein. | [*Philadelphia: William Dunlap.* 1760.] Folio, pp. 2.   L. C. P. 1679

KOFFLER. (J. F.) A | Letter | From a | Tradesman in Lancaster | to the | Merchants of the Cities of | Philadelphia, New- | York and Boston, re- | specting the Loan of Mo- | ney to the Government, with | some Remarks upon the | Consequence of the Re- | fusal by | John Frederick Koffler. | [*Philadelphia:*] *Printed [by Peter Miller & Co.?] in the Year* 1760. | 16mo. pp. (3), 14.   L. C. P. 1680

LAW. (W.) An | Extract | from a |Treatise|By William Law, M.A. | Called, | The Spirit of Prayer ; | Or, | The Soul rising out of the Vanity of | Time, into the Riches of Eternity. | Discovering the true Way of turning to God, | and of finding the Kingdom of Heaven | the Riches of Eternity in our Souls. | *Philadelphia:* | *Printed by B. Franklin, and D. Hall.* 1760. | 8vo, pp. 47.

A | LETTER | To the People of | Pennsylvania ; | Occasioned by the Assembly's passing | that Important Act, | for | Constituting the Judges | of the | Supream Courts and Common-Pleas | During Good Behaviour. | . . . | . . . | . . . | . . . | . . . . | *Philadelphia: Printed [by William Dunlap] in* MDCCLX. | 8vo. pp. 39. + The Second Edition. [*Ibid.*] pp. 39.   L. C. P.   1682

In the Brinley Catalogue the second edition is attributed to the press of Franklin and Hall. Both editions were advertised in the Pa. Gazette as published by W. Dunlap.

LOWRY. (J.) A | Journal | Of the Captivity of | Jean Lowry | and her | Children, | Giving an Account of her being taken by the | Indians, the 1st of April 1756, from | William Mc.Cord's, | In Rocky-Spring Settlement in | Pennsylvania, | With an Account of the Hardships she Suffered, &c. | *Philadelphia:* | *Printed by William Bradford, at* | *the Corner of Front and Market-Streets,* 1760. | 8vo. pp. 31.   L. C. P.   1683

Half the pamphlet, pp. 18–31, is taken up with "Disputes between the said Mrs. Lowry, and the French," on the subject of Religion.

[MACK. (ALEXANDER)] Eine | Anmuthige Erinnerung, zu einer | Christlichen Betrachtung, Von der Wunderbaren | Allgegenwart | des Allwissenden | Gottes. | [*Germantown: Christoph Saur.* 1760.] Sm. 8vo. pp. 7.   H. S. P.   1684

MARTIN. Copie eines Brief von Herr Martin. *Ephrata:* 1760.   1685

A MOST Remarkable | Prophecy, | concerning | Wars and Political Events ; | especially | The Glorious | King of Prussia. | Taken from an ancient Latin Manuscript said to | be deposited in the Bodleyan Library. | With | An Essay towards an Explanation. | [Cut.] | *Philadelphia,* | *Printed and Sold by Henry Miller, in Second-street, at the* | *second House on the left hand from Race-street.* | MDCCLX. | *Price Four-pence; or Three Shillings a Dozen.* | Sm. 4to. pp. 8.   L. C. P.   1686

Note 14 of the Explanation reads "Here it may be observed, that there is another more ancient Prophecy than this, which foretells, *That the* Electoral House of Brandenburg *shall one day attain to the Imperial Dignity.*"

A NARRATIVE of the Life, together with the last Speech, Confession and solemn Declaration of John Lewis; who was executed at Chester, on Saturday the 21st of September, 1760, for the most inhuman, barbarous and bloody Murder of his Wife; . . . . With his Letter to Mr. Raine, . . . concerning the Publication of the said Narrative: And a Penitenial Prayer, which he composed just before his Execution. *Philadelphia: Andrew Steuart.* 1760.   1687

ℜℰ𝔘=𝔈ℑℜ𝔊𝔈ℜℑ𝔒𝔗𝔒ℜ 𝔄mericanifcher 𝔈alender, auf das ℑahr 1761. *Philadelphia: Anton Armbruester.* 1760.   1688

THE | NEW-YEAR | Verses, | Of the Printers Lads, who carry, | about the Pennsylvania Gazette to | the Customers. [*Philadelphia: B. Franklin, and D. Hall.* 1760.] Folio, 1 leaf. L. C. P.   1689

NEW-YEAR Verses of the Carriers of the Pennsylvania Journal. *Philadelphia: William Bradford.* 1760.   1690

OLD | Mr. Dod's | Sayings. | [*Philadelphia: Printed by William Bradford.* 1760.] Sm. 8vo. pp. 12.   L. C. P.   1691

THE PENNSYLVANIA Gazette.   H. S. P.   1692

Numbers 1619 (Jan. 3, 1760) to 1670 (Dec. 25, 1760), four pages each. Title and imprint as in No. 1232, *supra,* except in No. 1670, in which the arms, &c., are omitted.

THE PENNSYLVANIA Journal. *Philadelphia: Printed and Sold by William Bradford, at the Sign of the Bible, the Corner-House of Front and Market-* | *Streets, where Persons may be supplied with this Paper at Ten Shillings a Year,* | *And where Advertisements are taken in.* | H. S. P.   1693

Numbers 891 (Jan. 3, 1760) to 942 (Dec. 25, 1760), four pages each.

THE PENNSYLVANIA Pocket Almanac for 1761. *Philadelphia: William Bradford.* 1760.   1694

POPE. (ALEXANDER) An | Essay | on | Man. | By | Alexander Pope, Esq. | Enlarged and Improved by the Author. | With Notes | By William Warberton, M. A. | *London Printed:* | *Philadelphia Re-printed, and sold by W. Dunlap,* | *At the Newest-Printing-Office, in Market-Street,* | M,DCC,LX. | 8vo. pp. 68, 1 plate. L. C. P.

𝕯𝕰𝕽 𝕻𝕾𝕬𝕷𝕿𝕰𝕽 des Königs und Propheten Davids.   Zweite Auflage. *Germantown: Christoph Saur.* 1760.   1696

Title from Seidensticker's Bibliography.

𝕻𝕾𝕬𝕷𝕿𝕰𝕽𝕾𝕻𝕵𝕰𝕷 Das Kleine | Davidische | Psalterspiel | Der | Kinder Zions, | Von | Alten und Neuen auserlesenen | Geistes-Gesängen | Allen wahren Heyls-begieri= | gen Säuglingen der Weisheit, | Insonder= heit aber | Denen Gemeinden des Herrn, zum | Dienst und Gebrauch mit Fleiß zusammen= | getragen, | Und in gegenwärtig-beliebiger Form | und Ordnung, | Nebst einem doppelten darzu nützlichen und der | Materien halben nöthigen | Register, | ans Licht gegeben. | *Germanton gedruckt bey Christoph Saur,* 1760. | 12mo. pp. (6), 547, (23).   H. S. P. 1697

SAUNDERS. (R.)   A Pocket Almanac for 1761.   By Richard Saunders.   *Philadelphia: B. Franklin, and D. Hall.* 1760.   1698

SAUNDERS.   Poor Richard improved: | Being an | Almanack | . . . | . . . | . . . | . . . | . . . | . . . | . . . | . . . | . . . | . . . . | For the | Year of our Lord 1761: | Being the First after Leap-Year. | . . . | . . . | . . . | . . . | . . . | . . . | . . . | . . . | . . . | . . . . | By Richard Saunders, Philom. | *Philadelphia:* | *Printed and Sold by B. Franklin, and D. Hall.* [1760.] | Sm. 8vo. pp. (36).   H. S. P.

SMITH. (W.)   A | Discourse | Concerning the Conversion | of the | Heathen Americans, | and | The final Propagation of Christianity and | the Sciences to the Ends of the Earth. | In Two Parts. | Part I. Preached before a voluntary Conven- | tion of the Episcopal Clergy of Pennsylva- | nia, and Places adjacent, at Philadelphia, | May 2d, 1760; and published at their joint | Request. | Part II. Preached before the Trustees, Masters | and

Scholars of the College and Academy of | Philadelphia, at the
first anniversary Com- | mencement. | By William Smith, D. D.
| Provost of said College and Academy. | *Philadelphia: Printed
by W. Dunlap,* | MDCCLX. | 8vo. Title, 1 leaf; Preface, &c. pp.
i–iii; Sermons, pp. 1–53; Advertisement, pp. (2).   1700

TENNENT. (G.) A | Persuasive | to | The Right Use of the
Passions in Religion; | or, | The Nature of Religious Zeal Ex-
plain'd | its Excellency and Importance Open'd | and Urg'd, | In
a | Sermon, | On Revelations iii, 19. | Preached at Philadelphia,
January 27th, 1760. | By Gilbert Tennent, | Minister of the Gos-
pel of Christ. | . . . | . . . | . . . | . . . | . . . . | *Philadelphia:* |
Printed and Sold by W. Dunlap, M,DCC,LX. | 8vo. pp. 43, (1). c.

THOMAS. (T.) The Pennsylvania Almanac for 1761. By
Thomas Thomas. *Philadelphia: William Dunlap.* 1760.   1702

TOBLER. (J.) [Cut.] 1761. | The Pennsylvania | Town and
Country-Man's | Almanack | For . . . 1761. | . . . | . . . | By
John Tobler Esq; | *Germantown: printed and sold by C. Sower.*
. . . | . . . | . . . | . . . . [1760.] | 16mo. pp. (40). H. S. P. 1703

VIRO Praeclarissimo | Ingenuis artibus, atque humanitate
perpolito, | Thomae Boone Armigero, | Provinciae Novae-Caesa-
riae Gubernatori, . . . | . . . | Reverendo aeque ac honorando D,
Samueli Davies, Collegii Neo-Caesariensis Præsidi, | . . . | . . .
| . . . | . . . | . . . | . . . | . . . . | Haec philosophemata, quae
(Numine adjurante) sunt desendenda, | Juvenes primi gradus in
artibus Candidi, | . . . | Habita publicis comitiis in Aula-
Nassovica apud Princeton viiivo calendas Octobris, A. D.
MDCCLX. *Ex typis Andreae Steuart.* | Folio, 1 leaf. L. C. P. 1704

VOTES and Proceedings of the House of Representatives of the
Province of Pennsylvania. Met at Philadelphia on the Fourteenth of October Anno Domini 1759, and continued by Adjournments. *Philadelphia: B. Franklin.* 1760. Folio.   1705

WAREING. (ELIJAH) On the Death of | John Wagstaffe. |
An elegiac Poem. | *Philadelphia: Printed (at the Desire of many
Friends) by Andrew Steuart, in Second-street.* 1760. | Folio, 1
leaf.   H. S. P. 1706

WATTS. (I.)   The | Psalms | of | David, | Imitated in the Language of the | New-Testament, | And applied to the | Christian State and Worship. | By I. Watts, D. D. | . . . | . . . | . . . | . . . . | *Philadelphia:* | *Printed by W. Dunlap, at the Newest-* | *Printing-Office, on the South Side of the* | *Jersey-Market,* MDCC-LX. | 24mo. pp. viii, 308, (19).   H. S. P.   1707

WEATHERWISE. (A.) Father Abraham's Almanac for 1761. By Abraham Weatherwise. *Philadelphia: William Dunlap.* 1760.   1708

1761.

ABEL. (T.)   A Treatise of Substensial Plain Trigonometry, applied to Navigation and Surveying. By Thomas Abel. *Philadelphia: Andrew Steuart.* 1761.   1709

𝕬𝕭𝕲𝕰𝕱𝕺𝕽𝕯𝕰𝕽𝕿𝕰 | Relation | der Erſcheinung | eines entleibten Geiſts | Dem Publico zur Nachricht getreulich | aus dem Mund derer, die von An= | fang bis ans Ende mit intereſſirt, | aufgeſchrieben. | . . . | . . . | . . . . | *Ephratæ Typis & Consensu Societatis,* | *Anno Domini* MDCCLXI. | Sm. 8vo. pp. 39.   H. S. P.   1710

AN ACCOUNT of the Births and Bu- | rials in Christ-Church Parish, in Philadelphia, | from December 25, 1760, to December 25, 1761. | By Caleb Cash, Clerk, and William Davis, Sexton. | [n. p. n. d.]   Folio, 1 leaf.   L. C. P.   1711

AGUECHEEK. (A.) The Universal American Almanac for 1762. By Andrew Aguecheek. *Philadelphia: Andrew Steuart.* 1761.   1712

AMERICA in Tears: A Pastoral Elegy, on the Death of His Most Sacred Majesty King George the Second. *Philadelphia: Andrew Steuart.* 1761.   1713

ANNO Regni | Georgii III. | Regis, | Magnæ Britanniæ, Franciæ & Hiberniæ, | Primo. | At a General Assembly of the Province of Penn- | sylvania, begun and holden at Philadelphia, |

the Fourteenth Day of October; Anno Domini 1760, in | the Thirty-
fourth Year of the Reign of our late Sove- | reign Lord George
II. by the Grace of ·God, | of Great-Britain, France and Ireland,
King, Defender | of the Faith, &c. | And from thence continued by
Adjournments to the Four- | teenth Day of March, 1761, in the
First Year of the | Reign of our Sovereign Lord George III.
&c. | [*Penn Arms.*] | *Philadelphia:* | *Printed and Sold by B. Frank-
lin, at the New-* | *Printing-Office, near the Market.* MDCCLXI. |
Folio, Title, 1 leaf; pp. 49–98. + And from thence continued . . .
to the Twen- | ty-third Day of April, 1761, . . . | . . . . | [*Ibid.*]
Title, 1 leaf; pp. 101–103. + And from thence continued . . .
to the Twen- | ty-sixth Day of September, 1761, . . . | . . . . |
[*Ibid.*]   Title, 1 leaf; pp. 107–125.   H. S. P.   1714

BLAIR. (J.) A Sermon Delivered at the Forks of Brandy-
wine April 22, 1761. At the Ordination of the Reverend Mr.
John Carmichael, Published at the request of the Congregation.
By John Blair, A. M. Minister of the Gospel at Fogg's Manor.
Philadelphia: William Bradford. 1761.   1715

A BRIDLE for the Ass; being a Second Letter to the Congregations of the Eighteen Presbyterian (or New-Light Ministers) who
wrote the late Contradictory Letter to the Archbishop of Canterbury; with some Remarks on the two Performances that have
appeared in their Defence.   By an old Covenanting and true Presbyterian Layman.   *Philadelphia: Andrew Steuart.* 1761.   1716

CATALOGUE of Books for sale by James Rivington. *Philadelphia: James Rivington.* 1761.   1717

THE CHILD'S New Spelling Book.   *Wilmington: James
Adams.* 1761.   1718

COLMAN. (G.)   The Jealous Wife.   By George Colman.
Philadelphia: James Rivington. 1761.   1719

THE COMPLETE Letter-Writer.   *Philadelphia: James Rivington.* 1761.   1720

Advertised in the Pa. Journal, Jan. 15, 1761, but perhaps referring to an im-
ported work.

THE CONDUCT of the Eighteen Presbyterian Ministers set in a clear Light. *Philadelphia: Andrew Steuart.* 1761. 12mo. pp. 19.

CONTINUATION | of the | Account | of the | Pennsylvania Hospital; | From the First of May 1754, to the | Fifth of May 1761. | With an alphabetical List of the Contributors, | and of the Legacies which have been bequeathed, | for Pro- | motion and Support thereof, from its first Rise to that Time. | . . . | . . . | . . . | . . . | . . . | . . . | . . . | . . . | . . . | . . . | . . . | . . . | *Philadelphia: | Printed by B. Franklin, and D. Hall.* MDCCLXI. | 4to. Title, 1 leaf; pp. 41–77.   1722

See No. 1363, *supra.*

DAVIES. (S.)   A | Sermon | delivered at | Nassau-Hall, | January 14, 1761. | On the Death of | His Late Majesty | King George II. | By Samuel Davies, A. M. | Late President of the College of New-Jersey. | Published by Request. | To which is prefixed, | A brief Account of the Life, Character, and | Death, of the Author. | By David Bostwick, A. M. | Minister of the Presbyterian Congregation in New-York. | *New-York, Printed: | Philadelphia Reprinted and Sold by William | Bradford, at the London Coffee-House,* | MDCCLXI. | 8vo. Half title, 1 leaf; Title, 1 leaf; pp. i-ix, 1-18.

DAVIES. A Valedictory Address to the Candidates for the Degree of Bachelor of Arts, delivered in Nassau-Hall, September 21, 1760. The Sunday before the Commencement, by Samuel Davies, A. M. late President of the College, deceased. *Philadelphia: William Bradford.* 1761.   1724

DILWORTH. (W. H.)   Das Leben | und Heroische Thaten | Des Königs von Preußen, | Friedrichs des III. Von seiner Geburt an, bis zu Ende | des 1760sten Jahrs, zusamt denen merck- | würdigsten Kriegs-Vergebenheiten welche | sich im vorigen Krieg mit Ihm zugetra- | gen haben; und dann auch dessen, was | in diesem jetzigen Krieg vorgefallen, so | weit Er mit drein verwickelt ist. | Zuerst in Englischer Sprache herausgegeben durch | W. H. Dilworth 1758. und nun ins Deutsche | übersetzt und vermehrt. | *Germantown, | Gedruckt und zu haben bey Christoph Saur.* 1761. | 16mo. pp. 288.   1725

THE DOCTRINE of Water Baptism fairly stated, according to Scripture: Wherein all the Objections of the Quakers are fully refuted, and that Doctrine cleared from their Cavils. In two Sermons, on Matthew xxviii, 19. Being an Answer to a Pamphlet lately handed about, against Water-Baptism. *Philadelphia: Andrew Steuart.* 1761.   1726

DODD. (W.) Practical Discourses, on the Miracles and Parables of our blessed Lord and Saviour Jesus Christ. *Philadelphia: James Rivington.* 1761.   1727

ELLIS. (E.) The Advice of Evan Ellis, late of Chester County, deceased, to his Daughter when at Sea. *Wilmington: James Adams.* 1761.   1728

AN EPISTLE from the Yearly Meeting. *Philadelphia:* 1761.

AN ENQUIRY into the value of Canada and Guadaloupe; in Answer to a late Pamphlet (supposed to be written by Dr. Franklin, and) called, The Interest of Great Britain Considered, with Regard to her Colonies, and the Acquisitions of Canada and Guadaloupe. By a British Gentlemen. *Philadelphia:?* 1761.

Advertised in the Pa. Gazette, July 16, 1761, as "This Day is published. Sold by James Rivington."

FOX. (T.) The Wilmington Almanac for 1762. By Thomas Fox. *Wilmington: James Adams.* 1761.   1731

GIBBONS. (T.) Divine Conduct vindicated, or the Operations of | God shown to be the Operations of Wisdom: | In the Substance of Two | Discourses | preached at | Haberdashers-Hall, | London, March 29, 1761; | Occasioned by the Decease of | The Rev. Mr. Samuel Davies, M. A. | And President of the College of Nassau-Hall in New-Jersey, | February 4, 1761. | By Thomas Gibbons, M. A. | In which are contained | Some Memoirs of Mr. Davies, and | some Extracts from his Letters. | . . . | . . . | . . . | . . . | . . . | . . . | . . . | . . . | . . . . | *London:* | *Printed for Thomas Field, at the Wheatsheaf, at the Corner* | *of Pater-noster Row, Cheapside:* | *And Sold by William Dunlap, at the Newert Printing-* | *Office, in Philadelphia.* 1761. | 8vo. pp. 31, (1). c. 1732

Advertised in the Pa. Gazette, Oct. 29, 1761, as "Just published by W. Dunlap."

GUYSE. (J.)   A Practical Exposition of the New-Testament in the Form of a Paraphrase; with occasional Notes in their Proper Places for further Explication and serious Recollections, at the close of each Chapter.   By Dr. John Guyse.   *Philadelphia: James Rivington.*   1761.   1733

HABERMANN. (J.)   Johann Habermann von Eger, weiland Prediger und Superintendenten in Zeitz, kleines Christlich Gebätbuch. *Germanton.   Gedruckt bey Christoph Saur.*   1761.   1734

Title from Seidensticker's Bibliography.

DER | HOCH=DEUTSCH | Americanische | Calender, | Auf das Jahr | . . . | . . . | 1762. | . . . | . . . | . . . | . . . | . . . | . . . | . . . | . . . | . . . | . . . | . . . . | Zum vier und zwanzigsten mal heraus gegeben. | *Germantown: Gedruckt und zu finden bey Christoph Saur.* | . . . | . . . . [1761.] | 4to. pp. (48).   H. S. P.   1735

HOPKINSON. (F.)   An | Exercise, | containing | A Dialogue and Ode | Sacred to the Memory of His late gracious Majesty, | George II. | Performed at the public Commencement in the College of | Philadelphia, May 23d, 1761. | The Ode written and set to Music | By Francis Hopkinson, Esq; M. A. in said College. | *Philadelphia:* | *Printed by W. Dunlap, in Market-Street,* MDCC-LXI. | Sm. 4to. pp. 8.   H. S. P.   1736

[HUSBANDS. (HERMAN)]   Some | Remarks | on | Religion, | With the Author's Experience in Pursuit thereof. | For the Consideration of all People; | Being the real Truth of what happened. | Simply delivered, without the Help of School-Words, or Dress | of Learning. | *Philadelphia:* | *Printed by William Bradford, for the Author.* | M,DCC,LXI. | 8vo. pp. 38.   L. C. P.   1737

The copy in the Philadalphia Library has the author's name noted on the title page in the handwriting of Du Simitiere. At the end of the tract it is said to have been " Written about the Year 1750."

JOHNSON. (J.)   The Advantages and Disadvantages of the Marriage State, as entered into with religious or irreligous Per-

sons; represented under the Similitude of a Dream. By the
Reverend Mr. John Johnson. The Sixth Edition. *Philadelphia:
Andrew Steuart.* 1761.   1738

DES | LANDMANNS ADVOCAT. | Das ist: | Kurzer Auszug |
aus solchen | Gesetzen von Pennsylvania und England, | welche daselbst
in völliger Kraft, und einem freyen Einwohner | auf dem Lande höchst
nöthig und nützlich zu wissen sind. | Enthaltend | Anweisungen, | Welcher-
gestalt der Landmann als ein Geschworener bey | Verhören und Rechts-
sprüchen, oder Juryman; als ein | Testaments vollzieher, oder Executor;
als ein Vormund, oder Guardian; als ein Friedenhalter, oder Constable;
| als ein Armenpfleger, oder Overseer of the Poor, u. s. w. sich zu be-
tragen hat. | Nebst viel andern Dingen, durch deren Wissenschaft der ge-
meine Mann seinen | schaden verhüten und seinen Nutzen befördern kan. |
Aus den Acten der Landsversammlung, oder Acts of | Assembly, und
andern bewährtesten Englischen Büchern | zusammen getragen | von einem
| Rechtsgelehrten: | Und zum Besten der hiesigen Deutschen, in ihre Mut-
tersprache übersetzt. | *Philadelphia, Gedruckt bey Henrich Miller, in
der Zwey-* | *ten-strasse, fuer den Verfasser.* 1761. | Sq. 8vo.

Collation: Title, 1 leaf; Dedication, pp. (2); Preface, pp. viii; text, 170, 1
folded leaf; Index, pp. (3); Corrigenda, 1 leaf.

LATIMER. (H.) Sermons. By the Right Reverend Master
Hugh Latimer, Bishop of Winchester. *Philadelphia: James
Rivington.* 1761.   1740

LETTER of a Farmer in answer to The Conduct of the
Eighteen Presbyterian Ministers set in a clear Light. *Philadelphia:* 1761.   1741

Title from Haven's List.

LOTTERY. Pettey's Island | Lottery, | For Effects to the full
Value of 10,000 Dollars, or £ 3750, | Without any Deduction. |
[*Philadelphia: W. Dunlap.* 1761.] Folio, 1 leaf. L. C. P. 1742

LYON. (J.) Urania, | or | A Choice Collection of Psalm-
Tunes, Anthems, and Hymns, | From the most approv'd Authors,
with some Entirely New; | in Two, Three, and Four, parts |
The whole Peculiarly adapted to the Use of | Churches, and

Private Families. | To which are Prefix'd | The Plainest & most Necessary Rules of Psalmody. | By James Lyon, A. B. | [*Phila-delphia:* 1761.] Oblong 8vo. H. S. P. 1743

Collation : Engraved title, 1 leaf; Dedication, pp. 2; Index, 1 leaf; Sub-scribers, pp. (3); Rules, &c. pp. i–xii, tunes, pp. 1–198. Title, rules and tunes engraved on copper by Henry Dawkins. "This book was much larger than any previous work that had been published in the colonies. Report says that it ruined the publisher."—*Hood's History of Music,* 159.

LYTTELTON. (G.) Observations | on the | Conversion | and | Apostleship | of | St. Paul, | By the Honourable | George Lyt-tleton, Esq ; | Member of Parliament, and one of the Com- | mis-sioners of the Treasury. | In a | Letter to Gilbert West, Esq ; | *London, Printed :* | *Philadelphia, Reprinted by Henry Miller,* | *in Second-street, next to the corner of Race-street.* | MDCCLXI. | Sm. 8vo. pp. 79. L. C. P. 1744

THE | MECHANICK'S | Address | to the | Farmer : | Being a short Reply to some of | the Layman's Remarks on the | Eighteen Presbyterian Ministers | Letter to the Arch-bishop. | *Philadelphia :* | *Printed by Andrew Steuart, at the* | *Bible-in-Heart, in Second-street.* 1761. | Sm. 8vo. pp. 14. L. C. P. 1745

THE MERCHANTS and Trader's Security. *Wilmington : James Adams.* 1761. 1746

MILTON. (A.) The Farmer's Companion ; instructing how to run Land without a Compass, and to plat the same in an easy Manner. Also a Supplement thereto, directing how any Person may tell the Time of Day by a Walking Stick, or a Piece of Board, and thereby set off any Course of the Compass. By Abraham Milton, of Kent County, Maryland. *Philadelphia : Andrew Steuart.* 1761. 1747

MINUTES | of | Conferences, | held at | Easton, | In August, 1761. | With the Chief Saschems and Warriors of the | Onondagoes, Cayugas, | Oneidas, Nanticokes, | Mohickons, Delawares, | Tutel-oes, Conoys. | [*Penn Arms.*] | *Philadelphia :* | *Printed and Sold by B. Franklin, and D. Hall, at the* | *New-Printing-Office, near the Market.* MDCCLXI. | Folio, pp. 18. L. C. P. 1748

THE MIRACULOUS Power of Clothes and Dignity of the Taylors. Being an Essay on the Words, Clothes make Men. A Satire Translated from the German. *Philadelphia: Printed and Sold by Henry Miller.* 1761. 1749

DIE NATURALISATIONSFORM derjenigen, welche ohne Eid mit dem Quäkerattest naturalisirt werden. *Germantown: Christoph Saur.* 1761. 1750

Title from Seidensticker's Bibliography.

NEU-EINGERICHTETER Americanischer Calender, auf das Jahr 1762. *Philadelphia: Anton Armbruester.* 1761. 1751

DAS NEUE | Testament | Unsers | Herrn und Heylandes | Jesu Christi, | Verteutscht | Von | D. Martin Luther. | Mit | Jedes Capitels kurtzen | Summarien. | Auch beygefügten vielen richtigen | Parallelen. | *Germanton.* | *Gedruckt und zu finden bey Christoph Saur*, 1761. | 12mo. pp. (4), 562, (4). H. S. P. 1752

A NEW List of the Army in North-America, with the Rank of the Officers in the Regiment and Army, carefully corrected to April 1761. *Philadelphia: James Rivington.* 1761. 1753

NEW-YEAR Verses of the Carriers of the Pennsylvania Gazette. *Philadelphia: B. Franklin and D. Hall.* 1761. 1754

NEW-YEAR Verses of the Carriers of the Pennsylvania Journal. *Philadelphia: William Bradford.* 1761. 1755

AN ODE on the Prospect of Peace. *Philadelphia: Henry Miller.* 1761. 1756

THE PENNSYLVANIA Gazette. H. S. P. 1757

Numbers 1671 (Jan. 1, 1761) to 1723 (Dec. 31, 1761), four pages each, with extras of two pages each to Numbers 1671–74, 1676–81, 1684, 1686–90, 1692–95, and 1697–1723; "Supplements" of 4 pages to Numbers 1682, 1691, and 1696, and one of two pages to No. 1685. No. 1687 is misnumbered 1689.

THE PENNSYLVANIA Journal. H. S. P. 1758

Numbers 943 (Jan. 1, 1761) to 995 (Dec. 31, 1761), four pages each, with a "Supplement" of two pages to No. 965. Title and imprint as in No. 1693, *supra.*

THE | PENNSYLVANIA | Pocket Almanack, | For the Year 1762. | Calculated for the Use of the Province | of Pennsylvania, and the neighbour- | ing Provinces. | *Philadelphia:* | *Printed and Sold by W. Bradford,* | *at the London Coffee-House.* [1761.] | 24mo. pp. (24).   1759

PROCLAMATION. G. [*Royal Arms.*] R. | By the Honourable | James Hamilton, Esq; | Lieutenant-Governor, and Commander in Chief of the Province of Pennsylvania, and | the Counties of New-Castle, Kent and Sussex, on Delaware, | A Proclamation. | *Philadelphia: Printed by B. Franklin, and D. Hall.* [1761.] | Folio, 1 leaf.   H. S. P.   1760

Offering bounties to recruits for the Pennsylvania Regiments.

PROCLAMATION. [*Royal Arms.*] | By the Honourable | James Hamilton, Esq; | Lieutenant-Governor and Commander in Chief of the Province of Pennsylvania, and | Counties of New-Castle, Kent and Sussex, on Delaware, | A Proclamation. | *Philadelphia: Printed by B. Franklin, and D. Hall.* 1761. | Folio, 1 leaf.

Against settlers entering upon lands not purchased from the Indians, on the Delaware River, dated Feb. 20, 1761.

READING No Preaching; or, a Letter to a Young Clergyman, from a Friend in London, concerning the unwarrantable Practice of Reading the Gospel, instead of Preaching it. *Philadelphia: Andrew Steuart.* 1761.   1762

SAUNDERS. (R.) A Pocket | Almanack | For the Year 1762. | Fitted to the Use of Penn- | sylvania, and the neighbour- | ing Provinces. | With several useful Additions. | By R. Saunders, Phil. | *Philadelphia:* | *Printed and sold by B. Franklin,* | *and D. Hall.* [1761.] | 24mo. pp. (24).   1763

SAUNDERS. Poor Richard improved: | Being an | Almanack | . . . | . . . | . . . | . . . | . . . | . . . | . . . | . . . | . . . | . . . . | For the | Year of our Lord 1762: | Being the Second after Leap-Year. | . . . | . . . | . . . | . . | . . . | . . . | . . . | . . . | . . . . | By Richard Saunders, Philom. | *Philadelphia:* | *Printed and Sold by B. Franklin, and D. Hall.* [1761.] | Sm. 8vo. pp. (36).   H. S. P.

A | SECOND Letter | To the Congregations of the | Eighteen Presbyterian (or New-Light) | Ministers, | Who wrote the late Contradictory Letter to the | Archbishop of Canterbury ; | With some Remarks on the | Two Performances | That have appeared in their Defence. | By an old Covenanting and true Presbyterian Laymen. | ... | .... | *Philadelphia:* | *Printed by Andrew Steuart, at the Bible-in-Heart in* | *Second-street:* 1761. | ... | ... | ... | .... | Sm. 8vo. pp. 32.   c. 1765

A | SHORT, Easy, | and | Comprehensive | Method | of | Prayer. | Translated from the German. | And published for a father Pro- | motion, Knowledge and Benefit | of Inward Prayer, | By a Lover of Internal Devotion. | *Philadelphia,* | *Printed by Henry Miller, in Second-street, next to the Corner of Race-street.* | MDCCLXI. | 12mo. pp. 36.   N. Y. H. S. 1766

SMITH. (W.) The Great Duty of Public Worship, and of erecting and setting apart proper Places for that Purpose. A Sermon, preached in St. Peter's Church, Philadelphia, on Friday, September 4th, 1761. Being the Day appointed for the First Performance of Divine Worship in the said Church. To which is prefixed, an Account of the whole Service used on that Occasion. By William Smith, D. D. Published at the Desire of the Church-Wardens and Vestry. *Philadelphia:* *W. Dunlap*, MDCC-LXI. 8vo. pp. x, 5–41.   1767

SMOLLET. (T.) A History of the War in America, Germany, and the East-Indies. By Tobias Smollet. A new Edition. Two Volumes. *Philadelphia: James Rivington.* 1761.   1768

STEINER. (J. C.) Schuldigſtes | Liebes= und Ehren= | Denkmahl, | Unſerm weyland | Allergnädigſten und Glorwürdigſten Könige | von Großbritanien | Georg dem Zweyten, | nach Seiner Majeſtät tödlichem Hinſchiede, | ſo erfolgt den 25ſten October 1760, | aufgerichtet | in der Hochdeutſch=Reformirten Gemeine zu Philadelphia, | nach Anleitung | des Bildes Moſes des Knechts des Herrn, | in einer | öffentlichen Trauerrede, über die Worte Deut. 34 : 5, 7, 8. | von Johann Conrad Steiner, | Reformirten Prediger zu Philadelphia, | den erſten Februar, 1761. |

Philadelphia, Gedruckt und zu finden bey Henrich Miller, in der Zweytenstrasse, im zweyten Hause auf der linken | hand von der Reesstrasse. [1761.] | Sq. 8vo. pp. 31.   H. S. P.   1769

STEUART. (A.)   The | Gentleman and Citizen's | Pocket Almanack, | By Andrew Steuart, Bookseller. | For the Year 1762. | Fitted to the use of Pennsylvania and | the neighbouring Provinces. | Containing | Many useful Lists and Tables, | not in any other Almanack printed | on the Continent. | *Philadelphia: | Printed by Andrew Steuart, at the | Bible-in-Heart, in Second-street.* [1761.] | 24mo. pp. (48).   1770

TENNENT. (G.)   A | Sermon | On 1 Chronicles xxix. 28. | Occasioned by the Death of | King George the Second, | Of happy Memory, who departed this Life on the 25th Day of | October, in the Year of our Lord, 1760, in the 77th Year of | his Age, and the 34th of his Reign, beloved and honored by his | Subjects, for his Eminent-Royal-Virtues. | Together, | With some brief Hints, of the amiable Character of His Majesty | King George the Third, | Now seated on the British Throne, and the auspicious Omens, that | attend his infant Reign. | Preached | At Philadelphia, January 25th, 1761, and published at the request | of the Audience. | By Gilbert Tennent, Minister of the Gospel of Christ. | . . . | . . . | . . . | . . . | . . . | . . . | . . . | . . . | . . . | . . . | . . . | . . . | . . . | . . . . | *Philadelphia: | Printed by W. Dunlap,* MDCCLXI. | 8vo. pp. 17   H. S. P.   1771

THOMAS. (T.)   The Pennsylvania Almanac for 1762. By Thomas Thomas.   *Philadelphia: William Dunlap.* 1761.   1772

TOBLER. (J.)   The Pennsylvania Town and Country-Man's Almanac for 1762.   *Germantown: Christopher Sower.*? 1761.

A TRUE Copy of a Genuine Letter, sent to the Archbishop of Canterbury by Eighteen Presbyterian Ministers in America; With some Remarks thereon, in another Letter to the Congregations of the said Ministers. By an old Covernanting and true Presbyterian Layman. *Philadelphia: Andrew Steuart.* 1761.

TRYON. (T.) Some Memoirs of the Life of Mr. Thomas Tryon, late of London, Merchant. Written by Himself. Together with some Rules and Orders, proper to be observed by all such as would train up and govern either Families or Servants in Cleanness, Temperance and Innocency. *Philadelphia: William Dunlap.* 1761.   1775

VIRIS Præcellentissimis, | Thomæ Penn ac Richardo Penn, Armigeris, | Provinciæ Pennsylvaniæ, nec non Comitatuum Novi Castelli, Cantii & Sussexiæ ad Fluvium Delaware, veris atque solis Proprietariis; | Viro dignissimo, Literis humanioribus ornatissimo | Jacobo Hamilton, Armigero, | Prædictæ Provinciæ et Comitatuum, Vice-Gubernatori præclarissimo, nec non hujus Collegii & Academiæ Philadelphiensis Curatori; | . . . | . . . | . . . | . . . | . . . . | Hæc Philosophemata sub Præfecti Moderamine (Deo opt. maxo favente) discutienda, | Juvenes in Artibus initiati, | . . . | . . . | . . . | . . . . | [*Philadelphia:*] *Ex Typis Gulielmi Dunlap.* | [1761.] Foli, 1 leaf.   H. S. P.   1776

VOTES | and | Proceedings | of the | House of Representatives | of the | Province of Pennsylvania, | Met at Philadelphia, on the Fourteenth of October, Anno | Domini 1760, and continued by Adjournments. | [*Penn Arms.*] | [*Philadelphia:*] | *Printed and Sold by B. Franklin, at the New-Printing-Office,* | *near the Market.* MDCCLXI. | Folio, pp. 80.   ·   H. S. P.   1777

WALKER. (—.) An Account of the Voyages and Cruises of Commodore Walker. *Philadelphia:* 1761.   1778

Title from Haven's List.

WEATHERWISE. (A.) Father Abraham's | Almanac, . . . | . . . | For the Year of our Lord. | 1762. [32 lines.] | By Abraham Weatherwise, Gent. | *Philadelphia: Printed by W. Dunlap, at the* | *Newest-Printing-Office, in Market-Street.* [1761.] | Sm. 8vo. pp. (36).   H. S. P.   1779

DAS | WUNDER | ohne Maßen: | Wie sich hat martern laßen | der Schöpfer fürs Geschöpf; | Und wie sich | der hochheilge Gott | für | Sünder und Rebellen | gegeben in den Tod. | Oder, | Die Leidens= und

Todesgeſchichte des | Herrn der Herrlichkeit. | Aus den vier Evangeliſten kürzlich zuſammen gezogen | von einem | Bekenner und Verehrer Jeſu des Gekreuzigten. | *Philadelphia,* | *Gedruckt und zu finden bey Henrich Miller,* | *in der Zweyten-strasse, im zweyten Hause auf der linken hand* | *von der Ecke der Rees-strasse.* | 1761. | 16mo. pp. 16.   1780

DIE | WUNDERTHAETIGE Kraft | der | Kleider, | und | Hohe Würde | der | Kleidermacher: | Vorgeſtellet, | nach Anleitung des Sprüch= worts: | Kleider machen Leute; | von einem | Bemerker der Denk= und Handelweiſe | der Menſchen. | *Philadelphia,* | *Gedruckt und zu fin- den bey Henrich Miller,* | *in der Zweyten-strasse, im zweyten Hause auf der linken hand* | *von der Ecke der Rees-strasse.* | 1761. | 16mo. pp. 16.   H. S. P.   1781

1762.

AN ACCOUNT of the Births and Bu- | rials in Christ-Church Parish, in Philadelphia, | from December 25, 1761, to Decem- ber 25, 1762. | By Caleb Cash, Clerk, and James Weyley, Sexton. | [n. p. n. d.] Folio, 1 leaf.   L. C. P.   1782

AGUECHEEK. (A.) The Universal American Almanac for 1763. By Andrew Aguecheek. *Philadelphia: Andrew Steuart.* 1762.   1783

ANNO Regni | Georgii III. | Regis, | Magnæ Britanniæ, Franciæ & Hiberniæ, | Secundo. | At a General Assembly of the Province of Penn- | sylvania, begun and holden at Philadelphia, | the Fourteenth Day of October, Anno Domini 1761, in | the First Year of the Reign of our Sovereign Lord | George III. by the Grace of God, of Great- | Britain, France and Ireland, King, Defender of the | Faith, &c. | And from thence continued by Adjournments to the Seven- | teenth Day of February, 1762. | [*Penn Arms.*] | *Philadelphia:* | *Printed and Sold by B. Franklin, at the New-* | *Printing-Office, near the Market.* MDCCLXII. | Folio, Title, 1 leaf; pp. 129–183. + And from thence continued . . . to the | Twenty-sixth Day of March, 1762. | [*Ibid.*] Title, 1 leaf; pp. 187–211. + And from thence continued . . . to the | Third Day of May, 1762. | [*Ibid.*] Title, 1 leaf; pp. 215–220.   H. S. P.

[BENEZET. (ANTHONY)] A Short | Account | Of that Part of | Africa, | Inhabited by the | Negroes; | With Respect to the Fertility of the Coun- | try; the good Disposition of many of the Na- | tives, and the Manner by which the Slave | Trade is carried on. | Extracted from several Authors, in order to shew | the Iniquity of that Trade, and the Falsity of the | Arguments usually advanced in its Vindication. | With a Quotation from George Wallis's System of | the Laws, &c. and a large Extract from a Pamphlet, | lately published in London, on the Subject of the Slave | Trade. | . . . | . . . | . . . | . . . | . . . | . . . | . . . . | *Philadelphia : | Printed in the Year* M,DCC,LXII. | 16mo. pp. 56.   N. Y. H. S.   1785

This is the first edition, and was probably printed by W. Dunlap, for James Rivington, who advertises it for sale in the Pa. Gazette, Feb. 11, 1762.

[BENEZET.] A Short | Account | Of that Part of | Africa, | Inhabited by the | Negroes. | With Respect to the Fertility of the Country ; | and good Disposition of many of the Natives, and | the Manner by which the Slave Trade | is carried on. | Extracted from divers Authors, in order to shew | the Iniquity of that Trade, and the Falsity of the Argu- | ments usually advanced in its Vindication. | With Quotations from the Writings of several Per- | sons of Note, viz. George Wallis, Francis Hutche- | son, and James Foster, and a large Extract from a Pam- | phlet, lately published in London, on the Subject of the | Slave Trade. | The Second Edition, with large Additions and Amendments. | . . . | . . . | . . . | . . . | . . . | . . . | . . . | . . . | . . . | . . . | . . . | . . . . | *Philadelphia: | Printed by W. Dunlap, in the Year* MDCC-LXII. | Sm. 8vo. pp. 80.   H. S. P.   1786

CAPTAIN O'Blunder. *Philadelphia: Andrew Steuart.* 1762.

THE LARGER CATECHISM agreed upon by the Assembly of Divines at Westminster. *Philadelphia: Andrew Steuart.* 1762.

THE SHORTER CATECHISM agreed upon by the Assembly of Divines at Westminster. *Philadelphia: Andrew Steuart.* 1762.

CATHARINE and Petruchio. A Tragedy. *Philadelphia: Andrew Steuart.* 1762.   1790

THE | CHARTERS | and | Acts of Assembly | of the | Province | of | Pennsylvania. | In Two Volumes. | Vol. I. | Containing the Charters of the said Province, and the City, | Boroughs and Towns thereof: The Titles of all the Laws of | the said Province, since its first Establishment down to the Year 1700 : | The Acts of the said Assembly from the Year 1700 to 1743, now | in Force; and the Royal Confirmations and Repeals of | the said Acts. | Compared with the Public Records. | [*Penn Arms.*] | *Philadelphia : | Printed by Peter Miller and Comp.* MDCCLXII. | Folio.   H. S. P.   1791

Collation : Title and authorization, pp. (2) ; Charters, etc., pp. 1–21 ; Acts to 1700, pp. 1–4 ; Acts 1700–1742, pp. 1–164. Vol. II., Title, 1 leaf; Titles, etc., pp. iii ; Acts to 1759, pp. 1–116. Appendix, Title, 1 leaf; text, 1–18 ; Index, 1–32
The titles to the second volume and appendix are as follows :
The | Charters | and | Acts of Assembly | of the | Province | of | Pennsylvania. | Vol. II. | Containing the Acts of Assembly of the said Province, from the | Year 1744 to 1759, now in Force : A Collection of all the Laws | that have been formerly in Force within this Province, for Regulating of Descents and Transferring the Property of Lands, but are since | expired, altered, or repealed : from the Establishment of the Province, down | to this present Time. | Compared with the Public Records. | Together with | An Index, referring to the Matters | contained in both the Volumes. | [*Penn Arms.*] | *Philadelphia,* | *Printed by Peter Miller and Comp.* MDCCLXII. |
An | Appendix | Containing such | Acts of Assembly, | As have been formerly in Force within this Province, | For Regulating of Descents, | And Transferring the Property of Lands, &c. | But since, expired, altered, or repealed. | [*Penn Arms.*] | *Philadelphia: | Printed by Peter Miller, and Comp.* M,DCC,LXII. |
Edited by Lewis Weiss, and Charles Brockden, but generally known as "big Peter Miller."

THE | CHARTERS | and | Acts of Assembly | of the | Province | of | Pennsylvania, | In Two Volumes. | Vol. I. | Containing the Charters of the said Pro- | vince, and the City, Boroughs and Towns | thereof: | The Titles of all the Laws of | the said Province, since its first Establishment | down to the Year 1700: The Acts of the said | Assembly from the Year 1700 to 1743, now | in Force; and the Royal Confirmations | and Repeals of the said Acts. | Compared with the Public Records. | *Philadelphia,* | *Printed by Peter Miller and Comp.* MDCCLXII. | 16mo. L. 1792

Collation : Title and authorization, pp. (2) ; text, pp. 1–653 ; Errata, 1 leaf ; Vol. II.   Title, 1 leaf ; text, pp. i–xii, 1–464 ; Appendix, Title, 1 leaf ; text, pp.

1–71 ; Index, pp. 127. The Titles to Vol. II, the Appendix and Index are as follows : The | Charters | and | Acts of Assembly | of the | Province | of | Pennsylvania. | Vol. II. | Containing the Acts of Assembly of | the said Province from the Year 1744 to 1759, | now in Force : A Collection of all the | Laws that have been formerly in Force within | this Province for Regulating of Descents and Transferring the Property of Lands, but | are since expired, altered, or repealed : from the | Establishment of the Province down to the present | Time. | Compared with the Public Records. | Together with | An Index, referring to the Matters | contained in both the Volumes. | *Philadelphia,* | *Printed by Peter Miller and Comp.* MDCCLXII. |

An | Appendix. | Containing such | Acts of Assembly, | As have been formerly in Force | within this Province, | For Regulating of Descents, | And Transferring the Property of | Lands, &c. | But since expired, altered or repealed. | *Philadelphia :* | *Printed by P. Miller and Comp.* M, DCC, LXII. |

An | Abridgment | of the | Laws of Pennsylvania, | In Manner of an | Index. | *Philadelphia.* | *Printed by Peter Miller, and Company.* | MDCCLXII. |

THE CONTRIVANCES. A Comedy. *Philadelphia: Andrew Steuart.* 1762.   1793

THE | COUNTRYMAN'S | Lamentation, | On the Neglect of | A Proper Education | of | Children ; | With an Address to the Inhabitants | of | New-Jersey. | . . . | . . . | . . . | . . . | . . . . | *Philadelphia :* | *Printed and Sold by W. Dunlap, for the* | *Author,* MDCCLXII. | 8vo. pp. 52.   L. C. P.   1794

CRISP. (S.) Two | Letters | written by | Samuel Crisp, | About the Year 1702, | To some of his Acquaintance, upon his | Change from a Chaplain of the Church | of England, to join the People called | Quakers. | . . . . | *Philadelphia :* | *Printed by and for Andrew Steuart, at the Bible-* | *in-Heart, in Second-street, near Black-Horse-Alley.* | *Price 4 d. single, or 2 s. 6 d. a Dozen, to such as buy to sell* | *again, or give away.* | *Sold also by Samuel Garwood, in the Jersies.* | 16mo. pp. 16.   H. S. P.   1795

THE CYDER-MAKER'S Instructor. *Philadelphia: Andrew Steuart.* 1762.   1796

DAILY Conversation with God : | Exemplify'd in the | Holy Life | of | Armelle Nicholas, | A poor ignorant Country Maid in France, com- | monly known by the Name of Good Armelle ; |

who departed this Life, at Bretaigne, in the | Year 1671. | Translated from the French. | . . . | . . . | . . . | . . . | . . . | . . . | . . . | . . . | . . . | . . . | . . . . | Wilmington, | Printed by James Adams, in Market-street, 1762. | Sm. 8vo. pp. 16.   H. S. P.   1797

THE DOUBLE Disappointment; or, the Humours of Phelim O'Blunderoo, Esq; A New Farce. Philadelphia: Andrew Steuart. 1762.   1798

EDGAR and Emmerline. A Tragedy. Philadelphia: Andrew Steuart. 1762.   1799

ELLWOOD. (T.) Davideis. The life of David, King of Israel; A Sacred Poem, in five Books. By Thomas Ellwood. Philadelphia: B. Franklin and D. Hall. 1762.   1800

ES ift noch recht am End. Ephrata : 1762.   1801

[EVANS. (NATHANIEL)] Ode, | On the late | Glorious Successes | Of his | Majesty's Arms, | And present Greatness | Of the English Nation. | Philadelphia: | Printed and Sold by William Dunlap, M,DCC,LXII. | Sq. 8vo. pp. 14.   L. C. P.   1802

FOX. (T.) The Wilmington Almanac for 1763. By Thomas Fox. Wilmington: James Adams. 1762.   1803

[FRANTZ. (AUGUST HERMAN)] Der heilige und ſichere Glaubens= weg eines Evangeliſchen Chriſten. The holy and sure way of Faith of an evangelical Christian. Philadelphia. H. Miller. 1762.

Title from Seidensticker's Bibliography. Printed in English and German.

GEISTLICHER Irrgarten, mit Vier Gnadenbrunnen: | Philadelphia, gedruckt bey Henrich Miller, im Jahr nach der Erloesung aus dem Irrgarten und Eroeffnung der Himmelsthor 1762. | Folio, 1 leaf.

GERMAN Newspaper. Philadelphia: Anthony Armbruster. 1762.   1806

"All Gentlemen and others that will favor me with their Advertisements (as I publish a German Paper every week on Friday) shall be reasonably served. Anthony Armbruster."—Pa. Gazette, Sept. 9, 1762.

GESSNER. (S.) The Death of Abel. In Five Books. By Solomon Gessner. *Philadelphia: William Bradford.* 1762. 1807

GODFREY. (T.) The | Court of Fancy; | A | Poem. | By Thomas Godfrey. | . . . | . . . | . . . | . . . | *Philadelphia:* | *Printed and Sold by William Dunlap,* M,DCC,LXII. | Sm. 4to. pp. 24. L. C. P. 1808

HABERMANN. (J.) Johann Habermanns Gebät=Buch. [Diese Ausgabe ist in größerer Schrift.] *Germantown. Gedruckt und zu finden bey Christoph Saur.* 1762. 1809

Title from Seidensticker's Bibliography.

HALL. ([Joseph ?]) The Christian: Laid forth in his whole Disposition and Carriage. And a short Catechism. By Bishop Hall. *Philadelphia: Andrew Steuart.* 1762. 1810

HISTORICAL Memorial of the Negociations of France and England from the 26th of March, 1761, to the 20th of September, of the same year, with the vouchers. Translated from the French. *Philadelphia:* 1761. 1811

Title from Haven's List.

DER | HOCH=DEUTSCH | Americanische | Calender, | Auf das Jahr | . . . | . . . . | 1763 | . . . | . . . | . . . | . . . | . . . | . . . | . . . | . . . | . . . | . . . | . . . | . . . . | Zum Fünff und zwanzigsten mal heraus gegeben. | *Germantown: Gedruckt und zu finden bey Christoph Saur.* | . . . | . . . . [1762.] | 4to. pp. (48). H. S. P. 1812

[HOPKINSON. (Francis)] An | Exercise, | Containing | A Dialogue and Ode | On the Accession of His present gracious Majesty, | George III. | Performed at the public Commencement in the College of | Philadelphia, May 18th, 1762. | *Philadelphia:* | *Printed by W. Dunlap, in Market-Street,* M,DCC,LXII, | 4to. pp. 8. H. S. P. 1813

HOPKINSON. Science. | A | Poem. | By | Francis Hopkinson, Esq; | . . . | . . . . | *Philadelphia:* | *Printed by William Dunlap, in Market-Street,* | MDCCLXII. | 4to. pp. 19. L. C. P. 1814

HOPKINSON. Science. | A | Poem. | By Francis Hopkin-son. | . . . | . . . . | *Philadelphia : Printed, and Sold by Andrew* | *Steuart, at the Bible-in-Heart, in Second-street.* | MDCCLXII. | Sm. 8vo. pp. 8.   L. C. P. 1815

    This edition was a piracy, see Hopkinson's advertisement in the Pa. Gazette March 18, 1762.

IMRIE'S Letters. *Philadelphia : Andrew Steuart.* 1762. 1816

JEMMY Carson's Collection [of Ballads?] *Philadelphia : Andrew Steuart.* 1762.   1817

    Advertised in the Pa. Gazette, Dec. 2, 1762.

ЈЄТ3Т ist mein Bieler Schmerz. *Ephrata.* 1762.   1818

JOSEPH of Arimathea. *Philadelphia : Andrew Steuart.* 1762.

THE JOVIAL Crew. A Farce. *Philadelphia : Andrew Steuart.* 1762.   1820

KATECHJSMUS oder kurzer Unterricht christlicher Lehre wie der= selbe in denen Reformirten Kirchen und Schulen der Churfürstlichen Pfalz auch anderwärts getrieben wird. *Philadelphia : Gedruckt bey Peter Miller u. Comp.* 1762.   1821

    Title from Seidensticker's Bibliography.

KLAGEN Eines Theils der Evangelisch=Lutherischen Gemeindeglieder zu Philadelphia wider einige dermalige Aeltesten der Gemeine. *Philadel-phia : Gedruckt bey H. Miller.* 1762. Folio, pp. 4. 1762. 1822

    Title from Seidensticker's Bibliography.

LAMPEN. (F.) Dr. Fred. Lampens Wahrheitsmilch. Auf neu nachgesehen, ꝛc. Mit der Vorrede des Predigers der Ref. Hoch Teutschen Gemeinde zu Amwell in New Jersey Dr. Casper Staples, unter Vorwis= sen der Ehrw. Penna. Coetus. *Philadelphia : Anton Armbruester.* 1762.   1823

A LETTER from a Gentleman in England to his Friend in Philadelphia ; giving him his Opinion of the College in that City. *Philadelphia : Andrew Steuart.* 1762.   1824

LILLIPUT. A Farce. *Philadelphia: Andrew Steuart.* 1762.

LLOYD. (—.) Arcadia: Or, the Shepherd's Wedding. A Dramatic Pastoral. As it is Performed at the Theatre Royal. By the Rev. Mr. Lloyd. The Music Composed by Mr. Stanley. *Philadelphia: Andrew Steuart.* 1762.   1826

LOVE his own Rival. A Comedy. *Philadelphia: Andrew Steuart.* 1762.   1827

THE | MANNERS of the Times ; | A | Satire. | In two Parts. | By Philadelphiensis. | . . . | . . . . | *Philadelphia:* | *Printed and Sold by William Dunlap*, M,DCC,LXII. | Sq. 8vo. pp. 16.   H. S. P.

𝔙𝔒𝔏𝔏𝔖𝔗𝔄𝔈𝔑𝔇𝔍𝔊𝔈𝔖 𝔐𝔄𝔯𝔅𝔘𝔯𝔊𝔈𝔯 Gejang=Buch, zur Uebung der Gottjeligfeit, in 649 Chrijtlichen und Trojtreichen Pjalmen und Ge= jängen Hrn. D. Martin Luthers. Und andrer Gottjeliger Lehrer, Or= dentlich in XII. Theile verfaffet, Und mit nöthigen Regijtern auch einer Verzeichniß verjehen, unter welche Titul die im Anhang befindlichen Lieder gehörig: Auch zur beförderung des jo Kirchen= als Privat=Gottesdienjtes, Mit erbaulichen Morgen=Abend=Buß=Bericht= und Communion=Gebätlein vermehret. *Germanton: Gedruckt und zu finden bey Christoph Saur.* 1762. 12mo. pp. 527, (14), 96, 1 plate.   1829

THE | MILITARY Glory | of | Great-Britain, | an | Enter- tainment, | given by the late candidates for | Bachelor's Degree, | At the close of the | Anniversary Commencement, held | in | Nassau-Hall, | New-Jersey | September 29th, 1762. | *Philadel- phia:* | *Printed by William Bradford*, M,DCC,LXII. | Sq. 8vo. pp. 15, and 5 folded leaves of music.   H. S. P. 1830

MURTAGH O'Lavery. *Philadelphia: Andrew Steuart.* 1762.

A NARRATIVE of the Unhappy Life and Miserable End of Samuel Stoddard, late of the County of Burlington, and Province of West New-Jersey ; who was tried at a Supreme Court, held at Burlington, aforesaid, on Saturday, the Sixth of November 1762, for the barbarous, cruel and inhuman Murder of Jacob Cole ; of which crime he was found guilty, and, according to sentence, was executed at Burlington, on Tuesday, the 23d of the same Month. *Philadelphia: Andrew Steuart.* 1762.   1832

NEU=EJNGERJCHTETER Americanischer Calender auf das Jahr 1763. *Philadelphia: Anton Armbruester.* 1762.   1833

NEU=EJNGERJCHTETES | GESANG=BUCH | in sich haltend | eine | Sammlung | (mehrentheils alter) | schöner lehr=reicher und erbaulicher | Lieder, | Welche von langer Zeit her bey den Bekennern | und Liebhabern der Glorien und Wahrheit | Jesu Christi biß anjeŧo in Uibung | gewesen: | Nach den Haupt=Stücken der Christli= | chen Lehr und Glaubens eingetheilet, | und | Mit einem Verzeichniß der Titel | und dreyen Nüŧlichen Registern | versehen. | Anjeŧo also zusammen getragen, | und | Zum Lobe Gottes und heilsamen | Erbauung im Christenthum, | ans Licht gegeben. | *Germantown, gedruckt bey Christoph Saur, | auf Kosten vereinigter Freunden*, 1762. | 16mo. pp. xxiii, (3), 760, (40).   1834

NEU=vermehrtes | Gesäng der einsamen | Turtel=Taube, zur gemeinschaftlichen Erbauung ge= | sammelt und ans Licht gegeben. | [*Cut.*] | *Ephrata Typis Societatis Anno* 1762. | 16mo. Title 1 leaf; Vorrede, pp. (4); text, pp. 1–329; Register, pp. (3); Additional Hymns, leaves.   1835

DER NEUESTE, Verbessert= und Zuverläßige | Americanische | Calender | Auf das 1763ste Jahr Christi, | Welches ein gemein Jahr von 365 Tagen ist. | Darin enthalten | Die Wochen=Monats= und Merkwürdige Tage; des Monden | Auf= und Untergang; seine Zeichen, Grade, und Viertel; die Aspecten der | Planeten, samt der Witterung; des Siebengestirns Aufgang, Südplaŧ | und Untergang; Auf= und Untergang der Sonnen; nebst der | Fluth oder dem hohen Wasser zu Philadelphia; | Und andere gewöhnliche Calender=Arbeit. | Wie auch | Geschichten, Sittenlehren, lustige und angenehme Erzählungen, ꝛc. ꝛc. | Vornemlich nach dem Pennsylvanischen Horizont berechnet; | Jedoch in den angrenzenden Landschaften ohne merklichen Unterscheid zu gebrauchen. | Zum Erstenmal heraus gegeben. | *Philadelphia, Gedruckt und zu finden bey Henrich Miller, in der Zweyten-strasse.* | . . . | . . . | . . . . [1762.] | Sm. 4to. pp. (40).   H. S. P.   1836

NEW-YEAR Verses of the Carriers of the Pennsylvania Gazette. *Philadelphia: B. Franklin, and D. Hall.* 1762.   1837

NEW-YEAR Verses of the Carriers of the Pennsylvania Journal. *Philadelphia: William Bradford.* 1762.   1838

THE OLD Maid.   A Comedy.   *Philadelphia: Andrew Steuart.*
1762.   1839

NOSUM Nosorum : | Or, | A New Treatise | on | Large Noses.
Philadelphia : | *Printed [by Andrew Steuart] for the Society of
Noses.* | M.DCC.LXII. | Sm. 8vo. pp. 8.   H. S. P.   1840

A satire on the Presbyterian and Quaker factions.   The date may be a misprint for 1764.

A | PANEGYRICK. | By Strephon. | . . . | . . . | . . . | . . . . |
Philadelphia : | *Printed and Sold by William Dunlap,* M,DCC,-
LXII. | Sq. 8vo. pp. 11.   L. C. P.   1841

THE PENNSYLVANIA Gazette.   1842

Numbers 1724 (Jan. 7, 1762) to 1775 (Dec. 30, 1762), four pages each, with
"Supplements" of two pages each to Numbers 1724, 1731, 1738, 1739, 1751, 1762,
and 1770.

THE PENNSYLVANIA Journal.   H. S. P.   1843

Numbers 996 (Jan. 7, 1762) to 1047 (Dec. 30, 1762), four pages each, with extra
half sheets of two pages each to Numbers 1003, 1009, 1014, and 1015.   Title and
imprint as in No. 1693, *supra.*

THE PENNSYLVANIA Pocket Almanac for 1763.   *Philadelphia : William Bradford.*   1762.   1844

POTTS. (J.)   Confusion is Fallen, and a Seal of the Gospel is
opened.   Being five Discourses on contrary Subjects, proving each
other by infallible Demonstrations; one of which is a Map of
Purgatory, made out between Scripture Parables and Part of the
Sermon Christ preached to the Spirits in Prison.   By John Potts,
of Cumberland County, Pennsylvania.   *Ephrata :?* 1762.   1845

𝕯𝕰𝕽 | 𝖕𝖘𝖆𝖑𝖙𝖊𝖗 | Des Königs und Propheten | Davids, | ver-
teutscht von D. Martin Luther | Mit kurtzen Summarien oder | Inhalt
jedes Psalmen; | Mit | Bielen Parallelen oder gleichen Schrifft-Stellen.
| *Philadelphia, gedruckt und zu finden bey Nicolaus* | *Hasselbach,
in der Second-strasse, zwischen der Ræsse-* | *und Wein-strasse.* 1762.
| Sm. 8vo. pp. 239. 9.   c.   1846

𝕯𝕰𝕽 𝖂𝕾𝕬𝕷𝕿𝕰𝕽. *Germantown: Christoph Saur.* 1762. 1847

Title from Seidensticker's Bibliography.

THE REGISTER Office. A Comedy. *Philadelphia: Andrew Steuart.* 1762.   1848

SAUNDERS. (R.) A Pocket | Almanack | For the Year 1763. | ... | ... | ... | .... | By R. Saunders, Phil. | *Philadelphia:* | *Printed and sold by B. Franklin,* | *and D. Hall.* [1762.] | 24mo. pp. (24).   1849

SAUNDERS. Poor Richard, improved. Being an Almanac for 1763. By Richard Saunders, Philom. *Philadelphia: B. Franklin, and D. Hall.* [1762.]   1850

THE SHAM Beggar. A Farce. *Philadelphia: Andrew Steuart.* 1762.   1851

A | SHORT Introduction | to | Grammar. | For the Use of the | College and Academy | In Philadelphia. | Being a New Edition of | Whittenhall's Latin Grammar, | With Many | Alterations, Additions and Amendments | From antient and late Grammarians. | ... | ... | .... | *Philadelphia:* | *Printed by Andrew Steuart, for the College* | *and Academy of Philadelphia, and Sold* | *at his Printing-Office at the Bible-in-* | *Heart, in Second-Street ; and by the rest* | *of the Book-Sellers, in Philadelphia, New-* | *York, &c.* | MDCC-LXII. | Sm. 8vo. pp. iv, 137. (4).   H. S. P. 1852

[SMALRIDGE. (George)] The Art of Preaching, in imitation of Horace's Art of Poetry. *Philadelphia: Andrew Steuart.* 1762.   1853

SMITH. (W.) The last Summons. | A | Sermon | Preached in Christ-Church, | Philadelphia ; | On Sunday, January 10, 1762. | At the Funeral of | The Rev. Robert Jenney, L. L. D. | Rector of the said Church. | By William Smith, D. D. | Provost of the College and Academy of Philadelphia. | *Philadelphia: Printed and sold by A. Steuart, at the* | *Bible-in-Heart,* MDCCLXII. | *Sold also by W. Bradford, D. Hall, W.* | *Dunlap and J. Rivington ; and by H.* | *Gaine, in New-York.* | 16mo. pp. 16.   N. Y. H. S. 1854

SPELLING Book. In German. *Philadelphia: Henry Miller.* 1761. 1855

Miller printed 2000 copies for the Moravians.

THE SPIRIT of Contradiction. A Comedy. *Philadelphia: Andrew Steuart.* 1762. 1856

STEUART. (A.) The | Gentleman and Citizen's | Pocket-Almanack, | By Andrew Steuart, Bookseller. | For the Year 1763. | Fitted to the Use of Pennsylvania and | the neighbouring Provinces. | Containing | Many useful Lists and Tables, | not in any other Almanack printed | on the Continent. | This Almanack contains more than | double the Quantity of any other Pocket- | Almanack printed in this Place. | *Philadelphia: | Printed by Andrew Steuart, at the | Bible-in-Heart, in Second-street.* [1762.] | 24mo. pp. (48). 1857

TOBLER. (J.) The Pennsylvania Town and Countryman's Almanac for 1763. *Germantown: Christopher Sower.*? 1763. 1858

VIRIS Præcellentissimis, | Thomæ Penn ac Richardo Penn, Armigeris, | Provinciæ Pennsylvaniæ, . . . Proprietariis; | . . . | Jacobo Hamilton, Armigero, | Prædictæ Provinciæ . . . Vice-Gubernatori præclarissimo, nec non hujus Collegii & Academiæ Philadelphiensis Curatori; | . . . | . . . | . . . | . . . | . . . | . . . | . . . | . . . . | Hæc Philosophemata sub Vice-Præfecti Moderamine . . . discutienda; | Juvenes in artibus initiati, | . . . | . . . | . . . . | [*Philadelphia:*] *Typis Henrici Milleri, in vico vulgo dicti Second-street.* [1765.] | Folio, 1 leaf. H. S. P. 1859

VOTES | and | Proceedings | of the | House of Representatives | of the | Province of Pennsylvania, | Met at Philadelphia, on the Fourteenth of October, Anno | Domini 1761, and continued by Adjournments. | [*Penn Arms.*] | *Philadelphia: | Printed and Sold by B. Franklin, at the New-Printing-Office, | near the Market.* MDCCLXII. | Folio, pp. 58, (1). H. S. P. 1860

WEATHERWISE. (A.) Father Abraham's Almanac for 1763. By Abraham Weatherwise. *Philadelphia: William Dunlap.* 1762.

𝕯𝕰ℜ 𝖂𝕺𝕰𝕮𝕳𝕰ℜ𝕿𝕷𝕵𝕮𝕳𝕰 𝕻𝖍𝖎𝖑𝖆𝖉𝖊𝖑𝖕𝖍𝖎𝖘𝖈𝖍𝖊 𝕾𝖙𝖆𝖆𝖙𝖘𝖇𝖔𝖙𝖊. *Philadelphia: Henrich Miller*. 1762. Folio.   1862

The full title of the earliest issue of this paper (No. 60) with which I have met is given in the following note kindly contributed by Mr. John W. Jordan :

John Henry Miller, better known as Henry Miller, born in Waldeck, 1702, was apprenticed to a printer in Switzerland, published a paper there, and subsequently uniting with the Moravians, managed their publication office at Marienborn. His first visit to Pennsylvania was made in company with Zinzendorff, in 1741, and his second in 1751, when he was engaged by Franklin to superintend his German printing, and afterwards by William Bradford. With S. Holland, in January, 1752, he published "The Lancaster Gazette," but he retired five months afterwards. Returning from Europe in 1760, with new printing materials he opened an office on the west side of Second, two doors from Race street, where in January of 1762, he published "Der Wöchentliche | Philadelphische Staatsbote. | Mit den neusten Fremdem und Einheimisch Politischen Nachrichten; | Samt den | von Zeit zu Zeit in der Kirche und Gelehrten Welt sich ereignenden Merkwürdigkeiten. | Diese Zeitung wird alle Montage ausgegeben, für Sechs Schillinge des Jahrs, bey Henrich Miller, Buchdrucker, | zwischen der Wein und Rees-strasse, in der Zweyten-strasse." | The cut of a Post-boy, holding in his hand a script on which is *Novæ*, in the centre of the title was added in No. 157, Jan. 14, 1764, but in No. 226, Feb. 23, 1767, a Post-horn was substituted for the script. No. 199, Oct. 31, 1765, is called "Ein Abschieds Geschenk." Miller says he finds "himself under the necessity of discontinuing his paper for awhile, but thinks it his duty to thank the public in general and the merchants in particular for the generous encouragement they have given it; and at the same time requests the favor of their custom hereafter, in any stamp-free printing work or translating." The publication was resumed on Nov. 18, 1765, and on Dec. 2, of the same year, the imprint, slightly changed, was removed to the bottom of the fourth page. The next change in the title was made with No. 311, Jan. 1768, to "Der Wöchentliche Pennsylvanische Staatsbote," etc. With No. 696, another change was made to "Henrich Millers Pennsylvanische Staatsbote," etc., the cut of the Post boy removed, and the size of the paper reduced, but it was issued semi-weekly on Tuesdays and Fridays. July 9, 1776, No. 813, a double sheet was issued, containing the full text of the Declaration of Independence, in German, displayed in all the typographical wealth of the office. July 30, No. 819, it was again issued weekly on Tuesdays ; after December 19, No. 838, on Thursdays, and from Jan. 8, 1777, to May 26, 1779, on Wednesdays. The last issue of the Staatsbote prior to occupation of the city by British was No. 877, Sept. 17, 1777, and the first after the evacuation No. 878, Aug. 5, 1778. In May of 1779, Miller disposed of his paper to Steiner and Cist, and in No. 920, May 26, published his farewell address. The paper contained four pages, folio, with frequent supplements of two pages. During the Revolution it not unfrequently contained only two pages. The Library Company of Philadelphia possesses a nearly complete file of this paper from April, 1763, until the close of its career. It was succeeded by "Die Philadelphische Correspondenz," issued at first by Steiner and Cist, and afterwards by Melchoir Steiner. He died at Bethlehem, Pa., March 31, 1782.

WOOLMAN. (J.)   Considerations | on keeping | Negroes; | Recommehded to the Professors of | Christianity, of every denomination. | Part Second. | By John Woolman. | . . . | . . . | . . . | . . . . | *Philadelphia:* | *Printed by B. Franklin, and D. Hall.* 1762. | 16mo. pp. 52.   1863

WUDRIAN. (M. W.)   M. Valentin Wudrians seel. | Creutz-Schule, | In sich haltend: | Eine schöne Christliche Unterweisung von dem | lieben Creutz; | Vor alle | Creutz-Brüder und | Schwestern, | Als durch welches Mittel sie sich in allerhand | zustoßendem Creutz, Trübsal, Kranck- | heit Noth und Tod kräfftiglich aufhelffen | und aus Gottes Wort trösten mögen; | Nebst einem zu End eines jeden Capitels an- | gehängten Ge- | spräch zwischen Christo | und der Seelen. | Zusammen getragen von einem wolgeprüfften Creutz-Bruder und Nach- | folger Jesu Christi. | *Ephrata Drucks u. Verlags der Bruederschaft.* | Anno 1762. | 16mo. pp. (10), 465, (3).   H. S. P.   1864

1763.

AN ACCOUNT of the Births and Burials in St. Peter's | and Christ-Church Parish, in Philadelphia, from De- | cember 25, 1762, to December 25, 1763.   By Caleb | Cash, Clerk, and James Wey-ley, Sexton. | [n. p. n. d.]   Folio, 1 leaf.   L. C. P.   1865

AN | ADDRESS | to the | Freeholders | of | New-Jersey, | On the Subject of | Public Salaries. | *Philadelphia:* | *Printed and sold by Andrew Steuart, at the Bible-in-Heart, in* | *Second-street: Sold also at most of the Stores in the Jersies.* | MDCCLXIII. | 8vo. pp. 24.   L. C. P.   1866

AGUECHEEK. (A.)   The Universal American Almanac for 1764.   By Andrew Aguecheek.   *Philadelphia: Andrew Steuart.* 1763.   1867

ALL'S Well! or an Address to the public, occasioned by "Methodism Anatomiz'd; or the" (Unreasonable) "Alarm to Pennsylvania," &c.   To which is suffix'd A Word or Two for the sole Benefit of the Author of that Alarm.   *Philadelphia: Andrew Steuart.*   1763.   1868

ANNO Regni | Georgii III. | Regis, | Magnæ Britanniæ, Franciæ & Hiberniæ, | Tertio. | At a General Assembly of the Province of Penn- | sylvania, begun and holden at Philadelphia, | the Fourteenth Day of October, Anno Domini 1762, in | the Second Year of the Reign of our Sovereign Lord | George III. by the Grace of God, of Great- | Britain, France and Ireland, King, Defender of the | Faith, &c. | And from thence continued by Adjournments to the | Fourth Day of March, 1763. | [*Penn Arms.*] | *Philadelphia:* | *Printed and Sold by B. Franklin, at the New-* | *Printing-Office, near the Market.* MDCCLXIII. | Folio, Title, 1 leaf; pp. 223–276. + And from thence continued . . . to the | Eight Day of July, 1763. | [*Ibid.*] Title, 1 leaf; pp. 279–286. + And from thence continued . . . to the | Thirtieth Day of September, 1763. | [*Ibid.*] Title, 1 leaf; pp. 289–296.   H. S. P.   1869

ANNO Regni | Georgii III. | Regis, | Magnæ Britanniæ, Franciæ & Hiberniæ, | Tertio. | At a General Assembly of the Province of Penn- | sylvania, begun and holden at Philadelphia, | the Fourteenth Day of October, Anno Domini 1763, in | the Third Year of the Reign of our Sovereign Lord | George III. by the Grace of God, of Great- | Britain, France and Ireland, King, Defender of the | Faith, &c. | And from thence continued by Adjournments to the | Twenty-second Day of October, 1763. | [*Penn Arms.*] | *Philadelphia:* | *Printed and Sold by B. Franklin, at the New-* | *Printing-Office, near the Market.* MDCCLXIII. | Folio, Title, 1 leaf; pp. 299–311.   H. S. P.   1870

THE | ASS | in the | Lyon's Skin; | Luckily discover'd | By his Braying. | . . . | . . . | . . . | . . . | . . . . | *Philadelphia:* *Printed and Sold by Andrew Steuart, in* | *Second-street.* 1763. | Sm. 8vo. pp. 8.   L. C. P.   1871

A reply to " Errata ; or, the Art of Printing incorrectly."

AN AUTHENTICK Account of the Proceedings against John Wilkes, Esq; *Philadelphia: William Dunlap.* 1763.   1872

BALBA. (A. A.) Gruendlicher Unterricht von den Metallen, Darinnen beschrieben wird, wie sie werden in der erden generirt; und was man insgemein dabey findet. In zwey Büchern. Vormals im Spaniſchen beſchrieben durch Albaro Alonſo Barba, Pfarrherr zu St. Bernhards Kirchſpiel in der Kaiſerlichen Stadt Potoſi in dem Königreich Peru, in Weſt=Indien; im Jahr 1664. Hernach in das Englandiſche überſetzt durch Edward, Graff von Sanpwich, Anno 1669. Und nun um ſeiner Vortrefflichkeit willen zum erſtenmal ins Hoch=teutſche überſetzt, und zum druck befördert, durch G. R. Dieſer Kunſt beflieſſenen. Nebſt einem neuen anhang betreffend obige materie. *Ephrata: Gedruckt durch I. Georg Zeisiger,* Anno 1763. 12mo. pp. 198 +, 1 plate.   1873

BAXTER. (R.) The Saint's Everlasting Rest: Or, a Treatise of the Blessed State of the Saints in their Enjoyment of God in Heaven. By Mr. Richard Baxter. Abridged by Benjamin Fawcett. The Second Edition. *Philadelphia: William Bradford.* 1763.   1874

[BENEZET. (ANTHONY)] Eine | kurtze vorſtellung des theils von | Africa, | Welches bewohnt wird von | Negroes. | Darinnen beſchrieben wird die fruchtbarkeit des= | ſelben landes, die gutartigkeit deſſen einwoh= ner, | und wie man daſelbſt den ſclaven=handel treibt. | Ausgezogen aus verſchiedenen Authoren, um | die ungerechtigkeit ſolchen handels und die falſch= | heit derer gründen, womit er behauptet wird, | antag zu legen. | Nebſt anführung mancher ſchrifftlichen zeugnüſſen von ver= | ſchiedenen nahmhafften perſonen als: Georg Wallis, | Frantz Hutſchinſon und Jacob Foſter, und einem | auszug eines in London neulich gedruckten büchleins, | welches auch von gedachtem ſclaven=handels handelt. | . . . | . . . | . . . | . . . . | *Ephrata Drucks der Societat auf kosten et-* | *licher freunden Anno Domini* MDCCLXIII. | 16mo. pp. 107.   H. S. P.   1875

[BENEZET. (A.)] A Short Account of that Part of Africa inhabited by the Negroes. The Third Edition. *Philadelphia: William Dunlap.* 1763.   1876

BIBLIA, | Das iſt: | Die | Heilige Schrift | Altes und Neues | Tes= taments, | Nach der Teutſchen Ueberſetzung | D. Martin Luthers, | Mit jedes Capitels kurtzen Summarien, auch | beygefügten vielen und richtigen Parallelen; | Nebſt einem Anhang | Des dritten und vierten Buchs Esrä und des | dritten Buchs der Maccabäer. | *Germantown:* | *Gedruckt bey Christoph Saur,* 1763. | 4to. pp. (4), 992, 277, (3).   H. S. P.   1877

A BRIEF Account of the Life of the late Reverend Caleb Smith, A. M. Minister of the Gospel at Newark Mountains; who died October 22, 1762. *Philadelphia: William Dunlap.* 1763. 1878

A | BRIEF Instruction | in the | Principles | of the | Christian Religion, | Agreeable to the | Confession of Faith, put forth by the Elders | and Brethren of many Congregations of Chri- | stians (Baptized upon Profession of their Faith) | in London, and in the Country. | To which is added, | The Proofs thereof, out of the Scriptures, in Words at | Length. | The Seventh Edition, Corrected. | . . . | . . . | . . . | . . . | *Wilmington,* | *Printed by James Adams, in Market-street,* 1763. | 16mo. pp. 48. 1879

BROWN. (J.) An address to the principal inhabitants of the North American Colonies, on occasion of the Peace. Together with a Sermon preach'd at St. Paul's on Sunday the 6th of March 1763, on occasion of the Brief for the establishment of the Colleges of Philadelphia and New York. By John Brown, D. D., Vicar of Newcastle. *Philadelphia: Andrew Steuart.* 1763. 1880

CALENDER auf das Jahr 1764. *Gedruckt bey N. Hasselbach, Techesnut-Hill.* 1763. 1881

CATECHISMUS, | Oder | Anfänglicher Unterricht | Christlicher | Glaubens= | Lehre; | Allen Christlichen Glaubens=Schülern, | Jung oder Alt, | Nöthig und Nützlich sich darin zu üben. | . . . | . . . | . . . | . . . | . . . | . . . | . . . . | *Philadelphia,* | *Gedruckt bey Henrich Miller, in der | Zweyten-Strasse.* 1763. | 12mo. pp. (4), 146. H. S. P. 1882

A CUDGELL to drive the Devil out of every Christian Place of Worship: Being a Second Edition (with necessary Improvements, which now render the sense entirely plain) of the Lawfulness, Excellency and Advantage, of Instrumental Music, in the public Worship of God, but chiefly of Organs. *Philadelphia: Andrew Steuart.* 1763. 1883

DER KLEINE DARMSTÄDTISCHE | Catechismus | Herrn D. Martin Luthers | nebst beygefügten Fragstücken für diejen= | ige sonderlich welche christlichen Gebrauch nach | confirmiret worden und hieraus zum erſten | mahl der heilige Abendmahl gebrauchen. | *Germanton. Gedruckt bey Christoph Saur.* 1763. 16mo. 1884

[DEFOE. (DANIEL)] The | Dreadful Visitation | in | A short Account of the | Progress and Effects | of the | Plague, | The last Time it spread in the City of | London in the Year 1655 extracted from | the Memoirs of a Person who resided there, | during the whole Time of that Infection. | With some Thoughts on the Advantages which | would result to Christianity, if a Spirit of Impartiality | and true Charity was suffered to preside amongst the | several religious Denominations, &c. | . . . | . . . | . . . . | *Germantown: Printed by Chr. Sower.* 1763. | 16mo. pp. 16. 1885

DELAWARE. Laws | of the | Government | of | New-Castle, Kent and Sussex, | Upon Delaware. | Vol. II. | [*Royal Arms.*] | *Wilmington,* | *Printed by James Adams, in Market-street,* 1763. | Folio. H. S. P. 1886

Collation : Title, 1 leaf; Authorization, 1 leaf; Titles, pp. i-iv ; text, pp. 1–81.

A | DIALOGUE | on | Peace, | an | Entertainment, | Given by the Senior Class at the | Anniversary Commencement, | Held at Nassau-Hall | September 28th, 1763. | *Philadelphia:* | *Printed by William Bradford,* M,DCC,LXIII. | Sm. 4to. pp. 27. L. C. P.

DUCHÉ. (J.) The Life and Death of the Righteous. | A | Sermon, | preached at | Christ-Church, Philadelphia, | On Sunday February the 13th, 1763, | At the Funeral of | Mr. Evan Morgan. | By Jacob Duché, M. A. | One of the Ministers of the united Churches of | Christ-Church, and St. Peter's, Philadelphia, | and Chaplain to the Right Honourable the Earl | of Stirling. | *Philadelphia:* | *Printed by B. Franklin, and D. Hall.* | MDCCLXIII. | 8vo. pp. 24. H. S. P. 1888

EDWARDS. (M.) A | Sermon, | Preached, in the college of Philadelphia, at the | ordination of the Rev'd Samuel Jones, A.B. | By Morgan Edwards, A. M. | Minister of the Baptist Church in the said City. | To which are annexed, A narrative of the | ordination ; and, A charge delivered | on the occasion. | *Philadelphia:* | *Printed by Andrew Steuart, at the Bible-in-Heart, in* | *Second-Street.* | M,DCC,LXIII. | Sm. 8vo. pp. 48. H. S. P. 1889

ERRATA; | or, the | Art of Printing incorrectly: | Plainly set forth, | By a Variety of | Examples | Taken from a | Latin Grammar, | Lately printed | By Andrew Steuart, | For the Use of the | College and Academy of this City. | . . . | . . . | . . . . | *Philadelphia,* [*William Bradford.*] M.DCC.LXIII. | + The Second Edition. [*Ibid.*] Sm. 8vo. pp. 23.   H. S. P.   1890

AN | EXERCISE, | containing | A Dialogue and Ode | on Peace. | Performed at the public Commencement in the | College of Philadelphia, May 17th, 1763. | . . . | . . . | . . . | . . . | . . . . | *Philadelphia :* | *Printed by Andrew Steuart, at the Bible-in-Heart,* | *in Second-street,* M,DCC,LXIII. | 8vo. pp. 8.   L. C. P.   1891

The Dialogue was written by the Rev. Nath. Evans and the Ode by Dr. Paul Jackson, of Chester.

FINLEY. (J.)   An Essay on the Gospel Ministry.   Wherein the Nature of this Ministry, the Propriety of employing Men therein, the Importance of it, the Qualifications requisite in a Gospel Minister and the Means of preserving an able and faithful Ministry, and preventing its being corrupted, are briefly considered.   By James Finley, V.D.M.   To which are added, Three Emphatical Addresses; The First to a Clergyman; the Second from a Father to his Sons intending the Ministry, and the Third to the Laity.   *Wilmington : James Adams.*   1763.   1892

FOX. (T.)   The Wilmington Almanac for 1764.   By Thomas Fox.   *Wilmington : James Adams.*   1763.   1893

FRANCKEL. (D. H.)   A Thanksgiving | Sermon, | for the | Important and Astonishing | Victory | Obtain'd on the Fifth of December, M,DCC,LVII, | By the Glorious King of Prussia. | Over the united and far superior Forces of the | Austrians, in Silesia: | Preached on | The Sabbath of the Tenth of said Month, | at the | Synagogue of the Jews, in Berlin. | By David Hirchel Franckel, | Arch-Rabbi. | Translated from the German Original, printed at Berlin. | *Philadelphia :* | *Printed by Andrew Steuart, and sold at his Printing-* | *Office, at the Bible-in-Heart in Second-street.* 1763. | Sm. 8vo. pp. 16.   L. C. P.   1894

FUNCK. (H.) Eine | Restitution, | Oder eine | Erklärung | einiger Haupt=puncten des Gesetzes : | Wie es durch Christum erfüllet ist, und vollkommen vol= | endet wird werden an seinem grossen Tage ; Nach In= | halt der Heiligen Schrift, des Neuen und Alten Testa= | ments. | Aufgesetzet in 25 Theil | durch | Einen Lehrer des Neuen und Alten Testaments, in der Gemein | der Gläubigen in Jesum Christum : die man mit dem Bey=namen | nennet die Wieder=täuffer oder Menonisten. | Henrich Funck | ... | ... | ... | .... | Verlegt und zum Druck befordert durch die von Henrich Funcks | unterlassenen Kindern. | *Philadelphia,* | *Gedruckt bey Anton Armbruester in Moravien Ally.* 1763. | Sq. 8vo. Title and Vorrede, pp. (7); text, pp. 1–308, (1).　　H. S. P.　1895

GESANG=BUCH. Neu=vermehrt= und vollständiges | Gesang=Buch, | Worinnen sowohl die | Psalmen Davids, | Nach | D. Ambrosii Lob= wassers, | Uebersetzung hin und wieder verbessert, | Als auch | 730. aus= erlesener alter und neuer | Geistreichen Liedern | begriffen sind, | Welche anjetzo sämtlich | in denen Reformirten Kirchen | der Hessisch=Hanauisch= Pfältzisch=Pensilvanischen | und mehreren andern angräntzenden Landen zu singen ge= | bräuchlich, in nützlicher Ordnung eingetheilt, | Auch | Mit dem Heydelbergischen Catechismo und | erbaulichen Gebätern versehen. | Zweyte Auflage. | *Germantown,* | *Gedruckt und zu finden bey Christoph Saur,* 1763. | 24mo.　　H. S. P.　1896

　　　Collation: 1 Plate; title, etc. pp. (2); text, pp. 1–208; Register, pp. (2); Geistreicher Lieder, pp. 1–536; Register, pp. (10); Heidelbergischer Catechismus, etc., pp. 1–24; Evangelia und Episteln, pp. 1–82, (1). See No. 1258, *supra*, for the title to the Geistreicher Lieder, and No. 1301, *supra*, for the first edition.

GRUBÉ. (J. A.) Essay of a Delaware Hymn Book. By Rev. B. A. Grubé. *Bethlehem : J. Brandmiller.* 1763.?　　　　1897

　　　See Pa. Mag. Hist. and Biog., Vol. VI., p. 250.

GRUBÉ. A Harmony of the Gospels, translated in the Delaware Language by Rev. B. A. Grubé. *Bethlehem : J. Brandmiller.* 1763.　　　　　　　　　　　　　　　　　　　　　　1898

HARKER. (S.) An Appeal from the Synod of New York and Philadelphia, to the Christian World by the Reverend Samuel Harker. Written by himself. *Philadelphia : Printed by William Dunlap.* M,DCC,LXIII. 8vo. pp. 40.　　　　　1899

HARKER. Predestination consistent with General Liberty: Or the Scheme of the Covenant of Grace. By Samuel Harker, Minister of the Gospel at Black River, in New-Jersey. *Philadelphia: William Dunlap.* 1763. 1900

𝕯𝕰𝕽 | 𝕳𝕺𝕮𝕳=𝕯𝕰𝖀𝕿𝕾𝕳 | Americaniſche | Calender, | Auf das Jahr | . . . | . . . | 1764. | (Welches ein Schalt=Jahr von 366 Tagen iſt.) | . . . | . . . | . . . | . . . | . . . | . . . | . . . | . . . | . . . | . . . | Zum ſechs und zwantzigſten mal heraus gegeben. *Germantown: Gedruckt und zu finden bey Christoph Saur.* | . . . | . . . . [1763.] | 4to. pp. (48). H. S. P. 1901

[HOPKINSON. (Francis)] A | Collection of Psalm Tunes, | with a few | Anthems and Hymns, | Some of them Entirely New, | for the Use | of the United Churches | of | Christ Church and St. Peter's Church | in | Philadelphia, | 1763. | [*Philadelphia: W. Dunlap.*?] Oblong 4to. H. S. P. 1902

Collation: Engraved title, 1 leaf; Dedication, pp. (2); Introduction to the Art of Psalmody, v–ix; Engraved Music (in 3 parts) xxii leaves. The dedication—"To the Reverend Mr. Richard Peters, Rector of the United Churches of Christ Church and St. Peter's Church, in Philadelphia"—says "this Attempt to the Improvement of our Psalmody, . . . [is] made . . . in as clear and easy a Manner as possible, so that children, with very little attention, may understand them." The minutes of the Vestry of the United Churches contain, in the year 1764, a resolution of thanks to Francis Hopkinson for his efforts to "instruct the children of the united congregations the art of psalmody." The music was probably engraved by Henry Dawkins.

IMPARTIAL Reflections to be considered by the King, his Ministers, and the People of Great Britain; containing impartial Observations on the Quantity of Goods produced in the British and French Colonies in America, and exported from thence yearly. *Philadelphia: Rivington and Brown.* 1763. 1903

I[NGLIS.] (J[ohn]) By the way of | A Scripture Interpretation. | Theism: | A | Prophesy: | Or, | Prophetical Dissertation. | Predicting and declaring | The Coming of the expected Messiah, in the | Character of Lord and King; | The | Setting up of a National Theocracy, in the | Calling of the Jews, and Redemption | of the Gentile Church. | Part I. | Consisting of | An Astro-Theological Unfolding of certain | formerly obscure, but highly-interesting and | capital Points of Doctrine. | Adapted to the present Crisis of Affairs. | By J - - - I - - - - - - . | . . . | . . . | . . . | . . . | . . . | . . . | . . . | . . . | . . . | . . . . | *Philadelphia* : | *Printed for the Author.* | [*by William Dunlap.*] MDCCLXIII. | 8vo. Title, 1 leaf; Contents, pp. (2); A Lesson, pp. (2); Introduction, pp. i-li; An Enquiry, &c., pp. 281, (1); Errata, 1 leaf; 1 Plate.   H. S. P.   1904

LAND Office, Philadelphia, March 10. 1763. | [n. p. 1763.] 4to. 1 leaf.   H. S. P.   1905

Notice signed William Peters to persons in the Lower Counties that a Warrant from the Land Office must be obtained before entry be made upon any vacant lands.

THE | LAWFULNESS, Excellency, and Advantage | of | Instrumental Musick | in the | Public Worship of God | Urg'd and Enforc'd, | From Scripture, and the Example of the far | greater Part of Christians in all Ages. | Address'd | To all (particularly the Presbyterians and Baptists) who | have hitherto been taught to look upon the Use of | Instrumental Musick in the Worship of God | as Unlawful. | By a Presbyterian. | . . . | . . . . | *Philadelphia* : | *Printed and sold by William Dunlap, at the Newest* | *Printing-Office, in Market-Street.* M,DCC,LXIII. | 8vo. Half title, 1 leaf; pp. 38.   H. S. P.   1906

A second edition was advertised in the Pa. Gazette, June 16, 1763. See No. 1883, *supra*.

METHODISM anatomiz'd ; | or an | Alarm to Pennsylvania. | By a Lover of True Piety, | In Opposition to Enthusiasm. | With some Remarks on a Discourse | deliver'd September 24th, 1763. | . . . | . . . . | [*Philadelphia* :] *Printed for the Author, and sold by John* | *Morris, at the Green-Man in Fishamble-* | *street.* MDCCLXIII. | 16mo. pp. 16.   L. C. P.   1907

MINUTES | of | Conferences, | held at | Lancaster, | In August, 1762. | With the Sachems and Warriors of several Tribes of | Northern and Western Indians. | [*Penn Arms.*] | *Philadelphia* : | *Printed and Sold by B. Franklin, and D. Hall, at the* | *New-Printing-Office, near the Market.* MDCCLXIII. | Folio, pp. 36.

NEU=EJNGERJCHTETER Americanischer Calender, auf das Jahr 1764. *Philadelphia: Anton Armbruester.* 1763.   1909

DAS NEUE | Testament | Unsers | Herrn und Heylandes | Jesu Christi, | Verteutscht | Von | D. Martin Luther. | Mit | Jedes Capitels kurtzen | Summarien. | Auch beygefügten vielen richtigen | Parallelen. | *Germantown | Gedruckt und zu finden bey Christoph Saur,* 1763. | 12mo. pp. (4), 679, (3).   H. S. P. 1910

DER NEUESTE, Verbessert= und Zuverläßige | Americanische | Ca= lender | Auf das 1764ste Jahr Christi, | Welches ein Schalt=Jahr von 366 Tagen ist. | . . . | . . . | . . . | . . . | . . . | . . . | . . . | . . . | . . . | . . . . | Zum Zweytenmal herausgegeben. | *Philadelphia, Ge= druckt und zu finden bey Henrich Miller, in der Zweyten-strasse* . . . | . . . | . . . . [1763.] | Sm. 4to. pp. (48).   H. S. P. 1911

NEW-YEAR Verses of the Carriers of the Pennsylvania Ga- zette. *Philadelphia: B. Franklin, and D. Hall.* 1763.   1912

NEW-YEAR Verses of the Carriers of the Pennsylvania Jour- nal. *Philadelphia: William Bradford.* 1763.   1913

THE PENNSYLVANIA Gazette.   1914

Numbers 1776 (Jan. 6, 1763) to 1827 (Dec. 29, 1763), four pages each, with "Supplements" of two pages to Numbers 1800 and 1819.

THE PENNSYLVANIA Journal.   H. S. P. 1915

Numbers 1048 (Jan 6, 1763) to 1099 (Dec. 29, 1763), four pages each, with extra half sheets of two pages each to Numbers 1082, 1084, 1086, 1087, 1089, 1090, 1091, and 1093 to 1098. Title and imprint as in No. 1693, *supra.*

THE PENNSYLVANIA Pocket Almanac for 1764. *Philadel- phia: William Bradford.* 1763.   1916

A | PROPHECY, | lately | Discovered; | In which are pre- dicted | Many Great and Terrible | Events. | . . . | . . . | . . . . | [*Philadelphia:*] *Printed,* [*by A. Armbruster*] *in the* 1763d *Year of the* | *Christian Æra.* | 16mo. pp. 14.   L. C. P. 1917

[RITZEMA. (JOHANNES)] Aan den | Eerwaarden | Do. Johannes Leydt, | Predikant in N. Brunswyk, &c. | *in Te Philadelphia, Gedruckt by Hendrik Miller, | in de Twede Straat.* | MDCCLXIII. | 8vo. pp. 38.   H. S. P. 1918

SAUNDERS. (R.) A Pocket Almanac for 1764. By Richard Saunders, Phil. *Philadelphia: B. Franklin, and D. Hall.* 1763.

SAUNDERS. Poor Richard improved : | Being an | Almanack | . . . | . . . | . . . | . . . | . . . | . . . | . . . | . . . | . . . | . . . . | For the | Year of our Lord 1764: | Being Bissextile, or Leap-Year. | . . . | . . . | . . . | . . . | . . . | . . . | . . . | . . . | . . . | By Richard Saunders, Philom. | *Philadelphia:* | *Printed and Sold by B. Franklin, and D. Hall.* [1763.] | Sm. 8vo. pp. (36). H. S. P.

SCHABALIE. (J. P.) Die Wanblenbe Seel, Durch Johann Philip Schabalie in Niederlaenbischer Sprach beschrieben; anjetzo aber in bie Hochteutsche Sprach übersetzt von B. B. B. *Germanton: Gedruckt und zu finden, bey Christoph Saur,* 1763. 12mo. pp. 463 +. 1921

A | SHORT, Easy, | and | Comprehensive | Method | of | Prayer. | Translated from the German. | And published for a farther Promo- | tion, Knowledge and Benefit of In- | ward Prayer. | By a Lover of Internal Devotion. | The Second Edition with Addition. | *Germantown,* | *Printed by Christopher Sower.* | MDCC-LXIII. | 12mo. pp. 34.   H. S. P. 1922

STEINER. (J. C.) Die Herrliche | Erscheinung | bes | Herrn Jesu | zum Allgemeinen | Welt=Gericht, | Samt | besselben Folgen | für die Gerechten unb Ungerechten, | auf bie endlose Ewigkeit : | In Achtzehn Predigten, | Nach Anleitung ber eigenen Worte bes zukünftigen | Richters Jesu, bey Matth. XXV. 31, u. s. s. | vorgestellet, | Unb | wie zur Auf= munterung ber Frommen, also zum | Schrecken unb Erweckung ber Gott= losen, | angepriesen von | Johann Conrab Steiner, | weyland Reformir= ten Prebiger zu Philabelphia. | Nebst ber | bem sel. Verfasser am 7ten Julii bes verflossenen Jahrs | gehaltenen Leichen=Rebe; unb Kurzen Nach= | richt von bessen Lebens=Umstänben. | *Philadelphia,* | *Gedruckt bey Henrich Miller, in der Zweyten Strasse.* | 1763. | 8vo. pp. (8), 478.

STEUART. (A.) The | Gentleman and Citizen's | Pocket-Almanack, | By Andrew Steuart, Bookseller. | For the Year 1764. | Fitted to the Use of Pennsylvania and | the neighboring Provinces. | Containing | Many useful Lists and Tables, | not in any other Almanack printed | on the Continent. | This Almanack contains more than | double the Quantity of any other Pocket- | Almanack printed in this Place. | *Philadelphia:* | *Printed by Andrew Steuart, at the* | *Bible-in-Heart, in Second-street.* [1763.] | 24mo. pp. (48).   1924

THE SUFFICIENCY of the Spirit's Teaching, without Humane Learning: Or a Treatise tending to prove Humane Learning to be No Help to the Spiritual Understanding of the Word of God. *Wilmington: James Adams.* 1763.   1925

THORNE. (W.) A New Set of Copies, in large Modern Round text, for the Use of School. By William Thorne, Writing-Master and Accomptant in Philadelphia. *Philadelphia: B. Franklin, and D. Hall.* 1763.   1926

TOBLER. (J.) The Pennsylvania Town and Countryman's Almanac for 1764. By John Tobler. *Wilmington: James Adams.* 1763.   1927

TODD. (J.) An humble Attempt towards the Improvement | of Psalmody: | The | Propriety, | Necessity and Use, | Of | Evangelical | Psalms, | in | Christian Worship. | Delivered at a Meeting of the Presbytery of Hanover in Virginia, | October 6th, 1762. By John Todd, A. M. | . . . | . . . | . . . | . . . | . . . | . . . | . . . . | *Philadelphia:* | *Printed by Andrew Steuart, at the* *Bible-in-Heart, in Second-* | *Street,* MDCCLXIII. | Sm. 8vo. pp. 40.   H. S. P.

A TRUE Copy of an inimitable and incomprehensible Doggrel | Poem, sent by Parson All-sense, alias Smallsense, alias, | Nonsense, to D. J. Dove, at Germantown-School. | [*Philadelphia:*] *Printed by Black-Beard,* [*Andrew Steuart.*] 1763. | Folio, 1 leaf.   L. C. P.

TUNES in Three Parts. *Philadelphia: Anthony Armrbuster.* 1763.   ˙ 1930

See No. 1764 for the second edition.

VIRIS Præcellentissimis, | Thomæ Pennac Richardo Penn, Armigeris, | Provinciæ Pennsylvaniæ, . . . Proprietariis ; | . . . | Jacobo Hamilton, Armigero, | Prædictæ Provinciæ . . . Vice-Gubernatori præclarissimo, nec non hujus Collegii & Academiæ Philadelphiensis Curatori ; | . . . | . . . | . . . | . . . | . . . | . . . | . . . . | Hæc Philosophemata sub Vice-Præfecti Moderamini . . . discutienda ; Jurenes in artibus initiati, | . . . | . . . | . . . . | [*Philadelphia :*] *Typis Henrici Milleri.* . . . [1763.] | Folio, 1 leaf.   H. S. P.   1931

See No. 1859, *supra.*

VOTES | and | Proceedings | of the | House of Representatives | of the | Province of Pennsylvania, | Met at Philadelphia, on the Fourteenth of October, Anno | Domini 1762, and continued by Adjournments. | [*Penn Arms.*] | *Philadelphia :* | *Printed and Sold by B. Franklin, at the New Printing-Office,* | *near the Market.* MDCCLXIII. | Folio, pp. 67, (1).   H. S. P.   1932

WEATHERWISE. (A.)   Father Abraham's Almanac for 1764. By Abraham Weatherwise.   *Philadelphia: William Dunlap.* 1763.   1933

WHITEFIELD. (G.) Observations | on some | Fatal Mistakes, | In a Book lately published, and intitled, | The Doctrine of Grace ; or, The | Office and Operation of the Holy | Spirit vindicated from the Insults of | Infidelity, and the Abuses of Fanaticism. | By Dr. William Warburton, Lord Bishop | of Gloucester. | In a Letter to a Friend. | By George Whitefield, A.M. | late of Pembroke College, Oxford, and Chap- | lain to the Countess of Huntingdon. | . . . | . . . | . . . | . . . . | *London, printed :* | *Philadelphia, reprinted, by William* | *Bradford, at the Corner of Market and Front-* | *Street,* MDCCLXIII. | 12mo. pp. 24.   L. C. P.   1934

ZEUGNIS der Wahrheit | Oder: | eines Christen | Gedancken | von der vergangenen | und von der künfftigen | Reformation. | *Erstlich in Franckfurt und Leipzig 1760, nun aber zu* | *Germantown gedruckt bey Chr. Saur,* 1763. | 16mo. pp. 40.   H. S. P.   1935

END OF VOLUME I.